Real World QuarkXPress 6

for Macintosh and Windows

by David Blatner

PEACHPIT
PRESS

A PARALLAX
PRODUCTION

Real World QuarkXPress 6

Formerly known as *The QuarkXPress Book*
by David Blatner

Peachpit Press
1249 Eighth Street
Berkeley, CA 94710
510 / 524-2178
800 / 283-9444
510 / 524-2221 (fax)

Find us on the World Wide Web at: http://www.peachpit.com
To report errors, please send a note to errata@peachpit.com

Peachpit Press is a division of Pearson Education

Editor: Nancy Davis
Production Coordinator: Lisa Brazieal
Interior design and production: moo.com
Cover design: Gee + Chung Design
Cover Illustration: Diane Fenster

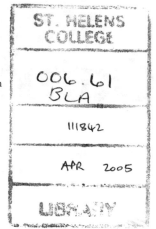

Permissions

The following photographs were used with permission of Special Collections Division, University of Washington Libraries. Figure 10-7 on page 561, photo by A. Curtis, negative no. 4103; Figure 10-22 on page 581, photo by Todd, negative no. 10511.

Notice of Rights

Notice of Liability

Trademarks

ISBN 0-321-19959-6
9 8 7 6 5 4 3
Printed and bound in the United States of America

Real World QuarkXPress 6

FOR MACINTOSH AND WINDOWS

preface

THE
AMAZON
EXPLORERS

▼ ▼

"You're doing what?"

"We've got one QuarkXPress document here to print the borders for each page, and then in this other document we have all the text in galleys. We tried to put them together, but because we don't know the program well enough, it's faster just to use our production people for pasteup."

"If you're just going to paste it up, why are you using QuarkXPress at all?"

"A consultant suggested we buy a computer and QuarkXPress. But we haven't had a chance to really learn it. Besides, QuarkXPress lets us make really good borders."

It was a story I had heard before. Designers, ad agencies, small and large businesses continue to buy computers and copies of QuarkXPress with the idea that everything was going to be easier, faster, and cooler. All that can be true, but let's face it: QuarkXPress is not a magical solution. Desktop publishing requires knowledge, experience, and expertise.

It seems there is a need for a consultant who not only knows the computer and graphic design, but also one who can sit there, patiently, and—at 11 PM—walk with you through building a better registration mark, making a drop cap, or explaining how master pages work. All for a low-cost flat fee. That consultant is this book.

▼ ▼

The Early Days

But how did this book come to be? What possessed me to write over 250,000 words on a piece of computer software? Let's start at the beginning of my QuarkXPress story.

The early days of desktop publishing were much simpler than they are now. When a new program came out, we publishers asked some basic, hard-hitting questions.

▶ Can you put text on a page?

▶ Can you put graphics on a page?

▶ Does the page print?

Once we had a satisfactory answer to those three questions, we could get down to brass tacks, ripping it to pieces to make it do all the things it wasn't designed to do. It was a wild time, much like trudging through the Amazon forests with only a machete and a match.

To be blunt, I'm not ordinarily the quiet type. So it is telling that, when I saw the first copy of QuarkXPress 1.0, all I could say was, "Wow." Here was, at last, a program to use instead of PageMaker. No more eyeballing the measurements, or relying on built-in algorithms. Those were the PageMaker 1.2 days, and XPress was a glimmer of hope in the dark ages.

After many years of suffering system crashes, blank pages coming out of the printer, PostScript errors, and dealing with clients and designers who wanted the impossible (yesterday, please), I learned just about everything there was to know about this complex piece of software.

Making Pages

I was not (and am not) a designer. My strength has always been the ability to use all my QuarkXPress tips and tricks to make good-looking pages quickly and efficiently. And back in 1990, I knew it was finally time to put finger to keyboard and get this information out to you, the real-world users of QuarkXPress.

Over the last 13 years, I've squirreled away every trick and tip I could find, storing them up for the next edition, or the one after that. Everything I've collected, right up to the time I made PDF files of this edition, I have managed to squeeze into this book.

But books full of tips and tricks tell just half the story. And I think the simple menu-by-menu approach that most computer books use deserves the phrase "tastes filling, less great!" I knew there should be much more.

My idea was to roll together tips and tricks, a full overview of the program, and in-depth discussions of core concepts behind using QuarkXPress in the real world. So, I've included discussions on fonts, PostScript printing, color models, and much more, alongside examples of how I've been using QuarkXPress for the past 16 years. I also describe the way QuarkXPress operates and how to take advantage of its sometimes strange methods.

Of course, this is a lot of information for a single book. But what did you shell out $44.99 for? Chopped liver? No, this book is meant not only to be read, but to be used. I wanted to include a Post-It pad so you could mark the pages you'll use the most, but it didn't work out. Don't let that stop you, though.

▼ ▼

About this Book

Although I expect you to know the basics of using a Macintosh or Microsoft Windows (moving the mouse, pulling down menus, and so on), I have purposely taken a wide spectrum of potential readers into account, from off-the-shelf beginners to seasoned professionals. I did this because I've found that those seasoned professionals are delighted to learn new tricks, techniques, and concepts, and people who have used computers very little sometimes surprise me with their intuitive grasp of the Big Picture.

Remember, this book was written for you. It's designed to work for you—as your personal consultant—whoever you are. It's also designed to help you get a sure footing on a sometimes uneven path and to help you make pages like the pros.

Organization

I have organized this book to reflect what I think QuarkXPress is all about: producing final camera-ready output from your computer. So I start with an overview of the program, move on to building a structure for the document, then discuss the basics—such as putting text and pictures on a page. Next I move into some fine-tuning aspects of QuarkXPress, and finally to printing. And, because so many people now must output their files both to paper and to the Internet, I have also included a chapter on Web publishing. That's the speed-reading rundown; now here's a play-by-play of the chapters.

▶ **INTRODUCTION.** In the Introduction, I lay out QuarkXPress on the table, telling you what it is and what it does. I also run down each of the new features in version 6.

▶ **CHAPTER 1: LEARN QUARKXPRESS IN 30 MINUTES.** One of the most frequently-asked-for additions to this book has been a step-by-step beginner's guide to learning QuarkXPress. If you're brand new to XPress, this chapter, which takes a hands-on approach to learning the program, should be perfect for you.

▶ **CHAPTER 2: QUARKXPRESS BASICS.** The first step in understanding QuarkXPress is learning about its structure from the ground up. This involves an investigation of QuarkXPress's menus, palettes, and dialog boxes. Advanced users tell me they find features and techniques in this chapter that they never knew.

▶ **CHAPTER 3: TOOLS OF THE TRADE.** Every vocation has its tools, and we desktop publishers are no different. This chapter offers an in-depth study of each tool in QuarkXPress's Tool palette, how to use it, and why.

▶ **CHAPTER 4: BUILDING A DOCUMENT.** Without a sturdy foundation, your document won't be reliable or flexible when you need it to be. This chapter discusses the basics of making earthquake-proof infrastructures for your pages: opening a new project, creating master pages, and setting up column guides and linking for text flow.

▶ **CHAPTER 5: WORD PROCESSING.** If you wanted a drawing program, you would have bought one. Words are what most people use QuarkXPress for, and this chapter is where words start. I talk here about simple text input, working with word processors, the Find/Change feature, and checking spelling.

▶ **CHAPTER 6: TYPE AND TYPOGRAPHY.** Once you've got those words in the computer, what do you do with them? Chapter 6 discusses the details of formatting text into type—fonts, sizes, styles, indents, drop caps—all the things that turn text into type.

▶ **CHAPTER 7: COPY FLOW.** You bought the computer, so why not let it do the work for you? This chapter explains how to use style sheets and XPress Tags to automate aspects of copy processing, and how to use importing and exporting effectively.

▶ **CHAPTER 8: LONG DOCUMENTS.** QuarkXPress 6 incorporates three major features that help you when working with long documents: lists, indexes, and the Book palette. Here, I discuss each of these in detail and offer suggestions for how to use them effectively.

▶ **CHAPTER 9: PICTURES.** Who reads text anymore? I like to look at the pictures. And pictures are what Chapter 9 is all about. I discuss every relevant graphics file format and how to work with each in your documents. I also cover rotating, skewing, and other manipulations of images.

► **CHAPTER 10: FINE-TUNING IMAGES.** In this chapter, I look at brightness, contrast, and halftoning for bitmapped images such as scans. I also explore XPress 6's clipping feature and how it works with TIFF images.

► **CHAPTER 11: WHERE TEXT MEETS GRAPHICS.** This is the frontierland: the border between the two well-discussed worlds of type and pictures. Life gets different on the edge, and in this chapter I discuss how to handle it with grace—using inline boxes, paragraph rules, and the text runaround features.

► **CHAPTER 12: COLOR.** QuarkXPress is well-known for its powerful color capabilities. Chapter 12 covers color models, building a custom color palette, applying colors, and the first steps in understanding color separation.

► **CHAPTER 13: PRINTING.** This chapter is where everything I've talked about is leading: getting your document out of the machine and onto film or paper. Here, I cover every step of printing, including the details of the Print dialog box, the finer points of service bureaus, and troubleshooting your print job.

► **CHAPTER 14: GOING ONLINE WITH QUARKXPRESS.** Many of the new features in version 6 involve building Web pages. Here I explain how to use these tools as well as explore making Acrobat PDF files for print or the Web from within QuarkXPress.

► **APPENDIX A: COLOR MANAGEMENT.** Color management is all about improving the correspondence between colors on screen, on color printer output, and on printed results from offset printing. The QuarkCMS XTension is covered in detail in this appendix.

► **APPENDIX B: MACINTOSH VS. WINDOWS.** More and more people are using QuarkXPress in a cross-platform environment. In Appendix B, I explore the ins and outs of moving files between the two programs and operating systems.

► **APPENDIX C: XTENSIONS AND RESOURCES.** Where do you go when QuarkXPress isn't doing what you want? This appendix offers suggestions for many popular XTensions, as well as both print and Web-based resources you should know about.

▶ **APPENDIX D: SCRIPTING.** In Appendix D, I cover the wild world of scripting QuarkXPress using AppleScript on the Macintosh. Don't worry, I'm not really a programmer myself; if *I* can understand this stuff, so can you.

▶ **APPENDIX E: XML TOOLS.** If you make books, magazines, or newspapers, you need to know about XML. It's the hot new thing in the industry, but it's certainly the hardest thing you can do in QuarkXPress today.

▶ **APPENDIX F: XPRESS TAGS.** If you use XPress Tags (which I discuss in Chapter 7, *Copy Flow*), you will no doubt need a reference to the many obscure and arcane codes. I've laid them all out here.

▶ **APPENDIX G: ANSI CODES.** In order to type certain special characters in QuarkXPress for Windows, you need to know each character's ANSI code. I'm forever forgetting them, so I built a list of them, which I've included here.

Finding What You Need

There are many ways to read this book. First, there's the cover-to-cover approach. This is the best way to get every morsel I have included. On the other hand, that method doesn't seem to work for some people. As I said, this book is meant to be used, right off the shelf, no batteries required.

I've done everything in my power to make it easy to find topics throughout this book. However, there's so much information that sometimes you might not know where to look. The table of contents breaks each chapter down into first- and second-level headings, so you can jump to a particular topic fast.

If you are primarily looking for the new version-6 features, you should take a look at the description of new features in the Introduction. That will also tell you where in the book I describe the feature fully.

Finally, if you can't find what you're looking for, or are trying to find an explanation for a single concept, try the index.

Faith

Just to be honest with you, there's almost no way to explain one feature in QuarkXPress without explaining all the rest at the same time. But that would make for a pretty confusing book. Instead, I'm asking you to take minor leaps of faith along the path of reading these chapters. If I mention a term or function you don't understand, trust me that I'll explain it all in due time. If you are able to do that, you will find that what I am discussing all makes sense. For example, I'm not going to talk about the details of creating a new document until the fourth chapter, *Building a Document*, even though I need to talk about working with documents in Chapter 2, *QuarkXPress Basics*.

▼ ▼

Acknowledgments

No book is an island. So many people have directly and indirectly contributed to this book's production that I would have to publish a second volume to thank them all. However, I want to thank some folks directly.

Behind the scenes. Several other writers have worked on pieces of this book. Specifically, Patti Schulze wrote a large chunk of the material involving XPress's Web features, and Steve Werner contributed greatly to several sections, including layout spaces, tables, and making PDF files. Sandee Cohen, Phil Gaskill, Kass Johns, Keith Stimely, Bob Weibel, and Eric Taub contributed significantly to earlier editions. Jeff Tolbert was instrumental in capturing on-screen images. Bruce Fraser, my coauthor on *Real World Photoshop*, also provided technical editing and reality checks.

The infrastructure makes it great. A great thanks to the people at Quark who put out XPress.

A special thanks to Cyndie Shaffstall of The Power XChange; Jay Nelson at *Design Tools Monthly*; Diane Burns; John Cruise; Doug Peltonen; Sal Soghoian; and Sandy Bozek of Apple Computer.

And many thanks go to all the people who wrote, called, and e-mailed me their comments and suggestions. I've tried to incorporate their ideas into this seventh edition.

The People Who Made This Book

Throughout the process of developing this edition, I have been surrounded and supported by quality people, including Steve Roth, who edited the first few editions of this book. Cindy Bell of Design Language, Kris Fulsaas, and Agen Schmitz were excellent in making sure my t's were dotted and i's crossed, and — most of all — making sure that I didn't sound like a fool. Also important have been Glenn "industry pundit" Fleishman, Jeff Carlson of Never Enough Coffee Creations, and Larry "Mr. Analog" Chen.

I want to thank my publisher, Nancy Ruenzel, and my editor at Peachpit, Nancy Davis. In fact, everyone at Peachpit has been great, including Lisa "fill or kill" Brazieal, Mimi Heft, Kim Lombardi, Gary-Paul Prince, Scott Cowlin, and Trish Booth. Special appreciation also goes to Ted Nace, the original publisher at Peachpit– I gave it the wings, but he made it fly.

And, finally, there are those people even further behind the scenes who helped along the road. Vincent Dorn at LaserWrite in Palo Alto, who said, "Hey, let's go to Burger King." Steve Herold at LaserGraphics in Seattle, who said, "Meet Steve Roth." All my parents; my wife, Debbie Carlson, and son, Gabriel; Alisa, Paul, and Camille Piette; Suzanne and Damian Carlson-Prandini; and other friends who were such a support over the past few decades. It wouldn't have happened without you.

Thanks.

David Blatner
Seattle, Washington

OVERVIEW

▼ ▼

Preface		v
Introduction		1
Chapter 1	Learn QuarkXPress in 30 Minutes	11
Chapter 2	QuarkXPress Basics	43
Chapter 3	Tools of the Trade	113
Chapter 4	Building a Document	243
Chapter 5	Word Processing	285
Chapter 6	Type and Typography	307
Chapter 7	Copy Flow	421
Chapter 8	Long Documents	463
Chapter 9	Pictures	503
Chapter 10	Fine-Tuning Images	547
Chapter 11	Where Text Meets Graphics	585
Chapter 12	Color	613
Chapter 13	Printing	671
Chapter 14	Going Online with QuarkXPress	737
Appendix A	Color Management	805
Appendix B	Macintosh vs. Windows	831
Appendix C	XTensions and Resources	841
Appendix D	Scripting	847
Appendix E	XML Tools	861
Appendix F	XPress Tags	879
Appendix G	ANSI Codes	885
Index		893

CONTENTS

▼ ▼

Introduction   QuarkXPress:The Big Picture 1

The Birth of an Upgrade 1

    The History 2

    If You Skipped the QuarkXPress 5 Upgrade 5

    What's New In QuarkXPress 6 7

Hardware and System Software Requirements 8

▼ ▼

Chapter 1   Learn QuarkXPress in 30 Minutes 11

Pages, Views and Guides 12

    Creating a New File 12

    Working in the Window 14

    Working with the Tool Palette 15

    Zooming Around 15

    Adding Pages 17

    Adding Guides 17

    Saving 18

Text and Text Formatting 20

    Drawing a Text Box 20

    Modifying a Text Box 21

    Typing Text 22

    Formatting Text 22

    Importing Text 23

    Linking Text Boxes 24

    Multicolumn Text Boxes 25

    Character Formatting 27

    Leading 28

    Paragraph Formatting 29

    New-Line Character 30

Graphics, Colors, Frames, and Lines 31
    Drawing a Picture Box 31
    Importing Graphics 32
    Runaround 33
    Resizing and Rotating Graphics 34
    Adding Color 35
    Adding a Frame 36
    Drawing Lines 37
Printing 38
    Printing on Your Desktop 38
    Sending to a Service Bureau 39
How to Really Sound Like You Know What You're Talking About 41

▼ ▼

Chapter 2   **QuarkXPress Basics** 43
First Steps in Quarking 44
    Other Files 45
Know Thy Program 47
    About That About Box 47
    XPress Preferences 48
    XTensions 51
    Keyboard Shortcuts 57
File Management 57
    Opening Documents 58
    Closing Documents 58
    Saving Your Document 59
    Templates 63
    Multiple Documents 64
QuarkXPress's Interface 65
    Menus 66
    Palettes 68
    Dialog Boxes 74
    By the Numbers 76
    Context-Sensitive Menus 77
After You Click OK 79
    Revert to Saved 79
    Undo and Multiple Undo 80
    Cancel and Interruptible Redraw 82
Getting Around Your Document 82
    Scrolling 83
    Zooming 84
    Moving from Page to Page 87

Manipulating Your Layout 89
    Menu Manipulations 89
    Thumbnails 90
    Page Layout Palette 91
    Moving Items Between Documents 92
    Moving Pages Between Documents 92
Changing Defaults 93
Layout and Application Preferences 93
    Display Preferences 94
    Interactive Preferences 98
    Save Preferences 101
    Undo Preferences 102
    XTensions Manager Preferences 102
    File List and Default Path Preferences 103
    Full Res Preview Preferences 104
    Index Preferences 104
    Jabberwocky Preferences 104
    PDF Preferences 104
    Fraction/Price Preferences 105
    General Preferences 105
    Measurements Preferences 107
    Paragraph and Character Preferences 109
    Tool Preferences 109
    Trapping Preferences 111
    Quark CMS Preferences 111
    Layers Preferences 111
QuarkXPress from Zero to Sixty 112

▼ ▼

Chapter 3   Tools of the Trade 113

Items and Contents 113
    Selecting Items 115
Item Creation Tools 117
    Making Boxes 119
    Changing Box Type 124
    Lines and Arrows 124
    Text Paths 127
Bézier Boxes and Lines 132
    Understanding Bézier Controls 133
    Bézier and Freehand Tools 136
    Drawing with the Pen Tools 139
    Editing Bézier Paths 145
    Scissors Tool 153
    Merge Commands 153

Splitting Compound Objects 160
Transforming Boxes and Lines 160
Converting Text to Paths 164
Manipulating Items. 167
Moving Items. 167
Resizing and Reshaping Items 168
Rotating Items 171
Skewing Items 173
Flipping Out 173
Locking Items 174
Suppress Printout and Suppress Picture Printout 175
Duplicating Items 175
Deleting Items 178
Relationships Between Items 179
Layering Items. 179
Grouping Objects 180
Modifying Grouped Objects. 181
Constraining 183
Aligning and Distributing Objects 185
Synchronize Text 190
Synching and Unsynching Text 190
Limitations of Synchronizing 193
The Layers Palette. 193
Making Layers 194
Assigning Layers. 195
Moving and Deleting Layers. 197
Layer Attributes 199
Layer Preferences 201
Linking 202
Linking Text Boxes. 202
Unlinking Text Boxes 203
Copying Linked Text Boxes 204
Guides and Rulers. 204
Rulers 205
Guides 206
Snap to Guides. 209
Frames, Dashes, and Stripes 210
Frames 210
Creating Custom Dashes and Stripes 214
Frame Editor 222
Tables 222
Building Tables. 223
Changing Rows and Columns. 226

Formatting Cells 229

Formatting the Table Box 230

Formatting Gridlines 230

Convert Table to Text or Group 232

Default Preference Settings 233

Tables for Web Layouts 234

Libraries 235

Manipulating Libraries 235

Adding and Moving Library Entries 236

Removing Library Items 237

Labeling Library Items 237

Saving Libraries 239

Appending Settings 240

Moving On 241

▼ ▼

Chapter 4   **Building a Document** 243

Building a New Document 244

Page Size 245

Margin Guides 246

Column Guides 247

Facing Pages 248

Automatic Text Box 248

Projects and Layouts 250

Projects 251

Layouts 251

Creating a New Layout 251

Working with Layouts 252

Layout Limitations 253

Master Pages: Elementary 254

What Master Pages Are Good For 254

How QuarkXPress Does Masters 256

Your First Master Page 257

Automatic Text Boxes 259

Master Guides 259

Automatic Text-Link Icon 260

Automatic Text-Link Box 260

Modifying Automatic Text-Link Boxes 261

Creating Multiple Automatic Text-Link Boxes 262

Unlinking Automatic Text-Link Boxes 262

Master Pages and Document Pages 262

Changing Master-Page Items 262

Applying Master Pages to Document Pages 266

Master Pages and the Page Layout Palette 267

    Page Layout Palette 268

    Applying Master Pages 271

Making Pages 272

    Insert Pages. 272

    Document-Layout Insertions 273

Modifying Your Pages. 275

    Changing Page Size 275

    Changing Facing Pages. 276

    Changing Margins and Guides 276

Automatic Page Insertion 276

    Text Linking 277

Multipage Spreads 277

Sections and Page Numbering 278

    Changing Your Starting Page Number 279

    Changing the Page-Numbering Style 280

    Prefixes 280

Automatic "Continued . . ." Pagination 281

    To Create a "Continued on . . ." Message 281

Foundations 283

▼ ▼

Chapter 5   **Word Processing** 285

Entering and Editing Text 285

    Selecting and Navigating. 286

    Deleting Text 288

    Drag-and-Drop Text 288

Importing Text 290

    What Filters Are, and How to Use Them. 291

Finding and Changing 292

    Where QuarkXPress Looks 292

    Specifying Text 293

    Specifying Attributes 295

    What to Find, What to Change 296

    Type Styles 297

    Going to It 298

Spelling Checker 299

    Checking a Word. 300

    Checking a Selection 300

    Checking a Story. 300

    Checking a Layout/Master Page 302

    Auxiliary Dictionaries. 303

Watching Your Words 305

▼ ▼

Chapter 6   **Type and Typography** 307

Fonts and Font Management 308

   Missing Fonts 310

   Font Usage 311

Character Formatting 313

   Selecting a Typeface. 313

   Font Size 315

Type Styles 316

   Styling by Attributes Versus Font Choice 319

Color and Shade. 321

Horizontal and Vertical Scaling. 322

Kerning and Tracking. 324

   Kerning 325

   Tracking. 328

   Wordspacing 330

   Baseline Shift. 331

Paragraph Formatting 332

Alignment 333

   Horizontal Alignment 333

   Vertical Alignment 335

Indents 340

Leading 344

   Specifying Leading 344

   Leading Methods 346

   Leading Modes. 348

Space Before and After 351

First Baseline. 352

Tabs 353

   Setting Tab Stops 356

   Changing and Deleting Tab Stops 358

   Tab Leaders. 359

   Right Indent Tab. 360

Hyphenation and Justification 361

   The Basics of H&J 361

   Auto Hyphenation. 362

   Justification. 364

   Forced Justification 366

Setting Your Own H&J 367

   Creating an H&J Setting 367

   Deleting and Appending H&Js 367

   Applying an H&J Setting 369

Widow and Orphan Control. 372
   Keep With Next ¶ 372
   Keep Lines Together 373
Baseline Grid. 375
   Maintain Leading 378
Fine-Tuning Type 378
   Typographic Preferences. 379
Kerning and Tracking Tables 382
   Kerning Tables 382
   Tracking Tables 385
Tweaking Hyphenation 388
   Hyphenation Method. 388
   Suggested Hyphenation 388
   Hyphenation Exceptions. 389
Special Characters 391
   Formatting Characters 391
   Punctuation and Symbols 397
   Foreign Punctuation and Accents 403
   Math Symbols and the Symbol Font. 403
   Dingbats 405
Typographic Special Effects 408
   Fractions 408
   Initial Caps 411
   Shadow Type Alternatives 418
   Pricing. 419
Text Greeking 420
Putting It Together 420

▼ ▼

Chapter 7   **Copy Flow** 421
   Managing Copy 421
   Working Smart 422
Style Sheets. 423
   A Style Is a Style Sheet Is a Style. 423
   The Benefits of Style Sheets 423
   Local Formatting Versus Formatting with Styles. 424
   Tagging Paragraphs 426
   Defining Styles 429
   Creating a New Paragraph Style. 430
   Normal Style and No Style 434
   Appending Styles 437
   Deleting (and Replacing) Styles. 440
   Basing One Style on Another 440

Next Style 442
Character-Based Styles 443
What Word Processor to Use 448
How QuarkXPress Style Sheets Work with Word 449
Exporting Text 452
How to Export Text 453
Pitfalls 453
A Solution: XPress Tags 454
Why Use XPress Tags? 455
How to Use XPress Tags 455
BBEdit and Other Text Editors 461
Getting Your Stories Straight 462

▼ ▼

Chapter 8   Long Documents

Chapter 8   **Long Documents** 463
Books 464
Building a Book 465
Editing Your Book's Documents 468
Synchronizing Your Book 471
Page Numbering and Sections 473
Printing Books 475
Lists 475
Setting Up a List 476
The Lists Palette 478
Building and Rebuilding Lists 481
Indexes 482
Adding a New First-Level Index Entry 483
Cross-References (X-refs) 489
Adding a New Reference to an Entry 490
Adding a New Second-Level Index Entry 490
Deleting an Entry 492
Editing Index Entries 492
Index Preferences 494
Building the Index 496
Indexing Books and Projects 500
Putting It Together 501

▼ ▼

Chapter 9   Pictures

Chapter 9   **Pictures** 503
Graphic File Formats 504
Bitmapped Images 504
Object-Oriented Graphics 507
File Types 508

Importing Pictures into QuarkXPress 516

Pasting Pictures 516

Get Picture 517

What Happened to My Picture?. 518

Working with Pictures 520

Moving Your Picture Around 520

Cropping 521

Resizing Your Picture 523

Rotating, Skewing, and Distorting 524

Picture Management. 528

To Represent 528

Picture Usage. 529

Dynamically Updating Images 534

Auto Picture Import. 534

Edit Original 535

Object Linking and Embedding (OLE). 536

Preview Quality, Greeking, and Suppression. 536

Picture Greeking. 536

Suppress Printout 537

Full Resolution Preview 537

Page as Picture. 539

Page and Spread 539

Scale 540

Bleed. 540

Format. 541

Transparent Page 542

Space 542

Preview 542

Data and OPI. 543

A Warning. 545

Image on the Half Shell 546

▼ ▼

Chapter 10   **Fine-Tuning Images**. 547

The Picture File 548

Bitmapped Images 548

Modifying Images. 549

Importing High-Resolution TIFF Graphics 549

The Style Menu 550

Contrast. 554

Picture Contrast Specifications 555

Color. 561

Clipping Paths 564
   Applying a Clipping Path 564
   Clipping Caveats. 569
   Clipping Options 569
   Editing the Clipping Path 577
Halftones 579
Many Colorful Shades of Gray 584

Chapter 11   **Where Text Meets Graphics** 585
Transparency 586
Text Runaround 586
   Runaround Type. 586
   Editing the Runaround 593
   Inverting the Text Wrap. 596
   Running Text On Both Sides of an Object 596
Anchored Boxes 598
   Turning a Box into a Character 598
   Modifying Anchored Boxes 599
   Working with Anchored Boxes 603
Paragraph Rules 607
   Rule Above/Rule Below. 607
Poking and Prodding 612

Chapter 12   **Color** 613
What You See and What You Get 614
Describing Color 615
   Spot Versus Process Color 615
   Color Models. 618
   Color-Matching Systems. 620
Specifying Color 625
   The Color List 625
   Show. 626
   New 627
   Edit. 631
   Duplicate 632
   Delete 632
   Append 633
   Edit Trap 635
   Save 635
   Cancel 635
Multi-Ink Colors. 635
   Building a Multi-Ink Color 636

Special Colors 638

    Registration. 638

    Indeterminate 639

Colors Palette 640

Blending Colors 641

Trapping 647

    Trapping Preferences 649

    Custom Color-Pair Trap Settings 654

    Object-Level Trapping 660

    Trapping to Multiple Colors 664

Color from Outside Sources 665

    Object-Oriented EPS Files 665

    What You Can and Cannot Change 666

    Bitmapped Images 667

Deciding to Work in Color 670

▼ ▼

Chapter 13   Printing

Printing 671

PostScript. 672

Deciphering the Print Dialog Box 673

    Choosing a Printer: Macintosh versus Windows. 673

    The Pages You Want 675

    Print Status 677

The Document Tab 678

    Tiling. 687

The Page Setup Tab 689

    Printer Description 689

    Paper Specifications 691

    Roll-Fed Printer Specifications 694

The Output Tab 695

The Options Tab 700

    Picture Output 702

The Layers Tab 705

Setting Bleeds 706

The OPI Tab 708

The Preview Tab 708

Page Setup, Printer, and Properties 710

    Macintosh: Page Setup and Printer 710

    Windows: Properties 712

Print Styles 713

Color Separations 716

    The Basics of Color Separation 716

    Printing Color Separations. 716

The Rosette. 717

The Color Halftone Settings 718

Working with an Imaging Center. 720

How to Send Your File 721

Sending QuarkXPress Files 722

Checklists for Sending QuarkXPress Files. 723

Collect for Output. 724

Sending a PostScript Dump 725

Printing to Disk: Macintosh 727

Printing to Disk: Windows 729

Checklist for Sending PostScript Dumps 730

Troubleshooting. 731

Graphics Look Awful 731

General Fixes. 732

Big Ugly White Gaps Appear Between Colors 734

Wrong Screen Frequency 734

Document Settings 734

Fonts Come Out Wrong 735

Registration Problems 735

"Job Finished" 735

▼ ▼

Chapter 14   **Going Online with QuarkXPress**. 737

HTML and Web Browsers 739

Exporting Your Content 741

Web Documents and File Structure 742

Setting up Folders. 743

Creating Web Pages. 744

Setting Up File Paths 748

Page Properties 749

Building the Web Page 753

Text Boxes. 754

Converting Text to a Graphic 754

Defining CSS Font Families 758

Picture Boxes. 759

Tables and Lines. 761

Previewing Your Pages 761

Hyperlinks 762

About URLs. 763

The Hyperlinks Palette 764

Creating Named Anchors 766

Rollover Images 767

Two-Position Rollovers 769

Cascading Menus 771
    Creating the Menus 771
    Attaching the Menus 773
Image Maps 774
HTML Forms. 775
    Define the Form 776
    The File Select Tool 779
    Text Fields 780
    Lists and Popup Menus 782
    Checkboxes and Radio Buttons. 786
    Buttons 787
Exporting Your Page as HTML 789
    Tables in HTML 791
Importing HTML 792
XPress Page as Picture 793
Acrobat PDF Files 796
    Creating a PDF File 797
    Export Layout as PDF. 799
The Future of Publishing 804

▼ ▼

Appendix A   **Color Management**. 805
Managing Color 806
Before You Use QuarkCMS 813
Using QuarkCMS 815
The QuarkCMS XTension 816
Telling QuarkCMS About Pictures 820
Using Hexachrome Color 824
Color Management at Print Time 825
Pros and Cons 829

▼ ▼

Appendix B   **Macintosh vs. Windows** 831
File Names, Types, and Creators 832
What Does (and Doesn't) Transfer 834
Modern Myths. 840

▼ ▼

Appendix C   **XTensions and Resources** 841

▼ ▼

Appendix D   **Scripting** 847
Macros Versus Scripting 848
Getting Scripting Information 850

Writing a Script 851

Looking at a Script 856

Stuff You Should Know About 858

▼ ▼

Appendix E   **XML Tools** 861

Separating Content and Form 863

XML Basics 865

Quark's XML Tools 871

▼ ▼

Appendix F   **XPress Tags** 879

▼ ▼

Appendix G   **ANSI Codes** 885

▼ ▼

Colophon 891

Where to Reach Me 892

Index 893

QuarkXPress: The Big Picture

Trying to figure out just what type of program QuarkXPress is reminds me of a scene from an old *Saturday Night Live* episode, when a couple bickered over their new purchase. "It's a floor wax," said one. "No, it's a dessert topping," replied the other. The answer soon became clear: "It's a floor wax *and* a dessert topping." QuarkXPress is a program with the same predicament. Some people insist it's a typesetting application. Others bet their bottom dollar that it's a Web-design tool. Still others make XPress a way of life.

The truth is that QuarkXPress is all these things, and more. However, no matter how you use it, it is never more than a tool. And a tool is never more than the person behind it.

Here in the Introduction, I talk about the big picture: the history of QuarkXPress from version 1.0 through version 6. Most importantly, I set the stage for the real thrust of this book: how to use QuarkXPress to its fullest.

The Birth of an Upgrade

If you've never watched an artist create an image with oil paints, you may not understand what all the fuss and expense is about. When you see the end result, it's easy to think that they just picked up a brush and painted the whole

1

thing. What you'd be missing is the hours of slowly building, changing, covering, modifying, pondering, and dreaming. Half of what makes a piece of art special is the *process* of its creation.

Art isn't the only thing that is born out of process. Computer software is very similar. And so it's with great admiration that I can look forward to each new revision of QuarkXPress, where code has been modified, other parts ripped out and replaced with something better, and then—in fits of inspiration—whole new features are added, making the final piece (at least for this version) one step better, more usable, and simply *cooler* (see Figure I-1).

Version 6 of QuarkXPress has, from its announcement, been met with mixed criticism. Some people rave about the dozen or so new features, believing the ability to build Web pages from within a page-layout program will save them hundreds of hours a year. Others stare blankly at you if you mention the upgrade and ask why, after almost two years since the last major release, the Quark engineers were so thoughtless as to leave out fundamental features such as a Scaling palette, or drop shadows.

I admit to holding both opinions: I believe QuarkXPress 6 is a major step forward in page-layout, offering extraordinary new features that I would be loath to give up. It's funny, but even some of the seemingly smallest new abilities or changes to interface are clearly a big win over previous editions. On the other hand, I keep a list on my desktop called "ThingsThatAnnoyMeAbout-XPress6" in which I let myself complain about both big-ticket items—such as why doesn't XPress have a Story Editor, like PageMaker—and the small stuff, too—keystrokes that used to be fast in version 3.x but now slow you down in later versions.

The History

If you're a new user to QuarkXPress, the past probably holds little meaning for you because all you want to do is jump in and start using the product as it works today. However, many of you have probably been using XPress for a while (three years? seven years? more?) and it's worth taking a step back every now and again to look at where we've been and how far QuarkXPress has come.

I've been writing about QuarkXPress since version 3.0, but I still remember using version 1.10, back in 1987, when just getting the page to print was considered a feature. The jump to version 2.0 felt pretty big, but it wasn't earth-shaking. In fact, it wasn't until 1990's release of version 3.0 that QuarkXPress really grew into a world-class page-layout tool. Version 3.0 introduced XPress users to the pasteboard metaphor, the polygon tool (for pictures only), and a major interface-lift that turned heads and started winning converts. Still, when version 3.0 shipped, there were only a handful of service bureaus around the

Figure I-1
Evolution of
the species

Version 1.10

Version 2.12

Version 3.3

Figure I-1
Evolution of
the species
(continued)

Version 4

Version 5

country that would accept XPress files; PageMaker was the dominant force in the industry and you were a rebel if you even mentioned Quark.

In version 3.1, we saw new features like automatic ligatures, color blends. In 3.2, Quark got rid of the XPress Data file which was driving service bureaus crazy, introduced EfiColor's color management system (which fell with a thud for most people), added new style sheet features, scripting, math features in the palettes, and—for some people the biggest feature of all—a Microsoft

Figure I-1
Evolution of
the species
(continued)

Version 6

Windows version of QuarkXPress. Version 3.3 was really only a minor upgrade, but it shocked the world with its polygonal text boxes, letting you sculpt text blocks into any shape you wanted. Most importantly, throughout all these versions, those wacky Quark engineers have kept fixing bugs that users would find, always trying for a more perfect application.

It took seven years for Quark to make the leap from version 3.0 to version 4.0, but the cool new features were worth the wait: Bézier curves, type on a curve, character-level style sheets, editable clipping paths (including the ability to make any embedded path a clipping path), custom line and dash styles, and more.

If You Skipped the QuarkXPress 5 Upgrade

Quark won't share the actual number of users who upgraded to version 5, but from all indications, it didn't exactly overwhelm their shipping department. If you were one of those who just stuck with version 4, let me share with you the big feature improvements that appeared in version 5, as these were, of course, all rolled into version 6 as well.

▶ **WEB DOCUMENTS.** The majority of new features in QuarkXPress 5 related to the ability to make and export HTML Web pages, including interactive rollovers (graphics that change when the cursor is on top of them), image maps (specifying areas of a graphic that are "hot links"), and form elements (checkboxes, buttons, text entry fields, and so on). See page 737.

▶ **TABLE TOOL.** People have been asking for a way to make tables in QuarkXPress for over ten years. Ask no further. The Table tool lets you create all kinds of cool-looking tables. You can even embed these tables into text boxes so that they flow with your stories. See page 222.

▶ **LAYERS PALETTE.** The Layers palette is another long-standing item off the wish-list. If you know how to use the Layers palette in Adobe Illustrator or Macromedia FreeHand, you'll pick this up in no time. See page 193.

▶ **CONTEXT-SENSITIVE MENUS.** I love context-sensitive menus: those menus that popup when you Control-click (Mac) or right-mouse-button-click (Windows) on something. Version 4 had one context-sensitive menu (in the Style Sheets palette). Version 5 implemented lots more. See page 77.

▶ **VISUAL INDICATORS.** You may see little icons in the upper-right corner of various objects; don't worry, that's just the visual indicator feature, which lets you know on which layer each object is sitting, as well as if an object is a special item like a Web form. See page 196.

▶ **HYPERLINKS.** The Hyperlinks palette lets you assign links to Web pages or to pages within your document. You can then use these hyperlinks to navigate in exported HTML or PDF files. See page 762.

▶ **COLLECTING FONTS.** QuarkXPress 4 let you collect linked graphics before sending your files to a service bureau; now XPress finally collects the fonts and color profiles that you used. See page 724.

▶ **CHARACTER LISTS.** The primary limitation of the Lists feature in QuarkXPress 4 was that it only let you use paragraph styles. Now you can also use character styles. See page 475.

▶ **SCRIPTS MENU.** If you use QuarkXPress on a Macintosh, you should be using AppleScripts, especially now that Quark has added a scripts menu. Quark even threw in a bunch of free scripts you can use. See page 847.

▶ **INTERFACE IMPROVEMENTS.** There are a number of other small improvements to the interface of QuarkXPress. For instance, the Colors palette now displays whether a color is a process or spot color (see page 640), you can search for colored text in the Find/Change palette (see page 292), and the Preferences dialog box is now easier to navigate (see page 93).

As I said, there are many more features than this. Stuff like Transparent EPS, multiple text insets, improved indexing, and print dialog box enhancements. Don't worry, I cover them all in the next 900-odd pages.

What's New In QuarkXPress 6

So what's new in QuarkXPress 6? A lot. Following is a list of what I consider to be the most important changes, though the ones that are most important to your workflow may be different than the ones that get me all excited. (I'm not going to list every little niggling feature that's different between the last version and this one; if you need that, take a look at the What's New addendum that comes with XPress.)

▶ **NATIVE OS X.** The most obvious change in XPress 6 is that it now runs natively under Mac OS X and Windows XP. This isn't as big a deal on Windows as it is on the Macintosh, where OS X users no longer have to use XPress in Classic mode. Another significant change to the interface is that the palette controls now live in the Window menu rather than the View menu. See page 65.

▶ **LAYOUT SPACES.** Let's say you're creating a business card, a Web page, and a brochure for a client. Wouldn't it be cool if you could put all those pages (which share similar designs and text, but have very different page sizes and layout needs) in the same document? That's what the Layout Spaces feature is all about: combining documents into the same document. See page 250.

▶ **MULTIPLE UNDO.** It took 15 years and a lot of Jolt Cola (or Mahacola, for those software engineers in India), but Quark finally got around to letting us undo more than one action. See page 80.

▶ **EXPORT PDF.** QuarkXPress no longer requires Acrobat Distiller to create PDF files because now it ships with its own "distiller" software. XPress still writes PostScript to disk and then distills it, however. See page 796.

▶ **NEW WEB FEATURES.** Quark is fixated on the idea that users want to use XPress to create Web pages, so they've added some more cool Web features to version 6, including the ability to create two-position rollovers, hyperlinks to other pages in the document, hierarchical families of fonts, and cascading menus. See page 769.

▶ **PASTE IN PLACE.** This little feature is hardly worth noting except that it's something I've wanted for years: The ability to copy an object, then paste it on a different page but in the same place. See page 176.

▶ **FULL RESOLUTION PREVIEW.** People have complained about the screen previews of images in QuarkXPress forever. Now, fewer people will be complaining because the Full Resolution Preview feature improves the onscreen display dramatically for both bitmapped and vector images. However, you need to register your software to get the XTensions that provide this functionality. See page 537.

▶ **SYNCHRONIZE TEXT.** Do you use the same text over and over in the same document, or across multiple layout spaces in a project? Synchronize Text lets you mirror text from one place to another so if you change it in one place it changes everyplace else. See page 190.

▶ **MINI IMPROVEMENTS.** Version 6 offers incremental improvements to a number of areas throughout the program. For example, you can now select all the items on a layer (page 197), link text cells together in a table (page 225), control which hyperlinks display in the Hyperlinks palette (page 764), and print composite color better using DeviceN color (page 697).

On the other hand, there are some tradeoffs, too. If you use any third-party XTensions, you'll have to get updates, as they won't work with this version of XPress. That could be a problem, since a number of XTension developers have no intention of updating their software.

▼ ▼

Requirements

To take advantage of all these great new features in QuarkXPress, you need, at a minimum, a dual processor G5 or a 9 GHz Pentium VI computer with 4 GB of RAM, a 120-gigabyte hard disk drive, a 600 MB magneto-optical drive, a 32-bit color drum scanner, a high-res imagesetter with a PostScript 3 RIP, a 1200-by-600-dpi laser printer, a 23-inch Barco color monitor with 24-bit video and graphics accelerator cards, and, of course, an NTSC video capture board and genlock control panel.

Just kidding! You can actually get by with some pretty limited hardware. But, as few things are more frustrating than being all psyched up to start something only to discover that you can't, for lack of an essential component, here's a résumé of the components you need to know about.

Hardware and System Software

While early versions of QuarkXPress for the Macintosh could run on almost any Macintosh sold in the past 15 years (with a minimum of a 68020 processor), version 6 now requires operating system 10.2 or later, which itself requires a fast G3, G4, or G5 Macintosh with a lot of RAM. In order to print or create PDF files you also must have a PostScript printer driver loaded. In order to install XPress on your hard drive, you have to have about 400 MB of free space.

If you use Windows, your PC had better be a 300 Mhz Pentium or better, running Windows 2000 or Windows XP. You also need a minimum of 128 MB of RAM and 300 MB of free hard disk space.

Of course, on either platform you need a mouse (or some other pointing device) and a keyboard. Plus, note that while QuarkXPress 6 does print on non-PostScript printers, it is optimized to print best on a PostScript printer.

Keyboards

QuarkXPress is a keyboard- and mouse-intensive program. You'll be spending a lot of your time selecting items or text, dragging, or choosing menus. If you have an extended keyboard—one that has the 15 function keys, page up and down keys, and a keypad—you can save yourself hours (or days!) by using built-in shortcuts. You can also assign style sheets to keys (this is where the keypad comes in handy). And if you get a utility like CE Software's QuicKeys (for Mac or Windows), you can use the keyboard even more effectively. While I like the ergonomic nature of adjustable keyboards, I don't find them as helpful in production work because they put the function and page keys in a separate unit that's hard to position well.

Hard Disks

The Iron Law of Hard Disk Storage is that your needs expand to equal and then exceed the storage capacity available. Get the biggest hard disk you can. If you think you'll never need more than a gigabyte of storage, then get double that. You may be sorry later if you don't. Most of the new computers don't come with anything smaller than a 30 GB hard drive anyway; you don't need that much for QuarkXPress files, but if you do Photoshop work, too, that's a pretty good minimum.

Random Access Memory

RAM is good. Put as much into your computer as you possibly can afford. If you're doing serious publishing, chances are you'll want to run QuarkXPress along with several other applications, and probably want 512 MB of RAM or even a gigabyte. If you do a lot of Photoshop work, you'll always wish you have more (I don't recommend people use Photoshop and QuarkXPress on the same system without a minimum of 512 MB, and preferably more like 1 GB). You'll want the extra RAM to move around smoothly when you have those programs open along with much-needed system extensions. The more color work you're doing, the more RAM you should have.

▼ ▼

QuarkXPress and You

Version 6 of QuarkXPress is clearly a pretty impressive package. But don't let it intimidate you. Remember, QuarkXPress is not only a machete, it's a Swiss Army machete. If you want to use it for writing letters home, you can do it. If you want to create glossy four-color magazines, you can do that too. The tool is powerful enough to get the job done, but sometimes—if you're trying to get through that Amazon jungle—you need to wield your machete accurately and efficiently.

Let's look at how it's done.

1

LEARN QUARKXPRESS
IN 30 MINUTES

"Here's a copy of QuarkXPress; our consultant says it's easy to learn, so I'm sure you'll be able to lay out the annual report by Friday. Right?"

If you've ever heard these words, you know the true meaning of the word *panic*. Fortunately, you've come to the right place. This chapter will give you everything you need to know to work with XPress in just 30 minutes. Well . . . maybe not *everything* you need. Obviously there's much more to XPress than I can cover in one short chapter. I've been working with this program for over 15 years and I'm still picking up new techniques. But if you're like most people you need to roll up your sleeves and get started working in XPress as soon as possible. That's what this chapter is for.

I've put together a simple XPress document that you will create yourself, step by step, as you read through the chapter. Working through the project will give you a sense of what QuarkXPress 6 is all about, and will help you understand many of the topics covered in the rest of the book.

The project is a simple one-fold brochure for a mythical product called "Gold Standard" (see Figure 1-1). If it'll help, try to visualize yourself as a designer or production artist working for the Gold Standard company; you've got 30 minutes to build this basic brochure.

Before you start working, you need to get the materials for the brochure: the product illustration, the company logo, and the text. If you have access to the

Figure 1-1

The one-fold brochure
you're going to create

Internet, you can download these materials from the *Real World QuarkXPress* Web site (*www.peachpit.com/blatner/*). There's also a finished version of the brochure for you to open to see if you've followed the steps correctly.

Don't worry if you don't have access to the Web. You can use other materials you have on your computer. For instance, if you've got a picture of your cousin on his vacation, use that instead of the product illustration. Use a picture of your dog instead of the company logo. And use any text file—like a letter from your Mom—for the text. It doesn't matter if you don't replicate the project exactly as shown, just as long as you understand the principles.

▼ ▼

Pages, Views and Guides

In this section of the project you create a new file for the project, make sure the margins are correct, add some guides, add a page, and navigate around your document.

Creating a New File

Before you can begin working, you need to launch QuarkXPress and create a new document.

1. Launch QuarkXPress by double-clicking on the application icon. (See Figure 1-2; see page 44 for information on installing XPress.)

2. When the application has opened (after you see the menus and a couple of palettes), choose Project from the New submenu (under the File menu). The New Project dialog box appears (see Figures 1-3 and 1-4).

Figure 1-2

QuarkXPress at home in its folder

Figure 1-3

Creating a new document

Figure 1-4

The New Project dialog box

Portrait

Landscape

3. As we'll see in Chapter 4, *Building Documents,* each document can contain several layouts. The New Project dialog box lets you name the first layout and determine whether it should be a Print layout or a Web layout. In this case, choose Print from the Layout Type popup menu. I cover Web layouts in Chapter 14, *Going Online with QuarkXPress.*

4. Make sure the document size is set to US Letter. Click on the landscape orientation icon. This will set the dimensions.

> Width: 11 inches
> Height: 8.5 inches

5. Make sure that both the Facing Pages and Automatic Text Box checkboxes are turned off—that is, they don't have an X through them. (For more information about working with Facing Pages and Automatic Text Boxes, see page 248.)

6. You also need to set the margins and columns as follows.

> Top: .5 inch (use the " mark for inches)
> Bottom: .5 inch
> Left: .5 inch
> Right: .5 inch
> Columns: 2
> Gutter Width: 1 inch

7. Click OK. This creates your new XPress document with a single page, margins at .5 inch around the edge of the page, and two columns on the page.

▼ ▼

Tip: Use the Tab Key in Fields. You can jump from one field to the next in any dialog box by pressing the Tab key. For instance, in the New Document dialog box you were just in, you could have pressed Tab to jump to any field you wanted to change. You can go to the previous field by pressing Shift-Tab.

▼ ▼

Working in the Window

Depending on how XPress was used by the last person to use it on your machine, you may need to change some things on the screen.

1. To see everything in your window, choose Fit in Window from the View menu. (This is so important that you should start using its keyboard shortcut: Command-zero or Ctrl-zero.)

2. If you do not see the Tool palette on your screen, choose Show Tools from the Window menu.

3. If you don't see the Measurements palette on your screen, choose Show Measurements from the Window menu.

4. If you don't see the Page Layout palette on your screen, choose Show Page Layout from the Window menu. Your screen should look like the illustration in Figure 1-5.

Figure 1-5
The document window

Tool palette

Pasteboard

Measurements
palette

Margin guides

Page Layout palette

Working with the Tool Palette

Some of the tools (such as the Item tool and Content tool) are always visible in the Tool palette. Other tools (such as the Oval Text Box tool) are hidden, and are visible only if you click on the icon in the Tool palette.

▶ To choose one of the visible tools, click the icon for that tool in the Tool palette (see Figure 1-6). The tool will be highlighted.

▶ To choose one of the hidden tools, press on one of the tool icons with a small triangle in the upper-right corner, and then drag over to the right to choose the tool.

Chapter 3, *Tools of the Trade*, discusses XPress's tools in detail.

Zooming Around

As you're working in XPress, you constantly zoom in and out to see very small details on your page or to look at the page as a whole. Fortunately, XPress provides many different ways to zoom in and out. (See page 82 for all the ways to change the page views.)

Figure 1-6

The Tool palette with the popout tools visible

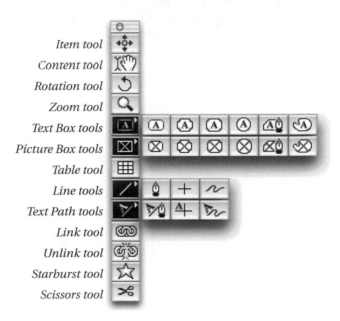

Item tool

Content tool

Rotation tool

Zoom tool

Text Box tools

Picture Box tools

Table tool

Line tools

Text Path tools

Link tool

Unlink tool

Starburst tool

Scissors tool

1. Select the Zoom tool in the Tool palette.

2. Position the Zoom tool cursor over the upper-left corner of the page and click several times. Each click magnifies your view. (If you don't see anything when you zoom in, you may be looking at the middle of the page. Use the scroll bars to adjust the view.)

3. Hold down the Option (or Alt) key. Notice that the Zoom tool cursor changes from a plus sign to a minus sign. Click several times to zoom out from the view of the page.

4. Release the Option (or Alt) key and position the Zoom tool cursor inside the page. Then drag with the Zoom tool to create a small square. When you release the mouse, you zoom in on the area you just marqueed. (This will be more useful when you actually have something on your page!)

5. Double-click on the magnification percentage in the lower-left corner of the window (see Figure 1-7). Enter "80" and then press the Return or Enter key. XPress switches to 80-percent magnification view.

Figure 1-7

The Magnification level box

Adding Pages

Every new QuarkXPress layout opens with one page already in place. Since this brochure will be printed on two sides of the page, you need to add a page to your document. (See page 272 for more information on adding pages to and deleting pages from a document.)

1. In the Page Layout palette, click on the small rectangular page icon at the top, labeled "A-Master A" (see Figure 1-8).

2. Drag the icon down under the first page. Release the mouse when you see the plain rectangle under the page. The second page is automatically created for you right where you drop the icon. (If you drop the new page in the wrong place, just drag it to where you want it in the palette.)

You can also choose Insert from the Page menu to add a page, but it's a good idea to get in the habit of using the Page Layout palette as early as you can.

Figure 1-8

Dragging a master page to create a new page

Drag this down to add a new page

Page-one icon

Adding a new page

Adding Guides

To make it easier for you to lay out the various elements you're going to put on your page, you need to place some guides.

1. Double-click on the page-one icon in the Page Layout palette to make sure you are on that page.

2. You can add guides by pulling them from one of the rulers at either the left or the top of the page. If you can't see the rulers, choose Show Rulers from the View menu. Move your mouse over to the vertical ruler and

press. You should see a little two-headed arrow appear on the ruler (see Figure 1-9).

Figure 1-9
Pulling a guide out
from the ruler

3. Drag the two-headed arrow out from the ruler and let go when the guideline is at the 5.5-inch mark on the top ruler (watch the guide line against the ruler). A colored guide appears where you let go. You can also position guides by watching the Measurements palette.

4. Because you need a guide on page two, double-click on page two in the Page Layout, and repeat step 3. (See page 254 to see how master pages can automate this process.)

▼ ▼

Tip: Working with Guides. To reposition a guide, just move your cursor over the guide, click, and drag the guide to the new position. In general, you should have the Item tool selected to do this. To delete a guide, drag it outside the document window (any side will do). You can make your guides invisible by choosing Hide Guides from the View menu (then choose Show Guides to turn them back on). For more information about guides, see page 204.

▼ ▼

Tip: What Page Are You on? Quark has a quirk when it comes to showing what page you are on. When you look at Figure 1-10, at first it seems like you're looking at page one. After all, that's what the page number in the lower-left corner says. However, notice the thin gray line at the top of the window? That means the previous page's pasteboard is visible. *That* is page one. The page you're looking at is page two.

▼ ▼

Saving

You've done enough work that you need to save your file.

1. Choose Save or Save As from the File menu (they're both the same for new, unsaved documents). QuarkXPress displays the Save As dialog box (see Figure 1-11).

Figure 1-10

Page numbering

Page one

Page two

Figure 1-11

Save As dialog box

The document gets saved in this folder.

2. Name your file *Gold Brochure*, and choose a folder to put your file in—not in the QuarkXPress folder!

3. Leave the Type as Project and the Version set to 6.0. (For more information on alternate settings, see page 59.)

4. If you turn on the Include Preview checkbox, you'll see a thumbnail preview of page one each time you open the document.

For the rest of this project, you should continue to save your work at whatever intervals you feel comfortable with.

▼ ▼

Text and Text Formatting

In order to put text on your page, you must first create a text box. In this section of the project you'll create several text boxes, add text to those boxes by typing as well as importing text from a file on disk, and you'll link the text boxes together so that the text flows from one box to another. Finally, you'll format the text using various fonts, sizes, and so on.

Drawing a Text Box

When you launch a word processing program, you can start typing right away. QuarkXPress is different: it requires you to put your text into text boxes. You create a text box using one of the Text Box tools.

1. Double-click on the first page in the Page Layout palette to make sure you are working on that page.

2. Select the Rectangle Text Box tool in the Tool palette (that's the one with square corners and the little "A" in it).

3. Move the cursor over to the right side of the page. Your cursor should change to a plus sign. Press and drag like in Figure 1-12. Don't worry yet about the precise size or location of the box.

4. Release the mouse when you've completed the drag. You should see a box with no text—just a blinking insertion point. If there isn't a blink-

Figure 1-12

Dragging to
create a text box

Press here

Path of drag

Release here

ing cursor, then you'll need to select the Content tool in the Tool palette (the one with the hand icon).

▼ ▼

Tip: Item Tool Versus Content Tool. One of the most frustrating parts about learning QuarkXPress is remembering the difference between the Item and the Content tool. The Item tool is the first tool in the Tool palette (the technical term is "the pointy thingy"). You use it to manipulate items on your page. For instance, to move the whole text box to a different location, you'd use the Item tool. Also, to delete an item, you can press Delete when you have the Item tool selected (or choose Delete from the Item menu).

The second tool in the tool palette is the Content tool, which lets you change the *content* of the page items. For instance, if you don't see a blinking insertion point in your new text box, it's probably because you have the Item tool selected. In order to type in the text box, you've got to have the Content tool selected.

Note that when you make a box (like the text box you just made), XPress almost always automatically chooses the Item or Content tool for you, depending on which one you used last.

▼ ▼

Modifying a Text Box

You can change the size of a text box at any time by dragging any of the eight handles located on the corners and sides of the text box. (For more tips on working with text boxes, see page 167.)

1. Move your cursor over to the small black handle at the top side of the text box (it doesn't matter what tool you have selected). Your cursor should change to a "finger" (see Figure 1-13). This indicates that you can resize the box.

2. Click and drag with the finger cursor, moving the handle so that the top of the box sits at the 2-inch mark. (You can get a precise measurement

Figure 1-13
The finger cursor

by watching either the guideline in the vertical ruler or the Y coordinate in the Measurements palette.)

3. Next, position the left side of the box at the 6-inch mark of the horizontal ruler. Note that the edge of the box will probably snap to the column guide you placed there earlier.

4. Position the right side of the box at the 10.5-inch mark (this should snap to the right margin guide).

5. Position the bottom side of the box at the 6.5-inch mark of the vertical ruler.

Typing Text

Now that you have a text box on your page, you can start typing in the box (remember that you need to select the Content tool first).

1. So that you can better see the text you're about to type, choose Actual Size from the View menu. (If you still have difficulty reading the text, try zooming in closer.)

2. Type the words, "Introducing a whole new standard in home medicine" into the box. (Don't type the quotation marks.)

3. If you make an error typing, you can use any of the normal text-editing techniques to modify the text (like using the Delete or Backspace key, double-clicking on a word to select it, and so on).

4. When you're done, leave the insertion point blinking inside the text box. Do not click outside the text box to deselect the box. (We're not done with that text yet!)

Formatting Text

The text you have created comes in with the default formatting from the Normal style sheet, which is almost never what you really want. However, you can change the formatting of your text at any time.

1. To select all the text in the text box, choose Select All from the Edit menu (or type Command-A or Ctrl-A). This highlights all the text in the text box (text in a text box is called a *story*, even if there's only one little paragraph like this).

2. You can choose a font from one of two places: the Style menu or the Measurements palette. Let's use the second choice: click on the little

Figure 1-14

Text formatting in the
Measurements palette

Alignment icons: Flush left, Centered,   *Font*   *Point size*
Flush right, Justified, and Force justified

triangle next to the font name in the Measurements palette (see Figure 1-14). A list of the available typefaces appears.

3. Choose any serif typeface (such as Garamond, Times, or Palatino).

4. The point size popup menu in the Measurements palette displays a list of point sizes, but the one we want is not included. You can enter the point size you want by selecting the point size and typing in the number "50". Then press Return or Enter.

5. Finally, click on the Centered alignment icon in the Measurements palette. The text centers itself within the text box.

Importing Text

While the text on the first page is short, most of the time you'll find yourself working with text that is saved in a word-processing file. (For more on how to import text files, see page 290.)

1. Go to the second page and draw a 2-inch-tall text box that extends from the left margin to the right margin of the page. Use the Item tool to move the text box so that the top of the box sits at the top margin of the page.

2. With the insertion point blinking in the text box (switch to the Content tool), choose Get Text from the File menu. The Get Text dialog box appears (see Figure 1-15).

3. Use the dialog box to find the file *Brochure.txt* from the files you downloaded. (If you weren't able to download that file, use some other text file that is about two pages in length.)

4. Click OK to import the text. (If you receive a message that you're missing fonts, don't worry about it—you'll be changing the typeface for the text anyway.)

Figure 1-15

Get Text dialog box

Linking Text Boxes

The text you have imported is too long to fit in the little text box you've made. You can always tell when there's more text than can fit in a box by the red overset mark at the lower-right corner of the text box (see Figure 1-16). Rather than change the size of the box to fit the text, we're going to build another bigger text box, and then link the two text boxes together so that the text flows from one into the other.

1. Draw a second text box on the left side of page two. This text box should extend from the left margin to the 5-inch column guideline. The box should start at the 4-inch mark on the vertical ruler and stop at the bottom margin.

2. While this text box is still selected, choose Duplicate from the Item menu. This creates a copy of the text box and offsets it slightly. Use the Item tool to position this duplicate on the right side of page two (place it so that it mirrors the left side of the page).

Figure 1-16

Overset mark

The overset mark tells us there's more text than can fit in the box.

3. Choose the Link tool in the Tool palette (the one that looks like a little chain of doughnuts). Click on the first box on the page (the wide one at the top) with the Link tool. The outside edge of the box begins to animate, to tell you that it's selected.

4. Then click on the empty text box on the left side of the page. An arrow flashes momentarily between the two boxes, and the continuation of the text appears in the second box (see Figure 1-17).

5. Choose the Link tool again; click first on the text box on the left side of the page and then on the empty box on the right side of the page. The text is now linked from the top box to the left box and then to the right box.

Figure 1-17
Linking text boxes

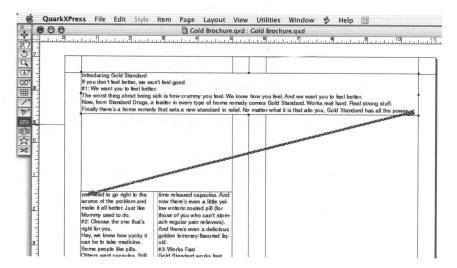

▼ ▼

Tip: Rules for Linking Text. Linked text boxes don't have to be on the same page. After you click once with the Link tool, you can scroll to another page and click on the next text box. You cannot link two boxes that each have text in them; you can only link if one box is empty. For more information on working with linked text boxes, see page 202.

▼ ▼

Multicolumn Text Boxes

Text boxes are one way to divide text into different areas on the page. However, you can also have multiple columns within a text box. QuarkXPress gives you two different ways to set columns within a text box (we're going to use both methods here).

1. Click on the text box on the lower-left side of the page (you can use either the Item tool or the Content tool for this).

2. In the Measurements palette, change the number in the "Cols" field from 1 to 2 (see Figure 1-18). Press the Return or Enter key to apply the change. Two columns appear in the text box.

3. Click on the text box on the lower-right side of the page. Choose Modify from the Item menu and then click on the Text tab (see Figure 1-19).

4. Change the Columns field to 2 and then click the Apply button to see the change (you can move the dialog box out of the way if it's covering the text box). Now press OK to apply the change.

Don't worry if your text doesn't fill all the columns right now (or if there's another overset mark). You've still got more formatting to do.

▼ ▼

Tip: Setting the Gutter Width. One of the advantages of choosing Modify from the Item menu when setting your columns is that you can change the gutter width, which is the amount of space between the two columns of the text box.

▼ ▼

Figure 1-18
Columns setting in the
Measurements palette

Number of columns

Figure 1-19
Item Modify Text
dialog box

Character Formatting

The text you have imported needs to be formatted. While you could use the formatting options in the Measurements palette, let's take a look at a few other ways you can format text.

1. First, make sure you have the Content tool selected, and then press Command-A (or Ctrl-A) to select all the text in the story. Change the typeface to the same font you used on page one.

2. To deselect all the text, click once somewhere inside the text box. Now, to select just the first line of text, place your cursor over that line of text and click three times. This should select the words "Introducing Gold Standard." (Note that clicking once places the text cursor, twice selects a word, three times selects a line, and four times selects a paragraph.)

3. Choose Character from the Style menu to open the Character Attributes dialog box. This is where you can format and apply all the attributes for the selected line of text (see Figure 1-20).

4. Click the All Caps box and then click the Apply button to see the change.

5. Use the Size field to enter a size that's about 42 points. Click the Apply button. If your text extends past one line, reduce the point size until the selected line of text fills the width of a single line. When you're done, click OK.

6. Triple-click on the second line: "If you don't feel better, we won't feel good." Use the Character Attributes dialog box again to set the point size to 24.

7. Use the finger cursor to move the bottom edge of the top text box up, changing the height so that only these two lines are in the box. This

Figure 1-20
Character Attributes
dialog box

forces the text down to the other boxes. You can make the other boxes slightly larger to fill the extra space, if you want.

8. Select the next line: "#1: We want you to feel better" (you can quadruple-click to select it all quickly). Click on the large K icon toward the right side of the Measurements palette; this changes the line to all caps. Now set the point size to 13.

9. Select each of the numbered lines on the page and change them so they match the text in step 8.

▼ ▼

Tip: Style Sheets Stop Drudgery. By the time you finish formatting each of the numbered paragraphs in the text, you're probably feeling like there's got to be a better way to format text. There is. QuarkXPress has a feature called Style Sheets that makes formatting text much faster. For more information about style sheets, see page 423.

▼ ▼

Leading

Each character in a line of text sits on a *baseline*. Leading (pronounced *ledding*) is the amount of space from one baseline to the next. The greater the leading, the more space between the lines. The text in your project currently has an "auto" amount of leading applied. However, for reasons I describe in Chapter 6, *Type and Typography*, you should usually avoid auto leading. Instead, here's how you can apply an absolute leading value.

1. Click so that your insertion point is blinking in the first line of the second text box (the one on the left).

2. Scroll over to the lower-right corner of the page and Shift-click on the last line of the text box. This selects the text from the first line to the last.

3. Click on either the increase- or decrease-leading arrow in the Measurements palette until the amount reads 14. This tightens up the space between the lines. If no number appears in the leading field of the palette, you can also simply replace the leading value with the number 14 (see Figure 1-21).

▼ ▼

Tip: Paragraph Attributes Don't Need Selections. Character attributes in QuarkXPress are those typographic attributes that you can apply to a single character—things like font, size, color, baseline shift, and so on. On the other hand, paragraph attributes—like leading, indents, and so on—can only be applied to a whole paragraph. The upshot is that if you want to change a para-

Figure 1-21
Leading arrows

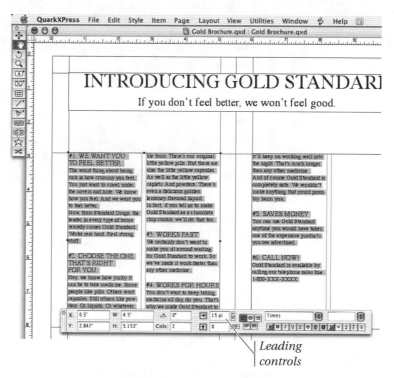

Leading controls

graph attribute, you can select just part of the paragraph or even just have your insertion point blinking inside the paragraph. XPress is smart enough to know that the change applies to the whole paragraph.

▼ ▼

Paragraph Formatting

There are other paragraph attributes besides leading. While you can find some of the other paragraph attributes in the Measurements palette, you can find them *all* in the Paragraph Attributes dialog box (select Formats from the Style menu).

1. Select the subhead labeled #2, and then choose Formats from the Style menu (see Figure 1-22).

2. Change the amount in the Space Before field to .25 inches. Then click OK to see the change.

3. Do the same for all the other numbered subheads, too.

▼ ▼

Tip: When No Space Is Added. If a paragraph is at the top of a column when you add Space Before, XPress won't add any space. If the paragraph is at the bottom of a column, XPress won't add any space after. It turns out that this

Figure 1-22

Paragraph Attributes
dialog box

behavior is normal and almost always what you really want, but it confuses beginners, so I wanted to point it out.

▼ ▼

New-Line Character

Some of the lines in your text may break in places where you don't want them to. While you could hit the Return or Enter key to break the line, that would split the paragraph into two, which may cause formatting problems. Instead, try using a new-line character, which lets you break a line without creating a new paragraph.

1. Choose Show Invisibles from the View menu. This lets you see invisible formatting characters such as the new-line character, spaces, tabs, carriage returns, and so on. (See Figure 1-23; for more information on other special characters, see page 391.)

2. Click to place the text cursor where you want to break the line. For this exercise, go to the first page and place the text cursor just to the left of a word that is hyphenated (if there aren't any hyphenated words on the first page, find one on the second page).

Figure 1-23

The new-line character

#1: WE WANT YOU ↵
TO FEEL BETTER.¶
The worst thing about being
sick is how crummy you feel.

When Show Invisibles is on, you can see characters like the new-line character and returns.

3. Hold down the Shift key and press Return—*not* the Enter key. (Computers that run Microsoft Windows often don't have a Return key; in this case, use the Enter key that is *not* part of the numeric keypad; that key is used for something else in XPress.)

Graphics, Colors, Frames, and Lines

Congratulations! You've almost completed your project. In this section you'll create picture boxes that hold the graphics for the brochure, import images, size them, and position them on your page. You will also add some color to the document, as well as special frames and lines.

Drawing a Picture Box

Just as text boxes hold text, picture boxes hold pictures. So before you import a graphic, you need to create a picture box to hold that image.

1. Click on the Rectangle Picture Box tool in the Tool palette.

2. Move your cursor to the middle of page two and draw a box approximately 2.5 inches tall and wide. (Don't worry about getting it exact; you'll change the size later.)

3. When you release the cursor you should see an × through the box, indicating that you have created a picture box (see Figure 1-24).

Figure 1-24
An empty picture box

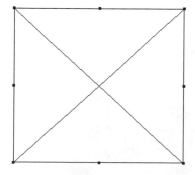

4. If you do not see an ×, you need to choose Show Guides from the View menu. If you still don't see an ×, then you haven't created a picture box. Choose Delete from the Item menu and make sure you choose the Rectangle Picture Box tool; then redraw the picture box.

Importing Graphics

Once you've created a picture box, you can bring a graphic into it. This graphic can come from an illustration program like Adobe Illustrator or Macromedia FreeHand. Or it can come from an image-editing program like Adobe Photoshop. (For more information on working with graphics from other programs, see page 516.)

1. With the picture box still selected, choose Get Picture from the File menu. Note that in earlier versions of XPress you had to have the Content tool selected when importing a graphic; now you can use either the Content or the Item tool.

2. When the Get Picture dialog box appears, find the file called *Gold Package.tif* from the files you downloaded. If you don't have those files, find any TIFF or EPS graphic on your hard drive. Then click Open to import the image.

3. Move your cursor into the middle of the picture box and notice that the cursor changes into a flat hand. When you click and drag the mouse with this cursor, you can move the graphic around within the picture box (see Figure 1-25).

4. The picture box is currently too small to show the entire package. Drag out the sides of the picture box until the box is big enough for the graphic (if you're using the Gold Standard image, the box should be about 4 inches wide, and 3.5 inches tall).

5. Positioning the graphic in the middle of the box using the hand cursor is slow and not very accurate. Instead, press Command-Shift-M (or Ctrl-Shift-M) to center the graphic in the picture box. (That's M for "Mathematical Middle"!)

Figure 1-25

The hand cursor repositions graphics within the picture box

6. Now that you've got the graphic in the right-size box, you may need to move the box itself around. Switch to the Item tool (the top tool in the Tool palette) and move your cursor over the picture box. A four-headed arrow appears with which you can drag the box around. Move the picture box so that its top is at the 2.75-inch mark. Make sure the graphic is at least partly over the text.

7. Position the center of the box on the 5.5-inch guide. (You can accomplish this visually by aligning the center handles of the box on the guide.)

▼ ▼

Tip: Wait Before You Drag. As you resize or move objects, wait a moment after you press the mouse button down and before you start to drag. This will let you see the text dynamically reflow around objects as you move them. This lets you know, as you move the objects, how your layout will look. (If you have friends or coworkers who started with earlier versions, they may not know about this feature. You can amaze them with your expertise.)

▼ ▼

Runaround

If you could transport a group of typesetters through time from twenty years ago to today, the thing that would astound them most would probably be the ease with which we can wrap text around objects on a page. Back in those days, to get text to run around the shape of a picture took hours of inserting special codes at the end of every line. With QuarkXPress you can do it in a matter of seconds. (For more details on text runaround and clipping paths, see page 564 and 586.)

Whenever you place an object on top of a text box, that object can force the text below to run around it (also known as "text wrap"). In this case, the text is wrapping around the picture box, but you could just as easily wrap text around another text box or a line.

1. Select the picture box and choose Runaround from the Item menu (or press Command-T or Ctrl-T). The Modify dialog box appears with the Runaround tab selected (see Figure 1-26).

2. Currently, the runaround is set to Item (this is the default value), which means that the underlying text runs around the edges of the picture box itself. Choose Auto Image from the Type popup menu. This tells XPress to automatically find the outside edge of the picture and use it for the runaround.

Figure 1-26

The Runaround
tab of the Modify
dialog box

3. Press the Apply button (not the OK button) to see what this does to
    your layout. Notice that the text is too close to the image.

4. Change the Outset amount to 14 points. Then press the Apply button
    again. The text moves away with a 14-point gap between it and the
    graphic. Click the OK button to apply the runaround.

Resizing and Rotating Graphics

Because this brochure is a mailing piece for the Standard Drug company, we
need to add a logo on the left side of page one, and make sure the logo is the
proper size and orientation.

1. Here's a new way to move between pages in your document: click on
    the small page popup menu at the bottom left of your document win-
    dow. A small page list will appear (see Figure 1-27). Choose page one
    from the list.

2. Draw a picture box on the left side of page one. Make the dimensions
    of the picture box about 1.25 inches wide by about 1 inch tall. (You can
    watch the Measurements palette as you draw the box, to get the proper
    size.)

3. Use Get Picture (from the File menu) to import the *Logo.eps* file. Again:
    If you don't have this graphic, you can use another picture.

4. This logo is way too big for the picture box. However, rather than
    change the size of the box, let's change the size of the image. Change

Figure 1-27
The page popup list

the X% field in the Measurements palette from 100 to 50 (you don't have to type the percent character). Press the Tab key to jump to the Y% field and change the number there to 50, too. Press the Return or Enter key to apply these values.

5. The logo needs to be rotated. Double-click on the angle field in the Measurements palette and change 0° to -90 (you don't have to type the degree symbol; see Figure 1-28). Press the Return or Enter key to apply the value. (If XPress tells you that "the item cannot be positioned off the pasteboard," set the rotation back to zero, move the item farther down on the page, and then try to rotate it back to 90 degrees again.)

6. Use the Item tool to position the picture box in the corner under the top margin and next to the guide at the 5-inch mark.

Figure 1-28
The Picture Box
Measurements palette

Box rotation   *Horizontal and vertical scaling*

Adding Color

Right now the only color on page two comes from the graphic. Let's add some more color to that page by setting the background color of the top text box.

1. Move to page two and click on the top text box. Choose Modify from the Item menu (or press Command-M or Ctrl-M). The Modify dialog box appears (see Figure 1-29).

2. Choose Yellow from the Box Color popup menu. (For more information on creating your own colors, see page 625.)

3. A solid-yellow text box is a bit too bright for this piece, so select 50 percent from the Shade popup menu.

4. Click the Apply button to see how the color is added to the background of the text box. (Feel free to move the dialog box out of the way to see the page, but don't click OK yet.)

Figure 1-29

The Modify
dialog box

Tip: Use the Colors Palette. The Colors palette allows you to apply colors without using the Modify dialog box or menus. Choose Show Colors from the Window menu to open the palette. For more information, see page 640.

Adding a Frame

The text box at the top of page two (the same one you're working on now) needs a frame around it. Fortunately, it is very easy to add a frame to a text or picture box. (For more on working with frames, see page 210.)

1. While you're still in the Modify dialog box, click on the Frame tab (see Figure 1-30).

2. Change the amount in the Width field to 8 points and click the Apply button. A solid black frame appears around the text box.

3. Press on the Style popup menu and choose the style called Thin-Thick, then click the Apply button again. The frame changes to a double-line.

4. In the area of the dialog box labeled Gap, change the color to Yellow and set the shade to 50 percent. This helps the frame appear to be part of the text box. Click OK to apply all the changes.

Note that changing the frame changes the amount of space inside the text box, which may cause text reflow. If you need to, adjust the size of the text box or the size of the text so that the text fits correctly.

Figure 1-30

The Frame dialog box

Drawing Lines

QuarkXPress has two types of elements: boxes and lines. Lines can be decorative (like arrows, dashed patterns, and so on) or paths that hold text. For your project, you'll create two basic lines as graphic elements at the top and bottom of page one.

1. Switch to page one and select the Orthogonal Line tool in the Tool palette (that's the one that looks like a plus sign). "Orthogonal" just means that you can only draw horizontal or vertical lines. The tool next to it lets you draw diagonal lines, too.

2. Drag the Orthogonal Line tool across the top margin of page one, starting from the 6-inch guide and ending at the right margin. When you let go, you may not be able to see the line because the guide is sitting on top of it.

3. In the Measurements palette, choose "8 pt" from the Line width pop-up menu (see Figure 1-31). The line becomes thicker.

4. Choose the style called Thin-Thick from the Line style popup menu in the Measurements palette.

5. Duplicate the line by choosing Duplicate from the Item menu (or pressing Command-D or Ctrl-D).

Figure 1-31
The Measurements
palette for lines

Line width   *Line style*

6. Move the line down to the bottom margin so that it aligns with the same margins as the line at the top (get in the habit of switching to the Item tool to move objects on your page).

7. Change the line style to Thick-Thin in the Measurements palette (see Figure 1-32).

Figure 1-32
The final page, with lines

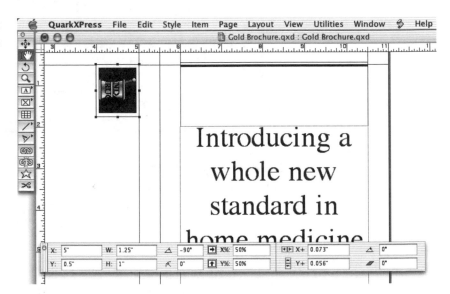

Printing

That's it! You've finished the brochure. Now all you need to worry about is printing it. There are two ways to print a QuarkXPress document. You could print the file directly to a desktop printer connected to your computer. Or you could send the file to a print shop or service bureau for special (high-resolution) output.

Printing on Your Desktop

QuarkXPress is designed to be used with a PostScript printer. If your printer cannot print PostScript, you may obtain unexpected results (that's a diplomatic way to say that your printed page might appear quite unlike what you see on screen). Nonetheless, whatever printer you have, the steps to print a document are very much the same. (See page 671 for more information on printing.)

1. Select Print from the File menu. The Print dialog box appears (see Figure 1-33).

2. Choose the number of copies (of each page) you want to print in the Copies field.

3. If you only wanted to print page one, you could enter the number "1" in the Pages field. However, because you want to print both pages of this document, leave the field set to All.

4. Click on the Setup tab. You should always check the Setup tab to make sure it's properly configured. For instance, because your document is wider than it is tall, you should select the Landscape ("sideways") orientation icon. Also, make sure you have the proper printer selected on the Printer Description popup menu. Most of the problems people have when printing are due to selecting the wrong printer here. If your particular printer doesn't appear, choose one that is similar to it, or choose Generic B&W from the list.

5. Press the Print button to start printing.

Figure 1-33
The Print dialog box
(It looks a bit different on
Windows, but it's basically
the same)

Sending to a Service Bureau

Desktop printers do not have the high-quality resolution necessary for professional printing. If you are going to have your file printed by a commercial print shop, you need to send your QuarkXPress document to the print shop or service bureau. (Some service bureaus require that you export an Acrobat PDF file; if that's the case, see page 797.) However, there are a few steps you can take to make sure that the file will print properly when it gets there.

1. Choose Usage from the Utilities menu and then select the Fonts tab. This shows you a list of the fonts that you have used in the document (see Figure 1-34).

Figure 1-34

The fonts used in the document

2. Make a note of those fonts. Your service bureau will want to know that information.

3. Select the Pictures tab of the same dialog box. This displays a list of the graphics used in the document (see Figure 1-35).

Figure 1-35

The pictures used in the document

4. Make sure the Status column shows OK for each picture. If it shows Missing or Modified, you need to update the pictures in the file. (See page 529 for more information about this dialog box.)

5. Finally, when you send the file to the service bureau (on disk or via e-mail or whatever), make sure you send both the QuarkXPress file *and*

the pictures used in the document. If you do not send the pictures, your service bureau will not be able to print your file properly. That's because XPress doesn't actually import pictures into your file; it only brings in a low-resolution preview image and creates a *link* to the high-resolution image on your disk.

▼ ▼

How to Really Sound Like You Know What You're Talking About

Well, it only took 30 minutes, but you've already learned most of what you need to build basic pages in QuarkXPress. However, just in case you've got a job interview tomorrow, you may need a few buzz words to throw around. If you have the list below and the information in the rest of the book tucked away, you should become a QuarkXPert in no time!

XTensions. XTensions are software that add functionality to QuarkXPress (they sit in the XTension folder, inside the QuarkXPress folder). Some XTensions come with QuarkXPress, some are free, and others are bought from third-party developers (see page 841). For instance, there's no way to lock a guideline in XPress, but there's a free XTension that you can download from the Internet that lets you do it. Note that XTensions that worked with earlier versions of XPress do not work with version 6.

Bézier tools. Bézier (pronounced "beh-zi-ay") tools let you create boxes and lines with curves, just like in Adobe Illustrator and in Macromedia FreeHand (see page 132).

Book. You can create a special document called a "Book" that appears on screen like a palette; you can then add XPress documents to the Book. The idea is that documents in a Book should act like a single publication, like chapters of a real book (see page 464).

Libraries. Another kind of special document is the library, which, when opened, also appears on screen like a palette. You can store page items in libraries that you'll use multiple times. For example, you could put a picture box that contains your company's logo in a library; then when you want to use that item, you can simply drag the picture box out onto your page (for more info, see page 235).

Master pages. Objects that you want to put on multiple pages in your document can be put on a master page. Your document pages are each linked to a master page, so if you put a red box on the Master Page A, every document page that is linked to that master page will have a red box on it, too (see page 254). A better example is automatic page numbering; you can put an automatic page number on a master page, and the proper page number appears on every page, so you don't have to put it there manually (see page 278).

Trapping. Trapping is a procedure that compensates for the misregistration that can happen when printing multiple colors (see page 647).

PPDs. PostScript Printer Description files (PPDs) are files that include information about printers; QuarkXPress uses these when it prints.

Kerning and tracking. Kerning changes the space between two letters; tracking lets you change the space between several characters in a row (this is more properly called "range kerning"; see page 324).

H&Js. Hyphenation and Justification (H&Js) settings are used to control the look of type as well as to turn automatic hyphenation on and off (see page 361).

Clipping. A clipping path is for cutting out parts of a picture you don't want to appear on your page. For instance, if you had a picture of your friend Bob standing on a beach, you could draw a clipping path around him, and the beach surroundings would disappear (see page 564).

2

QuarkXPress Basics

Whoever thought that something called a "gooey" would ever be so important to the way we use a computer? While most of the world clutched their crib sheets to remember "how-to" keyboard codes for saving a document, moving to the end of a line, or drawing a box, a few visionary researchers came upon a simple idea: a *graphical user interface*, or GUI ("gooey"). "Why not," these researchers asked, "make using a computer more intuitive?" These researchers developed the underpinnings of the Macintosh GUI, which in turn laid the groundwork for desktop publishing to take off.

The basics of the Macintosh and Windows GUIs are simple: create an environment in which somebody can get the most out of a computer without having to remember too much, or even think too much in order to get the job done. The GUI comes between the person using the computer and the computer itself. For example, when you want to move a file from one disk to another, you click on it and drag it across the screen. The GUI handles all the internal computer stuff for you.

When you work with QuarkXPress, you work with the Macintosh or Windows GUI. You don't have to remember long arcane codes or read a computer language, or even understand what's going on behind the scenes. Certainly, the more you know about how computers work, the better you can use them. However, this book is not meant for programmers. This book, like QuarkXPress, is—to steal a line from Apple—"for the rest of us."

I hear mumbling in the halls: "Who cares about gooey users and interfaces? I just want to use the program." Well, hold on; you can't tell the players without a program, and you can't effectively use QuarkXPress without understanding how it relates to you. So I'll play emcee and introduce the players: the members of the QuarkXPress interface.

▼ ▼

First Steps in Quarking

I'm going to start with a quick discussion of installing and upgrading QuarkXPress. In versions 3 and 4 of XPress, the upgrader was a completely different package than the installer; with XPress 5, everyone got an installer. Now XPress 6 returns to the good ol' days, and you'll receive either an upgrader or an installer.

If you're like me, you bypass the manual entirely and just start shoving disks into the computer to see what there is to see. You'll find that all the peripheral files for the program are located intact on the CD-ROM, while the program itself is compressed. The installer is the only thing that can piece together and decompress the application onto your hard drive. But if you want to copy the other filters, XTensions, or files over by hand later, you can do that, too. (I just let the installer do it for me; it's much easier and it knows where all the proper files are.)

Remember to keep your serial number and validation code nearby when installing it, and don't throw these away. If you ever need to reinstall the software (I have to about once every six months or so, when weird things start popping up), you'll need this information.

▼ ▼

Tip: Starting Over from Scratch. If something goes horribly wrong when you're installing your copy of QuarkXPress, and you need to cancel the procedure in the middle (or your machine crashes, effectively cancelling it for you), then I strongly suggest that you throw away all the XPress files on your hard disk and just start over from scratch. It's not a good idea to leave half-baked copies of the program lying about on your computer.

▼ ▼

Tip: Starting Clean. It's a good idea to remove all previous versions of QuarkXPress from your Windows machine before installing version 6. Technically, you can have more than one on your hard drive, but if you later use the built-in Windows Add/Remove Programs utility to de-install any of the versions of XPress, it may get confused and delete files that are also being used for the other version. I simultaneously run multiple versions of XPress on my Macintosh all the time, though.

▼ ▼

Patchers. Instead of releasing a full new update of the program, the folks at Quark sometimes just release a patcher. For example, version 4.0 was a little buggy (okay, so it was *really* buggy), but Quark quickly released a patcher for it that updated it to version 4.01, and then another that updated to 4.02, and so on. By the time you read this, Quark will almost certainly have released "micro-updates" for version 6 that fix bugs or add small features. It's worth checking with Quark every now and again (*www.quark.com*).

Quark License Administrator. For 10 years Quark has promised companies with heaps o' copies of XPress a network administration program to help manage them all. Finally, they've delivered with the Quark License Administrator. If you have five or more copies of XPress on your network, you should probably take a look at getting a site license so that you can use this tool. The details are outside the scope of this book, but one thing is important: Make sure you install the administration software before installing your copies of QuarkXPress.

Other Files

When the installer is done doing its thing, you'll find a slew of files on your hard disk. These include several files for getting text from word processors, a dictionary, and several other files that help XPress do its business. Figure 2-1 shows a folder containing QuarkXPress and its application files.

Most of the files are in the QuarkXPress program folder, though XPress does install some files (including its Preferences files) elsewhere on your system. If you need to find those files, use the operating system's Find feature to search for the word "Quark".

Required Components. There are a dozen or so folders inside the QuarkXPress folder, including Color (which holds all the color libraries; more on that in Chapter 12, *Color*), Documents (which consists of the User Guide and other documentation in Acrobat PDF format), and Help (in which the thousands of files for Quark's Help system live). The files inside the Required Components folder are actually parts of QuarkXPress itself; they're features like the Table tool and the ability to import JPEG files. They're so important that the program won't run without them present.

Figure 2-1
Standard
QuarkXPress
folders

Fortunately, you never have to worry about these files. Just leave them alone and forget they're even there. The reason Quark put them there was that it makes updating those features much easier; if, for example, they rewrite the Layers palette to be cooler, they can easily write an update program that replaces the one inside your folder with the new version.

▼ ▼

Tip: No Allocating RAM to QuarkXPress. On the Macintosh, in operating systems 9.2 and earlier, programs had to ask the system for a specific amount of RAM (memory) when they first launched. However, OS X manages RAM dynamically, adjusting the amount of RAM each program needs on the fly. The good news is that you no longer need to increase the RAM allocation to QuarkXPress 6. The bad news is that XPress 6 wants much more RAM than version 4 or 5 did—where XPress 5 could get by with 32 Mb, and XPress 4 was happy in 10 or 12 Mb, you probably want a minimum of 128 Mb of RAM in your computer to handle XPress 6. I personally wouldn't use it on a machine that had less than 256 Mb, and 512 Mb is preferable. Good thing RAM is cheap!

▼ ▼

Tip: Turnkey QuarkXPress. You can get XPress to start automatically whenever you start up your computer. On the Macintosh, add QuarkXPress to the list in the Login Items panel of the System Preferences application. In Windows, you can put a blank document or a shortcut to QuarkXPress in the Startup folder (it's inside the Programs folder, in the Start Menu folder, in the Windows folder).

▼ ▼

Know Thy Program

Before I go any further into the wild world of QuarkXPress, I think it's necessary to take a quick look at four parts of the program: the Environment dialog box, the XPress Preferences file, XTensions, and keyboard shortcuts. The first can help you figure out where you are; the second helps XPress remember where it is. The third, XTensions, let you extend the functionality of the program. And the fourth is all about making you super-efficient.

About That About Box

There are times when it's helpful to know the state of your Mac or PC. One of those times is when you're on the telephone with Quark technical support. Another is when you're troubleshooting a weird problem yourself. QuarkXPress can tell you about itself and its environment via the Environment dialog box (see Figure 2-2). You can get to this dialog box in several ways.

▶ ABOUT QUARKXPRESS. On the Macintosh, hold down the Option key and choose About QuarkXPress from the Application menu (that's the one labelled "QuarkXPress"). In Windows, hold down the Alt key and choose About QuarkXPress from the Help menu.

▶ HELP. If you have an extended keyboard on your Macintosh, you can press Option-Help. (The Help key is up near the Delete and Page Up keys.)

▶ LAPTOP KEYSTROKES. If you work on a Macintosh laptop, try Command-Option-Control-E.

The Environment dialog box tells you familiar information about your system and your version of QuarkXPress. It also displays a list of XTensions that you have currently running, and if you click on one, you'll see the XTension's serial number (if it has one; most don't). Lastly, try clicking on the User Reg. Info button at the bottom of the dialog box. This button should open a new XPress document and fill a text box with all the information that the software sent to Quark when you registered your product. I find this interesting, but not particularly helpful.

Figure 2-2
QuarkXPress
Environment
dialog box

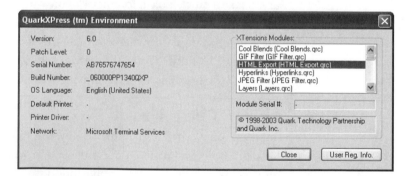

XPress Preferences

Most programs are accompanied by a preferences file in which they store various default settings, and QuarkXPress is no different—though it is a little different than most applications, in that it has 18 different preference files. The basic XPress Preferences file remembers almost everything, from where you last placed the palettes on-screen to whether you like your measurements displayed in picas or inches. Most of the settings it remembers are controls that you can set in the various preferences dialog boxes (I'll discuss these in "Changing Defaults," later in this chapter). Other settings it remembers reflect mysterious internal machinations and aren't worth worrying about.

In earlier versions of XPress, there was only one preferences file and it was stored loose in the QuarkXPress folder. Now, there are 18 preferences files, and they're all stored in the Preferences folder. (In Mac OS X, the Preferences folder is in the Library folder, which is in the user folder. In Windows, these files live in the Quark folder, inside the Application Data folder, which is a hidden folder inside the Documents and Settings directory.) On the Mac, all XPress preference files have the .prf file name extension.

Troubleshooting. One thing you should be aware of, however, is that the XPress Preferences file can become corrupt. It's not common, but it does happen; and when it does, XPress may start acting strangely. It's hard to say what "strangely" means, but I've seen menus appear in the wrong place, dialog boxes display garbled text, and so on. When strange stuff like this appears, here's what I do.

1. Quit QuarkXPress and relaunch it. Often that clears things up.

2. If it doesn't make things better, quit again and drag the QuarkXPress program icon, the Required Components folder, and the library file (OmniCore.Mach-O.r.dylib) into another folder or out onto the desktop and launch the program from there.

3. From here, XPress can't find the XPress Preferences file or its XTensions, so it creates a new, fresh XPress Preferences folder.

4. If the problem persists, then it probably has something to do with the operating system, a font, a picture, or the file itself. However, if the problem goes away, it almost certainly has something to do with one of the prefrences files or an XTension. Unless I just recently installed an XTension (see "XTensions," below), my first guess is usually the XPress Preferences file. So I quit again, move those four items back to their normal folder, and move the XPress Preferences file into another folder (or throw it in the trash).

5. Again, QuarkXPress creates a fresh preferences file when you launch. If the trouble still has not gone away, then the problem is almost certainly with an XTension or the program itself.

▼ ▼

Tip: Resetting and Switching Preferences. The XPress Preferences file remembers all sorts of information about how QuarkXPress behaves.

▶ Hyphenation exceptions and edits to the kerning and tracking tables (see Chapter 6, *Type and Typography*, for more on these)

▶ Default document preferences that you have set up in the Preferences dialog box

▶ Application preferences set up in the Preferences dialog box

▶ Default settings for colors, H&J settings, print styles, style sheets, and lists ("default" meaning the settings that appear whenever you create a new document)

▶ Positions of the program's palettes (including whether they're open or closed)

As I noted above, if you delete the XPress Preferences file (or move it so that the program can't find it), then QuarkXPress creates a clean new one for you. This is a great method for starting over from scratch. However, note that you lose all the above settings.

The fact that these settings are stored in the preferences file means that you can actually have two or more XPress Preferences files with varying information. For instance, you could keep a special XPress Preferences file for a certain client with specific kerning and hyphenation needs. Of course, you can only have one in the QuarkXPress folder at a time, but the other one(s) can be hidden inside another folder until you want to switch them. However, you do have to quit and relaunch QuarkXPress for the new settings to take effect.

▼ ▼

Tip: Sharing Your Preferences. If you're the bossy type (or perhaps you're just the boss), you might want everyone else in your work group to share the same preferences as you. No problem: just copy your XPress Preferences file into their preferences folders. Unfortunately, you can't move an XPress Preferences file from a Macintosh to a PC or vice versa.

▼ ▼

Tip: Save and Back Up Those Preferences. XPress only saves its default preferences when you quit the program. That means if you set up the program the way you want it and then the system crashes, your customization work is lost. If you want to customize QuarkXPress, do it, then quit and relaunch the program.

Also, if you do a lot of editing to the kerning or tracking tables or hyphenation exceptions (see Chapter 6, *Type and Typography*), you should probably consider keeping a backup of your XPress Preferences file, just in case it goes south someday. (Or, in case the boss from the previous tip decides to overwrite your file without saving it.)

▼ ▼

Tip: Environment Easter Egg. Try holding down the Command, Option, and Shift keys and clicking in the Environment dialog box for an insight into who at Quark contributed to QuarkXPress 6 over the years (see Figure 2-3). Next time you go to Seybold or some other trade show, perhaps you'll recognize them at the Quark booth. In Windows, turn on Caps Lock, and then click while pressing Control and Shift.

Figure 2-3

Hidden "easter egg" pictures in the Environment dialog box

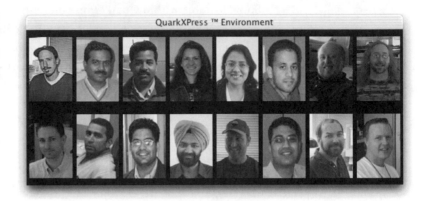

▼ ▼

XTensions

Here's an aspect of QuarkXPress that I think is so hot and amazing that I couldn't think of a nasty thing to say about it even if I tried. Quark has built in a system so that programmers can write add-on modules (XTensions) to work with QuarkXPress. There are over 300 developers around the world creating these XTensions (some people call these "plug-ins"). Some cost $5,000 and are designed for a very limited market, such as large newspapers. Others are free, and can (and should) be used by anyone using QuarkXPress. Appendix C, *XTensions and Resources*, provides more information about how to get your hands on XTensions.

In order to use an XTension, all you have to do is place it in the XTension folder, which is inside the QuarkXPress folder. When you start up QuarkXPress the XTension does its thing, whatever that may be. Usually, XTensions add an item to a menu, or even add a whole new menu. Most XTensions add items to the Utilities menu, because they are utilities. For example, years ago Quark released a free XTension called Type Tricks, which, among other things, added a feature called Line Check to the Utility menu (see "Line Check," in Chapter 6, *Type and Typography*). TypeTricks now ships with XPress 6.

▼ ▼

Tip: Old XTensions, New Product. Most XTensions that worked with XPress 3 would also work for XPress 4, but none of them work with XPress 5. Most, but not all, XTensions that were written for XPress 4 could be used with XPress 5.

However, *no* XTensions that worked with any previous version will work with XPress 6. All XTensions must be rewritten to function with this new version. You can blame the folks at Quark or the developers or anyone else you like, but the cause comes down to "progress," and it just keeps marching on.

▼ ▼

Some features within QuarkXPress are entirely based on XTensions, like indexing, kerning and tracking tables, and the color management system. As we'll see in Chapter 6, *Type and Typography*, and Chapter 9, *Pictures*, XTensions are also used as filters that enable QuarkXPress to read or write certain text and graphics file formats. For example, without the MS-Word XTension, XPress can't read or write files in the Microsoft Word format.

Here's a quick rundown on the various XTensions that ship with QuarkXPress on the Macintosh and Windows platforms.

- ▶ **AVENUE.QUARK.** Lets you use XPress's XML export features, including tagging objects on your page (see Appendix E, *XML Tools* for more on XML).

- ▶ **COMPRESSED IMAGE IMPORT.** This XTension knows how to interpret various image compression formats—primarily LZW compression in TIFF files. Without this XTension, you won't be able to read those kinds of files.

- ▶ **CUSTOM BLEEDS.** Lets you set custom bleed amounts in the Print and Save as EPS dialog boxes.

- ▶ **ERROR REPORTING.** This Windows-only XTension tells XPress to write a file to disk whenever the program crashes. In theory, you could send this file to Quark to help them debug the problem. In reality, you should probably just ignore this unless Quark tech support actually instructs you otherwise.

- ▶ **DEJA VU.** The Deja Vu XTension remembers what XPress files you've recently worked on as well as what folders you've recently used in the Get Picture, Get Text, and Open dialog boxes. When Deja Vu is loaded, you'll see a list of recently-opened files in the Open submenu (under the File menu), as well as File List and Default Path panels in the Preferences dialog box (see "Layout and Application Preferences" later in this chapter).

- ▶ **EPS PREVIEW.** This XTension works in conjunction with the Full Res Preview XTension to let XPress display full resolution previews of EPS images. Quark's current policy is to only send you this XTension after you have registered your copy of QuarkXPress.

▶ **FULL RES PREVIEW.** The Full Res Preview XTension lets you display high-resolution and vector images at the resolution of the screen, even when you zoom in. I discuss this more in Chapter 9, *Pictures*.

▶ **GUIDE MANAGER.** The Guide Manager XTension takes a very basic concept (letting you place and delete guides on your pages) and makes it incredibly complicated. See "Guides," in Chapter 3, *Tools of the Trade*.

▶ **HTML TEXT IMPORT.** With this XTension, XPress can import simple HTML files just as though they were regular word-processor files.

▶ **IMAGEMAP.** This lets you create image maps in Web layouts.

▶ **INDEX.** Enables the various indexing features, such as the Index palette (see Chapter 8, *Long Documents*).

▶ **ITEM SEQUENCE.** This is part of the avenue.quark XML tagging functionality. If you don't use XML, you don't need this active.

▶ **JABBERWOCKY.** I love the Jabberwocky XTension! It lets you fill any text box (or chain of text boxes) with random text much more interesting than the ol' Lorum Ipsum stuff. You can control Jabberwocky's language in the Jabberwocky panel of the Preferences dialog box and the Jabberwocky Sets feature under the Edit menu.

▶ **KERN-TRACK EDITOR.** Lets you edit kerning and tracking tables (appears in the Utilities menu). See "Fine Tuning Type" in Chapter 6, *Type and Typography*.

▶ **MS-WORD 6-2000 FILTER.** Lets you import and export Microsoft Word files. Quark is constantly updating their MS Word import filter; it's a good idea to check the Quark Web site regularly to see if there's a new one available.

▶ **OPI.** If you use an OPI workflow (where low-quality pictures get swapped out for high-quality images at print time), you need this XTension active. It adds OPI features to the Print and Save as EPS dialog boxes.

▶ **PDF FILTER.** Whenever you see the word "filter," remember it means both import *and* export. This filter lets you import Acrobat PDF files into picture boxes and export your pages in the PDF format.

▶ **PNG FILTER.** Do you use the PNG file format? Not many people do yet (it's primarily used for Web graphics), but if you do, you need this XTension.

▶ **QUARK CMS.** Enables the color management system, which is covered in Appendix A, *Color Management.*

▶ **RTF FILTER.** The ability to import Rich Text Format (RTF) files is new in the Macintosh version of XPress. RTF is a standard exchange format for formatted text. If your word processor isn't supported by XPress, see if it will export in the RTF format.

▶ **SCISSORS.** After I complained to a Quark engineer that the Bézier line tools really needed a scissors tool, he sat down and wrote up the Scissors tool over a weekend. It ended up being an XTension instead of being built-in to the program, but that's okay. I discuss this more in Chapter 3, *Tools of the Trade.*

▶ **SCRIPT.** This Macintosh-only XTension not only makes QuarkXPress scriptable, but it lets you run AppleScripts from within the program, via the Script menu (see Appendix D, *Scripting*).

▶ **SHAPE OF THINGS.** The Shape of Things XTension adds a Starburst tool to the Tools palette. To define the starburst (number of sides, how far inset every other point should be, and so on), double-click on the tool. Then draw a box with the tool the size you want the starburst to be. I find this very clunky, but it works in a pinch.

▶ **SUPER STEP AND REPEAT.** The Super Step and Repeat XTension adds a feature (of the same name) to the Edit menu that lets you create duplicates of any object (or objects) while offsetting, skewing, scaling, and rotating. See "Duplicating Items," in Chapter 3, *Tools of the Trade.*

▶ **TYPE TRICKS.** This XTension adds several features and macros to XPress, including Make Fraction, Make Price, Custom Underline, Remove Manual Kerning, Word Spacing, and Line Check. I cover these all in Chapter 6, *Type and Typography.*

▶ **WORDPERFECT FILTER.** Lets you import and export files in the WordPerfect format.

▶ **XML IMPORT.** This lets you import XML files into your QuarkXPress documents (see Appendix E, *XML Tools,* for more on this process).

▶ **XPRESS TAGS FILTER.** Lets you import and export files in the XPress Tags format. See Chapter 7, *Copy Flow,* for more information on XPress Tags and why they're so cool.

Disabling XTensions. You don't need all those XTensions loaded in QuarkXPress at the same time. XTensions don't take up much hard disk space, so it's hardly worth throwing them away (though if you do, and someday you find you need them again, you'll find them on the QuarkXPress installation CD-ROM). But it is worth disabling XTensions that you don't use because they slow down the program at launch time, and they take up extra RAM while you're using XPress.

For instance, if you only use Microsoft Word as your text editor, go ahead and disable the WordPerfect text filter. If you never use PNG images (I don't know anyone who does), disable that XTension.

There are two ways to skin a banana . . . er, I mean disable an XTension. First, if you haven't launched XPress yet, you can manually move the XTension file from the XTension folder into any other folder (preferably the XTension Disabled folder). Or, if you're already in QuarkXPress, you can use the XTensions Manager by selecting it from the Utilities menu (see Figure 2-4). Either way, the changes you make only take effect when you launch QuarkXPress.

Figure 2-4
XTensions Manager

XTensions Manager. The XTensions Manager dialog box is simple, at heart: all it does is move XTensions back and forth between the XTension and the XTension Disabled folders. As I said earlier, you can do the same thing yourself by hand, but this is easier and usually faster.

You can disable or enable an XTension by turning on or off the checkbox next to it in the Enable column (just click once on the checkbox to toggle its setting). If you want to disable or enable more than one XTension at a time, you could use the Shift (for contiguous selections in the list) or Command (for discontiguous selections) keys to select them and then choose On or Off from the Enable popup menu (though this is usually more trouble than it's worth).

There are six other controls in the XTensions Manager dialog box.

▶ **ABOUT.** I'm forever forgetting what some of my XTensions do, who developed them, and so on. You can find out all this (and more) by selecting an XTension and clicking the About button (see Figure 2-5).

Figure 2-5
About XTensions

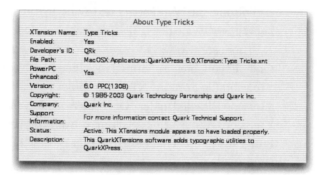

▶ **SAVE AS.** QuarkXPress lets you build sets of XTensions that you can recall at any time in the XTensions Manager dialog box. To create a set, first enable the XTensions you want to be loaded and disable those you don't. Then, click the Save As button and name the set. If you want to make a change to a set you've made, select it in the Set popup menu, make the changes (enable or disable the XTensions), and then use Save As to save it with the same name (XPress asks you if you really want to replace the old set with this new one).

▶ **SET.** The Set popup menu lets you choose which set you want active in the XTensions Manager dialog box. There are two sets by default: All Enabled and All Disabled.

▶ **EXPORT.** The sets you create are saved in the XPress Preferences file, but you can save a set to disk, too, by clicking Export.

▶ **IMPORT.** Once you have saved a set to disk, you can import it into a different version of XPress by clicking the Import button.

▶ **DELETE.** How difficult could Delete be? Just select the set you want to delete and click the Delete button. Now, that wasn't so bad, was it?

▼ ▼

Tip: Last-Minute XTension Changes. You can open the XTensions Manager while you're launching QuarkXPress by holding down the spacebar as soon as you see the QuarkXPress introductory splash screen (keep holding it down until you see the XTensions Manager dialog box). Here, you can turn on or off XTensions or sets of XTensions without having to quit and restart XPress.

If you find yourself holding down the spacebar too frequently, you might consider telling XPress to always open the XTensions Manager dialog box at program launch. You can do this on the XTensions Manager tab of the Preferences dialog box (see "Changing Defaults," later in this chapter).

▼ ▼

Keyboard Shortcuts

People often ask me what they can do to speed up their work. If you think the answer is buying a new computer or getting more RAM, you get three demerits. The best way to speed up your work is to speed *you* up, and the best way to speed you up is for you to learn as many keyboard shortcuts as you can. I'm talking about typing Command-N (or Control-N on Windows) instead of going to the File menu each time you need to create a document.

One look at the tear-out keyboard charts in the back of the book will tell you that there are a lot of shortcuts in XPress. But the built-in keyboard shortcuts don't let you do everything. Keystrokes can't select Export Layout as PDF, for instance, or add a page to a layout. That's why I bought QuicKeys from CE Software (*www.cesoft.com*)—one for Macintosh and one for Windows—which lets me build my own keyboard-activated macros.

For those who don't know what making macros is all about, let me elucidate. Macros are miniprograms that you can build that tell the computer to do a set of actions: type a key, pull down a menu, hide an application, and so on. Macros don't have to be as simple as just selecting a menu item, though. For example, one macro I have selects a paragraph, applies a style, puts an extra rule above the paragraph, and places a special character after the paragraph's last word. One keystroke sets the macro off and running.

Anytime you find yourself doing the same sequence of events repeatedly, you should think to yourself, "I could write a QuicKey to do this." For more on macros and scripting, take a look at Appendix D, *Scripting*.

▼ ▼

File Management

Getting a good grasp on file management is essential to working most efficiently and happily with QuarkXPress. When I talk about file management with QuarkXPress, I am talking primarily about opening, closing, and saving your documents. These are pretty basic concepts, so if you've used other Macintosh or Windows programs, you should feel right at home with these actions.

Opening Documents

I won't talk in depth about creating new files until Chapter 4, *Building a Document*. However, here I do want to talk about opening them. (In case you don't have any to play with, there are several QuarkXPress documents available on the installation disc.)

There are three ways to open an existing QuarkXPress document. You can double-click on the document's icon, which launches QuarkXPress and opens the file. Or, you can drag the document's icon onto the QuarkXPress icon (or an alias on the Macintosh—a shortcut on Windows—for QuarkXPress). If you are in QuarkXPress, you can select Open from the File menu (or press Command-O or Control-O).

▼ ▼

Tip: Salvaging Damaged Documents. Yes, it does happen from time to time that QuarkXPress may corrupt a document. Sometimes, what appears to be a perfectly good document one day will give you grief the next. The worst is when you try to open a file and get a Bad File Format (70) or Unexpected End of File error.

First, if you can open it, try using the Save As command to save the document to a new file. This can sometimes help, since as you work on a document, it can become larger and more complicated as you edit text and arrange elements. Save As makes a "clean" copy of the file, without this information.

The next thing I'd try is the Markztools XTension from Markzware (*www.markzware.com*). This XTension can sometimes repair files that seem irreparable.

If you have a QuarkXPress document so badly corrupted that you can't even open it, and Markztools can't help either, you may at least be able to salvage some of the text by opening the XPress file using a word processor or text editor. For instance, BBEdit is a popular text editor on the Mac that can open just about anything. You'll be able to see all the text in the document, though it will appear garbled in places, and it'll be completely unformatted.

▼ ▼

Closing Documents

You have four choices for closing a document.

► Click the close box of the document window.

► Press Command-W (this is Mac only).

► Choose Close from the File menu.

► Select Quit from the same menu. (Of course, this choice not only closes the file, but it also quits QuarkXPress.)

If changes have been made to the document since the last time you saved it, you'll see an alert box asking you if you want to save those changes.

▼ ▼

Tip: Closing Up Shop. If you want to quickly close all open documents, you can either press Command-Option-W or Option-click the Close box. In Windows you have to press Alt-W and then press the letter A (which selects Close All from the Window menu).

▼ ▼

Saving Your Document

Until you save your document to a disk, it exists only in the computer's temporary memory (called RAM), ready to disappear forever in the event of a power disruption or system crash. You should save any new document as soon as it opens, and make frequent saves during your work session. All it takes is Command-S (Ctrl-S). I suggest developing it into a nervous tic. I cannot tell you how many times I and my clients have lost hours of work because we didn't save frequently enough. I even made a little sign to post above my computer that says, "Save Every 10 Minutes." You can also use Quark's Auto Save feature (see "Auto Save," below).

Let's look at the commands in QuarkXPress that let you save your documents, along with two other powerful features: one for autosaving and one for making backups.

Save. If you want to save your document with the same name that it already has, you can select Save from the File menu (or press Command-S or Ctrl-S). If you haven't yet saved your document, and it is unnamed, selecting Save automatically acts like Save As.

Save As. Selecting Save As from the File menu (or pressing Command-Option-S or Ctrl-Alt-S) lets you save the document you're working on under a different name. For example, I often save different versions of a document, with each version number attached to the file name. The first one might be called "Brochure1.qxd", the next "Brochure2.qxd", and so on. Whenever I decide to create a new version, I choose Save As from the File menu, which brings up the Save As dialog box (see Figure 2-6). I type in a file name (or edit the one that's there), then click the Save button to save it to disk. If you decide to do this, remember to delete earlier versions as soon as you decide you don't need them anymore, or else your hard disk will burst at the seams.

File management is an issue that too many people just don't seem to "get." The Save As dialog box is a key ingredient in file management. The important issue here is that your document is saved to whatever folder is open in the Save

Figure 2-6
The Save As dialog box
(Macintosh and Windows)

As dialog box. If you want your document saved in a folder called Current Jobs, you must navigate your way to that folder.

You have three choices to make (in Windows, only two) when saving a file to disk with the Save As dialog box.

▶ **PREVIEW.** On the Macintosh, you can save a first-page preview along with your document by checking Include Preview in the Save As dialog box. Note that the only way to add a preview to a document you've already saved is to resave it using Save As. Adding a preview to a document only adds about 5 K or 10 K to the total size of the document, so there's almost no reason not to turn this on.

▶ **TYPE.** The Type popup menu lets you choose between Document and Template. Document is for regular files. I discuss templates later in this section.

▶ **VERSION.** The last option lets you save the file as either a 5.0 or a 6.0 file. While it's nice that Quark has given us the option to save a file in the 5.0 format, you'd better be careful if you do (see the following tip).

▼ ▼

Tip: Saving As a 5.0 File. Beware! Saving your file in a 5.0 format can be hazardous to your health (and the health of your document). It's not that the folks at Quark are trying to make your life miserable, it's just that you can do things in XPress 6 that XPress 5 just doesn't understand. The only things you really need to watch out for, however, are tables and some Web features. XPress 5 didn't let you link table cells together, so if you have done this (see "Tables" in Chapter 3, *Tools of the Trade*), you should select each of your tables and choose Convert Table to Group before saving in the earlier version.

In general, if you're going to save your document in the 5.0 format, you should always use Save As and then keep the 6.0 version unharmed and unchanged. Also, if you do perform this maneuver, make sure you open the document again and compare the before and after versions carefully. (You have to close the document and reopen it in order to see the changes.)

▼ ▼

Tip: It Never Hurts to Save As. As you work on an XPress document, constant edits and revisions can cause the file to grow a little and increase the risk that an unforeseen disaster (cosmic rays? dust-sucking CPU fans?) could corrupt the file. You can guard against this file bloat by occasionally using the Save As command. You can save with the same name or a different one; either way, the file usually shrinks a little to its proper size because all the "garbage" has been swept away. Note that if you have Auto Save turned on, XPress is performing this Save As feature for you behind the scenes, so you don't have to worry about it.

▼ ▼

Auto Save. At first glance, Auto Save looks like a yawner. As it turns out, it's anything but. There are plenty of commercial and shareware utilities that will automatically save a document you're working on, as you're working on it. But all these utilities work by generating the equivalent of QuarkXPress's Save command at predefined intervals. Now suppose you mistakenly delete all of a story; then, before you can Undo your deletion, your autosave utility kicks in, saving your document (and your mistake) for all eternity—or until you fix your mistake, or lose your job because of it! For this reason, I've stayed away from autosaving utilities.

Until now. The folks at Quark really got the design of this feature right. You turn on Auto Save by checking it in the Save tab of the Preferences dialog box (see "Changing Defaults," later in this chapter), and you can specify any interval you want between saves (the default is every five minutes). But—and here's the great part—Auto Save doesn't automatically overwrite your original file. That only happens when you use the Save command. So if you use the Revert to Saved command, you revert to the last saved version of your original file—just as you would expect—*not* to the last Auto Saved one (see "Revert to Saved," below).

Auto Save exists to help you recover from a dreaded system crash or network communications failure. (When you lose the connection to your file server with a file open, sometimes QuarkXPress refuses to let you do a Save As.) After you have a crash, you can restart QuarkXPress and open the Auto Saved file. (On the Macintosh, the file gets ".AutoSave" appended to its name. On Windows, it has the .asv file-name extension.)

Whenever QuarkXPress does an autosave, it creates a file in the same folder as your document; this file keeps track of every change you've made since the last time you saved the document. Whenever you save your document, the program deletes the incremental file, and then it starts over again.

The problem with Auto Save is that it creates a file the same size as the one you're working on. If your file is 100 MB large, then you'd better have at least 100 MB available for the autosaved version, too.

▼ ▼

Tip: Auto Save Saves the Day. If you have Auto Save turned on and QuarkXPress freezes up, there's a small chance that the function will still be working in the background. That means that if you wait for a little while instead of rebooting immediately, XPress might save all the work you've done since the last Auto Save. If Auto Save is set to save every five minutes, then wait five minutes after the freeze before restarting the machine. It doesn't always work, but when it does, it's like a cool glass of water on a hot day.

▼ ▼

Auto Backup. Until recently, revision control with QuarkXPress has been strictly up to you. If you wanted to keep previous versions of a document, you had to be sure to copy them to another location, or use Save As frequently, slightly changing the name of your file each time. (I name my files with version numbers: 1.1, 2.4, etc.) Now those days are gone.

You can use Auto Backup (also found on the Save tab of the Preferences dialog box, under the Edit menu; or press Command-Option-Shift-Y or Ctrl-Alt-Shift-Y) to tell QuarkXPress to keep up to 100 previous versions of your document on disk (the default is five). By clicking the Destination button, you can specify exactly where you want revisions to be stored. The default, "<document folder>", is simply the folder in which your original document resides.

If you ever need to open a previous version of a file, just look in the destination folder. The file with the highest number appended to its name is the most recent revision. Note that it's often a good idea to change the backup destination folder to a different hard drive, just in case the one you're working on decides to leap off your desk.

▼ ▼

Tip: Fill 'Er Up with Backups. After working with Auto Backup for a couple of weeks, you may find your hard drive mysteriously filling up. Remember, those backup files (as many per file as you've specified in Preferences) don't go away by themselves. You need to delete them when you're done with them. One suggestion: Set your Auto Backup to save to a special backup folder on a seldom-used drive.

▼ ▼

Templates

To some people, the concept of templates seems shrouded in more mystery than the Druids of old. Here's an area that seems complicated because people make it complicated. But it's not.

You have the choice of saving your document as a template when you're in the Save As dialog box. When a file is saved as a template, nothing changes except that you cannot accidentally save over it. For example, let's say you create a document and save it as a normal document called "Newsletter Template". Then, a couple of days later you go back into the document and create the newsletter: you make changes, flow text in, and place pictures. You then select Save from the File menu. The file, "Newsletter Template", is modified with the changes you made, and there is no way to "go back" to the original untouched file (unless you've made a backup somewhere).

Okay, now let's say you create that same "Newsletter Template", then save it as a template by choosing Template from the Type popup menu in the Save As dialog box. The next time you open the file, it opens with a name like "Document1" so if you select Save, you get the Save As dialog box.

▼ ▼

Tip: Resaving Templates. If QuarkXPress gives you the Save As dialog box when you try to save a document specified as a template, how can you change the template itself? Simple. You can replace the old template with a new one by giving it exactly the same name in the Save As dialog box. (Don't forget to click the Template button if you still want it to be a template.)

▼ ▼

Tip: Alternate Templates. The Macintosh operating system offers an alternate way of making templates: stationery pads. To make an XPress document a stationery pad, you can select its icon in the Finder, choose Get Info, and then turn on the Stationery Pad checkbox. The next time you open the document, the operating system asks you what you want to name your new document and where you want to save it. This is kind of like automatically opening the file and immediately doing a Save As. Stationery Pad isn't only for QuarkXPress documents; any Macintosh document can be made into a template using this Get Info feature.

▼ ▼

Multiple Documents

QuarkXPress lets you open up to 25 document windows at a time. However, the actual number and size of documents you can have open depends on both the amount of memory available and the number of other files open.

Window management. Having so many document windows open at once could mean massive clutter and confusion (especially for people like me, who think that the "desktop metaphor" was created to let us make our virtual desktop as messy as our physical one); fortunately, Quark provides two solutions.

First, XPress lists all open document windows in the Windows menu. Just selecting a document name makes it active, which is particularly convenient if the file you want happens to be hidden under a slew of other windows.

Second, XPress offers two features alongside the list of document windows: Stack Documents and Tile Documents (see Figure 2-7). The Stack Documents command arranges your windows somewhat like a slightly fanned hand of cards. There's always at least a tiny smidgen of each window showing, even the hindmost one, so you can select any window by clicking on it.

Tiling resizes every document window so that each takes up an equal portion of your computer's screen. So if you have three document windows, the Tile Documents command sizes and arranges them so that each takes up one-third of your screen. I often use this when dragging objects or pages from one document to another.

▼ ▼

Tip: Windows Menu Shortcut. The Windows menu sure is useful, but there's an even easier shortcut on the Macintosh: Hold down the Shift key and click on the title bar of your active document window; up pops a replica of the documents under the Windows menu, from which you can select any window or stack or tile them all (see Figure 2-8). What better place for a Windows menu than in a window itself? (This doesn't work on the Windows platform.)

▼ ▼

Tip: Tiling to Multiple Monitors. It turns out that if you have more than one monitor attached to your Mac, you can have QuarkXPress tile documents so that the tiling spreads across all your available monitors. So if you have two

Figure 2-7

The Windows menu

Figure 2-8

Popup menu from
the title bar of a
document window

monitors and four open documents, two documents will appear in each monitor. You can turn on this feature by checking the Tile to Multiple Monitors box in the Display tab of the Preferences dialog box (it's on by default; note that this is currently a Mac-only feature). If you turn off this option, QuarkXPress tiles all the open documents to only your main monitor (the one that's displaying the menu bar).

▼ ▼

QuarkXPress's Interface

While working in QuarkXPress, you have access to its powerful tools and features through several areas: menus, palettes, dialog boxes, keystrokes, and context-sensitive menus. Let's look carefully at each of these methods and how you can use them.

Menus

There are several conventions used in QuarkXPress's menus. One is the hierarchical menu, which I call a submenu. These allow multiple items to be, literally, offshoots of the primary menu item. Another convention is the checkmark. A checkmark next to a menu item shows that the feature is enabled or activated. Selecting that item turns the feature off—or disables it—and the checkmark goes away. If a menu item has an ellipsis (...) after it, you know that selecting it will bring up a dialog box. Finally, menus show the main keystroke shortcut for a menu item. Figure 2-9 shows these three menu conventions. Other conventions are discussed as needed throughout the book.

I don't need to talk a great deal here about menus and what's on them because I discuss their contents throughout the book. However, you should note that certain types of features fall under particular menus. Let's go through a quick rundown.

▶ FILE. Items on the File menu relate to disk files (entire documents). Commands to open, save, and print files are located here.

▶ EDIT. The Edit menu contains features for changing items within QuarkXPress. The last section of the Edit menu contains features to edit internal defaults on a document- or application-wide level, such as the color palette, the text style sheets, and specifications for each tool on the Tool palette (see "Tool palette," later in this chapter).

▶ STYLE. The Style menu changes depending on what item you have selected on your document page. Selecting a picture box results in one Style menu, selecting a text box results in a different one, and selecting rules (lines) results in a third menu. The items on the Style menu enable you to change specific style attributes of the selected item.

▶ ITEM. Whereas the Style menu contains commands for changing the contents of a picture or text box, the Item menu's commands change the box or rule itself. For example, changing the style of a picture box's contents might involve changing the shade of a picture. Changing an attribute of the box itself may involve changing the frame thickness of the picture box.

▶ PAGE. The Page menu is devoted to entire pages in your document layout. Controls for master pages (see Chapter 4, *Building a Document*)

Figure 2-9

Menu conventions

Checkmark

Keystroke shortcut

Submenu symbol

are located here, as well as several features for adding, deleting, and navigating among pages.

▶ **LAYOUT.** XPress 6 lets you include more than one layout space in a single document (I discuss making layout spaces in Chapter 4, *Building a Document*), and the Layout menu lets you control these layouts—adding new ones, deleting them, and so on.

▶ **VIEW.** Almost every feature based on what you see and how you see it is located in the View menu. This menu also includes several other items, such as Show Guides, that involve QuarkXPress's interface. I discuss these later in this chapter.

▶ **UTILITIES.** This menu is, in many ways, a catchall that contains assorted goodies for helping make pages. The spelling checker, kerning tables, the feature that tells you what pictures and fonts you've used, and so forth are kept here. Also, most XTensions add items to the Utilities menu, so the more XTensions you have, the longer this menu.

▶ **WINDOW.** The Window menu lists all your open documents and all the available palettes.

▶ **SCRIPT.** The Macintosh version of QuarkXPress has a Script menu (when the Script XTension is active). When XPress is first launched, any compiled Applescripts present in the Scripts folder (inside the QuarkXPress folder) are added to this menu. Folders within the Scripts folder become submenus inside this menu.

Palettes

One of the key elements in QuarkXPress's user interface is the palette structure. A palette in QuarkXPress is similar to a painter's palette insofar as a palette contains a selection of usable and changeable items that you can put wherever suits you best. A left-handed painter may hold a paint palette in her right hand, while a short ambidextrous painter might place the palette on the floor. QuarkXPress has several palettes, each with a different function, which can be placed anywhere you like on the screen. They're additional windows on the screen that, although they can overlap one another, never go "behind" a document window (that's why they're sometimes called *floating* palettes).

You can manipulate palettes in the same manner as you would move a document window. For example, to move a palette, drag the window from its top shaded area. To close a palette, click the Close box in the upper-left corner (upper-right corner in Windows). Also, two palettes I'll talk about in a moment (the Page Layout palette and the Libraries palette) have Zoom boxes in their upper-right corners. Click on the Zoom box once and the palette expands; again, and it reduces in size.

QuarkXPress comes with eleven palettes: Tool, Measurements, Page Layout, Style Sheets, Layers, Colors, Hyperlinks, Trap Information, Lists, Synchronize Text, and Index (see Figure 2-10). The avenue.quark XTension also adds the Placeholders and Sequences palettes. Libraries and Books also appear as palettes. When you first launch QuarkXPress, you can see two of these seven: the Tool palette and the Measurements palette.

QuarkXPress remembers which palettes are open or closed and where each palette is placed, so palettes show up where you left them next time you launch the program.

Let's take a look at each of these palettes.

Tool palette. The Tool palette is the most elementary and functional of the palettes. There's not a lot you can do without it. Here you have the tools for making boxes in which you place your pictures and text, tools for rotating, tools for drawing lines, and tools for linking the text boxes together to allow the flow of text. Selecting a tool is easy: just click on it (see "Tip: Keyboard Palettes," below). I won't go into each tool here, as I discuss them in some depth in Chapter 3, *Tools of the Trade*.

▼ ▼

Tip: Enlarge or Reduce Your Tool Palette. QuarkXPress has a slew of tools in the tool palette and, to accommodate them all, it places many of them inside popout menus (some people call these "fly-out menus"). When you click on any tool that has a little triangle in its upper-right corner and you hold the

Figure 2-10
QuarkXPress's
palettes

Measurements palette

Tool palette

*Synchronized Text
palette*

*Page Layout
palette*

Style Sheets palette

Index palette

Colors palette

Trap Information palette

*Lists
palette*

Layers palette

Hyperlinks palette

mouse button down for a moment, a popout menu offers a number of other, similar tools.

If you have a lot of screen real estate, you can pull these other tools out of the popup menus and add them to the main Tool palette by holding down the Control key (on both Macintosh and Windows) when you click on the tool. (That is, hold it down when you click on the popout menu, and only let go after you've selected the tool you want.)

Conversely, you can put these tools back into popout menus by Control-clicking on them. It all depends on whether you want a long or a short palette (see Figure 2-11).

Figure 2-11
The Tool palette: The long and the short of it

Measurements palette. Like the Style menu, the Measurements palette is dynamic: it changes depending on what sort of item is selected. Text boxes have one type of Measurements palette, Picture boxes have a second type, and rules and lines have a third type (see Figure 2-12). Which tool from the Tool palette you have selected also has an effect on how the Measurements palette looks. The Measurements palette's purpose in life is to show you an item's vital

Figure 2-12

The Measurements palette's displays for the three kinds of item selections

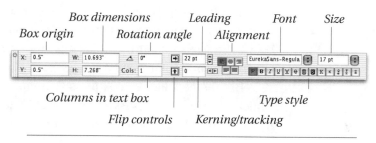

For text boxes

Box origin — *Box dimensions* — *Rotation angle* — *Leading* — *Alignment* — *Font* — *Size*

Columns in text box — *Flip controls* — *Kerning/tracking* — *Type style*

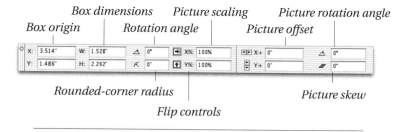

For picture boxes

Box origin — *Box dimensions* — *Rotation angle* — *Picture scaling* — *Picture offset* — *Picture rotation angle*

Rounded-corner radius — *Flip controls* — *Picture skew*

For lines (rules)

Line origin — *Line rotation* — *Line mode* — *Line weight* — *Line style* — *End caps*

Line length

statistics and save you a trip to the Style or Item menu for making changes to those page elements.

For example, if you select a text box, the Measurements palette shows the dimensions of the text box, the coordinate of its upper-left corner, the number of columns in the box, the rotation angle of the box, and the style, font, and size of the text you've selected in the box.

Not only does the Measurements palette display this information, but you can click on an item in the palette and change it. For example, if you want to rotate a picture box 10 degrees, you replace the "0" with "10" and then press either Return or Enter. (Pressing Return or Enter tells QuarkXPress that you've finished; it's like clicking an OK button.)

Note that the left half of a Measurements palette displays information about a page element (an "item"), and the right half displays information about the contents or the style of the item (see "Items and Contents" in Chapter 3, *Tools of the Trade*).

▼ ▼

Tip: Keyboard Palettes. You can access and select items on either the Tool palette or the Measurements palette by using keyboard commands. To show or hide the Tool palette, press the F8 key (assuming you have an extended keyboard). To select the next tool down on the Tool palette, press Command-Control-Tab or Option-F8 (in Windows, press Control-Alt-Tab or Control-F8). To select the next higher tool, press Command-Control-Shift-Tab or Shift-Option-F8 (in Windows, press Control-Alt-Shift-Tab or Control-Shift-F8). If you have closed (hidden) the Tool palette, you can open it by pressing any of these key commands.

You also can use the Tab key to move through the Measurements palette. You can jump to the first item on this palette by pressing Command-Option-M (or Ctrl-Alt-M; this also opens the palette, if it was closed).

I find it much faster to toggle between items on the Tool palette using keystrokes, especially when moving between the Content tool and the Item tool. And I hardly ever use the mouse to click in the Measurements palette, preferring instead to press Command-Option-M (Ctrl-Alt-M), then tabbing through the items until I get where I want. You can also press F9 to show and hide the Measurements palette.

▼ ▼

Tip: Jump to Fonts. Changing from one font to another is often a real hassle, but it's much less so with of my favorite keyboard shortcuts: Command-Shift-Option-M (or Ctrl-Alt-Shift-M; the same as jumping to the Measurements palette, but adding the Shift key).

▼ ▼

Page Layout palette. You can find the Page Layout palette by selecting Show Page Layout from the View menu (or pressing the F10 key). In earlier versions of XPress this was called the Document Layout palette. This palette displays a graphic representation of your document, page by page. When you first start using it, it's slightly weird, but the more you work with it, the more you realize how amazingly cool it is.

I discuss the Page Layout palette in "Manipulating Your Document," later in this chapter (and again, in greater detail, in Chapter 4, *Building a Document*), but—in a nutshell—you can use this palette for creating, deleting, and shuffling pages, assigning master pages, and creating multipage spreads. Generally, many of the functions of the Page menu can be performed by dragging icons in the Page Layout palette.

Style Sheets palette. The principle is simple: Whenever you're working with text, you can apply, edit, and view style sheets on the fly by using the Style Sheets palette. This palette lists all the paragraph and character styles in your document, along with their keyboard shortcuts if they have any. (If you have lots of styles, you can make the palette larger or just scroll through them.) I discuss the Style Sheets palette (including what style sheets are, if you don't know already) in Chapter 7, *Copy Flow*.

Colors palette. Just like styles, you can apply and edit colors with a click, using the Colors palette. This floating palette contains a list of every available color, along with a tint-percentage control and three icons. Depending on what tool and object you have selected, some icons are grayed out. When you select a text box, the icons represent frame color, text color, and background color for that box. When you select a line, two icons gray out, and only the line-color icon remains. I cover this in more detail in Chapter 12, *Color*.

Trap Information palette. Unlike most palettes in QuarkXPress, in which you have the option either to use them or to use menu items, the Trap Information palette is the only way that you can use object-by-object trapping (I cover trapping in detail in Chapter 12, *Color*). The palette shows you the current trap information for a selected page object, gives you "reasons" why it's trapping the object that way, and lets you change that object's trap value. Unless you change the trap value, the Trap Information palette displays all objects at their default trap.

Lists palette. The Lists palette displays collections of paragraphs in your document or book that are tagged with specific style sheets (determined by the list specification). I cover lists and how you can make tables of contents with them in Chapter 8, *Long Documents*.

Synchronize Text palette. The Synchronize Text palette lets you "link" text boxes of text together in such a way that when you change the text in one box, the synchronized boxes mirror the change. I discuss synchronized text in Chapter 3, *Tools of the Trade*.

Profile Information palette. Quark's color management system (CMS) lets you view and change color device profiles on an image-by-image basis in the Profile Information palette. This palette only appears in the View menu when you have the Quark CMS XTension loaded, and it's only active when the color management system is turned on. I cover this palette and why you'd want to use it in Appendix A, *Color Management*.

Index palette. I cover the Index palette and indexing documents in general in Chapter 8, *Long Documents*. Suffice it to say that the Index palette is your one and only ticket to getting an index in QuarkXPress (other than using some other commercial XTension). It is only available when the Index XTension is loaded and active.

Libraries palette. Here's another QuarkXPress feature that I discuss in much greater detail later in Chapter 3, *Tools of the Trade* (I'm not trying to tease; I'm just taking things one step at a time). A library looks like a simple palette, but it has some very powerful uses. You can have more than one Libraries palette open at a time (each floating palette represents one Library file), and you are able to store up to 2,000 items in each library. Libraries are slightly different from other palettes in that they're not accessed by the View menu; you use the New Library command to create them, and the standard Open dialog box to access them (both under the File menu).

Books palette. Books are like libraries in some ways, except they're collections of documents rather than items. Books let you tie together multiple documents that have a common purpose, like chapters in a book or spreads in a magazine. I cover books and the Books palette in Chapter 8, *Long Documents*.

Layers palette. Objects in XPress are always above or below one another. The Layers palette makes this relationship among items more obvious by letting you create named layers on which you can put your lines, text boxes, picture boxes, and tables. I'll cover layers in detail in Chapter 3, *Tools of the Trade*.

Hyperlinks palette. Both Web layouts and Acrobat PDF documents can take advantage of hyperlinks, which are "hot links" that, when clicked, take you somewhere. The Hyperlinks palette lets you store all the hyperlinks in your document so you can use them and re-use them quickly. I discuss hyperlinks in great detail in Chapter 14, *Going Online with QuarkXPress*.

Dialog Boxes

You can perform almost every function in QuarkXPress with only the palettes and the menus. However, it is rarely efficient to work this way. Dialog boxes are areas in which you can usually change many specifications for an item at one time. For example, Figure 2-13 shows the Modify dialog box for a text box. In this dialog box, you can modify any or every item quickly, then click the OK button to make those changes take effect.

Dialog box terminology. Here's a quick lesson in terminology, if you're unfamiliar with dialog boxes. The area in which you enter a value is called a *field*. Oftentimes there are *checkboxes* that can be checked on or off, or grayed out if undefined. Many dialog boxes also contain *popup menus*, which act much

Figure 2-13
A typical dialog box

Tabs

Checkbox   *Fields*   *Button*   *Popup menu*

like the menus at the top of the screen: just position the cursor on them, press the mouse button, and drag the mouse up or down until you have selected the item you want. Then let go of the mouse button.

Typically, dialog boxes have two buttons: OK and Cancel. Clicking OK closes the dialog box and puts your changes into effect. Clicking Cancel closes the dialog box and ignores the changes you've made. Some dialog boxes have a Save option, which acts as an OK button. Other dialog boxes have an Apply button. Clicking this button temporarily applies the settings you've made to the document so that you can see them. If you like what you see, you can then click OK. If you don't like it, you can usually press Command-Z (Ctrl-Z) to revert the dialog box to the last setting. In any case, you can click Cancel to rid yourself of the dialog box and the changes you've made, even after applying them (see "Undo and Multiple Undo," later in this chapter).

▼ ▼

Tip: Pushing Your Buttons. Almost every button in QuarkXPress's dialog boxes can be replaced with a keystroke. The keystroke is usually the first letter in the button's name. For example, if a dialog box has Yes and No buttons, you can select them by pressing Command-Y and Command-N (or just press Y or N in Windows). When you're checking spelling, you can select the Skip button by pressing Command-S (Alt-S in Windows). Note that any button that is highlighted (has a darker border than a normal button) can be selected by pressing Enter or Return. (This is usually the OK button, but might be something else, such as Find Next in the Find/Change dialog box.) You can press Cancel by pressing Command-period on the Macintosh or Esc in Windows.

▼ ▼

Tip: Switch Tabs. You can switch among the tabs in a tabbed dialog box in the same way you switch from one tool to the next in the Tool palette: either click ing on one or pressing Command-Control-Tab (Ctrl-Alt-Tab) or Command-Control-Shift-Tab (Ctrl-Alt-Shift-Tab).

▼ ▼

Tip: Continuous Apply. As I said earlier, the Apply button temporarily applies the change you made in a dialog box. You can then decide whether you want to actually make that change, revert, or cancel the operation entirely. Even though pressing Command-A (Alt-A in Windows) speeds up the process some, I often find it helpful to be in a Continuous Apply mode by pressing Command-Option-A or holding down the Option key while clicking Apply (hold down Alt while clicking Apply in Windows). This highlights the Apply button (turns it black), as if you were holding the button down continuously. Now, every change you make in the dialog box is immediately applied to your page item. You can still press Command-Z (Ctrl-Z) to undo the last change, or Command-period or Esc to cancel the dialog box. To turn off Continuous Apply, just press Command-Option-A (or Alt-click) again.

▼ ▼

By the Numbers

Unless you raise horses and measure everything in "hands," chances are that you and QuarkXPress share a common measurement system. QuarkXPress understands measurements in points, picas, inches, ciceros, centimeters, agates, and millimeters. (You can even type measurements in Qs, which is used in some Asian countries—1 Q is a quarter of a millimeter.) You can always use these measurement units, no matter what the default setting is (see "Changing Defaults," later in this chapter). Table 2-1 shows how to specify a value for each system.

The mathematical abilities of most people I know have degenerated to the point of having to use calculators to "be fruitful and multiply." Realizing this, Quark incorporated into every entry field the ability to calculate. You can specify measurements with a plus or minus sign to build simple equations using one or more measurement units. For example, if a measurement was set to "10p" and you wanted to add 4 centimeters, you could type "10p+4cm". Similarly, if you wanted to take away one pica, two points, you could type "10p-1p2". Note that the first example mixes measurement systems; you don't have to be consistent here because the program does all the math for you.

You can also use * (the asterisk) for multiplication and / (the slash) for division in any field. If you have a text box that measures 4.323 inches and you want to make it two-thirds as wide, just add "*2/3" to the right of the inch

Table 2-1

Measurement systems

YOU CAN SPEC . . .	BY TYPING . . .	EXAMPLES
points	pt or p	6pt or p6
picas	p	10p or 2p6 (2 picas, 6 points)
inches (decimal)	"	6" or 6.5" or 6.888832"
ciceros	c	2c or 6c3 (6 ciceros, 3 points)
centimeters	cm	3cm
millimeters	mm	210mm
Q (Japanese unit)	Q	4Q
agates	ag	10ag

mark. Or, if you want to make a picture box 120 percent of its current size, just type "*1.2" after the width measurement. Remember that you can mix up and match all the measurements, too; so even "3p+24mm/3*9" is valid (though I can't think why you'd need it).

▼ ▼

Tip: Fractions in Arithmetic. Here are two unconventional ways to use arithmetic in QuarkXPress: fractions and placing items on a preset grid.

To get an eighth of a pica, you can type "1p/8" (one eighth of a pica is, of course, the same as one pica divided by eight). To place a text box at 3 7/8 inches from the left side of the page, place it at "3" ┤7"/8" (XPress does the division or multiplication in an equation first, then the addition or subtraction).

Similarly, let's say you're using a strict leading grid and you want to put a picture box exactly 20 lines down. If the grid is based on 13-point leading, you can set the vertical origin of the box to "13pt*20" (leading value times the number of lines down the page).

▼ ▼

Context-Sensitive Menus

QuarkXPress 5 introduced context-sensitive menus to QuarkXPress. Context-sensitive menus—menus that appear wherever your cursor is, and which change depending on what you're clicking on—have been around in other programs for over a decade, but Quark is a little slow to join the party. (Actually, to be fair, the Style Sheets palette did have a context-sensitive menu in version 4.x.) On the Macintosh, you can activate the context-sensitive menu by Control-clicking; in Windows, you simply click with the right mouse button. What you click on determines what kind of menu you get (see Figure 2-14).

I think context-sensitive menus are one of the best ways to boost your productivity in XPress, right up there with learning the keyboard shortcuts. Just get in the habit of Control-clicking (or right-mouse-button-clicking) on things. I

Figure 2-14
Context-sensitive menus

Click on text box

Click on picture box

Click on Style Sheets palette

Click on line

Click on Colors palette

Click on Hyperlinks palette

Click on ruler

Click on Layers palette

*Click on Page
Layout palette*

Click on page

Click on Lists palette

Figure 2-14
Context-sensitive menus
(continued)

Click on table

Click on Synchronized Text palette

wish there were even more menus, so I could apply text formatting or align objects on the fly. Oh well. There's always another version in the future.

After You Click OK

Mistakes are common in the world of desktop publishing. In fact, one of the great benefits of working on a computer, in my opinion, is that I can make as many mistakes as I want and always recover from them. In QuarkXPress, there are several methods to recover from a mistake or a decision you later regret.

Revert to Saved

As I said above, no changes are permanent until you save them to disk. If you want to discard all changes made to a document since the last save, you can do it by closing the document (choose Close from the File menu) and telling QuarkXPress that you don't want to save the changes. Or, if you wish to continue working on it without interruption, choose Revert to Saved from the File menu. For example, if—in the name of improvement—you have managed to mess up your document beyond redemption, you can revert to the version that you last saved.

Tip: Revert to Last Minisave. The Auto Save feature I talked about above goes by another name, too: PageMaker calls these things minisaves.

Sometimes you want to use a minisave as something other than crash insurance. You can actually revert to the last autosave instead of going back all the way to the last full save (for instance, if you like the changes you made five minutes ago, but not the ones you made 10 minutes ago). Just hold down the Option key when you select Revert from the File menu.

▼ ▼

Undo and Multiple Undo

Since I'm on the topic of reverting back and ignoring changes to the document, we really need to take a quick detour and look at the Undo commands. Undo is found under the Edit menu, and is a staple of all quality programs. If you make a mistake, you can almost always Undo it.

New in QuarkXPress 6 is the ability to undo more than one thing at a time. In fact, you can undo up to the last 30 things you did to your file, either one at a time, or in bunches of steps. To undo a single action, press Command-Z (Ctrl-Z). To undo more than one action at a time, click and hold down the mouse button on the Undo popup menu in the lower-left corner of the document window. The Undo popup menu lists all the undoable actions you've performed recently, labeling them cryptically, like "Undo Line Change," "Undo Typing," or "Undo Text Box Change" (see Figure 2-15).

XPress also lets you *redo* steps after undoing them. By default, pressing Command-Z (or Ctrl-Y in Windows) redoes the last action you undid. Similarly, you can choose more than one action to redo from the Redo popup menu (next to the Undo popup menu). Redo is helpful when you're not sure whether you want to make a change—you can undo the change, then redo it for a "before and after" effect.

Note that each layout space has its own undo list, so if you make a change on the first layout, switch to the second layout and make another change, and then try to undo twice, you'll only undo the change on the second layout. So XPress actually has a maximum of 30 undo steps per layout. However, also note that XPress forgets the undo list when you quit or close a document.

Undo Preferences. If you count carefully, you'll find that, out of the box, XPress only remembers the last 20 things you do, while earlier I said it should remember 30. You can make it remember *up to* 30 by changing the value in the Undo panel of the Preferences dialog box (press Command-Option-Shift-Y or Ctrl-Alt-Shift-Y). Remember that each additional step you want XPress to remember takes some extra RAM. In a memory-tight situation, you might reduce this value to 5 or 10 steps. In general, 20 is a pretty good default.

The Undo panel of the dialog box also lets you specify which keyboard shortcut you want to use for the Redo command. You have three choices:

Figure 2-15
Undo and Redo
popup menus

Undo

Redo

Clicking on the Undo popup menu lets you undo more than one action at a time.

Command-Shift-Z, Command-Z, and Command Y (or Ctrl-Shfit-Z, Ctrl-Z, and Ctrl-Y). This is handy for two reasons. First, if you're used to the way some other program (like Microsoft Word) does it, you can match XPress to that method. Second, if you choose anything other than Command-Z (Ctrl-Z), then you can undo multiple steps with Command-Z (Ctrl-Z) and then redo multiple steps with whichever other keyboard shortcut you choose. If both Undo and Redo are set to Command-Z (Ctrl-Z), the shortcut only undoes the last action.

When you can't Undo it. Unfortunately, there are a number of things that you'd expect to be able to undo that you can't. For instance, if you insert or delete a page, XPress can't undo that. XPress can't undo adding or moving a guide. Nor can it undo something you've changed on a master page once you've returned to the document page. Plus, sometimes if you do something that is undoable, it wipes out the undo list so you can't undo anything you did before that action. This is one reason I do a lot of saving (so I can always perform a Revert to Save if I need to).

Text and type styles. QuarkXPress bundles together any text actions that you do at the same time so that if you select Undo, all the changes get undone at once. That means typing a bunch of text into a text box counts as one Undo step, but as soon as you move the cursor and start typing someplace else, you begin a new undo step. For example, if you type three words, then move back a word and add a letter, XPress resets its Undo "memory" so an Undo would only remove the added letters. This can be frustrating if you don't really know what's going on because it seems like it forgets stuff. It's not forgetful; we are.

Similarly, all the typographic styles you apply to text count as one Undo step until you move the cursor. Here's an example: If you select a word and make it bold and italic and small caps and change the font size four times (I'll show you how to do all that later in the book), and then press Command-Z (Ctrl-Z), QuarkXPress reverts to how the text was before you applied any type styles. You can't just undo the last font size change you made.

Cancel and Interruptible Redraw

You can get yourself out of a bad situation in every dialog box or palette in QuarkXPress by remembering the ubiquitous and powerful features: Command-period or Esc (Cancel) and Command-Z (Undo). For instance, if you change the x or y coordinates for a text box, and then decide what you're doing is a mistake, you can undo it even before the change takes place. Pressing Command-Z (Ctrl-Z) reverts to the previous state and keeps the field highlighted. Pressing Command-period or Esc reverts and takes you out of the palette or dialog box altogether.

Interruptible Redraw. QuarkXPress has a "hidden" feature that can make life much better: interruptible screen redraw. If you have 43 pictures and text boxes on your page and it's taking forever to draw them, you can press Command-period (or Esc) to cancel the redraw. QuarkXPress stops drawing as soon as it finishes drawing the next object (that's slightly different from some other programs, such as Adobe Photoshop, which stop immediately).

You can also interrupt screen redraw by selecting a menu item or typing any other keyboard shortcut. Note that screen redraw is only relevant when the Off-screen Draw option is turned off in Preferences (see "Changing Defaults," later in this chapter).

▼ ▼

Tip: Forcing Screen Redraw. As I'm talking about screen redraw, I should probably also mention that Command-Option-period (Macintosh) and Shift-Esc (Windows) will force XPress to redraw the screen. I find this useful because XPress has various persistent problems (bugs) that cause it, on occasion, to update the screen improperly. Often, if something just looks weird (like "what's that line doing there?" or "my text isn't supposed to look like that"), just force a screen redraw and the problem goes away.

▼ ▼

Getting Around Your Document

QuarkXPress shows you the pages in your document as though they were all spread out in order on a giant white pasteboard. However, unless you happen to work on an enormous screen, you never get to see much of the pasteboard at one time. Let's look at how you can move around to see different parts of a page, and different pages within your document.

Scrolling

The first step in moving around within your document is scrolling. *Scrolling* refers to using the horizontal and vertical scroll bars on the right and bottom sides of the document window to move your page (see Figure 2-16). If you click the arrow at the top of the vertical scroll bar, you move a bit "up" your page (closer to the top). If you click the left arrow in the horizontal scroll bar, you move to the left on your page, and so on.

I find that many people never get past this elementary level of scrolling. This is conceivably the slowest method you could use. I implore you to look at the alternatives.

You can move large distances in your document by moving the little white box (some people call it the "scroll elevator") in the scroll bars. Clicking in the gray area moves you by one screen at a time. You can also use keystrokes to move around the screen vertically. Table 2-2 shows you how to do this.

▼ ▼

Tip: Scroll Speed. If you do use the scroll bar arrows to get around, you definitely want to examine the Scroll Speed feature in the Preferences dialog box. This feature lets you control how far each click in a scroll-bar arrow takes you. For example, if you have the Scroll Speed set to Fast, then clicking an arrow may move you an entire screen or more. If you have it set to Slow, a click may move the screen one or two pixels.

Don't confuse Scroll Speed with Speed Scroll. I cover the latter in "Changing Defaults," later in this chapter.

Figure 2-16
Document window

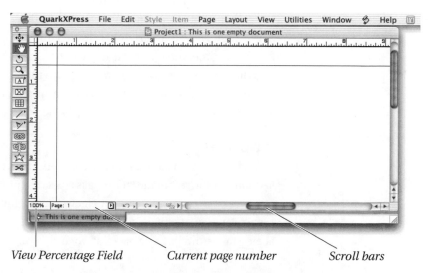

View Percentage Field   *Current page number*   *Scroll bars*

To move . . .	Press . . .	Extended keyboards, press . . .
Up one screen	Control-K	Page Up
Down one screen	Control-L	Page Down
Start of document	Control-A	Home
End of document	Control-D	End
First page	Control-Shift-A	Shift-Home
Last page	Control-Shift-D	Shift-End
Next page	Control-Shift-L	Shift-Page Down
Previous page	Control-Shift-K	Shift-Page Up

▼ ▼

Tip: Live Scrolling. When you drag the white box along the scroll bar, it's often difficult to tell how far on the page or the document you've gone. This is because the vertical scroll bar represents the entire length of your document, and the horizontal scroll bar represents the full width of the pasteboard. If you have multipage spreads in your document, the pasteboard can be very large (see more on spreads in Chapter 4, *Building a Document*). But if you hold down the Option/Alt key while you drag the box, the screen scrolls with you, so you can see how far you're going (this is called *live scrolling*).

You can enable live scrolling on a permanent basis by checking in the Live Scroll box in the Interactive tab of the Preferences dialog box. With that feature turned on, Option-dragging (Alt-dragging) on the scroll bar box makes the document *not* live scroll.

▼ ▼

Tip: Use the Grabber Hand. The Grabber Hand is arguably the most important tool in QuarkXPress. The problem with the scroll bars is that you can only scroll in one direction at a time. It's a hassle: down a little, over to the left, down a little more, now to the right, and so on. But if you hold down the Option/Alt key at any time, the cursor turns into the Grabber Hand, and when you click and drag, the page moves where you move the Grabber Hand. Try it! I think it's one of the greatest methods for getting around the page.

▼ ▼

Zooming

If you have a brand-new 90-inch HDTV monitor, you may not need to read this section. For the rest of us, zooming is a necessity of life. When you zoom in and out on a page, you are using an electronic magnifying glass, first enlarging a particular area of a page, and then reducing your screen view so that you are seeing the entire page or pages at once.

QuarkXPress lets you magnify or reduce your screen view from 10 percent to 800 percent, in steps of 0.1 percent. You can jump between several preset views quickly by selecting them from the View menu or by using keystrokes.

▼ ▼

Tip: Maximum Zoom Power. If you switch back and forth between the Macintosh and Windows, as I do, you'll quickly notice that although you can always zoom in to 800 percent on the Macintosh, you generally can't get any closer than 692 percent in Windows. What's the deal? It has to do with screen resolution. QuarkXPress for Windows assumes your screen resolution is about 96 ppi (pixels per inch), though you can change this value in the Preferences dialog box (see "Changing Defaults," later in this chapter). If you lower the screen resolution setting in XPress, the program lets you zoom in more (at 72 ppi, you can zoom in to a full 800 percent). If you raise the resolution setting, you can zoom in less.

As for the Macintosh, QuarkXPress is stuck believing that your screen is displaying 72 ppi, no matter what the resolution truly is. Oh well.

▼ ▼

View menu. The View menu lists zooming values of Fit in Window, 50%, 75%, Actual Size (which is 100 percent), 200%, and Thumbnails. Fit in Window adjusts the zoom percentage to fit whatever size window you have open at the time. If you're working with facing pages, then the scale is set to fit a two-page spread in the window. Thumbnails zooms way back so that you can see a bunch of pages at the same time (but it does more than that; see "Thumbnails," later in this chapter).

When you select a magnification from the View menu, QuarkXPress automatically zooms to the percentage you want and centers the current page in your window. If any item on the page you're looking at is selected when you switch magnifications, QuarkXPress centers that item in the window. Or, if the item is on the pasteboard, the program centers it if any part of the item is showing when you switch views.

For example, if you select a short rule on a page while viewing at Fit in Window size, and then select Actual Size, QuarkXPress zooms in and centers that rule on your screen. If the selected item is a text box and you have the Content tool selected, the program centers the cursor or whatever text is highlighted. This makes zooming in and out on a page much easier: if you're editing some text, you can use Fit in Window to see the "big picture," then select Actual Size to zoom back to where your cursor is in the text.

▼ ▼

Tip: Accidental Zooming. You've probably had it happen to you already: You select Fit in Window from the View menu, and suddenly you jump to a different page. It's really not as strange as it seems. Fit in Window always fits the current page in the window. But what's the current page? It's the page that is touching the upper-left corner of the document window. If just a tiny bit of the previous page is showing at the top or left of the window, that's the one that will get centered on-screen.

▼ ▼

Zoom tool. You can also use the Zoom tool on the Tool palette for your quick zooming pleasure. Sorry, did I say "quick?" I hardly find clicking in the Tool palette, then on my document, then back in the Tool palette a "quick" procedure. However, we're in luck because there's a keystroke: On the Macintosh, if you hold down the Control and Shift keys, you get a Zoom In tool; add the Option key, and you get a Zoom Out tool. (In earlier versions, it was simply the Control key; in fact, if you like the old way, you can bring it back in the Interactive panel of the Preferences dialog box; see "Changing Defaults," later in this chapter.)

In Windows, you have to press both Control and the spacebar to zoom in; Control-Alt-spacebar provides the Zoom Out tool. (If you have a text box selected, make sure you press the Control key before the spacebar, or else you'll type a space character.)

Each time you click on your page with the Zoom tool, QuarkXPress zooms in or out by a particular percentage. The increments that it uses can be controlled in the Tool Preferences dialog box (see "Changing Defaults," later in this chapter).

Keystroke zooming. If I can avoid using the menus, I usually do; they're almost never the most efficient method of working. So when it comes to zooming, I much prefer to use keystrokes and clicks. Table 2-3 shows the basic keystrokes and keystroke-and-click combinations for zooming in and out.

▼ ▼

Tip: Fit More in Your Window. If you select Fit in Window from the View menu or press Command-zero (Ctrl-zero), QuarkXPress fits the current page to the window. However, if you hold down the Option key while selecting Fit in Window (or press Command-Option-zero or Ctrl-Alt-zero), it zooms to fit the entire width of the pasteboard into the window.

This feature has a fun corollary: If you don't need a big pasteboard around your facing-pages layout, you can shrink down its width to 10 percent or 20 percent of the page width (this is a setting in the Preferences dialog box). Now when you press Command-Option-zero (Ctrl-Alt-zero), you get the equivalent of "fit spread in window."

▼ ▼

Table 2-3

Zooming

PRESS . . .	TO GO TO OR TOGGLE . . .
Command-1/Ctrl-1	Actual Size
Command-0/Ctrl-0	Fit in Window
Command-Option-0/Ctrl-Alt-1	Fit pasteboard in window
Command-Option-click/Ctrl-Alt-click	Between Actual Size and 200%

Magnification field. Another of my favorite methods for zooming in and out is by adjusting the View Percent field in the lower-left corner of the document window. Note that when you're in Actual Size, this field shows "100%". Whenever you zoom in or out, this field changes. Well, you can change it yourself by clicking in the field (or highlight the field by pressing Control-V on the Mac, or Control-Alt-V in Windows), typing a percentage, and pressing Enter or Return. You can also type T for Thumbnails or M for Maximum (usually 800% on the Mac and 692% on Windows).

Zoom marquee. There's no doubt that my favorite zooming technique is to hold down the Control key (to get the Zoom tool), and drag a marquee around a specific area (in Windows, press Control-spacebar). When you let go of the mouse button, QuarkXPress zooms into that area at the precise percentage necessary to fit it in the window. (I like to call this "magdrag," for magnification-drag.) So if you're at Actual Size and drag a marquee around one word, QuarkXPress can zoom in to 600 percent and center that word on your screen. You can use this to zoom out, too, by dragging a marquee that's larger than your screen (the screen scrolls along as you drag the marquee), but I don't find this as useful.

Moving from Page to Page

In the last section I talked about moving around your page using scrolling and zooming. Because every page in your layout sits on one big pasteboard, these same techniques work for moving around within your layout. You can scroll from one page to another using the scroll bars and the Grabber hand, and so on. But let's be frank: This is not the fastest way to get around. It might help in moving around a two-page spread, but not for moving around a 200-page book. Instead, there are ways to move by whole pages at a time, or to jump to the page you want.

Extended keyboards. If you have an extended keyboard (I recommend these for serious desktop publishers), you can move one page forward or back by pressing Shift-Page Up or Shift-Page Down (on the Macintosh you can replace the Shift key with the Command key if you like). If you don't have an extended keyboard on the Mac, Control-Shift-K and Control-Shift-L also move one page at a time.

You may find yourself wanting to jump to the very beginning or end of your layout. On a Macintosh, you can press the Shift-Home key or Shift-End (or, on non-extended keyboards on the Mac, press Control-Shift-A or Control-Shift-D). In Windows, press Control-Page Up or Control-Page Down to jump to the first or last page of the layout, respectively.

Moving to a specific page. If you're trying to get to a page somewhere in the middle of your document, there are four methods to get there quickly.

▶ Double-click the page icon in the Page Layout palette or single-click the page number below the icon (I discuss this palette in more detail in Chapter 4, *Building a Document*).

▶ You can change the page number field in the lower-left corner of the document window. This is a minor hassle because you have to select the page number and then change it, but it's not too bad.

▶ You can choose a page by clicking on the popup menu next to the page number field in the lower-left corner of the document window, and dragging until you get to the page (see Figure 2-17).

▶ You can select Go To from the Page menu (or, better yet, press Command-J or Ctrl-J). Note that if the page you want to go to is in a differently named section, you have to type the name exactly as it's listed in the lower-right corner of the document window. For instance, if you're using Roman numerals and you want to jump to the fourth page, you have to type "iv". (See "Sections and Page Numbering," in Chapter 4, *Building a Document*, as well as the next tip.)

Figure 2-17
Popup pages

▼ ▼

Tip: Jump to Absolute Page Numbers. If you play around with sections and page numbers, you may find yourself in a quagmire when you try to print a page range. For example, let's say your layout begins on page 56 and you want to print the 16th through the 20th pages. You could sit around and try to figure out what numbers to plug in to the Print dialog box's page range fields, or you could just type "+16" and "+20". The plus sign before the number means that the numbers are absolute; the first page is "+1", the second page is "+2", and so on.

This is also helpful when moving to a page using Go To page. You can quickly jump to the 20th page by typing "+20".

▼ ▼

Note that for any of the keystrokes I've outlined here, there is a menu item in the Page menu. I think working with a mouse and menus is fast, but there is no doubt that once you start working with keystrokes, moving around your document becomes lightning-fast.

▼ ▼

Manipulating Your Layout

Okay, now that I've covered how you can move around your document, let's talk about how you can insert, delete, and move pages within your layout. There are three good ways to handle these tasks in QuarkXPress: menu items, thumbnails, and the Page Layout palette. Let's look at each one of these.

Menu Manipulations

As I said much earlier in this chapter, the Page menu holds QuarkXPress's page-manipulation tools. In this section we're primarily interested in the first three menu items: Insert, Delete, and Move. I'm holding off on a discussion of inserting pages until another chapter (see "Making Pages," in Chapter 4, *Building a Document*), so I'll talk about the last two.

Delete. When you choose Delete from the Page menu, QuarkXPress displays the Delete dialog box. This is a simple dialog box asking you which page or pages to delete. If you only want to delete one, just type it in the From field. If you want to delete consecutive pages, then type the page range in the From and To fields.

Move. If you want to move a page or a range of pages, you can select Move from the Page menu. Here you can specify which page or pages to move, and where to move them (see Figure 2-18). For example, if you want to move pages 15 through 21 to after the last page in your layout, you can type "15" in the first field, "21" in the second field, and click To End of Layout. You also can specify a move to before or after a specific page.

Figure 2-18
The Move Pages
dialog box

▼ ▼

Tip: Doing It to the End. QuarkXPress is smarter than the average computer program. In fact, it's slowly learning plain English. For example, if you want
to delete from one page to the end of the layout, but you don't know what the
last page number is, you can type "end" in the Thru field of the Delete dialog
box. This also works in the Move Pages dialog box. For instance, you can move
from page 15 to the end of the layout by typing "15" and "end" in the fields.

▼ ▼

Thumbnails

You can see a thumbnail view of your layout in the same way as you select any
other percentage scaling view: from the View menu. (Or by typing "T" into the
Magnification field in the lower-left corner of the document window. Actually
you can type "T", "Th", "Thu", "Thum", or "Thumb"—it just depends on how
much you feel like flinging your fingers across the keyboard.) Although you can
use this to look at your layout as thumbnails (it's like looking at it in 10-percent
viewing mode), Thumbnails is actually more useful as a tool for moving pages.

To move a page in Thumbnails mode, select the page and drag it to where
you want it. While moving a page around in Thumbnails mode, you'll find the
cursor turning into two different icons. The first looks like a minipage. If you
let go of the mouse button with this icon displayed, the page is moved, but it's
added as a spread. That is, the rest of the pages won't shuffle and reflow (see
"Multipage Spreads" in Chapter 4, *Building a Document*).

The second icon, a black arrow, appears when you move the cursor directly to the left of or under another page. This arrow means that the page will be
placed directly before or after a specific page. Letting go of the mouse button
when you have this arrow cursor reflows the pages in the layout. This is the
same as moving pages using Move from the Page menu.

▼ ▼

Tip: Selecting Multiple Pages. It's easy to select more than one page at a
time in Thumbnails mode or in the Page Layout palette (more on the latter in
the next section). If the pages are consecutive (pages four through nine, for
example), click the first page in the range, hold down the Shift key, and click the
last page in the range. Every page between the two is selected (this is just like
selecting text).

You can select nonconsecutive pages (such as pages one, three, and nine) while in Thumbnails mode or in the Page Layout palette by holding down the Command/Ctrl key while clicking on each page.

▼ ▼

Page Layout Palette

The Page Layout palette (this was called the Document Layout palette in earlier versions) is one of the key elements in working efficiently with multipage documents. You can move pages, delete them, insert new ones, create and apply master pages, and more, with a quick drag of an icon. Let's look at how you can use this palette to delete and move pages.

To open the Page Layout palette, select Show Page Layout from the View menu (see Figure 2-19). For our purposes right now, you only need to think about two parts of the palette: the page icons and the icons in the upper-right corner. I'll get into more advanced uses (applying master pages, for instance) in Chapter 4, *Building a Document*.

Moving pages within the Page Layout palette is just like moving them in Thumbnails mode, except that you can't see what's on the pages. Simply select the page or pages that you want to move, and drag them to their destinations. QuarkXPress uses the same icons here as in Thumbnails mode. That is, the little page icon means that you're creating a spread, and the right and down arrow icons mean that you're moving the pages into the flow (the other pages displace to accommodate the moved page).

Deleting a page with the Page Layout palette is even simpler than deleting a file while on the Mac desktop or Windows Explorer: just select the page(s) and click the Delete icon (on the Mac, it's the little trash can; in Windows, it's the icon with the "X" through it). However, do note that in QuarkXPress you

Figure 2-19
The Page
Layout palette

— Blank pages and duplicate/delete area

— Master pages area

— Document layout area

cannot undo these actions and retrieve a page that you throw away. Obviously, it's worth being extra careful in this area.

Moving Items Between Documents

You don't have to stop at moving items and pages just within your layout. You can move them from one document to another faster than you can say, "Maybe it's time to get a larger monitor for my computer."

To move a page item from one document to another, you must have both documents open and visible on your screen. This is difficult on small screens. I find the Tile Documents feature (under the Window menu) useful for this. Then, with the Item tool select the item you want to move (or hold down the Command/Ctrl key to get the Item tool temporarily), and drag it across.

If you pause between the document windows, you may find the first document starts to scroll. Don't worry, it's just QuarkXPress not realizing that you want to move it all the way into the second document. Just move the item a little farther and the scrolling should stop. Once you let go of the mouse button, the item is copied over into the new document. Note that I say "copied." The item is not actually moved; rather, it is copied from one into the other. To get rid of it in the first document, just delete it (Command-K or Ctrl-K).

Of course, there is always the old standby method for getting items from one document to another: Copy and Paste. Here, you want to make sure that you have the Item tool selected while in both documents, or else XPress won't know that you want to copy or paste the item itself.

Moving Pages Between Documents

Versions 1 and 2 of QuarkXPress sported a Get Document function, which was extremely useful. First of all, it let you copy whole pages from one document to another. Secondly, it let you access pages from a different document without actually opening it (this was often helpful in retrieving corrupted files). Unfortunately, the Get Document feature is long gone.

Taking its place is a feature that lets you actually drag a page from one document into another, as long as both documents are in Thumbnails view. (Hold down the Option key and select Tile to put *all* documents into Thumbnails mode.) This is especially handy if you like to see the pages that you're copying before you copy them. In fact, Quark's tech support still recommends this as a preferred method for saving documents that are becoming corrupted.

▼ ▼

Tip: Moving Background Windows. If you're working on a Macintosh and you need to resize and move your document windows in order to drag across page items or even full pages, you might find it helpful to know that you can move a window without actually selecting it. That is, normally, if you click on a window, that window is brought to the front (it becomes *active*). You can move a window without bringing it to the front by holding down the Command key while you click and drag the bar at its top. Actually, this isn't a QuarkXPress feature; it's a Macintosh feature.

Changing Defaults

Each and every one of you reading this book is different, and you all have different ways of using QuarkXPress. Fortunately, Quark has given you a mess of options for customizing the internal default settings. A *default setting* is a value or indicates a way of doing something; QuarkXPress uses the default value or method unless you specifically choose something else.

For example, the factory default setting for picture and text boxes is that they are created with no border frame around them (see "Frames, Dashes, and Stripes," in Chapter 3, *Tools of the Trade*). But if you're so inclined, you can modify QuarkXPress so that every text box you create is automatically framed with a two-point line. In this way, you can customize your work environment so that it best suits you.

Default settings range from how guides are displayed on the screen to how QuarkXPress builds small caps characters. In version 4, Quark consolidated a number of different preferences dialog boxes into two: Application Preferences and Document Preferences. In version 5, they went even further and merged these into a single Preferences dialog box. On the Macintosh, you can find the Preferences feature under the Application menu (the one labelled "QuarkXPress"). In Windows, you can find the Preferences feature in the Edit menu.

XTensions can add their own preferences to this submenu, as well. For instance, Quark's Type Tricks XTension (which comes with XPress 6) adds a preference that lets you set defaults for its Fraction and Price feature. Similarly, the Index and QuarkCMS XTensions that ship with XPress also add their own panels to the Preferences dialog box, too. Let's take a look at the Preferences dialog box here.

Layout and Application Preferences

The Preferences dialog box (press Command-Option-Shift-Y on the Macintosh or Ctrl-Alt-Shift-Y in Windows) contains preferences that affect the ways your layout and the program act. The dialog box is broken down into 23 different panels (also called tabs), each of which contains a mess o' preferences you can set. (There may be more or fewer than this, depending on what XTensions you have installed.) The first section of panels are application preferences; the last section of panels are layout preferences. The difference is important.

Application preferences affect how XPress works on your particular computer. The settings aren't saved with your layouts, so if you move them to another computer, they may appear slightly different. This isn't bad, because we're talking about general changes such as the color of the margin guides and the width of the pasteboard.

Layout preferences only affect the current layout. Even if you have other layouts or documents open at the same time, the change is made to only the one that is active. However, if no documents are open when you change this dialog box, then you are setting new defaults for the whole program and that change is made to every new layout you create from then on (it doesn't change layouts you've already made). These changes are stored in the XPress Preferences file, and are used when creating new documents or layouts.

Let's take a close look at each preference setting in each panel of this dialog box. However, note that I won't cover the avenue.quark, Browsers, or Street Post panels here; instead, I'll hold off until Chapter 14, *Going Online with QuarkXPress* to cover the HTML stuff and Appendix E, *XML Tools* to cover the other the XML features.

Display Preferences

The first panel, Display, lets you control how your document pages and your images appear on-screen (see Figure 2-20). The controls are slightly different between the Macintosh and Windows versions.

Guide Colors. The controls at the top of the Display tab let you change the colors of QuarkXPress's three types of guide lines: Margin, Ruler, and Grid (this control is available for both Macintosh and Windows). The Margin guides are the lines that show where the page margins are. The Ruler guides are the guides you can pull out onto the page. And the Grid guides are the lines that the program shows you when you have Show Baseline Grid enabled (see Chapter 6, *Type and Typography*). Of course, if your monitor only displays grays, then this control only affects the shade of gray you'll see.

Tile to Multiple Monitors. Here's where you tell QuarkXPress whether you want it to consider *all* the monitors you have plugged into your computer when it tiles open documents. Unless you have more than one monitor hooked up, you should just leave this turned off. Currently, this is a Macintosh-only feature.

Figure 2-20
The Display panel
of the Preferences
dialog box
(XPress for Windows
versus Macintosh)

Full-screen Documents. Checking this box lets you zoom windows to fill your entire screen; unchecking it leaves room for the Tool and Measurements palettes. I typically leave this turned off, but why should you listen to me? The options are here to make your life easier. This is currently a Macintosh-only feature, as well.

Off-screen Draw. I guess some Mac-heads don't like seeing QuarkXPress draw each page object one at a time (the slower the Macintosh, the slower the redraw). When Off-Screen Draw is turned on (it is, by default), QuarkXPress redraws all the items "behind the scenes" and shows them to you all at once.

I like to turn this off, so I can see what's taking so long and stop it if I want (see "Interruptible Redraw," earlier in this chapter). It takes just as long either way, so it really comes down to how you like your computer to behave.

Opaque Text Box Editing. Back in QuarkXPress 3.x, the program always made text boxes opaque when you selected them with the Content tool. In XPress 4, the folks at Quark changed the behavior so that the box was transparent (if it had a background color of None). Some liked it the old way because it let you edit the contents of a box free of any distractions caused by other page elements. Some liked it the new way because they wanted to edit the content of text boxes and see what was behind them at the same time. Now, in XPress 6 you have a choice: When you turn on the Opaque Text Box Editing checkbox (it is off by default), XPress returns to its old opaque, version 3.x behavior.

Color TIFFs/Gray TIFFs. The Color TIFFs and Gray TIFFs popup menus (these appear on both Macintosh and Windows) let you control how QuarkXPress builds screen previews for TIFF images when you import them. As you'll see in Chapter 9, *Pictures*, a TIFF picture doesn't have a built-in preview, so XPress has to build one for it when you import it. These preferences *only* affect how images look on screen and on non-PostScript printers (like a desktop inkjet).

In QuarkXPress 3.x and 4.x, Color TIFF was set to 8-bit (256 colors) and Gray TIFF was set to 16 Levels of gray. This kept file sizes small and page drawing snappy, but it left users unhappy because image quality was poor. So in XPress 5, the folks at Quark increased the default value for Color TIFF to 32-bit (on the Macintosh it's 32-bit, in Windows it's 24-bit, but they're really pretty much the same thing), and for Gray TIFF to 256 levels of grays. The result: much better-looking pictures on screen, but *much* larger file sizes and sometimes slower performance. This is the main reason that QuarkXPress 5 and 6 documents are typically much larger in file size than those from version 4.

If you are creating Web layouts with XPress, the 32-bit Color TIFF preference is great. However, for print layouts I tend to change this back to 8-bit. The screen quality isn't as good, but everything else seems to run more smoothly. When I care a lot about image quality (like when I want to adjust a clipping path around an imported image), I turn on the High Res Preview feature (see Chapter 9, *Pictures*).

Pasteboard Width. That pasteboard around a layout's pages is great, but I usually find it a little too large (and—depending on the job—occasionally too small). Fortunately, I can control how wide the pasteboard is by specifying a percentage in the Pasteboard Width field. The default value of 100 percent tells

QuarkXPress to make each side of the pasteboard the same width as one page in the layout. That is, if you have an 8.5-by-11-inch page, each side of the pasteboard is 8.5 inches wide. Changing the Pasteboard Width to 50 percent makes the pasteboard half that width.

Unfortunately, there's still no way to change the height of the pasteboard, so it's stuck at a half-inch above and below your page. I keep hoping that Quark will change this, but no luck yet.

▼ ▼

Tip: PasteboardXT. Many of the world's religions teach us that it's important to be mindful of every step, as the slightest wrongdoing can cause a great disaster. Case in point: A small XTension developer released a shareware XTension almost ten years ago called PasteboardXT that lets you change the height of your pasteboard. It's a great idea, and everyone wanted this feature, so they downloaded it from the Internet and America Online and Compuserve and they passed it around in their offices and schools . . . . But this version of PasteboardXT had an interesting flaw: it was a *required* XTension. That means that if you use this XTension while working on a document, then you save the document and give it to me, I have to have the XTension, too, or else I won't be able to open your document.

Many of the world's religions also tend to frown on the four-letter words that people used when they discovered this problem. The developer realized his wrongdoing, and quickly released a newer version of PasteboardXT that no longer acted as a required XTension. The time between wrongdoing and redemption was not great, perhaps a few months. The effect, on the other hand, has been staggering.

The "PasteboardXT problem" has been far and away the biggest hassle for desktop publishers in the history of desktop publishing. Hundreds of thousands of people have been affected by that one error, even though the solution to the problem is incredibly simple: If you use any newer version of the XTension, open the file and resave it; the requirement is removed. Or, you can open the file and resave it with the Pasteboard XTerminator XTension loaded (you can get both of these at *www.markzware.com*).

What does this lesson teach us?

▼ ▼

Show All Alerts. QuarkXPress has a number of alert dialog boxes which pop up from time to time—like the one that appears whenever you press the Printer button in the Print dialog box. Most of these annoying dialog boxes have a checkbox that says "Don't Show This Again." Almost everyone turns this checkbox on, and they never see those alerts again. However, if you click this button in the Display panel of the Preferences dialog box, those alerts will come back. Pretty exciting, huh?

Display DPI Value. Earlier in this chapter, I mentioned that the limitation on how far you could magnify your page on a Windows machine depended on your Display DPI Value. This control is a Windows-only setting (though I have no idea why; Macintoshes can have as widely variable screen resolution as PCs), and it lets you more closely match your page size in QuarkXPress to your monitor's resolution. Because most PC monitors average around 96 ppi, this is the default value in the Preferences dialog box.

The idea is that if you hold up a physical ruler to the screen, one inch on the ruler should equal (more or less) one inch on QuarkXPress's ruler. If it doesn't you can adjust the Display DPI Value. Larger values make XPress's ruler larger; lower values make XPress's ruler smaller. If you don't care about matching the screen to reality, you can adjust at will (or just leave it alone).

Interactive Preferences

The Interactive panel of the Preferences dialog box is a grab bag of options that controls XPress's screen display and what happens when you navigate around your document (see Figure 2-21). Again, these are all Application preferences, so they affect your whole program, not just individual layouts or documents.

Speed Scroll. Here's a wonderful enhancement to XPress that makes me want to bow down and give thanks in the general direction of Denver (where Quark lives). When Speed Scroll is turned on (it is by default), QuarkXPress automatically greeks the display of pictures, graphics, and blends as you scroll through a layout. Only when you stop scrolling does it take the time to properly display these elements.

This may not sound like a big improvement at first, but if you've died of boredom while scrolling through a long document with lots of big four-color TIFFs, you'll appreciate how much time Speed Scroll can save you (that is, unless you *like* taking a coffee break while you scroll). I turn this on and leave it on.

Scroll Speed. Yep, now there's Speed Scroll *and* Scroll Speed. It's not confusing, is it? As I discussed earlier in the "Scrolling" section, Scroll Speed controls how fast QuarkXPress scrolls when you use the scroll bars. Note that the default Scroll Speed control setting is pretty slow. Increasing the speed (by clicking on the right arrow) can make a drastic difference in how quickly you can make your pages (although this won't speed up screen redraw).

Figure 2-21

The Interactive panel
of the Preferences
dialog box

Live Scroll. My editor keeps telling me not to be redundant in my writing. And since I already gave my *spiel* about Live Scroll earlier in this chapter (see "Scrolling"), here I'll just say: Yes, this is a great feature, and it's great to have it built right in, but it's nowhere near as cool as the Grabber Hand.

Smart Quotes. This option both turns on the Smart Quotes feature and lets you specify which characters will be used for open and closed quotes. Smart Quotes works by looking to the left of the insertion point to determine if an open or closed quote character should go there. If the character to the left is a white space character, such as a spaceband, tab key, or return, QuarkXPress enters an open single or double quote when you press the ' or " key.

The popup menu lets you choose some alternative quote characters, including various double quotes, Spanish alternatives, and inside and outside guillemet (French quote mark) combinations, which can be useful if you're formatting foreign-language documents (see Figure 2-22).

Figure 2-22

Different kinds of Smart
Quotes available

> "This is an example of Smart Quotes," he said.
>
> "This is a different kind of Smart Quotes," he added.
>
> „Here's yet another kind of Smart Quotes," he continued.
>
> «These quotes are called guillemets,» he went on.
>
> »So are these, but they're reversed,« he concluded.

The main place where Smart Quotes isn't so smart is when you're typing apostrophes at the beginning of a word—"In late '93," for instance. Watch out for these. (See "Tip: Getting Your Quotes Straight," in Chapter 6, *Type and Typography*, for a lesson on how to type curly and straight quotes quickly.)

▼ ▼

Tip: Toggling Smart Quotes. Smart Quotes is really cool if you type a lot in QuarkXPress. However, if you ever want to enter a single or double "neutral" straight quote character, it's a hassle to turn off Smart Quotes first. Instead, hold down the Control key when typing the quote (single or double). When Smart Quotes is on, you get a straight quote; when it's off, you get a curly quote.

▼ ▼

Delayed Item Dragging. Normally, when you click on an object and drag it somewhere on your page, XPress just shows you a gray outline of the item you're moving. If you're performing a quick move, this is probably all you really need. But if you're trying to position something carefully, then you usually need to see the object itself. If you click the mouse button down on top of the object and hold it down for a moment before you drag it, the object flashes quickly. That's your sign that when you drag it, you'll be able to see the picture or the text or whatever.

The Delayed Item Dragging option on the Interactive tab lets you control two things. First, the Delay field lets you specify how long you need to hold the mouse button down on an object before XPress flips into this mode. You can type anything from 0.1 second (almost instantaneous) to five seconds (why even bother?). I prefer about 0.5 second, but you should play around with it and see what suits you best.

Second, you have to choose between Show Contents and Live Refresh. The default, Live Refresh, is a wonderful feature that forces XPress to reflow text as you move objects over it. For example, let's say you're trying to set the width of a text box so that the text flows just perfectly in it. You can click on one of the side handles and wait for a moment for the effect to kick in. The cursor changes to the Live Refresh cursor (it looks like a little starburst). Now the text reflows automatically as you drag the handle.

The other setting, Show Contents, is simply a way to turn Live Refresh off, so that when you click-hold-and-drag you can see the object but it doesn't affect text flow (at least not while you're dragging). The only time I would choose this is when I'm working on a slower computer (Live Refresh does take extra processing power).

Page Range Separators. How do you type "from page four through page nine, plus page 12" in the Print dialog box? You use page range separators. The default separators are the hyphen and the comma: "4-9, 12". However, you can change this to any other two symbols you like. I can't think of a good reason to ever alter this preference.

Control Key Activates. By default, you get a context-sensitive menu when you click with the Control key on the Macintosh and you get the Zoom tool (temporarily) when you Control-Shift-click. You can reverse this behavior in the Interactive panel of the Preferences dialog box by selecting Zoom in the Control Key Activates section. Old fuddy-duddies like me who want XPress to act like it did back in versions 3.x and 4.x use this feature.

Drag and Drop Text. Drag and Drop Text lets you drag selected text from one place in a text box to another. I cover this in detail in Chapter 5, *Word Processing*.

Show Tool Tips. When the Show Tool Tips option is on (it is, by default) and your cursor hovers over a tool in the Tool palette for a moment, XPress displays a little tag that tells you the name of the tool. It seems like every piece of software on the market has to have this feature these days. Maybe it's useful in other software, but it's annoying in XPress. I turn this off and leave it off. (Obviously it doesn't hurt to leave it on, though.)

Save Preferences

What gets saved, when is it saved, and where does it get saved? Those are the questions answered on the Save tab of the Preferences dialog box (see Figure 2-23). Most of these features are discussed elsewhere in the book, so I won't cover them in detail here.

Auto Save and Auto Backup. Auto Save ensures that you don't lose too much work because of a system crash or other unexpected event. Auto Backup helps you carry out the chore of keeping backups by making copies of your documents when you save them. Both of these are covered in detail in "Saving," earlier in this chapter.

Auto Library Save. I discuss libraries and how to use them in the next chapter, *Tools of the Trade*. However, one thing you should know up front: Libraries are only saved when you close or quit QuarkXPress . . . unless you enable Auto Library Save. This makes XPress save the library every time you add an item to it. It slows down production a little, but it's worth it as a safety measure.

Fortunately, in XPress 4 and 5, Auto Libaray Save is turned on by default. Now the only time I turn it off is when I need to add a lot of items to a library

Figure 2-23

The Save panel
of the Preferences
dialog box

at the same time (so it doesn't stop to save the file between each item). Then I
turn it right back on.

Save Document Position. When Save Document Position is on (it is, by
default), QuarkXPress saves some extra information with your document:
where the window was when you saved the file, what view percentage you
were at, and how large the document window was. I leave this option turned
on most of the time, but I sure wish it did more, like remember what page I was
on when I last left the document, and even where on the page I was zoomed
in. Oh well.

Undo Preferences

The Undo panel of the Preferences dialog box lets you specify the number of
actions XPress remembers. It also lets you choose a keyboard shortcut for the
Redo command. (When will Quark make all keyboard shortcuts editable?) I
covered Undo preferences in more depth earlier in this chapter.

XTensions Manager Preferences

The XTensions Manager panel only offers one control: Show XTensions
Manager at Startup (see Figure 2-24). This lets you specify the conditions on
which you want the XTensions Manager dialog box to appear upon launching
XPress. You do have three choices within this control, though. (Also, see "Tip:
Last-Minute XTension Changes," earlier in this chapter.)

Figure 2-24

The XTensions
Manager panel

▶ The default, "When Error loading XTensions occurs," tells XPress to open the dialog box if something goes wrong with an XTension at launch time; for instance, if it's an old XTension and is going to cause trouble with this version of XPress.

▶ The feature called "When XTension folder changes" tells XPress to open the dialog box whenever it notices that you've added or removed an XTension from the XTension folder. I leave this turned off; after all, if I added or removed an XTension, I probably did it for a good reason.

▶ The third option, "Always," is pretty self-explanatory: Every time you launch XPress, the dialog box appears.

File List and Default Path Preferences

The Deja Vu XTension (which ships with XPress) adds two panels to the Preferences dialog box: File List and Default Path. The first, File List, lets you specify how many recently-used documents XPress remembers and where you'd like them listed (either at the bottom of the File menu or in the Open submenu, under the File menu). Which you choose is entirely up to you and your aesthetic. XPress also gives you the option of alphabetizing the names and displaying the full file path (the folders in which the file is nested) rather than just the file name. I generally increase the number of files to 5 or 6, but I leave the other settings alone.

The Default Path panel lets you specify default folders (or "directories," if you prefer that word) for four different dialog boxes: Open, Save/Save As, Get

Text, and Get Picture. These features are really helpful when you're working on a long project in which all the text is in one folder, all the pictures are in another folder, and you're constantly going to be opening and saving files from a specific folder. Once you've set these in the Preferences dialog box, XPress always brings up these folders first; then, on the occassions that you need a picture or text from somewhere else, you can navigate to it manually.

The problem is that the Default Path settings are application preferences rather than layout preferences, so if you have two or more projects you're working on at the same time, this doesn't really help you much.

Full Res Preview Preferences

While I cover the Full Res Preview feature fully in Chapter 9, *Pictures*, here's the quick low-down version: The first time you turn on Full Resolution from the Preview Resolution submenu (under the Item menu), the program writes a cache file to disk—the next time you turn it on for a picture, XPress reads the cache file, which is faster than recreating the high-res version. The Full Res Preview panel of the Preferences dialog box lets you control how the program handles these cache files—where they reside and how much disk space you'll allow them to take up—as well as under what circumstances XPress should actually display the full-res previews.

Index Preferences

The Index panel of the Preferences dialog box lets you fine-tune the look of your index. I cover indexing in detail in Chapter 8, *Long Documents*.

Jabberwocky Preferences

The Jabberwocky XTension lets you fill text boxes with random text. You can use the Jabberwocky panel of the Preferences dialog box to choose what language to "jabber" in, as well as whether the text should appear in prose (full sentences and paragraphs) or verse (short lines, like a poem).

PDF Preferences

The PDF panel of the Preferences dialog box controls how PDF files are created when you choose Export Layout as PDF from the Export submenu (under the File menu (see Figure 2-25 and Chapter 14, *Going Online with QuarkXPress*).

Workflow. If you only make PDF files occasionally, you'll probably be happy leaving Workflow set to Direct to PDF. This tells XPress to write the PostScript to disk, then immediately use its built-in Jaws software to distill the file into a PDF file.

Figure 2-25
The PDF panel
of the Preferences
dialog box

On the other hand, if you make a lot of PDF files or you want to use Acrobat Distiller for some reason, it's usually faster to just let XPress write the PostScript to disk and then distill all those files later, when you take a lunch break. In that case, choose Create PostScript File for Later Distilling. One other option: If you use Distiller's Watched Folder feature (which automatically distills any PostScript file that appears in a particular folder), then you should turn on the Use Watched Folder checkbox in XPress's Preferences dialog box and direct XPress to that folder (click the Select button). That "watched folder" could even be on a server somewhere.

Default Options. I cover all the details of the PDF Export Options dialog box in Chapter 14, *Going Online with QuarkXPress*, so suffice it to say that you can change the default settings in this dialog box by clicking the Options button on the PDF panel of the Preferences dialog box. For example, if you're tired of typing your name in the Author field, you can set it up once here and not worry about it again.

Fraction/Price Preferences

The Type Tricks XTension adds a panel to the Preferences dialog box which lets you control how it builds "automatic" fractions and prices. I cover this in more depth in Chapter 6, *Type and Typography*.

General Preferences

The General panel of the Preferences dialog box is the catchall, with controls ranging from how guides appear to what happens when you reapply master pages to pages (see Figure 2-26). Some of these preferences have been part of QuarkXPress for 15 years!

Note that these are all Layout preferences, so they only affect the currently-open layout (or all future documents, if no document is currently open). I cover just about all of these in other places in the book, so forgive me if I rush through their descriptions here.

Greek Text Below. Computer screens aren't very good at displaying tiny text, and it often takes too long to display it anyway. Greek Text Below lets you turn this text "off" so you just see gray lines where the text should be (see "Text Greeking," in Chapter 6, *Type and Typography*).

Greek Pictures. Tired of seeing all those pictures on your screen? Slow screen redraw got you down? Turn 'em off with the Greek Pictures control (see "Greeking and Suppression," in Chapter 9, *Pictures*).

Guides. When you pull a guide out onto your page (see "Guides and Rulers," in the next chapter), this control determines whether it sits on top of your page objects or below them. (Hint: Leave this set to In Front.) The Snap Distance is how close an object has to get before it snaps to the guide (when Snap to Guides is turned on in the View menu).

Master Page Items. QuarkXPress may reapply a master page to your document page on various occasions. This control lets you choose what happens to

Figure 2-26

The General panel of the Preferences dialog box

the master page items in these cases (see "Master Pages and Document Pages," in Chapter 4, *Building a Document*).

Auto Picture Import. Picture management is an important topic in QuarkXPress. Auto Picture Import lets you automatically re-import pictures that have changed on disk since the last time you saved the document (see "Picture Usage," in Chapter 9, *Pictures*). Strangely, although this is a layout preference, it appears to apply to all the layouts in a document. Be careful with this one!

Framing. You can place borders around text boxes and picture boxes, but do you want the frame to sit on the outside or the inside of the box? (See "Frames, Dashes, and Stripes" in Chapter 3, *Tools of the Trade*.)

Hyperlinks. Don't like the default magenta and blue colors that XPress uses to mark where anchors and hyperlinks are? You can change their on-screen appearance in the Hyperlinks section of the Preferences dialog box. This is as useful as changing your guide color—that is, it's only useful if you have an allergy to the colors. Otherwise, leave them alone. I cover hyperlinks and anchors in detail in Chapter 14, *Going Online with QuarkXPress*.

Auto Page Insertion. When you import a large amount of text into an automatic text box, XPress may add pages to your document. Here's where you can control this behavior. (See "Automatic Page Insertion," in Chapter 4, *Building a Document*.)

Auto Constrain. If you've never used Auto Constrain, don't start now. It sets up parent/child relationships between boxes that are drawn inside boxes, and it harkens back to the very early days of QuarkXPress (see "Constraining," in the next chapter).

Measurements Preferences

The Measurements panel of the Preferences dialog box (see Figure 2-27) lets you control the rulers and measurements in your document.

Horizontal Measure and Vertical Measure. These two popup menus let you tell XPress what measurement system you like using (see "Guides and Rulers," in Chapter 3, *Tools of the Trade*). Version 4 added the ability to use agates. Remember that even if these popup menus are set to inches, you can always specify measurements in picas or centimeters or any other system.

Figure 2-27
The Measurements
panel of the Preferences
dialog box

Points/Inch. Somebody, sometime, somewhere along the line, decided that PostScript should measure 72 points to an inch. However, as it turns out, printers and graphic designers have always measured just *over* 72 points to the inch. QuarkXPress, being the power-rich program it is, gives you the choice of how you want to measure points. If you have a burning need to work in a traditional measurement setting, you can change the value of the Points/Inch field in the Preferences dialog box to 72.27. I tend toward progress and think that people should just throw out their old rulers and embrace a new standard. Thus, I leave it at 72 points per inch.

Ciceros/Cm. A cicero, in case you're like me (*Americanus stupidus*), is a measurement in the Didot system, used primarily in France and other continental European countries. Just as a pica equals 12 points, the cicero equals 12 points. The difference? Differently sized points. A Didot point equals 0.01483 inch instead of the American-British 0.01383 inch. Anyway, the only really important thing about all this is that QuarkXPress defaults to 2.1967 ciceros per centimeter. This is close enough to a traditional cicero (you can do the math).

Note that if you want to work with Didot points more directly, you should probably also change Points/Inch, above, to 67.43.

Item Coordinates. The ruler that runs across the top of your page can measure the width of your page or the entire spread (see "Guides and Rulers," in the next chapter).

Paragraph and Character Preferences

I spend a good long time covering all the features that appear on the Paragraph and Character tabs in "Typographic Preferences," in Chapter 6, *Type and Typography*, so please forgive me if I punt on their descriptions here. Suffice it to say that these two tabs offer controls that affect how QuarkXPress handles its typography, and without understanding (and setting) some of these features, you're going to bang your head against a wall trying to get good type.

Tool Preferences

The features on the Tools tab of the Preferences dialog box can really help you reduce the monotony of page layout (see Figure 2-28). Perhaps every time you draw a line you change its thickness to 0.5 point. Or perhaps every time you create a text box, you set the Text Inset value to zero or the background color to None. Instead of making the change hundreds of times, just make it once by changing the way the various tools in the Tool palette work.

You can use the settings on the Tool tab to change the default settings for any of the item-creation tools on the Tool palette, plus the Zoom tool (I discuss each of these tools and how best to use them in the next chapter, *Tools of the Trade*). To change a default for an item-creation tool (the tools that create picture boxes, text boxes, or lines), select the tool's icon in the list of tools along the left side of the tab, and then click the Modify button.

Let's take a look at what each button on this tab does.

Modify. When you click the Modify button, XPress opens a dialog box that looks very similar to the Modify dialog box you normally get in QuarkXPress (if you're not familiar with the Modify dialog box, see "Manipulating Your Items," in Chapter 3, *Tools of the Trade*). There are, however, several differences. For instance, there's no Clipping tab because you can't control the default settings for picture clipping (it's always an object-by-object control). Also, fields such as Origin Across and Origin Down are grayed out because those are always going to be different for every box you make.

Use Default Prefs. If you've made changes to a tool's default preferences (by using Modify), you can return it to the factory settings by selecting the tool from the Tool list and clicking Use Default Prefs. For example, if you have to make 35 text boxes, each with a yellow background and a cyan frame, you could change the Rectangular Text Box tool to have these settings, then make the 35 boxes, and then reset the tool by coming back to the Tool tab and clicking this button.

Figure 2-28

The Tools panel
of the Preferences
dialog box

Select Similar Types. If you select any of the text box creation tools and click the Similar Types button, XPress highlights *all* the text box creation tools (the rectangular one, the oval one, the freehand one, and so on). Chances are, if you're going to change the default setting of a line or a box, you'll probably want to make the change for all the similar tools at the same time. Note that you can always select or deselect additional tools from the Tools list by Command/Ctrl-clicking on them.

Select Simliar Shapes. You want all your oval boxes to have a border, but not your rectangular ones? No problem. Select one of the oval box tools and then click the Similar Shapes button. Now when you click Modify, you're changing the settings for just the oval boxes. Note that the Modify dialog box is pretty limited when you select multiple tools that are of different types. For instance, if a text box and a picture box are selected when you click Modify, you can only change a couple of settings, like the box's Background color, and its Frame size and style.

Default Tool Palette. Back in the tip "Enlarge or Reduce Your Tool Palette," I told you how you could move tools around so that your palette would take up more or less space on-screen. If you ever tire of the way you've arranged your Tool palette, just come to the Tools tab of the Preferences dialog box and click the Default Tool Palette button. QuarkXPress resets the tools to their original state again.

View Scale. The last area of the Tools tab, labelled "View Scale," is only active when you select the Zoom tool from the Tools list. This area lets you change the minimum and maximum values that XPress allows you to zoom on your page. However, because these values are already set at their extremes (10 percent to 800 percent), I don't see any good reason to change them. However, I do often change the Increment setting, which controls how far XPress zooms in or out with each click of the Zoom tool (see "Zooming," earlier in this chapter). Because the default setting of 25 percent is pretty paltry, I usually use a more substantial value, like 75 percent or 100 percent, so that when I magnify my page, it really magnifies.

▼ ▼

Tip: Get to Those Tool Preferences Quickly. As you probably can tell, I do almost anything to avoid actually making a selection from a menu. I just find that other methods are faster for me, and they should be for you, too. For example, you can jump to the Tool Preferences dialog box by double-clicking on a tool in the Tool palette. This automatically highlights the tool you chose, and you're ready to make your change.

▼ ▼

Trapping Preferences

Trapping is a complicated issue that can compensate for errors made when printing colors on a printing press. I'm going to skip the features you can find in the Trapping panel of the Preferences dialog box because I discuss them at length in Chapter 12, *Color*.

Quark CMS Preferences

The Quark CMS (Color Management System) XTension has its own panel inside the Preferences dialog box. This is where you turn the color management system on or off (it's off by default), set up what color profiles you want to use for RGB and CMYK colors, and tell the program whether to color manage what you see on screen. I cover these settings in detail in Appendix A, *Color Management*.

Layers Preferences

The Layers palette lets you manage how objects on your page stack up, print, and display on screen (see "The Layers Palette" in Chapter 3, *Tools of the Trade*). The default settings for each new layer in your layout can be controlled here in the Layers panel of the Preferences dialog box (see Figure 2-29).

Figure 2-29
The Layers panel
of the Preferences
dialog box

QuarkXPress from Zero to Sixty

QuarkXPress is an incredibly complex program that lets you create in minutes what it would take hours to do using more traditional methods. Its saving grace is the graphical user interface (GUI, or "gooey"), which offers a user-friendly method of navigating around your document and making changes. We've just begun looking at the myriad of features in QuarkXPress, but with these basics, you'll be up and running in no time.

In the next chapter we take another step further, exploring the tools that QuarkXPress offers, how best to use them, and how to manipulate the various text boxes and lines that you can create on your pages.

3

TOOLS OF THE TRADE

Have you noticed that we typically identify people's professions by the tools they use? I have only to mention some tool, and a vocation comes to mind: A hammer and nails. A cold stethoscope. A blackboard and chalk. A printing press. We don't think of a hairdresser as standing around waving his arms but, rather, wielding a pair of scissors or a razor.

Every trade has a toolbox with which they must make a living, and you and I are no different. Our toolbox is our computer—or, more specifically, QuarkXPress—and the tools inside are the subject of this chapter. Like all tools, these take some time to learn, and it's not until you really start using them regularly that you begin to learn their secrets.

In the last chapter I primarily talked about QuarkXPress's general interface: this does this, that does that. Now my emphasis shifts toward the practical. Let's look at each tool on the Tool palette in turn.

▼ ▼

Items and Contents

If you only learn one thing from this chapter, it should be the difference between items and contents. This is a concept that some people find difficult to understand, but it is really pretty simple. Moreover, the concept of items and contents is central to working efficiently in QuarkXPress.

Let's take it from the beginning. In order to put text on a page, you must place it in a text box. To put a graphic image on a page, you must place it in a picture box. Text boxes act as a sort of corral that holds all the words. There's almost no way a word can get outside the bounds of a text box. Picture boxes act as a sort of window through which you can see a picture. In both cases, the content of the box is different from the box itself.

Boxes are *items*. What goes inside them is *content*. Similarly, a line is an item, and the text you place on it is content. You can modify either one, but you need to use the correct tool at the correct time.

Item tool. The Item tool (or "Pointer tool"; though sometimes it's called by its technical name: "the pointy-thingy"; see Figure 3-1) is the first tool on the Tool palette. It's used for selecting and moving items (picture and text boxes, rules, and so on). You can use the Item tool by either choosing it from the Tool palette or by holding down the Command (Ctrl) key while any other tool is selected (though you can't select or work with multiple items with this Command key trick). I discuss all the things you can do with items later in this chapter, in "Manipulating Items."

Content tool. The second tool on the Tool palette is the Content tool (sometimes called the "Hand tool"). This tool is used for adding, deleting, or modifying the contents of a text or picture box or a text path. Note that its palette icon consists of a text-insertion mark and a hand. When you have selected this tool from the Tool palette, XPress turns the cursor into one of these icons, depending on what sort of box you have highlighted (as we see in Chapter 9, *Pictures*, the hand is for moving images around in a picture box).

Figure 3-1
The Item and
Content tools

Item tool
Content tool

▼ ▼

Tip: Opaque versus Transparent Backgrounds. In the good old days, QuarkXPress always made text and picture boxes opaque when you selected them with the Content tool. For some, this was always annoying because you couldn't change the content in a box and see what was behind the box at the same time. Other people thought this was a great system because it let you edit the contents of a box free of distractions caused by other page elements.

In version 4 the first group won, and when you selected the Content tool, boxes that have a background of None (that is, they're transparent) remained transparent. Fortunately, now you have the option of either behavior: The default works like XPress 4, but if you turn on the Opaque Text Box Editing checkbox in the Display panel of the Preferences dialog box (Command-Option-Shift-Y or Ctrl-Alt-Shift-Y), XPress behaves like it did in earlier versions.

▼ ▼

Tip: Blurring Lines Between Tools. Apparently a lot of people had difficulty remembering which tool—Item or Content—to use for certain tasks, so the folks at Quark loosened the reins a little. You can now perform several tasks that you could never do in QuarkXPress 3.

▶ You can import pictures into picture boxes when the Item tool is selected.

▶ You can change various attributes of pictures using the Style menu and the Measurements palette when the Item tool is selected.

▶ When you have the Content tool selected, you can select multiple objects by Shift-clicking on them or by dragging a marquee around them (see "Selecting Items," below).

Of course, the people who were most upset by these changes were trainers, consultants, and writers. Most people who use XPress daily hardly think about these changes which just make life a little easier.

Note that almost all the other restrictions for these two tools remain: You still need to use the Content tool to import or edit text and to move pictures around within the picture box.

▼ ▼

Selecting Items

The most basic action you can take with a page item in QuarkXPress is to select it. Once again: To select and modify an item itself, you generally need to use the Item tool. To select and modify the contents of a picture or text box, you need to use the Content tool.

You can select more than one item at a time with either the Item or the Content tool. However, the Content tool acts just like the Item tool when you have two or more items selected (the cursor even changes to the Item tool cursor). There are two ways to select more than one item on your page: Shift-clicking and dragging a marquee.

Shift-click. You can select multiple items by Shift-clicking on them with either the Item or Content tool. If you have more than one item selected and you want to deselect one, you can Shift-click on it again (Shift-clicking acts as a toggle for selecting and deselecting).

▼ ▼

Tip: Grab Down Deep. There are plenty of times I've found that I need to reach through one or more objects on my page and grab a box or line that's been covered up. Moving everything on top is a real hassle. Instead, you can select through page items to get hold of objects that are behind them. Hold down the Command-Option-Shift (Ctrl-Alt-Shift) keys while clicking with either the Item or Content tool to select the object one layer down. The second click selects the object on the next layer down, and so on.

▼ ▼

Marquee. If you drag with the Item tool, you can select more than one item in one fell swoop. This is called dragging a *marquee* because QuarkXPress shows you a dotted line around the area that you're dragging over. Every picture box, text box, and line that falls within this marqueed area gets selected, even if the marquee only touches it slightly.

I love the ability to drag a marquee out with the Item tool in order to select multiple objects. It's fast, it's effective, and it picks up everything in its path. However, sometimes it even picks up things you don't want it to pick up. For example, let's say you have an automatic text box on your page and then place some picture boxes on it. If you drag a marquee across the page to select the picture boxes, chances are you'll select the text box, too. You may not notice this at first, but if you group the selection or start dragging it off into a library or someplace else, you'll be taking the text box along for the ride. This spells havoc (press Command/Ctrl-Z to undo the last action).

So, just a quick lesson from people who've been there: Watch out for what you select and group. And if you do select more than you want, remember that you can deselect items by holding down the Shift key and clicking on them.

▼ ▼

Tip: Deselecting En Masse. To deselect one or more objects, you typically need to click a white area on the page (someplace where there are no other objects). However, there's a faster way: You can deselect every selected page item in one stroke by pressing Tab when the Item tool is selected. I find this really helpful when I'm zoomed in on the page and can't tell what's selected and what isn't. When you have the Content tool selected, the Tab key means something different: If a text box is selected, the Tab key types a tab character. But if you've selected more than one object, the Content tool acts just like the Item tool, so the Tab key deselects them.

▼ ▼

Tip: Select All. There's a third way to select more than one object on your page at a time. If you want to select all the page items, you can press Command-A (Ctrl-A). However, this only works when you have the Item tool selected. (When you have the Content tool selected, Command-A or Ctrl-A means "select all the text in a text box.")

▼ ▼

Item Creation Tools

The name of the QuarkXPress game is page layout, so we'd better start laying out some pages. There are five kinds of items you can put on your page: text box, picture box, contentless box, lines, and text paths. I spend much of the rest of the book discussing how to put content inside these objects and what to do with it once it's there, so I'd better spend some time now exploring the items themselves, how to make them, and how to edit them for your needs.

In this section, I discuss the various tools you can use to create page items. There are more tools than ever in this version of the program, so many that the folks at Quark decided to hide some of them inside popout menus in the Tool palette (see Figure 3-2, as well as "Palettes," in Chapter 2, *QuarkXPress Basics*, for more information on how to move these tools in and out of the popout menus).

Note that because the Bézier drawing tools have their own set of problems and solutions, I'm going to hold off on discussing them until the next section.

▼ ▼

Tip: Keeping Your Tools Around. After you use a tool (any tool other than the Zoom tool), the Tool palette automatically reverts back to either the Content or the Item tool (depending on which of the two you last used). This becomes a hassle if you want to use the same tool again. Instead, you can hold down the Option (Alt) key as you select a tool. The tool remains selected until you choose another one.

▼ ▼

Figure 3-2

The item creation tools

For the sake of the illustration, I've pulled all the tools out of their popout menus and into one long palette.

Item tool

Content tool

Rotation tool

Zoom tool

Rectangular Text Box tool

Rounded Corner Text Box tool

Photographic Corner Text Box tool

Beveled Corner Text Box tool

Oval Text Box tool

Bézier Pen Text Box tool

Freehand Bézier Text Box tool

Rectangular Picture Box tool

Rounded Corner Picture Box tool

Photographic Corner Picture Box tool

Beveled Corner Picture Box tool

Oval Picture Box tool

Bézier Pen Picture Box tool

FreeHand Bézier Picture Box tool

Table tool

Orthogonal Line tool

Bézier Pen Line tool

Diagonal Line tool

Freehand Bézier Line tool

Diagonal Text Path tool

Bézier Pen Text Path tool

Orthogonal Text Path tool

Freehand Bézier Text Path tool

Text Link tool

Text Unlink tool

Starburst tool

Scissors tool

Making Boxes

In earlier versions of XPress, when you wanted a box, you had to clearly specify what kind of box it was—a text box or a picture box—and you had to pick a different tool to create each. And that was it; there was no switching once you had drawn the box. What's more, there were a slew of tools for making different-shaped picture boxes and only one (rectangular) for making text boxes.

But life is better now. XPress offers all the same tools for both text boxes and picture boxes, and although you still have to pick one or the other when drawing a box on your page, you can switch it from picture to text and back again. There's even a new kind of box, called a contentless box, which I talk about in just a little bit.

Creating a box is simple: Choose one of the box tools from the Tool palette, and then click and drag on your page. You can see exactly how large your box is by watching the width and height values on the Measurements palette. Note that you can keep the box square (or circular, if you're using the Oval Text Box tool or the Oval Picture Box tool) by holding down the Shift key while dragging.

All boxes—as items—have a number of basic attributes that you can display and change.

▶ Position on the page

▶ Size (height and width)

▶ Background Color

▶ Corner Radius

▶ Box angle and skew

▶ Suppress Printout

▶ Frame size and Style

Of course, text boxes and picture boxes each have a few of their own characteristics, as well, and the Measurements palette and Modify dialog box both change to accommodate these differences.

▶ Columns (text box only)

▶ Text inset (text box only)

▶ Text angle and skew (text box only)

▶ Picture angle and skew (picture box only)

▶ Suppress Picture Printout (picture box only)

Let's take a quick look at some of these box attributes. I don't cover them all in this section, but don't worry: I cover them all by the time the chapter is through.

(There are several other items in the Modify dialog box and the Measurements palette, too—for instance, the scale of pictures, text runaround, and so on. I hold off discussing these until later in the book, mostly in Chapter 6, *Type and Typography*, Chapter 9, *Pictures*, and Chapter 11, *Where Text Meets Graphics*.)

▼ ▼

Tip: That Ol' Modify Dialog Box. I use the Modify dialog box for text boxes, picture boxes, lines, and text paths so often that I'm glad to have some variance in how I get to it. You can open the Modify dialog box for a page element in several ways (see Figure 3-3).

▶ Select the item with either the Content or the Item tool and choose Modify from the Item menu. This is for people who work by the hour.

▶ Select the item with either the Content or the Item tool and press Command-M (Ctrl-M). This is great if both hands are on the keyboard.

▶ You can Control-click on an item (or right-click on Windows) to display a context-sensitive popup menu in which you can choose Modify.

▶ Double-click on the page element with the Item tool. (Remember, you can hold down the Command or Ctrl key to temporarily work with the Item tool.) This is my favorite method, as I almost always work with one hand on the keyboard and one on the mouse.

Once you're in the dialog box, you can tab through the fields to get to the value you want to change. After a while, you memorize how many tabs it takes to get to a field, and you can press Command-M, Tab, Tab, Tab, Tab, Tab, type the value, press Return, and be out of there before QuarkXPress has time to catch up with you. That's when you know you're becoming an XPress Demon.

▼ ▼

Position and size. All boxes are positioned by their upper-left corner. This point is called their *origin*. The first two fields in the Modify dialog box and the Measurements palette are Origin Across and Origin Down. However, unless your box is rectangular, the origin is not necessarily where you think it is because the origin is based on the box's bounding box—the smallest rectangle that could completely enclose the item (see Figure 3-4).

Figure 3-3
The Modify
dialog box

*The Modify dialog
box changes
depending on
what you have
selected*

Figure 3-4
Bounding box
and position

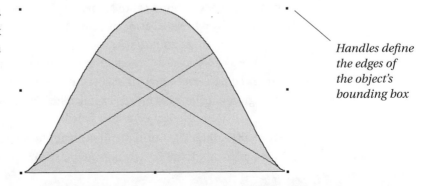

*Handles define
the edges of
the object's
bounding box*

Note that if you've rotated the box, it still thinks of the original upper-left corner as its origin. So if you rotate 90 degrees counterclockwise, the lower-left corner (formerly the upper-left corner) is still the origin point.

The size of the box is then specified by its width and height (the distances to the right and down from the origin). These values, too, are calculated from the item's bounding box.

▼ ▼

Tip: Quick, Accurate Boxes. Some people tend toward a visual approach to creating and sizing boxes in QuarkXPress, while others work with a more mathematical or coordinate-based method. Fortunately, both work equally well. You can click and drag page elements out to the size you want them, if you prefer to make a decision based on seeing what it looks like.

Or, if you're working on a grid, you can draw a box to any size, and then jump into the Measurements palette or Modify dialog box to specify the exact origin coordinates, the width, and the height.

▼ ▼

Tip: Moving an Item's Origin. One of the features I've always coveted in Adobe PageMaker and Adobe InDesign is the ability to set the origin of a page element from a number of locations, rather than just the upper-left corner. Until QuarkXPress does the same, I can only offer a somewhat weak workaround for specifying alternate origins: use the built-in math functions. To set the right side of a box at a specific location, subtract the width of the box from the location's coordinate. For example, to set the right side of a 12-pica-wide box at the 2.75-inch mark, type "2.75"-12p" into the x-origin field of the Measurements palette.

To set the location for the center of a box, divide the box width by two and then subtract it from the coordinate. For example, if you want the center of a 16-pica-wide box to be at the 18-centimeter mark, you can type "18cm-16p/2". (XPress does division first, then performs the subtraction).

▼ ▼

Background color. Every picture and text box has a background color, or can have a background set to None. Any background color other than None and White can be set to a specific tint. Note that zero percent of a color is not transparent; it's opaque white.

A box can also have a blend of two colors in its background (I discuss creating, editing, and applying colors and blends in Chapter 12, *Color*). Both background colors and blends are specified in the Modify dialog box.

Corner Radius. The Corner Radius attribute is applicable to all boxes except those made with the Bézier tools (which I discuss later in this chapter). The

Corner Radius feature in the Modify dialog box lets you set how rounded the corners should be (see Figure 3-5). (On the Beveled Corner box tools, it sets the size of the bevels.) In fact, because you can turn a rectangular box into a rounded-corner box just by setting its Corner Radius, I think there's little reason to ever use the Rounded Corner box tools.

Besides, and to be frank, rounded-corner boxes are one of the most obvious giveaways that you created your document using a Macintosh or Windows machine. Some of the all-time worst designs that have come off of a desktop computer use rounded-corner picture boxes. I really dislike them. But, then again, it's your design, and you can do what you like with it.

Figure 3-5
Corner Radius defines
how rounded
the corners are

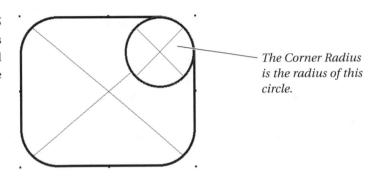

The Corner Radius is the radius of this circle.

Columns. While the previous several items were applicable to all boxes, the Columns attribute is text-box-specific. Text boxes can be divided into a maximum of 30 columns. Each column's size is determined by the size of the *gutter* (blank space) between columns. You can set the gutter width only in the Modify dialog box, although you can set the number of columns in either this dialog box or the Measurements palette.

Note that you cannot have columns with negative widths: the number of columns you can have is determined by the gutter width. For example, if your gutter width is 1 pica and your text box is 20 picas wide, you cannot have more than 20 columns; however, that many columns would leave no room for text.

Text Inset. The last attribute particular to text boxes is Text Inset. The Text Inset value determines how far your text is placed inside the four sides of the text box. For example, a Text Inset value of zero places the text right up against the side of the text box. A text inset value of "3cm" places the text no closer than 3 centimeters from the side of the box.

The default setting for text inset used to be 1 point because the folks at Quark noticed that text set flush against the side of a box is hard to read.

Fortunately, Quark's engineers came to their senses in version 6 and changed the default value to zero points (so the edge of the text is at the same place as the edge of the box). You can change this default setting for your text boxes to zero or any other value (see "Changing Defaults," in Chapter 2, *Quark-XPress Basics*). Or you can do it a box at a time in the Modify dialog box.

Note that you can now also specify the Text Inset value for each of the four sides rather than simply one value for all sides. To change the text inset on a side-by-side basis, turn on the Multiple Insets checkbox.

Changing Box Type

As I mentioned earlier, you can change a picture box into a text box and vice versa. The trick is the Content submenu (under the Item menu or in the context-sensitive menu). This submenu offers three choices when you have a box selected: Text, Picture, and None. Text and Picture are self-explanatory, though you should note that if there's something in your box (some text or a picture), changing the box type deletes it. The None setting leads us to a feature that first appeared in XPress 4: the contentless box.

Contentless boxes. It took 10 years for the engineers at Quark to figure out that we sometimes put boxes on our pages not to contain text or a graphic, but just for the sake of a background color (sometimes known as a tint build). In the past, you had to use a picture box or a text box to do this, with annoying side effects: Empty picture boxes display a big "X" in them; and text boxes, when covered by other boxes, display an overset mark, even if there's no text in them to overset.

Fortunately, QuarkXPress offers contentless boxes, which you can use just for this purpose. To get a contentless box, select a picture or a text box and choose None from the Content submenu (under the Item menu).

Unfortunately, while there used to be a way to get contentless box tools in the Tool palette—in version 4, you could open the Tool tab of the Preferences dialog box and Command-click (Ctrl-click) on the Default Tool Palette button—this feature disappeared in versions 5 and 6.

Lines and Arrows

The Tool palette contains four tools to draw lines and arrows on your page. To be precise, you really only draw lines, but those lines can be styled in several fashions, and they can have arrowheads and tailfeathers. You can create a line with any thickness between 0.001 point and 864 points (that's a pretty thick line—more than 11 inches thick), at any angle, and apply various styles and colors to it. Like boxes, you can view and change these attributes in the Modify dialog box and—for some—the Measurements palette.

Two of the tools are based on Bézier curves, and I discuss them in "Bézier Boxes and Lines," later in this chapter. The other two tools are the Diagonal Line tool and the Orthogonal Line tool.

Diagonal Line tool. The Diagonal Line tool can make a line at any angle. If you hold down the Shift key while dragging out the line, you can constrain the line to 45 or 90 degrees. Don't worry if the line looks jaggy on-screen; that will smooth out when the file is printed.

Orthogonal Line tool. For those of you who aren't in arm's reach of a dictionary, *orthogonal* means that the lines you draw with this tool can only be horizontal or vertical. This tool is somewhat redundant, given that you can make orthogonal lines easily with the Diagonal Line tool and the Shift key. However, I guess it's nice to have this option.

Line weight. I always use the word "weight" or "thickness" rather than "width," which is what QuarkXPress uses to describe lines. (When I talk about the width of horizontal lines, people often think I'm talking about length.) The line thickness is centered on the line. That is, if you specify a 6-point line, 3 points fall on one side of the line, and 3 points fall on the other side.

This value appears in three places: the Style menu, the Modify dialog box, and the Measurements palette. Even better, you can press Command-Shift-\ or Ctrl-Shift-\ (backslash) to bring up the Line Width field in the Modify dialog box. Table 3-1 shows several other ways to change a line's weight with keystrokes. (You can use the same keystrokes to specify type size.)

▼ ▼

Tip: Don't Use Hairlines. You have the option to select Hairline when choosing a line thickness. Don't. Traditionally, a hairline is the thinnest possible line you can print. On a low-resolution desktop printer, this is pretty

Table 3-1 Changing line weight	To...	Press...
	Increase weight by preset amount	Command-Shift-period *or* Ctrl-Shift-period
	Increase weight by one point	Command-Shift-Option-period *or* Ctrl-Alt-Shift-period
	Decrease weight by preset amount	Command-Shift-comma *or* Ctrl-Shift-comma
	Decrease weight by one point	Command-Shift-Option-comma *or* Ctrl-Alt-Shift-comma

thin, but on an imagesetter it's often too small to be seen. When you print your document, QuarkXPress actually replaces hairlines with 0.125 point rules so you don't get caught in this trap.

However, sometimes the program goofs up: When XPress 4.0 first shipped, many users went ballistic because the program had stopped catching and replacing hairline-width rules. Quark quickly fixed the "problem," so current versions work just fine. Nonetheless, it's always better to specify the thickness of your lines rather than rely on a program to do it.

▼ ▼

Color and shade. You can set the line's color to any color in the document (see Chapter 12, *Color*), then tint it to any value from zero to 100 percent, in 0.1-percent increments (zero percent is white). These specifications are available in the Modify dialog box, the Colors palette, or the Style menu.

Style and endcaps. Lines don't have to be boring; spice them up with a new style, or add endcaps to turn them into arrows. You can choose one of 11 different line styles and one of six endcap combinations by selecting them from two popup menus in the Modify dialog box, the Style menu, or the Measurements palette (see Figure 3-6).

Six of the line styles are stripes (multiple parallel lines) and four are dashes (lines with gaps). I discuss stripes and dashes, including how to make your own styles, in "Frames, Dashes, and Stripes," later in this chapter. For now, however, suffice it to say that when you specify a thicker line, the dash or stripe gets proportionally thicker, too (just as you'd expect).

Even though you have six endcap styles to choose from, the choice really comes down to either with arrowheads and tailfeathers, or without them. You can't edit the style of these endcaps, so you're stuck with what's built into the program.

Figure 3-6
Line styles

Note that if you choose an arrowhead that points to the right, the arrowhead you get might point to the left. The reason is that the arrowhead style pointing to the right actually means "put an arrow at the *end* of the line." XPress remembers how you drew the line—where you first clicked is the beginning of the line, and where you let go of the mouse button is the end. (This is different from the way it worked in earlier versions.) If the arrow is pointing the wrong way, just select the opposite direction in the Arrowhead popup menu.

Text Paths

The ability to put text on a path is, for many people, alone worth the price to upgrade from version 3. In the past, you had to switch to an illustration program to create this effect, then save the text as a graphic, then import it into a picture box . . . and then if you wanted to edit it, you had to go back to the original program, and so on. Well, no longer!

QuarkXPress offers four text-path tools that appear and act almost identically to the four line tools that I just discussed. While the two Bézier text-path tools are the ones you will probably use the most often, I discuss those in the next section ("Bézier Boxes and Lines"). Let's start, instead, with the two simple text-path tools: the Diagonal Text Path tool and the Orthogonal Text Path tool. And then let's look at how you can customize the text on the path to get the effect you're looking for.

▼ ▼

Tip: Converting Lines to Text Paths. Just as you can convert a picture box to a line box and back again, you can make any regular line a text path by choosing Text in the Content submenu (under the Item menu). What this literally means is that lines can have content, too. In fact, in many ways a text path acts just like a text box that holds just a single line of text.

To change a text path to a regular line, choose None from the Content submenu.

▼ ▼

Drawing with the text-path tools. When you draw a path with a text-path tool, XPress immediately switches to the Content tool, letting you type along the line (see Figure 3-7). If you hold down the Shift key when you're drawing the path, the line is constrained to a horizontal, vertical, or 45-degree angle (which makes the Orthogonal Text Path tool a bit redundant).

If you want to edit the text on the path, watch the cursor carefully when you click or drag over the path. Depending on where you place the cursor, the cursor's appearance changes. If you put it directly over the line, you may get the Edit Segment cursor (I cover this in "Bézier Boxes and Lines," later in this chapter). Put it over an endpoint, you'll get the Move Point cursor. It's only over certain parts of the line that you see the Edit Text "I-beam" cursor.

Once again, text on a path acts just like it's in a text box, so you can use all the text editing features that I discuss in Chapter 5, *Word Processing*, Chapter 6, *Type and Typography*, and Chapter 7, *Copy Flow*. In fact, when you select the text path with the Content tool, the Measurements palette appears almost exactly the same as it does with text boxes; with the Item tool, the palette appears as though you had a line selected.

Figure 3-7
Drawing with the
text-path tools

Overset text
(path is too small)

Selecting text
on a path

Line width and style. By default, the text paths themselves have a thickness of Hairline and a color of None, which makes them invisible. The text on the path, of course, is a different matter. Every now and again, primarily for special effects, you'll want to change the line's style and weight (see Figure 3-8). You can do so with the same features as with normal lines: the Style menu, the Measurements palette, and the Modify dialog box.

Text Orientation. Text paths have a special tab in the Modify dialog box that lets you specify text-path options (see Figure 3-9). The first control you have over text on a text path is the orientation of the text. There are four options, though I should note that none of these has any effect on text paths you create with the Diagonal or Orthogonal Text Path tool. They only affect Bézier text paths. In fact, you can't even convert a diagonal or orthogonal text path to a Bézier curve in order to use these; rather, you have to actually create a new path with the Bézier text-path tools.

▶ FOLLOW THE CURVE. The first, and default, setting for Text Orientation forces each character to rotate along the curve. What that means is that each character of text isn't actually curved, even if the path is a Bézier path, but the overall effect is that of a curve (see Figure 3-10). This is what most people want 95 percent of the time.

▶ **WARP WITH THE CURVE.** The second option (the one in the upper-right corner) warps the text along the curve, resulting in a quasi-three-dimensional effect. What XPress is really doing is both skewing and rotating each character based on the slope of the curve. First it rotates it along the curve (as in the last option) and then it skews it forward or backward so that the character remains upright. This is useful primarily for special effects.

▶ **SKEW WITH THE CURVE.** The third option (in the lower-left corner) skews each character based on the slope of the curve, but doesn't rotate it. The result is . . . well, strange at best. When the curve is sloping up to the right, XPress skews the text to the left; when the curve goes down to the right, XPress skews the text to the right; if your curve doubles back and heads to the left, the text is flipped and skewed. I bet someone out there has come up with a good use for this, but I haven't.

Figure 3-8
Changing the line style on text paths

The text path is styled with a thick triple line

Figure 3-9
Text-path options

Figure 3-10
Text Orientation

Note that the thin gray
lines are included here just
for illustration
purposes

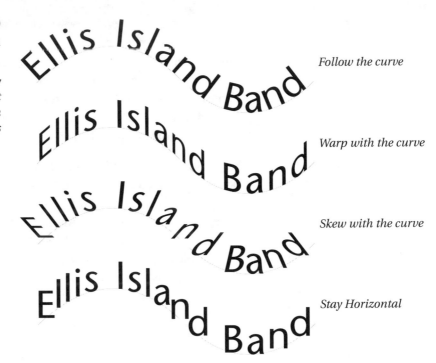

Follow the curve

Warp with the curve

Skew with the curve

Stay Horizontal

▶ STAY HORIZONTAL. The last option ensures that each character is not skewed or rotated as it makes its way along the path.

Text Alignment. The next control on the Text Path tab of the Modify dialog box is Text Alignment, which lets you specify what part of the text should align with what part of the path. For instance, the default setting is for the baseline of the text to align with the top of the line (see Figure 3-11). Of course, because the default line is only 0.25 point thick, there is very little difference between aligning to the top or the bottom of the line. If you make the line thicker, however, this makes a difference. (You can make the line thicker and still set the Color to None, making it invisible.)

If you set the Align Text popup menu to Ascent, however, then XPress moves the text down so that the highest ascender in the typeface (like the top part of a lowercase "k") aligns with the line. You can also choose Center (which centers the font's lower-case characters—its x-height—on the line) or Descent (which aligns the lowest descender of the font—like the bottom part of a lowercase "y"—to the line).

Which setting you should choose depends entirely on your situation, the text, and the type of curve. I find that it's often worth testing two or three different settings here until I get the effect I like most (remember the Apply button so you don't have to keep leaving the dialog box each time you try a new setting).

Flip Text. The last control in the Modify dialog box that applies to text paths is Flip Text, which doesn't so much flip the text as much as it flips what XPress thinks of as the path. That is, when this is turned on, QuarkXPress starts the text from the last point on the path instead of the first, and the top and bottom sides of the path are reversed (see Figure 3-12). The result is usually a mirror image of the original—except that XPress doesn't mirror the text itself, only the text flow. I find that when I use Flip Text, I almost always have to adjust the Text Alignment settings to accommodate it.

▼ ▼

Tip: Positioning the Text on the Curve. As I've said before, text on a path acts the same as text in a text box. This means that if you don't like the posi-

Figure 3-11
Text Alignment

Align Text: Baseline,
Align with Line: Top

Align Text: Baseline,
Align with Line: Bottom

Align Text: Ascent,
Align with Line: Top

Align Text: Center,
Align with Line: Center

Figure 3-12
Flip Text

tion of the text on your path, you can use the settings in the Paragraph Formats dialog box, like Left Indent and Horizontal Alignment. For example, if you want text to be centered on the path, just place the cursor in the text and change the Alignment to Centered (Command-Shift-C or Ctrl-Shift-C).

You can also add or remove space between characters along the path using kerning and tracking (see Figure 3-13). I discuss all these typographic controls in Chapter 6, *Type and Typography*.

Figure 3-13
Formatting text
on a curve

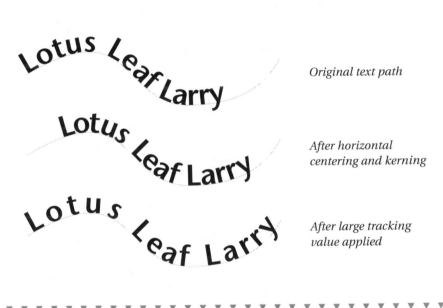

Original text path

After horizontal
centering and kerning

After large tracking
value applied

Bézier Boxes and Lines

For most people working in desktop publishing, the addition of Bézier curves to QuarkXPress version 4 was a joyous event. It means that we no longer had to leave QuarkXPress and open an illustration program just to set some text on a path, or draw a simple shape such as a heart to put a graphic in. Creating these kinds of elements has always been a hassle, and editing them was even worse. XPress's tools make editing paths and shapes much easier.

If you are familiar with the Bézier controls in programs such as Adobe Illustrator or Macromedia FreeHand, you will find the controls in XPress to be similar. As in those programs, the Bézier shapes are drawn with a Pen tool. And as in those programs, there are anchor points with handles to control the curves of the Bézier shapes. However, there are some features in QuarkXPress that are unique. This means that you may not be able to pick up the QuarkXPress Pen tools and start drawing immediately. You may need to retrain your fingers for the QuarkXPress tools.

If you have never worked with Bézier tools you may find them a little daunting. More than one student has given up learning the "dreaded Pen" tool in desktop illustration programs. Hang in there! Mastering the Bézier tools in QuarkXPress enables you to create the most sophisticated and interesting artwork and designs.

A word of caution: The Bézier tools in QuarkXPress are not a substitute for illustration programs such as Illustrator or FreeHand. The Bézier tools in QuarkXPress are for *basic* things like putting text on a path, converting text into masks, or creating simple shapes and logos. If you are working on complex illustrations, you will almost certainly find more powerful tools in a dedicated illustration program. Of course, having said that, people will probably start sending me all sorts of sophisticated artwork created solely in QuarkXPress. And I will be very impressed. (But I won't change my opinion.)

Understanding Bézier Controls

Why are they called "Bézier" controls? Because they were created by a French mathematician named Pierre Etienne Bézier (1910–1999). For those of you who never took French, his name is pronounced *Bay-zee-EH*. What Monsieur Bézier did was create a mathematical system to define the shape of curves.

Before Bézier, drafting was performed by painfully plotting dozens or even hundreds of points on a curve. Après Bézier, the entire curve could be described with one very short description including two coordinates points and their "control handles" (I'll explain handles in a minute). Not only are these curves easy to describe mathematically, but they lend themselves to a very simple user interface as well.

There are three different aspects to Bézier curves: points, segments, and control handles.

Bézier points. There are three different types of Bézier points in QuarkXPress: smooth points, symmetrical points, and corner points. Each one creates a different type of shape (see Figure 3-14).

> ▶ **SMOOTH POINTS.** Smooth points create curves with smooth transitions. The top of a roller coaster is a good example of a smooth curve. There is no abrupt change from the curve going up to the one going down, so you say the transition is "smooth." When you select a smooth point on a curve, it's indicated by a diamond dot.

> ▶ **SYMMETRICAL POINTS.** Symmetrical points are the same as smooth points except that the shape on one side of the curve is always equal to the shape on the other side. The curve created by a swinging pendulum is a good example of a symmetical point. The left side of the

Figure 3-14

The different types of
Bézier points

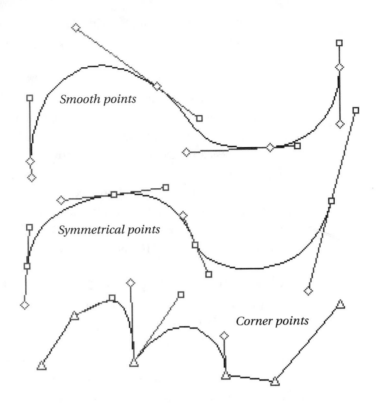

Smooth points

Symmetrical points

Corner points

arc created by the pendulum is equal to the right side of the arc. Symmetical points that are selected are indicated on the path by a square dot.

▶ **CORNER POINTS.** Corner points abruptly change their direction. The path of a ball bouncing is a good example of a path with a corner point. The top arc of the path is smooth, but the point where the ball hits the ground is a corner point because the path changes its shape abruptly. When you select a corner point, it appears on the path as a triangle dot.

Segments. Segments are the connections—or lines—between points (see Figure 3-15). There are two different types of segments in QuarkXPress: curved segments and straight segments.

▶ **CURVED SEGMENTS.** Curved segments are those that have a curved shape. They can be created between any two types of points.

▶ **STRAIGHT SEGMENTS.** Straight segments are (surprise!) those that have no curve to them. A straight segment can only be created between two corner points.

Figure 3-15

The two different types
of Bézier segments

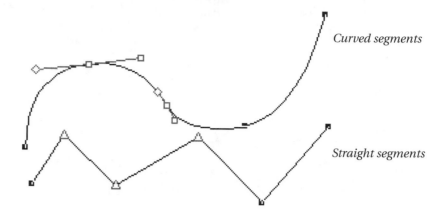

Curved segments

Straight segments

Control handles. Control handles tell curves where to go. Technically, the control handle defines the tangent to the curve, but I like to think of it more like the control handle saying "come toward this direction." As you draw or edit the points of Bézier curves, you see colored lines extending out from your points (see Figure 3-16). These are the control handles for the points. (Control handles are used solely to define the shape of the object. They don't print.) As you drag the handles around, the curve changes.

Smooth and symmetrical points always have two control handles (one on each side of the point). Corner points, on the other hand, can have two handles, one handle, or even no handles. Actually, even when it looks like there's no handle, there really is one . . . it's just that the handle has a length of zero, so it's sitting exactly on top of the corner point.

Every control handle is either an "In" handle or an "Out" handle, depending on which side of the point it sits on. They have exactly the same function, but it's useful to differentiate between them when talking about how to draw these curves and also when editing them. The In control handle has a small diamond at the end of the handle; the Out control handle has a square.

▼ ▼

Tip: Best Bézier Techniques. If you have worked with Bézier tools in programs such as Illustrator or FreeHand, you are most likely aware of the principles of creating smooth, clean Bézier shapes. However, if all this is new to you, there are a few basic principles you should keep in mind as you create your Bézier shapes. This ensures that your layouts look their best and print without any problems.

▶ **USE FEWER POINTS.** Try to keep the number of points on a Bézier shape to a minimum. For instance, the arc of a pendulum actually needs only two points to define it. An egg only needs four. The fewer the number of points on your shapes, the easier it is to create smooth curves (see Figure 3-17).

Figure 3-16
The two different types of
Control handles

"In" handle

"Out" handle

Figure 3-17
Limiting points

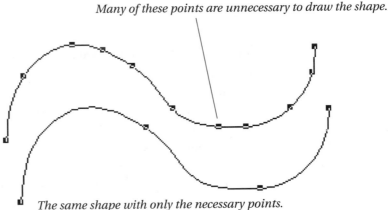

Many of these points are unnecessary to draw the shape.

The same shape with only the necessary points.

▶ **AVOID HUGE CONTROL HANDLES.** The control handles for curves define the shape of the curve. The longer the handle, the greater the curve. However, you should try to limit the length of the handle to approximately one-third the length of the curve segment (see Figure 3-18). This ensures that drawing and editing the curve will be as easy as possible, as well as ensuring smooth transitions from one point to the next. Don't get obsessive about this rule; it's just a guideline, and often you need to break guidelines to get the effect you want.

▶ **ANTICIPATE EDITING CHOICES.** As you create Bézier shapes, try to anticipate where you might want to have a point to edit later on. For instance, if you are following the shape of an arm, you might want to have a point at the elbow, rather than have just one segement that extends from shoulder to wrist. That way you have the ability later on to change the shape with the new point.

Bézier and Freehand Tools

QuarkXPress offers two kinds of tools that create Bézier shapes: the pen tools and the freehand tools. (I use the word "freehand" to describe how they

Figure 3-18

Limit length of
control handles

*Try to limit control
handles to one-third the
length of the arc.*

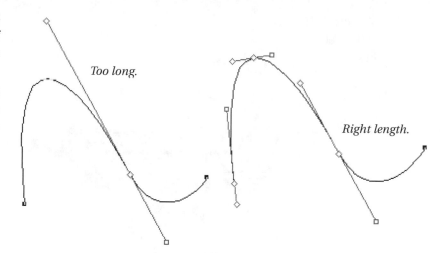

Too long.

Right length.

work; they don't have anything to do with Macromedia's FreeHand drawing program.) However, these two tools each come in five flavors—text box, picture box, contentless box, line, and text path—for a total of 10 different Bézier tools (see Figure 3-19).

Pen tools let you create shapes by precisely placing Bézier points and manipulating the control handles as you create the shape. The freehand tools let you draw a shape freeform, by eye; XPress then traces your path, figuring out where the points and control handles should be positioned.

▼ ▼

Tip: Comparing Bézier and Freehand Tools. If you find the pen-based Bézier tools hard to learn, you may be tempted to only use the freehand tools instead. Don't do it. No matter how steady your hand, you will still almost never get the curve you want with one of the freehand tools. Plus, the freehand tools only create curved segments, not straight segments. This means that the freehand tools can create the curves at the top of a tombstone, but not the straight sides. For that you need the pen tools.

Most people don't have the hands of a surgeon, and the paths created by the freehand tools follow every jiggle and bump of your mouse (see Figure 3-20), so unless you're extremely lucky, your paths will have extra points where you don't need them—or may not have enough points where you do need them.

Use the freehand tools only if you have not learned how to draw with the equivalent Bézier pen tool. And then be prepared to spend a good deal of time manually editing and reshaping the path by moving, adding, and deleting points. But then set aside some time later on to practice working with the pen tools.

▼ ▼

Figure 3-19
The Bézier and freehand tools in the toolbox

Figure 3-20
Objects drawn with Bézier tools are much smoother than those drawn with the freehand tools.

Bézier heart   *Freehand heart*

▼ ▼

Tip: Automatically Closing Bézier and Freehand Boxes. When you use one of the Bézier box tools (to create a picture box, a text box, or a content-less box), you have to close the path you draw. There are three ways to close a path, thus finishing the box.

► You can finish the box by clicking on the first point in the path.

► You can double-click on the last point, to have XPress close the path for you. The last point (the one where you double-clicked) is a corner point.

▶ When you're drawing with one of the pen tools, the box closes as soon as you choose another tool from the toolbox. If you're using one of the freehand tools, the path closes as soon as you release the mouse button.

▼ ▼

Tip: Finishing Bézier Lines. I have long wished for a line tool that could draw more than one segment at a time. Well, the Bézier line and text-path tools extend far beyond my humble request. With them, you can draw all manner of lines on your pages, and then place text along the path. But there's one puzzling problem: how do you tell XPress that you're finished drawing at the end of the line?

With the freehand tools, it's easy: you just let go of the mouse button. With the pen tools, it's less obvious: you have to either double-click (which adds a corner point as the last point on the path), or choose another tool. If I've got my left hand on the keyboard (I typically do), I just press Command-Control-Tab (or Control-Alt-Tab in Windows) to switch to the next tool on the tool palette. Or, if you can reach, Shift-F8 tells XPress to switch to the Content tool.

▼ ▼

Drawing with the Pen Tools

Okay, it's time to get down to business with some exercises that should help you learn to use the various Bézier tools. I'm going to walk you quickly through three sets of step-by-step instructions that use the three types of Bézier points.

Here's three suggestions to keep in mind as you're working. First, watch how the cursor changes depending on where it is located and what function it is performing (see Table 3-2). Second, watch the shape of the points on the path. Those shapes are also clues as to the type of path being created. Finally, while you're learning to use the Bézier tools, give yourself a large, open page to work on. Don't try to cramp your artwork into a tight little space.

Drawing corner points. The easiest type of point to draw with the pen tools is a corner point connected to a straight segment. So this first exercise is to draw a diamond shape that consists of only four corner points (see Figure 3-21). If you used earlier versions of QuarkXPress, you'll find that drawing corner points is, at its simplest, just like making a polygonal picture box.

1. Select the Bézier Pen Picture Box tool. (Although these lessons apply to all the Bézier pen tools, I use the picture box tools here.)

Table 3-2	IF YOU WANT TO . . .	LOOK FOR THIS CURSOR . . .
Bézier cursor clues	Move a point	
	Move or extend a control handle	
	Add point to a path	
	Delete a point or handle	
	Close a path	
	Move or modify a segment	
	Convert between Smooth and Corner points	

2. Position your mouse where the left point of the diamond should be located, and click. You should see a little colored dot indicating that you have placed the first point. (If the color of the dot looks familiar, it's because Bézier paths are colored the same as your Margin guides as you're drawing them; for more information see "Changing Default Preferences," in Chapter 2, *QuarkXPress Basics*.)

3. Move your mouse to where the top point of the diamond should be located, and click. You should see another colored dot with a colored line connecting the first and second points.

4. Now do the same for the right point and the bottom point of the diamond.

5. Finally, as you place your mouse over the first point you created, the cursor should change to a rounded-corner rectangle. Click to close the box. Or, alternately, remember that you can close the path automatically simply by switching to another tool.

Congratulations! You have just created a diamond shape with a Bézier pen tool.

Drawing a curved object. The second-easiest type of point to draw is a smooth point connected to another smooth point. This exercise is to draw a bean shape, which consists of only easy smooth points (see Figure 3-22).

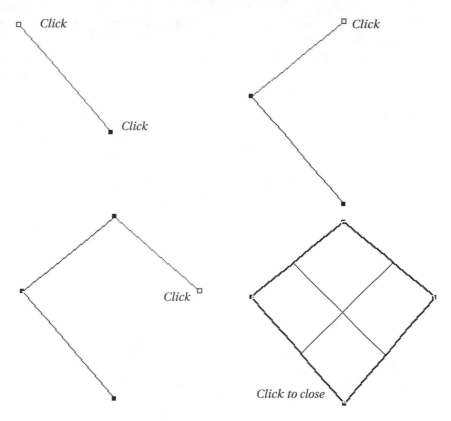

Figure 3-21

Drawing a straight-segment object

1. Select the Bézier Pen Picture Box tool.

2. Position your mouse where the left curve of the bean should be located. Press down on the mouse and drag up. You should see a colored dot with two control handles. Stop dragging when the Out control handle extends about 1.5 inches out from the colored dot.

3. Move your mouse to where the top point of the bean should be located. Press and drag down and to the right at approximately a 30-degree angle. Stop dragging when the Out control handle extends about 1.5 inches out from the colored dot. You'll see an arc connecting the first and second dots.

4. Move your mouse to where the middle curve of the bean should be located. Press and drag straight down. Stop dragging when the Out control handle extends about 0.5 inch out from the colored dot. You will see an arc connecting the second and third dots.

5. Move your mouse down to where the bottom curve of the bean should be located. Press and drag down and to the left at approximately a 30-degree angle. Stop dragging when the Out control handle

Figure 3-22

Drawing a curved-segment object

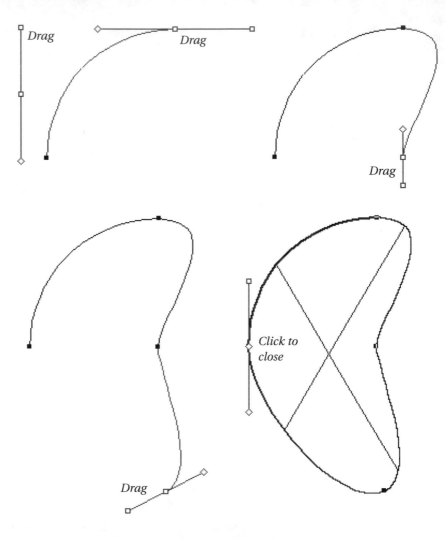

extends about 1.5 inches out from the colored dot. You will see an arc connecting the third and fourth dots.

6. Move your mouse back to the first point you created and click once to close the path with a curved segment.

Well done! You have just created a bean shape with a Bézier pen tool. However, if you don't like what you have created, don't delete it. In the next section, I discuss how you can edit the points, segments, and control handles on your curve.

▼ ▼

Tip: Constraining with the Shift Key. As you draw, if you hold the Shift key, you can constrain your pen-tool actions to 45-degree increments. This helps you make sure that straight-line segments are perfectly horizontal, vertical, or on 45-degree angles. If you press Shift when you click with the pen tool, the new point is added on the same horizontal, vertical, or diagonal (45-degree) orientation from the last point. If you press Shift while you drag (after you click, but while the mouse button is still held down), the control handles are similarly constrained.

▼ ▼

Tip: Watch the Measurements Palette. The Measurements palette shows the position, length, and angle of each of the points and control handles as you draw them. Keep an eye on the amounts as you draw. While you can always go back and edit the handles and points later, it helps to see what you're doing as you do it.

▼ ▼

Drawing a combination object. The previous two exercises contained only one type of point each. But shapes in the real world are much more complicated, consisting of objects with combinations of points and combinations of segments. In this exercise we'll draw a baseball field shape (or, if you prefer, an ice cream cone shape), which consists of both corner and smooth points (see Figure 3-23).

1. Select the Bézier Pen Picture Box tool.

2. Position your mouse where the home plate of the field should be located, and click to create a corner point.

3. Move your mouse to where third base should be. Click to create another corner point with a straight segment, connecting home to third.

4. Now we're going to begin a curve, so you need to add an Out handle to the point you just made. (Remember that I said corner points can have control handles that sit right on top of the point? Here's how you drag it out.) Hold down the Command (Ctrl) key and move the cursor on top of the third-base point. When the cursor is directly over the point, the cursor looks like a finger with a small black dot. If you click and drag now, you'll move the point itself.

   Move the cursor to the other side of the point from the line segment you've already drawn by one or two screen pixels, and the cursor changes to a finger with a white dot (see Figure 3-24). Now when you click and drag, you're manipulating the control handle, not the point itself. (It's a subtle cursor change, but a crucial one.)

5. Drag straight up to extend the Out handle from the point.

Figure 3-23

Drawing a combination-segment object

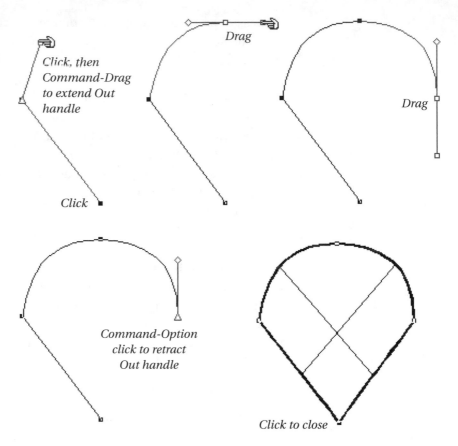

Click, then
Command-Drag
to extend Out
handle

Drag

Click

Drag

Command-Option
click to retract
Out handle

Click to close

6. Move your mouse to where the top of the outfield would be. Click and drag to the right to create a smooth point at the top of the curve.

7. Move your mouse over to where first base should be. Since you need to complete the curve of the outfield, click and then drag straight down; this creates both In and Out handles on this point.

8. The final segment of the shape is a straight line, so you need to remove the Out handle from the point you just made. Hold down both the Command and Option (or Ctrl-Alt) keys and click on the Out handle to "delete" it. (It looks like you're deleting it, but you're really just retracting it so that it sits on top of the point itself.)

9. To finish the field, move your mouse down to the first point and click.

Well, take me out to the ballgame! You've just created a baseball-field shape. Don't worry if your field is a little asymmetrical. You can always edit the points and handles of your shape later on. Or tell everyone it's a field in San Francisco.

Pen and keyboard actions for Bézier tools. Table 3-3 lists a summary of the mouse and keyboard actions for drawing with any of the Bézier tools. I find that sometimes it's not worth the trouble to get the shape right the first time, so I draw smooth points everywhere and then edit them later.

Figure 3-24
Close up detail on the cursor showing how it will move the control handle rather than the point itself

Table 3-3
Mouse and keyboard actions for drawing

To create a . . .	. . . do this
Smooth point	Drag
Corner point with no handles	Click
Corner point with only an In handle	Drag, then Command-Option-click on the Out handle
Corner point with only an Out handle	Click, then Command-drag out the Out handle
Corner point with both In and Out handles	Drag, then Command-Option to retract the Out handle, then Command-drag to extend a new Out handle (or—Macintosh only—Drag, then Command-Control-drag the Out handle)

Editing Bézier Paths

Once you've created a path, that doesn't mean you have to live with it exactly the way you first drew it. (Otherwise, the world would be full of asymmetrical baseball fields!) XPress offers several tools to let you modify points and paths either by eye or by using precise numeric entries.

Selecting points. Before you can modify a point on a path, you have to select it. And in order to select a point on a path, Edit Shape must be turned on (select Shape from the Edit submenu, under the Item menu). When Edit Shape is turned on, you can see (and edit) the points on the curve. When it's off, you can only manipulate the object's bounding box (see Figure 3-25).

To select a point on a path, select the object first, and then click on the point (you can use either the Item or Content tool for this). Unfortunately,

Figure 3-25
Edit Shape

When Edit Shape is on,
you can edit the points.

When Edit Shape is off, you
can only change the height
and width of the object.

dragging a marquee over a point does not select it; you have to click right on it. When I'm trying to get something done quickly, I often find myself accidentally moving the point when I click on it. Be careful of this, and keep one hand on the Command-Z (Ctrl-Z) keys so you can Undo the action as necessary.

There are several ways to select more than one point on the path.

▸ You can hold down the Shift key and click on the additional points.

▸ Clicking on a segment between two points automatically selects the two points on either end of the segment.

▸ You can double-click on a point to select all the points in the path. (If the path is a compound path—that is, there is more than one independent path within the total path—you can select all the points on all the paths by triple-clicking.)

Dragging points and segments. Once you have selected a point or points on your path, you can move or edit it (them) by dragging with either the Item or Content tool. Again, watch the cursor for clues: The cursor that looks like a hand with a black dot indicates that you're going to move the selected point. The Item tool cursor ("the pointy-thingy") indicates that you're going to move the entire object rather than individual points. The hand with a white dot means you're going to drag a cursor handle. (Actually, to be more precise, the white dot is either a white square or a white diamond, depending on whether you're on top of an In or an Out handle.)

There is one other cursor you'll see: the hand cursor with a little line next to it. This indicates that you can move the segment between two points (see Figure 3-26). What happens when you click and drag, however, depends on the type of points at the ends of the segment.

Figure 3-26
Moving segments

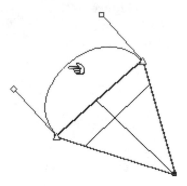

Dragging a straight-line segment   *Dragging a curved segment*

▶ If the two points are corner points, dragging the segment actually moves both points.

▶ If one or both of the points are smooth or symmetrical, the points don't move when you drag the segment. Instead, the control handles adjust accordingly.

Sometimes it's just too much of a hassle to adjust the control handles to create the curve I'm looking for, so I just grab the segment I'm editing and drag it to where I want it to go. This way, QuarkXPress does all the work in figuring out the correct positions for the control handles.

▼ ▼

Tip: Snap Points to Guides. Dragging points around your page is an inexact science at best, even if you want the Measurements palette for feedback on your page coordinates. If I know exactly where I want to place a point, I often drag out horizontal and/or vertical page guides to that coordinate. Then, when I drag the point on the curve, it snaps to the guide, ensuring its location. Unfortunately, Snap to Guide doesn't work on control handles.

▼ ▼

Changing points in the Measurements palette. Designers working in illustration programs usually like to move things around by eye. However, many XPress users want or need to work with more numerical precision. Fortunately, the Measurements palette lets you see and modify all the attributes of points on your curve: their type, their position, and the position of their control handles (see Figure 3-27). I'll hold off on changing point type for now, and focus just on altering point and handle position.

▶ **POINT POSITION.** When you select a single point on your curve, the right side of the Measurements palette displays its position in the XP

Figure 3-27

Bézier points in the
Measurements palette

X and Y axis coordinate of the point

In handle angle
and length

Out handle
angle and
length

and YP fields. If you're trying to make a small change to a point's position, it's usually much easier to do it here than to drag the point around.

▶ HANDLE POSITION. At first, the way the Measurements palette displays the positions of a point's control handles seems odd, but it turns out to be incredibly intuitive and useful. The In handle (the white diamond) and the Out handle (the white square) are represented by their angle and their length. As for all angles in XPress, this angle value increases counterclockwise. That is, zero degrees leads horizontally to the right of the point on the curve, 90 degrees points directly up, and so on.

Of course, when you change either the angle or the length of one control handle, it may change the other's as well, depending on the type of the point. Corner points have fully independent handles. The handles on smooth points can have different lengths, but their angles always add up to 180 degrees. And both the lengths and the angles are locked to each other in symmetrical points.

▼ ▼

Tip: Getting Consistent Curves. I find it unfortunate that the Space/Align feature can't align individual points on a curve. The next best thing, then, is to align the points by selecting them and then entering a proper value for their XP or XY coordinate, or for their control handles. Don't forget that Copy and Paste work within the Measurements palette, so you can Copy the XP coordinate from one point and Paste it in the XP field for another point.

▼ ▼

Tip: Precision Point Placement. When you have the Item tool selected, the arrow keys nudge things around your page. Therefore, if you want to move a point on a curve 1 point (about 0.014 inch) up, just select it with the Item tool and press the Up Arrow key. Nope, this doesn't work for control handles.

▼ ▼

Tip: Bézier Math. Strangely enough, I've always liked math (see my 1997 book *The Joy of* π, if you doubt me). However, I have to admit that I've become quite rusty at basic math due to the proliferation of calculators in my life. Fortunately, all of my favorite mathematical tricks can be applied to the numerical settings for Bézier points. For instance, if you want a point to move 2 picas down, you would type "+2p" after the YP coordinate value and then press the Return key. Similarly, you can cut the length of a control handle in half by typing "/2" after the handle length.

▼ ▼

Adding and deleting points. It's easy to add or remove a point on your path: just Option-click (Alt-click). The same keystroke adds or removes points, depending on where you click. Note that the kind of point that XPress adds depends on the type of segment you're clicking on: if it's a straight-line segment, XPress adds a corner point; otherwise, it adds a smooth point. Basically, the program tries to alter the shape of the Bézier curve as little as possible when you add a point.

Changing a point type. Gertrude Stein would never have said that a curve is a curve is a curve, because she knew that you could change the type of a point with a click of a button or the flick of a keystroke. Once you have selected a point on a curve, you can change its type in one of four ways (see Figure 3-28).

▶ ITEM MENU. You can select a point type from the Point/Segment Type submenu (under the Item menu; see Figure 3-29). This is by far the slowest method.

▶ MEASUREMENTS PALETTE. You can click on a point type in the Measurements palette.

▶ KEYSTROKE. You can press Option-F1, -F2, or -F3 to change the selected point to a corner, smooth, or symmetrical point, respectively. (Use the Control key in Windows.)

▶ CLICK AND DRAG. If you're the interactive type, you might like the ability to click or click-and-drag on a point or a control handle with the Control key held down (Control and Shift in Windows). This works whether you have the Item or Content tool selected. If you Control-click on a smooth or symmetrical point, its control handles are retracted to a length of zero and it becomes a corner point. You can also turn a smooth or symmetrical point into a corner point by Control-dragging one of its control handles. This method doesn't retract the handles (see Figure 3-30).

Figure 3-28
Changing the
type of a point

*Symmetrical and
smooth points
converted to corner
points don't change
their appearance. That
is because changing the
point type only unlocks
the control handle
lengths and angles. You
can then manually
adjust the handles.*

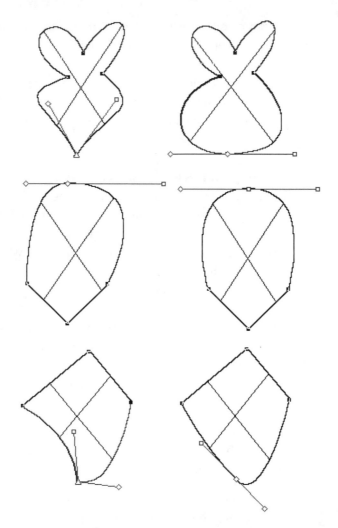

Conversely, you can change a corner point into a smooth point by holding down the Control key (again, Control-Alt in Windows) and clicking and dragging on the point itself. This extends the control handles as you drag.

▼ ▼

Tip: Converting Multiple Points. If you have selected a single point on your curve, the icon for that type of point is highlighted in the Measurements palette. You can then convert the point from one type to another by clicking on one of the other icons. However, if you have more than one type of point selected, no one icon is selected. You can still click on any one of the icons to convert all of the selected points. I find this helpful when smoothing out the paths created by the freehand tools.

▼ ▼

Figure 3-29
Point types

Figure 3-30
Dragging smooth points
into corner points

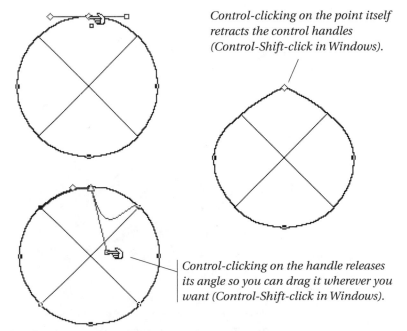

*Control-clicking on the point itself
retracts the control handles
(Control-Shift-click in Windows).*

*Control-clicking on the handle releases
its angle so you can drag it wherever you
want (Control-Shift-click in Windows).*

Changing a segment type. Just as you may want to modify the type of a
point, you might consider changing the type of a segment from straight to
curved, or vice versa. To do this, you need to select the segment (either click
on it or select the points on either side of the segment). Then you can select

Straight Segment or Curved Segment from the Point/Segment Type sub-menu (under the Item menu)—this is the slow way; or you can click on the Straight or Curved Segment icon in the Measurements palette. A third choice: press Option-Shift-F1 to get a straight segment, or Option-Shift-F2 to get a curved segment (Control-Shift-F1 and Control-Shift-F2, respectively, in Windows).

When you convert a segment from curved to straight, any control handles that extended into the segment are retracted. This usually radically changes the appearance of the path (see Figure 3-31).

When you convert a segment from straight to curved, however, the appearance of the segment doesn't change at all. Two control handles are simply added to the points at the end of the segment; you can then drag these control handles to create the curve.

Figure 3-31
Changing the
type of segments

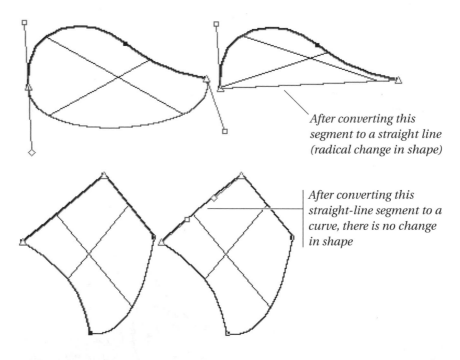

After converting this segment to a straight line (radical change in shape)

After converting this straight-line segment to a curve, there is no change in shape

▼ ▼

Tip: Flipping Shapes Around. As I've said before, the Bézier controls in QuarkXPress are hardly as sophisticated as those in dedicated illustration programs. But often there are workarounds for features that XPress is missing. For instance, although XPress has no way of mirroring (some people call this reflecting) a shape, you can use this short technique to achieve the effect (see Figure 3-32).

Figure 3-32
Flipping an object

Before the flip   *Dragging the side handle over*   *After resetting the item's width*

1. Turn off Edit Shape in the Edit submenu (under the Item menu) so you see the object's bounding box.

2. Select the value in the width (W) field in the Measurements palette and Copy it.

3. Drag one of the left or right side handles across the object until it crosses the opposite side of the shape. Now the shape is mirrored, but it's distorted.

4. Select the width field in the Measurements palette again, and Paste in the value on the clipboard.

Of course, if you want to flip the shape vertically, you would Copy and Paste the height field rather than the width field.

▼ ▼

Scissors Tool

When you have the Scissors XTension active (it is installed by default), XPress adds a Scissors tool to the bottom of the Tool palette. The Scissors tool lets you cut boxes and lines. For instance, if you click in the middle of a line, XPress splits the line into two lines at that point. If you click in the middle of a text path, XPress splits it into two text paths and automatically links them together (as though you had linked them with the Text Link tool). The Scissors tool also converts text boxes into text paths (see "Tip: Text Boxes to Text Paths," later in this chapter).

Merge Commands

Okay, I admit it: I couldn't draw my way out of a paper bag. There just seems to be a disconnect between the part of my brain that knows what it wants and the part that can use these tools. Because of this, I often combine various oval and rectangular boxes to create the shapes I want. QuarkXPress makes this easy with the various features under the Merge submenu (under the Item menu); see Figure 3-33. The Merge commands allow you to join separate shapes into one, or to have one shape act like a cookie cutter on another.

Figure 3-33

The Merge commands

In order to use the Merge features, you have to select two or more boxes or lines. After selecting one of the Merge features, you'll end up with one box (even if the original objects were lines, your final shape is always a box—the one exception is the Join Endpoints command). If the original items have different background colors, the final box takes on the background color of the back-most object. Similarly, if the original boxes have imported text or graphics, only the text or the graphic in the back-most object is kept (see Figure 3-34).

There are seven features in the Merge submenu: Intersection, Union, Difference, Reverse Difference, Exclusive Or, Combine, and Join Endpoints. (As we'll see in a moment, Join Endpoints is only available when you have two lines selected.)

Figure 3-35 contains some examples of various effects you can create with the Merge features. After reading the following descriptions, can you tell how each one was created?

Figure 3-34
The Merge commands
in action

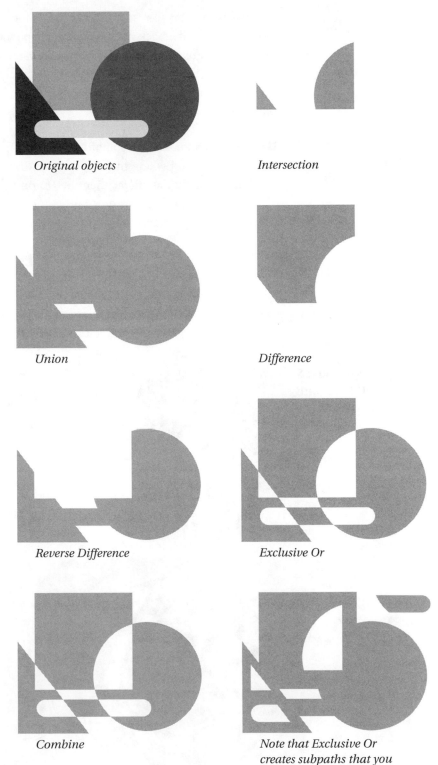

Original objects

Intersection

Union

Difference

Reverse Difference

Exclusive Or

Combine

*Note that Exclusive Or
creates subpaths that you
can move around.*

Intersection. The Intersection command looks for the areas where the objects overlap the back-most object. It keeps those areas and then deletes all the other areas of the shapes. If the front-most objects are separate, the remaining objects will also be separate. A single object that has separate, individual paths is called a *compound object*, or a *compound path* (see Figure 3-36).

Union. The Union feature combines all the shapes into one object, and no hole is left behind where they overlapped. If some of the original shapes aren't overlapping the others, then the Union command leaves the objects separate, but they all act as one compound object. (In fact, if none of the original objects overlap, then Union is identical to the Combine command.)

Difference. The Difference command uses the front object as a cookie cutter on the back-most object. The result is that the shape of the front object is cut out of the back-most object, even if that means punching a hole in the middle of it. (If you select two concentric circles and choose Difference, you end up with the shape of a bagel with a see-through hole in the center.)

Figure 3-35
Special effects with
the Merge features

Reverse Difference. The Reverse Difference command reverses the previous command. That is, Reverse Difference creates a union of all the selected objects except the back-most one. It then cuts out the shape of the back-most object from this front-most union.

Exclusive Or. The Exclusive Or feature builds a transparent hole wherever the shapes overlap. This hole is a compound path that you can move around later if you want (see "Tip: Moving Pieces of Compound Objects," below). If you select two objects, one of which is completely enclosed by the other, Exclusive Or is identical to Difference. If the objects don't overlap at all, the result is identical to Union. But if the objects are only partially overlapping, you get really wacky results. I've tried for months to think of a practical use for this feature, to no avail. If you find it indispensible for some reason, let me know.

Combine. The Combine command creates an effect visually identical to the Exclusive Or command. Also like Exclusive Or, if two objects are fully contained within each other, it's identical to Difference; if the objects are not overlapping, it's identical to Union. The big difference is that if the shapes are partially overlapping, each original item is maintained as a separate path within the compound object. That is, XPress won't create any new paths for

Figure 3-36
Compound objects

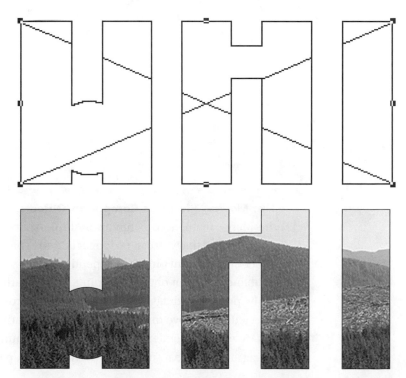

you, as it does with Exclusive Or. This becomes relevant if you try to edit the paths later.

Join Endpoints. The last item on the Merge submenu, Join Endpoints, is only available when you have two lines or text paths selected. There's one other condition for Join Endpoints to work, however: two end points (one on each path) must be placed on top of each other. (Actually, they can be within 6 points of each other.) As soon as you select Join Endpoints, XPress merges the two points into one corner point (moving each of them slightly, if necessary; see Figure 3-37).

Join Endpoints doesn't work with only Bézier lines. You can join a Bézier Text Path to an Orthogonal line, or join together two Orthogonal lines to create a new Bézier line, and so on. The only requirement is that both objects be open lines. As I said earlier, if you join different types or styles of lines, the resulting path takes on the attributes of the back object. For instance, regular lines are converted to text paths if the back-most object is a text path.

Figure 3-37
Join Endpoints command

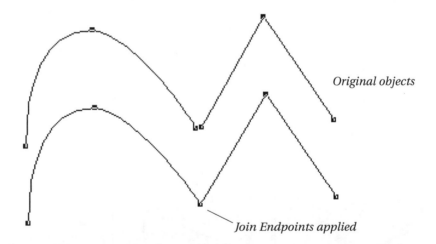

Original objects

Join Endpoints applied

▼ ▼

Tip: Moving Pieces of Compound Objects. Just because you use one of the Merge features to combine multiple shapes into a compound object doesn't mean that you can no longer edit the shapes. As I said earlier, you can select all the points in an independent path within a compound path by double-clicking on one of the points on the path. Now when you move one of the points (by dragging it or pressing an Arrow key when the Item tool is selected), you move the whole independent path (see Figure 3-38).

Moving independent paths within a compound object can provide interesting and strange results if you partially overlap one path over another, but

Figure 3-38
Moving a path within a
compound object

 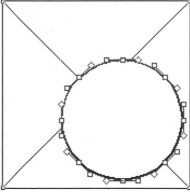

This is one object with   *Here, the points on the subpath*
a hole in the middle.   *have been selected and moved.*

after playing with it for a little while you'll find ways of controlling the effects
to get the look you want.

▼ ▼

Tip: Creating Symmetrical Objects. It turns out that many of the shapes
people want to create are symmetrical, and yet drawing symmetrical objects
is not the easiest thing to do. Here's one technique to get symmetrical objects
on your page.

1. Create one-half of the symmetrical object.

2. Duplicate the object using Step and Repeat with the Vertical and
   Horizontal Offsets both set to zero.

3. Mirror this duplicate object (see "Tip: Flipping Shapes Around," earlier in this chapter).

4. Move the duplicate item into place (remember, you can hold down
   the Shift key while dragging an item to constrain it horizontally or
   vertically).

5. Select the two objects and use Union (if the items are boxes) or Join
   Endpoints (if they're lines) to combine them into a single object.

After you create the symmetrical object, you often need to do a little
cleanup (removing points, for instance), but the result is almost always better than if you tried to draw the shape by hand. Note that you can also draw
one-half of a symmetrical box by drawing a path, using this technique, and
then converting the path into a box (see "Transforming Boxes and Lines,"
later in this section).

▼ ▼

Splitting Compound Objects

So now you know how to merge shapes together, and you've seen how this sometimes results in compound objects. There's got to be a way to pull these compound paths apart again. Indeed there is. You've got two choices in the Split submenu (under the Item menu): Split Outside Paths and Split All Paths. Which you use depends on what you've got and what you're trying to achieve.

Split All Paths simply separates every independent path within a compound object into its own object. Split Outside Paths, on the other hand, only splits up paths that aren't surrounded by other paths. For instance, let's say you've used the Union feature to make two bagels sitting next to each other. Split All Paths would turn this into four separate ovals. Split Outside Paths would turn it into two bagels, because the "holes" in each bagel are fully enclosed, and so they don't get separated (see Figure 3-39).

Transforming Boxes and Lines

Once you have created a text box, picture box, contentless box, or line, you can change it into some other form using the Shape submenu under the Item menu (see Figure 3-40). For example, if you made a rectangular picture box on your page, you could turn it into an oval by first selecting the picture box and then selecting the oval picture box icon in the Shape submenu.

I can't say that I've ever used some of the items in the Shape submenu for anything other than a good chuckle . . . for instance, the beveled-corner box and the photo-frame box. But you might have some use for them, and if you do, remember that the "depth" of the bevel or the concave curve is determined by the Corner Radius setting (in the Measurements palette or the Modify dialog box).

Instead, I most often use the Shape feature to convert boxes to lines or vice versa.

Converting boxes to paths. You can convert any kind of box into a line by selecting one of the three line shapes in the Shapes submenu: diagonal, orthogonal, or Bézier.

> ▶ DIAGONAL LINE. When you convert a box into a diagonal line, XPress replaces the box with a line that stretches from the upper-left corner to the lower-right corner of the box's bounding rectangle (the bounding rectangle is the smallest rectangle that completely encloses the box shape). If you can find a good use for this, more power to you.

> ▶ ORTHOGONAL LINE. Selecting the orthogonal line is actually even less useful: you just get a horizontal line that spans the width of the box.

Figure 3-39
Split commands

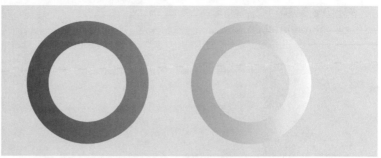

Original objects: one compound path made of two "bagels."

After Split Outside Paths, we get two bagels.

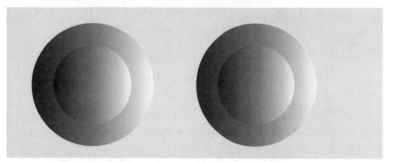

After Split All Paths, we get four objects, each with a blend.

▶ **BÉZIER LINE.** Choosing the Bézier line is where you hit pay dirt. When you select this option, the outline of the box you have selected becomes a Bézier line. Of course, Bézier lines are always open paths, so even though the path probably appears closed, it has a beginning and an ending point. (It's sometimes difficult to find an endpoint . . . look for any one point on the path that looks even slightly different from the others. If you still can't find one, and you really need to, just start clicking and moving points—and then selecting Undo if it's not an endpoint—until you find the right place.)

Note that if the box had a dash or stripe selected as a frame, that same style is applied to the resulting path. (Of course, the special

Figure 3-40

Shape submenu

bitmapped frames can't be applied to lines; see "Frames, Dashes, and Stripes," later in this chapter.)

Note that you cannot currently undo a change from a box to a path. Because of this, I usually make a duplicate of the box before converting the original.

▼ ▼

Tip: Watch Out for Shape Changes. When you use the above technique to change a framed box into a line, you need to watch out for two things. First, the size of the box generally changes. This is because frames are run on the inside or outside of a box, but lines "grow" on both sides of its centerline. Take that dimension shift into consideration as you make your initial box.

The second thing to watch for is notches in your frame. Again, lines are always open paths, so a thick frame (which turns into a thick line width) may have a notch in it where the two endpoints meet (see Figure 3-41).

▼ ▼

Tip: Text Boxes to Text Paths. If you want to set some text in a circle, you need a circular text path. Unfortunately, it's a pain in the eyeball to draw a perfect circle with the Bézier text-path tool. Here's a better way: Make a circular text box and type in it the text you want on the path. Now, choose the Bézier line from the Shape submenu under the Item menu (that's the one that looks like a squiggle). The text box becomes a text path, and the contents of the box become the contents of the path (see Figure 3-42). It's as easy as that.

Well, actually, it's never as easy as "that." There is one more step: You must change the color of the line to None in order to make it invisible (unless you want to be able to see the text on a path *and* the path itself). Note that the best way to specify exactly where on the path you want the text to begin is to click on that point with the Scissors tool. This automatically converts the box into a path and starts the text at that point.

▼ ▼

Converting paths to boxes. If you select a line and choose one of the regular boxes from the Shape submenu—such as the rectangular or oval box—

Figure 3-41
Converting a framed
box to a line

*Note the notch in at
what is now the
beginning of the
path. Also, the box
has become larger
because of the path.*

Figure 3-42
Text boxes to text paths

XPress replaces your line with a box of this shape (the size of the box is determined by the line's bounding rectangle). This isn't particularly interesting. What is interesting is what happens when you choose the Bézier box from the Shape submenu.

If you simply select the Bézier shape, XPress converts the outline of the path into a box. For instance, if you have a straight line 1 inch long and 8 points thick, the result is a rectangular box that is 1 inch long and 8 points wide (see Figure 3-43). Obviously, it doesn't make much sense to do this for thin lines.

If you hold down the Option (Alt) key when selecting the Bézier box shape, XPress does something completely different: it closes the path for you. If the line had a line style (dots, dashes, or whatever), QuarkXPress applies that style as the box's frame.

▼ ▼

Tip: Converting Dashes and Stripes to Bézier Boxes. I think the ability to convert a line to a box, in which XPress actually builds the box based on the outline of the line, is really amazing. To me, the best part about it is that line styles—such as dots, stripes, or arrowheads—are also converted, usually becoming a compound object. If you want, you can then select Split All Paths to further manipulate each of the individual Bézier paths of the shape.

Again, this sort of thing makes the most sense when you are working with thick lines. Once you've got a box based on the line, you can fill it with a color, a blend, text, or a picture (see Figure 3-44).

▼ ▼

Switching shapes back and forth. Just because you can convert one box shape into another, or change lines to boxes and vice versa, don't get the idea that it's always reversible. In fact, it's pretty rare that once you've changed an object from one shape into another, you'll ever be able to get it back to the original shape again.

Converting Text to Paths

Digital typefaces, as we'll see in Chapter 6, *Type and Typography*, generally contain mathematical outlines of each character in the font. These outlines are scalable, so that you can view or print them at any resolution or size and they'll always be smooth. Wouldn't it be cool if you could also convert those outlines into QuarkXPress Bézier boxes? You can.

To convert text to a box, select the text with the Content tool and choose Text to Box from the Style menu (see Figure 3-45). There are, of course, a few caveats. You can only convert up to a single line of text at a time. You can only convert fonts for which you have the outline files installed (even then, some

Figure 3-43
Converting paths
to boxes

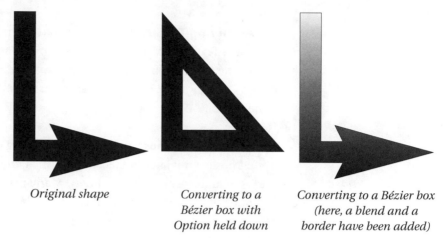

Original shape

*Converting to a
Bézier box with
Option held down*

*Converting to a Bézier box
(here, a blend and a
border have been added)*

Figure 3-44
Converting line styles
to Bézier boxes

*Here, the striped line has
been converted into a
Bézier box and a blend
placed in it.*

fonts don't seem to convert well, particularly the TrueType system fonts like Chicago or Geneva on the Macintosh). Finally, while you can convert a lot of characters at the same time, it doesn't mean that you'll actually get them to print later. Keep it simple.

If you have selected more than one character of text, they are all convert-ed into a single picture box. You can then use Split Outside Paths to separate them into individual characters, if you'd like. Whether you split them or not, you can use all the editing features I've discussed to manipulate the outlines. After all, these are picture boxes now.

Also, note that I use the term *convert.* However, I should probably say *cre-ate,* because the original text is not deleted from the text box (although see the next tip).

▼ ▼

Tip: Anchoring Text Outlines. If you hold down the Option (Alt) key when you select Text to Box from the Style menu, XPress actually replaces your selected text with the Bézier box, anchoring it in the text as an inline graphic (see Chapter 11, *Where Text Meets Graphics*, for more information on inline boxes).

▼ ▼

Tip: Careful with Those Frames. I'm not going to discuss putting borders around boxes until later in this chapter (in "Frames, Dashes, and Stripes"), but I should make one comment now: Many people don't realize that when they put a border around a box, it can actually change the shape of the box. If Framing is set to Outside on the General tab of the Preferences dialog box, adding a frame will actually expand the boundaries of the box itself. If the border is too thick, the edges of the box may bump into each other, permanently altering the shape of the box (see Figure 3-46).

Figure 3-45
Creating Bézier
paths from text

Figure 3-46
Frames can sometimes
change the shape of
boxes

The original text, converted to a box

*After a frame is applied
(Framing set to Outside)*

*When the frame is removed or
reduced in size, you can see that the
box outlines have been altered.*

Manipulating Items

Once you've created a page element (item) such as a picture box or a line, what can you do with it? A lot. In this section I talk about how to move, rotate, skew, resize, reshape, lock, duplicate, suppress the printout of, and delete items. Remember that I'm talking only about the items themselves here, so you often need to select the items with the Item tool to make most of these changes.

Moving Items

You can move a page element in several ways. First, if you're an interactive type, you can select the Item tool, then click on the object and drag it. Or, if you have the Content tool selected, you can get the Item tool temporarily by holding down the Command (Ctrl) key, which lets you move an item, too. (However, note that if you have more than one object selected, Command-dragging or Ctrl-dragging with the Content tool moves a single item in the group, not the whole group.)

The second method for moving an item is by changing its origin coordinates in the Measurements palette or the Modify dialog box. I find this method especially useful if I need to move the item a specific amount. For example, let's say I have a text box with its origin at 1 inch across and 1 inch down. If I want to move the text box horizontally 18 picas, I change the Origin Across coordinate in the Measurements palette to "1"+18p", then press Enter. The box automatically moves over.

A third method for moving items is by selecting them and pressing the Arrow keys on the keyboard. Each time you press an Arrow key, the item moves one point in that direction. Holding down the Option (Alt) key when you press an Arrow key moves the item 0.1 point.

Tip: Techniques for Item Placement. If you have a style of placing and sizing your page elements—such as lines and picture boxes—that works for you, stick to it. Nonetheless, here are some basic guides that I find helpful.

▶ Use picas and points for everything except basic page size. These are the standard units among designers and printers, and allow precision without having to deal with numbers like 0.08334 inch (which is 6 points, or 0.5 pica). If you're working with type, this also makes it easier since type is generally specified in picas and points.

▶ Try to use round numbers for most of your measurements. Creating or moving a box at the Fit in Window size usually gives you measurements that have coordinates out to the thousandth of a point, such as

"6p3.462". It might seem like a picky detail, but, in the long run, it can come in handy to either create your boxes at Actual Size and then resize them if needed, or—if you must work at a reduced or enlarged view—go into the Measurements palette or the Modify dialog box (double-click on the box or press Command-M or Ctrl-M) and change the coordinates and the sizes to round numbers.

▶ Use oval- or Bézier-shaped picture boxes only when you must have that shape. Using a rectangle or square box for the majority of your pictures can cut your printing time to half or a third of what it takes when you use ovals.

▼ ▼

Tip: Viewing Changes As You Make Them. It's always a hassle to move, resize, or rotate a box, because while you're doing it, QuarkXPress only shows you the outline of the box rather than the whole box. Or does it?

If you hold the mouse button down on a picture-box handle for about half a second before dragging it, you can see the picture crop (or scale, if you have the Command or Ctrl key held down, too) as you move the handle. Similarly, if you move or rotate the box, you can see the text or picture rotate while dragging if you simply pause for about half a second before starting to drag. No, you don't have to count out half a second; just wait until you see the object flash quickly before you start dragging. (The exact amount of time is determined by the Delayed Item Dragging value on the Interactive tab in the Preferences dialog box.)

▼ ▼

Tip: Moving an Item's Origin. Adobe PageMaker and Adobe InDesign both let you set the origin of a page element from any of its corners or its center, rather than just the upper-left corner. Until QuarkXPress does the same, I can only offer a somewhat weak workaround for specifying alternate origins: use the built-in math functions. If you want the right side of a 12-pica-wide picture box to be set at the 2.75-inch mark, type "2.75"-12p" into the x-origin field of the Measurements palette. That is, simply subtract the width of the box from the right point. Or, if you want the center of a 16-pica-wide text box to be at the 18-centimeter mark, you can type "18cm-16p/2".

▼ ▼

Resizing and Reshaping Items

Resizing an object means changing its width and height, while reshaping it may involve moving points around, like turning a rectangle into a triangle. Both are easy to do, but how you go about doing it depends on the type of object you have selected. (Resizing and reshaping a group of items are special-case scenarios that I cover in "Modifying Grouped Objects," later in this chapter.)

Resizing boxes. The most basic shapes are the non-Bézier boxes, like the rectangle and the oval. To resize these, you once again have a choice between using QuarkXPress's interactive click-and-drag style or working in measurements.

▶ RESIZING BY DRAGGING. To resize by clicking and dragging, you place the screen cursor over one of the box's handles. Boxes have eight handles (one on each side, one on each corner) that you can drag to resize. Dragging a side handle resizes the box in one direction—horizontally or vertically. Dragging a corner handle resizes the box in two directions (horizontally *and* vertically). Of course, as I discussed earlier in this chapter, if the shape is a Bézier box, you need to turn off Edit Shape (in the Edit submenu under the Item menu) to see these handles.

Also, note that XPress lets you "flip" a box, resulting in a mirror of the original, by dragging one of the side handles across the box and past the opposite handle (see "Tip: Flipping Shapes Around," earlier in this chapter).

▶ RESIZING BY THE NUMBERS. The second method of resizing and reshaping boxes is by changing their height and width values. These values are located in both the Modify dialog box and the Measurements palette. Unless you're a wizard at math, it's difficult to keep an object's aspect (width-to-height) ratio this way (see "Tip: Proportional Resizing by the Numbers," below). Instead, this is a great way to make a box exactly the size you want it. For example, if you want an 8-by-10-inch picture box, you can draw one to any size you'd like, then change its width and height coordinates to 8 inches and 10 inches.

▼ ▼

Tip: Maintain the Ratios. In order to maintain an item's width and height ratio while stretching it, you can hold down the Option (Alt) and Shift keys while dragging. If you want to constrain the box into a square or circle, just hold down the Shift key while dragging. (If the object were rectangular or oval, it would snap into a square or a circle.)

▼ ▼

Tip: Proportional Resizing by the Numbers. Don't forget that QuarkXPress can do a lot of math work for you. This can come in handy in situations in which you're trying to resize items on a page. For example, if you know that the 1-by-2-inch box (2 inches tall) on the page should be 5 inches wide, you can type "5"" into the width box. But what do you put in the height box? If you want to keep the aspect ratio, you can let the program do a little math for you: just type "*newwidth/oldwidth" after the height value. In this example, you'd type "*5/2" after the height. This multiplies the value by the percentage change in width (if you divide 5 by 2, you get a 250-percent change, or 2.5 times the value).

Remember that you cannot divide by a measurement, so you cannot type something like "*5"/18p". You would have to type "5"/1.5" (1.5 is 18p in inches).

▼ ▼

Bézier boxes and lines. I discussed editing Bézier lines and boxes earlier in this chapter. The one thing I want to reemphasize is to pay attention to the Edit Shape feature (in the Shape submenu, under the Item menu; or toggle it on and off with Shift-F4, or F10 in Windows). When this is on, you can edit the individual Bézier points, control handles, and segments. When it's off, you can only change the overall size (height and width) of the item.

Lines. Most people define lines by their two endpoints (I'm only referring to straight lines with two endpoints, including those made with the Diagonal Text Path tool). However, QuarkXPress can define any line in four different ways. Each line description is called a *mode*, and it shows up in both the Modify dialog box and the Measurements palette (see Figure 3-47). The four modes are as follows.

▶ **ENDPOINTS.** This mode describes the line by two sets of coordinates, x1,y1 and x2,y2. In the Modify dialog box, these are called the First Across and First Down, or the Last Across and Last Down.

▶ **LEFT POINT.** In Left Point mode, QuarkXPress describes a line by three values: its endpoint (from wherever you started the line when dragging is its first point), its length, and its angle. An angle of zero degrees is always a horizontal line; as the angle increases, the line

Figure 3-47
Line modes

rotates counterclockwise, so that 45 degrees is a diagonal up and to the right, and 90 degrees is vertical.

▶ **RIGHT POINT.** QuarkXPress uses the same three values for the Right Point mode, except that it uses the coordinate of the last point on the line (wherever you let go of the mouse button).

▶ **MIDPOINT.** The fourth mode, Midpoint, defines lines by their length and angle based on the coordinate of the center point. That is, if a line is 2 inches long, QuarkXPress draws the line 1 inch out on either side from the midpoint, at the specified angle.

You can define a line while in one mode, modify it in another, and move it with another.

For example, let's say you draw a line someplace on your page. You then find you want to rotate it slightly. You have the choice to rotate the line from its left point, right point, or midpoint by selecting the proper mode from the Measurements palette or the Modify dialog box, then changing the line's rotation value. If you want to move just the left point of the line by 3 points (and leave the other point stationary), you can switch to Endpoints mode and alter the x2,x2 coordinate.

To resize a line by a given percentage, you can multiply its length by the percentage. If you want a line to be 120 percent as long, just multiply the length value in the Measurements palette or Modify dialog box by 1.2. To make it half as long, multiply by 0.5 or divide by two.

▼ ▼

Tip: Constraining Lines Along an Angle. We all know that you can hold down the Shift key while you draw out a line, to constrain the line horizontally or vertically. However, if you hold down the Shift key while resizing it (dragging one of its endpoints), XPress constrains it along its angle of rotation (or its angle plus 45 degrees, or plus 90 degrees).

Note that this is different from earlier versions of the program, in which holding down the Shift key while resizing would constrain a line to a vertical or horizontal position. Now the only way to force a diagonal line into an orthogonal line is to set its angle to zero or 90 degrees.

▼ ▼

Rotating Items

You can rotate an item numerically using the Modify dialog box or the Measurements palette, or by eye with the Rotation tool (the third item in the Tool palette). Note that positive rotation values rotate the object counterclockwise; negative values rotate it clockwise (this is arguably counterintuitive). Most objects are rotated from their center. This center may not be where you think it is, however, because the center is defined as the middle of the object's bounding box.

Lines are the main exception when it comes to the center of rotation. Lines rotate differently depending on their Mode (see "Lines," above). For example, if a line is in Left Point mode when you specify a rotation, the line rotates around the first endpoint.

If you are more visually minded, you can rotate items using the Rotation tool.

1. Select a page item.

2. Choose the Rotation tool from the Tool palette.

3. Click where you want the center of rotation, but don't let the mouse button go yet.

4. Drag the Rotation tool. As you drag, the object is rotated in the direction you drag. The farther from the center of rotation you drag, the more precise the rotation can be.

I rarely use this tool in a production setting, but that's just my bias. It may suit you well. However, it's significantly harder to control the rotation by using the tool rather than by entering a specific value.

▼ ▼

Tip: Rotate Around a Single Point. Let's say you want to rotate 10 objects around a particular point. If the point is in the middle of the 10 objects, you've got no problem: select them all and type the rotation value into the Measurements palette. But what if the point isn't in the middle of the group of objects? Here are two ways to do it.

▶ You can use the Rotation tool. This is, in fact, the only time I ever use this tool. Select the objects, select the tool, click the point around which you want to rotate, and drag the mouse around until you get the angle you want. This is perfectly good if you don't need a specific angle, but trying to rotate a bunch of objects to exactly 30 degrees like this is nearly impossible.

▶ I like this method instead: Draw a big picture box that surrounds all the objects you want to rotate. Make sure the center of the box is where you want to rotate from (when Show Guides is turned on, you can see the center point; it's where the diagonal lines join). Select all the objects you want to rotate, along with the picture box. Then type the rotation value into the Measurements palette. XPress rotates around the center of the biggest box that surrounds all the objects.

▼ ▼

Skewing Items

QuarkXPress lets you skew boxes and their contents. As I discuss in Chapter 9, *Pictures*, skewing is the same as rotating the vertical axis and not the horizontal one. If you skew a text box or a picture box, the text or picture within the box is skewed to the same angle. You can skew a box by typing a value into the Skew field on the Box tab of the Modify dialog box (it only lets you enter values between -75 and 75 degrees). Enter a positive number to skew the box and its contents to the right; a negative number skews them to the left.

If you need to spice up your afternoon, you can skew the contents of a box separately from the box itself (you can find Text Skew on the Text tab and Picture Skew on the Picture tab of the Modify dialog box).

Skewing boxes isn't something you need to do every day, but by combining QuarkXPress's ability to skew and rotate text boxes, you can create some interesting effects, like a three-dimensional cube with angled text on each side (see Figure 3-48).

Figure 3-48
Box skew

Flipping Out

It used to be that if you wanted to flip a picture or text along the vertical or horizontal axis—so that you could mirror it on facing pages, for instance—you had to dive into a graphics program, flip the image, save it as a picture, then bring it into your QuarkXPress document.

Well, no longer. Just select the object, then go to the Style menu and choose Flip Vertical or Flip Horizontal. Note that you have to use the Content tool to do this, as this is actually mirroring the contents of the box rather than the box itself. Not only does this command let you flip pictures and text, but flipped text remains fully editable (to do this, you have to practice reading the newspaper in the mirror).

You can also use the icons for flipping contents in the Measurements palette (see Figure 3-49). The top icon controls horizontal flipping; the lower one controls vertical flipping.

Figure 3-49

Flip Horizontal
and Vertical

Locking Items

There are times when you want an item to stay how and where it is. For example, if you've painstakingly placed multiple text boxes on your page, you may not want someone else who will be working on your page to move or resize them accidentally. You can lock any page item down to its spot, making it invulnerable to being moved or resized with the Item tool. Just select the item with either the Item or the Content tool and choose Lock from the Item menu (or press Command-L or Ctrl-L).

If an item is locked, the Item tool cursor turns into a padlock when passed over it. You cannot move it by clicking and dragging either the item or its control handles. I find this feature especially helpful when I'm working on a complex page and don't want an accidental click here or a drag there to ruin my work.

However, just because you lock something does not mean that it won't move or change. If you select the box with the Item tool and your cat jumps onto your keyboard, pressing one of the Arrow keys, the box moves. If you use the Space/Align feature, QuarkXPress ignores the Locked status and moves the object (this *really* bugs me). And you can easily change the coordinate of the item's origin or its height or width in the Measurements palette . . . that changes the item, too. You can even delete locked items. The *only* thing that Lock stops you from doing is dragging the box.

Oh yes, you can also always change the contents of an item; locking only affects the item, not the contents within.

To unlock an item, select it and press Command-L (Ctrl-L) again (or choose Unlock from the Item menu).

Suppress Printout and Suppress Picture Printout

If you turn on Suppress Printout (in the Modify dialog box) for any object on your page, QuarkXPress won't print that object. Ever. Period. This is helpful when you want nonprinting notes to be placed in your layout, or for setting runaround objects that affect your text but don't print out on your final page. (However, just because the object doesn't print doesn't mean the text runaround goes away; see Chapter 11, *Where Text Meets Graphics*.)

When you have a picture box selected, the Modify dialog box also offers a second checkbox: Suppress Picture Printout. If you check this one, it keeps the picture from printing, but the box itself still prints. The difference? If the picture has a frame around it, the frame prints and the picture doesn't.

▼ ▼

Tip: Post-it Notes. If your QuarkXPress documents need to move from one person to another, you may want to add comments to certain objects or areas of a page. By taking advantage of QuarkXPress's ability to suppress the printout of any item, you can easily create noticeable, but nonprinting, electronic "Post-it" notes, to contain comments and suggestions about an individual document (see Figure 3-50).

Create a text box and enter the text of the note. Give the box a background of 100-percent yellow, a runaround of None, and turn on Suppress Printout in the Text Box Specifications dialog box (so as not to affect the printing of the document).

Figure 3-50

Post-it notes

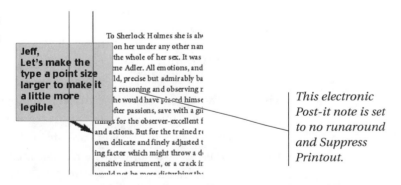

▼ ▼

Duplicating Items

When I stand around watching over their shoulders as people work, one of the most common suggestions I make is to use the Duplicate and Step and Repeat features more often. If you need to make two text boxes, it's rarely worth the trouble to draw both of them; just make one and then duplicate it.

There are three ways to duplicate a page element: Copy and Paste it, Duplicate it, or use Step and Repeat.

Copy and Paste. Selecting an item, copying it, and pasting it (Command-C and Command-V or Ctrl-C and Ctrl-V) is the most common way people learn to duplicate objects, though it's not always the most efficient or precise way. Many people get confused when they Copy and Paste picture and text boxes, because they don't use the correct tools. Remember that you should use the Item tool when working with *items* (boxes, lines, and text paths), and the Content tool when working with the *contents* of boxes or text paths. If you have the Content tool selected and you try to copy a text box, you only copy text. Copying with the Item tool actually copies the text box. (See "Tip: Copy the Opposite," below.)

When you Paste a page item, the program places it in the middle of your screen or as close as it can get it on whatever spread you're currently on (however, see "Tip: Paste in Place," below). This little detail has been known to trip up even advanced users of XPress, because the page you're looking at is not always the page you're currently on. If even only a little sliver of the previous spread is touching the upper-left corner of the document window (where the two rulers meet), Pasting places the object on *that* spread, not the one that takes up most of your screen.

▼ ▼

Tip: Paste in Place. Both PageMaker and InDesign have long had a feature called Paste in Place, or "power pasting," which pastes an object at the same place on the page as you copied or cut it from. QuarkXPress 6 finally incorporates this very helpful feature. It's hiding in plain view in the Edit menu, but few XPress users notice it there. Alternately, you can press Command-Option-Shift-V (Ctrl-Alt-Shift-V).

▼ ▼

Tip: Copy the Opposite. As I said earlier, whether the Command-C (Ctrl-C) keystroke Copies the page item or the contents within the page item depends entirely on whether you have the Item or the Content tool selected. However, you can also Copy the item itself when you have the Content tool by pressing Command-Option-C (Ctrl-Alt-C). For example, if you have the Content tool selected and you want to Copy a whole text box, you can press Command-Option-C (Ctrl-Alt-C).

▼ ▼

Duplicate. Choosing Duplicate from the Item menu (or pressing Command-D or Ctrl-D) duplicates whatever item(s) you have selected. The default setting for Duplicate is to offset the duplicate item ¼ inch down and to the right from the original object, but Duplicate always uses whatever horizontal and vertical offsets you last used in Step and Repeat.

Step and Repeat. The Step and Repeat feature can best be described as a powerhouse, and I wish every program had it. The Step and Repeat command (under the Item menu, or press Command-Option-D or Ctrl-Alt-D) lets you select one or more objects and duplicate them with specific horizontal and vertical offsets as many times as you like.

For example, if you want 35 vertical lines, each 9 points away from each other across the page, draw one line and then choose Step and Repeat from the Item menu. In the Step and Repeat dialog box, enter "34" in the Repeat Count field (you already have the first one made), "9pt" in the Horizontal Offset field, and "0" in the Vertical Offset field. After you use Step and Repeat, you can press Command-Z (Ctrl-Z) to Undo all of the duplications.

Both Duplicate and Step and Repeat have certain limitations. First, you cannot duplicate an item so that any part of it falls off the pasteboard. If you are working with constrained items (see "Constraining," below), you cannot duplicate them so that any of the copies would fall outside of the constraining box. And while any items you duplicate from within a constrained group become part of that constrained group, note that duplicating an item from a set of grouped objects does not result in the copy being part of the group.

Super Step and Repeat. What started out as a frivolous little free XTension that you could download from the Quark Web site is now a frivolous little XTension that comes bundled with XPress. The Super Step and Repeat feature in the Item menu (which appears when the XTension of the same name is active), not only offsets duplicate objects, but skews, scales, and rotates the duplicates, too. I'm sure that someone, somewhere is somehow using this XTension in money-making ways, but I just turn this XTension off so I'm not tempted to sit around playing with it rather than getting my work done.

▼ ▼

Tip: Clone Item. If you're a Macromedia FreeHand user, you're probably familiar with the Command-= (Ctrl-=) keystroke to duplicate an item without any offset. This is called *cloning*. I use this all the time when I'm building pages in QuarkXPress.

First, I use Step and Repeat to copy an object with the Horizontal and Vertical Offset fields both set to zero. Now, next time I want to clone something, I just press Command-D (or Ctrl-D, which always uses the last offsets I typed in Step and Repeat). This works as long as I don't change the Offsets or quit XPress.

▼ ▼

▼ ▼

Tip: Moving Objects to Other Documents. QuarkXPress's ability to drag objects around the page (or from one page to another) doesn't stop at the boundaries of the document window. You can use the Item tool to drag an object or group of objects to another document (see "Moving Items Between Documents," in Chapter 2, *QuarkXPress Basics*). Of course, you need to have both documents open and visible on the screen to do this, so you cannot drag and drop from one layout space to another.

▼ ▼

Deleting Items

As I suggested above, there is a difference between deleting the contents of a picture or text box and deleting the box itself. When the contents of a box (such as a picture or text) are deleted, the box still remains. When the box itself is deleted, everything goes. There are three basic ways to delete a page item.

▶ I think the easiest way to delete a page item is to select it (with either the Item or Content tool) and press Command-K (Ctrl-K). This is the same as selecting Delete from the Item menu.

▶ The second-easiest way to delete an item is to select it with the Item tool and press the Delete key on your keyboard. Remember that if you use the Content tool, you delete the text or picture rather than the box.

▶ A third way to delete an item is to select it with the Item tool and select Cut or Clear from the Edit menu. Of course, cutting it actually saves the item on the Clipboard so that you can place it somewhere else later.

The only one of these methods that works for deleting a single item from a group is Command-K (Ctrl-K). That's because to remove this kind of page item, you must first select it with the Content tool (or else you end up deleting the entire group).

▼ ▼

Tip: Alien Deletions. Computer software has a long history of "Easter eggs": wacky little useless features that programmers include late at night after too many hours of staring at the screen. QuarkXPress has a couple good Easter eggs (I mentioned one of them already, in Chapter 2, *QuarkXPress Basics*). My favorite is the little Martian that walks out on your screen and kills an object on your page (see Figure 3-51). You can call this little fella up from the depths by pressing Command-Option-Shift-K; or you can hold down the

Figure 3-51
The Martian

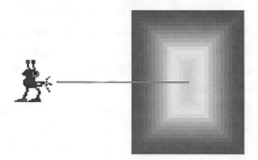

modifiers while selecting Delete from the Item menu. (Versions 4 and 5 offer an additional alien creature, too, but he only appears once every five or six times you use the keystroke.)

Unfortunately, the Martian is a Macintosh-only Easter egg. However, the same keystroke (Ctrl-Alt-Shift-K) provides a different sort of Easter egg on Windows: the deleted object melts down your screen with a wonderful gurgling sound.

Relationships Between Items

Page-layout programs like QuarkXPress are designed so that you can put a number of text and picture objects on a page. That's the whole point. And anytime you have more than one object on a page, you're going to be concerned about the relationships between those objects. For instance, if you have a block of text and a picture next to it, you probably have an idea about how you want those two items to relate: Do they align on their left edges? Are they centered next to each other? Should the picture always follow the text?

Curiously, some page-layout software developers don't understand this fundamental element of page layout, and they haven't included tools for handling these relationships in their programs. Fortunately for us, however, Quark *does* understand.

In this section I talk about controlling relationships between items: layering, grouping, constraining, and, finally, their position on the page relative to other page elements.

Layering Items

QuarkXPress, like most desktop publishing programs, handles multiple objects on a page by *layering* them. Each page item (picture box, text box, contentless box, text path, or line) is always on a higher or lower layer than the other page items. This is also called a *stacking order*. This is generally an intuitive approach to working with page elements; it's just what you would do if each of the objects were on a little piece of paper in front of you. When you're placing objects on your page, you work from the bottom of the stacking order up. The first object you place is the bottom-most object, the second object is on top of it, and so on.

If none of your page elements touch or overlap one another, then layering has almost no relevance to you. However, when they do touch or overlap in some way, you want to be able to control which objects overlap which. The primary methods for controlling the stacking order are the Bring to Front and Send to Back commands in the Item menu.

Bring to Front and Send to Back function as sweeping controls, moving a selected object all the way to the back or all the way to the front layer. When you hold down the Option key while selecting the Item menu, the Send to Back and Bring to Front items become Send Backward and Bring Forward. (Note that these are always visible in Windows, so you don't have to hold down a modifier key.) Note that you can also use the function keys to move things up and down through layers (see Table 3-4).

For even more control over how your objects stack up, you can also create multiple layers in the Layers palette; I discuss that in "The Layers Palette," later in this chapter.

Table 3-4
Layering keystrokes

Press . . .	To . . .
F5	Bring to Front
Shift-F5	Send to Back
Option-F5 (Ctrl-F5)	Bring Forward
Shift-Option-F5 (Shift-Ctrl-F5)	Send Backward

Grouping Objects

Objects on a page are rarely lone creatures. Often, they like to bunch together to form single units, like organic cells grouping to form a vital organ in your body. Similarly, you can create groups of page items. A group of objects can include any number of boxes and/or lines. When you select one member of the group with the Item tool, the whole group gets selected. Or, you can select and modify individual members of the group with the Content tool. Here's what you do.

1. Using the Item or Content tool, select the items you want grouped. You can hold down the Shift key to select multiple items. Or, you can drag a marquee over or around the objects (any object that the marquee touches is selected).

2. Select Group from the Item menu or press Command-G (Ctrl-G).

It's that easy. When the group is selected with the Item tool, a dotted line shows the bounding box of the grouped objects (see Figure 3-52).

To ungroup the objects, select the grouped object with the Item tool and select Ungroup from the Item menu (or press Command-U or Ctrl-U).

Figure 3-52
Grouped objects

Bounding box shows the grouped objects

▼ ▼

Tip: Multilevel Grouping. Not only can you group multiple objects, but you can group multiple groups, or groups and objects. This means that you can build levels of grouped objects. For example, on a catalog page you may have six picture boxes, each with a caption in a text box. You can group each caption box with its picture box, then select these six grouped objects and group them together. Later, if you ungroup the six objects, each picture box is still grouped with its caption box.

▼ ▼

Modifying Grouped Objects

As I mentioned above, once you have grouped a set of objects, you can still modify each of them using the Content tool. Just select the element and change it. Each item can be rotated, resized, or edited just as usual. To move a single object in a grouped selection, hold down the Command (Ctrl) key to get a temporary Item tool. Then move the object where you want it and release the Command (Ctrl) key.

The group Modify dialog box. QuarkXPress lets you do some pretty nifty things with grouped items. If you select Modify from the Item menu (or press Command/Ctrl-M, or double-click on the group with the Item tool), QuarkXPress gives you a special Modify dialog box for the group. Which controls you see in this Modify dialog box depends on whether every object in a group is the same type of object (all rules, all text boxes, or whatever).

Some features in this group Modify dialog box are always available, like Origin Across and Origin Down, which determine the upper-left corner of the bounding box for the whole group. Angle, too, sets the rotation for the group, as though the group were a single object.

If you change a value in the group Modify dialog box, you change that value for every one of the objects in the group. For example, if you specify a background color for the grouped objects, the background color is applied to all the boxes and lines in the group. If you set the Picture Angle to 20 degrees for a group of picture boxes, the items in each of the picture boxes are rotated within their boxes (see Chapter 9, *Pictures*).

You can turn on the Suppress Printout option for a group of mixed objects, and each of the objects in the group has its Suppress Printout checkbox turned on. Similarly, you can add or change the frame around a group of objects, as long as they're all boxes. If you later ungroup the objects, the settings you made while they were grouped remain.

Note that if you have any lines (rules) in the group, changing the background color of the group affects the color of the line itself.

There's one rule that applies to modifying groups of objects that I still can't figure out: You can't open the Modify dialog box for a group of objects when one group is nested inside another. You have to ungroup the objects, and regroup them individually. Strange.

Scaling groups. The engineers at Quark snuck a little feature into the program without much ado: the ability to scale groups of objects. I'm surprised they were so quiet about it, as it's a wonderful step forward. But it's not quite a leap forward yet—you'll see why in a moment.

To scale several objects at once, you first have to group them. Next, you can drag one of the group's corner or side handles. When you let go, all the objects in the group are scaled proportionally. There are, as always, a few options you can take advantage of.

▶ If you hold down the Command (Ctrl) key when you drag, any content (text and pictures) inside boxes or lines within the group is also scaled.

▶ If you hold down Option (or Alt) and Shift when you drag, the group is scaled proportionally. (Again, add the Command or Ctrl key to scale the contents proportionally, too.)

▶ If you only hold down the Shift key, the group is constrained into a square (not particularly useful, but it's good to know the option is there).

▶ You can type values in the height or width fields in the Measurements palette. This forces the whole group to fit within that size. For exam-

ple, if you need to fit three picture boxes within a 10-centimeter column, you could type "10 cm" in the width field. Of course, it's easy to
scale the items disproportionately when you do this (see "Tip:
Proportional Resizing by the Numbers," earlier in this chapter). Also,
note that this scales the boxes, but not their contents.

Remember that you can scale by a percentage by using XPress's
built-in math functions. For instance, if you want each item in the
group to be 130-percent larger, type "*1.3" after the current width and
height values.

The ability to scale groups was added to QuarkXPress 4 almost as an
afterthought, and sadly, this limited feature didn't get any better in XPress 5
or 6. There are a number of features that XPress doesn't scale when you scale
a group and its contents, such as the values for Space Before, Indent, Rule
Above, and so on. These may be bugs, but they just shore up my opinion that
XPress needs a *real* scaling tool, much like those offered in some of the
XTension packages, like Gluon's ProScale.

Constraining

Ten years ago, if you asked a QuarkXPress user what one feature they would
have sold their grandmother to get rid of, they would invariably have said,
"Parent-and-child boxes." Back in versions 1 and 2 of XPress, these parent-
and-child boxes made it nearly impossible to be flexible with page design
because boxes became "trapped" inside other boxes. These constraints were
actually rather useful and accessible when you got accustomed to them. But
there were many times when what I really needed was a choice of whether to
enable it or not. Parent-and-child constraints are still in QuarkXPress, but
thank goodness they *are* now an option rather than a rule.

Let's be clear here for those not familiar with this feature. I'm not talking
about the type of constraining that people usually talk about (and that I've
mentioned earlier in this chapter) that refers to holding down the Shift key
to constrain the movement of an object to a 45- or 90-degree angle. This is a
different sort of constraint.

Parent-and-child box constraints remind me of a baby's playpen (this is
probably some leftover childhood trauma, but I don't want to go into it). A
playpen is basically a box that is a structure in its own right. However, you
can place objects (or babies) into it, and they can't get out unless you physically take them out.

Similarly, a parent box is a text or picture box that has certain structural
constraints so that any items that are created or placed inside its boundaries
("child" items) can't easily get outside those boundaries. Imagine a text box

that was specified as a parent box. It acts as a normal text box. However, when you draw a line inside it using one of the Line tools, that line cannot be moved or resized to extend outside the text box. The only way you can get it out is by cutting it and pasting it elsewhere.

I know it sounds awful, but, as I said, there are some great applications. For example, building a table by adding vertical and horizontal rules to a text box is aided if those rules don't slip away when you move the box (child items always move with their parents). Also, if you have a specific area in which all items must remain, creating a parental constraint makes sure that you don't accidentally mess up your specifications when your eyes are bleary at three in the morning.

You can create parent-and-child box constraints in two ways: automatic constraints and manual constraints. Let's look at each of these.

Automatic constraints. Automatic constraints were the standard for early versions of QuarkXPress. With automatic constraints on, all picture and text boxes act as parent constraint boxes. You can turn automatic constraints on and off by checking the Auto Constraint box in the Preferences dialog box. You can turn on Auto Constraint when every box you create is to be a parent or a child box, and then turn it off to create "normal" boxes and items.

Note that the parent box and the child items are grouped when you select them with the Item tool. To unconstrain these items, see "Manual constraints," below.

Manual constraints. If you prefer, you can apply your own parent-and-child box constraints to a set of objects by manually constraining them. It's easy to do.

1. Make sure the page elements you want to be child items are totally within the boundaries of the box you want to be the parent box.

2. Make sure the soon-to-be-parent box is behind each of the objects that are soon to be constrained. Parent boxes must be on a lower layer than their children. You can think of the playpen analogy: the playpen must be under—and surrounding—the child.

3. Select and group the child and parent objects and boxes (see "Modifying Grouped Objects," earlier in this chapter).

4. Select Constrain from the Item menu.

Those objects that are on top of the parent box and that are in that group are constrained to the boundaries of the parent box.

You can unconstrain this group of objects by clicking on the parent-and-child group with the Item tool and selecting either Unconstrain or Ungroup from the Item menu. Unconstrain removes the constraints, but leaves the items grouped. Ungroup removes both the grouping and constraining specifications. (You can't have parent-and-child constraints without grouping.)

Aligning and Distributing Objects

Before I knew how cool the Space/Align feature was, I simply didn't know how badly I needed it. Now I use it all the time; once you know about it, you probably will, too. Space/Align is, in some ways, the control center for setting up object relationships on your page. Let's look at why.

The whole idea of Space/Align is to move page items around to create certain relationships between them. The tools you have to work with are Between, Space, and Distribute Evenly. Here's what you do.

1. Select all the items that you want to relate to one another. For instance, if you want two items to align along their left edges, select both of them.

2. Select Space/Align from the Item menu and determine the nature of the relationship. Are you trying to align the objects vertically or horizontally? Or both? Turn on the appropriate checkboxes in the dialog box.

3. Decide whether you want to align or distribute the objects. I'll talk about the difference in just a moment. If you're aligning the objects, select Space and enter the amount of space you want between the items; if you're distributing them, select Distribute Evenly.

4. Tell QuarkXPress what part of the objects you want to align or distribute. For example: the left edges of two boxes, or the tops of a few lines, or the centers of five mixed items.

Starting with the second step, let's take a look at each of these.

Vertical/Horizontal. If you select some objects, then choose Space/Align from the Item menu (or press Command-comma or Ctrl-comma), you'll see the Space/Align Items dialog box (see Figure 3-53). This dialog box is broken down into Horizontal and Vertical sections, and you can use one or the other—or both—by clicking their respective checkboxes.

Space. Enabling the Space control (by clicking the radio button in front of it) lets you align objects. The value in the Space field determines how far apart

Figure 3-53

The Space/Align
dialog box

the objects should align. A value of zero (which is the default) means "align exactly." For example, let's say you want to line up the left edges of two boxes. If you specify "0p" as the Space value, the left edge of the first box is at the same place as the left edge of the second box. If you specify "5p" as the Space value, the left edge of the first box is placed 5 picas from the left edge of the second box (see Figure 3-54).

But which box moves? The top-most or left-most items always stay stationary; they are the reference points for alignment. Other page elements move to align with them.

As I said, I use alignment all the time. If I have four text boxes that I want to line up on their right edges, I no longer have to draw guides or figure measurements. Now, I just select them all and align their right edges with Space set to zero.

▼ ▼

Tip: Use Apply in Space/Align. Let's face it: the Space/Align dialog box is a case study in horrible user interface and is so confusing that many people avoid it just so they don't have to figure out how it works. One of the most important techniques for using the Space/Align features is to *always* click on the Apply button (or press Command-A or Ctrl-A) before leaving the dialog box. This way, you can see the effect of your Space/Align settings, and—if something unexpected happened—you can change them. Sure, you can usually undo any alignment you've made after you leave the dialog box, but why take the effort when you can check out your changes in advance?

▼ ▼

Tip: Spacing with Percentages. You don't have to type an absolute value into the Space field. You can type a percentage, too. For instance, if you want the tops of two lines to be twice as far apart as they already are, you can type "200%" and click OK. When you're working in percentages, the Apply button has an additional function: it lets you apply that percentage more than once. If you type "150%" and click Apply, the objects are spaced one and a half times their existing distance. Then, if you click Apply again, they're moved *another* one and a half times, and so on.

▼ ▼

Distribute Evenly. Let's say you have three picture boxes and you want the space between them to be equal. It could take nigh-on forever to figure out exactly where to move the middle box so that you've got equal space on each side. Instead, you can let the Distribute Evenly feature do it for you. I find distribution helpful when I have a number of items that are all the same size, but are scattered around the page (see Figure 3-55).

Distribute Evenly always takes the left-most and right-most, or the top-most and bottom-most, page elements that you have selected (depending on whether you're aligning vertically, horizontally, or both) and uses them as the distribution boundaries. In other words, those objects don't move, but all the other objects that you selected do move.

Between. The last step in the process outlined above is figuring out what part of the objects you want to align or distribute. Your choices are the edges (Top, Bottom, Right, and Left), the Center, and the object itself (called Item). You choose any one of these by selecting it from the Between popup menu. Of course, the Horizontal section only lets you choose Left Edges, Right Edges, or Centers, while the Vertical section only lets you choose Top Edges, Bottom Edges, or Centers.

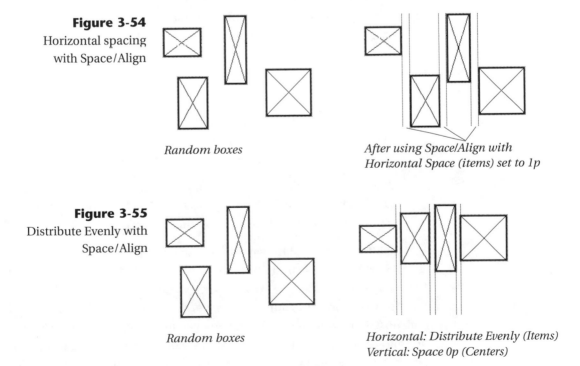

Figure 3-54
Horizontal spacing with Space/Align

Random boxes

After using Space/Align with Horizontal Space (items) set to 1p

Figure 3-55
Distribute Evenly with Space/Align

Random boxes

Horizontal: Distribute Evenly (Items) Vertical: Space 0p (Centers)

Distribute Evenly leaves the farthest left and right items in the same place, while dividing the rest of the space between all of the intermediate items.

The concept of aligning or distributing objects based on Item is sometimes confusing to people. Item refers to the bounding box of the page element. So, for example, horizontally aligning two text boxes with Space set to zero and Between set to Item results in the right side of one being aligned with the left side of the second. Another way to say this is that there is zero space between the items.

And note that I said this is based on the *bounding box* of the object, which is the smallest rectangle that can enclose the entire object. This may result in alignment that you might not expect, especially when you're working with rotated or oddly shaped Bézier picture boxes. Typically, when you're distributing objects, you'll use Item as the Between setting.

If you have multiple objects on a page, and you want to center all of them on top of each other, you can apply both a vertical and a horizontal alignment to them, with Centers selected in the Between popup menu, and Space set to zero.

▼ ▼

Tip: Measuring from Picture Box to First Baseline. I worked on a job a few years ago where the art director insisted that the first baseline of each caption under an illustration sit exactly two picas from the bottom of the picture. This is exactly the kind of thing that can drive you nutty trying to figure out, and it's exactly the kind of thing that QuarkXPress can do for you somewhat automatically (saving you from a life of frustration and mental anxiety). Instead of measuring each and every caption and picture box, try this method.

1. Use Space/Align to align the text (caption) and picture (illustration) boxes with no space between them. That means set the Vertical Space field to zero space between Items. You can also set the horizontal alignment, if that's required (I usually center them, for instance).

2. Set the first baseline of the caption's text box to the value you're looking for. In this case, it'd be two picas (see "First Baseline" in Chapter 6, *Type and Typography,* for more on this feature).

Voilà! The baseline of the caption is sitting two picas from the top of the text box, which is the same as the bottom of the picture box (see Figure 3-56).

▼ ▼

Tip: Space/Aligning Groups. The Space/Align feature is one of the coolest and most underused tools in XPress. You can use it to set up all sorts of relationships between items on your pages. For instance, you can tell two objects to be exactly two picas apart; or to place an equal amount of space

Figure 3-56
First baseline
to bottom of
picture box

*General Abraham
Meshugga before the
great battle.*

*From baseline
to box is 1p3*

horizontally between four pictures; or to align 50 different lines along their left edges.

One of the lesser-known features within the Space/Align function, however, is how it deals with groups. If you select three boxes and set them to vertically center, then all three boxes gets centered. However, if you group two of those boxes first, then XPress centers the loose box with the group of boxes.

▼ ▼

Tip: Centering an Object on the Page. There are three ways I use to center an object on a page. The first uses the Measurements palette.

1. Select the object, and in the x-origin field of the Measurements palette, type the page width minus the object width. If the object was four inches wide on an 8.5-inch page, you'd type "8.5"-4"".

2. Type the page height minus the object height in the y-origin of the palette.

3. Go back to the x- and y-origin fields and divide those values by two (type "/2" or "*.5" after what's there already).

The second method uses Space/Align.

1. Draw a box the same size as the page. I usually draw any ol' sized box, type zeros into the x- and y-origin of the Measurements palette, and the page size into the height and width fields.

2. Send this box to the back (don't forget the shortcut: Shift-F5).

3. Shift-select the object or group of objects you want to center (so that they're selected along with the background box).

4. Use Space/Align to align the centers of all the objects, vertically and horizontally.

5. Delete the page-sized box you drew.

If the objects you're centering are all grouped together, the whole group gets centered on the page. Otherwise, each individual object gets centered (they'll all overlap).

The third method is the simplest: use the Align to Page feature in the XPert Tools XTension (see Appendix C, *XTensions and Resources*).

Synchronize Text

Synchronized text is text that is designated to remain "in synch," across multiple layouts within the same project, or even among multiple text boxes within the same layout. (I discuss projects and layouts in Chapter 4, *Building Documents*.) When synchronized text is changed in one place, it automatically changes in every other place that it appears. For example, let's say you synchronize the addresses in three layouts in a project: a letterhead, an envelope, and a business card. Then when you change the address in the letterhead, the address also changes in the other two layouts, too. Since XPress 6 supports both print and Web layouts in a project, you can even synchronize text between both print and Web pages.

Synchronizing text is kind of like storing text in a library (see "Libraries," later in this chapter). You first have to create one instance of the text and add it to the Synchronized Text palette; then you can drag it out of the synchronize palette for each instance where you want the text (see Figure 3-57).

Synching and Unsynching Text

Before you can synchronize text in two or more text boxes, you have to add it to the Synchronized Text palette (select Show Synchronized Text from the

Figure 3-57
Synchronizing text

Window menu to open the palette). Select any text box or text path with text in it and click the Synchronize Text button on the palette. (You can also choose Synchronize from the Style menu or the context menu). XPress will ask you to give this block of text a name; you can use any name you want, as this text just appears in the palette as a label representing the block of text. When you click OK, the label name appears as a new entry in the middle section of the palette.

You can store many blocks of synchronized text within the same project. The Synchronized Text palette displays a label name for each block, and also displays the names of the layouts where the synchronized text is used.

Inserting text. Once you've got text in the Synchronized Text palette, you can use it in another text box by clicking an insertion point in any text box or text path on any layout in the same project, selecting a label name in the Synchronized Text palette, and clicking the Insert Text into Text Box button. Similarly, you can simply drag and drop the label name over the box or path. Now the text is "synched." If you've already got text in the box or path, XPress asks if you're sure you want to replace the contents. (Synchronized text has to be the only thing in a text box or text path.)

You can recognize text boxes or text paths that have synchronized text because their handles look like they've been electrified (they have little lightning bolts in them).

Editing text. When you need to change synchronized text, just select it in any of the boxes or paths where it's used and edit it as usual. (There is no "master" box; any synchronized box will do.) It changes immediately in all of its instances—even several times on the same page if you've used it more than once.

Note that only the text (the actual letters and numbers and symbols) is synchronized. The text formatting is not synchronized. When you first synchronize text it copies the formatting of the original, but you can reformat the text in each text box for a different look, and it'll still remain synchronized. For instance, you might want some text to appear in one font and size on a brochure (print layout) but in a totally different font and size in a Web page (Web layout).

Editing the text label. You can edit the name of the synchronized text label at any time. Simply select the label name on the Synchronized Text palette, and either click the Edit Name button or choose Edit Name from the context menu (Control-click or right-button click on the label).

Unsynchronizing text. Sometimes you might need to "unsynch" either one instance or all the instances of a synchronized text block. For example, if you've synchronized addresses in all your layouts but the address for the business card has to be listed in a more condensed way. Since all synched text blocks must share exactly the same content, you'll have to unsynchronize that box on the business card layout; the other instances remain synchronized. To do this, select the text box or text path with the Content tool. Then choose Unsynchronize Text from the Style menu or the context menu.

If you want to unsynchronize all instances of a synchronized text block, select the label name in the Synchronized Text palette and then either click the Unsynchronize All button, or choose Unsynchronize All from the context menu. The label name remains (in case you want to use it again), but all the instances of the formerly "synched" text can now be edited independently. (If you need to resynchronize the text again, just drag the label name over one or more text boxes.)

Removing the text and label. Synchronized text remains saved in the Synchronized Text palette, whether it's used or not, until you remove it. To remove the text from the project, select the label name for the synchronized text, and click the Remove Item button (or choose Remove Content Item from the context menu). This both removes the label from the palette and unsynchronizes all the text boxes, so you can now edit them independently.

▼ ▼

Tip: Store "Boiler-plate" Text. You can store text in a project even if you don't intend to use it right away. You may know that certain blocks of text will be used in each of the layouts of a project. Place your text in a dummy text box and synchronize it in the Synchronized Text palette. Then delete the text box and the label remains in the palette ready to insert it in your layouts as you need it.

Limitations of Synchronizing

While you'll find many useful ways to use this feature, you should also be aware of its limitations. The synchronize text feature always includes all the text in the text box. You can't include just part of it. Each instance of the text must be exactly the same (except you can change the formatting in each instance).

Text on a master page can't be synchronized, nor can text with anchored items. There is also no way to synchronize text between different projects (all the layouts that use the text must exist within the same project).

I wish that Quark had also included the ability to synchronize graphics as well as text. Maybe we'll get that in the next version.

▼ ▼

The Layers Palette

The Layers palette helps you work in a more organized manner when building your documents by letting you separate each part of your layout into its own layer. For instance, you could put all your pictures boxes on one layer and text boxes on a different layer. Then, your copy editor could hide all the pictures in order to focus better on the text. Or, in a document that will be distributed in two countries, you could put English text on one layer and Spanish on a second layer. Because only visible layers are output when you print, you could hide the Spanish layer when printing the English text, and vice versa.

You can also use layers as a way to play around with a new design concept while keeping other parts of your layout intact and not compromised, like a trial-and-error playground. For instance, if your picture boxes were all on one layer, you could duplicate that layer, hide the original layer, then play with those pictures all you want, knowing that if it doesn't work out, you can just delete this duplicate layer and go back to your first idea.

Layers have long been a staple of illustration programs like Adobe Illustrator and Macromedia FreeHand; in fact, if you've used layers in those programs, you'll be right at home using the Layers palette in QuarkXPress.

The Default Layer and master pages. Before I get into the details of creating and manipulating layers, I need to mention two kinds of layers that appear in every document you create. The first is the Default Layer, which cannot be deleted. This is the layer that your objects live on when you don't specify any other layer—it's the basic layer that you're probably used to from earlier versions of XPress.

The other "layer" is the master page layer. While the Default Layer appears as a separate layer in the Layers palette, this one does not. Sadly, there is no way to assign master page objects other layers while viewing the master page (see Chapter 4, *Building a Document,* for more on master pages). Instead, when you place an object (a box, line, or whatever) on a master page, XPress always assigns it to the Default Layer, but on your document pages these objects appear *below* the other objects on your Default Layer—as though there were a separate master page layer.

Of course, you can always select a master page item on your document page and assign it to another layer, but that breaks the link between this item and the master page (so changes to this item on your master page won't change this object on your document page anymore).

Making Layers

You can control everything having to do with layers in the Layers palette (select Show Layers from the Window menu; see Figure 3-58). To make a new layer, click on the New Layer button (that's the one that looks like sweat is flying off it). Layers always appear named "Layer 1", "Layer 2", and so on, but it's easy to change these names (I'll cover that in a moment). Note that you can have up to 256 layers in your layout (including the Default Layer), but I recommend keeping your layers to a minimum whenever possible, for the sake of simplicity.

Figure 3-58
The Layers palette

▼ ▼

Tip: Layers of Context. Don't forget that you can use context menus in the Layers palette (Control-click on the Mac, or right-button-click in Windows). The context menu in the Layers palette (see Figure 3-59) is very useful when dealing with layers, and lets you create a new layer; delete, edit, or duplicate the layer you clicked on; hide other or all layers; show other or all layers; lock other or all layers; and delete unused layers.

▼ ▼

Figure 3-59
Layers palette's
context menu

Assigning Layers

When you draw out a box, table, or line, it is automatically added to whatever layer you have selected in the Layers palette. The selected layer always has a little pencil icon visible to the right of the layer name, indicating that you can write to that layer (see Figure 3-60). If you create something on the wrong layer, don't worry; it can easily be moved.

As soon as an object appears on a layer (any layer other than the Default Layer), XPress adds a little colored icon in its corner, called a *visual indicator* (see Figure 3-61). Visual indicators let you see which layers are assigned to your items by matching the color of the drop-shadowed colored rectangle to the color assigned to the layer in the Layers palette. The visual indicators won't print; they're for your onscreen reference only. However, if these visual indicators are driving you batty, you can make them go away by choosing Hide Visual Indicators from the View menu.

Figure 3-60
Icons in the
Layers palette

Visible

Pencil icon shows which layer is currently active

Currently selected object is on this layer

This layer is locked

Switching layers. You can move one or more items from one layer to another by selecting the object(s) and clicking the Move Item to Layer button in the Layers palette. This displays the Move Items dialog box (see Figure 3-62), where you can pick the destination layer. XPress always moves the item(s) to the exact same page coordinates on the new layer.

Another way to move one or more selected objects is to drag the Active Item icon (it looks like a small box of squares in the far right column of the Layers palette) to the desired layer. If that icon is confusing, note that it's a miniature version of the standard eight handles around a selected item on your page—that is, the "active item."

▼ ▼

Tip: Duplicating Among Layers. If you want the same object to be on more than one layer, you can hold down the Control key (on both Macintosh and Windows) while dragging the Active Item icon from one layer to another. Multiple items on the same layer can also be duplicated.

▼ ▼

A third method to move items from one layer to another is using Cut or Copy and Paste. This is the slowest method (you have to select the object, cut

Figure 3-61
Visual indicators

These little icons tell you which layer the object is on. They aren't elegant, but they do the job.

Figure 3-62
Moving items from
one layer to another

it, click on a different layer in the palette, and then select Paste). Worse, the object is always centered on the screen when you paste it rather than ending up with the same page coordinates.

Of course, when you move an item to a new layer, the object assumes the attributes of that new layer. That is, if the target layer is turned off (is invisible), then that object will suddenly disappear when you assign the layer.

▼ ▼

Tip: Watch for Grouped Items. The Layers palette works independently of the Group feature, so grouped objects can have different items on different layers. That is, you can select one object in a group and move it to a different layer from the other items in the group. Similarly, you can select items from different layers and group them. This may or may not be a good thing, depending on how you work.

▼ ▼

Tip: Select All Items. Those sneaky folks at Quark added a feature to the Layers palette that few users ever find: You can tell XPress to select all the items on a given layer by choosing Select Items on Layer from the context-sensitive menu (Control-click on a layer in the palette on the Macintosh, right-click in Windows).

▼ ▼

Moving and Deleting Layers

Adding page items to your layers is only half the fun! You also need to be able to manipulate the layers themselves: moving them up and down, merging them together, duplicating them, and deleting them.

Moving layers up and down. To change the stacking order of your layers (moving a layer makes objects on that layer appear above or below objects on other layers), you can hold down the Option key (Mac) or the Alt key (Windows) while dragging a layer up or down in the Layers palette.

Note that the Send to Back, Send Backward, Bring to Front, and Bring Forward features in the Item menu only work *within* a layer, not across the layers. That is, choosing Bring to Front makes the selected object the topmost item on its layer, but won't move the object from one layer to another.

Merging layers. You may decide at some point during that creative process we call page layout that your file just doesn't need so many layers. Fortunately, you can merge layers together, so that the objects on two or more layers all end up on one happy layer. To merge two or more layers, select more than one (unlocked) layer for merging by Shift- or Command-clicking (Ctrl-clicking) in the Layers palette. Then press the Merge Layers button to display the Merge Layers dialog box (see Figure 3-63). Here you must decide which layer will be the new home to all the items from these selected layers.

Figure 3-63

Merging layers

Duplicating layers. You can duplicate a layer (make a copy of the layer and all its contents) with the context-sensitive menu: Control-click (Macintosh) or right-button-click (Windows) on the layer you want to duplicate, and then select Duplicate Layer. However, if that layer has one or more linked text boxes, you may get a result you don't expect.

▶ If you duplicate a box containing the first box of two or more linked boxes, the contents of the entire linked story will be copied into that box and will be displayed with the standard overflow symbol.

▶ If you duplicate a layer with a middle box from a linked chain of boxes, all of the copy from that box and any successive copy will be copied into that box with an overflow symbol. The copy contained in boxes from linked boxes *preceding* that box disappears from the new layer.

▶ If you duplicate a layer containing only the end box in a linked set of boxes, only the copy from that box will be duplicated into that box.

These results are just the same as if you used the Copy and Paste, Duplicate, or Step and Repeat features on a linked text box.

Duplicating layers between documents. Need to get one or more layers from one document into another? No problem: when you drag an object from one document into another, the object's layer comes with it. The same thing happens when you drag a page from one document into another (when both files are in Thumbnails view). If you need all the objects on a layer to come across, too, then make sure you first choose Select Items on Layer from the Layer palette's context menu. Unfortunately, there's no way to duplicate layers from one layout space to another within a project (because you can't drag-and-drop between layouts).

If you don't want a layer to come with a dragged object, make sure you assign the Default Layer to that object before dragging it. By the way, if the target document already contains a layer with the same name in the Layers palette, XPress adds an asterisk symbol to the layer's name.

Deleting layers. To delete a layer, select the layer you no longer want and click the Delete button in the Layers palette. QuarkXPress displays a dialog box asking if you want to delete the items on that layer or move those items to another layer (see Figure 3-64).

▼ ▼

Tip: Watch What You Delete. As a safety measure, before you delete a layer, make the other layers invisible (see "Tip: Hide Other Layers," below). This way, you'll be sure of what you are deleting on that layer.

▼ ▼

Figure 3-64
Deleting a layer

Layer Attributes

Every layer has six attributes: Name, Color, Suppress Printout, Locked, Visible, and Keep Runaround. You can turn on and off the Visible and the Locked attributes by clicking in the first two columns of the Layers palette (the columns with the eyeball and the padlock at the top). You can change all six attributes by double-clicking on the layer in the Layers palette to bring up the Layer Attributes dialog box (see Figure 3-65).

> ▶ NAME. As soon as you create a layer, it's a good idea to change its name to something more descriptive than "Layer 1."

> ▶ COLOR. The Color attribute affects that layer's Visual Indicator; it has no effect on the color of that layer's objects or printing or anything like that. I rarely change a layer's color. One exception is when I'm making a Notes layer (a layer for notes to myself or other folks work-

Figure 3-65

The Layer Attributes
dialog box

ing on this layout), which I often change to either a bright green or a light blue. (The blue reminds me of "non-repro blue," like the old days before desktop computerized page layout.)

▶ **SUPPRESS PRINTOUT.** Turning on the Suppress Printout checkbox in the Layer Attributes dialog box is basically the same as selecting all the objects on that layer and turning on the Suppress Printout checkbox in the Modify dialog box (see "Suppress Printout and Suppress Picture Printout," earlier in this chapter). This is helpful for a Notes layer or any other time when you want something to be visible on screen but not on the printed page. Note that you can also control which layers will print from the Layers tab of the Print dialog box (see Chapter 13, *Printing*).

▶ **LOCKED.** In earlier versions, turning on the Locked checkbox was the same as selecting the items on that layer and selecting Lock from the Item menu. As you know from "Locking Items," earlier in this chapter, the Lock feature isn't particularly robust. Fortunately, now when you turn on the Locked checkbox (or click in the Locked column of the Layers palette), XPress *really* locks the items on that layer—you can't even select these items anymore. Text and picture boxes on locked layers are still affected by Find/Change and Picture Usage, however.

▶ **VISIBLE.** The most commonly-used layer attribute is Visible, which determines whether you can see the items on this layer. Of course, items on an invisible layer will not print either, so this is a fast way to switch among layers you want to print and those that you don't.

▶ **KEEP RUNAROUND.** Let's say you have a picture box on a layer, and that picture box has a runaround setting that forces text to flow around it (see "Text Runaround" in Chapter 11, *Where Text Meets Graphics*). The Keep Runaround attribute tells XPress what you want to do about text runaround when this layer is invisible. When it's turned on (it is by deafult), the objects on that layer still force text to wrap around them. If you turn this off, then the text wrap on other layers will change depending on whether the layer is visible or not. For instance, if your document has a Spanish layer and an English layer, you probably want the text to flow differently depending on which language is visible.

▼ ▼

Tip: Hide Other Layers. Do you want to make all your layers invisible except one? No problem: Control-click in the eyeball column of the layer you want visible. If you Control-click in the Locked column, XPress locks all the other layers but that one. (This lets you lock all your layers: Control-click and then click in the Lock column of the layer.)

▼ ▼

Layer Preferences

If you don't like the default settings in the Layer Attributes dialog box, you can change them in the Layer panel of the Preferences dialog box (Command-Option-Shift-Y or Ctrl-Alt-Shift-Y; see Figure 3-66). Of course, you can't change the Name or Color attributes here, as those are different for every layer. However, you can turn on or off the Visible, Locked, Suppress Printout, and Keep Runaround checkboxes.

Like other layout preferences, if you change these settings while your file is open, only that file is affected. If you change the settings with no docu-

Figure 3-66
Layers preferences

ment open, then all newly created documents from that time forward will reflect the new settings.

▼ ▼

Linking

I need to introduce a concept here that is crucial to working with text boxes: *linking*. Links, sometimes known as chains, are the connections between text boxes that allow text to flow from one into the other. You can have as many text boxes linked up as you like. There are two ways to link text boxes together: have QuarkXPress do it for you automatically, or do it yourself manually. I cover automatic text links in Chapter 4, *Building a Document*. I cover manual linking here.

Linking Text Boxes

Let's say you have two text boxes and the text in the first is overflowing (a text overflow is indicated by a little box with an "X" in it in the text box's lower-right corner), so you want to link it to the second text box. Here's what to do.

1. Choose the Linking tool from the Tool palette (it's the one that looks like three links in a chain).

2. Next, click on the first text box. A flashing dotted line should appear around it.

3. Finally, click on the second text box. When you select the second text box, an arrow should momentarily appear, connecting the first text box to the second. I call this the *text link arrow*. This happens even if the two text boxes are on different pages.

That's it. The boxes are now linked, and text flows between them. If you want to link another box to your text chain, just follow the same procedure: click on the second text box, then on the third, and so on. You cannot link a box to another box that has text in it unless the second box is already part of the chain.

If you want to add a text box to the middle of a text chain, first click on a box that is already linked, and then click on the text box you want to add. The text now flows from the original chain through your added text box and continues on to the original chain (see Figure 3-67).

▼ ▼

Tip: Getting Rid of the Flashes. Many people seem to get flustered when they've selected a text box with the Linking tool and then decide they don't

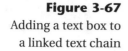

Adding a text box to
a linked text chain

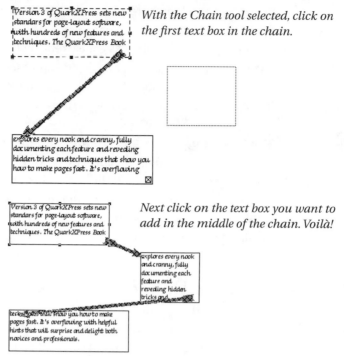

*With the Chain tool selected, click on
the first text box in the chain.*

*Next click on the text box you want to
add in the middle of the chain. Voilà!*

want to follow through and link the box to anything after all. The text box is just sitting there flashing, seeming to call for some special action. Nope, no action is required. You can either click someplace where there's no text box, or just switch tools, and the flashing stops.

▼ ▼

Tip: Linking with Text Paths. I've said it before, and I'll say it again: text paths are just like one-line-tall text boxes. And, as such, you can use the text linking tools to link to and from them. You can even put them on a master page and use them as automatic text boxes (again, more on these in the next chapter).

▼ ▼

Unlinking Text Boxes

If you want to remove a link between two text boxes, use the Unlinking tool from the Tool palette. The process is simple. Let's say you have a link between two text boxes that you want to sever. First, click on one of the text boxes with the Unlinking tool. As soon as you click on it, you should see the plaid gray arrow linking the two boxes. Then click on either the arrowhead or the tailfeathers of this text link arrow. The arrow disappears and the link is gone.

If other page items are on top of the text link arrow's arrowhead and tail-feathers, you may not be able to click it. This always seems to happen at 1 a.m., after everything else has gone wrong on the project, and this is the last straw. Nonetheless, the way I solve this problem is to rearrange the layers using Move to Front and Move to Back, or to temporarily shift the obstructing objects in order to get to one of the two.

▼ ▼

Tip: Unlinking a Text Box from the Middle of a Chain. If you unlink a text box from the middle of a chain by clicking on the arrowhead or tailfeathers with the Unlinking tool, the entire text chain is broken at that point. Instead, you can tell QuarkXPress to remove a text box from the text chain without breaking the rest of the flow by selecting the Unlinking tool, then holding down the Shift key while clicking on the box you want to remove.

▼ ▼

Copying Linked Text Boxes

I really love the ability to easily copy objects between documents (or between pages or layouts in a document). However, you may bump into some limitations when you try to copy linked boxes.

You can copy one or more text boxes from a chain of linked text boxes, and QuarkXPress copies, along with it, the entire text chain from that box on. None of the text preceding that box in the chain is copied—only the text from the ensuing linked boxes (and any overflow text). It'd be nice if QuarkXPress could automatically break the chains when you copy, bringing to the new document only the text within the box you're moving (if you'd like, that is). But we have to leave them refinements to work on for the next version.

There's one other way to copy linked boxes, especially when the boxes are on multiple pages. If both documents are in Thumbnails view, you can drag-copy multiple pages from one document to another. In this case, links between boxes on different pages are also maintained in your target document, even if you didn't grab all the text boxes in the chain.

▼ ▼

Guides and Rulers

When you are working on your layout, you usually have rulers on the top and left side of the window. This not only gives you a perspective on where you are on the page, but it's a great visual aid in selecting coordinates. Let's say you want to change the size of a picture box by dragging a corner handle. If you're visually inclined, you may not want to bother with referring to the Measurements palette while you drag. Instead, if you watch the rulers, you'll see that gray lines show the left, right, top, and bottom edges as the box moves.

Rulers

You can turn the rulers on and off by selecting Show or Hide Rulers from the View menu, or by pressing Command-R (Ctrl-R). The only time you really need to turn the rulers off, though, is when you want to get a slightly larger view of the page. Otherwise, just leave them on.

You can specify which measurement system you want to use for your rulers in the Preferences dialog box (from the Edit menu, or press Command-Option-Shift-Y or Ctrl-Alt-Shift-Y). The vertical and horizontal rulers don't have to use the same measurement system. For example, you can set Horizontal Measure to inches and Vertical Measure to picas. That would just confuse me, so I generally keep both the same (I always use picas).

The values you choose in the Preferences dialog box are not only used on the rulers, but also throughout the Measurements palette and Modify dialog box. For example, if you change the Vertical Measure to ciceros, then every vertical measurement shows up in ciceros and points. You can still type in measurements using other units—see Table 2-2 in Chapter 2, *QuarkXPress Basics*—but QuarkXPress always converts them.

Item Coordinates. If you're using facing pages or multipage spreads, the ruler can measure from the upper-left corner of each page in the spread or from the upper-left corner of the whole spread. For instance, let's say you have two letter-size pages in a facing spread (like in a magazine). If you set the Item Coordinates popup menu in the Preferences dialog box to Page (the default value when you install QuarkXPress), the horizontal ruler goes from zero to 8.5 inches on the left page, and then starts at zero again for the right page.

If you change Item Coordinates to Spread, the horizontal ruler stretches across the entire spread, beginning with zero and ending with 17 inches (two times 8.5). I almost always leave this control set to Page, but every now and again I change it to Spread, so that I can measure where objects sit across the spread.

Adjusting the rulers. You can change more than just the measurements you see in the rulers and how far the measurements reach; you can also change where the rulers measure from. Typically, the zero points of the horizontal and vertical rulers begin at the upper-left corner of the page or spread. But you can move the origin—called the "zero, zero point"—of the rulers by clicking in the little square area where the rulers meet and dragging to where you want the origin to be.

There are two great reasons to use this feature. First, this is how you control what prints out when you're manually tiling a document (see Chapter 13, *Printing*). Second, you might need to measure a number of objects from some point on the page that's not the upper-left corner. For instance, you can set the ruler origins to the bottom-left corner instead, so that the measurements run up the page instead of down.

When you're ready to reset the ruler origins, click that same little white box at the juncture of the rulers just once. The zero points are set back to where they started.

Visual accuracy. Rulers are visually accurate. That means, when a box or a rule looks like it is directly over a tick mark in the ruler, it really is. For example, if you want to visually place a box at the 2-inch mark (as opposed to using the Measurements palette), you can follow the gray lines in the rulers as you drag the box. When the gray line is over the 2-inch mark, the box is truly at 2 inches, even when you're at a view of other than 100 percent, or if you've changed the Points/Inch value. Note that if you have Inches Decimal selected as your vertical or horizontal measurement in the Preferences dialog box, you get 20 tick marks in each inch (each is 0.05 inch); if you select Inches, the rulers only have 16 tick marks (each is 0.0625 inch).

This might not seem like a big deal, but in some earlier versions, you could never really be sure unless you checked the Measurements palette or the Modify dialog box. It might have been at 1.998 or 2.01 inches.

▼ ▼

Tip: The Portable Ruler. Sometimes, you need to verify that two objects are a precise distance apart. A quick way to do this is to make a picture or text box with the runaround set to None. Then use the Measurements palette to make the box's height or width the distance you want to check. Move the box over to the page objects, and compare their spacing to the box size (see Figure 3-68). Then just delete or move away your temporary measurement box. Of course, if you want to align two page items so that they are an exact distance apart, you'd probably want to use Space/Align instead.

▼ ▼

Guides

Back in the good old days, before we all started laying out pages by sitting in front of little plastic boxes, no one worked without guides. We had blueline

Figure 3-68

The portable ruler

guides on paste-up boards, straightedge guides on drafting tables for making sure we were aligning items correctly, and transparent rulers to ensure that we were measuring type and rules correctly. I certainly didn't throw away any of that stuff when I bought my computer—they still come in handy pretty often. However, QuarkXPress gives me all those tools electronically.

You can add a vertical or a horizontal guide to your page by clicking one of the rulers and dragging onto the page.

▼ ▼

Tip: Page versus Pasteboard Guides. It turns out that there are two sorts of guides in QuarkXPress: page guides and pasteboard guides. If you drag a guide out and release the mouse button when the cursor is over the page, you get a *page guide*: it runs the length of the page from top to bottom or from side to side. It doesn't cross over a spread or onto the pasteboard or anywhere beyond the page. If you let the mouse button go while it's over the pasteboard, however, you get a *pasteboard guide* that runs the length of the whole spread and all the way across the pasteboard. Note that you can't put pasteboard guides on master pages (I cover master pages more in the next chapter).

▼ ▼

Guides don't print, so it doesn't matter where you place them on your page. However, you may want to adjust the guides to fall in front of or behind opaque text or picture boxes. You can do this by changing the Guides setting in the Preferences dialog box. Your two choices are Behind and In Front (I always leave this setting on the latter).

Once you've placed a guide on your page, you can move it by clicking the guide and dragging it to where you want it. Note that if you have the Content tool selected, you have to click in an area where there are no other items in order to move a guide. Otherwise, XPress doesn't know if you're clicking on the guide or the contents of a box. Alternately, you can switch to the Item tool, or hold down the Command or Ctrl key (to get the Item tool temporarily). With the Item tool, you can always grab and move it.

The Measurements palette displays the coordinate of where the guide is while the guide is moving (unfortunately, once you let go of the guide, there is no way to find out where it sits on the page (the measurement) without "grabbing" it again—and probably moving, too).

To remove a guide from your page, grab it and drag it out of the window. That means you can drag it back into either ruler, or off to the right or bottom of the window, whichever is closest to where your cursor is at the time.

▼ ▼

Tip: Moving Guides Deselects Objects. You may or may not have noticed that when you have two or more objects selected and you go and move a guide, the objects are automatically deselected. What a pain! If you only have one object selected, it works just fine. Here's a quick workaround that Kristen Kollath-Harris developed back when she worked as one of those great tech support folks: hold down the Shift key while you move the guide. That way XPress won't deselect the objects.

▼ ▼

Tip: Getting Rid of Ruler Guides. No matter how easy it is to move guides around, it's always a hassle to add 20 guides to a page and then remove them one at a time. Well, take a shortcut: hold down the Option (Alt) key while clicking once in the horizontal ruler, and all the horizontal guides disappear. Option-clicking (Alt-clicking) in the vertical ruler has the same effect on vertical guides.

Actually, it's one step more complex than this. If the page touches the ruler when you Option-click (Alt-click) on it, only the page guides disappear (the ones running the length of the page). If the pasteboard touches the ruler, only the pasteboard guides go away (the ones running across the whole pasteboard).

▼ ▼

Tip: Dashed Guides. If you change QuarkXPress's ruler guides to solid Black (zero RGB) in the Preferences dialog box, the guides become dashed lines. Some people like 'em that way, it turns out. For solid black guides, set the color to 99 percent black.

▼ ▼

Tip: Scale-Specific Guides. Here's one of my favorite "hidden" features in QuarkXPress: If you hold down the Shift key while dragging a ruler guide onto your page or spread, it becomes magnification-specific. That is, if you pull it out in Actual Size view, you'll only be able to see it at Actual Size view or a higher (more zoomed-in) magnification. If you zoom out (let's say to Fit in Window view), it disappears. This is great for those times when you want to see a thumbnail of the page without guides, but need the guides to work with.

▼ ▼

Snap to Guides

One of the most important values of guides is that page items can snap to them. All guides have this feature, including margin and column guides (I'll talk more about those in Chapter 4, *Building a Document*). You can turn Snap to Guides on and off by selecting it in the View menu. For example, if you have five picture boxes that you want to align, you can pull out a guide to the position you want it, and—if Snap to Guides is enabled in the View menu—as the picture boxes are moved next to the guides, they snap to that exact spot.

On the other hand, there are times when you probably want to disable Snap to Guides—so just select it again from the View menu, or use the Shift-F7 shortcut. For example, if you are working with a box or a line that is very close to a column guide, it may snap to the guide when you don't want it to. Just turn off Snap to Guides. Generally, however, I leave this feature on.

The distance at which a guide pulls an item in, snapping it to the guide position, is determined by a control in the Preferences dialog box (Command-Shift-Option-Y or Ctrl-Alt-Shift-Y). The default value is 6 points.

▼ ▼

Tip: Snapping Line Edges to Guides. When you drag a line close enough, it snaps to the guide. But what part of the line snaps? Whereas a box or a group always snaps to a guide based on its bounding box, there are different rules for lines. Lines built with the Diagonal and Orthogonal Line tools always snap to guides at their endpoints. Bézier lines, on the other hand, generally snap like boxes—at the edges of their bounding boxes. If your line is thin, like 0.5 point, it hardly matters where it's snapping. If it's thick, though, it could make a big difference.

You can force a diagonal or orthogonal line to snap at its edge instead of its endpoints by selecting it along with another object. For instance, you could draw a little dummy picture box above a line, select both the line and the box, and then drag them both close above the guide. This lets you snap the bottom of the line to the guide; then you can delete the picture box you made.

You can force a point on a Bézier line to snap to a guide by selecting it first. If you want to move the whole line, select all the points (double-click on any point on the curve) before dragging the point you're trying to align.

▼ ▼

▼ ▼

Frames, Dashes, and Stripes

There are times when you want to put a picture on your wall with a frame, and there are times when you just tape it up frameless. When you're making pages, there are times when you want a frame around a text, picture, or contentless box, and there are times when you don't. Similarly, there are times when you want to apply a custom line style to a path (see "Lines and Arrows," earlier in this chapter).

In this section, I explore how to place borders around boxes and then how to build custom line styles that you can use either as frames on boxes or as line styles.

Frames

All boxes have frames, but by default the frame thickness is zero width, which is the same as no frame at all. You can add a frame to a box by selecting it, choosing Frame from the Item menu (or pressing Command-B or Ctrl-B), and then increasing the frame thickness to anything above zero.

The Frame tab of the Modify dialog box contains fields and popup menus that let you specify the weight, color, gap color, shade, and line style of your frame (see Figure 3-69). Color and shade are self-explanatory, but I should talk a little about frame styles, gap color, and thickness.

Frame style. In addition to the normal solid black line, XPress offers 10 PostScript-styled frames and nine bitmapped frames (see Figure 3-70). I encourage you to avoid the bitmapped frames with names like Yearbook, Deco Shadow, and Maze. These frames generally print incredibly slowly and often look jaggy because they're based on black-and-white bitmapped images rather than smooth, PostScript vector lines (see "Frame Editor," below, as well as Chapter 9, *Pictures*, for more information on bitmapped versus vector images). These bitmapped frames are only available on rectangular boxes anyway; if you select a Bézier, oval, beveled, or photo-frame-shaped box, the bitmapped frames disappear.

Earlier versions of QuarkXPress for Windows didn't have these bitmapped frames, but for the sake of consistency Quark added them to version 4. I would have been just as happy if they left them out. However, if you do use one of them, I encourage you to choose the frame thickness that is outlined in the Width popup menu; any other width may look odd or cause trouble at print time.

The PostScript lines are made up of dashed or striped lines. I describe how you can edit these or make your own below.

Figure 3-69
The Frame tab of the
Modify dialog box

Figure 3-70
Default frame styles

*These jaggy bitmapped
frames are now available
on Windows, but I still
don't recommend
using them.*

Gap color. All the PostScript frame styles (other than the basic solid line) have gap areas—dashed lines have gaps between the dashes, stripes have gaps between the stripes. The Gap section of the Frame tab lets you specify what color those gaps should be. At first, this feature appears really frivolous and designed for silly special effects. But on closer inspection, you'll see that it's actually a quite important role when using these frame styles because it lets you choose whether the gap should be transparent (color of None) or opaque (any other color; see Figure 3-71).

Figure 3-71
Gap color

Gap color set to None ———

Gap color set to White ———

Frame weight. Quark calls the thickness of a frame its "width." I'm used to calling it the *weight*. No matter what you call it, it's the thickness of the line making up the frame. And, similar to lines, if the line weight is not thick enough, the frame style may not show up properly (a triple line set to 0.5 point generally comes out looking just like a single 0.5-point line).

Frames can grow from the box edge in, or from the box edge out. That is, a 10-point frame is measured from the edge of the box to either the outside or inside. This is different from lines: their weight is measured from their center (a 10-point line falls 5 points on one side of the line and 5 points on the other).

You can control which side of the box edge the frame falls on with the Framing popup menu in the Preferences dialog box (from the Edit menu, or press Command-Shift-Option-Y or Ctrl-Alt-Shift-Y). Choosing Inside from this menu places frames on the inside of boxes; Outside places them on the outside. The confusing thing is that even when you have Frames set to Outside, the frame looks like it's falling on the inside. That's because QuarkXPress actually makes the box itself a little bigger to set the frame correctly *as though* it were an Inside frame. I think this method is sort of a pain in the butt, so I always leave it set to Inside.

Note that you can create a frame on a box while in the Inside mode, then change the mode to Outside, and subsequent frames are built on the outside of boxes (or vice versa). Existing boxes don't change when you change the preferences.

▼ ▼

Tip: Fancy Borders. Okay, I admit that I'm a graphics snob, but I just don't like the "special" bitmapped frames that XPress offers. Instead, if I want a nice border, I build it in an illustration program such as FreeHand or Illustrator or use a typographic frame. While typographic frames are pretty obscure, they're cool! For example, you can create a nice border using characters from an ornamental typeface such as Adobe Caslon Ornaments (see Figure 3-72).

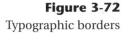

Tip: Spreading or Choking with Frames. It's easy to make concentric circles in QuarkXPress: After making a single circle, duplicate it, scale it larger, and then use Space/Align (Command-comma or Ctrl-comma) to align the circles to their centers. However, it's significantly harder to make non-regular shapes or letters concentric. Here's one way to do it.

1. If you're using text, first convert it to outlines by selecting Text to Box from the Style menu.

2. Use Step And Repeat with offsets set to zero to "clone" the object (make a duplicate exactly on top of itself).

3. In the General tab of the Preferences dialog box (Command-Option-Shift-Y or Ctrl-Alt-Shift-Y), set Framing to Outside and click OK.

4. Now use the Border feature (Command-B or Ctrl-B) to add a frame around the object you want to make larger. Note that when you set Framing to Outside, XPress doesn't just put the frame on the outside of the object, it actually makes the object bigger and then puts the frame on the inside. Weird? Very!

5. Now return to the Preferences dialog box and set Framing to Inside and press OK.

6. Select the enlarged object and set the border thickness to something small (like 1 point). Instead of the outside of the frame shrinking back

Figure 3-72
Typographic borders

in, the inside of the frame "shrinks out," so that what's left is a bloated version of the original shape.

7. Finally, select Send to Back from the Item menu so you can see the original object centered inside this new "bloated" version (see Figure 3-73).

You can "choke" objects (make them concentrically smaller) by following just the opposite procedure: First add a somewhat thick frame while the Framing preference is set to Inside, change Framing to Outside, and then set the frame smaller again.

As you can probably tell, this trick is really forcing XPress to do something that it wasn't really meant to do, and you'll find that it won't work at all in some circumstances. The key is to watch out for sharp corners. For instance, typefaces with serifs don't work well at all because they have much sharper corners than the bulky san serif type faces. It's pretty obvious when the trick won't work: the edges shoot out in very improbable directions (see Figure 3-74). (Of course, you might find this an interesting design element to work with if you're producing something for a punk rock band.)

▼ ▼

Creating Custom Dashes and Stripes

Those dashed and striped PostScript patterns that you can use as frames around boxes or as line styles are great, but no matter which one I pick, I find myself wanting to change it, if even just a little. This may be my own peculiar compulsive nature (I prefer to think of it as my "style"), but fortunately, QuarkXPress lets me tweak these styles to my heart's content with the Dashes & Stripes feature.

To create your own line style, or to edit one of the built-in styles, select Dashes & Stripes from the Edit menu (see Figure 3-75). Like style sheets, H&J settings, and colors (each of which I discuss later in this book), when you edit Dashes & Stripes while a document is open, the change applies to that document only. If no documents are open when you make a change, it applies to all new documents that you create from then on, but not to previously saved documents.

▼ ▼

Tip: Edit the Presets. As you'll see, it's really easy to create new dash and stripe styles. However, it's almost always a good idea to edit a pre-existing style rather than to start from scratch. You can edit a style by clicking on it in the Dashes & Stripes dialog box and clicking Edit or Duplicate. I prefer using Duplicate so that I don't change the original style (I might want to use it later).

Figure 3-73
Making concentric
objects

This is made of four objects: the original type converted to text, two "bloated" versions, and one "choked" version.

Figure 3-74
When good tricks go bad

This would have worked with an outside frame of one or two points, but XPress just can't deal with big frames around sharp corners.

Figure 3-75

The Dashes & Stripes
dialog box

▼ ▼

Tip: What Styles Have You Used? The Show popup menu lets you change
which dash and stripe styles XPress lists in the Dashes & Stripes dialog box.
The Show popup menu lists four options other than the default setting, All
Dashes & Stripes: Dashes, Stripes, All Dashes & Stripes Used, All Dashes &
Stripes Not Used. Unless you have created a lot of styles, you probably won't
find yourself using this popup menu. Nonetheless, there is one thing to
watch out for: if you use one of these styles as a box frame, and then decide
not to use a frame at all (that is, you set the frame thickness to zero), that
style still appears in the All Dashes & Stripes Used setting.

▼ ▼

Dashes. To create a new dash style, select Dash from the popup menu that
appears when you click on the New button (the button is actually a popup
menu in disguise). The Edit Dash dialog box appears complex at first, but,
like most features in QuarkXPress, it's easy if you take it one piece at a time.

  ▶ RULER AREA. Dashes are defined by a repeating pattern of segments.
     For instance, a basic dash is made of two segments: a solid line fol-
     lowed by a gap. A more complex line might be made by combining
     two or three different-length lines separated by gaps (see Figure 3-
     76). The ruler area at the top of the Edit Dash dialog box lets you spec-
     ify the size of these segments. To specify the beginning or ending
     point of a segment, click in the ruler; or you can define the full length
     of a segment by clicking and dragging. (The values in the ruler change
     depending on the Repeat Every popup menu setting; see below.)

     If you like the length of a segment, but not where it sits in the full
     length of the pattern, you can click on the segment itself (as opposed
     to the arrow markers in the ruler) and drag it to the left or to the right.
     Note that the only time you would want to add more than a single

segment marker is if you want a non-regular pattern—that is, a pattern like "thin, thick, thin, thick," and so on.

▶ **POSITION.** If you click on one of the segment markers in the ruler area, its value appears in the Position field. You can also add a segment marker to the ruler by typing a value here and clicking Add. I find this much more efficient than clicking and dragging in the ruler area, though the interactive method is usually more fun.

▶ **PREVIEW.** You can see approximately how the dash pattern will appear in the Preview area of the dialog box. The slider control to the

Figure 3-76

Dashes

This custom dash pattern results in this line

This custom dash pattern results in this line

left of the preview line lets you see how the pattern appears in thinner or thicker lines. Remember, however, that you're still only seeing a low-resolution screen preview of the dash; often, especially in dash patterns with really thin lines, what you see on-screen may be significantly different from what you get on paper.

▶ **REPEATS EVERY.** Contrary to intuition, the Repeats Every control lets you set the length of the repeating pattern. There are two options in the popup menu to the right of the Repeats Every field: "Times Width" and "Points." When this is set to "Times Width" (it is by default), the length of the pattern is determined by the thickness of the line or frame—so as the line gets thicker, the pattern becomes longer (see Figure 3-77). For instance, let's say you set Repeats Every to 3. If you apply this to a 6-point-thick line, the pattern you specify in the ruler area is 18 points long (3 × 6). If you decrease the line weight to 3 points, the dash reduces, too, to 9 points (3 × 3).

Figure 3-77
Repeat Every

Repeats every 3 times width

Repeats every 6 times width

Repeats every 3 times width (but thicker line)

Repeats every 9 points

On the other hand, you may not want the distance between the patterns to shift when you change the line weight. You can accomplish this by changing the popup menu to "Points." Now, the Repeats Every value specifies an absolute width for the pattern—if you say the pattern is 10 points long, that's how long it'll be (see "Stretch to Corners").

▶ **MITER.** The Miter setting determines what the line style does when it hits a corner. If you apply this dash only to a smooth line or a rounded-corner box, the Miter control has no effect at all. There are three options in the Miter popup menu: sharp corner, rounded corner, and beveled corner (see Figure 3-78). (Miter is actually controlled by PostScript itself, not QuarkXPress.)

Figure 3-78
Miter

Sharp corner miter   *Round corner miter*   *Bevel corner miter*

▶ **ENDCAP.** Endcap is another PostScript-level feature, and it lets you choose the look of each line segment within the dash (see Figure 3-79). The basic distinction is square ends versus round ends, though you also have the choice of whether the endcap extends past the edge of the segment.

Figure 3-79
Endcap

▶ **STRETCH TO CORNERS.** When you turn on the last control in the Edit Dash dialog box, Stretch to Corners, you're giving QuarkXPress the leeway to adjust the Repeat Every setting so that your pattern reaches from one end of your path to the other, or from one corner of your frame to another (see Figure 3-80). For instance, imagine XPress repeating the pattern along your line; when it gets to the end, it might only be able to fit half the pattern in. If Stretch to Corners is on, the program adjusts the pattern. In general, it adjusts it so slightly that you wouldn't even notice, though it is obvious on occasion, depending on the pattern, the line thickness, and the length of the line. Nonetheless, I always turn Stretch to Corners on and only turn it off when the effect is displeasing on my pages.

▼ ▼

Tip: Watch Your Dashed Corners. Thick box frames and thin dash patterns don't always match when it comes to the corners. The problem isn't QuarkXPress's; it's just that the thin dashes don't meet up properly in the corners. QuarkXPress tries to adjust, but it doesn't always work. I wish I could

Figure 3-80
Stretch to Corners

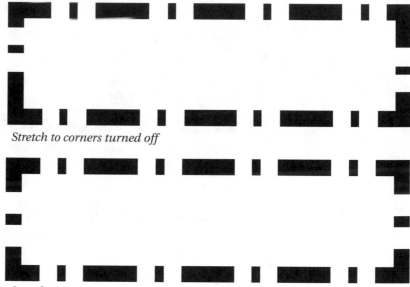

Stretch to corners turned off

Stretch to corners turned on

offer you a solution, but instead I can only say, "Watch out," and suggest that you change the dash pattern or the line thickness if it becomes a problem.

▼ ▼

Stripes. You can create the second type of custom PostScript line style by selecting Stripe from the New popup menu in the Dashes & Stripes dialog box. The Edit Stripe dialog box is slightly less imposing than the last we explored, and its functionality is very similar (see Figure 3-81). The primary difference, of course, is that you end up with a stripe, in which the line segments and gaps run along the path, as opposed to dashes, which run perpendicularly.

There are four options in the Edit Stripe dialog box: ruler area, Position, Preview, and Miter.

> ▶ **RULER AREA.** Stripes are defined by separating the width of your path into smaller lines and gaps. You can specify the width of these subpaths by placing width markers in the ruler area of the Edit Stripe dialog box. As with dashes, you can click in the ruler area to place a marker, or click and drag to specify the thickness of a subpath. If you like the width of the subpath, but not the vertical placement, you can click on the subpath (not the index markers) and drag it up or down.

> ▶ **POSITION.** When building or editing a stripe, it's always a good idea to watch the Position field, which gives you feedback as you click or

Figure 3-81
Edit Stripe

drag markers in the ruler area. You can also add markers at specific places in the ruler area by typing them here.

▶ **PREVIEW.** The Preview area offers an example of what your stripe will look like when applied to a path or a line. I recommend setting the slider to the largest line setting, as typical low-resolution monitors can't hope to give you a good approximation on the thinner lines.

▶ **MITER.** As with the dash pattern, the Miter setting controls what happens to the stripe at corners. Let's say you choose the rounded-corner Miter setting; if you apply this stripe to a rectangular picture box, the four corners will each be rounded slightly, even though the Corner Radius setting in the Modify dialog box is set to zero. (In fact, they're slightly rounded because this value is set to zero; if you increase the Corner Radius value, the Miter goes away.) In general, I use the default sharp-corner Miter unless I'm trying to achieve some special effect with the stripe.

Moving dashes and stripes around. You can make custom dashes and stripes all you like, but if you make them in one document, how do you get them into another? There are two ways to move Dashes & Stripes styles between documents.

▶ **MOVE AN ITEM.** If you apply a custom dash or stripe to a line, or set it as a frame style for a box, you can copy that item from one document to another and the custom style comes with it. Even if you then delete the item, the custom style remains. Remember, you can copy items from one document to another with Copy and Paste, or by dragging it between the two document windows.

▶ **APPEND.** You can also move a line style from one document to another by clicking the Append button in the Dashes & Stripes dialog box. XPress asks you for the document you want to copy from, and then asks you for the Dashes & Stripes setting you want to copy. Note that the Append feature also appears under the File menu, though if you choose it there, you can append style sheets, lists, H&J settings, and colors, too.

▼ ▼

Tip: Comparing Dashes & Stripes. Sometimes it's really hard to tell the difference between two dashes or two stripes. Fortunately, QuarkXPress offers a built-in comparison feature. First, select the two styles you want to compare from the list in the Dashes & Stripes dialog box (you can select two discontiguous items from the list by holding down the Command or Ctrl key). Then, Option-click (Alt-click) on the Append button (when you hold down the Option key, this button changes into a Compare button).

▼ ▼

Frame Editor

A quick history lesson: QuarkXPress, before version 5, used to ship with a little utility called Frame Editor that let you create borders or frames that you can apply to rectangular boxes. Unfortunately, all the frames you could make were bitmapped, like the horrible Deco and Ornate frames that ship with XPress. That means that rather than defining a border with smooth lines and curves, you have to use dots in a bitmap (see Chapter 9, *Pictures*, for more information on the differences between object-oriented and bitmapped images). The biggest problem with this is that diagonal and curved lines appear jaggy at almost any size. Fortunately, Quark no longer ships the Frame Editor.

▼ ▼

Tables

Building tables in QuarkXPress has long been painful without buying a third-party XTension. Fortunately, XPress now has a Table tool which lets you create simple tables quickly and painlessly. Whether you need a table for financial data in an annual report, a form for ordering supplies, or a chart listing this week's Top Ten Pop Songs, the Table tool will make your life a happier place.

Table Terms. In order for you make and use tables, you need to understand some table terminlogy.

- ▶ A *cell* is one box of information within a table. Tables consist of a grid of cells, and cells are always picture or text boxes.

- ▶ A *field* is the contents of one cell; in XPress, cells can contain either text, pictures, or be blank.

- ▶ A *row* is a horizontal series of cells in a table (there is normally more than one row in a table).

- ▶ A *column* is a vertical series of cells in a table (there is normally more than one column in a table).

- ▶ A *table* is the entire unit, all columns and rows containing cells.

- ▶ A *delimiter* is a text character that tells XPress to separate one field from the next. The primary delimiter characters are usually a tab and a new paragraph character, but it can also be a comma, a space, or any other character. You only need to worry about delimiters when converting text into a table or a table into text (I'll cover both of these later in this section).

It's important to remember that tables in QuarkXPress are actually just grids of text and picture boxes separated by regular ol' lines. You could manually make a table with boxes and lines, but it would take much longer than using the Table tool and you wouldn't be able to take advantage of a few special table features (like combining cells together).

Building Tables

You can make a table anywhere on your page (or pasteboard) by selecting the Table tool from the Tool palette (that's the one that looks like a small fly-swatter) and dragging out a box, just like you would any picture or text box. The program immediately displays the Table Properties dialog box, in which you can enter the number of columns and rows you want in the table, as well as whether you want the cells to be text or picture boxes (see Figure 3-82). Don't worry, you can always change the cell type, or insert (or delete) rows and columns later. You can even change the tab order of your cells and link the cells together. I'll discuss these features soon.

Once you have drawn a table, you can insert text or pictures into each cell, just as though each cell were a text or picture box (which, as I said

Figure 3-82
Drawing a new table

before, it actually is). So you can click in the cell with the Content tool and either type or use Get Text or Get Picture. If you have linked your cells together (see "Linking Text Cells," below), any text you type or import flows from cell to cell. If you have not, it only flows into the cell in which the text cursor is flashing.

Convert Text to Table. QuarkXPress lets you turn any selected block of text into a table by choosing Convert Text to Table from the Item menu. This gives you the Convert Text to Table dialog box (see Figure 3-83), which lets you specify the row and column delimiters, and the order you want the table filled. XPress automatically calculates the number of columns and rows, so you don't have to type those (though you can override these numbers if you dare).

Figure 3-83
Convert Text to Table

Let's say you need to format some data from Microsoft Excel. You can tell Excel to export the data using a tab-delimited format, which places tabs between each field and a paragraph return at the end of each row. Import that text file into XPress, select it, specify these delimiters, and press OK. QuarkXPress does the rest and builds a table object on your page, placing the proper fields in each cell. The original text box is still there; if you don't want it anymore, you'll have to delete it yourself.

Note that some comma-delimited text files use a format in which any fields that actually contain commas are surrounded by quotations marks. Currently, XPress cannot deal with these kinds of files, so it's much better to use tab-delimited text whenever possible.

QuarkXPress also lets you convert a table into text; I'll cover that later in this section.

Setting tab order. XPress lets you specify the table's "tab order"—the order in which you jump from cell to cell. You can select this option in the Table Properties dialog box when you first create the table, or when you use the Convert Text to Table command. Or you can change it later by selecting the table and choosing Modify from the Item menu, and clicking the Table tab. Normally, you'll accept the default (from left to right in the first row, and then downward through the rows). However, you can also choose one of three other orderings: Right to Left, Top Down; Top Down, Left to Right; and Top Down, Right to Left (sorry, I can't find any way to start the data at the bottom and tab upward).

▼ ▼

Tip: Jump to Next Cell. When the text cursor is in a cell, you can jump to the next text cell by pressing Control-Option-Tab (Ctrl-Alt-Tab)—that's Control, not Command for you Macintosh folks.

▼ ▼

Linking text cells. While XPress 5 didn't allow any linking of text cells in a table, XPress 6 is more flexible, letting you link text cells within a table together, or to any other text box or text cell. You can link cells automatically, following a specified link order, or linked manually in any order you want.

To link cells automatically, turn on the Link Cells option in the Table Properties dialog box when creating a table. Then choose one of four choices from the Link Order popup menu—the same orderings as in the Tab Order popup menu. Text placed into a table cell flows from cell to cell in the link order. If you forget to set this when you first create the table, you can select Link Text Cells from the Table submenu (in the Item menu or the context menu) while the Item tool is selected. Then you can choose the link order in the Table tab of the Modify dialog box. However, you can't apply automatic linking when there's already text in the cells.

Since text table cells are really text boxes, you can also use the Linking tool to manually link cells together. Use the Linking and Unlinking tools as I describe earlier in this chapter. You can also link text between cells in a table and any other text box.

Of course, if you link the cells in your table and then try to enter text in the third cell over, the text appears in the first cell. That is, linked cells act just like linked text boxes. This confuses even advanced users.

Note that if you later save your document as an XPress 5 file, the links will be lost. To avoid this problem, select Convert Table to Group from the Table submenu (in the Item menu or the context menu; see "Convert Table to Text or Group," later in this section).

Changing Rows and Columns

Now that you have a table, it's time to start formatting it: changing the size of the table, adding or removing columns or rows, combining and splitting cells, and changing the size of columns or rows.

Resizing the table. There are two ways to resize your table: you can drag one of the table's corner or side handles, or you can drag the edge of the table itself. The difference between these two methods is important. If you drag a corner or side handle, XPress changes *all* the cells in the table. For instance, if you pull the right side handle out, you change the width of every cell in the table.

You can hold down a modifier key while dragging a side or corner handle, too. If you hold down the Shift key while you drag, the table is resized to a square. The Command (Ctrl) key resizes the contents of each cell along with the table (Command-Option-Shift-drag or Ctrl-Alt-Shift-drag resizes the table and keeps the same height-width proportion.)

If, however, you click and drag the *edge* of the table (on any point where there isn't a handle), then you extend only the cells along that edge (see Figure 3-84).

Deleting columns and rows. To delete a column or row, you need to select a whole column or row of cells. To do this, select the table with the Content tool and then move the cursor just outside the table until the cursor icon changes to a horizontal or vertical black arrow. Clicking when you see this cursor results in a whole row or column being selected. Once you have selected a row or column, you can delete it by selecting Delete from the Table submenu (under the Item menu, or in the context-sensitive menu).

Figure 3-84
Resizing your tables

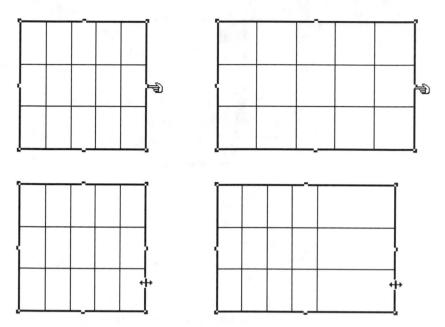

To select more than one contiguous column or row, drag the black-arrow cursor over additional columns or rows. To select discontinuous columns or rows, hold down the Shift key as you select each column or row.

Adding columns or rows. To add a new column or row, use the Content tool and place the cursor in a table cell. Now select Insert Row or Insert Column from the Table submenu (under the Item menu, or in the context-sensitive menu). Either way, XPress displays the Insert dialog box, which lets you choose how many rows or columns you want to add, as well as where the new rows or columns should be added (see Figure 3-85). If you turn on the Keep Attributes option, the added cells take on the formatting of the selected cell. When this option is off, you just get default, no-format cells.

Combining and splitting cells. Cells don't have to be exactly one row tall or one column wide. You can make a cell span across multiple rows or columns by selecting two or more cells and combining them. To select more than one cell in a table, Shift-click on each cell you want selected. Or, you can also just drag the Content tool over two or more cells to select them all. If you select a cell by accident, you can Shift-click on it to deselect it. Then, when you've selected two or more cells in a row or column, choose the Combine Cells feature from the Table submenu (in the Item menu, or in the context-sensitive menu). Combining cells eliminates all content from all selected cells except the one in the upper-left-most selected cell. That content will fill the newly combined cell.

Figure 3-85

Inserting rows or
columns

If you later decide that you want combined cells returned to their original appearance, you can split them. Select the combined cell and choose
Split Cell from the Table submenu (in the Item menu, or in the context-sensitive menu). Note that you can only split cells you've already combined; not
regular cells.

▼ ▼

Tip: Combining Breaks Links. When you have cells in a table that are
linked together, combining cells removes the combined cell from the linking
order. To check the new linking order, click on the table with the Unlinking
tool, and the linking arrows are displayed. Use the Linking tool to reestablish
links the way you would like. (On the other hand, if you use the Split Cell
command on a combined cell, the links are maintained.)

▼ ▼

Changing row and column size. You can resize a single row or column by
dragging the gridlines between the rows and columns with the Content tool.
This can be a little tricky; you have to move the cursor over the gridline until
you see it change into a cross-like double-headed arrow. Once you see that
cursor, you can click and drag the gridline.

Note that QuarkXPress has no way to automatically resize column or row
boundaries based on the content of the cells. Maybe in a later version of the
program it will offer an auto-expand feature.

There's one other way to change your row or column size: place the cursor in a cell and open the Modify dialog box (select Modify from the Item
menu, press Command-M (Ctrl-M), or Command/Ctrl-double-click on the
table). Here, switch to the Cell tab and set the height or width of this cell—
changing it for this one cell changes it for all the cells in that row or column.

If you have more than one cell selected, you can click the Distribute
Evenly button in the Cell tab of the Modify dialog box to equalize the rows or
columns. That is, it takes the total width or height of the cells and divides it
up equally for each row or column you have selected. This is extremely use-

ful when you want several rows or columns to be the same width but aren't sure exactly what that width should be.

Maintain Geometry. When you select a table and open the Modify dialog box, you'll notice a feature called Maintain Geometry on the Table tab (see Figure 3-86). You can also select this option from the Table submenu (in the Item menu, or in the context-sensitive menu). When this checkbox is turned on, XPress will not change the size of the table when you add or remove rows or columns—it simply resizes the remaining rows and columns proportionally. It also maintains the table dimensions when you change row or column size. If you leave this feature turned off, then the table size actually changes when you add or remove columns.

Also, when Maintain Geometry is turned on, you cannot resize a table by dragging one of its outside edges. You can, however, still use the corner or side handles.

Formatting Cells

Remember that each cell in a table is just a picture box or a text box, and you can do almost anything to a cell that you would to an ordinary box. For instance, to change a cell from a text box into a picture box, place the cursor inside it and choose Picture from the Content submenu (under the Item menu or the context-sensitive menu).

Similarly, to change the background color of the cell, you can use the Color palette or the Modify dialog box. You can even format a cell to have a background of None or a gradient.

Figure 3-86
The Table tab of the
Modify dialog box

Here's something you can do to cells in a table that you cannot do with regular picture or text boxes: You can apply formatting to the contents of more than one cell at a time. For example, if you want to apply a paragraph style to all the cells in a row, you can select that row (see "Changing Rows and Columns," above) and click on the style in the Style Sheets palette. If you want your headings to be rotated in the cells, you can select that row, open the Modify dialog box, and change the Text Angle field.

Formatting the Table Box

There is another box which contains the cells of a table and which is behind them, called the table box. However, by default, table cells have a white background so you can't normally see it. To change the color of the table box itself, pick a color in the Table tab of the Modify dialog box or select the table with the Item tool and then pick a color from the Colors palette. Now, if you change the background color of the cells to None either by selecting them or changing the table preferences (see below), you can see the table box's color. By default, the table box itself has a transparent background so you can see through it to objects below.

The table box also has a frame that surrounds the table. You can change its properties by first selecting the table with the Item tool, and then choosing Modify from the Item menu, and selecting the Frame tab.

Formatting Gridlines

Now that you know how to format the stuff inside cells, it's time to format the stuff around them: the gridlines. There are three ways to select the gridlines.

▶ You can select the table with the Item tool (instead of the Content tool) and open the Modify dialog box (press Command/Ctrl-M). Choose the Grid tab of the Modify dialog box (see Figure 3-87), and then click on one of the buttons along the right side of the dialog box: vertical gridlines, horizontal gridlines, or all gridlines.

▶ With the Content tool selected, you can choose Select Vertical, Select Horizontal, Select Borders, or Select All from the Gridlines submenu (under the Item menu, or in the context-sensitive menu). When you choose Select Borders, XPress selects the four outer sides of the table.

▶ You can choose one or more gridlines in your table by Shift-clicking on them with the Content tool.

Once you have one or more gridlines selected, you can specify color, style, and width in the Grid tab of the Modify dialog box. Or, if the Modify dialog box isn't open, you can change these settings in the Style menu or the con-

Figure 3-87
The Grid tab of the
Modify dialog box

text-sensitive menu. Remember that the gridlines are exactly like regular lines in XPress, so you can use custom dashes and stripes, change the gap color, or whatever else you choose to do.

Sometimes you'll want to make a table that has no gridlines—where the cells abut each other with no lines in between. To do this, select the lines you want to change and set their color to None. Note that when you have transparent gridlines, you're looking at the table box; if you've changed the table box's color, then you'll see this color "peeking through" the gridline.

▼ ▼

Tip: Matching Gap Color. If you use a dashed or striped gridline style in your table, I recommend setting the Gap Color to the same color as the background color of the cells. This way the gaps will match the background color and not appear as white.

▼ ▼

Tip: One-Celled Tables. Have you ever wanted to draw a text box with different line thicknesses on each side? Or a box that only has a border on three sides? Try this trick, suggested by Quark's Darin Overstreet: Make a table with only one column and one row, and then select each side individually (Shift-click on it) and change its color, style, or width (see Figure 3-88). To make a box with a border on only three sides, select the fourth side and change its color to None.

▼ ▼

Tip: Making Combs. Here's another fun table trick: you can make a comb (one of those segmented fill-in-the-blanks boxes that are ubiquitous on forms) by creating a table with multiple columns and only one row. Then

Shift-click on the top gridline to select it and set its color to None. (See an example in Figure 3-89.)

Figure 3-88
One-celled tables

Figure 3-89
Table combs

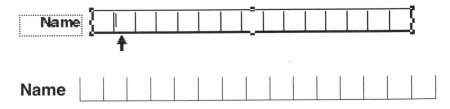

Convert Table to Text or Group

You can extract the contents of a selected table into a single text box by choosing Convert Table to Text from the Table submenu (under the Item menu or in the context-sensitive menu). XPress gives you choices regarding delimiter characters (what to put between the contents of each cell), the text extraction order, and the choice to delete the table once converted (see Figure 3-90).

When you click OK the program generates a new text box with the contents from the table, separated by delimiters (usually tab characters). You can position this text box someplace on your page, or use Save Text (from the File menu) to export the text to disk. For instance, you might want to export the table to disk as a text file if your client or accounting department needs a text version of your table to import into a spreadsheet.

Picture cells in your table get automatically converted to anchored picture boxes when you extract the data with Convert Table to Text.

You can also convert a table to a group of text boxes by selecting Convert Table to Group from the Table submenu (under the Item menu or the con-

Figure 3-90
Convert Table to Text

text-sensitive menu). The table is replaced with grouped boxes. You might do this if you were saving back to QuarkXPress 5 format when you're using features not supported by that version.

▼ ▼

Tip: Switching Rows and Columns. You've spent two hours setting up a table, and suddenly your art director says, "Make all the rows into columns and vice versa." Before you throw something at him, try this trick. Select the table and choose Convert Table to Text from the Table submenu (under the Item menu). In the Convert Table to Text dialog box, turn off the Delete Table checkbox (you may need the original later), and set the Text Extraction Order to Left to Right, Top Down (the one with the "Z" icon). Click OK, select all the text in the resulting text box (Command-A or Ctrl-A), and then choose Convert Text to Table from the Item menu. This time, change the Cell Fill Order to Top Down, Left to Right (the icon looks like a backward "N"). Your new table should have the same content as the first, but with the rows and columns switched. Unfortunately, XPress has no way to copy the gridline and cell background color formatting from one table to another, so you'll have to do that manually.

▼ ▼

Default Preference Settings

Are you tired of changing the gridlines in all your tables to half a point instead of one point? Do the cells in your tables always have the same background color? Do you want your table text to be vertically centered in your table's cells? Don't tire yourself by change these manually every time you make a table; instead, double-click on the Table tool to open the Tool tab of the Preferences dialog box, and click Modify to change the Table tool's default settings (see Figure 3-91).

Of course, like other document preferences, if a document is open when you change these settings, it affects just that one document. To change the application's default settings for any newly created documents, change these defaults with no documents open.

Figure 3-91

Table tool preferences

This dialog box lets you change defaults for both text and picture cells.

Note that these preferences affect both how tables appear when you draw them with the Table tool *and* when XPress makes a table for you using the Convert Text to Table feature.

Tables for Web Layouts

While I don't cover building Web layouts and exporting to HTML until Chapter 14, *Going Online With QuarkXPress*, it's worth noting here that you can use the Table tool to produce tables in Web layouts. Then, when you export HTML from your Web layout, XPress automatically converts your table into an HTML table. However, because HTML tables have severe restrictions, XPress simply won't let you do much formatting to tables that you create in a Web layout. For instance, gridlines must be a minimum of 2 pixels, you cannot change their color or style, and you cannot rotate text in a cell.

Therefore, if you want to use any of the more fancy table formatting, you must first turn on the Convert Table to Graphic checkbox in the Modify dialog box. This way, XPress exports your table as a picture (typically a GIF image) instead of an HTML table. If you turn your print layout into a Web layout, QuarkXPress turns this checkbox on by default.

▼ ▼

Libraries

QuarkXPress lets you keep libraries full of items: picture boxes, text boxes, lines, groups of objects, and so on. These libraries are saved as external files on disk. For example, while writing this book, I placed each piece of artwork in a library, grouped with figure numbers, captions, and callouts. The artwork was later dragged out of the library by the production team onto the QuarkXPress pages. This increased the chance that nothing too weird would happen when making pages, and decreased the time it took to produce a chapter.

Note that a library holds page items, plus their contents. For example, you could place a text box with a particular headline in a particular style in a library. However, picture boxes in libraries don't fully embed their pictures. If a picture was imported using Get Picture, the library only remembers the link to the external file, rather than the file itself. So, although my artwork could be stored in a library, I still had to move all of my EPS and TIFF files from disk to disk (if you are lost, don't worry; I talk about all these issues in Chapter 9, *Pictures*).

You can have more than 10 libraries open at a time (I haven't found an upper limit yet), and each library can hold up to 2,000 entries. You can even label each library entry for quick access. Let's look at how all of this is done.

▼ ▼

Tip: Libraries from Different Versions. Remember that a library is just an XPress document with a thumbnail preview; if you open an older-version library in a newer version of XPress, you'll no longer be able to open the library in the older version of the program. I speak from sad experience on this one, by the way. Yes, it can happen to you.

▼ ▼

Manipulating Libraries

Libraries are, in many ways, just like QuarkXPress documents. Putting an item in a library is like putting it on a separate page of a document. The analogy follows in creating and opening libraries, as well. You can create a new library by selecting Library from the New submenu in the File menu (or by pressing Command-Option-N or Ctrl-Alt-N). And to open a library, you select it in the Open dialog box (the program recognizes it as a library automatically, so you don't have to do anything special). Once you choose a library, QuarkXPress brings it up on your screen as a palette.

As I mentioned back in the last chapter, palettes work much like other windows (in fact, I often call them windoids). For example, you close a palette like a window, by clicking the Close box in the upper-left corner (upper-right in Windows). The palette floats, so you can move the palette wherever you like on your screen. You also can expand the palette by clicking the Zoom box in the upper-right corner of the window. Note that this type of zooming doesn't have anything to do with a percentage scaling view. The first time you click on it, the palette fills your screen. The second time, it decreases back to "normal" size. You also can resize the windoid by clicking and dragging the lower-right resizing box, just like a normal window.

Adding and Moving Library Entries

You'll hardly believe how easy it is to add and remove library entries. To add a page item to an open library, just click on the item with the Item tool (or hold down the Command (Ctrl) key to get a temporary Item tool), and drag the item across into the library. When you're in the library, your mouse cursor turns into a pair of glasses (don't ask me why; all the librarians I know wear contacts), and two triangular arrows point to your position in the library. When you let go of the mouse button, the item you're dragging is inserted in the library at the location these pointers indicate. That is, you can position your page item (or an existing library item) anywhere in the library by dragging it into place.

You also can add an item to a library by using Cut or Copy and Paste. You need to use the Item tool to cut or copy an item from the page, but you can use either the Item or Content tool to paste it in a library. Just click in the position where you want the item to go, then press Command-V (or Ctrl-V; or select Paste from the Edit menu). When picking a place to paste the item, click between two items, so that you can see the positioning arrows. If you click on an item in the library before pasting, you are telling QuarkXPress to replace that item with this new one.

Note that although I'm saying you can add "an item" to the library, that one item can contain a number of page items. If you want, you can select picture boxes, text boxes, and lines—whether grouped or not—and put them all into the same library item.

After you add an item to a library, then you can see a thumbnail-size representation of it (see Figure 3-92). This representation is highlighted, and you won't be able to do any work on your page until you click someplace other than the library.

You can move an item in a library from one position to another by clicking on it and dragging it to a new position. If you have more items in your library than will fit in the palette, you may have some difficulty, because the library doesn't automatically scroll as you drag. I use one of two methods to get around this. First, you can cut and paste items, as I described above.

Figure 3-92
Adding an item
to a library

The arrows or lines show where the item will be inserted.

Each item is reduced to a thumbnail representation.

Second, you can click the Zoom box to expand the size, reposition the item, and rezoom the box down to a small palette.

Removing Library Items

To take an item from an open library and place it on a page, click on it with either the Item or Content tool and drag it onto your page. This doesn't remove the item from the library; it makes a copy of it on your page. It's similar to dragging something from one document to another. If you want to delete an item from a library, click on it, then select Clear from the Edit menu (or press the Delete key). You also can use Cut from the Edit menu (Command-X or Ctrl-X), which removes the item and places it on the Clipboard. QuarkXPress always warns you before totally removing something from a library, because you can't Undo afterward.

Labeling Library Items

Imagine having 150 different items in a library and trying to find just the ones that are pictures of baby seals. Remember that all you can see on the screen is a tiny thumbnail representation of the items. Luckily, you have labeled each library item with a foolproof system, and you are just a popup menu item away from finding those baby seals.

Every item in a library may be labeled either for identification purposes or to group items together (or both). With your library items labeled, you can access the library items by a single label, multiple labels, and more.

To assign a label to a library item, double-click on its thumbnail representation. Up comes the Library Entry dialog box. In this dialog box, there is only one field in which you can type the label. After you add one label to an item, the popup menu in this dialog box is enabled (see Figure 3-93). This popup menu lists each of the previous labels you've assigned (see "Tip: Grouping Library Items," below).

After you have labeled items in your library, you can select from among them with the popup menu at the top of the Library palette (see Figure 3-94). This acts as a kind of electronic card catalog. There are always two items in this popup menu: All and Unlabeled. Selecting All shows you every item in the library. Selecting Unlabeled displays only the items that have not yet been labeled. Any other labels that you have assigned to library items also appear on this popup menu. If you select one of these, you only see items that have been assigned that label.

Then, if you select a second label from the popup menu, that label is added to the category you're already looking at. The name on the popup menu changes to Mixed Labels, which tells you that more than one label is being displayed. You can deselect one label category by rechoosing it from the popup menu (that is, these labels in the popup menu act as on-and-off toggle switches). You can deselect all the subcategories by choosing All from the popup menu.

Figure 3-93
The Library Entry dialog box

Figure 3-94
Selecting a subcategory in the library

▼ ▼

Tip: Grouping Library Items. As I mentioned above, you can group library items together (this isn't the same as grouping items on the page). You do this by giving them the same label. For example, if you have a bunch of lines that you use a lot for one magazine, you might label them all "Mag Lines." Then, when you need one, you simply pull down the Library palette's popup menu and select that label.

However, if each one of the item's labels isn't exactly the same, QuarkXPress won't know to group them together. Instead of typing the same label over and over again for each item, you can just type it once. Then use the popup menu in the Library Entry dialog box to choose that item each time you want to assign it to an item within the library. This is faster, and you avoid typos.

▼ ▼

Saving Libraries

No matter how hard you try, you won't find a command to save the library file. This can be disconcerting, to say the least. What happens to all those items if you can't save them?

In previous versions of XPress, QuarkXPress would save a library only when you quit the program or closed your current document. This is generally unacceptable, because people work for long periods without quitting or closing a document (during the production of the first edition of this book, one person lost over an hour's worth of work because of a system crash before the library was saved).

Fortunately, you can turn on the Auto Library Save feature in the Preferences dialog box. This feature, which is on by default, forces QuarkXPress to save a library every time you place a new item in it. This may slow down your work a little if you're adding a number of items, but it could also save you lots of time if something should go wrong.

Once a library is saved on disk, you can move it from one computer to another. However, note that you cannot move it from a Macintosh to a PC or vice versa. This is an unfortunate limitation due to the way QuarkXPress saves the thumbnail images.

▼ ▼

Tip: Send Your Libraries, Not Your Pictures. If you're preparing templates and picture libraries so that someone else can do the actual page-layout work, remember that you might not need to send them the picture files on disk. QuarkXPress captures a low-resolution preview image for each picture when you imported it into a picture box, and that's saved within the library.

If you send just the library file, the person making pages can place, see, and print the screen representations. When the document file comes back to you, QuarkXPress remembers the locations of all the original graphics files on your disks, and uses those for printing.

▼ ▼

▼ ▼

Appending Settings

QuarkXPress lets you save groups of text or object formatting with a name, called *styles*. Styles (some people call these "presets" or "settings") aren't just for text; XPress lets you give names to special lines and dashes, hyphenation and justification settings, colors, hyperlinks, and much more. Most of the features that let you build these settings live at the bottom of the Edit menu. I'll cover how to make each of these styles in later chapters, but there's one topic about styles that I want to cover here: how to copy settings from one document to another.

You cannot copy and paste or drag-and-drop a setting itself, but you can apply a style to an object and move the object from one document to another. For instance, if you want to copy two colors, you could apply them to two objects, then copy those objects from one file to the next. However, if you need to copy a bunch of styles (paragraph styles, colors, hyperlinks, and so on) from one document to another, it's probably faster and easier to use the Append feature (under the File menu).

The Append feature lets you pick and choose any set of styles from a file on disk to copy into the currently-open document. When you select Append, XPress asks you first to pick a QuarkXPress file on disk, then it displays the Append dialog box (see Figure 3-95). To copy a style, first choose among the style types in the left column, then pick the styles you want and click the dialog box's right arrow button (or double-click the style name). You can pick more than one style from the list by Shift- or Command/Ctrl-clicking.

Append makes it easy to choose a bunch of styles—like four paragraph styles, two colors, and three special Dashes & Stripes—all in one shot.

Figure 3-95
The Append
dialog box

▼ ▼

Moving On

You now know the basics of how QuarkXPress relates to you, and the general concepts of how you can use its tools to make your pages. If you weren't familiar with these tools before, a little practice will turn you into a pro in no time. If you were familiar with them, I hope you now have increased your arsenal of high-caliber techniques.

Either way, you should now be ready to move into the next chapter, in which I move away from a freeform, throw-it-all-on-a-page style of working and introduce you to a few of the systematic methods in which you can build documents.

4

BUILDING A DOCUMENT

I find the design process really fascinating. The designer must meld rigid, mathematical specifications with flowing, flexible sensibilities. XPress works best when you use this mix. First, build the foundation of your document with precision. Second, place items on the page with creativity.

This chapter is about starting that process: building an infrastructure for your document. I call this "document construction." It's just like the construction of a building. First you decide on the building's specifications—how tall and wide you want it to be, and so on. Next you lay a foundation and build structural supports.

In QuarkXPress it's very similar. First you decide on specifications for the document—how tall and wide, whether it's double- or single-sided, and so on. Next you build the structures of the page—page elements that repeat, page numbering, and text flow. If you don't take these steps first, the foundation of your work will be unreliable—and your building might just fall down.

Step with me into the building mode. Our first stop is opening a new document.

QuarkXPress 6 introduces some new concepts to the construction process: Now when you create a new file, you're creating a project. Each project now consists of one or more layout spaces, which I usually just call layouts.

▼ ▼

Building a New Document

When you open QuarkXPress using the program defaults, you'll see a blank screen underneath the menu bar, with the Tool and Measurements palettes showing. To create a new document, choose New from the File submenu (or press Command-N or Ctrl-N). This brings up the New Project dialog box, shown in Figure 4-1. You're creating the default layout for your project. It is here that you determine a layout's type (print or Web). For print layouts, you're specifying the page dimensions, page margins, number of columns, the spacing between columns, and whether the pages are laid out facing each other. For Web layouts, you're describing the basic parameters of your Web page. I discuss creating Web pages in Chapter 14, *Going Online with QuarkXPress*.

Figure 4-1

The New Project dialog box

For print documents

For Web documents

Table 4-1

Preset page sizes

NAME	IN INCHES	IN PICAS/POINTS	IN MILLIMETERS
US Letter	8.5 by 11	51p by 66p	216 by 279.4
US Legal	8.5 by 14	51p by 84p	216 by 355.6
A4 Letter	8.27 by 11.69	49p7.3 by 70p1.9	210 by 297
B5 Letter	6.93 by 9.84	41p6.9 by 59p0.7	176 by 250
Tabloid	11 by 17	66p by 102p	279.4 by 431.8

The New Project dialog box is the "Checkpoint Charlie" for entering the new-document zone (walls may crumble, but metaphors remain). Note that there is nothing in the New Project dialog box that locks you in; you can make changes to these settings at any time, even after you've worked on the document a lot.

Let's take a detailed look at each of items in this dialog box.

Page Size

When you make your pass through the New Project dialog box on the way to creating a print document, you have the opportunity to determine the dimensions of its pages. The *default setting*—the one QuarkXPress chooses for you if you make no change to the settings in the dialog box—is a standard letter-size page: 8.5 by 11 inches (or A4 size in QuarkPassport). You can choose from five preset sizes, or you can choose a custom-size page by typing in the values yourself—from 1 by 1 inch to 48 by 48 inches. Table 4-1 shows the measurements for each of the preset choices in three common measurement units.

▼ ▼

Tip: Page Size Is Not Paper Size. Page Size in the New Project dialog box refers to the size of the pages you want as your finished output—it does not refer to the size of the paper going through your printer. These sizes may or may not be the same. In the Page Size area, type in the page dimensions of the actual piece you want to produce. For example, if you want to create a 7-by-9-inch book page, enter these values in the Width and Height fields, even if you're outputting to a laser printer capable of handling only letter-size pages.

▼ ▼

Tip: Exceeding Maximum Page Size. The maximum page size in XPress is 48 by 48 inches. If you need to exceed it, though, it's easy enough to do; it only requires a little arithmetic. Figure out the ratio of your required size to XPress's maximum, create your document at 48 by 48 (or 48 by whatever), and then type your ratio in the Reduce or Enlarge field in the Setup tab of the Print dialog box. You'll also have to use the inverse of your ratio on your desired point sizes and all other measurements, since they'll be printing larger than you've specced them.

For example, suppose you need a page size of 72 by 30 inches. Set up your page for 48 by 20 inches, type "150" in the Reduce or Enlarge field in Page Setup, and spec all your measurements, point sizes, and so on as two-thirds of your final, desired measurements.

▼ ▼

Margin Guides

The Margin Guides area allows you to specify the size of your margin on all four sides of a page: Top, Bottom, Left, and Right. When you work with facing pages (see below), Left and Right change to Inside and Outside. These margin guides can be used to define the *column area*. In the book-and-magazine trade, the column area is usually called the *live area*. It's the area within which the text and graphics usually sit (see Figure 4-2). Running heads, folios, and other repeating items sit outside the live area.

The term "live area" may be slightly misleading, however, because everything that's on a page gets printed, whether it's inside the margin guides or outside them—or even partially on the page and partially off it. Note that the margin guides are only that—guides. You can ignore them if you want. You should also note that these guides specify the size of the automatic text box (which I'll talk about later in this chapter).

There are some things about margin guides that make them unique. Although margin guides resemble ruler guides both in form and function, you cannot change the position of the margin guides by dragging them; you have to change them in the Master Guides dialog box (which is only available when a master page is showing). I look at making this kind of modification in "Modifying Your Pages," later in this chapter.

Figure 4-2
The Column,
or "live" area

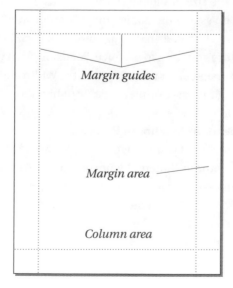

Margin guides

Margin area

Column area

Your document pages don't all have to have the same margin guides. But because margin guides are based on master pages, you have to create multiple master pages to have different margin guides. Once again, I defer discussion of this process until later in the chapter. For now, let's just concentrate on building one simple document.

By the way, note that these guides don't print. Nor do they limit what you can do on the page. They are simply part of the general infrastructure of the document, and are meant just to be guides. Not only can you change them at any time, but (as with the printed guides on blueline grid paper) you can disregard them entirely.

Column Guides

There's another kind of automatic guide you can place on a page: column guides. If you select a value larger than one in the Columns field in the New Project dialog box, the area between the margin guides is divided into columns. For example, if you want a page that has three columns of text on it, you can specify a value of "3" (see Figure 4-3).

Your next decision is the amount of gutter space. Sometimes people use the word "gutter" to refer to the inside page margin; this is different. In QuarkXPress, the *gutter* is the blank space between column guides.

Perhaps the best way to think about column guides is the concept of the page grid. Unfortunately, QuarkXPress can't create a true horizontal and vertical grid for your page. However, it can give you the tools to make one yourself. Column guides are the first part of that procedure; they allow you to place columns of space on a page. When Snap to Guides is selected from the View menu, items such as text boxes and lines "snap to" your column guides (see Chapter 2, *QuarkXPress Basics*).

Figure 4-3
Column guides

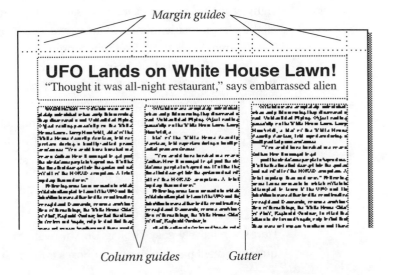

Margin guides

UFO Lands on White House Lawn!
"Thought it was all-night restaurant," says embarrassed alien

Column guides   Gutter

▼ ▼

Tip: Snap to Guides for Box Fitting. I often find it more helpful to draw separate text boxes for each column rather than to use one large text box separated into columns. If you have Snap to Guides turned on (on the View menu), you can quickly draw a text box that fills one column. This text box can be duplicated, then positioned in the next column, and so on, until each column is created.

Drawing multiple text boxes is also useful if you want each column to be a different width or height. When you're done making boxes, you can remove the column guides by using the Master Guides feature, or you can just leave them where they are.

▼ ▼

Facing Pages

The Facing Pages feature of the New Project dialog box (and the Layout Properties dialog box) deserves some special attention. At this stage in the game, you have two choices: single-sided pages or facing pages.

Single-sided pages. Single-sided pages are what most people generate from desktop-publishing equipment: single-sided pieces of paper. For example, handbills, posters, letters, memos, or one-page forms are all single-sided. In QuarkXPress a normal, single-sided document looks like a series of pages, each positioned directly underneath the previous one (see Figure 4-4).

Facing pages. Whereas nonfacing pages are destined to be single, facing pages are always married to another page (well, almost always). For example, pick up a book. Open it in the middle. The left page (the *verso*) faces the right page (the *recto*). In some books (like the one you're looking at), the left and right pages are almost exactly the same. However, most book pages have a slightly larger inside margin (*binding margin*) than the outside margin (*fore-edge margin*). This is to offset the amount of the page "lost" in the binding.

QuarkXPress displays facing pages next to each other on the screen (see Figure 4-5). For example, when you move from page two to page three you must scroll "across" rather than "down." Note that even page numbers always fall on the left; odd numbers always fall on the right.

If you check Facing Pages in the New Project dialog box, XPress sets up two master pages: a left and a right page. These can be almost completely different from each other (we'll see how soon).

Automatic Text Box

Here's a relatively easy choice: Do you want your first page and all subsequently added pages to have text boxes automatically placed on them? If so,

Figure 4-4

Single-sided pages

Figure 4-5

Facing pages

turn on the Automatic Text Box option. This is clearly the way to go if you're working with documents such as books or flyers that are mostly text. However, if you're designing an advertisement with text and pictures placed all over the page, there's really no good reason to use the Automatic Text Box feature.

If you do check Automatic Text Box, the text box that QuarkXPress makes for you is set to the same number of columns and gutter size that you specified in the Column Guides area, and it fills the page out to the margin guides. I discuss the Automatic Text Box checkbox in detail in "Automatic Text Boxes," later in this chapter.

▼ ▼

Tip: Check That New Project Dialog Box. QuarkXPress remembers what you selected in the New Project dialog box for the last document, and gives you the same thing next time you start on a new document. This can be helpful or it can be a drag (especially when one of your colleagues creates a 3-by-5-inch document just before you start working on a tabloid-sized job). You'll hear me say this throughout the book: Verify each dialog box as you go. Don't just assume that you want every default setting. Pay attention to those details and you'll rarely go wrong.

▼ ▼

Projects and Layouts

Before we proceed further with describing how to build your document, I need to talk a bit about the new concepts of projects and layouts introduced in QuarkXPress 6. XPress files created in earlier versions have one layout space, which I've always just called a document. Now, you can create multiple layouts in a single file, which can be a handy way of organizing related documents.

For example, you might be creating several documents for a client—a letterhead, an envelope, and a business card, as well as a simple Web site. You can store all of these as layouts in the same file, now called a project. Each layout can have its own page size, orientation, method of output, and so on.

Each project can contain as many as 25 layouts. Each layout is defined either as a print layout, which works essentially like a print document in QuarkXPress 4 or 5, or a Web layout, which is similar to the Web document in XPress 5.

A word of warning here: While projects are generally good things, keep in mind that files can become corrupted. If your project becomes corrupted, you'll lose all the documents which are contained in it.

Projects

A project is the file that is a container for your layouts. It also includes those attributes that can be exchanged between documents in the Append dialog boxes—style sheets, colors, H&Js, lists, dashes & stripes, and hyperlinks. For Web layouts, it also stores menus, font families, meta tags and cascading menus.

This means that in a project which contains a letterhead, envelope and business card, for example, that each layout shares the same colors, styles, and so on. And if you change the colors or style sheets in one layout, they'll be changed in the other layouts in the same project.

Within a project, you can also synchronize the text between two or more layouts using the new Synchronize Text palette. I discuss this in Chapter 5, *Word Processing*.

Layouts

A layout is a document that has a particular type of content—for output either in print or on the Web. It contains any of the QuarkXPress items that I describe throughout this book—text boxes, picture boxes, contentless boxes, lines and text paths. It also contains any guides created in that layout. Master pages and layers are also layout-specific; each layout in a project can have its own, different than any other layout in the same project.

Preferences are also stored individually in each layout. These include things like tool preferences, measurement units, and zoom settings. Hyphenation exceptions and settings in the Trap Information palette are layout-specific as well.

When you check spelling, or use the Find/Change dialog box or the Index palette, these operations only take place within the currently selected layout. Although a List definition can be used in any layout within a project, when you build a list, it only uses the currently active layout.

When you print, export to PDF, save a page as EPS, or collect for output, the action only affects the current layout.

Creating a New Layout

Once you have created a project (which always has one layout space in it), you can add new layouts to your file. However, see "Layout Limitations" below to decide whether a multi-layout project is appropriate for the kind of work you're doing.

To create a new layout, choose New from the Layout menu or Control-click (right-click) on the tab of a layout and choose New (see Figure 4-6). As you add

Figure 4-6
The Layout Space
context menu

layouts to your file each one shows as a tab with the layout name at the bottom of your project.

When you create a new layout, you see a dialog box exactly the same as when you create a new project, except that in the title bar it says New Layout.

Working with Layouts

To navigate from one layout to the next, click on the tab of the layout you want in the lower-left corner of the document window. (If not all the tabs are visible a popup menu appears at the right end of the tabs which allows you to select one.) You can also choose Previous, Next, First or Last in the Layout menu. There is also a Go To submenu in the Layout menu, where you can choose the name of the layout you want to view. Unfortunately, I haven't been able to find a keyboard shortcut to jump to a particular layout.

You can duplicate a layout by choosing Duplicate from the Layout menu. This duplicates all the elements of a layout, including master pages, layers, guides, and any items you have placed on the pages. However, items that are on the pasteboard, outside of the page area aren't included. Note that if you change the layout type—from Print to Web or vice versa—certain objects will be changed. I talk about conversions between media types in Chapter 14, *Going Online with QuarkXPress*.

Layout Properties. There is no longer a Document Setup command in QuarkXPress 6 as there was in earlier versions. Instead, each layout has its own properties. You can edit a layout's properties by choosing Layout Properties from the Layout menu or you can select Layout Properties from the context menu by Control-clicking (right-clicking) when you click on a layout's tab. Here you can change the layout size or orientation, and whether the layout has Facing Pages. You can even change a Print layout to Web layout (or *vice versa*), but objects may change. The Column Guides and Margin Guides for a layout are grayed. I describe how to change these options in "Modifying Your Pages," later in this chapter.

▼ ▼

Tip: Reducing Page Size. When duplicating layouts, if your new layout is smaller than the layout you're duplicating, you'll have the best luck if you change the size *after* making the new layout. Say, for example, that you've created a letterhead as your initial layout and now you want to create a notepad with similar elements but with a smaller size. If you reduce the page dimensions in the Layout Properties dialog box, XPress will likely not allow you to do it because certain items on your page will fall outside of the new pasteboard. Instead, choose the original page size when duplicating the page. Move the page items to fit them in the new dimensions, then use the Layout Properties command in the Layout menu to change the Page Size.

▼ ▼

Deleting Layouts. You can also delete a layout from a project. First make the layout you want to delete visible, then click Delete from the Layout menu or choose Delete from the context menu on the layout's tab. You'll be warned that the action can't be undone. If you click OK, the layout will be removed from the project.

▼ ▼

Tip: Bringing in Earlier Files. Opening a document from an earlier version of QuarkXPress opens it as project with one layout. To combine multiple XPress 4 or 5 documents into the same project, create a layout for each one, then switch each to Thumbnails mode from the View menu. Drag the pages from one document to another.

▼ ▼

Layout Limitations

You should be aware of some of the limitations of having multiple layouts within a project.

▶ You can't view two or more layouts at the same time.

▶ You can't drag-and-drop page items from layout to layout because you can't see more than one at a time. Instead, copy elements and then use Paste or Paste in Place from the Edit menu to duplicate items.

▶ If you're working with QuarkXPress's Book feature (see Chapter 8, *Long Documents*), you won't be able to work with projects that have multiple layouts. Book chapters can only contain projects with a single print layout.

▶ You can't copy guides or master pages between layouts. As a workaround, use the Duplicate command from the Layout menu when you begin creating a layout to duplicate guides and master pages from an existing layout.

You should think carefully before you create multiple layouts in a project. These work best for simple layouts that share common attributes like styles, colors, H&Js, and other attributes which can be appended. Because these attributes are shared at the project level, it makes it easy to keep them synchronized. Multi-layout projects also work well when you want to synchronize text (see Chapter 5, *Word Processing*).

Where multi-layout projects don't work well is when you need to have layouts where the precise positioning of elements is critical. Since layouts can't share master pages or copy guides, it's difficult to make sure that page items share the same page positioning.

Master Pages: Elementary

Master pages are the means of establishing repeating elements common to multiple pages within a document. For example, if you have one master page in a single-sided document, then what's on that master page shows up on every new page you create. In facing-page documents there are two master pages, one for the left page and one for the right. In this case, whatever you put on the "left" master page shows up on all the left document pages, and what is on the "right" master page shows up on all the right document pages.

What Master Pages Are Good For

Although your creativity in formatting master pages may be unlimited, master pages' most common uses are for running heads, repeating graphics, and automatic page numbers (see Figure 4-7). These items are perfect for master pages, because creating them for every page in your document would be a chore that Hercules would shudder at and Job would give up on.

Figure 4-7
Running heads
and footers

Automatic Page Numbering. I have a confession to make: Before I knew better, I would put "1" on the first page, "2" on the second page, and so on. When I deleted or added pages, I just took the time to renumber every page. That seemed reasonable enough. What else could I do?

QuarkXPress lets you set up automatic page numbering for an entire document (and as I discuss in Chapter 8, *Long Documents*, for multiple documents as well). You don't actually type any number on the master page. What you do is press the keystroke for the Current Box Page Number character (Command-3 or Ctrl-3). This inserts a placeholder character which is replaced by the page number when you're looking at a document page. In master pages, the page-number placeholder looks like this: <#>.

The number appears in whatever font, size, and style you choose on the master page. For example, if you set the <#> character to 9-point Futura, all the page numbers come out in that style. This can actually cause some confusion: If you choose a font like an Expert Set or a collection of dingbats, the numbers or the <#> characters might appear differently than you expect. But with normal typefaces, you'll see the numbers just like you'd think.

Remember, the Current Box Page Number character (Command-3 or, in Windows, Ctrl-3) is simply a character that you type, manipulate, or delete using keyboard commands. You also can type it alongside other text, to form text blocks that read "Page <#>", or "If you wanted to find pg. <#>, you found it."

These page numbers flow with your pages. For example, if you change page 23 to be your new page 10, every page in the document changes its position and numbering accordingly. Also, if you change the page-numbering scheme to Roman numerals or whatever (see "Sections and Page Numbering," later in this chapter), QuarkXPress automatically changes that style on every page.

Graphics and master pages. You can do anything with a graphic on a master page that you can do on a regular document page, including define it for text runarounds. You can be subtle and put a small graphic in your header or footer, or you can put a great big graphic in the background of every page (see Figure 4-8).

The thing to remember when you format master pages with graphics—whether as backgrounds or for runaround effects—is that what you place on the master page appears on every page of the document. If you only want a graphic on a few pages, you're best off either handling such things on a page-by-page basis in the regular document view, or creating different master pages to hold different graphics.

Figure 4-8

Placing a graphic on your master page

How QuarkXPress Does Masters

Master pages in QuarkXPress are totally different than PageMaker's or InDesign's. Elements on QuarkXPress's master pages show up on regular document pages not as view-only elements existing on an "underlay," but as real elements which you can edit just like any other page element. You can still go back and edit your master page, but whatever you change on a document page ("local changes") stays changed.

You can base document pages on a *formatted* or a *blank* master page (the latter is the QuarkXPress equivalent of turning a master page "off"). And you can have multiple master pages—up to 127—in any document, so you can base different document pages on different master pages. This is very useful if your document comprises multiple sections that require different looks.

I'm going to stick to the basics in this elementary section on QuarkXPress's master pages, because to throw the options and variables down on the table all at once might make things seem more complicated than they really are. Working with master pages isn't complicated if you take it step by step.

Your First Master Page

Two things happen simultaneously when you click OK in the New Project dialog box: QuarkXPress builds a master page called "A-Master A" and creates the first page of your default layout for you to work on. The master page and the document page are almost identical. If you turned on Facing Pages in the New dialog box, "A-Master A" has a left page and a right page; otherwise, it's just a single page.

There are three methods for switching between viewing the master pages of a document and the document itself.

▶ **PAGE LAYOUT PALETTE.** The icons for the master pages are located at the top of the Page Layout palette. (In earlier versions, this was called the Document Layout palette.) To jump to the master page you want, double-click on its icon (see Figure 4-9).

▶ **DISPLAY SUBMENU.** You can choose to work on either your document pages or your master pages by selecting one or the other from the Display submenu located under the Page menu (see Figure 4-10).

▶ **POPUP PAGE.** Clicking and dragging the page number popup menu in the lower-left corner of the document's window gives you a list of icons from which you can select any document page or master page (see Figure 4-11).

Figure 4-9
Viewing a
master page

Figure 4-10
Selecting a page
to look at

Figure 4-11
Popup pages

You can tell whether you're looking at a document page or a master page by three telltale signs.

▶ The page-number indicator in the lower-left corner of the document window tells you if you are looking at a document page or a master page.

▶ An automatic text-link icon is always in the upper-left corner of a master page. (Later in the chapter, I discuss what this is and how you use it.)

▶ While viewing a master page, you aren't able to perform certain functions that are usually available. For example, the Go To feature (Command-J or Ctrl-J) is disabled, as is Insert.

▼ ▼

Tip: Printing Master Pages. Printing master pages is simple enough, but people often can't figure out how to do it. The trick: you have to have the master page that you want printed showing when you select Print from the File menu. Note that this prints both the left and right pages if the document has facing pages (you can't print only the left or the right page alone). Unfortunately, this means that if you have 12 different master pages and you want them all to be printed, you have to print them one spread at a time.

▼ ▼

Automatic Text Boxes

Although master pages look very similar to normal document pages, there are some basic differences you need to be aware of. These are the master guides, the automatic text-link icon, and the automatic text-link box. Each of these features is integral to the construction of a well-built document in QuarkXPress.

Note that *automatic text-link icon* is my term for what Quark's documentation refers to as both the "Intact Chain Icon" and the "Broken Chain Icon." Similarly, my term *automatic text-link box* is referred to as the "automatic text box" in the Quark manuals. I think my terminology is more descriptive, so that's what I use. If you like theirs, then you can do a mental substitution.

Master Guides

I said earlier that you could change the margins and column guides after you set their values in the New Project dialog box. The Master Guides dialog box is the place to do this. You can get the Master Guides dialog box by selecting Master Guides from the Page menu when you're working on a master page (see Figure 4-12).

When you use the Master Guides dialog box to change the margin guides or the column guides, only the currently open master page changes. Later in this chapter, you'll learn about having multiple master pages; in that case, you can have different margins and columns for each master page in your document.

Figure 4-12
Master Guides
dialog box

Master Guides

Column Guides

Columns: 1

Gutter Width: 0.167"

Margin Guides

Top: 0.5"

Bottom: 0.5"

Inside: 0.5"

Outside: 0.5"

Cancel   OK

Note that when you change the margin guides or column guides using Master Guides, you affect the automatic text box on that page (if there is one). If the boundaries of the automatic text box reach to the margin guides (they always do, unless you've changed them), the boundaries are changed to match the new margins. Similarly, if you change the Columns field in the Master Guides dialog box, the automatic text box also gets altered (as long as you haven't changed its boundaries or column settings).

Automatic Text-Link Icon

The automatic text-link icon is the little picture of a chain in the upper-left corner of every master page. It is the gateway to QuarkXPress's automatic text-linking feature. This feature allows XPress to automatically link together text boxes that occur on each page. Of course, you can always link boxes together manually, but automatic text boxes are much faster. The automatic text-link icon works with the automatic text-link box, which I discuss next.

The automatic text-link icon is always either broken (disabled) or linked (enabled). You can use the Linking and Unlinking tools while you're viewing your master pages to switch automatic linking on and off (see below).

Automatic Text-Link Box

Another item of importance to master pages is the automatic text-link box. This is a text box that is linked through QuarkXPress's automatic linking mechanism. Automatic linking is the way that QuarkXPress links pages together. I know this sounds confusing. Let's look at an example.

Picture a one-page document with only one master page, called "A-Master A." If your text fills and overflows the text box on the first page, and your "A-Master A" has an automatic text-link box on it, then the program can automatically add a new page and link the overflow text onto the newly added page. If there is no automatic text-link box on the master page, then XPress does not link your first-page text box to anything, and you have to link things manually (see Chapter 2, *QuarkXPress Basics*).

There are two ways to get automatic text-link boxes on your master page.

▶ **AUTOMATIC TEXT BOX.** If you check Automatic Text Box in the New Project dialog box when you're creating a document (it is on by default), QuarkXPress places a text box on your first layout page and also on "A-Master A." The box on the master page is an automatic text-link box.

▶ **LINKING TO THE CHAIN.** You can create your own automatic text-link box by drawing a text box on your master page and then linking it to the automatic text-link icon. Select the Linking tool from the Tool palette, click on the automatic text-link icon in the upper-left corner of the page, then click on the text box you want automatically linked (see Figure 4-13). If you want both the left and right pages to contain automatic text-link boxes, you need to link each page's icon to a text box.

An automatic text-link box is a special-case text box. It is reserved solely for text that is typed on (or flowed into) document pages, so you cannot type any text in it while you're on the master page. This is different from other boxes that are on the master page, which can contain text or graphics (like running heads or automatic page numbers).

Figure 4-13
Manually linked
automatic text boxes

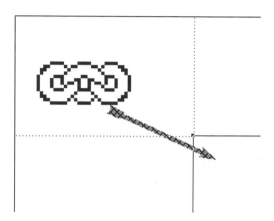

Modifying Automatic Text-Link Boxes

While you cannot type in automatic text-link boxes, you can make many formatting specifications for them. For example, you can specify the number of columns, width, height, background color, and frame. While QuarkXPress originally places automatic text-link boxes so that they fill the area outlined by the margin guides (with the number of columns specified for column guides), you can always move and resize them to suit your needs.

▼ ▼

Tip: Assigning a Startup Font. Although you cannot actually type in an automatic text-link box while in master-page viewing mode, you *can* assign character and paragraph formatting to the box. Just select the text box with the Content tool and specify the font, size, style, leading, and so on. You can even set the default style sheet for the box (see Chapter 7, *Copy Flow*). Then when you return to the document page, the text you type in that box appears in the font, style, and leading that you chose. Text that is imported into that box does not necessarily appear in that font, however.

▼ ▼

Creating Multiple Automatic Text-Link Boxes

You can actually have any number of automatic text-link boxes on a master page. That is, text could flow into one, then another, and then another before flowing onto the next page. What you have to do is link them all in the order in which you want text to flow into them. You define the first box as "automatic" using the procedures described above. Then you click in succession with the Linking tool on the boxes you want to define as automatic text-link boxes. This defines them as part of the automatic text chain. You'll see the linking arrows shoot out with each new link that you create. To continue the link from a left master page to a right master page, click on the right master's automatic text-link icon before joining any boxes found on the right master.

Don't get any fancy ideas about having two separate automatic text-link boxes on a page, each holding a different story (for instance, having two stories that flow side-by-side through a document). Nope. Can't do that with automatic text boxes (you can set that up by linking the boxes manually, of course).

Unlinking Automatic Text-Link Boxes

The easiest way to discard an automatic text-link box is to delete it (press Command-K or Ctrl-K). But if you want to keep the box and simply negate its definition as an automatic text-link box, you can do that using the Unlinking tool. First, click on the automatic text-link icon with the Unlinking tool, thereby showing the linking arrow. Next, click on the tail of the linking arrow to break the chain and turn the box into a "normal" master-page text box. In the case of multiple successively linked boxes, the automatic linking is broken wherever you've broken the chain from the icon, though other links remain.

▼ ▼

Master Pages and Document Pages

There is a subtle but certain link between your master pages and document pages that goes beyond one mirroring the other. Because QuarkXPress lets you change master-page items (also known simply as "master items") on your document pages (unlike PageMaker), you have extra power; but with that power comes—what else?—responsibility. The responsibility to pay attention to what you're doing. Here's why.

Changing Master-Page Items

After you have created a master page and applied it to a document page, you can manipulate the master-page items in either master-page or document view. Which view you're in when you make a change determines what effect the change has on your document.

Changes to master items on master pages. If you are in master-page view when you make a change to a master-page item, the change is reflected on every page in your layout that is based on that master page—unless you've already changed that item on particular layout pages (see Figure 4-14).

For example, let's say you have a running head that contains the name of the layout and the page number. You have created a 30-page document with this master page, so each page has that running head on it. If you change the running head because the document's title has changed, that change shows up on all 30 pages. The same thing happens if you change the typeface of the running head, or anything else about the master page.

Figure 4-14
Master Page changes

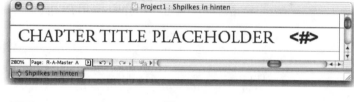

On a document page, the item shows up exactly as it appears on the Master Page with the correct page number inserted.

Edit this text for the running head on the document page.

If you then go back and change the text on the Master Pages . . .

. . . the running head remains the same on the document page.

In fact, if you deleted the running head's text box from the master page, it would be deleted from every document page based on that master page, too.

Changes to master items on document pages. However, if you change the running head on page 10 while you're in document view, and then rework the running head on the master page, the running head on every page *except* page 10 is changed. Page 10 remains unchanged because local page changes override the master-page change for that text box.

As long as no local page changes are made, if you delete the running head from the master page, the running head is deleted from every page of the document. But if a change has already been made locally to the running head on page 10, like in this example, then that running head on page 10 is *not* deleted. Even if you delete the whole master page, the text boxes that appear on document pages are deleted except for the one on page 10, which has been *locally* modified.

This keep-local-changes approach makes sense if you think about it, but it's often frustrating. For instance, if you forget that something is a master-page item and you change it even just a little, QuarkXPress notices and breaks the link between it and the master page. That's one reason why it's important to be clear on what's a master-page item and what's not. Note that if you change a master-page item on a document page (such as that running head in the earlier example) and then you change it back to exactly the way it was, QuarkXPress forgives and forgets that you ever changed it in the first place.

Content links and item links. Okay, let's take this one step further. It turns out that when it comes to master-page items, there are actually two kinds of links you can break: content links and item links. Let's say you have a text box with the word "Moose" in it on your master page. If you change the text on a document page, you break the content link. If you move the box (or change its size), you break the item link.

For instance, after changing the word "Moose" to "Elk" on page 23, let's say you go back to the master page and change "Moose" to "Bison" *and* change the size of the text box. Now, on every page but 23 the word gets updated to "Bison"—on page 23, the content link was broken, so it remains "Elk." But on every page, even page 23, the text-box size gets changed. It gets changed on page 23 because changing the text in a text box breaks the content link but not the item link, so changes to the item (the text box) itself are reflected (see Figure 4-15).

Okay, now let's say you change the color of the text box on page 19. Changing the background color breaks the item link (because you've affected the box itself), but not the content link. So if you move the box or change its size on the master page, it moves or resizes on all the pages except page 19.

Figure 4-15

Item and Content links
between master pages
and document pages

These two text boxes are on the document's master page. Any document pages based on this master page will also contain the same boxes.

Here, on a document page, I've made two changes: the font in one box and the placement of another box. The first change breaks the content link; the second breaks the item link.

Later, I change the background color of the boxes on the master page. (Note that this changes the item itself, not the content.)

Because I broke the item link for the second box, it doesn't get updated. The first box is updated because only the content link had been broken.

Now, back on the master page, I change the content of the boxes (in this case, by changing the font).

In this case, the first box is not updated because the content link had been broken. However, the second box is updated because the content link had not been broken (only the item link).

Note that if you delete an item on the master page, it will only be deleted from the document page if you have broken neither item nor content links. If this is totally confusing to you, don't worry; it's one of those things that you just have to try before you really understand.

Applying Master Pages to Document Pages

It's easy to assign a new master page to a document page (however, because you use the Page Layout palette to do it, I'm going to hold off discussing this until the next section, "Master Pages and the Page Layout Palette"). You can also reassign a master page to a document page—which is like stripping the master page off, and then applying it again. When you perform either of these tasks, master items from the current master page are generally deleted and replaced by the new master items. However, the one exception is when you have already locally modified a master item while you're on a document page.

One of two things can happen when you assign a master page to a document page that has locally edited master items, and the determining factor is the Master Page Items feature in the General panel of the Preferences dialog box (Command-Option-Shift-Y or Ctrl-Alt-Shift-Y). You have two choices: Delete Changes and Keep Changes.

Delete Changes. If Master Page Items is set to Delete Changes, when you reapply a master page to a document page, every master item on a page is deleted and replaced with new master items—even if changes have been made locally. This is a great way to "reset" the page if you have accidentally made changes to master items: reapply a master page to a document page while Delete Changes is set in the General Preferences dialog box. All the locally modified items are deleted and reset back to the original master items.

Keep Changes. The alternative to deleting locally modified master items is keeping them. When Keep Changes is selected in the General Preferences dialog box, QuarkXPress skips over any master items that you have modified (changed their position, size, shape, font, text, and so on). This is the default setting when you start a document.

Note that the Delete Changes and Keep Changes preferences have no effect if you simply edit a master-page item—only when you apply or reapply a master page to a document page. (I discussed editing master-page items in the last section.)

▼ ▼

Tip: When Are Master Pages Reapplied? One of the most frustrating occurrences to both beginning and experienced QuarkXPress users is the seemingly random way QuarkXPress automatically reapplies master pages to your document pages. However, there's really nothing random about it. Simply put, QuarkXPress automatically reapplies a master page every time a page switches sides in a facing-pages layout.

If you add one page before page four, then page four becomes page five, flipping from a left to a right page in the spread. In this case, QuarkXPress automatically reapplies the master page. The result can be chaos in your document, depending on what changes you've made to the master-page items. If you add two pages before page four, then QuarkXPress won't automatically reapply the master page at all. This is the main reason that I always try to add or delete pages in even increments when I'm working with facing pages.

▼ ▼

Summing It Up

And that's really all there is to how the master-page feature works. It's simple and ingenious, and any advanced things that you do with it are based on these operational principles.

▼ ▼

Master Pages and the Page Layout Palette

If you've gotten this far, you've learned the hardest stuff about QuarkXPress's master pages. Now it's time to take the next step and learn another level of control by using the following additional controls.

▶ Creating new master pages

▶ Creating new master pages based on existing ones

▶ Naming and ordering master pages

▶ Applying master pages to document pages

▶ Deleting master pages

There are many ways to use multiple master pages. For example, most books are separated into several sections, including front matter, body text, and index. Each section is paginated and formatted differently from the body, with different (or no) headers or footers. You can create a master page for each of these sections. Multiple master pages are almost required for magazine production, where you may have a plethora of different sections: front matter, regular article pages, photo features, full-page ads, and small-ad sections, to name a few.

Multiple master pages are accessible through the Page Layout palette. I introduced the Page Layout palette in Chapter 2, *QuarkXPress Basics*. Now I'm going to concentrate on how you can use it to work with your master pages.

Page Layout Palette

If you look at the Page Layout palette for the facing-page document in Figure 4-16, you'll see that it's divided vertically into four areas: creation and deletion, master page, document layout, and page number/section.

Figure 4-16

Page Layout palettes for a single-sided and a facing-pages document

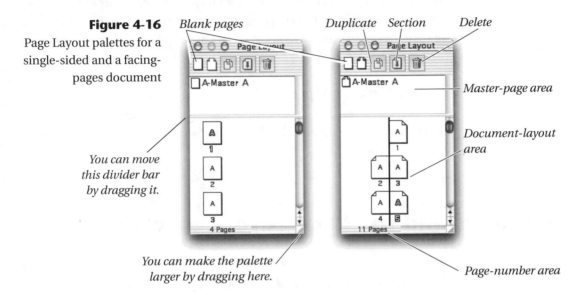

Blank pages   Duplicate   Section   Delete

Master-page area

Document-layout area

You can move this divider bar by dragging it.

You can make the palette larger by dragging here.

Page-number area

Creation and deletion area. At the top of the Page Layout palette is the creation and deletion area, which is used for creating, duplicating, and deleting both document and master pages. At the left, you see blank single-sided and facing-page icons (you can't edit these; they're always blank). Next to those icons are two buttons: one to duplicate master pages and the other to delete master or document pages. QuarkXPress 6 adds a button to open the Section dialog box, which I discuss in "Sections and Page Numbering" below.

There are two ways to create a new master page. First, you can drag a blank single-sided or facing-page icon into the master-page area (see Figure 4-17). Second, you can select a master page on the Page Layout palette and click the Duplicate button. There's only one way to delete a master page: select the master-page icon on the palette and click the Delete button (this also works for deleting document pages).

Note that deleting either a master or document page with the Delete button is not reversible with Undo (Command-Z or Ctrl-Z), so you should make sure you really want to do it.

▼ ▼

Tip: Avoiding Alerts. I don't know about you, but I often spout spontaneous invective when my computer alerts me to a dangerous procedure. Because I've used the program for so long, I *know* that what I'm doing can't be undone or is potentially lethal to my document. One example is the "Are you sure you want to delete these pages?" prompt when you click the Delete button in the Page Layout palette. QuarkXPress is trying to be helpful, because you can't reverse this action. But it typically just annoys me. However, if you Option-click (Alt-click) the Delete button, the pages are deleted without a prompt. Hoorah for progress.

Figure 4-17

Creating a new master page

Dragging a blank page to the master-page area changes the mouse icon to a page insertion symbol to indicate where the master page will be added.

▼ ▼

Tip: Retrieving Document-Layout Deletions. If you've deleted a master page from the Page Layout palette, the only way to get it back is by selecting Revert to Saved from the File menu. This, of course, only works if you've saved your document recently. Bear in mind that this method wipes out all changes you've made since your last save, so pause a moment and reflect before you jump into this last resort. (You can also revert to your last minisave—if you had Auto Save turned on in the Preferences dialog box—by holding down Option or Alt and selecting the Revert to Saved menu item.)

▼ ▼

You can also create document pages in this palette by dragging either one of the blank-page icons to the document area. (Of course, if your document is single-sided, the blank facing-pages icon will be grayed out . . . you can't add a facing page to a single-sided document.)

▼ ▼

Tip: Where Is the Page Added? Where you let go of the mouse button when you insert a page by dragging it into the Document area of the Page Layout palette determines where the page goes. If you drop the page when the cursor appears as a gray outline of a page, you're saying "Drop the page right here." This is how you can make a multipage spread (see "Multipage Spreads," later in this chapter).

On the other hand, if you let go of the mouse button when the cursor appears as a little black arrow, you're saying "Put the page here in the regular flow of the document." You get this black arrow cursor when you drag close to a page, but not on top of it.

▼ ▼

Master-page area. Just below the blank-document icons and the Delete and Duplicate buttons is the master-page area. Here's where you create, name, and access master pages. To create a new master page, as I said earlier, you can drag a blank-page icon into this area or select a master-page icon that's already in this area and click the Duplicate button. Duplicating another master page is the fastest way to make one master page that's based on another.

A default name is assigned to a master page when it's created: the first is "A-Master A," the second is "B-Master B," and so on. You can assign a new name to a master page by clicking on its name in the Page Layout palette (in Windows, you must double-click on the name). You can type up to three characters before a hyphen, and then up to 60 more. If you don't type a hyphen, XPress assigns a prefix and types a hyphen for you. The name you assign appears on menus throughout the program. The prefix (the characters before the hyphen) shows up in the page icons on the Page Layout palette.

If you create more master pages than you can see at once, you can drag on the divider bar between the master-page area and the document-layout area (like the split-window feature in Microsoft Word).

If you have more than two master pages, XPress lets you move them around by dragging their icons up and down. However, be careful: Dropping one master page on top of another tells XPress to make the second master page exactly like the first, wiping out the master-page items on that page in the process. (Fortunately, XPress alerts you first.) Instead, wait until you see the cursor change to a small black arrow; that means "Move the master page here."

Document-layout area. The largest part of the Page Layout palette is the document-layout area. This area shows icons of the document's pages, numbered and positioned in the order of their actual appearance in the document (see "Manipulating Your Layout" in Chapter 2, *QuarkXPress Basics*, for more on the document-layout area). Each page icon on the palette displays the master page it's based on. When you first create a new layout space, only one page is visible, and it is based on "A-Master A."

Remember that you can jump to a page in your document by double-clicking on its icon in this area.

Page-number area. In the lower-left corner of the Page Layout palette sits the page-number area. When no pages are selected on the Page Layout palette, this area displays the total number of pages in the document, but when you click on a page in the document-layout area, this area shows the page number (the page number of the currently selected page, not necessarily the one that you're looking at in the document window). This page number is the same as the number that sits under the page icon in the document-layout area of the palette. If you select more than one page on the palette, this area just shows you the number of pages. Not very helpful, and pretty boring (see "Tip: Absolute Page Numbers," later in this chapter).

Applying Master Pages

There are two ways to apply the formatting of a master page to an existing document page (I sometimes refer to this as "tagging a document page with a master page").

▶ You can drag a master-page icon on top of a document-page icon; it's OK to release the mouse button as soon as the page icon is highlighted. The document page assumes the formatting of that master page.

▶ You can select the page or pages to which you want to apply the master page (remember that you can Shift-click to select a range of pages, or Command-click (Ctrl-click) to select individual pages out of sequential order) and Option-click (Alt-click) on the desired master page in the master-page area. This is the only way to apply a master page to a number of pages at the same time.

Unmodified master items (from the old master page) are deleted and replaced with the new master items. Items that you have modified may or may not be deleted (see "Applying Master Pages to Document Pages," earlier in this chapter). You can also apply one master page to another by the same method.

If you don't want any master page applied to a particular page (if you want to turn master pages off for one page), you can apply one of the blank-document icons to it instead. Just do the same thing: either drop the blank-page icon on top of a document page in the palette, or Option-click (Alt-click) on the icon with the page(s) selected.

▼ ▼

Tip: Copying Master Pages. Have you ever wanted to copy a master page from one document to another? Kinda difficult, isn't it? Well, no, not really. Put both documents into Thumbnail viewing mode and drag a page from the first document into the second. The master page that was assigned to that document page comes along. Then you can delete the document page, and the master page stays in the second document. Unfortunately, the only way to copy a master page from one layout space to another is to first copy a page to a different document in a different window, and then copy it to the layout space.

▼ ▼

Making Pages

I've been discussing moving pages around and deleting them, but it's been slightly premature, as I hadn't yet gotten to adding new pages to a document. I cover that procedure here.

There are two ways to add pages to your document: using the Insert Pages dialog box or using the Page Layout palette.

Insert Pages

The first way you can add pages to your layout is by selecting Insert from the Pages menu. This brings up the Insert Pages dialog box (see Figure 4-18). You can also open the Insert Pages dialog box by Control-clicking/right-clicking on a page icon in the Page Layout palette and choosing Insert Pages from the context menu.

You can type the number of pages you want to add in the Insert field, and then select where you want those pages to be added. You have three choices: before a page, after a page, and at the end of the document. The first two require that you choose a page before or after which the page(s) should be added; the third requires no additional number, as it places the pages after the last page in the document.

Before you click OK, though, you need to think about two other things in this dialog box: the Link to Current Text Chain checkbox, and the Master Page choice. Let's look at these in reverse order.

Master Page choice. You can choose which master page you want your new pages to be based on by selecting one from the Master Page popup menu. Or, if you like, you can base new pages on blank single-sided or facing pages (of course, you can choose the latter only if you're working with a facing-page document).

Figure 4-18
The Insert Pages
dialog box

Link to Current Text Chain. If a text box is selected on your page, and the master page on which you are basing your inserted pages has an automatic text-link box, then you can have the inserted pages automatically linked with the text box you have selected. This is a potentially confusing concept, so let's look at it carefully.

Let's say you have a text box on a page, and it's overflowing with text. Let's also say that your master page "C-FeatureOpener" has an automatic text-link box on it that is enabled (linked to the automatic text-link icon).

1. Select the text box on the document page.

2. Select Insert from the Page menu.

3. Add a page based on master page "C-FeatureOpener" at the end of the document.

If you turn on the Link to Current Text Chain option in the Insert Pages dialog box, then the text from your document-page text box automatically links to your inserted pages. If you do not select Link to Current Text Chain, then the pages are still added, but there is no link between your text box and the text boxes on those pages. You can, however, link them up manually using the Link tool.

▼ ▼

Tip: Don't Make Documents Too Long. It's a good idea not to make documents too big. Extra-long documents increase the chances that you may run into the dreaded "Bad File Format" message that can mean a terminally corrupted file. If you must make a 1,000-page book, break it down into smaller segments! I don't really have any hard and fast rule about how big files should be, though. I tend to keep files under 5 or 10 MB in size, which for a book usually translates to under 100 pages; for a magazine or catalog it may be as few as 4 or 6 pages. Remember: never make a file longer than you'd care to recreate if you had to.

▼ ▼

Document-Layout Insertions

The second method for adding pages is to insert them via the Page Layout palette. Like everything else on this palette, you add pages by dragging icons. To add a page based on a master page, drag that master-page icon down to where you want it to be (before a page, after a page, at the end of a document, or as a page in a spread). If you don't want the page to be based on a master page, you can drag the single-sided or facing-page icon into place instead. (As mentioned above, you can only drag a facing-page icon if you are working with a facing-page document.)

If you want to add more than one page at a time, or want to add pages that are linked to the current text chain, then you must hold down the Option (Alt) key while clicking and dragging the page icon into place. When you let go of the icon, QuarkXPress opens the Insert Pages dialog box. You can select the appropriate items as described above.

▼ ▼

Tip: Unintentional Multipage Spreads. There are problems just waiting to unfurl when you move pages around in spreads. If you insert the pages next to an existing page, you may be unknowingly creating a multipage spread instead of adding pages the way you want. The trick is to be careful about what icons you see when you're dropping the page. If you see a page icon, you'll get a spread; if you see a black arrow icon, you'll add pages to the document flow.

▼ ▼

Tip: Bleeding over Spreads. Bleeding an object off a page is easy: you just place it off the edge of the page on to the pasteboard. But when you're working with a document in facing-page mode, you can't bleed an object off the right side of a left-hand page or the left side of a right-hand page because there's another page in the way. Fortunately, you can get around this obstacle by using the Page Layout palette. Let's say you want to bleed an object off the right side of page two (a left hand page).

1. Open the Page Layout palette or go into Thumbnails view.

2. Drag page three straight down until it's almost over page five, and let go when you see the small black arrow point downward.

The following pages should be pushed out of the way, but still retain their spread settings and page numbers (see Figure 4-19).

Figure 4-19
Setting up for a bleed into the gutter between pages

▼ ▼

Modifying Your Pages

Fortunately for desktop publishers, you can change the foundation of your document significantly more easily than a construction worker can change the foundation of a building. Not only can you modify your master pages in all sorts of ways, as we've seen, but you can modify the underlying page size, margins, column guides, and more. Let's look at each of these controls.

Changing Page Size

Even after you've clicked OK in the New Project dialog box and begun adding pages to a document, you can still change the page size for each layout space in your file by using the Layout Properties dialog box (choose Layout Properties from the Layout menu; see Figure 4-20). Note that this dialog box bears a striking resemblance to a portion of the New Project dialog box. The rules are just the same (see "Page Size," at the beginning of this chapter).

Your only real limitation in modifying page size is the size of any objects you have already placed on the page. QuarkXPress won't let you make a page so small that page elements would "fall off" the pasteboard (the size of the pasteboard surrounding each page is determined by the size of your document page). If this is a limiting factor, you may be able to work around the problem by adjusting the width of the pasteboard (see "Display Preferences," in Chapter 2, *QuarkXPress Basics*). The program also prevents you from making the document so small that the margin guides bump into each other. If that's the problem, first change the margin guides (I'll tell you how to do that in just a moment).

Figure 4-20
The Layout Properties
dialog box

Changing Facing Pages

You can use the Layout Properties dialog box to change one other page feature: facing pages. If you originally made your document single-sided, you can change to a facing-page document by checking Facing Pages in the Layout Properties dialog box. Facing-page documents can have both single-sided and facing-page master pages. When you turn on the Facing Pages option, the blank facing-page icon is enabled on the Page Layout palette; XPress does not, however, change your current master pages into facing-page master pages.

You cannot change a facing-page document to a single-sided document if you have any facing master pages. If you need to change a facing-page document to a single-sided layout (there's rarely a reason to do so), first delete all the facing master pages (select them from the Page Layout palette and click the Delete button), then turn off the Facing Pages checkbox in the Layout Properties dialog box.

Changing Margins and Guides

As I mentioned earlier, every page in your layout has the same margins until you create multiple master pages, each with different margins. When you first open a master page, its margin guides are set to the values you specified in the New Project dialog box. You can change these margins by selecting Master Guides from the Page menu. Remember that the Master Guides menu item is only available when a master page is being displayed.

Migrants from PageMaker should be aware that QuarkXPress's column guides cannot be repositioned by dragging them with the mouse. Instead, you change the Column Guides settings in the Master Guides dialog box. QuarkXPress lets you have a different number of columns and varied gutter sizes for each master page (all the columns must be the same width, however). If you want to have no column guides on a page, type "1" in the Columns field.

Automatic Page Insertion

Importing a long text document can be a harrowing experience when you're working with automatically linked text boxes. The text flows beyond page one and—it seems—into the netherworld. Where does the rest of the text go when the first text box is filled? QuarkXPress lets you control this with the Auto Page Insertion popup menu in the General panel of the Preferences dialog box. You have four choices: End of Story, End of Section, End of Document, and Off. The default setting (the way it's set up if you don't change anything) is End of Story.

End of Story. With the End of Story option selected, QuarkXPress inserts new pages right after the page containing the last text box in a story, and they bear the master-page formatting of the page that held that box. For instance, if your story starts on page one and jumps to page five, any text overflow from the page-five text box causes one or more pages to be inserted following page five, not page one.

End of Section. If you select End of Section, pages are inserted after the last page in a section (see "Sections and Page Numbering," below). Additional pages bear the master-page formatting of the last page in that section. Thus, if your page-one story jumps to page five, and page five is part of a section that ends with page eight, new pages inserted because of text overflow appear right after page eight.

End of Document. This option causes pages to be inserted after the last page of the document, no matter how long it is and regardless of any sections you might have set up. Inserted pages bear the master-page formatting of the last page of the document.

If you have only one story and one section in a document, then these three settings all have the same effect.

Off. When Auto Page Insertion is set to Off, QuarkXPress never adds pages automatically. Instead, you must add pages manually (see "Making Pages," earlier in this chapter). I often set Auto Page Insertion to Off when I get tired of XPress adding lots of new pages for me (this is also the setting I typically recommend to new users, who get skittish when XPress adds pages automatically). Then I'll insert pages as I need or want them, linking them manually or using the Insert Pages dialog box.

Text Linking

Remember, the Automatic Page Insertion feature only works if the master page that's getting inserted has an automatic text-link box. That makes sense, because pages are always inserted based on text flowing through the automatic text chain. You cannot have *automatic page insertion* without an *automatic text link,* and you cannot have that without an *automatic text-link box.*

▼ ▼

Multipage Spreads

Back when the rest of the world thought that facing-page spreads were pretty nifty, Quark came along and added the capability to build three-page spreads.

In fact, you can quickly and easily build a spread with four, five, or any number of pages, as long as the combined width of the pages doesn't exceed 48 inches.

Once again, this is a job for the Page Layout palette (this also works in Thumbnail mode). Spreads can be created in both facing-page and single-sided documents by dragging a page icon (either a new page or one already in the document) to the right side of a right page or to the left side of a left page. For this purpose, single-sided documents are considered to be made entirely of right pages, but there aren't many times that you'd be doing this with a single-sided document. The pasteboard (represented by the dark-gray area of the palette) automatically expands to accommodate the pages. Figure 4-21 shows an example of creating a three-page spread in a facing-page document.

Note that when you drag a page over to create a multipage spread, you shouldn't let go of the mouse button if you see the little black arrow icon. That'll reshuffle the file rather than build a spread. Instead, you should only let go when you see a dark page icon in the place where you want the spread page to be.

Figure 4-21
Making a three-page spread

Sections and Page Numbering

Earlier in this chapter I discussed how to apply automatic page numbering to your document's master pages. Here I talk about how to customize those page numbers and create multiple sections within a single document.

Ordinarily, a QuarkXPress document has one section. Page numbers start with the Arabic numeral "1" and go up consecutively, page by page. (I can't figure out why they're called Arabic numerals, because the numbers in Arabic are totally different; nonetheless, that's what normal, plain ol' numbers are called.)

However, by using the Section feature, you can change the starting page number, the page-number style, and you can add multiple sections that all have their own page-numbering style.

Changing Your Starting Page Number

Whenever you make a new section in your document, you're starting a new page-numbering scheme; in fact, that's really the only good reason for using sections.

For instance, let's say you're producing a book, and each chapter is saved in a separate QuarkXPress file. If the first chapter ends on page 32, you can tell QuarkXPress to start the page numbers in Chapter 2 at page 33, and so on. To do this, go to the first page of the document (the page on which you want to change the numbering), and select Section from the Page menu. Then turn on the Section Start checkbox. Type the starting page number for your document, and click OK (see Figure 4-22). XPress 6 gives you two more ways of opening the Section dialog box: You can click on the Section icon at the top of the Pages palette or Control-click (right-click) on a page icon on the Pages palette and select Section from the context menu.

Figure 4-22

Setting up a
new section

The first page of a new section always has an asterisk after its name. This doesn't print out. It's just a sign that QuarkXPress gives you on screen, saying that this is a section that's beginning.

You can have as many sections in a document as you want, each starting with a different page number. If you make the fifth page in your document a new section and set it to start on page 47, then your document's page numbering goes like this: "1, 2, 3, 4, 47, 48, 49 . . . ."

▼ ▼

Tip: Absolute Page Numbers. There is a hidden feature on the Page Layout palette: If you Option-click (Alt-click) on a page icon in the document-layout area of the palette, the page-number area displays the page's absolute number (for example, the 34th page in the document). This is extremely helpful when your pages are numbered in roman numerals or when you're using multiple sections.

▼ ▼

Tip: Starting on the Left. Do you want the first page of your document to be a left-hand page? If you've tried to simply delete page one, you've already found that page two jumps up to the right-hand page one spot. The problem is that left-hand pages are always numbered evenly in QuarkXPress. If you want page one to be on the left, use the Section dialog box to change its number to something even, like two. (Sorry, zero doesn't work!)

The problem is that only page one moves over to the left side; following pages don't follow along, and there's a blank spot where the second page should be (see Figure 4-23). Fortunately, you can drag (in the Page Layout palette) the second page up to the right of the first page. Don't let go of the mouse button when you see the page icon in the palette; make sure you see the small, black right arrow cursor first. Alternately, you can first assign page two to be the section start, and then delete page one.

▼ ▼

Changing the Page-Numbering Style

QuarkXPress lets you choose from five formats for numbering pages in the Section dialog box.

- ► Arabic numerals (1, 2, 3, 4, etc.)

- ► Uppercase Roman numerals (I, II, III, IV, etc.)

- ► Lowercase Roman numerals (i, ii, iii, iv, etc.)

- ► Capital letters (A, B, C, D, etc.)

- ► Lowercase letters (a, b, c, d, etc.)

To pick one of these numbering styles for a section, go to the first page in the section, select Section using one of the methods described above, and choose a numbering format from the Format popup menu.

Prefixes

Automatic page numbers can contain more than just a number in the five formats listed above. You can also add a prefix of up to four characters to the page

Figure 4-23
Starting with a left page

  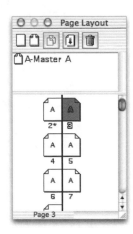

number. For example, you may want the page numbers in a book appendix to read "A-1," "A-2," and so on. The "A-" is a prefix to the Arabic numerals. You can type this kind of prefix in the Prefix field of the Section dialog box. This prefix not only appears on the Page Layout palette and in the automatic page numbers, it even shows up at the top of the page when you print with registration marks (see Chapter 13, *Printing*).

Automatic "Continued . . ." Pagination

In magazines and newspapers, where stories can jump from page six to 96, it is often helpful to have a "Continued on Page X" message at the bottom of the column from which text is jumping, and a "Continued from Page X" message at the top of the column to which it jumps. These are sometimes called "jump lines." QuarkXPress can't make these lines for you, but it can revise the page numbers in them automatically. This is useful because you may change links, or insert or delete new pages, or move the text boxes from one page to another, and each of these will require a change in the jump line's page numbers. If you use XPress's automatic page numbers, you won't have to go through every page and manually update the numbers.

To Create a "Continued on . . ." Message

It's easy to create these jump lines (see Figure 4-24) using the Previous Box Page Number and the Next Box Page Number characters: Command-2 and Command-4 (Ctrl-2 and Ctrl-4). If you press Command-4 (Ctrl-4) in a text box, XPress automatically replaces it with the page number of whatever page the current story links to. For instance, let's say the story on page one links to a text

Figure 4-24
Jump lines

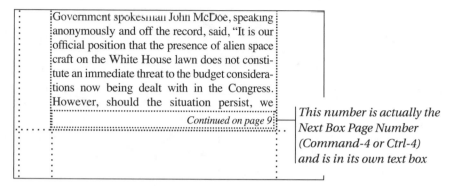

Government spokesman John McDoe, speaking anonymously and off the record, said, "It is our official position that the presence of alien space craft on the White House lawn does not consti- tute an immediate threat to the budget considera- tions now being dealt with in the Congress. However, should the situation persist, we

Continued on page 9

This number is actually the Next Box Page Number (Command-4 or Ctrl-4) and is in its own text box

box on page nine. If you press Command-4 (Ctrl-4) somewhere in the story on page one, XPress replaces it with the number "9" (the page to which the story links). Similarly, if you press Command-2 (Ctrl-2) somewhere in the story on page nine, QuarkXPress replaces it with the number "1" (the page from which the story links).

This is pretty cool, but it's not very useful because it's nearly impossible to include a "continued on page . . . " jump line in the middle of your story. It just doesn't work. So the folks at Quark built a hidden feature into these automat- ic page numbers: if either the Command-2 (Ctrl-2) or the Command-4 (Ctrl-4) character is in a text box that doesn't link to anything *and* if that text box is sitting on top of a text box that does link to something, then XPress uses the links in the lower text box to determine what numbers to use for the char- acters.

That means you can create a new little text box and type in it "Continued on page . . . " and then press Command-4 (Ctrl-4). If this text box is not on top of any other text boxes, the Command-4 (Ctrl-4) character is replaced with "<None>". However, in the example above, as soon as you drag it on top of the text box on page one, the number updates to show the number "9," because that's what the underlying story is linked to.

If your text links change, pages get shuffled or renumbered, or an act of god occurs, QuarkXPress always knows where your text is going to or coming from and it updates the Next Box Page Number and Previous Box Page Number characters.

Nonetheless, these jump lines can sometimes get confused. When QuarkXPress sees one of these jump lines, it looks at any text box that is behind the jump line. If there is more than one text box behind the jump-line text box, QuarkXPress chooses the one that is "closest" to it: the text box that is on the next layer down.

To create a "Continued from . . ." message. You can create a "Continued from . . ." jump line by following the same procedures for creating a "Continued on . . ." jump line, but you can place the new text box at the top of the column. When you come to the page number, press Command-2 (Ctrl-2) for the Previous Box Page Number character, which shows the page number of the previous text box in the chain. This number is also automatically updated as necessary.

Your messages don't have to read "Continued on . . ." and "Continued from . . . ." You can type any words you want—for instance, "Started on page <None>" or even "If you really care about finishing this story, you'll have to flip past the bulk of this magazine and go all the way to page "<None>", where you'll find it buried among the facial cream ads." What matters is that you type the relevant placeholder character somewhere in your message text box.

▼ ▼

Foundations

Like a construction worker on the job, you are now ready to build your pages with the understanding and confidence that you've got a strong infrastructure to hold the document up. First you can use the tools discussed in Chapter 3, *Tools of the Trade*, to build text and picture boxes on your master pages and document pages. And next you can fill those boxes with text and pictures; that's where I'm headed now.

5

WORD PROCESSING

When you think of QuarkXPress, you think of typography. But before you can set type in QuarkXPress, you somehow have to get the words onto your page. QuarkXPress has been a capable word processor in its own right. Style sheets, find and change, a spelling checker, and even drag-and-drop text editing are all elements that have made this program a competent—though not exceptional—word processor.

However, just because you can use QuarkXPress as a word processor doesn't mean that you should. In complex documents and on many lower-end computers, QuarkXPress can become so slow that a skilled typist can get ahead of it. In this chapter, I'll examine the strengths and the weaknesses of writing and editing in QuarkXPress, including its powerful Find/Change feature and its spelling checker (I'll cover style sheets in Chapter 7, *Copy Flow*).

▼ ▼

Entering and Editing Text

The most basic aspect of entering text into a QuarkXPress document is making sure that what you type shows up where you want it. QuarkXPress novices often become flustered when they open a document and start typing, only to find that nothing is happening. That's because to enter text, you must use the Content tool, and you must have selected a text box.

Selecting and Navigating

As I mentioned in the Preface, I assume that you're already familiar with the basic mouse and editing techniques used by almost every Macintosh and Windows application. However, QuarkXPress stretches beyond that interface, adding many features to the standard Macintosh and Windows methods of moving the insertion point and selecting text. One of the many things I like about QuarkXPress is that it provides more than one way to do the same thing; you can use either the mouse or the keyboard to select and to navigate.

Using the mouse. As with any program, you can select a range of text by dragging the pointer through it, or you can select a word by double-clicking on it. But QuarkXPress also has additional multiple-click selections (see Table 5-1). If you triple-click, you select a line of text. Quadruple-clicking selects a paragraph, and quintuple-clicking selects all the text in the active box's text chain. (I don't know about you, but clicking five times in succession is difficult for me; instead, I just press Command-A (Ctrl-A), which does the same thing.)

If you hold down the Shift key and click anywhere in your text chain, all the text from the previous location of the insertion point to the location of your click is selected.

If you select a range of text in a text box, then deselect the box and edit in other boxes, QuarkXPress remembers the selection. When you reselect that text box, the same text is still selected in it (this works until you close the document or quit XPress).

▼ ▼

Tip: Extend by Word. If you continue to press down on the mouse button after your final click, you can extend your selection by dragging. If you've selected a word by double-clicking, for instance, you can drag to select more text, word by word. And if you've selected a paragraph with four clicks, you can similarly drag to increase your selection, paragraph by paragraph.

▼ ▼

Table 5-1
Effects of multiple clicks

TO SELECT...	CLICK...
A word and contiguous punctuation	Twice
A line	Three times
A paragraph	Four times
An entire story	Five times

Using the keyboard. You can use the keyboard to duplicate most of the selections you can make with the mouse. You can also do many things with the keyboard that are not possible with the mouse alone (see Table 5-2). For instance, you can quickly jump to the beginning of a line just by pressing Command-Option-Left Arrow (Ctrl-Alt-Left Arrow).

Holding down the Shift key in combination with any of the keyboard movement commands selects all text between the insertion point's original location and the location to which the key combination sends it. In the example above, you could select all the text from the cursor point to the beginning of the line just by adding Shift to the keystroke.

▼ ▼

Tip: The Lazy Man's Way to Follow a Text Chain. You know that QuarkXPress has keystrokes that take you to the next or previous page in your layout, but what about a shortcut to go to the next page in a story? (If your story jumps to another page of your layout, as often happens in magazines and newspapers, this is important.) All you have to do is place the insertion point at the beginning or end of the story's text box on the current page. If you're at the beginning of the text box, press the Left or Up Arrow key to move the insertion point out of the current box to the previous box in the chain. If you're at the end of the box, similarly press the Right or Down Arrow key to jump the insertion point to the next box in the text chain.

As soon as you move the insertion point out of the current box, QuarkXPress follows it, scrolling automatically to the page containing the text box to which you've moved the insertion point. If possible, QuarkXPress even centers the box nicely in the document window.

▼ ▼

Table 5-2
Keyboard
text editing

TO MOVE TO THE . . .	PRESS . . .
Previous character	Left Arrow
Next character	Right Arrow
Previous line	Up Arrow
Next line	Down Arrow
Previous word	Command-/Ctrl-Left Arrow
Next word	Command-/Ctrl-Right Arrow
Start of line	Command-Option-/Ctrl-Alt-Left Arrow
End of line	Command-Option-/Ctrl-Alt-Right Arrow
Start of story	Command-Option-/Ctrl-Alt-Up Arrow
End of story	Command-Option-/Ctrl-Alt-Down Arrow

▼ ▼

Tip: Navigating Out of the Box. I find the ability to quickly jump to the beginning or end of a story by pressing Command-Option-Up Arrow or Command-Option-Down Arrow (Ctrl-Alt-Up Arrow or Ctrl-Alt-Down Arrow) especially handy. It can save you a lot of scrolling if you forget the exact page on which a story starts or finishes. Also, I use it all the time to quickly select all the text from the cursor to the beginning or end of the story by adding the Shift key. For instance, let's say you've got too much text in a text box and it overflows, producing an overset mark. You know that the overset text isn't important, so you want to delete it or move it to some other text box. You could use the text-linking tools, but it's sometimes faster to place the cursor after the last word in the text box and press Command-Option-Shift-Down Arrow (Ctrl-Alt-Down Arrow). This selects the overset text (even though you can't see it). Now you can delete it or cut it.

▼ ▼

Deleting Text

There are a number of ways to delete text in QuarkXPress (see Table 5-3). You can, of course, use the Delete key to delete text to the left of the insertion point, one character at a time, or to remove a text selection. QuarkXPress also lets you delete the character to the right of the insertion point by holding down the Shift key while pressing Delete. Similarly, Command-Delete (Ctrl-Delete) gets rid of the entire word to the left of the insertion point, and Command-Shift-Delete (Ctrl-Shift-Delete) removes the word to the right of the insertion point.

Drag-and-Drop Text

Drag-and-drop text editing is an easy way of copying or moving text from one location to another in a story, but it can cause trouble if you don't know how it works. To use drag-and-drop text editing, select some text, then drag the selection to another location in the text chain. As you move the mouse, you'll see an insertion point move along with it. When the insertion point reaches the place where you want the selected text to go, release the mouse button, and *presto!* Your text is cut from its original location and placed at the insertion point.

If you try this right now on your copy of XPress, it probably won't work because Drag and Drop is an option in the Preferences dialog box (Command-Y or Ctrl-Y, then switch to the Interactive tab), and by default it is turned off. If you like this feature, go ahead and turn it on.

You can also copy a selection, instead of just moving it, by holding down the Shift key as you drag. Note that any text you drag-move or drag-copy also gets placed on the Clipboard (replacing whatever was there). Also, at least for

Table 5-3

Keyboard deletions

To delete . . .	Press . . .
Previous character	Delete
Next character	Shift-Delete or Del key (Extended keyboard)
Previous word	Command-/Ctrl-Delete
Next word	Command-Shift-/Ctrl-Shift-Delete
Any select text	Delete

now, you can't drag-copy text between unlinked text boxes, or between documents—you can do it only within continuous text chains.

I rarely turn this feature on, not because I don't like it, but because I too often mess up my text when it's on by accidentally dragging a word or sentence when I don't mean to. This is the sort of feature that I'll turn on only when I need to use it; then I'll turn it off again.

▼ ▼

Tip: Speeding Up Text Entry. Unless there's a really good reason to do it, I don't recommend typing a lot of text directly into a text box in XPress. Obviously, XPress doesn't have important word-processing features like an outliner, renumbering, and so on. But perhaps the most important reason to consider using a word processor is speed. If you're working on an older (slower) computer, writing and editing text in QuarkXPress can seem incredibly slow. Entering text becomes so sluggish that the program can't keep up with even a moderately fast typist.

This happens because XPress has to do much more work than a typical word processor does whenever it must reflow text. If you're working on a long story that goes through several pages of linked boxes, and the text has to flow through and around other page elements, this complexity also adds to the computations that QuarkXPress must perform whenever you change or add text. Plus, XPress may have to compute kerning and other typographic styling, which slows it down further.

Nonetheless, if you need to type in XPress, here are a few things you can do to speed up the process. (Note that if you're working on a fast computer and you're not experiencing slow-downs, you can just go ahead and ignore these suggestions.)

▶ **Dummy text boxes.** Try typing or editing in a "dummy" text box in the pasteboard area of the page where you want to enter or change text. This is particularly helpful when the text box on the page is nonrectangular or the text has a complicated wrap around other objects. By typing in a plain ol' rectangular text box on the pasteboard, XPress doesn't have to work hard calculating how the text should wrap.

▶ HYPHENATION. Turning off Auto Hyphenation in each of your H&J sets can speed up XPress a little bit (see Chapter 6, *Type and Typography*). Don't forget to turn hyphenation back on when you're ready to proof or print your document.

▶ JUSTIFICATION. Don't set the horizontal alignment to Justified while you're typing. XPress has to do a lot of work to figure out how to justify the text each time you type a letter.

▶ KERNING. You might consider turning off automatic kerning in your document in the Preferences dialog box. This won't help a lot, but sometimes every little bit counts.

▼ ▼

Tip: Copy and Paste Commonly Used Characters. Typing bullets at the beginning of each line in a long list can drive anybody absolutely bonkers. The same thing goes with any commonly repeated character, especially if the character is in a different font or requires a hard-to-remember modifier key. Instead, just copy one of them and paste them wherever you need them. Yes, the Command-V (Ctrl-V) for pasting is also a keystroke, but it's easier than some keystrokes and certainly easier than changing the font, color, etc., all the time.

▼ ▼

Tip: Setting Text in All Caps. Never type two spaces after a period. Never type five spaces for an indent. Never cross the road without looking both ways. These are rules to live by, and if you follow them, they'll rarely steer you wrong. Here's another one: never type text in all capital letters in QuarkXPress. It's much more versatile to select any text you want capped and apply the All Caps type style (Command-Shift-K or Ctrl-Shift-K). Then, later, if you change your mind, you can countermand the style rather than having to retype all the text.

Of course, to every one of these rules there are exceptions. The exception to this one is when you're exporting the text as either ASCII text or another format that doesn't support the All Caps type style.

▼ ▼

Importing Text

More often than not, text is prepared in a word processor, then imported into a QuarkXPress document for final layout. The best way to get text into a text box in XPress is to import it using the Get Text command on the File menu. In order to access this command, you must have both a text box and the Content tool selected.

1. Position the insertion point where you want the text to be brought into the text box.

2. Choose Get Text from the File menu (Command-E or Ctrl-E).

3. When the Get Text dialog box appears, select one of the files listed. It displays all the files that are in word-processing formats that QuarkXPress can import (see the next section, "What Filters Are, and How to Use Them").

4. Press Return, or click the Open button.

While you're in the Get Text dialog box, you have two additional options for importing the file: Convert Quotes and Include Style Sheets.

▶ **Convert Quotes.** If you'd like QuarkXPress to automatically convert straight double and single quotes (" and ') to curly double and single quotes (" " and ' '), and double hyphens (--) to true em dashes (—), check Convert Quotes in the Get Text dialog box. I almost always leave this option turned on.

▶ **Include Style Sheets.** I almost always check the Include Style Sheets box so that XPress will include the file's style sheets (if there are any). Even if there aren't any style sheets specified in the word processing document, it's usually better to leave this option turned on, or else you may accidentally apply No Style to the text (see Chapter 7, *Copy Flow*, for more on style sheets and XPress Tags, and how this checkbox affects them both).

What Filters Are, and How to Use Them

QuarkXPress uses XTensions called filters to convert text to and from word-processing formats. Because they're XTensions, you can activate or deactivate them using the XTension Manager (see "XTensions" in Chapter 2, *QuarkXPress Basics*). There are also third-party word processing filters available that let you import various weird formats. Because these filters are XTensions, you can deactivate the filters you don't regularly use, making XPress load faster and require less RAM

While the MS Word filter usually works reasonably well, it is notoriously buggy, and you should periodically check to see if there's a new one available from the Quark Web site. Also, note that QuarkXPress now ships with an RTF filter which lets you import and export Rich Text Format files—if you have trouble importing a file from Microsoft Word or any other word processor, try saving it in the RTF format instead. In Chapter 7, *Copy Flow*, I explain why you should be careful about what word processor you use, and why I usually use Microsoft Word.

▼ ▼

Tip: Fast Saves from Word. This tip is really directed more at Microsoft Word, but because so many QuarkXPress users bring files in from Word (we do), I thought this was relevant: Never use Fast Save in Microsoft Word. Fast Save is a feature that saves time in saving documents, but increases trouble down the line (both in Word and in XPress). For instance, text can get "lost" from one save to another, and sometimes text doesn't import correctly into QuarkXPress when the file was fast saved. To get around Fast Save, go to the Preferences dialog box in Microsoft Word and turn off the Allow Fast Saves checkbox.

Finding and Changing

QuarkXPress has a powerful Find/Change feature that is too often overlooked and underused. You can use this feature to look for and change either text or formatting (or both at the same time), and it can do this within a story or throughout a layout.

Those of you who are familiar with XPress version 3 will notice two significant differences with the Find/Change feature. First, it is now a palette rather than a dialog box, so it always floats above your document (in earlier versions, it would often get lost behind other windows). Second, you can now search for and replace character and paragraph style sheets (I discuss style sheets at length in Chapter 7, *Copy Flow*).

Where QuarkXPress Looks

When it searches with the Find/Change feature, QuarkXPress can check either the entire text chain connected to the active text box, or it can look for and change text throughout an entire layout. (You cannot search more than one layout at a time.) If you have a text box selected, QuarkXPress searches through the story *from the location of the insertion point* to the end of the story (note that the button in the palette is called Find Next; that means "the next one after the cursor position").

There are two ways to search an entire story from the very beginning. First, you can put the insertion point at the very beginning of the story (press Command-Option-Up Arrow or Ctrl-Alt-Up Arrow). Better yet, you can leave the insertion point where it is in the story, and hold down the Option key to turn the Find Next button into the Find First button. (The fastest way to find the first instance of a word is to press Command-F or Ctrl-F to open or activate the Find/Change palette, type the word to be found, then press Option-Return or Option-Enter on the Macintosh, or Alt-Enter in Windows.)

If you want QuarkXPress to check all the text in the layout rather than just a single story, you must turn on the Layout checkbox in the Find/Change palette. When this option is turned on, XPress searches the top-most text box on a page first (in terms of layer order, not position on the page), which can be confusing if you're not sure which text boxes are "on top" of other text boxes.

Note that turning on the Layout option only searches one layout's pages; if you want to search the master pages, too, you have to do a separate search. If you're currently displaying a document's master pages, the Layout checkbox is labeled Masters, and you can use it to search all the layout's master pages at once.

Specifying Text

Generally, people want to search and replace text regardless of the text's formatting attributes. To do this, you can use the Find/Change palette as it first appears when you select the Find/Change command from the Edit menu (or press Command-F or Ctrl-F; see Figure 5-1). Enter the text you want QuarkXPress to find in the Find What field, then enter the replacement text in the Change To field.

Special characters. It's easy enough to search for normal words or phrases, but what about invisible characters? It turns out that you can enter certain special characters in the Find What and Change To fields with the aid of the Command or Ctrl key. For example, if you want to search for all the new-paragraph characters in a layout (what you get when you press Return at the end of a paragraph), you select the Find What field and press Command-Return (Ctrl-Enter). This appears in the field as "\p". You could just type "\p", but who needs to clutter up their brain with weird codes like that?

Table 5-4 shows characters you can enter in these fields, how to type them, and how they appear in the fields. Of course, because all these special characters use the backslash, to search for the backslash character itself in the Find

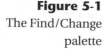

Figure 5-1
The Find/Change palette

Table 5-4

Typing special characters
in the Find/Change
palette

TO ENTER THIS CHARACTER . . .	PRESS . . .	OR TYPE . . .
Tab	Command-/Ctrl-Tab	\t
New paragraph	Command-/Ctrl-Return	\p
New line	Command-/Ctrl-Shift-Return	\n
New column	Command-/Ctrl-Enter	\c
New box	Command-/Ctrl-Shift-Enter	\b
Previous box page number	Command-/Ctrl-2	\2
Current box page number	Command-/Ctrl-3	\3
Next box page number	Command-/Ctrl-4	\4
Wildcard (single character)	Command-/Ctrl-?	\?
Backslash	Command-/Ctrl-\	\\
Punctuation space		\.
Flex space		\f

What or Change To fields you need to type the backslash twice, or press Command-\ (Ctrl-\).

Wildcards. You can use the wildcard character (\?) to represent any other character. This is useful if you're looking for a word you may have spelled different ways, such as "gray" and "grey." Instead of running two search operations to find all occurrences of this word, you could simply type "gr\?y" in the Find What field. You can get the wildcard character by pressing either Command-? (Ctrl-?) or by typing a backslash followed by a question mark.

Note that the wildcard character can only be used in the Find What field. QuarkXPress doesn't let you use it in the Change To field because the program's not sophisticated enough to do that kind of pattern-replacing.

Whole Word. Next to the Layout checkbox you'll find another one labeled Whole Word. Checking this box means that QuarkXPress only finds occurrences of the Find What text if it's a whole word. That means that the text can't be bounded by other text or numerals. So a Whole Word search for "ten" finds the word "ten" when it's bounded by spaces, punctuation, or special characters such as new-line or new-paragraph marks. It would *not* find "often," "tenuous," or "contentious." If you don't have Whole Word selected, QuarkXPress will find every occurrence of the text you entered, even if it's embedded in other text.

Ignore Case. If Ignore Case is turned on, QuarkXPress finds all occurrences of the text in the Find What field, regardless of whether the capitalization of the text found in the layout exactly matches what you typed into the Find What field. For example, if you entered "Help", QuarkXPress would find "Help", "HELP", and "help".

How QuarkXPress determines the case of characters it's replacing when Ignore Case is turned on depends on the capitalization of the text it finds in the layout.

▶ If the found text begins with an initial capital, or is in all uppercase or lowercase letters, QuarkXPress follows suit and similarly capitalizes the replacement text, no matter how you've capitalized it in the Change To field.

▶ If the found text doesn't match the above three cases, QuarkXPress capitalizes the replacement text exactly as you entered it in the Change To field.

For example, let's say you are searching for all examples of "QuarkXPress" and want to make sure the internal capital letters are proper. If you leave Ignore Case turned on, and the program finds "quarkxpress", it will not capitalize the proper characters. Turn off Ignore Case, and the feature replaces "quarkxpress" with "QuarkXPress", properly capitalized as you entered it.

▼ ▼

Tip: Searching for the Unsearchable. I mentioned earlier that you can look for invisible characters by typing certain codes. However, there are some characters XPress doesn't let you search for. For instance, you cannot enter the indent, the nonbreaking space, or the right-margin tab (Option-Tab) characters here.

If you have some heavy-duty searching and replacing to do with any of these characters, you can always export your story in XPress Tags format and search for the characters there. I cover XPress Tags more in Chapter 7, *Copy Flow*, including how to export and import this format. Once you know these basics, you can find the codes for these special characters in Appendix F, *XPress Tags*.

▼ ▼

Tip: Close the Find/Change Palette. You know you can open the Find/Change palette by pressing Command-F (Ctrl-F). Did you know you can close it by pressing Command-Option-F (Ctrl-Alt-F)?

▼ ▼

Specifying Attributes

As I said earlier, you can search for more than just text in QuarkXPress. You can search for text-formatting attributes (font, size, type style), too. If you want to search for formatting, uncheck the Ignore Attributes box in the Find/Change palette. When you turn this option off, the palette expands (see Figure 5-2). In addition to text fields under the Find What and Change To headings, there are areas on each side of the palette for specifying font, size, character style sheet, color, and type style.

What to Find, What to Change

When Ignore Attributes is turned off (that is, when you're searching for text formatting as well as text), each side of the Find/Change palette contains six options for searching or replacing: Text, Style Sheet, Font, Size, Color, and Type Style. The left side of the palette shows all the attributes that should be searched for; the right side is what the text should be changed to. The first five areas on each side of the palette—Text, Style Sheet, Font, Size, and Color—are simple to use; the sixth is only a little more complicated (see "Type Styles," below). If you want to specify something, make sure the area's checkbox is turned on. Then simply enter the text or point size in the appropriate fields, and/or select the font or style sheet from the appropriate popup menus.

On the left (Find What) side, the popup menus list only the fonts and style sheets actually used in the current layout; on the right (Change To) side, they list all the fonts and style sheets currently available.

There doesn't need to be a parallel between what you specify on the Find What side and on the Change To side. In fact, such asymmetrical searches offer some of the most intriguing possibilities for finding and changing in QuarkXPress.

You could easily, for example, find all occurrences of a company name and apply a character style sheet to them.

1. Type the company name into the Text field on the Find What side.

2. Uncheck the boxes for Style Sheet, Font, Size, Color, and Type Style on the left side of the palette. That tells the program to pay no attention to these attributes.

Figure 5-2
The Find/Change palette with Ignore Attributes turned off

3. Uncheck all the boxes on the right side of the palette except for Style Sheet. That tells QuarkXPress not to change any of these attributes when it finds the company name.

4. Check the Style Sheet box on the Change To side, and choose the character style sheet you want to apply.

This procedure searches for all occurrences of the text, no matter what formatting is applied, and replaces them with the same text but using a specific character style sheet (I cover text formatting in Chapter 6, *Type and Typography*, and style sheets in Chapter 7, *Copy Flow*).

Type Styles

Specifying type styles—bold, italic, and so on—in the Find/Change palette is a bit more complicated than what I described above; however, it's really not that bad once you get used to it. Once you turn on the Type Style option, the various formatting choices can be either on, off, or grayed out. Clicking an unchecked box makes it gray; clicking again turns it on; clicking a third time turns it off again (see Figure 5-3).

What do these various states mean? On the left side (the Find What side), a checked box means that you want QuarkXPress to find text set *only* in that style. An unchecked box means you *don't* want it to find text in that style. A gray box means that it doesn't matter if the text is formatted with that style or not; you want QuarkXPress to find text either way (see Table 5-5). Another way to look at it is that blank means "no," black means "yes," and gray means "I don't care."

The various checkboxes mean similar things on the right (Change To) side of the palette. Checking a style box means you want QuarkXPress to apply that style when it changes text that it finds. An unchecked box means you *don't* want that style to be present in the changed text (if it's there, QuarkXPress removes it). Leaving the box gray means that QuarkXPress doesn't do anything to that style. If it's already there, it stays there; if it's not, the program doesn't apply it.

Of course, a word can't simultaneously have both the Underline and Word Underline styles. So checking one unchecks the other, and graying one auto-

Table 5-5
Style controls in the Find/Change palette

Box is . . .	Means . . .
White or Up	Find or replace text without this attribute
Black or Down	Find or replace text with this attribute
Grayed	Find it either way, but leave it alone when replacing

Figure 5-3

Specifying type styles in the Find/Change palette

This says "search for all text that is Palatino with only the Bold style applied (but with or without Underline style) and set it to Stone Sans with only the Italic style.

Indifferent   Off   On

matically makes the other gray as well. Small Caps/All Caps and Superscript/Subscript work together similarly.

▼ ▼

Tip: Set Up Find/Change by Example. You can shave a few steps off your Find/Change process by placing the cursor in some text that's formatted the same as what you're looking for. If you place the cursor in a word that is in 23-point Times and then open the Find/Change palette, both the font and size are automatically chosen on the Find What side of the palette (you may still have to check the boxes next to them, though). This won't save a lot of time, but sometimes every little bit helps.

▼ ▼

Going to It

Now that you know how to specify what you want to find, what you want to change, and how to tell QuarkXPress where to search, you can use the four buttons at the bottom of the palette to begin finding and changing. When you first specify your Find/Change criteria, all buttons except Find Next are grayed out (see Figure 5-4). Hold down the Option key and click Find First, and QuarkXPress searches for the first occurrence of text matching your specifications in the current story or layout. It displays this text in the document window and selects it.

You then have a choice. Clicking Find Next again takes you to the next occurrence of text meeting your specifications, without changing the currently selected text. Clicking Change, then Find changes the selection as specified on the Change To side of the palette. QuarkXPress then looks for the next occurrence of matching text. The Change button changes the selected text and leaves it selected, and the Change All button tells XPress to search for and automatically change all occurrences in the story or layout. After QuarkXPress

Figure 5-4
The Find/Change
control buttons

*This changes to Find First
when you hold down the
Option key*

changes all occurrences, a dialog box comes up listing the number of changes made.

▼ ▼

Tip: Seeing Text as It Is Found. I find that after searching for a word, it is too often sitting right underneath the palette—so you can't see it. Very frustrating. Instead, if you're going to be doing a lot of searching and replacing, I suggest you move the palette to the top or bottom of your screen and resize your document window so that you can see both the palette and the document window at the same time.

If you are one of the unlucky sods who has a small-screen Macintosh, then try reducing the size of the palette by clicking the Zoom button in the box's upper-right corner (this is Mac-only, unfortunately). The reduced view shows only the buttons you need to navigate and change what you've specified (see Figure 5-5). Clicking the Zoom button again takes you back to the larger palette.

Figure 5-5
Shrinking the
Find/Change palette

▼ ▼

Spelling Checker

Of course, once you've got your text written or imported into QuarkXPress, you wouldn't want to print it without first running it through XPress's spelling checker. QuarkXPress comes with a 120,000-word dictionary (that's the file called XPress Dictionary), and you can create your own auxiliary dictionaries as well. The Check Spelling command is on the Utilities menu, and it allows you to check a selected word, a selection, a story, or a layout (see Figure 5-6).

Figure 5-6
The Check Spelling
submenu

Checking a Word

If you only want to check one word, you can select it (or you can just put the cursor anywhere within the word) and choose Word from the Check Spelling submenu (or press Command-L on the Macintosh; Control-W on Windows). The Check Word dialog box appears (see Figure 5-7), listing all the words in the XPress Dictionary (as well as in the open auxiliary dictionary, if there is one) that resemble the word you selected.

If the suspect word—the word you're checking is always called the *suspect* word, even if it's correctly spelled—appears in a dictionary, it shows up in the scrolling list and is selected automatically (this is different than some spelling checkers that actually tell you that the word is spelled right). This means, as far as QuarkXPress is concerned, that the word is spelled correctly; you can click the Done button to continue (on the Mac, press Command-period; in Windows, press Escape).

If the suspect word doesn't appear in an active dictionary, you can scroll through the list of words and select a replacement. Click on the proper word in the list, then click the Replace button (or press Return or Enter). The new spelling replaces the word in your story, and the Check Word box closes.

If QuarkXPress can't find any words that approximate the suspect word, it displays the message, "No similar words found." Click the Done button to close the Check Word dialog box.

Checking a Selection

QuarkXPress can also check the spelling of a selection: Simply select the text you want to check and type Command-L (Ctrl-L), or choose Selection from the Check Spelling submenu ("Word" changes to "Selection" when more than one word is selected in a text box).

Checking a Story

Typically, you're more likely to check a whole story rather than a single word or phrase. To do this, use the Content tool to select any text box that holds part of the story. Then select Story from the Check Spelling hierarchical menu (or press Command-Option-L on the Macintosh; Control-Alt-W on Windows). The Word Count dialog box appears, showing running totals as QuarkXPress scans the story, counting the total number of words, the total number of

Figure 5-7

Checking a word

unique words (each word counted once, no matter how many times it occurs), and the number of suspect words—ones that QuarkXPress can't find in its dictionary or in the open auxiliary dictionary, if there is one (see Figure 5-8).

When QuarkXPress is finished counting, click the OK button. If the program didn't find any suspect words, then this just returns you to your document. On the other hand, if it did catch one or more words, then the button brings up the Check Document dialog box. This dialog box displays suspect words one at a time, in the order in which they occur in the story. As each appears in the dialog box, QuarkXPress scrolls the document window to the suspect word, and highlights it so you can see it in the context in which it's used on the page. If a suspect word is used more than once in the story, QuarkXPress tells you how many times.

Changing the spelling. When you check the spelling of a whole story rather than just a word, QuarkXPress doesn't automatically show you possible replacement words. If you know the correct spelling for a suspect word, you can enter it in the Replace With field, and click the Replace button to have the new spelling replace the one in your document. Or if you do want QuarkXPress to look for possible spellings in the available dictionaries, you can click the Look up button (or press Command-L or Ctrl-L). QuarkXPress displays a list of possible alternatives in the scrolling text field. You can select an alternate spelling by clicking on it, then clicking the Replace button (or pressing Enter or Return). The new spelling replaces the suspect word in your layout, and QuarkXPress moves on to the next suspect word in the story. If there are no more suspect words, the Check Document dialog box closes.

Note that if QuarkXPress finds more than one occurrence of a suspect word, it will replace every occurrence of the word with the new spelling you choose.

Figure 5-8

Checking the spelling of a document

Skipping and keeping. To go to the next suspect word without changing the spelling of the current one, click the Skip button (Command-S or Ctrl-S, which usually means Save, but not here). To add the current suspect word to an auxiliary dictionary, click the Keep button (Command-K or Ctrl-K, which usually means Delete, but not in this dialog box). This button is only active when an auxiliary dictionary is open (see "Auxiliary Dictionaries," below).

▼ ▼

Tip: One-Letter Misspellings. I wonder how many years I used XPress's spelling checker before I finally figured out that it ignores one-letter words. That means that if you're typing quickly and press the wrong key—for instance, if you type "tie s yellow ribbon" rather than "tie a yellow ribbon"—XPress won't catch the word as misspelled. QuarkXPress also won't catch most abbreviations. If you type "tx" instead of "tax", XPress just thinks you mean "Texas," thus proving once more that there's nothing like the final once-over with a human eye for catching these little mistakes. (Note that this isn't only a limitation of QuarkXPress; many spelling checkers do the same thing.)

▼ ▼

Checking a Layout/Master Page

You can check the spelling of all the text in an entire layout by selecting Layout from the Check Spelling submenu (or by pressing Command-Option-Shift-L on the Macintosh; Control-Alt-Shift-W on Windows). QuarkXPress counts and checks all the words in your current layout, from first page to last. It displays the Word Count dialog box, then lets you change suspect words with a Check Document dialog box that is identical in layout and function to the Check Story dialog box.

Unfortunately, this procedure only checks the spelling on the real layout pages, not the master pages. To check spelling on master pages, you need to be viewing one of the master pages (it doesn't matter which, if you have more than one). When master pages are displayed, the Layout item on the submenu changes to Masters. By selecting this command you can check all the text on every master page in your layout, using a Check Masters dialog box that works just like the Check Story and Check Document dialog boxes.

Auxiliary Dictionaries

You can't add or change words in QuarkXPress's standard dictionary. You can, however, create and use an auxiliary dictionary, so you can have the program's spelling checker take into account specialized words that aren't in the standard dictionary. Note that you can only have one auxiliary dictionary open at a time for each layout in your document.

Creating or opening an auxiliary dictionary. To open an existing auxiliary dictionary, or to create a new one, select Auxiliary Dictionary from the Utilities menu. This opens the Auxiliary Dictionary dialog box. Select a dictionary stored on any mounted volume, and click the Open button.

You can also create a new auxiliary dictionary by navigating to the directory you want it, typing a file name in the field next to the New button, and then clicking the New button in this dialog box (see Figure 5-9).

Adding and removing words. When you first create an auxiliary dictionary, it's empty. There are two ways to add words to it. First, you can add words to the dictionary using the Keep button in the Check Story or Check Document dialog box. This button adds the current suspect word to your auxiliary dictionary. Another way to add words is with the Edit Auxiliary feature on the Utilities menu. This feature is only available when there's an auxiliary dictonary selected.

When you select Edit Auxiliary, a simple dialog box appears with a scrolling list of all the words in the currently open dictionary (see Figure 5-10). To add a new word, enter it in the text field and click the Add button. Words added to the dictionary cannot contain any spaces or punctuation (not even hyphens).

Words that have accents (or other foreign-language markings) were a no-no in the U.S. English version of QuarkXPress 3. Fortunately, QuarkXPress 4

Figure 5-9
The Auxiliary
Dictionary dialog box

changed that. Now if your name is García or Françoise, you can breathe more easily when you're checking spelling.

To remove a word from the dictionary, scroll through the list until you find the word. Select it by clicking on it, then click the Delete button.

▼ ▼

Tip: Adding All Suspect Words. Here's a fun way to add a bunch of words to your auxiliary dictionary, all at the same time. This only works if you've already selected an auxiliary dictionary for your layout, of course (choose Auxiliary Dictionary from the Utilities menu).

1. Create a text box with all the words that you want to add to the auxiliary dictionary.

2. Select Check Story from the Utilities menu, and when XPress displays the number of suspect words, click OK. (In this scenario, all the words in the story will be suspect words.)

3. In the Check Story dialog box, hold down the Option and Shift keys and click the Done button (on Windows, hold down Alt and Shift while clicking Close). This adds all the suspect words to the current auxiliary dictionary.

If you make a mistake or you want to make sure the words were added, select Edit Auxiliary in the Utilities menu.

▼ ▼

Figure 5-10
The Edit Auxiliary
Dictionary dialog box

Remembering dictionaries. If you open or create an auxiliary dictionary with a layout open, QuarkXPress automatically associates the two. Whenever you open the layout, QuarkXPress also opens the dictionary, until you either close that dictionary (by pressing Close in the Auxiliary Dictionary dialog box) or open a different one (this breaks the link with the first dictionary and makes a link with the new one).

You can also set up an auxiliary dictionary that will be applied to all subsequent new layouts by opening a dictionary while no documents are open. However, QuarkXPress may not be able to find an auxiliary dictionary if you move either the dictionary or a document associated with it—or sometimes even when you have a system crash while XPress is running—in which case, you'll receive an error message when you try to check spelling in your layout. If QuarkXPress loses track of the auxiliary dictionary, just go back and open it again.

Watching Your Words

By following the tips I've shown you here, you may not be able to have QuarkXPress write your stories for you, but you'll be able to get the very most out of the program's advanced word-processing features.

In the next chapter, you'll see how you can take those blocks of plain text that you've created and turn them into type, using QuarkXPress's extensive typographic controls.

6

TYPE AND
TYPOGRAPHY

There's an old husband's tale that says you can tell what a baby is going to grow up to become by the first real word she speaks. If she says "mama," she'll grow up to be a loving parent. If she says "teevee," chances are she'll be a couch potato. If she says "QuarkXPress," she'll become a designer.

There's no doubt—even if this tale is hogwash—that QuarkXPress is often the first word on a designer's lips when the topic of desktop publishing comes up. That's because no desktop-publishing application handles typesetting as powerfully as QuarkXPress does. In this chapter, I will discuss the many typographic controls that QuarkXPress puts at your fingertips. I'm going to start with the basics: typographic principles and fonts. However, professionals should at least skim over this section (the fundamentals of fonts are rarely taught, and many people find themselves in deep . . . uh . . . water at some point because of it).

Next, I'll discuss control of both character- and paragraph-level formatting, including—among many other items—kerning and tracking, hyphenation and justification, and typographic special effects.

If you're reading this book from cover to cover, expect to spend a little while here in this chapter. I've got a lot to talk about, and I expect that in the long run you'll find it rewarding.

▼ ▼

Fonts and Font Management

The word *font* now has several meanings. Historically, a font was a set of characters in a given typeface and size. Helvetica was a typeface, and 14-point Helvetica was a font. However, for the sake of simplicity, I'm following the path that has become popular over the past few years, defining both *typeface* and *font* as synonyms: a font or a typeface is a set of characters that share a common look.

For example, the text you're reading is in the Utopia font or typeface, while the headings for each section are in the Stone font or typeface. The more you learn about type and typography, the more you see its subtle nuances and personalities. But don't worry too much about that yet. Just start by seeing these basic differences.

There are four basic rules for working with fonts in professional desktop publishing:

▶ Use Type 1, PostScript fonts, or OpenType fonts.

▶ Try to avoid TrueType fonts.

▶ Use a font management utility.

▶ Be careful when choosing font styles.

Of course, with every rule there is at least one exception, and at least three instances where you should ignore the rule entirely. Nonetheless, here's a quick set of guidelines.

TrueType, PostScript, and OpenType. Just like there are lots of different kinds of word-processing file formats (Microsoft Word files are different than WordPerfect files, and so on), there are many different ways to digitally store font information. The two primary formats, however, are called TrueType and PostScript. Both Apple and Microsoft have really pushed the TrueType font format, and both Macs and PCs ship with a plethora of TrueType fonts already installed. You typically have to buy PostScript fonts from a vendor (like Adobe, Bitstream, or Monotype), or they may be copied to your system automatically when you install a program (like Adobe Type Manager, Adobe Photoshop, Adobe Acrobat, and so on) on your machine.

Another option is the OpenType format, which was jointly created by Microsoft and Adobe. The OpenType format was designed to be better than either TrueType or PostScript (also called Type 1) fonts. For instance, an OpenType font is made up of a single file that will work on a Macintosh or in Windows. Applications can also be written to take advantage of special

OpenType features, such as complex ligatures and automatic fractions. QuarkXPress has no special OpenType features yet, but I still consider OpenType the future of font technology, so it's worth exploring the use of this font type.

Most service bureaus wish that TrueType fonts would just go away because they have so much trouble printing them. Of course, TrueType is fine unless you're trying to do quality graphic design work, are working with other people, or are working with a service bureau. Printing these fonts has gotten easier, but as far as I'm concerned, it's still worth avoiding them. It's always tempting to use inexpensive or free fonts, but you almost always get what you pay for. If you're serious about desktop publishing, use PostScript or OpenType fonts.

Note that you no longer need to use Adobe Type Manager (ATM) in order to use PostScript fonts in XPress. (ATM rasterizes—"turns into bitmaps"—the mathematical outlines of PostScript fonts, so no matter how big you make them on screen, they always look nice and smooth. However, both Mac OS X and Windows XP rasterize PostScript fonts now.)

Type management utilities. If you only worked with two or three typefaces for the rest of your life, you'd never need to think about font management. However, most people doing any kind of publishing work commonly work with hundreds or thousands of fonts. Keeping these fonts in order is critical to working efficiently with QuarkXPress.

If you have more than 20 fonts on your hard drive, you should be using a font management utility. Period. These programs let you keep all your fonts together, either in one folder or in multiple folders anywhere you want on your hard drives. You can arrange fonts into groups, opening just the ones you want when you need them. In this way you keep your font menus short, speed up font selection, and keep your whole system lean.

Plus, most of these utilities are pretty cheap (between $30 and $150) so there's almost no reason not to have one around. Examples of font management utilities are Suitcase and Font Reserve from Extensis (*www.extensis.com*), MasterJuggler from Alsoft (*www.alsoft.com*). In fact, Mac OS X 10.3 will have a basic font management utility called FontBook built in (it had not been released by the time this book went to press). Which utility you should use depends on how many fonts you have (Font Reserve is best for thousands of fonts, while other utilities work better with fewer fonts).

Which Font to Choose. The fourth "rule" of fonts has to do with setting your fonts to bold, italic, and so on. The question often arises over whether people should choose bold and italic fonts from their font menus (if they're available) or get them by selecting bold or italic from the Style menu or the

Measurements palette. It's a good question. However, I'm going to punt on the answer for now; instead, I'll discuss it later in "Styling by Attributes Versus Font Choice."

Missing Fonts

When you open a document created with fonts that you don't currently have loaded on your system, XPress tells you that you're missing one or more fonts and gives you two choices: Continue and List Fonts (see Figure 6-1). (Of course, you'll rarely see this if you are using a font management utility which automatically activates missing fonts, such as Font Reserve or Extensis Suitcase.)

Continue. If you click the Continue button, XPress opens the document but displays the missing fonts on screen using system fonts (like Ariel or Geneva). If you select some text set in this missing font, you can see that the font field in the Measurements palette is blank because the proper font isn't available from the font list. Also, if you open Font Usage (see "Font Usage," below) or the Find/Change palette, you'll find a font called something like "{-2, Unknown}" or "{-122, MinionExpertRegular}".

Obviously, having a real font replaced with a system font doesn't make much sense, but if you're only perusing the document for overall design and you don't care about how the fonts look or how the text wraps from line to line, then this may be a reasonable option.

List Fonts. If you click the List Fonts button, XPress lists the missing fonts for you. To replace one of these missing fonts with a font that's available, select a typeface from the list, click the Replace button, then choose a replacement font. Note that this option replaces every instance of that font (within style sheet definitions, too). I'll sometimes replace fonts like this if I have a font that is close to the one specified in the document. For instance, I might replace a missing Goudy font with Palatino, since there is a similarity between these two oldstyle typefaces. Of course, because the character widths of these two fonts are different, line endings are almost sure to be different. Later, I would close the document without saving it, so that when I open it on a machine that has Goudy, the fonts will appear properly.

Printing missing fonts. You can also run into trouble when your computer has a screen font (also called a "bitmapped font") but no corresponding PostScript outline font (this isn't a problem with TrueType or OpenType fonts). In that case, when you print the document, XPress substitutes either a jaggy-looking bitmapped version of the font or Courier (that typewriter font). It's obviously important to have the outline fonts available.

Figure 6-1

Missing fonts

Font Usage

What's the fastest way to tell what fonts are being used in a layout that you have open? Choose Usage from the Utilities menu (on the Macintosh, press either F13 or Command-F6; press F2 on Windows). The Fonts tab in the Usage dialog box lists every font in a layout, lets you search for instances of that font, and lets you globally replace one font with another (see Figure 6-2).

Some people have complained that the Usage dialog box doesn't have enough search-and-replace abilities. Quark's answer: If you're trying to search and replace, you should use the Find/Change dialog box. It's hard to argue with that kind of logic.

Plus, there are three problems with using the Usage dialog box to search for and replace fonts.

▶ The Usage dialog box only displays fonts that are on the layout pages *or* the master pages, but not both at the same time. (Which one it displays depends on what pages are currently showing in the document window.)

▶ The Usage dialog box only displays fonts on the current layout space; if you have five layout spaces, you'll have to visit the dialog box five times.

▶ The Replace option in the Usage dialog box only replaces fonts on the layout page or the master pages (again, depending on which is showing), but it does not change fonts in the style sheet definitions. Let's say you use the font Matrix in a character style sheet and then apply that style to some text on a document page. If you try to replace Matrix with Garamond in the Usage dialog box, you'll only change the text on the

Figure 6-2

Font Usage

document page, not the actual definition of the style (it's the same as applying local formatting on top of the style). This is a mess.

Of course, the Find/Change palette has exactly the same three limitations, so global font replacements are not nearly as easy as you'd think.

More Information. You can find out more about a particular font in the Usage dialog box by selecting it and turning on the More Information checkbox. When this option is on, pay particular attention to the File Name and the Type. If you're not sure whether you're dealing with a PostScript or TrueType font, here's one great way to find out.

▼ ▼

Tip: Global Font Replacements. Let's say you've created a masterpiece in XPress—450 pages over six layout spaces, 47 style sheets, eight master pages. You've used the Franklin Gothic typeface family throughout the layout, sometimes applying it manually to text, sometimes using it in style sheet definitions. Now your art director demands (probably out of spite) that you replace Franklin Gothic with Univers. Unfortunately, there is no feature in XPress that lets you replace one font with another, at one fell swoop, on master pages, layout pages, and style sheets. Here's what I'd do.

1. Save the document and close it.

2. Turn off Franklin Gothic with your font management utility. (If you don't use a font management utility, then you'll have to manually "uninstall" the font from your system.) If your font management utility has an auto-activation feature (like Font Reserve or Suitcase) then make sure that feature is turned off.

3. Open the document again in XPress. When the program tells you that a font is missing, click the List Fonts button. Select Franklin Gothic from the list and click Replace. Choose Univers from the Replace pop-up menu, and click OK.

4. After the document is open and is displaying the first page, every instance of Franklin Gothic in your document will have been replaced with Univers, and you won't have to pull your hair out.

▼ ▼

Character Formatting

There are two types of typographic controls: character-based and paragraph-based. The character-based controls—typeface, size, color, bold, italic, and so on—are those that affect only the text characters you select. If you select only one word in a sentence and apply a character style to it, that word and only that word is changed. Paragraph-based controls let you change the formatting of the entire paragraph—left and right indents, tab settings, space before and after, and so on.

Let's talk about character formatting first—how you can change it, and why you'd want to.

Use the Content tool. The very first thing you need to know about controlling type in QuarkXPress is that you must have selected both the Content tool and the text box that contains the text you want to change. If you want to make a character-based change, you must select those characters you want to alter. If you want to make a paragraph-based change, you can select the paragraph (four mouse clicks) or a portion of the paragraph. You can even just have the cursor located anywhere within the paragraph. Just remember: If you want to change the content of a text box, use the Content tool.

Selecting a Typeface

Picking a typeface can be a very personal thing, fraught with implication and the anxiety of decision. If someone tells you they want their document set in 10-point Courier, it may be better just to stay quiet. However, once the choice is made, there are a number of ways to select the typeface. Let's look at each of them here.

The Style menu. Almost every typographic control can be accessed from the Style menu. Once you select the text you want to change, you can select the typeface name from the Font submenu.

The Measurements palette. If you would rather avoid submenus, you can select a typeface from the Measurements palette instead. Here you have two methods of selecting.

▶ You can click on the arrow popup menu to bring up a list of fonts. It is often quicker to select from this menu than from the Style menu because it's always visible and is not a hierarchical menu.

▶ You can type the name of the typeface you want. Do this by clicking to the left of the first character of the typeface name shown on the Measurements palette (or jump there quickly by pressing Command-Option-Shift-M or Ctrl-Alt-Shift-M), then typing a few characters of the typeface name you want. As soon as QuarkXPress recognizes the name, it inserts the rest of it for you.

For example, if you want to change from Helvetica to Avant Garde, click just to the left of the "H" and type "Ava." By the time you type these three letters, chances are XPress will recognize Avant Garde (as long as you have that font loaded). This is a boon to desktop publishers who have many fonts and are tired of scrolling down a list for five minutes to select Zapf Dingbats.

▼ ▼

Tip: Jumping Forward in the Menu. If your menu is really long and you want to jump to a certain point, you can use both methods of selecting a font in the Measurements palette. For example, if you're looking for Zapf Dingbats but can't remember how "Zapf" is spelled, you can type "Z" in the font field of the Measurements palette (remember, you can get there quickly by pressing Command-Option-Shift-M or Ctrl-Alt-Shift-M), then click on the popup menu. You're transported directly to the end of the list.

▼ ▼

Character Attributes. The Character Attributes dialog box is the Style menu and half the Measurements palette rolled into one, and is a simple keystroke away (Command/Ctrl-Shift-D; see Figure 6-3). Here you can change the typeface using all the same methods described in "The Measurements palette," above.

Find/Change and Font Usage. Let's say half your document is set in Helvetica and you want to change that copy to Futura. You can use either the Find/Change or the Font Usage dialog box to search for all instances of characters set in Helvetica, and replace them with Futura. I discuss the Find/Change dialog box in some detail in Chapter 5, *Word Processing*, and the Font Usage feature earlier in this chapter.

Figure 6-3
Character Attributes
dialog box

Font Size

Selecting a font is only half the battle; once you've done that, you typically need to change the size of the typeface. You use the same options for changing the type size as I described above: the Style menu, the Measurements palette, the Character Attributes dialog box, and the Find/Change dialog boxes (Font Usage doesn't let you change point size). In addition, you can use a set of keystrokes to make your selected text larger or smaller (see Table 6-1).

The preset point-size range that I mention in Table 6-1 is the same range listed on the Size menu: 7, 9, 10, 12, 14, 18, 24, 36, 48, 60, and 72. When you increase through the preset range with a keystroke, your character size jumps from one to the next on this list. I generally use Command/Ctrl-Shift-period and Command/Ctrl-Shift-comma (smaller and larger) to jump through the presets until I'm close to the size I want. Then I fine-tune the point size by adding the Option/Alt key to the keystroke, so that it moves only one point at a time.

▼ ▼

Tip: Precision Font Sizing. If you aren't satisfied with the preset font sizes, you can enter your own—in .001-point increments—in the Size field of the Character Attributes dialog box. You can get to this dialog box by selecting Other from the Size submenu or by pressing Command/Ctrl-Shift-\ (back-

Table 6-1
Font sizing keystrokes

PRESS ...	To ...
Command/Ctrl-Shift-period	Increase point size through a preset range
Command/Ctrl-Shift-comma	Decrease point size through a preset range
Command-Option-Shift-period *or* Ctrl-Alt-Shift-period	Increase point size in 1-point increments
Command-Option-Shift-comma *or* Ctrl-Alt-Shift-comma	Decrease point size in 1-point increments

slash). This is one of the keystrokes I use most often. (You could also use Command-Option-Shift-M or Ctrl-Alt-Shift-M and then press Tab to jump to the Font Size field on the Measurements palette.)

▼ ▼

Tip: Interactive Text Resizing. If you like working visually, you may not know exactly how large you want your text to be. You can resize text interactively by holding down the Command/Ctrl key while dragging on a handle (this also works with picture boxes; see Chapter 9, *Pictures*). As you resize the text box, the size of the text increases or decreases to fit your changes. Depending on how you reshape the box, the type size changes along with the type's horizontal or vertical scaling (see Figure 6-4).

Figure 6-4
Interactive text resizing

In addition to Command/Ctrl-key scaling, holding down Shift-Command (Ctrl-Shift) turns rectangular boxes into squares (scaling contents appropriately), and holding down Shift-Command-Option (Ctrl-Shift-Alt) scales the box and its contents but maintains existing horizontal and vertical proportions (this is usually what you'd want). And if you wait half a second after you click on a handle before you begin to drag, you can see the type change on screen as you drag (see "Tip: Viewing Changes as You Make Them" in Chapter 2, *QuarkXPress Basics*).

There are two catches to this funky feature. First, it only stretches type to the limits you could ordinarily stretch it to. You can't stretch type wider than 400 percent or larger than 720 points, because horizontal scaling and font size won't go any farther than that. Second, this scaling only works on unlinked text boxes, not on text boxes that are part of a longer story, as it's intended for use on headline and display type.

▼ ▼

Type Styles

QuarkXPress has 13 built-in attributes that you assign at a character level. Figure 6-5 gives samples of each of these, and examples of how to use each of them. These type attributes can be assigned to selected text in four ways, which are similar to how you assign typefaces and type size.

Character attributes. The slowest method of choosing a type style is by going to the Character Attributes dialog box (Command/Ctrl-Shift-D). The type styles in the Character Attributes dialog box are turned on and off by checking boxes. These checkboxes can be in one of three states: on, off, or indeterminate (gray).

▶ ON. An "X" in the checkbox means the style is selected for all the selected text.

▶ OFF. If the checkbox is blank, that style is not applied to any of the selected text.

▶ INDETERMINATE. A gray checkbox means that some of the characters that are currently selected have that style, and others don't. (See "Finding and Changing Type Styles" in Chapter 5, *Word Processing.*)

Style menu. Perhaps the second-slowest method of selecting a type style is to choose it from the Type Style submenu under the Style menu (see Figure 6-6).

Measurements palette. Each of the type styles is displayed by an icon on the Measurements palette (see Figure 6-7). The icons either display a sample of the style or give a graphic representation of it. For example, Superscript is shown by the numeral 2 over an up arrow. To select a type style, click on the icon. The icon acts as a toggle switch, so to turn the style off, you click on it again. If you have several type styles selected, you can rid yourself of them by clicking on the P (for Plain).

Note that the "indeterminate" state also appears on the Measurements palette; when you select text that contains more than one type style, the various icons appear gray. You can still turn them on and off by clicking on them.

Keystrokes. Each type style can be selected by a keystroke, as shown in Table 6-2. Once again, the styles are toggled on and off with each keystroke. I find keystrokes especially useful while typing directly into QuarkXPress; I can enter text and change styles while never taking my hands from the keyboard.

▼ ▼

Tip: Avoiding Some Styles. Just because XPress offers you a choice doesn't mean that you should take it. For instance, you should avoid using the Outline and Shadow type styles because they rarely look as good as you'd expect. XPress lets the operating system create these effects rather than building them

Figure 6 5
Type styles

Plain text

Italic

Bold

<u>Underlined (everything)</u>

<u>Word</u> <u>underlining</u>

~~Strike Thru~~

Outline

Shadow

ALL CAPS

Sᴍᴀʟʟ Cᴀᴘs

Su^{per}script .... (baseline shown as dotted line)

Sub$_{script}$ ....

Superior char^{acters}

Outline plus shadow

Small caps

Word underlining

Bold

Kindly Note:

The koala tea of Mᴏɪsʜᴇ <u>is</u> <u>not</u> **strained!**
That, however, has nothing *whatsoever* to
<u>do with</u> E=MC^2

Underlining   Superior character   Roman   Italic
(plain text)

itself, and the operating system is not very good at typographic effects (if it were, we'd all be using SimpleText or Windows Notepad for our typography). If you want these effects, you should build them using other XPress features.

You may or may not want to use the two underline styles and the strikethrough style, as well. They also fall into the "made by the system" category, so you have no control over things like how far the underline should be from the baseline, or how thick it should be (I discuss ways to create these effects more precisely, later in this chapter).

▼ ▼

Figure 6-6
Type Style submenu

Figure 6-7
Measurements palette
type styles

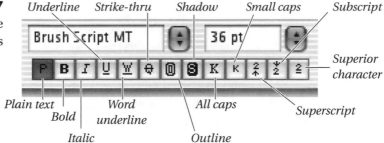

Styling by Attributes Versus Font Choice

On both the Macintosh and Windows operating systems, fonts are organized into families. For instance, the regular (roman), italic, bold, and bold italic styles of Bodoni all constitute a single family. Depending on your system setup, the font family may appear as a single name (Bodoni) or as several names (Bodoni Italic, Bodoni Bold, and so on).

There is an ongoing superstition in the design community that you should never just apply a type style (like just choosing Bold from the Style menu), and that you should instead always select the name of the styled font (like "Bodoni Bold") from the font list. This is hogwash.

In general, you can use either method—styling text either by applying style attributes, or by choosing the styled font itself. There are several drawbacks to applying a style attribute however.

▶ In order to simply click on Bold or Italic or whatever with confidence, you must know that the style you are choosing actually exists for that

Table 6-2

Type styles

KEYSTROKES	STYLE	EXAMPLE
Command/Ctrl-Shift-P	Plain text	Ecce Eduardus Ursus
Command/Ctrl-Shift-B	Bold	**Ecce Eduardus Ursus**
Command/Ctrl-Shift-I	Italic	*Ecce Eduardus Ursus*
Command/Ctrl-Shift-O	Outline	Ecce Eduardus Ursus
Command/Ctrl-Shift-S	Shadow	Ecce Eduardus Ursus
Command/Ctrl-Shift-/	Strikethrough	~~Ecce Eduardus Ursus~~
Command/Ctrl-Shift-U	Underline	<u>Ecce Eduardus Ursus</u>
Command/Ctrl-Shift-W	Word underline	<u>Ecce</u> <u>Eduardus</u> <u>Ursus</u>
Command/Ctrl-Shift-H	Small caps	Ecce Eduardus Ursus
Command/Ctrl-Shift-K	All caps	ECCE EDUARDUS URSUS
Command/Ctrl-Shift-=	Superscript	Ecce Eduardus Ursus
Command/Ctrl-Shift-–	Subscript	Ecce Eduardus Ursus
Command/Ctrl-Shift-V	Superior	Ecce Eduardus Ursus

font. For example, if your text is set in Symbol and you click on Italic, it may appear italic on screen, but you're taking a chance because there is no italic version of the Symbol font. The text is obliqued on screen, and may even be obliqued on your desktop laser printer; however, more often than not, the text will appear ugly or in the non-italic, roman face on an imagesetter.

▶ Some font families have more than just four faces; for example, Utopia (the typeface this text is set in) has a bold version, a semi-bold version, and a black version. If you select some Utopia text and press Command/Ctrl-Shift-B, do you know which bold version you're getting? If not, you shouldn't select your style this way. The key here is to know your typefaces inside and out before messing with the character styles.

▶ Fonts can become corrupted, and the connections with their other family members may be broken. In this case, you cannot choose character styles anymore. Often, replacing the font fixes the problem.

▶ You often don't even get the choice to select the "real styled font" because the operating system has hidden it from you (Microsoft Windows does this, for instance). In this case, you have to use character styles instead.

Which method is better? Choosing font style by formatting attribute is certainly faster, especially if you do it with keyboard commands. And it has the advantage of being font-independent. For example, if you've applied an italic formatting attribute to a range of your Bodoni text, and later decide to change your text face to Galliard, the italic formatting is retained.

On the other hand, if you choose the actual Bodoni Italic font for the emphasized range of text, when you make the change to Galliard, you get just Galliard and not Galliard Italic. Why? Because you simply switched from one font to another, and your text carried no formatting information. The original range was in an italic font with a Plain style attribute. To change fonts, you'd have to change Bodoni to Galliard, Bodoni Italic to Galliard Italic, Bodoni Bold to Galliard Bold, and so on.

No matter which method you use, I urge you to be consistent in your choice. There's little chance that something will go wrong if you change the type style in some places using style attributes and in other places using the actual fonts. However, it's best to be consistent.

▼ ▼

Color and Shade

You can quickly and easily change the color or the tint (shade) of a block of text. First, select the text and then select either the color from the Color submenu, or the tint value from the Shade submenu of the Style menu. You can also use the Colors palette to set both of these attributes (see Chapter 12, *Color*). The default tints are in multiples of 10 percent; however, you can assign a specific tint value by selecting Other from the Shade submenu, or by typing a value in the upper-right corner of the Colors palette (see Figure 6-8).

▼ ▼

Tip: Reversed Type. There is no specific command for reversed type—typically white-on-black type—as there is in Adobe PageMaker. But that doesn't mean you can't achieve that effect. Simply select the text and choose White from the Color submenu or from the Character Attributes dialog box (Command/Ctrl-Shift-D). If you want the reversed type to have a black back-

Figure 6-8

Assigning a color to type

ground, either place a black box behind it, or color the text box's background in the Modify dialog box (Command/Ctrl-M). (Also see "Tip: Reversed Type in Rules" in Chapter 11, *Where Text Meets Graphics*.)

▼ ▼

Horizontal and Vertical Scaling

Imagine that the characters in a typeface are rubber and stretchable. Now imagine stretching a typeface—one that took hundreds of hours to laboriously design at a specific width—to 160 percent of its size, warping the characters into something they were never meant to be. Now imagine the type designer's face contorting in horror as he or she sees what you've done to the type.

Okay, you get the idea: typefaces are designed to be a specific width, and shouldn't be messed with unless you have some really good reasons. What are some good reasons? The best reason of all is that you want the typeface to look that way. If you're responsible for the typographic design, then you can make any choices you want. Note that I'm not talking about your using 70-percent compression of Helvetica because you don't feel like buying another package from Adobe. I am talking about using Cheltenham compressed to 85 percent because it looks cool.

Another good reason to play with the horizontal scaling is if you need to make some body copy fit a particular space. Here I'm talking about changing the horizontal scaling of the text plus or minus two or three percent, not 10 or 20 percent. I'd be surprised if anyone other than the designer could see the difference of a few percent, especially at small sizes. But scaling Times Bold to 50 percent of its size to make it fit as a headline is a bad idea (see Figure 6-9).

After all these warnings, if you still want to play with the horizontal or vertical scaling of your type, you can do so using the Horizontal/Vertical Scale feature on the Style menu. (Vertical scaling first appeared in QuarkXPress 3.2; instead of stretching the type horizontally, it makes it taller while maintaining the same width.) First, select Horizontal or Vertical from the popup menu (you can't modify both at the same time). Entering values below 100 percent makes the text either narrower or shorter and squatter, depending on the Horizontal/Vertical setting; values above 100 percent stretch it wider or make it taller. You don't have to type a percent sign; just the number will do.

You can also alter horizontal and vertical scaling with keystrokes: Command/Ctrl-] (right square bracket) makes selected text wider in five-percent increments; Command/Ctrl-[(left square bracket) makes the selected text narrower in five-percent increments. (I remember the difference like this: the key on the left means narrow—or less; the key on the right means wider—or

Figure 6-9
Horizontal scaling of type

Got a problem?   *20 pt. Helvetica Condensed*

Check your compression.   *(Tracking: 0)*

Got a problem?   *20 pt. Helvetica (horizontal scaling: 60%)*

Check your compression.   *(Tracking: -3)*

Got a problem?   *20 pt. Helvetica bold (scaling: 60%)*

Check your compression.   *(Tracking: -2)*

*Times bold with horizontal scaling of 50% —
but with the inter-word spaces not compressed*

Rats! Squashed again!

*Times bold with horizontal scaling of 50% — inter-word spaces
also scaled to 50%. Tracking in both examples: -1*

Squashed! Rats again!

Times roman 10/11 — normal scaling

I began to experience an acute sense of panic when, despite
everyone's assurances to the contrary, I began to approach the
end of the line and found that I was not quite going to make
it.

Times roman — scaled to 99% (same line width)

I began to experience an acute sense of panic when, despite
everyone's assurances to the contrary, I began to approach the
end of the line and found that I was not quite going to make it.

---

more.) The keystrokes modify horizontal or vertical scaling depending on
which direction you last changed.

▼ ▼

Tip: Thoughts on Horizontal and Vertical Scaling. Here are just a few
more thoughts on the subject of horizontal and vertical scaling that you might
want to keep in mind.

▶ If you're going to use horizontal scaling, think carefully about the sort of typeface you're using. When you scale a font horizontally, the vertical strokes get thicker or thinner—depending on which way you're scaling—and the horizontal strokes stay the same width. A typeface that has thick verticals and thin horizontals (such as Bodoni) can become very odd-looking with just a little scaling. Faces that have only a little variation in stroke weight often handle scaling the best.

▶ Perhaps the worst kind of typeface to scale horizontally is script faces such as Berthold Script or Park Avenue. These are very delicate, and stretching them makes them look horrible and reduces their marginal legibility even further.

▶ Faces that are more square in nature, especially those with serifs, can handle being somewhat compressed with elegance. ITC Garamond, Cheltenham, and New Century Schoolbook, for instance, don't distort too badly until you drop below 90 percent or above 110 percent.

Kerning and Tracking

There are times in life when all those little letters on a page are just too far apart or too close together. The problem may be between two characters in 120-point display type, or it may be throughout an entire font. Whatever the problem, QuarkXPress can control it through the use of kerning and tracking. These two features are similar, but let's look at them one at a time.

Tip: Know Your Ems and Ens. Many typographic controls are specified using units of measure called *ems* and *ens*. (Some people call the en a "nut" to distinguish it aurally from an em.) These are not nearly as confusing as some people make them out to be. The default for the em in QuarkXPress is the width of two zeros side by side in the font and size you're working in. If that sounds weird, it's because it is. I can't figure out why they did it that way, but that's just the way it is. The width of an en space is half of an em space—the width of one zero.

Because this is so weird and unreasonable, Quark has added a checkbox on the Character tab of the Preferences dialog box labeled Standard Em Space. This sets the width of an em space to the same width that every other piece of software uses: the size of the typeface you're using. So if you're using 14-point Times with the Standard Em Space option turned on, the em space is 14 points wide. For consistency and a sense of doing the right thing, I recommend that you set this as your default (by changing the preference while no document is open).

If you're typing along and change point size, then the sizes of the em and en change as well. This can be a great aid. For example, if you change the size of a word after painstakingly kerning it, your kerning does not get lost or jumbled. The kerning was specified in fractions of an em, and therefore is scaled along with the type.

Em spaces and em dashes are not always equal in width. Usually they are (especially when Standard Em Space is turned on), but it really depends on what the typeface designer decided.

▼ ▼

Tip: What's 7/200 of an Em? Even though XPress defines kerning and other type-spacing values in ems, don't feel that you have to *think* in ems, unless you want to live and breathe typography. The important thing to remember is how the type looks, not all the numbers that get you there. When I'm working in QuarkXPress, I almost never think, "Oh, I'm going to change the kerning ¹⁄₂₀ of an em." I just say, "Oh, let's see how adding some kerning here would look." Focus on the results, and you'll get the feel for it pretty quickly.

▼ ▼

Kerning

Adjusting space between two characters is referred to as *kerning* or *pair kerning*. You'll sometimes find kerning defined purely as the removal of space between characters. In QuarkXPress, kerning can be either the removal or the *addition* of space—moving two characters closer together or farther apart. Figure 6-10 shows some examples of type, first unkerned and then kerned. The problem is made obvious here: too much space between characters can make words look uneven or unnatural.

QuarkXPress supports two kinds of kerning: automatic and manual. Type designers usually build into the font itself kerning-pair values that can be invoked automatically in QuarkXPress. Automatic kerning is global: it affects all instances of a character pair. Manual kerning is local: it affects only the pair selected.

Automatic. When I say "automatic," I mean really automatic: all you have to do is turn on the function, and QuarkXPress will make use of the font's built-in kerning pairs (actually, you don't even have to turn automatic kerning on, because it is on by default). It's up to font vendors to determine how many and which kerning pairs to include with a font, and which values to assign to them. Most fonts come with between 100 and 500 such pairs. Third parties also sell kerning pairs you can import.

There's almost no good reason to turn off automatic kerning altogether, but if you want to, the switch is on the Character tab in the Preferences dialog box. I wouldn't turn it off unless I were on a really slow machine and XPress was taking an inordinately long time flowing my text.

Manual. Figure 6-10 shows words in three renditions: with no kerning, with automatic kerning, and with manual kerning in addition to automatic kerning. The last looks best, doesn't it? (Please agree.)

Manual kerning in QuarkXPress is the adjustment of space between character pairs on a case-by-case basis. You make each adjustment in increments of fractions of an em space (see "Tip: Know Your Ems and Ens," above). Why anyone would want to kern to a precision of $\frac{1}{20,000}$ of an em space is beyond us, but QuarkXPress lets you do just that.

Manual kerning is usually reserved for larger type sizes for two reasons. First, it's harder to see poorly kerned pairs in smaller point sizes, so people say, "Why bother?" Second, you wouldn't want to go through a sizable amount of body text in the 8- to 14-point range, meticulously kerning pairs. It would take forever. Leave small type sizes to automatic kerning. If you don't like the built-in kerning pairs in a font, you can change them (see "Kerning and Tracking Tables," later in this chapter).

Manual kerning is a character-level attribute, but with a distinct difference from other character formatting. Instead of selecting the text you want to change, you place the cursor between two of the characters before you apply kerning (see Figure 6-11). If you select one or more characters, you end up

Figure 6-10
Kerned and
unkerned type

No automatic or manual kerning

DAVID WAVES!

Auto-kerning on; no manual kerning

DAVID WAVES!

Manual kerning applied to all character pairs

DAVID WAVES!

-15   -14   -6   -6   -7   -10   -5   -10   -5

Figure 6-11
Cursor placement
for kerning

Manual kerning with correct cursor placement

Incorrect cursor placement for manual kerning, but right for tracking

applying tracking rather than kerning (see "Tracking," below). Once you've clicked at an insertion point, you can control the space between the characters in four ways.

Kern or Character Attributes. You can select the Kern feature from the Style menu, which brings up the Character Attributes dialog box (you could type Command/Ctrl-Shift-D to get to this dialog box). Whole-number values typed in here represent units of $\frac{1}{200}$ em. For example, typing in "10" adds $\frac{10}{200}$ ($\frac{1}{20}$) of an em, and typing "-.1" removes $\frac{1}{2,000}$ of an em (typing a minus sign—a hyphen—before the value makes it negative). This is a really slow and painful way to apply kerning.

Measurements palette. The Measurements palette contains left-arrow and right-arrow icons that control tracking and kerning in text (they mean something different for pictures). Table 6-3 gives you a rundown on how to use them.

Keystrokes. I hate to take my hands off the keyboard while I'm working. Why should I, when I can do just about everything I need by pressing keystrokes? Table 6-4 shows the keystrokes you can use for kerning.

No matter which method you use to kern, you can see the kerning value in the Measurements palette (next to the left and right arrows) and in the Character Attributes dialog box.

▼ ▼

Tip: Kerning the Kerned. What shows up as the kern value when you want to kern a pair that is already kerned because of automatic kerning? Nothing. You'll still find a zero in the Kern Amount field. QuarkXPress regards the values applied by automatic kerning as the norm, so you don't have to worry

Table 6 3

Kerning control with the
Measurements palette
arrow icons

CLICK …	WHILE PRESSING …	TO …
Right Arrow		Increase space 10 units (1/20 em)
Right Arrow	Option/Alt	Increase space one unit (1/200 em)
Left Arrow		Decrease space 10 units (1/20 em)
Left Arrow	Option/Alt	Decrease space one unit (1/200 em)

about them. Of course, if you turn off automatic kerning after having applied manual kerning, your kerning values may be way off.

▼ ▼

Tip: Removing Manual Kerning. Have you ever been handed a file to which someone had spent many hours manually adding hundreds of kerning pairs? What if they really didn't know what they were doing, and you want to remove all that kerning before starting over? Fortunately, Quark has released a free XTension called Type Tricks. With this XTension installed, you'll see a feature on the Utilities menu called Remove Manual Kerning. Just select the range of text you want to affect, then select that from the menu. *Voilà!* All gone.

▼ ▼

Tracking

I know it's incredibly confusing, but it's true: There are two separate features in QuarkXPress called "Tracking." They're similar, but I need to break them down for clarity. The first is a character-level attribute, and I'm going to talk about it here. The second is a font-level attribute which changes the font as a whole, rather than just changing a set of characters, and I'll discuss it in great detail later in this chapter.

Character-level tracking. Tracking as a character-level attribute is the adjustment of space between all the character pairs in a range of text. It's sometimes called "track kerning" or "kern tracking," though I think the best name for it is *range kerning* (which is what it's called in PageMaker). The idea is simple: you can add or subtract space between many pairs of characters all at one time by using tracking controls (see Figure 6-12). These controls are so

Table 6-4

Kerning keystrokes

PRESS …	TO …
Command/Ctrl-Shift-}	Increase space 10 units (1/20 em)
Command-Option-Shift-} Ctrl-Alt-Shift-}	Increase space one unit (1/200 em)
Command/Ctrl-Shift-{	Decrease space 10 units (1/20 em)
Command-Option-Shift-{ Ctrl-Alt-Shift-{	Decrease space one unit (1/200 em)

similar to the kerning controls that I'm not even going to waste time and paper talking about them much.

You can control tracking by selecting a range of text and using the Measurements palette, the Track feature from the Style menu (this menu item changes from Kern to Track when you have more than one character selected), the Character Attributes dialog box, or the same keystrokes as if you were kerning. The reason all the controls are virtually the same is that QuarkXPress "decides" for you whether to kern or track, based on what is selected in the text box. In fact, though, these controls have the same function. One is applied to a single pair of characters; the other is applied to several or many pairs.

The crazy thing about this whole setup is that while kerning and tracking do the same thing, they are totally separate features. One result of this is that kerning and tracking are cumulative. For example, if you kern a character pair -10 units, then apply tracking of -10 units to those characters, the space between them ends up 20 units smaller than normal (which may be what you want; you just need to be aware of it). Also, if you track a word, then look at the kerning between two letters, it will look as though there were no kerning applied at all. If you're a former (or present) PageMaker user, this may really throw you for a loop.

Figure 6-12
Tracking text

Tracking: +7

Art directors *everywhere* were ignoring me until I realized what I needed: Much tighter tracking!

Tracking: -12

To England: That pre-cious stone set in a sil-ver sea

Tracking: 0. Copy doesn't fit.

To England: That precious stone set in a silver sea

Tracking: -4. Copy fits.

▼ ▼

Tip: When to Track. "Ah," I hear the reader sighing, "but what about some real-world tips?" Okay, let's set out some guidelines for you.

▶ If you're setting text in all capitals or in true small capitals from an Expert Set font, add between five and 10 units of space by tracking the word. Remember that you may not want to add tracking to the last character of the word (see "Tip: Tracking and the Single Word," below).

▶ Printing white text on a black background often requires a little extra tracking, too. That's because the negative (black) space makes the white characters seem closer together.

▶ Larger type needs to be tracked more tightly (with negative tracking values). Often, the larger the tighter, though there are aesthetic limits to this rule. Advertising headline copy will often be tracked until the characters just "kiss." You can automate this feature by setting up dynamic tracking tables, which I will discuss later in this chapter.

▶ A condensed typeface (such as Futura Condensed) can usually do with a little tighter tracking. Sometimes I'll apply a setting as small as -1 to a text block to make it hold together better.

▶ When you're setting justified text and you get bad line breaks, or if you have an extra word by itself at the end of a paragraph, you can track the whole paragraph plus or minus one or two units without it being too apparent. Sometimes that's just enough to fix these problems.

Remember, however, that no matter how solid a rule may be, you are obliged to break it if the finished design will be better.

▼ ▼

Tip: Tracking and the Single Word. The way tracking works, technically, is by adding or subtracting space to the right of each selected character. If you want to track a single word and don't want the space after the last character to be adjusted, you should select not the whole word, but only the characters up to the last letter. For example, if you want to apply 10-unit tracking to the word "obfuscation" without changing the space after the "n," you would only select the letters "obfuscatio" and then apply tracking.

▼ ▼

Wordspacing

Quark's free Type Tricks XTension adds one more option to character-level attributes: the ability to adjust kerning for spacebands within a selected range of text. As I discussed above, kerning is the adjustment of space between characters; it's often called "letterspacing," but I prefer to reserve that term for justification controls (which I'll talk about later in this chapter). What Quark is calling "wordspacing" here is really just changing the kerning between words (wherever it finds spacebands).

There are three conditions for adjusting wordspacing—spaceband kerning—over a selected range of text.

- ▶ You can only use keystrokes.

- ▶ You must have an extended keyboard.

- ▶ The Type Tricks XTension must be in your XTension folder (it must be currently active).

Table 6-5 shows the keystrokes you should use to adjust wordspacing. Note that adjusting wordspacing is no magic trick: QuarkXPress is simply adding and subtracting kerning from each spaceband (you can put the cursor between the spaceband and the first letter in a word to see how much space has been added).

There are two problems with adding wordspacing in this way. First, it's a pain to remove or change it (you can use Remove Manual Kerning as described earlier, but that will also remove any other kerning you've added). Second, at the timc of this writing, it doesn't appear to work in Windows properly. If we're lucky, Quark will come out with a version of this XTension that doesn't have this conflict.

Baseline Shift

The final character attribute I discuss here is *baseline shift*. The baseline is the imaginary line on which the type sits. Each line of text you're reading is made of characters sitting on a baseline. You can shift a character or a group of characters above or below the baseline using the Baseline Shift feature on the Style menu (see Figure 6-13).

Table 6-5
Keystrokes for wordspacing
(The Windows keyboard shortcuts weren't working as this book went to press)

PRESS...	TO...
Command-Control-Shift-] *or* Ctrl-Shift-]	Increase wordspacing 10 units
Command-Option-Control-Shift-] *or* Ctrl-Shift-]	Increase wordspacing one unit
Command-Control-Shift-[*or* Ctrl-Alt-Shift-[	Decrease wordspacing 10 units
Command-Option-Control-Shift-[*or* Ctrl-Alt-Shift-[	Decrease wordspacing one unit

Figure 6-13
Baseline shift

I DON'T NEED NO BASELINE SHIFT.

I FEEL A NEED FOR A SUPERSCRIPT.

OY. I'M FEELIN' KINDA UNSTABLE, WHAT WITH
ALL THIS BASELINE SHIFTING GOING ON.

Baseline shift is specified in points; negative values shift the character down, positive values shift it up. You can enter any value, up to three times the font size you're using, in hundredths of a point; for example, you can shift a character off the baseline 30 points in either direction if that character is in 10-point type.

Note that baseline shift is similar to kerning and tracking in an important way: even though you specify values in points rather than in fractions of an em, the value of the baseline shift changes along with the font size. For example, if you specify a 4-point baseline shift for 15-point type, when you double the font size to 30 points, the shifted character is "reshifted" to eight points ($2 \times 4 = 8$).

Paragraph Formatting

Character formatting is all very well and good, but when it comes to how text flows in a column, it don't make Bo Diddley squat. To handle text flow on a paragraph level, you have to use paragraph formatting. These controls include indents, leading, tabs, drop caps, and hyphenation and justification, as well as some esoteric functions such as Keep with Next ¶ and widow and orphan control. In this section, I'll discuss each of these features. In addition, as usual, I'll give lots of examples so you can see what I'm talking about.

Tip: Selecting Paragraphs. I often look over people's shoulders as they work, and what I see could scare a moose. One such scare is the technique of selecting a paragraph so that they can apply some paragraph formatting to it (leading, space before, or whatever). People think that they have to select the whole paragraph first. Not true! When you change paragraph formatting, you only need the cursor in the paragraph you want to change. That means you can have one word selected, or three sentences, or half of one paragraph and half of another, or whatever.

The central headquarters of paragraph formatting is the Paragraph Attributes dialog box (see Figure 6-14). Let's look at each feature of this dialog box in turn, and I'll branch off on tangents when I need to.

Alignment

Let's start with the most blatant paragraph attribute—its alignment. Most people are familiar with the five horizontal alignment options: left aligned, right aligned, justified, force justified, and centered. I will discuss each of these first, then move on to a less-known feature: vertical alignment.

Horizontal Alignment

If you've been involved with desktop typography long enough (a day or two), you'll know that different programs have different names for the same thing. For example, what QuarkXPress calls "left aligned" others may call "left justified" or "flush left/ragged right." I'm not going to start naming names, but QuarkXPress's terms are simpler and make more sense. For one thing, "justified" means only one thing: text that's flush to both left and right margins. "Fully justified" is redundant, and "left-justified" is . . . well, it just isn't. Figure 6-15 shows some examples of text with various horizontal alignments.

You can specify alignment for a paragraph in any of four ways.

Figure 6-14

The Paragraph
Attributes dialog box

▶ **PARAGRAPH ATTRIBUTES.** The Paragraph Attributes dialog box is always an option when you're changing paragraph formats. The control is a popup menu (see Figure 6-16). This, of course, is the slow way to apply formatting.

▶ **ALIGNMENT SUBMENU.** You can select the horizontal alignment you want from the Alignment submenu under the Style menu. This is pretty slow, too.

▶ **KEYSTROKES.** Note that the Alignment submenu lists a keystroke for each style. These are easy to remember, since they rely on first-letter mnemonics: hold down the Command/Ctrl and Shift keys and press "L" for Left, "R" for Right, "C" for Centered, and "J" for Justified. The keystroke for Forced Justify is a variant on Justified: Command-Option-Shift-J (Ctrl-Alt-Shift-J).

▶ **MEASUREMENTS PALETTE.** Perhaps the most simple alignment method of all is to use the Measurements palette. When you have an insertion point in a paragraph, XPress displays five icons representing the various alignment selections (see Figure 6-17). To change a paragraph's alignment, click on the one you want.

Figure 6-15
Horizontal alignment

We·have·heard·the·chimes·at·midnight.¶   *Left aligned*

A·hit!·A·palpable·hit!¶   *Centered*

I·am·too·much·i'·the·sun   *Right aligned*

Figure 6-16
Alignment control in
the Paragraph Attributes
dialog box

Paragraph Attributes

Formats | Tabs | Rules

Left Indent: 0p
First Line: 0p
Right Indent: 0p
Leading: 32 pt
Space Before: 0p
Space After: 0p
Alignment:
H&J:

Left
✓ Centered
Right
Justified
Forced

Drop Caps
Character Count: 1
Line Count: 3

Keep Lines Together
All Lines in ¶
Start: 2 End: 2

Keep with Next ¶
Lock to Baseline Grid

Apply   Cancel   OK

Figure 6-17
Horizontal alignment in
the Measurements palette

While left-aligned, right-aligned, and centered paragraphs are relatively straightforward, justified and force-justified text are a bit more complicated. Because of this, I'm putting off talking about justification and hyphenation until later in this chapter.

▼ ▼

Tip: Limit Your Alignments. I'm sure you would never do this. I know that you're a designer of reputation and flair. But I might as well mention this tip, just in case. Don't use left-aligned, right-aligned, centered, and justified text all on the same page unless you have a reasonable design sense and a signed note from your parent. Too often people let all this highfalutin' technology go to their heads and design their pages using every trick in the bag. Remember that there is strength in simplicity.

▼ ▼

Vertical Alignment

Vertical alignment is not really a paragraph attribute, but an attribute of each text box. Nonetheless, as vertical alignment is closely related to other paragraph attributes (leading in particular), I might as well bring this, too, into the discussion.

Just as horizontal alignment is the horizontal placement of the lines of text within a column, vertical alignment is the vertical placement of the text within its box. You can specify attributes similar to those used in horizontal alignment: Top, Bottom, Center, and Justified. The only place you can change this setting is on the Text tab in the Modify dialog box (Command/Ctrl-M, or double-click on the box with the Item tool selected). Here you're presented with a popup menu (see Figure 6-18).

Let's look briefly at each of the alignment possibilities.

Top. This is the default setting for text boxes. It's what you're probably used to if you use QuarkXPress regularly. The text starts at the top of the text box and,

Figure 6-18

Vertical Alignment in
the Modify dialog box

as you type, fills the box. Exactly where the text starts depends on the First Baseline control (discussed later in the chapter).

Centered. When Vertical Alignment is set to Centered, the text in the text box is vertically centered. That sounds trite, but I can't explain it any better. See Figure 6-19 for an example of this alignment. Note that blank lines can affect the positioning of the text in the text box; sometimes you have to delete them to get the text to look centered.

▼ ▼

Tip: Centering Text. Telling XPress to center text—either horizontally or vertically—may not result in your text looking perfectly centered. Why? Because the mathematical horizontal centering of text may not look as "right" as optical centering, especially if you have punctuation before or after the text. You can use invisible characters colored the same as whatever they're on top of (for example, white on top of a white background). Or you can use altered indentation (see "Indents," below) to change the way the text looks (see Figure 6-20). Remember, what looks right is more "right" than what the computer says.

In the case of vertical centering, text in all capitals or text in fonts such as Zapf Dingbats may not appear to be centered in the box. This is because QuarkXPress does not actually find the center of the characters you've typed. Instead, it uses the full height of the font, ascenders and descenders combined, to calculate proper placement. I suggest using baseline shift to move the characters around until they look the way you want them to.

▼ ▼

Figure 6-19

The four Vertical
Alignment settings

Edges of text box

Installing **KvetchWrite** is the absolute living essence of simplicity.

First, except on old S-100 systems, you will need to reformat your hard

disk. As you know, this is a short and simple procedure that anyone can do.

Next, remove Disk 27 from its fireproof container. If you forget the

Vertical alignment: Justified

Installing **KvetchWrite** is the absolute living essence of simplicity.
First, except on old S-100 systems, you will need to reformat your hard
disk. As you know, this is a short and simple procedure that anyone can do.
Next, remove Disk 27 from its fireproof container. If you forget the

Vertical alignment: Bottom

Installing **KvetchWrite** is the absolute living essence of simplicity.
First, except on old S-100 systems, you will need to reformat your hard
disk. As you know, this is a short and simple procedure that anyone can do.
Next, remove Disk 27 from its fireproof container. If you forget the

Vertical alignment: Top

Installing **KvetchWrite** is the absolute living essence of simplicity.
First, except on old S-100 systems, you will need to reformat your hard
disk. As you know, this is a short and simple procedure that anyone can do.
Next, remove Disk 27 from its fireproof container. If you forget the

Vertical alignment: Centered

Bottom. By specifying Bottom, you force the last line of text to the bottom of the box. Then as text flows into the text box, each line pushes the type higher in the box. Note that it is the bottom of the descender, not the baseline, that sits flush with the box's bottom.

Justified. "Justification" means here that the text will be flush with the top and bottom of the box. QuarkXPress puts the first line of the text box at the top, the last line at the bottom, and then adds or deletes space between interior lines. That means that there may be a lot of extra space between lines and paragraphs (the program overrides paragraph leading settings when necessary).

You can specify a maximum distance between paragraphs in a vertically justified text box by changing the Inter ¶ Max value on the Text tab in the Modify dialog box. A setting of zero, which is the default, tells QuarkXPress to distribute all space evenly by adding leading. A setting higher than zero lets the program add extra space between paragraphs rather than change your leading (this is usually preferable). Figure 6-21 shows some examples of vertically justified text with different Inter ¶ Max settings.

Figure 6-20
When centering is not centered

Vertical centering in the top example isn't optically even because the typeface isn't centered descender to cap height. The bottom example was centered by eye.

"Take your little brother swimming with a brick."

This is not visually centered because of the quotation marks.

"Take your little brother swimming with a brick."

This is adjusted by placing punctuation colored white on each line.

When Quark announced that XPress would support vertical justification, the press thought it would be the greatest thing since the transistor. My response to this is: If you set up your leading grids and text boxes correctly, you shouldn't need to have some computer going through your drawers, shuffling lines around. I wouldn't want a computer to marry my daughter (if I had one), and I don't want a computer changing my leading and paragraph spacing.

No matter how picky I am about correctly setting up my documents, I do admit that there are times when vertical justification comes in handy. For

Figure 6-21
Varying the
Inter ¶ Max setting

Ior, auritulus cinereus ille annosus Raili, solus in silvae angulo quodam carduoso stabat, pedibus late divaricatis, capite deflexo de rerum natura meditans.
"Cur?' cogitabat, modo "quemadmodum?'
Itaque Puo appropinquante Ior paulisper a meditatione desistere gavisus est ut maeste "Ut vales?' ei diceret.

Text is 10/11, Inter ¶ Max setting is zero points. The leading is ignored completely.

Gray line represents the text box.

Ior, auritulus cinereus ille annosus Raili, solus in silvae angulo quodam carduoso stabat, pedibus late divaricatis, capite deflexo de rerum natura meditans.

"Cur?' cogitabat, modo "quemadmodum?'

Itaque Puo appropinquante Ior paulisper a meditatione desistere gavisus est ut maeste "Ut vales?' ei diceret.

Text is 10/11, Inter ¶ Max setting is four points. The leading is adjusted slightly, while space is added between paragraphs.

Ior, auritulus cinereus ille annosus Raili, solus in silvae angulo quodam carduoso stabat, pedibus late divaricatis, capite deflexo de rerum natura meditans.

"Cur?' cogitabat, modo "quemadmodum?'

Itaque Puo appropinquante Ior paulisper a meditatione desistere gavisus est ut maeste "Ut vales?' ei diceret.

Text is 10/11, Inter ¶ Max setting is one pica. The leading is back to normal, and space is only added between paragraphs.

example, many newspapers constantly use this feature to "bottom out" their columns.

▼ ▼

Tip: When Vertical Justification Doesn't Work. Note that XPress will turn off vertical alignment in two instances: if the text box is not rectangular, or if some object is causing text runaround (see Chapter 11, *Where Text Meets Graphics*). In both these cases, the text box reverts to top alignment. I could explain the mathematical reasoning behind this, but suffice it to say that it would be incredibly difficult and time-consuming for XPress to align text vertically in these instances, so it just doesn't even try.

▼ ▼

Indents

Horizontal alignment depends entirely on where the left and right margins are. In a column of text, the margins are usually at the edges of the text box (or of the column, in a multicolumn text box). However, you may want the first line of every paragraph to be indented slightly. Or you might want the left or right margin to be somewhere other than the edge of the column. You control each of these by changing the values for paragraph indents.

▼ ▼

Tip: Watch the Text Inset. The default text inset for text boxes is one point, so your text will automatically be indented one point from each side of the box. Make sure to change the value in the Modify dialog box (Command/Ctrl-M) if you don't want the 1-point indent.

The best way to avoid this default problem is to close all documents, and double-click the Text Box tool. This brings up the Tool tab of the Preferences dialog box, where you can click the Modify button to change the Text Inset to zero. A text inset of zero sometimes makes the text a little hard to read on screen, because it bounces up against the side of the box; so you may or may not want to do this.

Note that some XTensions let you set the Text Inset differently for each side of the box: top, bottom, left, and right.

▼ ▼

QuarkXPress lets you change three indent values: Left Indent, Right Indent, and First Line indent. All three controls are located on the Formats tab in the Paragraph Attributes dialog box (Command-Shift-F or Ctrl-Shift-F; see Figure 6-22). I'll discuss each one and then talk about how you can use them in your documents.

Figure 6-22
The Indent settings

Left Indent. The Left Indent control specifies how far the paragraph sits from the left side of the text box or column guide. The Left Indent is actually measured from the Text Inset border, not from the side of the box. For example, if you want your paragraph to be indented exactly three picas from the side of the text box, and your Text Inset setting is four points, then your Left Indent should be "2p8" (3p - 4pt = 2p8).

Right Indent. The Right Indent control specifies how far the right edge of the paragraph will be positioned from the right edge of the text box or column guide (or the text box's Text Indent). For example, if you change the Right Indent to .5 inch, you can imagine an invisible line being drawn .5 inch from the right column guide. The text cannot move farther to the right than this line (see Figure 6-23).

First Line. Whatever you do, wherever you go, don't type five spaces to indent the first line of each paragraph. If you must, use a tab. If you want to avoid the problem completely, use a First Line indent. The First Line indent feature does exactly what it sounds like it would do: it indents only the first line of each paragraph.

How large your indent should be depends primarily on your design and on the typeface you are working with. If you are working with a typeface with a large x-height (the height of the lowercase "x" in relation to the height of the capital letters), you should use a larger first-line indent than if you are working with a typeface that has a small x-height. Book designers often use a one-

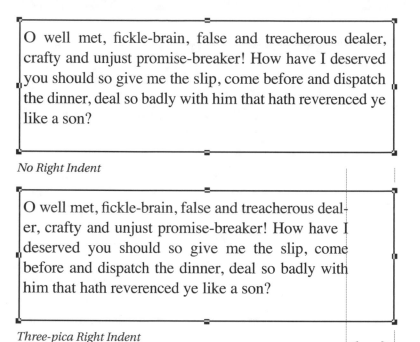

Figure 6-23
Right Indent

No Right Indent

Three-pica Right Indent

or two-em indent; if you're using 12-point type, the indent might be 12 points or 24 points.

▼ ▼

Tip: Hanging Indents. You can use Left Indent and First Line indent to create hanging indents (used for bullet lists and the like) by typing a negative number as the First Line indent. I often use "1p6" (one-and-a-half picas) for a left indent and "-1p6" for a first-line indent. This pushes the entire paragraph out to the 1p6 mark, and then pulls the first character (a bullet) back to the zero mark (see Figure 6-24). Typing a tab after the bullet skips over to the 1p6 mark whether or not I have a tab stop there (I'll discuss tabs and tab stops later in this chapter).

The benefit of hanging indents like this is that you don't have to painfully set your own returns after each line. If you set hard or soft returns after each line—I'll talk about the difference later in this chapter—and then you edit the text, or even change the typeface, it takes a long time to fix the text, removing the old returns and putting new ones in. This is horrible; if you had just used hanging indents instead, your problem would be solved automatically.

(You can also use an Indent Here character when creating hanging indents; I cover that in "Special Characters," later in this chapter.)

▼ ▼

Note that you don't have to specify any of the indents by typing numbers. While the Paragraph Attributes dialog box is open, you are shown a ruler along the top of the active text box (see Figure 6-25). This ruler contains three trian-gle markers: two on the left, and one on the right. You can move these icons by clicking and dragging them along the ruler.

The right triangle is the Right Indent. The bottom-left triangle is the Left Indent. The top-left triangle is the First Line indent. While moving these tri-angles around, the First Line indent moves as you change the Left Indent. For example, if you set a ¼-inch First Line indent, and then move the Left Indent triangle to ½ inch, the First Line indent moves with it to the ¾-inch point (½ inch plus ¼ inch).

▼ ▼

Tip: Formatting Past the Boundaries. As the old Zen master said, "Frustration dissipates like the morning fog when light is shed on the prob-lem." (Actually, I don't know any Zen masters, so I just made that up.) One frus-tration I've seen people get caught in is the issue of formatting beyond what you can see on screen. For example, when you open the Paragraph Attributes dialog box, QuarkXPress adds a ruler along the top of the text box so that you can manually add or edit the tab stops and indents. However, if the box is too wide, you can't see the left or right side of the ruler because it runs right out of the document window (see Figure 6-26).

However—and here's the shedding of the light—it turns out that if you click in that ruler and drag to the left or right, the page scrolls with you. Pretty soon you get to where you want to go and you can stop dragging. Note that when

Figure 6-24
Hanging indents

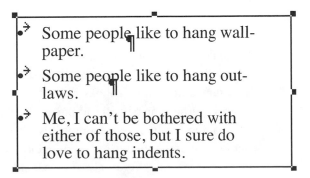

Figure 6-25
The text ruler associated with the Paragraph Attributes dialog box

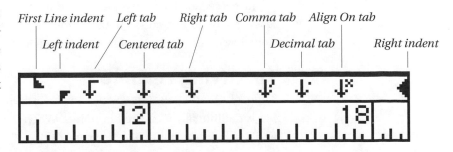

Figure 6-26

The too-wide ruler

If you select a wide block of text and bring up Paragraph Tabs, the ruler just runs right off the window.

you do this, you sometimes accidentally add a tab stop (I'll talk about tab stops later in this chapter), and you have to get rid of it by clicking on it and dragging it off the ruler.

Leading

If I could get one concept across to you in this chapter, I'd want it to be this: don't follow the defaults. By not following default values, you are forced to pay attention to how the type looks, rather than letting the computer do it for you. There is perhaps no better example of why this is important than leading.

Leading (pronounced "ledding") is the space between lines of type. The name originates from the lead strips or blocks used to add space between lines of metal type. QuarkXPress gives you considerable control over leading values for each paragraph, or it can "fly on automatic," specifying leading for you.

In this section I'll discuss the two modes and three methods for specifying leading. Pay close attention to the words "color" and "readability" in this section; they're the reasons designers bother to be so meticulous.

Specifying Leading

Although QuarkXPress lets you use any measurement system you want, leading is traditionally measured in points. When talking type, most typesetters and designers say things like, "Helvetica 10 on 12," and write it out as "10/12."

Designers who have grown accustomed to digital equipment (in other words, just about everybody) would say that "10/12" means setting 10-point type so that the baseline of one line is 12 points from the baseline of the next line (see Figure 6-27).

Figure 6-27
Specifying leading

Leading is a paragraph-level attribute; that is, you can specify only one leading value for each paragraph. You specify your leading in one of three ways: in the Paragraph Attributes dialog box (press Command-Shift-E (Ctrl-Shift-E) to open this dialog box and jump right to the Leading field), in the Measurements palette, or with keystrokes. Whereas in the first instance you can only type in the leading value, in the Measurements palette you can change leading in two ways (see Figure 6-28).

▶ You can select the leading value and replace it with whatever leading value you want.

▶ You can click the up or down arrow next to the leading value to increase or decrease the leading value in 1-point increments. Option/Alt-clicking increases or decreases in .1-point increments.

You can also use keyboard shortcuts to change a paragraph's leading; I've listed the four keystrokes in Table 6-6.

By the way, if you change leading in the Paragraph Attributes dialog box, you'll notice that XPress places a popup menu next to the Leading field. The popup menu doesn't really do anything, and I still can't figure out why they stuck it in there. Just ignore it.

Figure 6-28
Leading in the
Measurements palette

Table 6-6
Leading keystrokes

PRESS ...	To ...
Command/Ctrl-Shift-"	Increase leading in 1-point increments
Command-Option-Shift-" Ctrl-Alt-Shift-"	Increase leading in 0.1-point increments
Command/Ctrl-Shift-;	Decrease leading in 1-point increments
Command-Option-Shift-; Ctrl-Alt-Shift-;	Decrease leading in 0.1-point increments

Leading Methods

QuarkXPress lets you specify leading values in three ways: absolutely, automatically, and relatively. Let's look at these.

Absolute. Setting your leading in an absolute form makes your leading as steadfast as Gibraltar. If you specify 14-point leading, you get 14-point leading—no matter what size type the paragraph contains. If the type is bigger than the leading, the type overprints preceding lines. When, as in the example given above, someone talks about "10/12" type, this is what they're talking about.

QuarkXPress lets you type any absolute leading value between zero and 1,080 points (15 inches).

▼ ▼

Tip: True Zero Leading. If you set a paragraph's leading to zero, QuarkXPress decides that you really mean you want "automatic" leading (see below). But what if you really want no leading at all from baseline to baseline? If you set leading to .0001 points, the program rounds down to exactly zero. The next highest value is .001 points. The truth of the matter is that these are equivalent for all intents and purposes, but I wanted to be clear anyway.

Why would anyone want to use zero leading? Well, it wouldn't be common. Zero leading means that every line in the paragraph would be printed exactly on top of the line above it, making the whole paragraph be only one line tall. It's especially good for those postmodern designs where you don't really need to read any of the words.

▼ ▼

Automatic. Auto leading sets leading as a percentage of the largest font size on each line. This percentage is usually 20 percent greater than the font size. For example, if the largest font size on a given line is 10 points, then your leading will be set to 12 points (10, plus 20 percent of 10). If you change the font size to 12 points, then the leading changes to 14.4 points. Note that if you change only one character on a line to a larger font size, then that line alone will have a different leading value (which just *screams* "nonprofessional!"), even though Auto leading is a paragraph-wide feature (see Figure 6-29).

Auto leading is the default setting of any new text box. To choose it specifically, you can type either "Auto" or "0" as the leading value.

You can change the automatic-leading percentage value on the Paragraph tab in the Preferences dialog box. There are two things you should note about doing this, though. First, the change is layout-wide; you can't change the automatic leading percentage for only one paragraph or text box. Second, you must specify clearly what the automatic leading measurements are; that is, if you want a percent, you must type a percent sign. This is important because you can also specify automatic leading to be a relative value (more on relative values soon).

To be honest with you, I use automatic leading when I'm typing up grocery shopping lists (and sometimes when I'm writing a letter to my mom). But when I'm working on a professional project, I define the leading explicitly using absolute leading. Period. Many professional magazines, newspapers, and newsletters use automatic leading because they don't know any better, and then they blame QuarkXPress for outputting weird-looking text.

Relative. Whereas automatic leading generally determines the leading value based on a percentage of font size, relative leading determines leading by an absolute value. You specify relative leading by including the characters + or - (plus or minus—the minus sign is a hyphen) before your leading value. For example, applying a leading value of +3 to 12-point type results in 12/15 leading. If you change the font size to 22 points, you automatically get 22/25 leading (22 plus 3).

By typing a negative relative value, you can tighten up the leading. However, you have a limit: the height of a capital on the lower line cannot be higher than the baseline of the upper line (to get that effect, you have to use absolute leading).

The only time I use relative leading is when I am specifying *solid* leading—that is, when the leading equals the point size. Instead of keying in 30-point

Figure 6-29

Auto leading can result in irregular leading within a paragraph

Noodle. Oh! monstrous, dreadful, terrible! Oh! Oh! Deaf be my ears, for ever blind my eyes! **D**umb be my tongue! feet lame! all senses lost! Howl wolves, grunt bears, hiss snakes, shriek all ye ghosts!

King. What does the blockhead mean?

One character can throw the leading off.

leading for 30-point type, I type "+0". Then, if (or when) I change the font size, the leading changes with it.

Leading Modes

When specifying leading in QuarkXPress, you can work in one of two leading modes: Word Processing or Typesetting. You can select which mode to use on the Paragraph tab in the Preferences dialog box on the Edit menu.

Word Processing. Let's be straight here: even if you're using XPress only as a word processor, you shouldn't use Word Processing mode. There's just no point to it. Selecting Word Processing mode makes QuarkXPress use an ascent-to-ascent measurement. "Ascent to ascent" means that the leading value you specify will be measured from the top of a capital letter on one line to the top of a capital letter on the next line. The only reason Quark included this method was because many word-processing programs use it. You shouldn't, because the leading will change depending on the typeface you're using, and there's no way you can tell what the leading value actually is (this side of examining a font's ascent value using ResEdit or some font utility).

Typesetting. As I noted above, the proper way to specify leading on the Macintosh is to measure from the baseline of one line to the baseline of the next. QuarkXPress calls this Typesetting Mode. It's the program default; if someone has changed it, change it back and leave it alone.

▼ ▼

Tip: When Black and White Is Colorful. When designers and typesetters talk about the *color* of a page or of type, they aren't talking red, green, or blue. They're referring to the degree of darkness or lightness that the text projects. The color of text is directly related to the typeface, letterspacing, wordspacing, and leading. Other design elements, such as drop caps, graphic elements, or pullquotes, can have a significant effect on the color of a page. It's usually a good practice to maintain an even and balanced color across your page, unless you're trying to pull the viewer's eye (as opposed to pulling the viewer's leg) to one area or another (see Figure 6-30).

One way to see the color of a page or a block of type is to hold the printed page at some distance and squint. You can also turn the page over and hold it up to the light, so that you can see the text blocks without being distracted by the text itself.

▼ ▼

Tip: Leading Techniques. Here are a few tips and tricks for adjusting your leading. Remember, though, that ultimately it is how easily the text reads and

Figure 6-30

The color of text blocks

Eduardus ursus, amicis suis agnomine "Winnie ille Pu"—aut breviter "Pu"—notus, die quodam canticum semihiantibus labellis superbe eliquans

Stone Serif 9/12

Eduardus ursus, amicis suis agnomine "Winnie ille Pu"—aut breviter "Pu"—notus, die quodam canticum semihiantibus

Stone Serif bold 9/12

Eduardus ursus, amicis suis agnomine "Winnie ille Pu"—aut breviter "Pu"—notus, die quodam canticum semihiantibus labellis superbe

Helvetica 10/13

Eduardus ursus, amicis suis agnomine "Winnie ille Pu"—aut breviter "Pu"—notus, die quodam canticum semihiantibus labellis superbe eliquans

Garamond 10/13

Eduardus ursus, amicis suis agnomine "Winnie ille Pu"—aut breviter "Pu"—notus, die quodam canticum semihiantibus labellis superbe

Palatino with zero tracking

Eduardus ursus, amicis suis agnomine "Winnie ille Pu"—aut breviter "Pu"—notus, die quodam canticum semihiantibus labellis superbe eliquans

Palatino with -10 tracking

how comfortable the color is that counts. Figure 6-31 shows some samples for each of these suggestions.

▶ Increase the leading as you increase the line length. Solid leading may read fine with lines containing five words, but will be awful for lines containing 20 words.

▶ Generally use some extra leading for sans serif or bold type. It needs the extra room.

▶ Note the x-height of your typeface. Fonts with a small x-height can often be set tighter than those with a large x-height.

▶ Set display or headline type tightly. Big type can and should be set tightly, using either +0 relative leading or even absolute leading smaller than the point size you're using.

▶ When you're using really tight leading, be careful not to let the ascenders of one line touch the descenders of the line above it.

Of course, here's a corollary tip to all of these: break the rules if it makes the design look better!

Figure 6-31
Leading techniques

The longer a line, the more leading you'll need.

Look, s'pose some general or king is bone stupid and leads his men up a creek, then those men've got to be fearless, there's another virtue for you. S'pose he's stingy and hires too few soldiers, then they got to be a crowd of Hercule's. And s'pose he's slapdash and don't give a bugger, then they got to be clever as monkeys else their number's up.

9/9.5

9/11

Look, s'pose some general or king is bone stupid and leads his men up a creek, then those men've got to be fearless, there's another virtue for you. S'pose he's stingy and hires too few soldiers, then they got to be a crowd of Hercule's. And s'pose he's slapdash and don't give a bugger, then they got to be clever as monkeys else their number's up.

Fonts with small x-heights can be set tighter.

The misery of this one woman surges through my heart and marrow, and you grid imperturbed over the fate of thousands!

The misery of this one woman surges through my heart and marrow, and you grid imperturbed over the fate of thousands!

9/11.5

9/9.5

Display type can be set tightly.

The best thing since sliced bread

36/31

Watch out for your ascenders and descenders.

Cagney Jads

48/39

▼ ▼

Tip: From Automatic to Absolute. If you press Command-Shift-straight quote (Ctrl-Shift-') when the selected paragraph is set to Auto leading, XPress switches the leading to the absolute value that corresponds to the automatic value (it rounds to the nearest point). For instance, if you've got 10-point type and Auto leading is set to 20 percent, if you select a paragraph that has automatic leading and press Command-Shift-straight quote (Ctrl-Shift-'), XPress changes the leading to 12 points (120 percent of 10 points). This is the fastest way to switch from automatic to absolute leading.

▼ ▼

Space Before and After

Not only can you place interline space with leading, you can add space between paragraphs using the Space Before and Space After controls. You can find both of these controls in the Paragraph Attributes dialog box (Command-Shift-F or Ctrl-Shift-F).

While it is entirely your prerogative to use both Space Before and Space After, you normally will only need to use one or the other. Think about it: If you add equal space before and after a paragraph, it doubles the amount of space between each paragraph. I almost always use Space Before, but whichever you use is fine.

I've seen more than one designer become flustered when applying Space Before to the first paragraph in a text box. Nothing happens. Remember that Space Before has no effect on the first paragraph in a text box because it only adds space *between* two paragraphs. Fortunately, though, this is usually what you want. To add space before the first paragraph in a text box, use the First Baseline placement control (see "First Baseline," below).

▼ ▼

Tip: Adding Extra Space. Recently I witnessed one of my esteemed office-mates using multiple carriage returns to control the space between paragraphs, and I almost went apoplectic. Let's see if I can pound this idea into your head as strongly as I did by saying, "Don't use multiple spaces between words or punctuation!"

Don't ever use an extra carriage return to add space between paragraphs. Not only will you offend the people at Quark who spent long hours implementing the Space Before and Space After features, but you will—nine out of 10 times—mess yourself up with extra blank paragraphs hanging out at tops of columns or in other places where you don't want them. If you want a full line of space between paragraphs, apply it with Space Before or Space After in the Paragraph Attributes dialog box.

▼ ▼

Tip: Page Breaks. InDesign and PageMaker have a cool feature that I like: you can specify a paragraph attribute that forces the paragraph to start on a new column or page. That is, any paragraph tagged with this attribute will always start at the top of a page or column. As it turns out, you can do a similar thing in QuarkXPress by simply making the Space Before value in the Paragraph Attributes dialog box as large as the text column is tall. For example, if your text box is 45 picas tall, enter "45" in the Space Before field. You can set this as a paragraph style (see Chapter 7, *Copy Flow*) or as local formatting for particular paragraphs.

▼ ▼

First Baseline

The first line of a text box is always a tricky one for perfectionists. How far away from the top edge of the text box should the line sit? And how to get it there? Usually, QuarkXPress places the first line of text according to the text box's Text Inset value. For instance, if the Text Inset is set to 3 points, then the top of the first line of text is set 3 points away from the top edge of the box.

Typophiles will be happy to find that you can clarify what XPress uses as the "top of the first line of text" with the Minimum setting (found on the Text tab in the Modify dialog box). You can choose three values for the Minimum setting: Cap Height, Cap+Accent, and Ascent (see Figure 6-32).

Nonetheless, if you really care about the placement of your type, you may choose to use First Baseline Offset instead (also found in the Modify dialog box). First Baseline Offset lets you choose exactly how far from the top of the text box you want the first line of text to sit (measured from the baseline, of course). However, First Baseline Offset only kicks in when the distance from box edge to first baseline is smaller than the First Baseline Offset value.

For instance, if the baseline of the first line of text is 24 points from the top of the box when First Baseline Offset is set to zero (which is the default value), then First Baseline Offset won't do anything until you set the value higher than 24 points. If you set it to 30 points, then the baseline of the first line of text will sit at exactly 30 points from the top of the box. However, if you then go and change the text size to 60 points, XPress ignores the First Baseline Offset again and places the top of the text (as determined by the Minimum setting) at the Text Inset value.

Figure 6-32

The Minimum settings in
First Baseline Offset

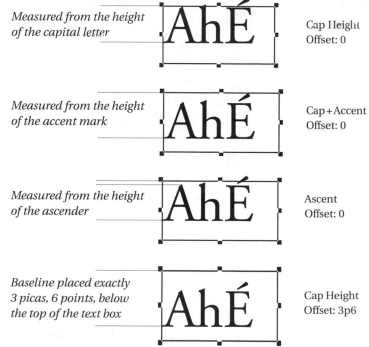

*Measured from the height
of the capital letter*

Cap Height
Offset: 0

*Measured from the height
of the accent mark*

Cap+Accent
Offset: 0

*Measured from the height
of the ascender*

Ascent
Offset: 0

*Baseline placed exactly
3 picas, 6 points, below
the top of the text box*

Cap Height
Offset: 3p6

Tip: Constant First Baselines. When you're working with a leading grid, you might be frustrated by where QuarkXPress places the first line in a text box. That's because XPress generally moves the baseline of the first line up or down to accommodate the size of the text, rather than sticking to your baseline grid (see Figure 6-33). But if you set the First Baseline value for the text box in the Modify dialog box, the first baseline always appears at the same place, and your leading grid isn't messed up. Note that the First Baseline value has to be bigger than the type itself in order for the line to be moved down.

So don't go adding multiple carriage returns or trying to do weird things with leading, space before, or baseline shift. Just use the First Baseline setting.

Tabs

If you've ever typed on a typewriter, you've probably encountered tabs. A tab is a jump-to signal in the form of a keyboard character. For example, if you're typing along and press the Tab key, the text cursor jumps to the next tab stop along the line. On a computer, the Tab key actually inserts an invisible character that you can delete or cut (or anything else you can do with characters).

Figure 6 33
First Baseline maintains
an even leading grid

Before

*Note that First Baseline
Offset aligns all the
columns of a text box*

After

You can place tab stops anywhere you like across the text column. Tab stops are paragraph-level formatting attributes, so each paragraph can have a different set of tab stops. If you don't specify your own tab stops, QuarkXPress sets default stops every half-inch across the text box.

▼ ▼

Tip: Don't Use Space Where You Really Want Tabs. Have you ever tried to align multiple columns using the spacebar? If you have, you have probably known frustration like no other frustration known to desktop publishers. I call it the "it-works-on-a-typewriter" syndrome. It's true; you can line up columns on a typewriter with spaces. But you shouldn't in desktop publishing. The reason has to do with fonts.

On most standard typewriters, the font you're using is a monospaced font. That means each and every character in the font is the same width. However, most typefaces on the Macintosh are *not* monospaced. Therefore, you cannot rely on an equal number of characters always spanning an equal distance. Figure 6-34 shows this phenomenon clearly. So don't use multiple spaces when you're trying to align columns. In fact, don't use multiple spaces ever. Use tabs.

▼ ▼

Tip: Multiple Tabs. If you are setting up a table and you want to place tabs between each column, follow the same rule as with spaces: don't type multiple tabs in a row to make your columns align. Set one tab stop for each column. Then press Tab once to jump from column to column.

▼ ▼

QuarkXPress lets you set seven types of tab stops using two different methods. Let's look at the types of tab stops first. They are: Left, Right, Center, Right

Figure 6-34

Using spaces
for alignment

Take one	from column "a"	and one	from column "b"
but here	you actually	have four	columns see?

Aligned with spaces (bad)

Take one	from column "a"	and one	from column "b"
but here	you actually	have four	columns see?

Aligned with tabs (good)

Indent, Decimal, Comma, and Align On. Figure 6-35 shows examples of most of these tab stops in a common situation—a table.

▶ **LEFT TAB STOP.** This is the type of tab stop you're used to from typewriters. The text after the tab continues as left-aligned. All tab stops are Left tab stops unless you specify them as another type.

▶ **RIGHT TAB STOP.** Tabbing to a Right tab stop causes the following text to be right aligned. That is, the text will be flush right against the tab stop.

▶ **CENTER TAB STOP.** Text typed after tabbing to a Center tab stop will center on that tab stop.

▶ **RIGHT INDENT TAB STOP.** Right Indent tabs don't show up on the pop-up menu because they're not really tab stops. You enter them in a text box with the Content tool selected by pressing Option/Alt-Tab. I'll talk about this more fully in just a moment.

▶ **DECIMAL, COMMA, AND ALIGN ON TAB STOPS.** These three tab stops act similarly. They act like a right tab until a special character is entered; then the following text is flush left. The decimal and comma tabs align on the first nonnumeric, nonpunctuation character. Selecting Align On brings up a one-character entry field; you can then enter the special character that acts as the tab stop.

▼ ▼

Tip: Formatting Tabs Quickly. One reader, Barry Simon, pointed out to me that you can sometimes format tab stops for a number of lines more easily by

Figure 6-35

Using tabs and tab stops

Acme Digital Frammis Corp.

"Have a wonderful day!"

1994 Customer Dissatisfaction as a Function of Product Color

Product Color	People Per Product	Units Sold	Unit Price ($)	Dissatisfaction Index*
Moon Maid	120/20	2001	12.95[a]	6.77
Stuck Pig	44/63	5877	19.95	13.32
Curmudgeon	56/56	31	6[b]	57.91
Haggis	1/100000	3	129.97	3244.36
		* Parts per million [a]Special discount [b]Sold to GK		

Left tab   *Align on "/"*   *Centered tab*   *Decimal tab*   *Right tab*

just working on a single line. If you set the proper tab settings for the first line, you can quickly apply those settings to the rest of the lines by selecting all the lines (including the first one), opening the Paragraph Attributes dialog box (Command-Shift-F or Command-Shift-T; Ctrl-Shift-F or Ctrl-Shift-T), and click-ing OK (or pressing Return). The tab setting for the first line is applied to the rest of the lines.

▼ ▼

Tip: Hanging Tabs. There's a subtle feature in the decimal tab function which you'll love if you ever create financial balance sheets. The decimal tab doesn't just line up decimals. Rather, QuarkXPress thinks of any nonnumber that falls after a number to be a decimal point, and aligns to it. For example, if you press Tab and type "94c2.4" on a line with a decimal tab, QuarkXPress aligns to the "c" rather than to the period.

I thought this was a bug until I realized how handy it could be. For exam-ple, if you are lining up numbers in a column, the negative-balance paren-theses hang outside the column. You can even create hanging footnotes, as long as they're not numbers (see the Unit Price column in Figure 6-35, above).

▼ ▼

Setting Tab Stops

To place a custom tab stop, open the Tabs tab in the Paragraph Attributes dia-log box, which you can find by choosing Tabs from the Style menu, or by pressing Command-Shift-T (Ctrl-Shift-T). When this dialog box is open, Quark-XPress places a ruler bar across the box of the text box you're working in (see Figure 6-36).

You can place a tab stop in one of two ways.

▶ You can click in the ruler above the text box and then choose what sort of tab stop you want by pressing one of the Tab stop buttons in the dialog box. (You can also choose the tab stop type before clicking in the ruler; it doesn't matter.)

▶ You can type a value into the Position field in the Paragraph Attributes dialog box and then choose what sort of tab stop you want it to be (or, again, you can choose the type first). Remember that you can type the value in a different measurement system than the ruler is displaying, or even use an equation to figure the position (see "Tip: Evenly Spaced Tab Stops," below). If you want to add another tab stop using this technique, click the Set button to "lock in" the tab stop (or press Command/Ctrl-S).

Don't forget the Apply button when setting tab stops. When you're setting up a table, you almost never get the tabs stops right the first time, so it's useful to click Apply (or press Command/Ctrl-A) to see how the tab stops will affect the paragraph before you close the dialog box.

Figure 6-36
Setting tab stops

▼ ▼

Tip: Evenly Spaced Tab Stops. Don't forget that you can use arithmetic in dialog box fields. This includes the Position field when you're setting tabs. If you want evenly spaced tabs, place each tab by adding an increment to the previous tab position. For instance, let's say you want a tab stop at .5 inch and every inch from there.

1. Type ".5" into the Position field (or ".5"" if your measurements aren't inches).

2. Press Command/Ctrl-S or click the Set button. This sets the tab stop in the paragraph without having to leave the Paragraph Attributes dialog box.

3. Position the cursor after the ".5" (you can just press the Right Arrow key) and type "+1".

4. Press Command/Ctrl-S or click Set again. (You can also press Command/Ctrl-A or click the Apply button.)

5. Continue until you have all the tab stops you need. When you're done, press OK.

Note that if the equation gets too long in the Position field, you can click on the last tab stop you added (the little arrow icon in the tab ruler). This simplifies the equation to save space.

My colleague Sandee Cohen pointed out that you can do a similar thing using multiplication and division. For example, if you wanted to set up tab stops at every .75-inch increment across a text box, you could set the first one at .75, then the second one at .75*2, the third at .75*3, and so on (clicking the Set button between each one).

You can even space out tab stops equally across a text box. Let's say you want five tab stops, and your text box is 35 picas wide. To set the first tab stop, type "35p/6" in the Position field (always divide by one more than the number of tab stops you want to end up with). To set the second tab stop, change this to "35p/6*2". Change the 2 to 3 for the third tab stop, and so on.

▼ ▼

Changing and Deleting Tab Stops

Once you have tab stops set for a paragraph, you can go back and edit them by dragging the tab-stop icons along the ruler in the Paragraph Attributes dialog box. Earlier versions of XPress only let you drag tab stops, but now you can edit a tab stop's position or type much more easily. The trick is to first select the tab stop you want to edit (click on it). Then you can press one of the tab-stop type buttons, change the position value, or edit the Fill Character (see "Tab Leaders," below). When you're done, click the Set, Apply, or OK button.

You can rid yourself of an unwanted tab stop by dragging the icon out of the ruler boundaries (see Figure 6-37). To clear all the tab stops for a paragraph, click the Clear All button in the Paragraph Attributes dialog box (or Option/Alt-click the ruler above the text box that appears when that dialog box is open).

Editing tab stops is one place that the continuous Apply feature is really helpful; as I pointed out in Chapter 2, *QuarkXPress Basics*, you can turn this feature on and off by Option/Alt-clicking the Apply button. When you turn it on, you can drag or edit tab stops and QuarkXPress updates the paragraph(s) automatically. This makes adjusting columns much faster and easier.

Figure 6-37
Dragging away a tab stop

Hey!⇥   You leave that tab stop alone!

Tab Leaders

A tab leader is a repeated character that fills the space created with the tab. The most common example is a table of contents, where the repeating period character fills the space between a chapter name and a page number. Each tab stop can have its own leader. In fact, in XPress, you can use either one or two repeating characters (see Figure 6-38).

To add a leader while creating a new tab stop, set the tab stop as described earlier, then—before you click Apply, Set, or OK—type the leader characters into the Fill Characters field. When you're done, click Set, Apply, or OK.

If the tab stop is already created and you want to change its leader, select the tab stop in the ruler above the text box, type the leader characters into the Fill Characters field, and then click Set, Apply, or OK.

Figure 6-38
Tab leaders

Moose attack ------------------on Golden Pond
A neverending §§§§§§§§§§§§ story of greed
Corruption ➭➭➭➭➭➭➭and extra-large boots.
Left-handed■■■■■■■■■■■■■■■■Windshifters!

Other characters used as tab leaders. In the second line, the size of the tab itself was reduced to 10 points. In the third and fourth lines, the tab character's font was changed to Zapf Dingbats.

▼ ▼

Tip: Adjusting Leaders. You don't have to be content with the size and font of a tab's leaders (otherwise called "fill characters"). If you want the characters to be smaller, select the tab character in the text (not the tab stop) and change its point size. If you want the characters to appear in another font, change the font of that tab character. People don't often think of the tab character as a character, but that's just what it is. If you turn on Show Invisibles (select it from the View menu), you can see the character as a little gray triangle.

Changing the font and size isn't all you can do; you can even change the amount of space between the leader characters. Select the tab space and adjust its tracking or kerning values. Typically, when you change the kerning value for a single character it only changes the space between it and the next character; however, in this case it changes the space between each of the leader characters (see Figure 6-39).

▼ ▼

Right Indent Tab

Trying to set a tab stop exactly at the right margin can be very frustrating. Even worse, if your right margin or the size of your text box changes, your tab stop doesn't follow along. Typing a Right Indent tab (Option-Tab on the Macintosh, Shift-Tab in Windows) fixes all that. This type of tab acts as though you've placed a right tab stop flush with the right margin of your paragraph. Plus, it moves as you adjust the margin or the text box. Inserting this type of tab effectively adds the tab and sets a variable tab stop at the same time. (I can hear the handful of people who "get it" sighing appreciatively in the background. Those of you who don't, just try it once and you'll understand.)

The Right Indent tab acts just like a tab character (you can even search for it the same way, using "\t"; see "Find/Change" in Chapter 5, *Word Processing*), though there's no way to set its own leader. It picks up the same leader as the previous tab stop in the paragraph. Note that you won't see a tab stop in the ruler that appears with the Paragraph Attributes dialog box; it's always set to the right margin, wherever that is. Also, you should note that Option-Tab (Shift-Tab in Windows) jumps past all other tab stops in that paragraph, all the way over to the right margin.

Figure 6-39

Adjusting the tracking of the tab leader characters

Period used as leader characters (18 points; same as other type on the line).

Moishe is ....not strange.

Oh yes . . . . he is, too.

Tab reduced to 10 points with a tracking value of 94.

Hyphenation and Justification

There are few things more dear to a typesetter's heart than hyphenation and justification—often called simply "H&J." Proper hyphenation and justification is often the most important single factor in the way a document looks. And if your H&J is bad . . . well, there's little that anyone can do (see Figure 6-40).

QuarkXPress has some very powerful controls over how it hyphenates and justifies text in a column. However, this is once more a situation where you won't want to rely on its default settings. Let's take a look at what H&J is all about, and then get into the details of how you can make it work for you.

The Basics of H&J

Although hyphenation and justification are entirely separate functions, they almost always go together. Almost always.

The idea behind both hyphenation and justification is to make text fit into a given space and still look as good as possible. It turns out that there are three basic ways to fit text without distorting it too much.

▶ Controlling the spacing between all the letters.

▶ Controlling the spacing between the words.

▶ Breaking the words at line endings by hyphenating.

Any one of these, if performed in excess, usually looks pretty awful. However, it is possible to mix them together in proper measure for a pleasing result.

Figure 6-40
Hyphenation and
Justification can
make a difference

Doing a good job with the program involves knowing a little something about good hyphenation and justification settings. If y'ain't got the good settings, you don't got the good-looking type, either. This paragraph, for example, is simply atrocious.

Doing an *especially* good job with the program involves taking the time to learn about its hyphenation and justification controls. You'll be glad you did.

▼ ▼

Tip: Check for Rivers. Often the first problem that arises when people set
their text to justified alignment is that their documents start looking like a
flood just hit; rivers of white space are flowing around little islands of words.
Because humans are so good at seeing patterns of lines (it's just how our brains
work), too much space between words is disturbing to the eye. I mentioned in
"Tip: When Black and White is Colorful" that turning the page over and holding it up to the light is a good way to check the color of a text block. It's also a
great way to check for rivers in your text. This way your eye isn't drawn toward
reading the words—just seeing the spaces.

▼ ▼

Although you can't adjust the algorithms that QuarkXPress uses for H&J,
you can change many variables that help in its decision making. These values
make up the Edit Hyphenation & Justification dialog box (see Figure 6-41),
found by first selecting H&Js from the Edit menu (or pressing Command-
Option-H or Ctrl-Alt-H), selecting the H&J to edit, and then clicking either the
New or Edit button.

Let's divide the controls in this dialog box into two groups—Auto
Hyphenation and Justification—and discuss them one at a time.

Auto Hyphenation

QuarkXPress can automatically hyphenate words at the end of a line, breaking
them into syllables according to an internal algorithm. When you first start up
the program, make sure that Auto Hyphenation is turned on (in earlier versions, the default setting was off, but XPress now usually turns it on). If it's off,
QuarkXPress won't hyphenate any words unless you type your own hyphens or
discretionary hyphens (see "Formatting Characters," later in this chapter). You
can turn on Auto Hyphenation in the Edit Hyphenation & Justification dialog
box (remember that if you turn it on when no documents are open, it stays on

Figure 6-41

The Edit Hyphenation &
Justification dialog box

for all subsequent files). When you enable hyphenation, several items become active. These features are the basic controls over QuarkXPress's internal hyphenating algorithms. Let's look at them one at a time.

Smallest Word. When QuarkXPress is attempting to hyphenate a line of text, it must decide which words are eligible for hyphenation. You can quickly discard most of the smaller words by specifying the smallest word QuarkXPress considers. For example, you might not want the word "many" to hyphenate at the end of a line. By setting the Smallest Word value to five or higher, you tell QuarkXPress to ignore this word, as well as any other word with fewer than five letters.

Minimum Before. The Minimum Before value specifies the number of letters in a word which must come before a hyphen break. Depending on your tastes and your level of pickiness, you might set this to two or three. Otherwise, words like "mnemonic" might break after the first "m." I find that most art directors prefer a minimum of three letters.

Minimum After. The Minimum After value determines the number of letters in a word that must come after a hyphenation break. Again, this value is based on aesthetics. Some people don't mind if the "ly" in "truly" sits all by itself on a line. (*The New York Times* breaks "doesn't" after the "s," but it's a newspaper, after all.) For most quality work, you would want a minimum setting of three. And never, ever, set it to one (the results are uglier than a vegetarian's face at a meat-packing plant).

Break Capitalized Words. This control is self-explanatory. You can tell QuarkXPress to either break capitalized words or not. The feature is there for those people who think that proper nouns should never be broken. I'm picky, but not that picky. (On the other hand, it is strange to see people's names hyphenated.)

Hyphens in a Row. One area in which I *am* that picky is the number of hyphens I allow in a row. For most work, I hate to see more than a single hyphen in a row down a justified column of text. QuarkXPress defaults to "unlimited," which is the same as typing zero. If you're creating newspapers, this might be appropriate. If you're making art books, be a bit more careful with your hyphens. I usually set this to two as a default and then go through and tweak the line breaks by hand.

Note that those wacky engineers at Quark placed a little popup menu next to this setting. Don't worry, it doesn't do anything; you can just ignore it.

Hyphenation Zone. Another way to limit the number of hyphens in a section of text is the Hyphenation Zone setting. While relatively simple in function, this feature is one of the more difficult to understand (it was for me, anyway).

The idea is that there's an invisible zone along the right margin of each block of text. If QuarkXPress is trying to break a word at the end of a line, it looks to see where the hyphenation zone is. If the word *before* the potentially hyphenated word falls inside the hyphenation zone, then QuarkXPress just gives up and pushes the word onto the next line (does not hyphenate it). If the previous word does not fall within the hyphenation zone, then QuarkXPress goes ahead with hyphenating the word (see Figure 6-42).

For example, if the words "robinus christophorus" came at the end of a line and QuarkXPress were about to hyphenate "christophorus," it would first look at the word "robinus" to see if any part of it fell inside the hyphenation zone. If it did, XPress wouldn't hyphenate "christophorus" at all; if it didn't, QuarkXPress would use its standard hyphenation algorithms to break the word appropriately.

Normally, Hyphenation Zone is set to zero units. This setting specifies no hyphenation zone, so all lines can have hyphenation up to the limit of the Hyphens in a Row value. Unless you really know what you're doing, there is little reason to change this value.

Figure 6-42
Hyphenation zone

Gray bar is for reference only

The effect of nonopposed interactive hypermedia contains the antithetical rhetorical conundrum irregardless of the particulant material

No hyphenation zone

The effect of nonopposed interactive hypermedia contains the antithetical rhetorical conundrum irregardless of the particulant

Hyphenation zone of four picas

"Of" and "antithetical" fall in the Hyphenation Zone, so the following words don't break.

Justification

As I mentioned above, justifying text is the process of adding or removing space across a line of text to keep it flush on the left and right. You can alter several of the parameters QuarkXPress uses for determining justification by changing values found in the Edit Hyphenation & Justification dialog box. These values are controlled in the Justification Method area. It's divided into values for wordspacing, letterspacing (called "character spacing" by Quark), and Flush Zone width, plus a checkbox for Single Word Justify. Let's look at each of these.

Wordspacing. As I described above in "Character Formatting," wordspacing determines the amount of space between words. In the case of justification, it describes the range of how large or small the spaces between words can be. You can specify Minimum, Optimum, and Maximum percentages of a normal space character. For example, a value of 80 percent allows a space between words that is 80 percent of a normal spaceband. (Note that the "normal" space is the spaceband width defined by the designer of the typeface; this can vary greatly between font families.)

Curiously, the default value for optimal wordspacing is 115 percent, which results in slightly more space than the font designer specified. I almost always specify a relatively loose minimum and maximum, such as 85 percent and 140 percent, but I change the optimum value to 100 percent. I do this because I'd rather have QuarkXPress add wordspacing than letterspacing. In general, however, some typefaces need tighter spacing; therefore, depending on the typeface, I might set Optimum to around 95 percent.

Character Spacing. You can also set Minimum, Optimum, and Maximum percentages for the spacing between characters. The percentages are based on the width of an en space (see "Formatting Characters," later in this chapter). Whereas 100 percent was normal for Word Spacing, zero percent is normal for Character Spacing, and should almost always be used as the Optimum setting.

I generally don't give QuarkXPress much freedom in adjusting letterspacing because I think the type designer probably knows more about what character widths should be than I do (and certainly more than QuarkXPress does). For example, I might set Minimum to -1 percent, Maximum to 4 percent and Optimum to zero percent. But here, again, is an area where you need to print out a few text blocks, preferably on an imagesetter, look at the color of the type, and decide for yourself.

I also try to keep this setting tight because loose letterspacing is difficult to read. Again, I'd rather add space between words than letters any day. Some typographers whom I greatly respect insist that letterspacing should always be set at "0/0/0" (that is, QuarkXPress should never change letterspacing). However, I'm from California originally, so I'm much looser than that.

▼ ▼

Tip: H&J Percentages Versus Tracking Units. My colleague Brad Walrod points out that each percentage of character spacing in the H&Js dialog box is basically the same as one unit of kerning or tracking. This enables you to perform a quick and easy test when you're trying to figure out what letterspacing you want in a document. If you're thinking about increasing the letterspacing value, use kerning to apply that same value to a paragraph of text, so you can see what it looks like.

As Brad says, "I guarantee that if you do this test you will never again use a maximum [letterspacing] value of 15 percent."

▼ ▼

Flush Zone. If you thought the Hyphenation Zone setting was obscure, you just hadn't heard about the Flush Zone yet. The Flush Zone setting does one thing, but does it very well: it determines whether the last line of a paragraph gets force justified or not.

The value you type in the field is the distance from the right margin that QuarkXPress checks. If the end of the line falls into that zone, the whole line gets justified. Of course, in many instances, you can just use the Forced Justify setting, so this feature isn't something I use much.

Single Word Justify. The Single Word Justify checkbox lets you tell QuarkXPress whether you want a word that falls on a justified line by itself to be force justified (see Figure 6-43). Newspapers will probably leave this turned on. Art directors of fancy foreign magazines might insist that it get turned off. Personally, I don't like how the word looks either way, and I'd just as soon have the sentence rewritten, or play with other character formatting to reflow the paragraph. This feature doesn't apply to the last line of a paragraph; you still need to use the Flush Zone or force justify to get those lines to justify.

Figure 6-43
Single Word Justify

A knock at the door! Quickly stuffing the long, slender, store-bought foodstuff into a drawer, he sprung blithely to receive his visitor, only to be greeted by thirty-six thousand members of the feared Fruit-and-Vegetablist Majority. He knew he was in trouble now.

A knock at the door! Quickly stuffing the long, slender, store-bought foodstuff into a drawer, he sprung blithely to receive his visitor, only to be greeted by thirty-six thousand members of the feared Fruit-and-Vegetablist Majority. He knew he was in trouble now.

In the example on the right, Single Word Justify is off. Note the phrase "Fruit-and-Vegetablist."

Forced Justification

Speaking of justification, when you select Forced (from the Style menu, the Measurements palette, or by pressing Command-Option-Shift-J or Ctrl-Alt-Shift-J), QuarkXPress forces every line in a paragraph to be justified, including lines that wouldn't ordinarily extend to the margin, such as the last line of a paragraph or even a single-line paragraph.

Forced justification has basically the same effect as creating a Hyphenation and Justification setting with a very large Flush Zone. It takes a lot of steps to define and apply such an H&J setting, however, so Quark has made it easy with the Forced mode.

Note that forced justification only works with full paragraphs, and QuarkXPress defines a full paragraph as ending with a return. Therefore, if you have a text box that has only one line in it, and that line doesn't end with a return, the program won't justify it.

Setting Your Own H&J

Different paragraphs in your document may need different hyphenation and justification settings. For example, you may want the paragraphs in the main body of your text to hyphenate normally, and text in sidebars or headlines to remain unhyphenated. You can use XPress's H&J feature to set up multiple H&J settings to be applied later at a paragraph level.

Creating an H&J Setting

When you choose H&Js from the Edit menu (or press Command-Option-H or Ctrl-Alt-H), the H&Js dialog box appears (see Figure 6-44). You can add, delete, edit, duplicate, or append H&J settings. The list on the left side of the dialog box shows the names of each H&J setting. A new layout only has one setting: Standard, which is the default setting for all text paragraphs.

You can add a new H&J setting in two ways.

▶ Click the New button to create a new H&J setting. Change the hyphenation and justification parameters as described above, give the setting a name, and click OK. The Edit H&Js dialog box you see when you click New is a duplicate of the Standard setting.

▶ Click first on a setting (such as Standard), and then click the Duplicate button. You can edit a duplicate of the setting you first clicked on. This is helpful for basing one H&J setting on another.

Deleting and Appending H&Js

To delete an H&J setting, first click on its name, then click the Delete button. If you've applied the H&J setting to any paragraph in the document, or to a style sheet, QuarkXPress prompts you for an H&J to replace it with. This is an easy way to merge several H&Js into a single one.

Figure 6-44

The H&Js dialog box

H&J settings are automatically available in all layouts in a project. However, if you have set up H&J settings in a different document, you can append them to your current document's list by clicking the Append button. After selecting the document to import from, the program lets you choose exactly which styles you want (see Figure 6-45). In case you don't know how the various H&Js are defined, XPress shows you the definitions in the Description area of the Append H&Js dialog box.

When you press OK in the Append H&Js dialog box, QuarkXPress checks to see if any incoming H&Js have the same name as those already in your document. If it finds such a conflict (and if the definition of the H&J is different in the two documents), it displays another alert dialog box and asks you what to do (see Figure 6-46). You've got four options, each a separate button.

▶ **RENAME.** You get to manually rename the H&J that's being imported with any other unused name.

▶ **AUTO-RENAME.** Automatically renames the incoming H&J with an asterisk at the beginning of its name. I'm sure there's a good reason for this option, but I've never figured it out.

▶ **USE NEW.** The incoming H&J setting overwrites the one already in the document. I usually use either this option or Rename.

▶ **USE EXISTING.** This is the same as cancelling the appending of the H&J; the old one (the one currently in the document) is retained and used. The only time you'd use this is if you didn't realize that there was a duplicate when you chose to append the H&J setting.

If you think there's going to be more than one conflicting style name, you may want to check the box marked Repeat For All Conflicts. This way, XPress handles the remaining conflicts in the same way.

Figure 6-45
Appending H&J settings

Of course, remember that there is also an Append feature on the File menu that you can use to import style sheets, colors, and H&Js at the same time. If you need to import both styles and colors, for instance, it's clearly efficient to do it with Append instead of in the Style Sheets dialog box.

▼ ▼

Tip: Copying H&Js with Copy and Paste. There's another way to move an H&J setting from one document to another: copy and paste a text box that contains a paragraph tagged with that H&J setting. However, if you move a setting this way, QuarkXPress won't do the same-name check described above. If there are differences between two H&J settings with the same name, the imported settings are just ignored (same as selecting Use Existing H&J).

▼ ▼

Applying an H&J Setting

Once you have created more than one H&J setting, you can choose which setting to use on a paragraph level by using the Paragraph Attributes dialog box. With the cursor in a paragraph, or with multiple paragraphs selected, you can select an H&J setting from the popup menu in the Paragraph Attributes dialog box (see Figure 6-47). You can also set the H&J setting in a style sheet (I talk more about Style Sheets in Chapter 7, *Copy Flow*).

▼ ▼

Tip: Tighter and Looser H&Js. Depending on the job I'm working on, I may have four or five different H&J settings in my document. Here are a few besides Standard that I often make myself and use.

▶ TIGHTER. This setting is the same as my Standard H&J, but with slightly smaller wordspacing and letterspacing values.

Figure 6-46

Conflicting H&J settings

Append Conflict ("Light")

This H&J is already in use. How would you like to resolve the conflict?

[Rename]   [Auto-Rename]

[Use New]   [Use Existing]

☐ Repeat For All Conflicts

Existing:

Name: Light; **Auto Hyphenation Disabled;** Hyphens in a Row: 2; Hyphenation Zone: 0"; Space Minimum: 95%; Optimal: 98%; Maximum: 110%; Character Minimum: -1%; Optimal: 0%; Maximum: 3%; Flush

New:

Name: Light; **Auto Hyphenation Enabled;   Smallest Word: 9; Minimum Before: 4;   Minimum After: 3;   Do Not Break Cap Words;** Hyphens in a Row: 2; Hyphenation Zone: 0"; Space Minimum:

[Cancel]

Figure 6-47

Applying an H&J setting

Paragraph Attributes

[Formats] Tabs Rules

Left Indent: [0p]

First Line: [0p]

Right Indent: [0p]

Leading: [15 pt] ⬍

Space Before: [0p]

Space After: [0p]

Alignment: [Left] ⬍

H&J:

☐ Drop Caps

Character Count: [1]

Line Count: [3]

☐ Keep Lines Together

◯ All Lines in ¶

◯ Start: [2] End: [2]

☐ Keep with Next ¶

☐ Lock to Baseline Grid

✓ Forced
Light
Off
Special
Standard

[Apply]   [Cancel]   [OK]

▶ **Looser.** Similar to Standard, but with slightly larger wordspacing and letterspacing values.

▶ **Heads.** I'll turn off Auto Hyphenation in this H&J setting, and set the wordspacing tightly, perhaps even to 75 percent.

▶ **No Hyphenation.** I'll usually have one H&J setting that is the same as Standard, but where Auto Hyphenation is turned off. This is the setting I use for subheads, for instance.

One of the most important things to remember when you're fooling around with these settings is the color of the page. If setting a tighter H&J makes one text block look noticeably darker than the rest of the page, you may need to manually alter the paragraph using tracking or kerning rather than let the H&J settings do it for you.

▼ ▼

Tip: Pseudo Insert Space with H&Js. Let's say you've got three words on a line. You want the first word to be flush left, the third word to be flush right, and you want equal space between each of these and the word in the middle (see Figure 6-48). You can do this by using forced justification and adjusting the H&J settings.

1. Create a new H&J setting called something mnemonic like "InsertSpace".

2. Make sure the letterspacing (labeled "Char") fields in the Justification Method area of the Edit H&Js dialog box are all set to zero. That means that XPress won't add extra space between any characters in the paragraph, only between words. You might need to increase the values in the wordspacing (labeled "Space") fields as well.

3. Save this new H&J setting.

4. Use the Paragraph Attributes dialog box (Command-Shift-F or Ctrl-Shift-F) to apply both the InsertSpace H&J setting and Forced alignment to the paragraph.

The paragraph should now be spread across the text box, with an equal amount of space between each word. If you want a normal word space between two words, use a punctuation space (Shift-space) or a flex space (Option-space on the Macintosh or Ctrl-Shift-5 in Windows) instead of a normal spaceband.

Figure 6-48
Inserting equal space between words

Here, no letterspacing is allowed, and a fixed-width space sits between the first two words.

The H&J setting is set so that no letterspacing can occur.

▼ ▼

Tip: Find/Change H&J settings. There's just no way to find and replace H&J settings throughout a document. Or is there? Let's say someone was working on your document and applied an H&J setting called "Really Tight" to paragraphs when you weren't looking. You want to clear this setting out. The trick is to select the setting you want to get rid of in the H&Js dialog box (in this case, choose Really Tight) and click the Delete button. XPress asks you which H&J to apply in its place. When you delete Really Tight from the H&J list, you can replace it with Standard, or something else. This effectively searches and replaces throughout the document: everywhere the Really Tight setting was applied, it gets changed to something else.

If you know you're going to need the H&J setting later, make sure you make a duplicate of it in the document or copy it into another document before you delete it!

▼ ▼

Widow and Orphan Control

I mean no disrespect to widows and orphans, but when it comes to typesetting, we must carefully control them, stamping out their very existence when we have the chance.

If you know what I'm talking about already, bear with me, or skip this paragraph (or test whether you can remember which is the widow and which is the orphan). A *widow* is the last line of a paragraph that winds up all by itself at the top of a column or page. An *orphan* is the first line of a paragraph that lands all by itself at the bottom of a column or page. I like the following mnemonic device: "widows" sounds like "windows," which are high up (top of the page), whereas "orphans" makes me think of tiny Oliver (who was small, and thus, at the bottom of the page).

Typesetters sometimes also refer to the single-word last line of a paragraph as either a widow or an orphan. To avoid the confusion, in my office I prefer to use the word *runt*.

All typographic widows and orphans are bad, but certain kinds are really bad—for example, a widow line that consists of only one word, or even the last part of a hyphenated word. Another related typographic horror is the subhead that stands alone with its following paragraph on the next page.

Fortunately, QuarkXPress has a set of controls that can easily prevent widows and orphans from sneaking into your document. The controls are the Keep With Next ¶ and Keep Lines Together features, and you can find them in the Paragraph Attributes dialog box (Command-Shift-F or Ctrl-Shift-F). Let's look at each of these.

Keep With Next ¶

The Keep With Next ¶ feature is perfect for ensuring that headings and the paragraphs that follow them are always kept together. If the paragraph is pushed onto a new column, a new page, or below an obstructing object, the heading follows right along (see Figure 6-49).

You may want to keep paragraphs together even when there are no sub-heads. For example, entries in a table or list that shouldn't be broken could each be set to Keep With Next ¶. In some earlier versions of XPress, the program would only keep two paragraphs together at a time; fortunately, that's changed, and you can keep a number of paragraphs together with this feature.

Keep Lines Together

The Keep Lines Together feature is the primary control over widows and orphans. When you check Keep Lines Together in the Paragraph Attributes dialog box, QuarkXPress expands the dialog box to give you control parameters in this area (see Figure 6-50). Let's look at these controls one at a time.

All Lines In ¶. You can keep every line in a paragraph together by checking All Lines In ¶. For example, if a paragraph spans across two pages, enabling All

Figure 6-49
Keep with Next ¶

This paragraph style does not have Keep with Next ¶ set.

This paragraph style does have Keep with Next ¶ set.

Figure 6-50
Keep Lines Together

Paragraph Attributes

Formats | Tabs | Rules

Left Indent: `0p`

First Line: `1p6`

Right Indent: `0p`

Leading: `12 pt`

Space Before: `p6`

Space After: `0p`

Alignment: `Left`

H&J: `Standard`

□ Drop Caps

Character Count: `1`

Line Count: `3`

☑ Keep Lines Together
   ○ All Lines in ¶
   ⦿ Start: `2` End: `2`

□ Keep with Next ¶

□ Lock to Baseline Grid

(Apply) (Cancel) (OK)

Lines In ¶ results in that entire paragraph being pushed onto the next page to keep it together.

It's easy to confound a computer. Do you remember that Star Trek episode in which a man forced a computer to commit suicide by instructing it to perform contradictory functions? Fortunately, XPress won't cause your Mac or PC to blow up if you specify All Lines In ¶ for a text block larger than your column. In cases like this, QuarkXPress simply pushes the whole paragraph out of the text box. (I've seen cases where people freak out because their text has disappeared, only to find out later that they had turned on both All Lines in ¶ and Keep with Next ¶ for every paragraph.)

Start. You don't have to specify that all the lines in a paragraph should be kept together. Instead, you can control the number of lines that should be kept together at the beginning and end of the paragraph.

The value you type in the Start field determines the minimum number of lines that QuarkXPress allows at the beginning of a paragraph. For example, specifying a two-line Start value causes paragraphs that fall at the end of a page to keep at least two lines on the first page before it breaks. If at least two lines of that paragraph cannot be placed on the page, then the entire paragraph is pushed over to the next page.

The Start feature is set up to eliminate orphans in your documents. If you don't want any single lines sitting at the bottom of a page, you can specify a value of 2 for the Start control (some designers insist that even two lines alone at the bottom of a page are ugly and may want to adjust the Start value to 3 or greater).

End. The value specified in the End field determines the minimum number of lines that QuarkXPress lets fall alone at the top of a column or after an obstruction. A value of 2 or greater rids you of unwanted widowed paragraphs (if a widow occurs, QuarkXPress "pulls" a line off the first page onto the second page or column).

▼ ▼

Tip: Other Widow and Orphan Controls. It's all very well and good to let QuarkXPress avoid widows, orphans, and runts for you, but you still need to painstakingly peruse each page of most documents, making adjustments as you go. You have many other tools to help you avoid widows and orphans. Here are some of my favorites.

▶ Adjust tracking by a very small amount over a range of text, but try to do at least a whole paragraph or a few complete lines so the color of the type doesn't vary within the paragraph. Often, nobody can tell if you've applied -.5 or -1 tracking to a paragraph or a page, but it might be enough to pull back a widow or a runt.

▶ Adjust horizontal scaling by a small amount, such as 99.5 percent or 100.5 percent.

▶ Make sure Auto Hyphenation and Auto Kern Above are turned on. Kerning can make a load of difference over a large area of text. Auto Hyphenation has to be changed in all of your H&Js, while Auto Kern Above affects the entire layout.

▶ Change your H&J's wordspacing to a smaller Optimal setting. If it's at 100 percent, try 98 percent. Of course, this changes every paragraph tagged with that H&J setting throughout your document.

▶ Set up different hyphenation and justification settings that you can apply to problem paragraphs. You might apply a tighter or a looser setting for one paragraph, for instance, or allow more hyphens in a row.

If none of these work for you, don't forget you can always just rewrite a sentence or two (if it's yours to rewrite). A quick rewrite can fix up just about any problem.

▼ ▼

Baseline Grid

In typography, the smallest change can make the biggest difference in a piece's impact. For example, look at a high-quality magazine page that has multiple columns. Chances are that each line of text has a common baseline with the text in the next column. Now look at a crummy newsletter. Place a rule across a page and you'll see lines of text all over the place. What's missing is an underlying grid. QuarkXPress's Baseline Grid feature lets you create a grid and lock each line of text to it. Nonetheless, while this is a powerful feature, I tend not to use it much; I'll explain why in a moment.

Each layout has its own Baseline Grid setting, which is pervasive throughout every page. However, whether a block of text actually locks to that grid is determined on a paragraph level.

Setting up the grid. XPress is clueless about your leading grid, so you need to set this up yourself. You can set the Baseline Grid value for the layout on the Paragraph tab in the Preferences dialog box. You have two controls over the Baseline Grid: the Start value and the Increment value. The Start value determines where this grid begins, measured from the top of the page. Set it to start at the first baseline of your body copy.

The Increment value determines the distance from one horizontal grid line to the next. Generally, this value is the same as the leading in the majority of your body copy. For example, if your body copy has a leading of 13 points, then you should type "13pt" as your Increment value. However, sometimes it's better to use half the body copy's leading; in this example, you might use a 6.5-point grid.

Assigning a baseline grid. To lock each line of a paragraph to the baseline grid that you have established, turn on the Lock to Baseline Grid checkbox in the Paragraph Attributes dialog box (Command-Shift-F or Ctrl-Shift-F). Note that the baseline grid overrides paragraph leading. That is, if your paragraph has a leading of 10 points, when you enable Lock to Baseline Grid each line snaps to the Increment value (13 points, in the example above). If your paragraph has a leading larger than the Increment value, each line snaps to the next grid value. In other words, your leading never gets tighter, but it can get pretty dang loose. If your Increment value is 13 points and your leading is 14 points, each line snaps to the following grid line, resulting in 26-point leading (see Figure 6-51).

Showing the grid. The baseline grid in QuarkXPress is usually invisible, so sometimes it's difficult to understand why text is sticking to weird baselines. However, you can see this underlying grid by selecting Show/Hide Baseline Grid from the View menu (or by pressing Option-F7 on the Macintosh or Ctrl-F7 on Windows). If you don't like the color of the baseline grid, you can set

Figure 6-51
Lock to Baseline Grid

With a 13-point Baseline Grid, type with 14-point leading locked to the grid gets bumped to the next grid increment.

But 13-point leading on a 13-point grid works perfectly.

it to whatever you want in the Preferences dialog box (Command-Option-Shift-Y or Ctrl-Alt-Shift-Y).

Note that the baseline-grid guides you see when you select Show Baseline Grid act just like ruler guides. They follow the Guides control in the Preferences dialog box as to whether they appear in front of or behind page items. And when Snap to Guides is turned on, page items snap to the baseline grid guides (when they're showing).

▼ ▼

Tip: Why I Rarely Use Lock to Baseline Grid. There is no doubt that a careful study and practice of baseline grids can make your document better looking. However, as I said earlier, I rarely use the Lock to Baseline Grid feature. The reason: you can get the same quality simply from being careful with your leading and text box placement. The key is to work with multiples of your leading grid.

For instance, if your body text has 15-point leading, then make sure your headlines and subheads also have 15- or 30-point leading. If you use Space Before or Space After, make sure those values are set only to 15, 30, or 45 points (or some other multiple of 15). Paragraphs in a list might have 7.5 points of space (half of 15) between them, and as long as there are always an even number of list items, the paragraphs after the list will always end up sitting right on the leading grid.

This might seem really limiting, but it's actually less so than using Lock to Baseline Grid. As long as you pay attention to the values for Leading, Space Before, and Space After, as well as turn on Maintain Leading (see below), you're pretty much assured that your baselines will align across columns and that your pages will look beautiful. Of course, it's always good to proof them, just in case.

▼ ▼

Maintain Leading

If you don't use baseline grids, but still want to maintain consistent leading on your page, you might want to look closely at the Maintain Leading feature. This feature—which I usually just leave turned on in the Preferences dialog box—ensures that each line in a text box is placed according to its leading value when another object (such as a picture box or a line) obstructs the text and moves text lines around.

When Maintain Leading is turned off, two things happen. First, the line of text following an obstruction abuts the bottom of that obstruction (or its text runaround, if the runaround value is larger than zero points; I talk about text runaround in Chapter 11, *Where Text Meets Graphics*). Second, the rest of the lines of text in that text box fall on a different leading grid than those above the obstruction do. This is much easier to see than to read (or write) about, so check out Figure 6-52. This feature has no effect on paragraphs that are already set to Lock to Baseline Grid.

Figure 6-52
Maintain Leading

In a recent survey of 1,231 inquiries which advertisers received from their space and time advertising, published by the Direct Mail Research Institute under the title, "How 1,231 Advertisers Handle Inquires by Mail," it was discovered that the average length of time

cool. But whether it did or not, the follow-up—

and especially the envelope used in the follow-up—had a fine opportunity for picking up the inter-

Here, Maintain Leading is turned off; the baselines don't match across columns.

In a recent survey of 1,231 inquiries which advertisers received from their space and time advertising, published by the Direct Mail Research Institute under the title, "How 1,231 Advertisers Handle Inquires by Mail," it was discovered that the average length of time required to follow up an inquiry is 8.87 days. The rest created in the adver-

cool. But whether it did or not, the follow-up—

and especially the envelope used in the follow-up—had a fine opportunity for picking up the inter-

Here, Maintain Leading is turned on and the columns align.

Fine-Tuning Type

Almost everything I've talked about in this chapter has been at a character or paragraph level. Here I'm going to talk about making typographic adjustments on a layout level. You have control over several areas at a layout level, including how superscript, subscript, superior, and small-caps characters are "built;" which words will hyphenate; and how XPress deals with ligatures, accents, and special spaces. You can also create custom automatic tracking and kerning tables, and run through an automatic check for typographic problem areas.

Let's look at how you can use these controls in your layouts.

Typographic Preferences

The Preferences dialog box (see Chapter 2, *QuarkXPress Basics*) lets you control the way QuarkXPress handles a number of its typographic features: superscript, subscript, superior, and small-caps characters, hyphenation, kerning, em spaces, baseline grid, leading, ligatures, and foreign-language accents (see Figure 6-53). Here's a run-down of all the different features in this dialog box, what they do, or where you can find information about them elsewhere in this book.

Remember that if you change items in the Document section of the Preferences dialog box with no documents open, the defaults are changed for every new layout you create from then on. And remember that all of the following are layout-wide preferences; you can't specify them for a particular story or paragraph.

Superscript and Subscript. Few people ever bother to get into the nitty-gritty of changing the way the Superscript and Subscript styles look, but the controls are on the Character tab in the Preferences dialog box if you ever want them. Both the Superscript and the Subscript controls are the same: Offset, VScale, and HScale. Some people try to fiddle with these values in order to make fractions; this is possible, but I recommend other fraction-making techniques instead (see "Typographic Special Effects," later in this chapter).

▶ OFFSET. You can determine how far from the baseline your superscript or subscript characters should move by altering the Offset amount. You specify Offset as a percentage of the text size. For example, if the offset for Subscript were set to 50 percent, then a subscript character would move 9 points down for 18-point type. You can specify any amount between one and 100 percent.

▶ VSCALE AND HSCALE. These terms are short for "vertical scale" and "horizontal scale," which are responsible for how tall and wide the superscript or subscript text is. The controls default to 100 percent, which I find much too large. I generally set both to a value between 70 and 80 percent, so that a superscript or subscript character doesn't stand out too much against the rest of the text. Here, too, you can set the value to anything between one and 100 percent.

Figure 6-53
Typographic preferences

Preferences

Application
  Display
  Interactive
  Save
  Undo
  XTensions Manager
  avenue.quark
  File List
  Default Path
  Full Res Preview
  Browsers
  Index
  Jabberwocky
  PDF
  Placeholders
  Fraction/Price
Project
  XML Import
Print Layout
  General
  Measurements
  Paragraph
  Character
  Tools
  Trapping
  Quark CMS
  Layers

Leading

Auto Leading: `20%`   ☑ Maintain Leading
Mode: ⊙ Typesetting   ○ Word Processing

Baseline Grid

Start: `3p`   Increment: `16 pt`

Hyphenation

Language	Method
U.S. English	Expanded

Cancel   OK

Preferences

Application
  Display
  Interactive
  Save
  Undo
  XTensions Manager
  avenue.quark
  File List
  Default Path
  Full Res Preview
  Browsers
  Index
  Jabberwocky
  PDF
  Placeholders
  Fraction/Price
Project
  XML Import
Print Layout
  General
  Measurements
  Paragraph
  Character
  Tools
  Trapping
  Quark CMS
  Layers

Superscript
Offset: `33%`
VScale: `100%`
HScale: `100%`

Subscript
Offset: `33%`
VScale: `100%`
HScale: `100%`

Small Caps
VScale: `75%`
HScale: `75%`

Superior
VScale: `50%`
HScale: `50%`

☐ Ligatures
Break Above: `1`   ☐ Not "ffi" or "ffl"

☑ Auto Kern Above: `4 pt`   ☐ Standard Em Space
Flex Space Width: `50%`   ☑ Accents for All Caps

Cancel   OK

Superior. You don't have to worry about the offset for superior characters because they are automatically set to be vertically flush with the cap height of that font. So the only modifications you can make here are to the vertical and horizontal scaling of the character. This is clearly an area of aesthetic choice. I tend to like the 50-percent default that QuarkXPress gives us; some people like to make the HScale slightly larger, such as 55 percent, so that the character has a little more weight.

Small Caps. You can also change the vertical and horizontal scaling of all characters set in the Small Caps character style in a layout. Though I think it would be nice to be able to set the characteristics of small caps on the character, paragraph, or story level, these layout-wide controls are usually good enough.

There are times when adjustable (or "fake") small caps are even better than traditional (or "true") small caps, such as those found in Expert Sets. For example, I know a designer who recently specified that all small caps in a book's body copy should be 8.5 points tall. The body text was 10-point Palatino, so the company producing the templates just changed the small-caps specifications to 85 percent in the horizontal direction (85 percent of 10-point type is 8.5-point type) and 90 percent in the vertical direction (making the characters slightly wider gives a slightly heavier—although stretched—look). A traditional small cap would not achieve this effect; however, it would probably keep the type color in the paragraph more consistent.

Accents for All Caps. This typographic refinement lets you specify whether accented lowercase characters keep their accents when you apply the All Caps character style to them. If this feature is turned on and you apply All Caps to the characters å, ë, ì, ó, û, QuarkXPress will give you Å, Ë, Ì, Ó, Û rather than A, E, I, O, U. Depending on the design of your document or what language you're working in, you may want to turn this feature on or off.

Leading Preferences. I talk about each of the Leading preferences earlier in this chapter. Leading Mode and Auto Leading are discussed in the section called "Leading" (you should always leave Leading Mode set to Typesetting). The Maintain Leading feature is discussed in the "Baseline Grid" section, where I said to just leave this setting turned on.

Auto Kern Above. Auto Kern Above is discussed in the "Automatic" section of "Kerning and Tracking." This is usually set to 4 points, which is very reasonable. (If you see a value higher than 4 here, you should probably lower it.)

Flex Space Width. See "Formatting Characters" in the "Special Characters" section, later in the chapter, for an explanation of this feature.

Hyphenation Method. I explore hyphenation methods a little later in the chapter, in "Tweaking Hyphenation." But I can give the rundown again now: just leave this set to Enhanced or Expanded (there's almost no reason to change it to Standard).

Baseline Grid. I wrote a whole section called "Baseline Grid" earlier in this chapter; check that out.

Standard Em Space. See "Tip: Know Your Ems and Ens," in the "Kerning and Tracking" section. The low-down: I like to turn this on.

Ligatures. I'll discuss ligatures later in this chapter in "Special Characters." My recommendation: turn it on. (Unfortunately, this feature doesn't exist on Windows.)

▼ ▼

Kerning and Tracking Tables

As I noted earlier in this chapter, most fonts include built-in kerning tables of 100 to 500 pairs. However, you can modify these pairs or add your own by using Quark's Kern/Track Editor XTension (it comes with QuarkXPress, though you have an option not to install it when you update or install QuarkXPress). Like all XTensions, you must make sure that this XTension is located in the XTension folder in order for it to work.

Modifying tracking and kerning tables is different from many of QuarkXPress's typographic controls in that it's font-specific. For example, if you alter the kerning table for Times Roman, those changes are in effect whenever you use Times Roman in any QuarkXPress document. However, the font itself is *not* altered on disk; so the changes don't show up when you're working in any other program.

The kerning modifications you make are stored both in the XPress Preferences file and in the document itself. That means that you can give the publication file to someone else and the custom values will stay with the document (when they open the file, they'll be prompted to choose whether or not they want to keep your preferences).

Kerning Tables

To modify a font's kerning table, choose Kerning Table Edit from the Utilities menu. This brings up the Kerning Table Edit dialog box, which presents a scrolling list of available fonts (note that this dialog box can take a long time to appear, depending on the number of fonts you have installed; see Figure 6-54). The list lets you choose the variants of each installed font (Plain, Bold, Italic, Bold Italic, and so on).

You have to edit kerning tables for individual fonts. This means that you cannot edit Palatino in its Plain style and expect all the Bold, Italic, and Bold Italic variants to be altered as well (see "Tip: Quick Kerning for Families," below).

After selecting a font from the list (you can jump through the list quickly by typing the first letter of the font name you want), click Edit to move to the Edit Kerning Table dialog box, where you can edit an existing pair, add a new pair to the list, or delete a pair (see Figure 6-55). You can also import and export lists of these kerning pairs in a text-file format. Let's look at how each of these operations is performed.

Adding a pair. You can add a new kerning pair to QuarkXPress's list in three steps.

1. Type the two characters in the Pair field. They appear in a preview window above the Value field. If there is already a kerning value set for this pair, it appears selected in the list of kerning pairs.

2. Type a kerning amount into the Value field. This value is specified in $\frac{1}{200}$ of an em (see "Tip: Know Your Ems and Ens," earlier in this chapter). The preview updates as soon as you enter new values.

3. Click the Add or Replace button.

That's all there is to it.

Editing a pair. You can adjust kerning pairs that you have created or that come predefined in the font by clicking on a pair in the Kerning Pairs table (or typing the two characters in the Pair field), and then modifying the number in the Value field. Once you have set the kern value you want, click the Replace button to add it back to the table.

Deleting or resetting a pair. If you don't like a kerning pair that you added, or you want to get rid of one that was built in, select the pair from the list and click the Delete button (or set the kern value to zero). Unfortunately, there is no way to reset a particular pair to its original value if you don't remember what it was. You can, however, reset the entire font back to its pure, original state by clicking the Reset button (of course, you lose all the other kerning pairs that you had built along the way).

Figure 6-54

The Kerning Table
Edit dialog box

Figure 6-55

Editing a kerning pair

Import/Export. There are those who know kerning pairs so well that they'd rather just type up a mess of them in a text-editing program and then import them all at once into QuarkXPress. You can do this by creating a text-only file within any text editor (such as Microsoft Word, BBEdit, or Windows Notepad) in the following format.

1. Type the kerning pair (the two letters).

2. Type a tab.

3. Type the kerning value in QuarkXPress's kerning units (1/200 of an em). Negative numbers mean negative kerning. Then just press Return to go to the next line.

4. Save the file as a text-only file. On Windows, save the file with a .KRN file-name extension.

5. Switch back to the Edit Kerning Table dialog box in QuarkXPress, and click the Import button to bring this text file in.

If you want to edit the kerning values that are already built into the font, you can first export those values by clicking the Export button. Then edit them and re-import them.

▼ ▼

Tip: Quick Kerning for Families. Applying kerning pairs to a number of faces can be very time-consuming and tiresome. You can speed up this process by using the Import feature to apply the same kerning tables to several typefaces. Once you've imported the kerning tables, you can go back and edit them to compensate for specifics of that typeface. Careful, though: the kerning values for an italic form of a typeface are going to be very different than the values for a roman form.

▼ ▼

Tip: Automatic Page Numbers Don't Kern. If you or the font designer has set up automatic kerning pairs for pairs of numerals, these pairs will *not* be kerned when they appear as automatic page numbers. QuarkXPress treats all automatic page numbers as single characters, even when they consist of multiple characters. Sadly, there's no ready fix for this one, except to use a typeface for page numbers in which the lack of automatic kerning won't cause an aesthetic headache.

▼ ▼

Tip: Un-Kerning Your Numbers. This tip puts a spin on what I think is a bug: applying the small caps style to numbers makes XPress ignore any kerning information you set up in its internal kerning tables for those numbers. On the positive side: If you kerned your digits using the Kern/Track Editor, and now you want to use that font in a tabular setting where you don't want the digits kerned after all, apply the small caps style to the digits. The numbers stay the same, but the kerning goes away!

Note that this trick doesn't work if you've used another method (a commercial font-editing program) to kern your font.

▼ ▼

Tracking Tables

Most fonts need to have tighter tracking applied to them in larger point sizes. You could change the tracking value for various display fonts by manually selecting the text and specifying a tracking value in the Character Attributes dialog box. However, QuarkXPress makes it easier for you by letting you create custom tracking tables for each font you use.

A tracking table tells QuarkXPress how much tracking to apply at various sizes of a font. This, too, is part of the Kern/Track Editor XTension that comes with XPress.

Here's an example to illustrate this feature. Let's say you're creating a template for a new magazine. You've decided to use Futura Bold for your headers, which are at a number of different sizes. You know that your largest header is 60 points and should have -20 tracking, and the smallest header is 12 points and should have no tracking. Here's what you do.

1. Select Tracking Edit from the Utilities menu.

2. Choose the font that you want to edit—in this case Futura Bold—and click the Edit button. If QuarkXPress recognizes the family as "merged," then it only shows you one family name rather than breaking it down into separate fonts. For instance, it shows you one Palatino selection rather than four Palatino fonts: roman, italic, bold, and bold italic. If the individual fonts are merged into one, the tracking gets applied to every font in the family. In font families that are not merged, you have to create tracking settings for each style variation—for example, one tracking table for "Bodoni," another for "B Bodoni Bold," and so on.

3. You see the Edit Tracking dialog box (Figure 6-56). The vertical axis represents tracking values from -100 to 100 in increments of $\frac{1}{200}$ of an em. The horizontal axis represents type sizes from 2 to 250 points; the farther to the right on the grid, the larger the type size is. The default setting is a horizontal bar at the zero-tracking level. In other words, this means that all point sizes start out with a tracking value of zero.

4. Click on the line at the 2-point size (on the far left). As you hold down the mouse button, you can see the graph values shown in the dialog box. Note that clicking on the graph places a new point on it. You can have up to four corner points on each graph. This first point I've added is the anchor at the zero-tracking level.

Figure 6-56

A tracking table graph

5. Click on the line at the 60-point size and drag the graph line down to the -20 tracking level. If I saved this now, then whenever you used Futura Bold, all sizes larger than 2 points would have negative tracking applied to them.

6. You can add a third control handle at the 12-point type size and set it to zero tracking. Now all type larger than 12 points has tracking applied; as the text gets larger, more and more tracking is applied.

To save your changes, click OK. Then if you're done with your tracking-table edits, click Save.

While editing a font's tracking table, you can start over by clicking the Reset button. You can always go back (even after you've saved) and click the Reset button to get the horizontal bar graph back.

Note that these tracking values are only applied to a font when Auto Kern Above is turned on. In fact, the tracking tables only apply to font sizes above the automatic-kerning limit which has been entered in the Auto Kern Above value field in the Preferences dialog box.

Like custom kerning, custom tracking is stored in your document as well as in your XPress Preferences file. So if you give one of your files with custom tracking to another person, they'll get an alert message when they open the document asking whether or not they want to retain the settings for tracking, kerning, and other customized values. As long as they click the Keep Document Settings button, the text in the file will be spaced exactly as it was on your system.

▼ ▼

Tip: Cleaning out Custom Settings. Because all your custom kerning and tracking tables are saved in the XPress Preferences file, you can "clean out" your system, ridding yourself of every edit you've made, by deleting this file and relaunching XPress (the program creates a fresh new preferences file if it doesn't find one at launch time). This removes other settings you've made, too, such as application-wide preferences and Suggested Hyphenation.

▼ ▼

Tip: Changing Custom Kerning and Tracking Settings. Perhaps you have different clients that prefer different sets of custom kerning and tracking tables. No problem. You can create a new XPress Preferences file for each client and hide them each in a separate folder or directory. When you want to switch from one to the other, just quit XPress, move the current XPress Preferences file into its folder, and replace it with the new one. Relaunch XPress, and you're set.

▼ ▼

Tweaking Hyphenation

Earlier in this chapter, I talked about how to create, edit, and apply H&J settings. However, you can fine-tune the program's hyphenation in a document with two tools and a preference: Hyphenation Exceptions, Suggested Hyphenation, and Hyphenation Method. Let's look briefly at each of these.

Hyphenation Method

In earlier versions of XPress, the program only used algorithms ("rules") to hyphenate its words. The result: some words didn't break properly and you got strange hyphenation. Over the years, XPress's algorithm slowly got better, and XPress started offering a choice between Standard and Enhanced algorithms (you can make the choice in the Paragraph tab of the Preferences dialog box).

The only reason to use Standard is if you are opening documents created in very old XPress files (pre-3.0) and you need them not to reflow. Similarly, if you're opening any version-3 files, XPress automatically applies the Enhanced setting to them, so that they don't reflow either.

QuarkXPress offers a third choice, however: Expanded hyphenation. In this setting, XPress checks words against a list in a built-in hyphenation dictionary; then, if it can't find the word, it uses a reasonably good algorithm to hyphenate it. There's no doubt that Expanded hyphenation is better, but it still ain't great, and there are many words that still hyphenate incorrectly.

So you should typically use Expanded hyphenation (unless you're working with old files and need them not to reflow), but you should check your document's hyphenation carefully nonetheless.

Suggested Hyphenation

The entire life's work of the Suggested Hyphenation feature is to help you figure out how QuarkXPress is going to hyphenate a word. First select a word (or put the cursor somewhere within or immediately to the right of a word). Next, choose Suggested Hyphenation from the Utilities menu (or press Command/Ctrl-H), and the program shows you how it would hyphenate that word (see Figure 6-57).

Figure 6-57
Suggested Hyphenation

All the algorithms that QuarkXPress uses to hyphenate words take into account the parameters set within the Edit Hyphenation & Justification dialog box (such as the number of entries in Break Capitalized Words, Minimum Before, and so on). For example, when Minimum Before is set to 3, the word "answer" does not appear hyphenated in the Suggested Hyphenation dialog box. However, if you change Minimum Before to 2, it does.

Hyphenation Exceptions

If you don't like the way XPress is hyphenating a word, you can override the program's algorithms by setting your own specific hyphenation in the Hyphenation Exceptions dialog box, which you access by selecting Hyphenation Exceptions from the Utilities menu. (Another way to override hyphenation is to use a discretionary hyphen, which I'll discuss in "Special Characters," later in this chapter.)

The first time you open the dialog box, the list is empty. To add a word, just type it in the available space, including hyphens where you want them. If you don't want a word to hyphenate at all, just don't put any hyphens in it (see Figure 6-58).

Once you've created some hyphenation exceptions, you can edit one of them by clicking on it, making the necessary change, and then clicking the Replace button (note that the Add button changes to a Replace button in this case). You can also delete an item on the list by selecting it and clicking the Delete button.

Hyphenation exceptions are stored with each layout in a project, and if you want the same exception in more than one layout you'll have to add it to each one individually. (If you edit this list while no documents are open, then the exceptions are stored in the XPress Preferences file, and get applied to all subsequent new layouts. Remember that if you set up a lot of hyphenation exceptions, you should keep a backup of your XPress Preferences file.)

Figure 6-58
Hyphenation Exceptions

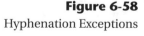

▼ ▼

Tip: Watch Those Hyphens. There's nothing like giving your document a good once-over before you print it out. One of the things you want to look for is a badly hyphenated word. Remember that QuarkXPress generally uses an algorithm to hyphenate words, and it doesn't always do it right. For example, QuarkXPress hyphenates the word "Transeurope" as "Transeur-ope" rather than "Trans-europe." If you find these problem words, you can either change them manually (by adding discretionary hyphens), or make a global change using Hyphenation Exceptions.

▼ ▼

Tip: Line Check. I can remember the day—no, days—when my final task before taking a 530-page book to the service bureau was to scroll laboriously though my QuarkXPress files, looking for and fixing any widows, orphans, and badly hyphenated words. Of course, each fix caused a reflow of all the text that followed, and so required more checking. Would that I'd had Quark's Type Tricks XTension, which adds a feature called Line Check to the Utilities menu. This handy feature automatically searches for typographically undesirable lines (see Figure 6-59).

Line Check searches through a layout looking for widows, orphans, automatically hyphenated words, manually hyphenated words, "loose" lines (justified lines that have exceeded the boundaries of the H&J settings), and text boxes that have overflowed. It won't fix them for you, but it sure does make cleaning up layouts at the last minute a less-harrowing experience.

At first, I typically deselect all boxes, and then choose Search Criteria from the Line Check submenu. Then I click the Count button (in the Search Criteria dialog box) to find how many instances of each "infraction" occur throughout

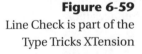

Figure 6-59

Line Check is part of the Type Tricks XTension

the layout. If I see that there are overflowed text boxes or orphans or widows or whatever, I start searching through the layout for them. Unfortunately, there's no way to jump from this dialog box to each instance; you can, however, place the cursor in a text box and select First Line from the Line Check submenu. If any instance of an orphan or widow (or whatever else you're looking for) occurs in that story, XPress highlights it. Then, to keep checking the story, select Next Line (or press Command/Ctrl-semicolon).

▼ ▼

Special Characters

If you're just using QuarkXPress to type letters to your Uncle Neil, you probably don't need this section. If you're doing just about anything else with it, stand by.

When you look at your computer keyboard, you see between 50 and 100 characters represented on the keys. What you don't see are the hundreds of special characters you can access with just a few keystrokes. In this section I'll look at some of those characters, including invisible "utility" characters, dingbats, math symbols, and special punctuation. By no means do you have to memorize most of these; instead, when you're actually working on documents, you may want to refer back to the tables I've included in this section.

Formatting Characters

The first set of characters we'll look at are invisible characters that are used for special formatting in your document. Several of these characters are visible when you select Show/Hide Invisibles from the View menu (or you can toggle them on and off by pressing Command/Ctrl-I). However, a few are not visible; you just have to remember where you put them. Let's take a look at what these characters are (see Table 6-7 for more information on these characters).

Return. Sometimes known as a "carriage return" or a "hard return," this is the key to press when you're at the end of a paragraph. In fact, the Return character separates paragraphs from each other. Most people don't think of the Return key as a character, but you can see it and select it with Show/Hide Invisibles turned on.

QuarkXPress is great at wrapping characters onto the next line, so don't press Return after each line like you would on a typewriter. Also, don't press Return twice in a row to add extra space between paragraphs. Instead, you should use Space Before and Space After (see "Space Before and After," earlier in this chapter).

Table 6-7
Invisible formatting
characters

NAME	INVISIBLES	MACINTOSH	WINDOWS
Return	¶	Return	Enter
Soft Return	↵	Shift-Return	Shift-Enter
Tab	→	Tab	Tab
Indent here	⏐	Command-\	Ctrl-\
Discretionary new line		Command-Return	Ctrl-Enter
Discretionary hyphen		Command-Hyphen	Ctrl-Hyphen
Nonbreaking hyphen		Command-=	Ctrl-=
Nonbreaking space		Command-space	Ctrl-5
New column	↓	Enter (keypad)	Enter (keypad)
New box	↧	Shift-Enter (keypad)	Shift-Enter (keypad)
En space		Option-space	Ctrl-Shift-6
Nonbreaking en space		Command-Option-space	Ctrl-Shift-Alt-6
Flex space		Option-Shift-space	Ctrl-Shift-5
Nonbreaking flex space		Command-Option-Shift-space	Ctrl-Shift-Alt-5
Current page number		Command-3	Ctrl-3
Previous text box page		Command-2	Ctrl-2
Next text box page number		Command-4	Ctrl-4

Soft Return. Holding down the Shift key while you press Return results in a soft return, often called the "new line" character. A soft return forces a new line without starting a new paragraph, with all its attendant attributes: Space Before and After, First Line Indent, paragraph rules, and so on. For example, I use soft returns for tabular text or for forcing a line break in justified or flush-left text. This is a character that takes some getting used to, but I recommend you play with it until you do, because it really comes in handy.

Tab. People also rarely think about tabs as separate characters, but that's just what they are. I talked about tabs in the section called "Tabs," earlier in this chapter, so all I need to say now is that you should really know your tabbing and never (never) use the spacebar to align columns. Also, you can see tab characters when Show Invisibles is turned on.

Indent Here. There's a great invisible formatting character called Indent Here, which you get by pressing Command/Ctrl-\ (backslash). This character causes the rest of the lines in a paragraph to indent to that character. I find this feature particularly useful for hanging punctuation or inline graphics, drop caps, or headings (see Figure 6-60).

Note that all the lines of the paragraph (after the Indent Here character) get indented, even if the paragraph spans two or more text boxes. The Indent Here character appears as a single vertical gray line when you turn on Show Invisibles from the View menu.

Some people use the Indent Here character to create hanging indents (like for bulleted lists). It's easy to do—just type a bullet, then a tab, then Command/Ctrl-\, and the rest of the paragraph is indented to the tab stop— but I don't like it as much as the trick where you set the Left Indent and First Line Indent (see "Tip: Hanging Indents," earlier in this chapter). The big difference? You can't specify an Indent Here character as part of a style sheet.

Discretionary hyphen. You remember that the Suggested Hyphenation feature lets you specify the hyphenation for a word, and wherever that word appears, it'll hyphenate the way you want. The discretionary-hyphen character (Command/Ctrl-hyphen) also lets you suggest hyphenation for a word, but it only works on a word-by-word basis. I use discretionary hyphens all the time when I'm finessing a document; if a line of text looks odd because XPress is

Figure 6-60

The Indent Here character

How do I love thee? Let me count the ways: ¶

1) This is the first one. I can't remember quite what it is, but I'm sure I mean well.¶

2) Here's the second one. Hmmm. Can't quite remember it, either, but now at the very least I know exactly how to ↵ use the Indent Here character.

Arrows indicate positions of Indent Here characters.

How do I love thee? Well, don't you think that's a bit of an impertinent question? I mean, if I'd asked *you* that, you'd have every right to throw me out. I mean, such nerve . . .

"We, the curmudgeonly, having solemnly sworn

being dumb in its hyphenation attempt, I'll throw in a discretionary-hyphen character where I think the word should hyphenate.

Note that typing a regular hyphen works just as well as a discretionary hyphen . . . at first. When you type a hyphen, XPress breaks the word at that spot (if the word is at the end of the line). But what happens if the text reflows for some reason (like if you add a word)? All of a sudden, you have hyphens scattered throughout your text (see Figure 6-61). If you use discretionary hyphens instead, they appear as real hyphens when they need to, but "disappear" when they're not needed (even Find/Change ignores the character).

▼ ▼

Tip: Stop Words from Breaking. Discretionary hyphens also play another role in QuarkXPress. If you place a discretionary hyphen immediately before a word, that word will never hyphenate at the end of a line. In other words, the discretionary hyphen also acts to turn hyphenation off for a single word.

▼ ▼

One problem arises when you want to remove a discretionary hyphen. Because you can't see this character (even when Show Invisibles is turned on), it's hard to select it and delete it. Try placing the cursor just before where you think the character is and using the arrow keys to move forward and backward. If there's a place where you hit the key but the cursor doesn't move, there might be an invisible character (like a discretionary hyphen) there.

Figure 6-61
Reflowed hyphens

Greetings, and congratulations on your purchase of **KvetchWrite**, the absolutely sensational new product for word processing, desktop publishing, object-oriented drawing, outline processing, flowchart creation, indexing, database management, telecommunications, and practically anything else you can imagine.

This is a regular automatic hyphen

Hard hyphens used here.

This text should have discretionary hyphens in it instead of hard hyphens.

Greetings, and congratulations on your purchase of **KvetchWrite**, the absolutely sensa-tional new product for word processing, desktop publishing, object-oriented draw-ing, outline processing, flowchart creation, indexing, database management, telecom-munications, and practically anything else you can imagine.

Another possibility is to use XPress Tags. If you export your story in XPress Tags format (see Chapter 7, *Copy Flow*, for more on this), you can find discretionary hyphens quickly. Just search for <\h> (the code for this character).

Nonbreaking hyphen. Sooner or later, you'll probably come upon a word which includes a hyphen, but which shouldn't be broken at the end of a line. For instance, you typically don't want figure references, such as "Figure 99-3," to break at line endings. The solution: you can use a nonbreaking hyphen by pressing Command/Ctrl-= (equals sign) instead of a normal hyphen.

Discretionary new line. You can place the discretionary-new-line character (Command-Return or Ctrl-Enter) within a word to suggest places to break that word if QuarkXPress needs to. It's much like a discretionary hyphen, but without the hyphen.

For example, if you type an en dash and feel comfortable about the surrounding words breaking at the end of a line, you can press Command/Ctrl-Return after the en dash (en dashes won't break without this, though em dashes will). If QuarkXPress determines that it needs to break the line at this point, it does. If it doesn't need to break the line there, it doesn't break it (and the character, being invisible, has no other effect on your text). Note that this character doesn't appear, even with Show Invisibles turned on.

Nonbreaking space. A nonbreaking space (on the Macintosh you can press Command-Space, Control-Space, or Command-5; on Windows, you can press Ctrl-5) looks just like a normal space character (and it expands and contracts as necessary in justified copy). However, it never breaks at the end of a line. A great use of this is in company names that include spaces, but shouldn't be broken over several lines (unless you absolutely have to).

New column and new box. If your text box contains multiple columns or is linked to other text boxes, you can use the New Column and New Box characters to force text to jump from one column or box to the next. Pressing Enter from your keyboard's numeric keypad forces a text jump to the next column. If the character is placed in the last (or only) column of a text box, it will force a jump to the next linked text box. Otherwise, pressing Shift-Enter forces a jump to the next linked text box.

En space. As I mentioned earlier in the chapter, an en is half an em, which— to QuarkXPress—equals either the width of two zeros or the height of the font you're working with (depending on how you've set up the Preferences dialog box). Pressing Option-spacebar results in an en space (on Windows, press

Control-Shift-6), which will not stretch in size in justified copy as much as a regular word space. (In other words, letterspacing still affects en spaces, though wordspacing values do not.) Command-Option-spacebar gives you an en space that doesn't break at the end of a line (on Windows, press Control-Alt-Shift-6). Note that an en space is rarely the same width as an en dash, even when Standard Em Space is turned on in the Preferences dialog box.

Flex space. When you press Option-Shift-space you get what's called a "flex space" (on Windows, press Control-Shift-5). You can specify how wide you want it to be (it flexes to your will). Also like the en space, once you specify its width, this space is fixed; it won't change width, even in justified text, unless you allow letterspacing in your H&J settings. (It's treated like just another character, so if QuarkXPress adds letterspacing in justified text, it adds it to the flex space, too. The space then expands.)

The control for this character's width is on the Character tab in the Preferences dialog box. The percentage is based on the width of an en space. Therefore the default value, 50 percent, is half an en space. 200 percent makes the flex space an em space. Note that when you change the width of a flex space in the Preferences dialog box, XPress changes the widths of flex spaces throughout that layout.

Punctuation space. The punctuation space (Shift-space)—sometimes called a thin space—is easy to confuse with the flex space while you're typing, and looks similar. They're both fixed-width characters, so they don't expand in justified type (unless you allow letterspacing in the H&J specs), but you can't specify the size of a punctuation space. Typically it's the same width as a comma or a period, but it's really up to the font designer. Punctuation spaces are often used in European typesetting, especially when setting numbers. You might type "1 024.35" (where a punctuation space—rather than a comma—is used as a delimiter).

Here's some typographic trivia for you: In some typefaces, the width of punctuation is set to the same width as the normal spaceband (which is often exactly half the width of a numeral in that font). In this case, the spaceband and the punctuation space are the same width, though one will stretch with wordspacing and one will not.

Page numbers. QuarkXPress lets you use three characters to display page numbering (see Table 6-8). As I noted in Chapter 4, *Building a Document,* these are not only page-dependent, but also text box–dependent. For example, you can place a text box with the next text-box character (Command/Ctrl-4) on top of a linked text box, and the page number will register the link of the text box

Table 6-8

Page-numbering
characters

PRESS ...	TO INSERT A CHARACTER REPRESENTING ...
Command/Ctrl-2	Previous text box
Command/Ctrl-3	Current text box
Command/Ctrl-4	Next text box

under it. The current text-box character (Command/Ctrl-3) is good for automatic page numbers on master pages; the previous text box character (Command/Ctrl-2) is good for "Continued from . . ." messages.

Punctuation and Symbols

A typographer shouldn't feel limited using a desktop computer. The typefaces from the major vendors (Adobe, Bitstream, Monotype, and so on) are loaded with the characters you need to create excellent type, including proper quotation marks, ligatures, and em dashes. If you aren't already a typographer, you'll want to pay careful attention to the tips and examples I provide here. Using some simple features—such as Smart Quotes and automatic ligatures—may make the difference between a piece that looks like it was desktop-published (in the worst sense of the phrase) and a piece that looks professional.

I can't discuss every special character that's included in a font, but I'll hit on a few of the important ones. Table 6-9 shows how to type each of these, plus a good number of additional characters.

Em and en dashes. An em dash, made by pressing Option-Shift-hyphen (on Windows, press Control-Shift-=), should be used in place of double hyphens to indicate a pause or a semiparenthetical. For example, don't type this: "Villainous-looking scoundrels - - eight of them." Instead, use an em dash. An em dash is named for how long it is (one em).

An en dash (Option-hyphen on Macintosh or Control-Alt-Shift-hyphen on Windows) should generally be used for duration and distance—replacing the word "to"—as in "August–September," "45–90 weeks long," and "the New York–Philadelphia leg of the trip." It's half as long as an em dash, so it doesn't stand out quite as much.

Note that QuarkXPress, if it needs to, breaks a line after an em dash when wrapping text, but not after an en dash (unless you put a discretionary soft return after it; see "Discretionary New Line," above).

▼ ▼

Tip: Narrowing Em Dashes. Perhaps typeface designers get overzealous every now and again with their characters. The em dash might certainly fall into this category, not in flourish but in width. Simply put, it's often just too wide. I'll sometimes make an em dash narrower by setting it to a horizontal

Table 6-9

Special punctuation and
symbols in most fonts

NAME	LOOKS LIKE	MACINTOSH	WINDOWS
Opening double quote	"	Option-[	Alt-0147
Closing double quote	"	Option-Shift-[	Alt-0148
Opening single quote	'	Option-]	Alt-0145
Closing single quote	'	Option-Shift-]	Alt-0146
Em dash	—	Option-Shift-hyphen	Ctrl-Shift-=
En dash	–	Option-hyphen	Ctrl-Shift-Alt-–
Ellipsis	…	Option-;	Alt-0133
Fraction bar	/	Option-Shift-1	N/A
Capital ligature AE	Æ	Option-Shift-'	Alt-0198
Small ligature ae	æ	Option-'	Alt-0230
Ligature fi	fi	Option-Shift-5	N/A
Ligature fl	fl	Option-Shift-6	N/A
Bullet	•	Option-8	Alt-0149
Copyright symbol	©	Option-G	Alt-Shift-C
Registered symbol	®	Option-R	Alt-Shift-R
Trademark symbol	™	Option-2	Alt-Shift-2
Degree mark	°	Option-Shift-8	Alt-0176
Section mark	§	Option-6	Alt-0167
Paragraph mark	¶	Option-7	Alt-0182
Dagger	†	Option-T	Alt-0134
Cents sign	¢	Option-4	Alt-0162

scaling of 75 or 80 percent of its original width. If you have a *lot* of them, you might consider doing this using XPress Tags: search for the em dash and replace with "<h80>—<h100>". I discuss XPress Tags and doing this kind of search in Chapter 7, *Copy Flow*.

▼ ▼

Ligatures. Ligatures are to typography what diphthongs are to language. They connects single characters together to make a single one. While many classic typefaces would contain up to 10 ligatures, typefaces on the Macintosh include only two basic ligatures (fi and fl), and Expert Sets from Adobe and other vendors usually have three more (ff, ffi, and ffl). Unfortunately, the folks at Microsoft didn't think ligatures were important enough to include in the Windows character set, so ligatures aren't available in most Windows fonts. Figure 6-62 shows ligatures in action.

The fact is, most programs make it a pain in the spleen to use ligatures. For instance, to get a ligature, you typically have to press an odd key combination

Figure 6-62
The fi and fl ligatures

Officially, the finalists
were affluent flounder *Without ligatures*

Officially, the finalists
were affluent flounder *With ligatures*

(Command-Shift-5 or Command-Shift-6 on the Macintosh). However, there are problems with using these "hard-coded" ligatures. If you type one of these characters in XPress, it won't be able to correctly spell-check or hyphenate it. Also, words with hard-coded ligatures in them might look strange in justified text if the program adds a lot of letterspacing. The final straw is that you can't easily edit the word (if you want to delete just the "f" or "i," you must retype both characters) or search for it in the Find/Change dialog box.

Fortunately, XPress has a great feature that gives you the best of all worlds: automatic ligatures. (Note that the Windows version of XPress doesn't include this feature because of limitations of Windows fonts.)

The key here is the Ligatures checkbox on the Character tab in the Preferences dialog box. When the Ligatures option is turned on, XPress automatically replaces every instance of "fi" and "fl" with the "fi" and "fl" ligatures. The wonderful thing about automatic ligatures is that spell-checking, searching, and hyphenation work just the way you'd hope they would because you're not typing weird special characters in the middle of words. You can even place your cursor between the "f" and the "i" in an automatic "fi" ligature because XPress still knows that it is two letters.

The Break Above field underneath the Ligatures checkbox becomes active when you turn automatic ligatures on. The number in this field tells QuarkXPress the letterspacing level above which to break the ligature apart. For example, suppose the field contains "1". If the ligature is kerned or tracked more than one unit, the ligature breaks apart, becoming two separate characters. If you change the number to "5", then QuarkXPress maintains the ligature until tracking or kerning has reached six units.

This is an important feature because you don't want two characters stuck together in "loose" text (the ligature stands out too much). This spacing limit also applies to justified text. That is, if you justify a text block by adding letterspacing, you're saying the ligatures may break into their single characters when necessary.

The last option in this area, called "Not ffi Or ffl," is for some finicky folks who think that those two particular combinations should not get the ligature treatment. I disagree, and I leave this option turned off.

Note that some fonts on the Macintosh have ligatures that look just like their character pair equivalents; this is especially true in sans serif typefaces, such as Helvetica. Also, some typefaces don't have built-in ligatures, and a few rare fonts have them but QuarkXPress doesn't "see" them. So the system's not foolproof, but it's still pretty good.

▼ ▼

Tip: Finding and Replacing Ligatures. If you're using QuarkXPress for Windows and you want ligatures, you'll have to manually search and replace the "fi" and "fl" combinations with the proper ligatures. If you do this, make sure you're careful about replacing them correctly. Especially make sure you turn off Ignore Case from the Find/Change dialog box. If you don't, the capitalized "Fi" or "Fl" combinations get changed, too! Remember that your search-and-replace strategy must also change the combination's font to the expert-set font containing the ligatures.

▼ ▼

Quotation Marks. The first tip-off that someone is green behind the ears in desktop publishing is his or her use of straight quotes instead of proper "printer's quotes." Straight quotes, which is what you get when you press the ' and " keys, should be used for notation of measurements (inches and feet) or for special typographic effect (some fonts' straight quotes look great in headline type). Printer's quotes, or curly quotes, should be used for English/American quotations. Quark has two features that have made it much easier to use curly quotes—Convert Quotes and Smart Quotes.

The Convert Quotes checkbox in the Get Text dialog box lets you convert all straight quotes into proper curly quotes when you import text. Second, you can turn on Smart Quotes in the Preferences dialog box. This automatically converts quotes as you type them. I always leave both of these turned on unless I specifically need to use straight quotes (see "Tip: Getting Your Quotes Straight," below).

Note that Smart Quotes can replace straight quotes with other sorts of quote marks (see "Tip: Get It Right for Overseas," below).

▼ ▼

Tip: Getting Your Quotes Straight. When Smart Quotes is turned on, every time you type a single or double quote it comes out curly. QuarkXPress is replacing the straight quote with the Option-[or Option-] and the Shift-Option-[or Shift-Option-] keys behind the scenes. (Those are Mac-only keystrokes.) However, if you really need a straight quote someplace, you can get it by pressing Control-' or Control-Shift-" (that's Control, *not* Command). On Windows, it's Control-' or Control-Alt-'. These keystrokes do just the opposite when Smart Quotes is turned off; then you get curly quotes. Unfortunately, this feature doesn't work with some foreign-language keyboard layouts (I've even had complaints about the UK keyboard not working in earlier versions of XPress).

▼ ▼

Registration, Copyright, and Trademark. The registration, copyright, and trademark characters are found on the Macintosh by pressing Option-R, Option-G, and Option-2 keys. In Windows, you should press Alt-Shift-R, Alt-Shift-C, and ANSI character code 0153 (see "Tip: ANSI Codes," below).

I have only one thing to say about using these characters: be careful with your sizing and positioning. I recommend immediately assigning the superior type style to the character, then determining whether it should be kerned or not (see Figure 6-63).

Figure 6-63
Special symbols

KvetchWrite™ is a product of No Accounting For Taste, Eh?® Documentation © Copyright 1990 No Class Productions.

Trademark and registration characters re-done as superior characters:

KvetchWrite!™ is a product of No Accounting For Taste, Eh?® Documentation © Copyright 1990 No Class Productions.

Registration mark kerned +12 to give it a little room to breathe.

Result without kerning: Eh?®

▼ ▼

Tip: Key Caps and Character Map. Anyone who can remember every character in a font, including all the special symbols and characters, is no one to borrow money from. I can never remember most of the characters I need, so I use Key Caps (on the Mac) and Character Map (on Windows). Both of these come free with your system—Key Caps is installed on the Apple menu, and Character Map is in the Accessories application group (see Figure 6-64).

To use Key Caps, select it from the Apple menu, then select the font you want to see from the Key Caps menu. When you hold down the Shift key, you see the map of all the uppercase characters. If you hold down the Option key, you see the Option characters, and so on. Click on the character you want to add to the text field at the top of the window. From there, you can copy and paste the character into a text box in XPress.

Character Map presents a table of characters for any font you choose. Simply double-click on the character you want (or click once and then click the Select button) to make the character appear in the Characters to Copy field. To enter the selected characters in XPress, click the Copy button, switch to your QuarkXPress document, place your insertion point, and paste (Control-V).

There are also a number of other shareware and freeware utilities on both Macintosh and Windows that let you find the character you need from a font even more easily than these two accessories do, but these usually work pretty well for me.

Figure 6-64

Key Caps and Character Map

Tip: ANSI Codes. Another way to type a character not found on your keyboard is to enter its Windows ANSI code (this is a Windows-only thing). First you need to look up the code, which you can find in Appendix G, *ANSI Codes,* or in your Windows manual. Notice that they're all four-digit codes, each beginning with a zero. Then, to enter the code, hold down the Alt key while you key in the code on your keyboard's numeric keypad.

The Character Map accessory in Windows also shows you the ANSI code in the lower-right corner when you click on a character.

Foreign Punctuation and Accents

Working in a foreign language is really a trip. Foreign languages have a different word for everything. Many foreign languages, like French and Spanish, contain accented characters that are built into fonts from the major type vendors. For example, you can type *élève* without switching to some obscure font. Table 6-10 lists the characters that you would most likely use in a foreign language.

Many people don't fully understand how to type these characters. Several of them aren't as easy as just pressing a key, or even a key with Option or Shift held down. For example, "é" is typed on a Macintosh by first typing Option-E, then typing the letter "e." It's a two-keystroke deal. On Windows, you can use the Character Map or type ANSI character code 0233 (as discussed above).

▼ ▼

Tip: Get It Right for Overseas. Here in the United States, I grew up with the ethnocentric viewpoint that the way I write and typeset is the way everybody does it. Not so. For example, single quotation marks are used in America where double quotation marks are used in Britain. In other European countries, my quotation marks are replaced with guillemets («, »). Note that Smart Quotes lets you set these to appear automatically when you press the quote keys. The Spanish language sets a question or an exclamation point at both the beginning (upside down) and at the end of sentences. Figure 6-65 shows examples of each of these styles.

If you do a lot of foreign-language work, and especially work that has multiple languages in the same document, you should check out Quark Passport—the multilingual version of QuarkXPress. This program lets you set a language as a paragraph attribute, and will then check spelling and hyphenate that language properly. It comes with about 12 languages built in. (You may run into some difficulties exchanging files in those languages with Passport if you don't have all the versions synchronized.)

Other languages, such as Hebrew, Farsi, Russian, and Greek, must be typed using a non-Roman font specific to that language, and may require specialized software. QuarkXPress is presently available in over 15 languages, including Japanese and German. (In case you're curious, Passport does not include Japanese.)

▼ ▼

Math Symbols and the Symbol Font

In my humble opinion, QuarkXPress is the wrong program in which to produce a mathematics textbook (though I know that it's been done). You can use utilities such as MathType from Design Science to help create equations, but

Table 6-10

Foreign accents
and punctuation

Name	Looks like	Macintosh	Windows
Left double guillemet	«	Option-\	Alt-0171
Right double guillemet	»	Option-Shift-\	Alt-0187
Left single guillemet	‹	Option-Shift-3	Alt-0139
Right single guillemet	›	Option-Shift-4	Alt-0155
Base double quote	„	Option-Shift-W	Alt-0132
Base single quote	‚	Option-Shift-0	Alt-0130
Question mark down	¿	Option-Shift-?	Alt-0191
Exclamation point down	¡	Option-1	Alt-0161
Acute vowel	áéíóúÁÉÍÓÚ	Option-E, then vowel	*
Umlaut vowel	äëïöüÄËÏÖÜ	Option-U, then vowel	*
Grave vowel	àèìòùÀÈÌÒÙ	Option-`, then vowel	*
Circumflex vowel	âêîôûÂÊÎÔÛ	Option-I, then vowel	*
Cedilla C	Ç	Option-Shift-C	Alt-0199
Cedilla c	ç	Option-C	Alt-0231
Capital slashed O	Ø	Option-Shift-O	Alt-0216
Small slashed o	ø	Option-O	Alt-0248
German ess (double s)	ß	Option-S	N/A
Dotless i	ı	Option-Shift-B	N/A
Tilde	˜	Option-Shift-M	Alt-0152
Tilde N	Ñ	Option-N, then Shift-N	Alt-0209
Tilde n	ñ	Option-N, then N	Alt-0241
Circumflex	ˆ	Option-Shift-N	Alt-0136
Macron	¯	Option-Shift-comma	N/A
Breve	˘	Option-Shift-period	N/A
Ring accent	°	Option-K	Alt-0176
Ring a	å	Option-A	Alt-0197
Ring A	Å	Option-Shift-A	Alt-0229
Dot accent	·	Option-H	N/A
Pound sterling	£	Option-3	Alt-0163
Yen	¥	Option-Y	Alt-0165

See Appendix G, ANSI codes, for the Windows equivalents.

they're not set up for doing heavy-duty math typesetting in XPress (not like the power tools in Adobe FrameMaker). Nonetheless, you can still do a pretty good job in QuarkXPress, as long as you don't have to produce 2,000 different equations in a document.

Figure 6-65
Foreign punctuation

The keys to doing a good job are using the correct symbols, and good typography. Most typefaces come with a wide variety of built-in math symbols. Table 6-11 provides a list of the most common of these and how to type them.

Almost any equation you'd want to typeset will require the Symbol font. Symbol is a Greek and math font that comes with your Macintosh or Windows system. It includes such characters as a multiplication sign (×), which you can create by pressing Option-Y (Mac) or Alt+0180 (Windows). Use Key Caps or Character Map, mentioned earlier, to examine the other characters in this typeface. Even better are pi fonts, such as Adobe's Universal News with Commercial Pi, which gives you better spacing and more flexible character weights. You can also purchase specialized math pi fonts, like Lucida Math.

Note that most Windows fonts include a multiplication character (Alt+0215) and division character (Alt+0247).

Dingbats

Letters, numbers, and symbols do not a funky design make. Ofttimes you need dingbats. Dingbats, or pi fonts, are collections of interesting and useful shapes, pictures, graphics, and so on. The most popular dingbat font by far is Zapf Dingbats—because it is included in most PostScript printers. Table 6-12 shows a listing of about a third of the Zapf Dingbats characters and how to type them. The other two-thirds are mostly variations on what is shown here.

Other examples of dingbat or pi fonts are Carta, Bundesbahn Pi, and Adobe Woodtype Ornaments (see Figure 6-66 for a few examples of various pi—or "dingbat"—fonts).

You can use these fonts for fun, but you'll more likely want to use them in a very functional way. Most people use them for bullets (those round Option-8 or Alt-Shift-8 bullets get boring pretty quickly). My favorite for this function is the lowercase "v" from Zapf Dingbats (❖).

Table 6-11

Commonly used
math symbols
(For Windows keystrokes,
please see Appendix G,
ANSI Codes.)

Name	Looks like	In most fonts	Symbol font
Division	÷	Option-/	Option-Shift-P
Plus or minus	±	Option-Shift-=	Option-Shift-=
Greater or equal	≥	Option-period	Option-period
Lesser or equal	≤	Option-comma	Option-3
Approximate equal	≈	Option-X	Option-9
Not equal	≠	Option-=	Option-P
Infinity	∞	Option-5	Option-8
Partial differential	∂	Option-D	Option-D
Integral	∫	Option-B	Option-Shift-;
Florin	ƒ	Option-F	Option-7
Capital omega	Ω	Option-Z	Shift-W
Capital delta	Δ	Option-J	Shift-D
Product	∏	Option-Shift-P	Shift-P
Summation	∑	Option-W	Shift-S
Pi	π	Option-P	P
Radical	√	Option-V	Option-/

You can also use these characters as graphics on your page. Don't forget you can shade and color different characters on your page to act as a background or foreground graphic.

▼ ▼

Tip: Ballot Boxes and Custom Dingbats. Many people create blank "ballot" boxes by typing a Zapf Dingbats lowercase "n" and setting it to outline style, or using the TrueType Wingdings font that comes with Windows. The problem with the first method is that imagesetting the outline often results in a hairline that is too thin to reproduce well. The only problem with the second method is that it's TrueType (I decidedly favor PostScript fonts for professional publishing). Nonetheless, there's a better option: anchored boxes (I'll cover this in much more detail in Chapter 11, *Where Text Meets Graphics*).

1. Create a picture box of any size.

2. Give the picture box a border (Command/Ctrl-B); I like to use .5 point.

3. Select the Item tool and cut the box (Command/Ctrl-X).

4. Using the Content tool, select where in the text you want the box to go, and then paste the box in there (Command/Ctrl-V).

5. Resize it to suit your needs.

Table 6-12

Useful characters
in Zapf Dingbats

NAME	SYMBOL	KEY OR KEYSTROKE
Shadow ballot box up	❑	O
Shadow ballot box down	❐	P
3D ballot box up	❑	Q
3D ballot box down	❐	R
Filled ballot box	■	N
Hollow ballot box	□	N (apply Outline style)
Opening great quote	"	Shift-]
Closing great quote	"	Option-N (Windows: Shift-tilde)
Opening single great quote	'	Shift-[
Closing single great quote	'	Shift-\
Great bullet	●	L
Great hollow bullet	○	L (apply Outline style)
Great shadow bullet	◗	M
Filled arrowhead	➤	Option-Shift-E (Windows: Alt-0228)
Right arrow	→	Option-] (Windows: Alt-0220)
Fat right arrow	➡	Option-Shift-U (Windows: Alt-0232)
3D right arrow	⇨	Option-Shift-I (Windows: Alt-0233)
Speeding right arrow	⇢	Option-Shift-7 (Windows: Alt-0224)
Triangle up	▲	S
Triangle down	▼	T
Love leaf	❦	Option-7 (Windows: Alt-0166)
X-mark	✘	8
Check-mark	✔	4
J'accuse	☞	Shift-=
Victory	✌	Comma
Scissors	✄	Shift-4
Pencil straight	✏	/
Pen nib	✎	1
Telephone	☎	Shift-5
Cross	✚	Shift-;
Star	★	Shift-H
Big asterisk	✳	Shift-Z
Snowflake	❄	D

Not only can you make box characters this way, but you can make any polygon, or anything else you can create within the application. Also, by importing a graphic into the picture box before you cut and paste it, you can create your own custom dingbats (Figure 6-67).

Figure 6-66
Some other dingbats

Whether traveling by 🚂, ⚓, or ✈, you should always 🚗 on the right side of THE road to get to the 🚂. Thank you! ✦ ✦ ✦ ✦

Symbols from Carta, Bundesbahn Pi, and Adobe Woodtype Ornaments.

Figure 6-67
Custom dingbats

And re*mem*ber! 👆 The *"cornier"* your Presentation, the less likely it is to be *Taken Seriously!*

Custom dingbat created by placing an EPS (Encapsulated PostScript) file within an anchored picture box. Picture box has been resized and its baseline shifted until the block of text looked appropriately corny.

☐ *Ballot box made with an outlined Zapf Dingbat ("n")*

☐ *Ballot box made with an anchored (square) picture box having a half-point (.5) frame.*

Typographic Special Effects

QuarkXPress is not a typographic special-effects program. But this does not mean that it can't give you the power to create many exciting effects with your type. In this section, I'm going to look at a few of the possibilities, like drop caps, rotated text, shadowed type, and type as a picture. But I can't cover everything that you can do. This, especially, is an area in which you have to play around.

Chapter 11, *Where Text Meets Graphics,* covers a few other special effects, such as text runaround, that you can create using QuarkXPress.

Fractions

Desktop publishing isn't so young that it doesn't have some hallowed traditions. One of the most hallowed is groaning in pain at the mention of creating fractions. But as with most traditions, you shouldn't let that frighten you off. The "fraction problem" in desktop publishing arises because most Macintosh fonts do not come with prebuilt fraction characters, and Windows fonts only have a small handful. (Windows fonts typically include three fractions—¼, ½, and ¾—which you type by pressing Alt+0188, 0189, and 0190, respectively).

You can create your own fractions in a number of ways. Let's take a look at each of these, and discuss why you'd want to use them.

Pseudo-fractions. You can create pseudo-fractions by typing in numbers separated by a slash. Let's be frank: they look awful, and are considered bad form. But in some cases, such as simple word-processed documents, they're perfectly acceptable. Opinion varies on how best to type these characters, especially when you have a fraction following a number. I generally like to add a hyphen between a number and its fraction. For example, one and one-half would be typed "1-1/2."

Don't try to use the fraction-bar character (Option-Shift-1 on the Macintosh, ANSI character code 0164 in the Symbol font on Windows) for this kind of fraction. It almost always bumps into the second number and looks like a *shmatta* (like junk).

Made fractions. You can create fractions—such as ½, ¾, or ²⁹⁄₃₂—by applying specific character-level formatting to each character in the fraction. The following example shows you how.

1. Type the pseudo-fraction; for example, "3/8." In this case, you should use the fraction-bar character (Option-Shift-1 on the Macintosh; on Windows, type Alt+0164 in the Symbol font) rather than the normal slash character.

2. Select the numerator—in this case, the "3"—and set it to the Superior style (Command-Shift-V or Ctrl-Shift-V).

3. Select the denominator—in this case, the "8"—and set it to the Superior *and* Subscript styles (Command-Shift-hyphen on the Macintosh; Control-Shift-9 on Windows).

4. Kern the fractions as desired.

If you don't like the size of the numerator and denominator, you can change the Superior settings on the Character tab in the Preferences dialog box. When a proper fraction follows a number, you probably don't want any sort of hyphen or even a space (see Figure 6-68).

Fractions via XTension. Quark's free Type Tricks XTension contains a feature that creates fractions for you. It essentially acts as a macro, changing the slash

Figure 6-68
Fractions

They tell me getting there is 3/8 of the fun.

A pseudo-fraction

I went to see *8-1/2* but only stayed for 2¾ of it.

A pseudo-fraction, followed by one created via the method noted in the text.

About ¼ of the time, I won't even give him a dime.

A fraction generated with Make Fraction (from the free TypeTricks XTension) plus some manual kerning within the fraction.

to a proper fraction bar, and changing the font size and kerning of the numerator and denominator. To let QuarkXPress make the fraction for you, follow these steps.

1. Type the fraction as two numbers separated by a slash.

2. Place the cursor in the fraction, or just to the right of it.

3. Select Make Fraction from the Type Style submenu.

Even though this feature is under the Style menu, Make Fraction is not really a character attribute; it's just a shortcut. Therefore, there's no way to undo the fraction using Undo. Note that on Windows, the fraction-bar character doesn't get substituted properly (Quark says that it does, but it doesn't), so you have to convert it yourself after making the fraction.

Personally, while many people go ga-ga over this feature, I find it only marginally faster than using the step-by-step method outlined above, and I like the results of the XTension less. (To be fair, you can control the results to some degree in the Fractions/Price panel of the Preferences dialog box.) Plus, if you change the font size of the fraction, the fraction made with styles changes dynamically, while the fraction made with the XTension has to be adjusted manually.

Stacked fractions. QuarkXPress also lets you create stacked fractions, such as $\frac{1}{4}$ and $\frac{3}{4}$. Here's a quick formula for making them.

1. Type the numerator and denominator, separated by an underline (Shift-hyphen).

2. Change the point size of these three characters to 40 or 50 percent of original size. For example, 12-point type gets changed to 5- or 6-point type.

3. Select the numerator and the underline, and apply a baseline shift equal to the point size.

4. Leave the numerator and the underline highlighted, and apply a tracking value of approximately -90 units.

5. At your discretion, apply extra kerning between the characters to achieve a more precise look. You may want to zoom to 800 percent, or print a test sheet.

Chances are, you'll need to adjust the numbers I provide for different typefaces and number combinations. Note that this method of creating stacked fractions only works when both numbers are single digits.

Expert Set fonts. Adobe and other companies have released expert set fonts that complement some of their normal font packages, such as Minion and Minion Expert. The Expert Sets contain some prebuilt fractions and a full set of correctly drawn and scaled superscript and subscript numerals, as well as the correct fraction bar for use with them. This really is the best way to make fractions, and it's what I used throughout this book. (An expert set font also contains oldstyle numerals, small capitals, and other special symbols and ligatures.) However, most fonts don't have Expert Sets; check with the font vendor for specifics.

Utilities. You can also create your own fraction fonts with a utility program such as Fontographer. This method allows you to use any font that you're already using to generate custom fraction characters. See Robin Williams's book, *How to Boss Your Fonts Around*, for details on creating a custom font.

Initial Caps

Initial Caps are enlarged characters at the beginning of a paragraph that lend a dramatic effect to chapter or section openings. There are four basic types of initial caps: raised, dropped, hanging, and anchored. Each of these styles is made considerably easier to create with the automatic drop-caps feature and the Indent Here character (Command/Ctrl-\).

Let's look at several initial caps and how they are made.

Standard raised caps. Raised caps can be created by enlarging the first letter of the paragraph (see Figure 6-69). It's important to use absolute leading when you create standard raised caps. If you don't, the first paragraph's leading gets thrown way off.

Hung raised caps. A spin-off of the standard raised cap is the hung raised cap (see Figure 6-70). You can hang the letter "off the side of the column" by placing an Indent Here character after it or creating a hanging indent with indents and tabs. The rest of the text block's lines all indent up to that point.

Standard drop caps. The Drop Caps control is located on the Formats tab in the Paragraph Attributes dialog box (see Figure 6-71). To create a drop cap in a paragraph, place the text cursor in the paragraph, press Command-Shift-F or

Figure 6-69
Standard raised caps

Unaccustomed as I am to public speaking . . . but that never did prevent me from running off endlessly at the mouth . . . you, sir! Stop that hideous snoring! But I digress . . .

14-point copy with a 30-point initial capital.

Figure 6-70
Hung raised caps

Unaccustomed as I am to public speaking . . . but that never did prevent me from running off endlessly at the mouth . . . you, sir! Stop that hideous snoring! But I digress . . .

14-point copy with a 30-point capital. Indent Here character has been placed to the immediate right of the raised cap.

Figure 6-71
Standard drop caps

Let it never be said that the Koala tea of Moishe is not strained. Should this be said, it is entirely possible that the very fabric of civilization would fall utterly into the hands of the

Drops Caps is set in the Paragraph Attributes dialog box. Note that the font size is replaced with a percentage.

☑ Drop Caps

Character Count: 1

Line Count: 3

Melior   100%

Ctrl-Shift-F (to bring up the dialog box), and turn on Drop Caps. You can then modify two parameters for this feature: Character Count and Line Count.

The character count is the number of characters made to drop. The line count is the number of lines that they drop. For example, specifying "3" in Character Count and "4" in Line Count makes the first three characters of the paragraph large enough to drop four lines down. You don't have to worry about sizing the character, aligning it, or specifying the space between the drop cap and the rest of the text. In this example, the baseline of the drop cap aligns with the fourth line, and the ascent of the drop cap aligns with the first line's ascent. Some fonts have ascents that are taller than their capital letters. This may make the process slightly more difficult, depending on the effect you're trying to achieve.

▼ ▼

Tip: Adjusting Space After Caps. I often find that I want to change the space between the initial cap and the text that's flowing around it. People have tried all sorts of weird workarounds for moving the two farther apart or closer together, but I prefer the simple method: add kerning between the drop cap and the character after it. The more kerning you add, the farther away the flow-around text is set. Negative kerning brings the text closer.

▼ ▼

Hanging drop caps. You can make these in the same way as the hanging raised caps: place an Indent Here character (Command/Ctrl-\) directly after the dropped character (see Figure 6-72). You can adjust the spacing between the drop cap and the following text by adjusting the kerning value between the drop cap and the next character (in this case, the Indent Here character).

Figure 6-72
Hanging drop caps

Three-line drop cap with Indent Here character placed here, creating hanging drop cap.

Let it never be said that the Koala tea of Moishe is not strained. Should this be said, it is entirely possible that the very fabric of civilization would fall utterly into the hands of itsworst

Scaled drop caps. XPress has one hidden feature that works on drop-cap characters and drop-cap characters only: percentage scaling. After creating a standard drop cap (as described above), you can select the drop-cap character(s) and change the point size to a percentage of the original drop-cap size. For example, Figure 6-73 shows a paragraph with the drop cap scaled to 150

Figure 6-73

Scaled drop caps

Let it never be said that the Koala tea of Moishe is not strained. Should this be said, it is entirely possible that the very fabric of civilization would fall utterly into the hands of its worst enemies, like that fellow whose name begins

The same, with the capital "L" enlarged to 150 percent of its normal size:

The Measurements palette reflects the change—again, as a percentage of the normal drop-cap size (not in points).

percent. You can change the percentage of the drop-cap character(s) to anything you want, and the baseline will always align with the text line to the right.

Anchored raised caps. Another way of making a raised cap is to create it in a separate text box, then anchor that box to the beginning of the paragraph (I discuss anchored text and picture boxes in Chapter 11, *Where Text Meets Graphics*). The raised cap in Figure 6-74 is actually a separate text box containing a large capital letter on a tinted background. The character is centered horizontally and vertically within the frame. I also applied other formatting to the initial cap, such as kerning and baseline shift.

Anchored drop caps. After creating an anchored raised cap, you can make it drop by selecting Ascent on the Box tab in the Modify dialog box (select the anchored box and press Command/Ctrl-M, or double-click on the anchored box).

Wraparound dropped caps. When you're using letters such as "W" or "A," you may want to wrap the paragraph text around the letter (see Figure 6-75). While you can use the Drop Cap option (along with a mess of other formatting), it's just easier to create the drop cap as a separate box and let XPress figure out the text runaround for you.

1. Create a new text box, type the initial-cap character, and format it the way you want it to look.

2. Select the initial-cap character and choose Text to Box from the Style menu. This converts the text into a picture box. You can now delete the original text box (the one that held the initial cap).

3. Unless you're going to put a picture inside the initial cap, choose None from the Content submenu (under the Item menu).

4. In the Modify dialog box (Command/Ctrl-M, or double-click with the Item tool), give the box a background color and set the Runaround to Item.

5. Move the initial-cap box into position over the paragraph.

This is only one of many variations on a theme for creating wraparound drop caps. Another is to use an initial cap brought in from an illustration program (as any sort of graphic file). You can then use QuarkXPress's automatic runaround or manual runaround feature to control the text runaround (I discuss text runaround in more detail in Chapter 11, *Where Text Meets Graphics*).

Figure 6-74
Anchored raised caps

We fully recognize that the message "Now formatting your hard disk. Have an *exceedingly* nice day," appearing during the **KvetchPaint** installation, is a bit alarming. Rest assured that it is a harmless prank by one of our programmers—who is, you can also rest assured, no longer with us. As soon as we can break the encryption he used, we will

Figure 6-75
Wrapping drop caps around pictures and picture boxes

With just a tin can and a piece of string you can find that a circle's perimeter is just over three times its diameter. With a good metal ruler, measuring by the tenth of a millimeter, you can even see that the ratio is just over 3.1415 to one. There are methods

Salivating in public is not only discouraged, but is, in fact, morally wrong. In fact, I think I could go so far as to say that the entire salivation process is, on occasion, a work of the devil. For example, when I see a chocolate sundæ, I know I should not eat it. My rational mind takes a very definite stand on that point. However, my salivary glands pay no mind.

Mixed-font caps. I've already cautioned you about using too many fonts on a page. But if there's ever a time to break the rules, it's with initial caps (see Figure 6-76). If you want your initial caps in a different font, simply change the font for those characters. However, note that when you change the initial cap's typeface, the character may not align properly with the rest of the text.

Multiple initial caps. Character Count in the Drop Caps feature lets you drop up to eight letters in your paragraph. So a drop cap could be a drop word, if you like (see Figure 6-77).

Playing with initial caps. Like I said, initial caps are great opportunities to play and come up with creative ideas. For instance, you could make a two-character automatic drop cap, and set the first character in some dingbat font. Change the color and tint of the dingbat, and then kern the second character back so that it sits on top of the dingbat (you may need to change the dingbat's baseline shift to make it look right). Can you re-create the initial-cap examples in Figure 6-78?

▼ ▼

Tip: Type in the Margin. In QuarkXPress, the edges of text boxes are usually inviolable. There's no margin release, no handy command for moving one line an eentsy bit over the edge. Or is there? This tip shows a clever way of fooling QuarkXPress into hanging text at the beginning of a line beyond the left margin of a column or text box (see Figure 6-79). The example I use is for a drop cap, but you could use it for hanging punctuation or any other character.

1. Instead of a single-character drop cap, specify a two-character drop cap, vertically spanning as many lines as you like.

2. Add a space to the left of the first character in the paragraph. If your paragraph is justified, this should be a space that doesn't get wider, such as Shift-spacebar.

3. Select the first character (I usually press Command/Ctrl-Up Arrow and then Shift-Right Arrow, which jumps the cursor to the beginning of the paragraph, then selects the first character) and apply negative tracking like crazy. You'll find you can tighten the tracking on that first character so much that the drop-cap character actually moves to the *left* of the space. Keep on tracking until the left edge of the character starts to disappear beyond the left edge of the text box. Adjust the tracking as necessary.

Although the first letter appears to be sliced off on the left side, it actually prints properly.

▼ ▼

Figure 6-76
Mixed font initial caps

Snell Roundhand   *Adobe Garamond*

Sconce, call you it? So you would leave battering, so I would rather have it a head. And you use these blows long, I must get a sconce for my head, and ensconce it too, or else I shall seek my wit in my shoulders. But, I pray, sir, why am I beaten?

Figure 6-77
Multiple initial caps

Five-character drop cap. Horizontal scaling of 75%; font size changed from 100% to 87.5%

Comma scaled down to 75% of normal font size, (it's less obtrusive that way).

What, gone in chafing, and clapped to the doors? Now I am every way shut out for a very bench-whistler; neither shall I have entertainment here or at home. I were best to go try some other friends.

Figure 6-78
More initial caps

A POOR MAN IS OBSERVED STARING in admiration at the large and ornate tombstone of the richest man in town. he shakes his head slowly and mutters, "Now, that's what I call living!"

Of course, the last time I went to one of those big banquets, I lost my wallet. I went up to the microphone and announced "Ladies and gentlemen, I've lost my wallet, with eight hundred dollars in it. Whoever finds it will get a reward of fifty dollars!"

Then a voice from the back of the room yelled out, "I'll give seventy-five!"

Figure 6-79

The amazing

hanging drop cap

Valen; if, by your art, you haves
Put the wild waters in this roar, allay them.
The sky it seems would pour down stinking pitch,
But that the sea, mounting to th'welkin's cheek,
Dashes the fire out. O, I have suffered
With those that I saw suffer! A brave vessel,
Who had, no doubt, some noble creature in her,
Dashed all to pieces.

——————————————— Edge of the text box

Shadow Type Alternatives

Applying the Shadow style to any range of selected type creates a generic shadow that cannot be customized. For example, you can't change its thickness, shade, or offset. Although this is a nice shadow effect on screen, its limitations make it not particularly useful for many purposes (plus, it often prints differently on different printers, so it's inconsistent).

You can have total control over your shadows by using duplicate text boxes. Here's one way to do it (see Figure 6-80).

1. Create a text box with some solid black text in it.

2. Duplicate the text box (Command/Ctrl-D).

3. Select the text within the second text box and modify it (change its color or tint, or something else about it).

4. Send the second text box to the back (choose Send to Back from the Item menu).

5. Set both the background color and the runaround of the top box to None. (Many people get confused at this last step, forgetting that if both the color and runaround aren't set to None, there's no way to see the text in the background box.)

You can then move the second text box around until you have it placed where you want it. Remember that you can click through the top text box by clicking with Command-Option-Shift (Ctrl-Alt-Shift) held down. You might also want to group the two text boxes together in order to move them as if they were one item.

▼ ▼

Tip: Shadow XTensions. There are several XTensions on the market that not only create drop shadows for you automatically, but they also build them faster and better than you can in XPress. The best known (and best period) is ShadowCaster from a lowly apprentice productions. If you have to build more

Figure 6-80
Shadows

Introducing
KVETCHWRITE
"You've tried the best, now try the rest!"
THREE

than one or two drop shadows in XPress each week, you should stop reading now and go buy it.

▼ ▼

Pricing

Quark's free Type Tricks XTension lets you automate one other common text-formatting function: pricing. It's simple to make a number into a price (see Figure 6-81). Just type the value, place the cursor within the number or just to the right of it, then select Make Price from the Type Style submenu under the Style menu. Note that all this feature does is delete the decimal point and apply the Superior and Underline styles to the digits after the decimal point. As with the Make Fractions feature, I'm not particularly excited about this little macro (I find that it's often faster to do this manually using keystrokes than it is to select the feature from the Style menu).

Nonetheless, you have several options for how QuarkXPress formats the character, including whether it should take out any decimal point you've included and whether the numbers after the decimal point (the cents) should have an underline or not. These controls are located in the Fraction/Price panel of the Preferences dialog box.

Figure 6-81
Make Price example
and preferences

"Okay, look, I'll give you $4.74 for it."
"How much did you say? I don't understand."
"I meant $4^{74}."
"Oh! Sure. It's a deal."

┌─Price────────────
│ ⊠ Underline Cents
│ ⊠ Delete Radix
└──────────────────

▼ ▼

Text Greeking

After all this talk about making text look better on the screen and on your printed output, you probably need a break from type. Let's talk about how to make type go away.

Designers have long worked with a concept known as *greeking*. Greeking is a method of drawing gray bars to represent blocks of text, rather than taking the time to image them all on the screen. QuarkXPress can greek text under a specific size limit, which you can define on the General tab in the Preferences dialog box. While the default value for text greeking is 7 points, you can set it anywhere from 2 to 720 points.

Unless you really want to see every character of every word at every size, there's hardly any reason to turn text greeking off. However, depending on what your page design is like, you may want to adjust the Greek Below values at different times. I typically set it to 4 or 5 points.

▼ ▼

Putting It Together

If you got through this entire chapter and are still not too bleary-eyed to read this, you must really be a QuarkXPress die-hard. After having learned about QuarkXPress's word-processing capabilities in the last chapter and what you can do to those words in this chapter, you're ready to move on to the theory and practice of style sheets and copy flow—automating all this formatting so you don't have to do it all manually every time you need it. There's working with type, and then there's working hard at type. I'm trying to get your work to be as easy as possible.

7

Copy Flow

As you've learned in preceding chapters, you can do all sorts of wonderful things to type in QuarkXPress. But there's more to the intelligent handling of your copy than simply setting it in exquisite type: you have to get the document produced on time.

In the development of a publication, copy is almost never static. For any number of reasons, you may have to make drastic changes in the formatting or content of the copy (usually at or beyond the last minute). Your success in meeting deadlines (and getting paid) can often depend on how carefully you've anticipated such changes. If you don't plan from the very beginning to manage the flow of your document's copy, it will surely end up managing you, and in ways you won't like.

Managing Copy

QuarkXPress has two very powerful tools for automating the formatting and management of your document's copy: style sheets and XPress Tags. Use them wisely, and you'll soon make your copy jump through hoops at the snap of your fingers (or the click of your mouse). Use them poorly, or not at all, and you'll be the one jumping through hoops, probably at three o'clock in the morning the night before a major job is due. In this chapter, I'll tell you how to make the best use of these features. The key is learning to work smart.

Working Smart

Simply put, there are two ways to handle your copy in QuarkXPress: the dumb way and the smart way. What's the main difference between the two? Working the smart way, you make the computer do as much of your work as possible. Working the dumb way, you take it on yourself to do the kind of mindless, repetitive tasks computers were meant to take off your hands—in this case, the repetitive formatting and reformatting of copy.

It takes a bit more time at first to set up a document to take advantage of XPress's automation, but it is well worth it if you ever need to make even the simplest layout-wide change in the way your text is formatted. Of course, if you're the kind of person who always gets everything right the first time, you'll never, ever need to change any formatting once you've entered it, so you may not find this chapter of much use. The rest of you should pay careful attention.

The dumb way. The dumb way to format your copy is the way you most likely learned earliest: by selecting text and directly applying various attributes. Want a paragraph to be centered? Go to the Style menu and center it. Need to change the typeface? Go to the Font menu and do it.

"What's so dumb about that?" you may ask. It's not that there's anything inherently wrong with applying formatting directly to your copy; it's just that by doing so, you doom yourself to performing the same selecting and modifying actions over and over again whenever you need to format another text element with the same attributes, and whenever you need to make major changes to your layout. If the paragraphs you've centered now have to be made flush left, you must again select and change each paragraph individually.

Another way of working dumb is to carefully format your text in QuarkXPress, and then when heavy editing is required, export the copy to a word processor, edit it, then re-import it into XPress. Suddenly you may notice that you've lost most of your special QuarkXPress formatting (such as horizontal scaling, superior characters, kerning, tracking, and so on), and it's time for another long, painstaking formatting pass through your document.

The smart way. The smart way to handle your copy is to take the time to be lazy. Make QuarkXPress's features work for you. By using style sheets, you can apply formatting faster than ever before. When the time comes to change an attribute (font, size, leading, or whatever), style sheets will exponentially speed up that process, too. Also, be sure to use XPress Tags if you export your text. This will retain your formatting information, even if you send stories out to be edited on a dreaded DOS or UNIX computer.

Let's jump in and look at how style sheets and XPress Tags can make your life a better place to be.

Style Sheets

A style sheet is a collection of text-formatting attributes with a name. For example, a style sheet named "Heading" might represent the following formatting: "14-point Helvetica Bold, centered, with half an inch of space before." Every time you apply that one style sheet to a paragraph, the paragraph is assigned all that formatting. You can create one style for titles, another for footnotes, and more styles for different levels of subheads. In fact, you can (and probably should) create a different style sheet for each and every different kind of paragraph in your layout, especially since there's no limit on the number of style sheets you can have in a document.

While XPress 3.x only had *paragraph style sheets* (styles that applied to an entire paragraph), version 4 introduced *character style sheets*. Character style sheets can be applied to a single character (or a word, or a sentence, or whatever). They're handy for run-in subheads, numbered lists where the number and period are in a typeface different from the text, and emphasis (like changing the font of all the company names in a layout). Again, if you're going to use the same character formatting more than once or twice in your document, you should create a character style sheet for that formatting.

The next step. In the following description, I'm first going to talk about paragraph styles, and then about character styles. Once you've got paragraph styles down pat, then character styles will be a piece of cake for you. Throughout the discussion, when I talk about style sheets, I will almost always mean both paragraph and character style sheets.

A Style Is a Style Sheet Is a Style

For some reason, Quark decided not to follow accepted terminology when it named its Style Sheets feature. It is commonly understood in publishing, both traditional and desktop, that the group of formatting attributes for a particular type of paragraph is called a "style." Plus, the list of all the styles in a layout is called a "style sheet."

However, in QuarkXPress language, each paragraph and character has its own so-called "style sheet," and the collection of these is also referred to as the "style sheet." Because of the confusion, I now tend to use the terms interchangeably. Forgive me, but after all, writing is an inexact science.

The Benefits of Style Sheets

Working with style sheets is smart for two reasons: applying formatting and changing formatting. I typically say that if your layout has more than two pages of text, you should definitely be using style sheets. (Don't feel that two pages is a minimum, though; *any* document is a suitable place to use style sheets, especially a document that you know will go through many rounds of revisions.) As with lots of other things (making backups, for example), think about the trade-offs you're talking about: more work up front to save some work downstream. It's up to you to decide whether it's worth doing.

Applying formatting. Let's say I've hired you to work on creating this book. I've specified three levels of headings, two kinds of paragraphs (normal indented paragraphs and the nonindented paragraphs that come right after headings, not to mention the run-in heads like in the paragraph you're reading right now), and a way that the figure numbers and titles should look. It's your job to apply those styles to all the text.

If you went through all 900 pages, fastidiously setting the font of each paragraph, the size of each paragraph, the alignment of each paragraph—and so on—I'd be calling you Rip Van Winkle before too long. Instead, you can define all the attributes for each paragraph in a style, then apply those attributes in one fell swoop by applying that style to a paragraph or to a range of paragraphs.

Changing formatting. Of course, the real nightmare would be when you hand me a draft copy of the book and I ask you to bring down the size of the headings half a point (of course, since we're in the design business, I'd wait to ask you until 5:00 PM on the Friday before Christmas). But if you're using styles, you'd smile and say "Sure thing!"

Whenever you make a change to the definition of a style, that change is automatically applied to every paragraph that uses that style. Because you've had the foresight to create a "Heading" style that is applied to every heading in the book, you need only change the attributes of that style—in this case, the point size—and it gets changed instantly throughout the entire layout.

Local Formatting Versus Formatting with Styles

A key point to remember about QuarkXPress paragraph styles is that the formatting contained in a style is applied to an entire paragraph. If the style calls for Times Roman, the entire paragraph will be in Times Roman. However, you can always override the style's font for specific text within the paragraph. This "local" or "hard" formatting remains, even if you change the style's font definition, or apply a different style sheet to the paragraph. (One exception: if a paragraph has the QuarkXPress option No Style applied to it, *all* local formatting will be wiped out when you apply a style to it. See "Normal Style and No

Style," later in this chapter.) In other words, hard formatting stays around for a long time, so you have to mind it carefully.

As I said earlier, you can also format just part of a paragraph with a character style; in this case, the character style you applied is also considered local formatting (because the character style you applied doesn't match the character style of the paragraph style . . . I'll discuss this more later in the chapter).

▼ ▼

Tip: Seeing Local Formatting. If there is any local formatting where the cursor is in the text (or in whatever text is selected), a plus sign appears to the left of the style's name in the Style Sheets palette. This is a handy way of knowing if you're looking at text formatted according to its style, or at formatting that's been applied locally (see Figure 7-1).

Local formatting is sometimes confusing for people, so here are a couple of examples of when you do and do not see the plus sign.

▶ If you apply local paragraph formatting to a paragraph—for instance, an automatic drop cap—the Style Sheets palette displays the plus sign next to the paragraph style, no matter where in the paragraph you place the cursor (because you've applied local formatting to the entire paragraph). There's no plus sign next to the text's character style sheet, however, because you have not changed any character formatting.

▶ If you change the point size of only three words in the paragraph, the plus sign appears only when the cursor is in that text. Local character formatting is always also local paragraph formatting because the paragraph style includes character formatting (I'll clarify this below).

The problem is that there's no way to see what the local formatting is—the plus sign appears the same whether you've changed a paragraph's font or its tracking (see "Tip: Totally Overriding Local Formatting," and "Tip: Find Local Formatting," later in this chapter).

▼ ▼

Figure 7-1
Local formatting flag

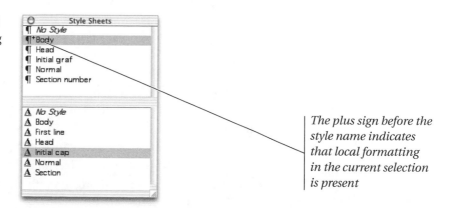

The plus sign before the style name indicates that local formatting in the current selection is present

Unfortunately, there is one instance in which QuarkXPress loses track of local formatting. If you apply a style to a paragraph that contains the same formatting attributes that you've used in local formatting, and then you apply a style with different formatting, your original local formatting will be lost.

For instance, assume you have a paragraph whose style calls for plain text (that is, neither bold nor italic), and you've made a few words in the paragraph bold. Next, you apply a style that makes *all* the text bold. Finally, you apply a style that *isn't* bold. All the text in the paragraph will no longer be bold, including the text to which you originally applied the bold formatting. This doesn't just apply to making text bold or italic, but to any local formatting which can also belong to a style: font, baseline shift, whatever.

The reason for this is simple: QuarkXPress only remembers local formatting by how it is *different* from the style applied to it. If you apply a style sheet that looks the same as the local formatting, it's not local formatting anymore (see Figure 7-2). (See "Tip: Removing Just Some Formatting," later in this chapter, for one way you can turn this "problem" into a "solution.")

Figure 7-2
How QuarkXPress loses
local formatting

Three words in
this paragraph
are bold.

Apply a style
which calls for all
text to be bold.

Now apply a style that calls
for plain text. See your local
formatting disappear.

Tagging Paragraphs

It's important to understand that there's a difference between paragraph formatting and the style name. When you apply a style to a paragraph, you're only *tagging* it with that name—essentially identifying *what it is*, not necessarily what it should look like. QuarkXPress has an internal style sheet list that tells it what collection of formatting should go with that name. If you tag the paragraph with a different name, the formatting automatically changes. Or if you change the attributes of the style sheet, QuarkXPress updates the formatting throughout the project (across all layout spaces).

Therefore, when you begin to work on a document, it's not really that important that the style sheets you use bear the correct formatting, since you can always change the attributes later. Once you've tagged all the paragraphs in your text, you can experiment by modifying their styles at your leisure.

There are three ways to apply style sheets—that is, to tag paragraphs—from within QuarkXPress: with the Style menu, with the Style Sheets palette, and with keystrokes.

Style menu. The most basic—and the slowest—method for applying a paragraph style is to select the style name from the Style Sheets submenu (under the Style menu; see Figure 7-3). Like any other paragraph formatting, your text selection or insertion point must be somewhere within the paragraph.

Figure 7-3
The Style Sheets
submenu

Style Sheets palette. The Style Sheets floating palette (select Show Style Sheets from the Window menu, or press F11) lets you apply, edit, and view styles on the fly without having to go to any menus (see Figure 7-4). The palette, which you can keep open on your screen all the time (or you can dismiss it when you don't want it, and call it back up by pressing F11 again), lists all the styles in your document along with their keyboard shortcuts, if they have any. If you have lots of styles, you can make the palette larger or just scroll through them.

Figure 7-4
The Style Sheets palette

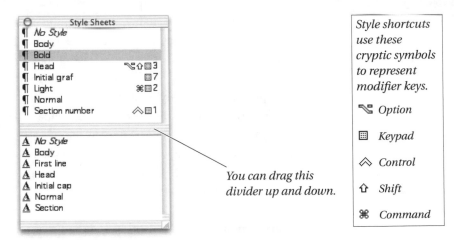

You can drag this
divider up and down.

*Style shortcuts
use these
cryptic symbols
to represent
modifier keys.*

⌥   *Option*

▦   *Keypad*

⌃   *Control*

⇧   *Shift*

⌘   *Command*

The beauty of this palette is that you can put it right next to (or on top of) your text box while you work. To apply a style to a paragraph, put the text cursor somewhere in that paragraph and click on the style in the palette. To apply No Style to a paragraph, click on No Style in the palette. The paragraph is no longer tagged with the style, but the formatting from the style remains as hard, local formatting (you should rarely use No Style; see "Normal Style and No Style," later in this chapter).

As you move your cursor through your text, the style sheet for each paragraph is highlighted in the Style Sheets palette; you can quickly see what styles are applied. This is especially helpful if local formatting overrides styles, or if you have two styles that are similar and you want to know if a paragraph is tagged with one or the other.

Keystrokes. The third method of applying styles to paragraphs is by using keystrokes. Each paragraph style can have its own keystroke, which you define for it (see "Creating a New Paragraph Style," below). Then you can select a paragraph and press that keystroke. In case you forget your keystrokes, they appear as reminders on both the Style Sheets submenu and the Style Sheets palette.

▼ ▼

Tip: Copying Attributes from One Paragraph to Another. You can copy all the paragraph formatting from one paragraph to another with a single mouse-click. First, place the cursor in the paragraph whose formatting you want to change, then Shift-Option-click (Shift-Alt-click) on the paragraph whose format you want to copy. (Note that both paragraphs have to be in the same story, but they do not have to be in the same text box.)

This copies all the paragraph formatting, including the paragraph's style sheet and any local paragraph formatting (margins, tabs, leading, space before or after). No local character formatting (font, size, bold, italic) in the destination paragraph is copied—only paragraph formatting.

▼ ▼

Defining Styles

To create or edit a paragraph style sheet, select Style Sheets from the Edit menu or press Shift-F11. This calls up the Style Sheets dialog box (see Figure 7-5). If you open this dialog box when a document is open, you'll see all the styles in that document. You can then use this dialog box to create, edit, and delete styles, and, by using the Append button, import some or all of the styles from another XPress document.

If you use the Style Sheets dialog box with no documents open, you can edit and add to QuarkXPress's default style-sheet list, which will then be automatically included in all new documents you create.

▼ ▼

Tip: A Quick Hop to Style Sheets. To edit a style, Command/Ctrl-click on that style in the Style Sheets palette. This brings up the Paragraph Style Sheets dialog box with the style name highlighted. Then you can click Edit, or press Return or Enter, to edit that style sheet (pressing Return or Enter here is often one step easier than clicking the Edit button).

▼ ▼

Tip: Showing Style Sheets. Quark did a significant facelift on the Style Sheets dialog box back in version 4 to accommodate character style. They also added the Show popup menu, which lets you determine which Style Sheets you want to display (several other features in XPress also have a Show popup menu feature, including Lists and Colors). There are five options on this popup menu.

Figure 7-5
The Style Sheets
dialog box

▶ **ALL STYLE SHEETS.** This is the default value, and simply displays every style sheet in the document.

▶ **PARAGRAPH STYLE SHEETS.** Many people complained about the addition of character styles as too confusing (personally, I don't know what they were talking about). Nonetheless, if you have a lot of styles and you only want to display the paragraph styles, choose this option.

▶ **CHARACTER STYLE SHEETS.** Opposite of the above, this option displays all the character styles and hides the paragraph styles.

▶ **STYLE SHEETS IN USE.** This is very useful. I often have many more style sheets in a document than I will typically use (the others are there just in case I need them). Choosing this option hides all those extras so they don't clutter up the dialog box.

▶ **STYLE SHEETS NOT USED.** I generally use this option when I feel like deleting all the unused styles.

Note that the Show popup menu has no effect on the Style Sheets palette. The palette always displays all the styles.

▼ ▼

Tip: Jump to a Style. If you have a *lot* of styles in your document, you're not going to want to slowly scroll through the list in the Style Sheets dialog box until you get to the one you want. Instead, just type the first letter or two of the style's name, and XPress jumps there.

▼ ▼

Creating a New Paragraph Style

Creating a new paragraph style sheet is as easy as one, two, three.

1. Create a paragraph in a text box (it can even be just some gibberish text in a dummy text box). Format it exactly the way you want the style sheet to be defined (both character and paragraph formatting), and place the cursor somewhere in the paragraph.

2. Go to the Style Sheets dialog box and click the New button (while this looks like a button, it's actually a popup menu). Choose Paragraph from the popup menu. (Or, if you want to copy another style, you can press the Duplicate button instead of New.)

3. Either way, the Edit Paragraph Style Sheet dialog box appears (see Figure 7-6). All the formatting from the paragraph you made is sucked into the dialog box, so you don't have to set it here. Enter the name of the new style in the Name field. Press OK, and then press Save to leave the dialog box.

Figure 7-6

The Edit Paragraph
Style Sheet dialog box

Make sure the text selection in step 1 doesn't include any text that is formatted in some other unwanted way—say, some words in bold or italic that you *don't* want to become part of the new style definition. In other words, this procedure picks up the paragraph *and* character attributes of where your insertion point (or selection) is, and uses them in defining your new style.

If you want to define a keystroke combination that will automatically apply the style, click in the Keyboard Equivalent field (in step 2), and press the combination you want. On the Macintosh, it's often a good idea to use a Function or keypad key in combination with the Control key, because you can be confident that keystrokes defined this way won't conflict with QuarkXPress's other key commands, almost none of which use the Control key (see the keyboard shortcuts tear-out card in the back of the book).

▼ ▼

Tip: Keys You Can Use for Style Shortcuts. You can only use certain keys for applying styles—the function keys (F1 through F15) and the numbers on the numeric keypad. In combination with the Control, Command, Shift, and Option (or Alt in Windows) keys, that allows for a lot of shortcuts. However, because QuarkXPress uses the function keys for its own shortcuts (both with and without Option/Alt and Shift), I suggest that you use function keys as style sheet hotkeys only in conjunction with the Control key.

There's no way to print a list of what keystrokes go with what styles (see "Tip: Printing Your Style Sheet," later in this chapter), so I just print a screen shot of the Style Sheets palette and tape it to my wall.

▼ ▼

Defining paragraph formatting. The step-by-step method above is a way to define a style by example, and it's the easiest and fastest way to make a style sheet. You can, however, also define a style sheet directly from within the Style Sheets dialog box. You need to learn this slower method, too, because it's how you edit styles and also how you can create style sheets when no document is open.

Once you've clicked the New button in the Style Sheets dialog box, selected Paragraph from the popup menu, and named your new style, you can define its paragraph formatting by setting values in the Formats, Tabs, or Rules tabs of the Edit Paragraph Style Sheet dialog box.

Character formatting in paragraph styles. Paragraph styles always include character formatting, too (like font, size, and so on). When you first create a paragraph style sheet, XPress assigns the Default character formatting. Personally, I think the word "default" is really confusing. In plain English, it means "Use the character formatting hidden inside the Character Attributes dialog box." It might help to remember that Default is the way that XPress version 3.x made style sheets (except that there was no Character Attributes dialog box back then).

You get to the Character Attributes dialog box by pressing the Edit button in the Edit Paragraph Style Sheet dialog box (see Figure 7-7). If you're building a paragraph style by example (as in the step-by-step outlined above), the character information here is the same as in your dummy "example" paragraph.

If you have already built other character style sheets (I'll cover how to do this later), you can replace Default with one of your own styles on the Style popup menu. The New button in the Edit Paragraph Style Sheet dialog box lets you create a new character style and apply it to this paragraph style in one fell swoop. If you've chosen a character style instead of Default, all the character attributes of that character style sheet are used in the paragraph-based style sheet you're defining.

In other words, you don't have to use character style sheets if you don't want to. You can create style sheets the old-fashioned XPress 3.x way by leaving the popup menu set to Default and pressing Edit to define the values. Just remember to think ahead, as building character styles and using them in paragraph styles may be more flexible down the line.

▼ ▼

Tip: Beware of the Edit Button. Watch out for the Edit button in the Edit Paragraph Style Sheet dialog box when you're using a character style *other* than Default. If you make an edit here, it edits the character style, too! Unfortunately, this makes it way too easy to change your character styles acci-

Figure 7-7
Character Attributes
in a paragraph style

*Click Edit to open the
Character Attributes
dialog box.*

dently (you might change them thinking that you're only editing the value for this paragraph style . . . not so).

▼ ▼

Editing style sheets. To edit a style sheet, select it from the list of styles in the Style Sheet dialog box and click the Edit button. You see the same tabbed dialog box as you did when you were creating the style sheet. Go ahead and make the changes you want, then press OK and finally press Save to leave the Style Sheets dialog box.

▼ ▼

Tip: Even Speedier Style Sheets. You can avoid the Style Sheets dialog box altogether by holding down the Control key and clicking on a style name in the Style Sheets palette (in Windows, click on any name in the palette with the right mouse button). The context-sensitive popup menu that appears lets you edit, duplicate, or delete the style that you clicked on (see Figure 7-8). Or you can create a new style by selecting New.

Figure 7-8
Shortcut to styles

Control-click or secondary button-click on the style name to get this popup menu.

Note that if you select New when clicking on one of the character styles, you'll create a new character style; if you click on one of the paragraph styles in the palette, you'll create a new paragraph style sheet. This is certainly the fastest way to create a style sheet, because you never have to look at the clunky Style Sheets dialog box.

▼ ▼

Tip: Removing Just Some Formatting. If you work with style sheets a lot (and who doesn't?), you should know about the Redefine Style XTension, which lets you change a style sheet definition based on changes on your document page. For example, if you want to change the font of your Heading1 style, just change one heading and then select Redefine Style. The XTension changes the definition for you based on your local formatting and the change ripples through the rest of the file. It's not free, but it's very inexpensive, and certainly worth the small cost.

▼ ▼

Normal Style and No Style

Every QuarkXPress document has a default style—the Normal style. This is the style automatically applied to all the text in a document if you don't specifically apply another style (if you type in a new text box, it's always in the Normal style). You can edit the Normal style just like any other.

No Style is different; applying it removes *all* style sheet information from a paragraph. (It doesn't remove your formatting, just any style sheet affiliation.) All the paragraph's formatting is then treated as hard local formatting. Normally, local formatting doesn't change when you apply a style to a paragraph. However, if the paragraph has No Style applied to it, subsequently applying a style sheet wipes out all local formatting. So if you have some words in italic, for instance, in a No Style paragraph, then applying any other style sheet to that paragraph will remove your italics (assuming that the new style sheet you've just applied is not itself defined as italic).

▼ ▼

Tip: Default Font. Tired of Helvetica or Arial being the font that appears by default when you create a new text box and type in it? The font you type in is defined in the "Normal" style sheet. To change the default font (or leading, or color, or any other paragraph or character formatting), modify your "Normal" style sheet. Simple as that. You can even change it when no documents are open to affect all subsequent files.

▼ ▼

Tip: To Use Normal or Not. In the past, I've always been wary of using the Normal style in my documents, always choosing instead to build other styles and use them. My reasoning had to do with the inability to find and change styles based on Normal or to append the Normal style from another document (there were other reasons, too). However, newer versions of XPress have rendered all my complaints obsolete, and there is little reason not to use the Normal style now. I still don't do it, but it's more out of tradition and superstition than practical sense.

▼ ▼

Tip: Totally Overriding Local Formatting. The fact that a paragraph that has No Style applied to it loses all local formatting (including bold and italic) when it's tagged with another Style Sheet is, more often than not, a pain in the butt and causes much confusion. However, there are some powerful uses for this feature, such as stripping out all local formatting that some dumbbell put in for no good reason.

Always on the lookout for a faster way to do something, I was pleased to find that I can apply "No Style" to a paragraph and then apply a style sheet in one stroke by Option/Alt-clicking on the style I want to apply in the Style Sheets palette.

▼ ▼

Tip: Removing Just Some Formatting. In the previous tip, we learned that "No Style" is great for eliminating all local formatting in a paragraph. However, what if you want to get rid of only *some* local formatting?

Instead of using "No Style" to get rid of all local formatting wherever it occurs, you can get clever with the way the document's paragraph styles are defined. The trick is that QuarkXPress is built in such a way that it only remembers local formatting that is different from the formatting in a paragraph style sheet. So, first change the style sheet so that it contains the formatting you want to remove, then remove that unwanted formatting from the style sheet.

This is much easier to understand with an example. Let's say you have a whole lot of text that has a "BodyText" style sheet applied to it, but some bozo selected the whole thing and changed the typeface to 18-point Futura (this kind of error happens a lot when you copy and paste text from one document to another and the style sheets are slightly different in each file).

The problem is that there are also words in the text that are made italic for emphasis. If you apply "No Style" to everything, then apply the "BodyText" style again, you would wipe out all italic attributes in the text, and you'd have to go back and reapply them by hand. However, using this technique saves the day (see Figure 7-9).

1. Edit the "BodyText" style so that its definition includes all the formatting that you *want to get rid of*. In this example, change the character formatting to 18-point Futura.

2. Save the change to the style sheet.

3. Edit the "BodyText" style again. This time, define it the way it was originally. In this example, you'd define it with the original typeface and size.

4. Save the change to the style sheet.

Now all the text is formatted properly: you've gotten all the text to be the original typeface and size, but you've retained the italic local formatting as well. You don't have to select the text; you just have to adjust the style sheets. (Of course, this tip relies on you knowing what local formatting has been applied to the text; if you don't know that, see "Tip: Finding Local Formatting," later in this chapter.)

Figure 7-9
Removing just the local formatting you don't want

She is like a <u>tree planted by streams</u> of water, that yields its *fruit* in its **season;** whose *leaf* does not wither, and everything she does shall *prosper*. The ungodly <u>are not so, but</u> are like **chaff** which the wind blows away.

1. Someone has gone in and changed some text to a different font and added underline style.

<u>She is like a tree planted by streams of water, that yields its *fruit* in its **season;** whose *leaf* does not wither, and everything she does shall *prosper*. The ungodly are not so, but are like **chaff** which the wind blows away.</u>

2. Change the paragraph style to match the local formatting.

She is like a tree planted by streams of water, that yields its fruit in its **season;** whose leaf does not wither, and everything she does shall prosper. The ungodly are not so, but are like **chaff** which the wind blows away.

3. Change the style back; the unwanted formatting is lost, but the desired local formatting remains.

▼ ▼

Tip: Redefining Tabs in Styles. Although you can define tabs within a style, it's a pain in the left buttock going back and forth between editing a style and looking at its effects on your page. An easier solution takes advantage of creating style sheets by example (see the previous tip) and the ability to merge styles. This tip assumes that you've already created a paragraph style sheet, and that you need to edit the tab stops.

1. Apply the style sheet to a paragraph (or select a paragraph that has the style already applied to it).

2. Change the tab stops of that paragraph to where you'd like them to be.

3. Create a new style sheet based on this new paragraph (see "Tip: Even Speedier Style Sheets" for the fastest way to do this). Name this style sheet slightly differently from the original style sheet (I usually just append the word "new").

4. Control-click (or on Windows machines, click with the right mouse button) on the name of the old style sheet, and choose Delete from the context-sensitive popup menu. When you're prompted with a dialog box asking for a replacement style, select the new style sheet and click OK.

5. Finally, Control-click (or click with the right mouse button) on the new style name, select Edit, and rename it without appending the word "new".

Of course, this isn't only for changing tabs. You can use this technique to change any element of a style sheet. However, note that this only works with a style that isn't based on another style, and it won't work with the Normal style.

▼ ▼

Tip: Giving Style Sheets a Color. Sometimes when I have lots of style sheets in a document, and they're all somewhat similar, I like to change the type color of each one. One might be blue, another might be red, and so on. This allows me to see on screen, at a glance, which style sheets have been applied where. Of course, if you do this, don't forget to change them all to the proper color before you go to final output.

▼ ▼

Appending Styles

The Append button in the Style Sheets dialog box lets you import styles from other QuarkXPress documents into your QuarkXPress project. After selecting the file from which you want to import, the program lets you choose exactly which styles you want (see Figure 7-10). In case you don't know what the incoming styles look like, XPress shows you the definitions in the Description area of the Append Style Sheets dialog box.

Because the incoming style sheet may include information about another style sheet (like a paragraph style that refers to a character style, or a style that is based on another), XPress always warns you that it may be importing more than you may have bargained for (see Figure 7-11). This dialog box becomes really annoying after you see it once or twice. Fortunately, the folks at Quark gave us an out: simply turn on the checkbox in the alert dialog box, and XPress refrains from displaying it again. Whether you turn the alert off or not, you should always check to see what styles have actually been imported.

When you press OK in the Append Style Sheets dialog box, QuarkXPress checks to see if any incoming styles have the same name as those already in your document. If it finds such a conflict, it displays another alert dialog box and asks you what to do (see Figure 7-12). You've got four options, each a separate button.

▶ **RENAME.** You get to manually rename the style that's being imported with any other unused name.

▶ **AUTO-RENAME.** Automatically renames the incoming style with an asterisk at the beginning of its name. I'm not sure why you'd use this, but I bet there's a good reason.

▶ **USE NEW.** The incoming style overwrites the one already in the document. I almost always use either Use New or Rename.

▶ **USE EXISTING.** This effectively cancels the appending of the style; the old one (the one currently in the document) is retained and used. The

Figure 7-10
Appending styles

Figure 7-11
XPress alerts you when
you're importing more
than you bargained for

Figure 7-12
Conflicting style
sheets alert

only time you'd use this is if you didn't realize that there was a duplicate when you chose to append the style.

If you think there's going to be more than one conflicting style name, you may want to turn on the checkbox marked Repeat for All Conflicts. This way, XPress handles the remaining conflicts in the same way.

Of course, remember that there is also an Append feature on the File menu that you can use to import style sheets, colors, and H&Js at the same time. If you need to import both styles and colors, for instance, it's clearly efficient to do it with Append instead of in the Style Sheets dialog box.

Appending with cut and paste. Another way to move a style from one QuarkXPress document to another is to copy text containing that style. You can use Copy and Paste, or you can drag a box containing the text from document to document. However, beware: QuarkXPress won't alert you to any style-name conflicts. Instead, it just throws away the incoming style's formatting information and replaces it with the existing style's attributes plus local formatting on top so that the text looks the same as it did in the source document. In other words, this is a good way to import a style or two, but it's often a lousy way to import text, especially when the style name already exists in the target document.

▼ ▼

Tip: Comparing Two Styles. I hate it when I have two styles that are very similar but I can't remember how they're different. Fortunately, QuarkXPress lets you compare two style sheets. Select two styles in the Style Sheets dialog box (click on one, and then Command/Ctrl-click on the other), then Option/Alt-click the Append button. (Actually, as soon as you hold down the Option/Alt key, you'll see the Append button change to a Compare button.) The result: a dialog box that lists each element of the two style sheets; the differences are highlighted in bold (see Figure 7-13). Of course, you can only compare two character styles or two paragraph styles; you can't mix and match.

▼ ▼

Tip: Find Local Formatting. Earlier I mentioned that there's no way to find out what local formatting someone has applied to text. That's not strictly true. You can figure out what local formatting is on a paragraph by creating a new style sheet based on the local formatting (just create a style while the cursor is in the text), then use the Compare button (see the previous tip) to compare the new style with the original style. The differences between the two indicate local formatting.

▼ ▼

Deleting (and Replacing) Styles

You can delete a style sheet by clicking the Delete button in the Style Sheets dialog box (Command/Ctrl-clicking lets you select and delete more than one style; Shift-Delete lets you select contiguous styles). If the style sheet has been applied somewhere in your document (or if it's referenced by another style sheet—see "Basing One Style on Another," below), XPress asks you if you want to replace the style with another one. That is, all the text that is tagged with the deleted style is assigned a new style sheet, rather than going to "No Style."

Basing One Style on Another

You can also base one style sheet on another. By basing many styles on, say, the Normal style, you can quickly change many elements in your document by simply changing the Normal style.

For example, let's say you want all your subheads to be the same as the "Heading 1" style, but with 14 points of space before, and horizontally centered. By basing the subhead style on the "Heading 1" style, you can ensure that every change you make to the "Heading 1" style is instantly reflected in the subhead style. If you change the "Heading 1" style's font from Helvetica to Franklin Gothic, the font of the subheads based on the "Heading 1" style automatically changes from Helvetica to Franklin Gothic as well.

(In this case, the "Heading 1" style sheet is the *parent style* and the subhead style based on it is called the *child style*.)

Figure 7-13

Comparing two styles

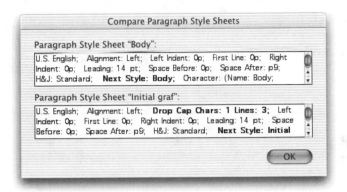

Here's how you can base one style on another.

1. Choose a style sheet from the Based On popup menu in the Edit Paragraph Style Sheet dialog box. In the case of the example above, choose Normal.

2. Edit the various tabs in the Edit Paragraph Style Sheet dialog box to change only those attributes you want to be different in the new style. In this example, you would change the Alignment and Space Before settings on the Formats tab of the dialog box. Watch out, though; changing the character formatting in the two styles can be a little tricky, so make sure you carefully read the "Character-Based Styles" section, later in this chapter.

3. Note that the description at the bottom of the Edit Paragraph Style Sheet dialog box lists the "based on" style along with all the additional formatting you've applied to the new style (see Figure 7-14). Click OK and then click Save to leave the Style Sheets dialog box.

If you plan your styles carefully, you can use the Based On feature to create nested hierarchies of styles based upon one another, so that a simple change to one style will be applied to all the styles based on it, and the styles based on those, *ad infinitum*. This "ripple effect" can be a great time-saver, so it's well worth your while to take greatest advantage of it.

▼ ▼

Tip: Based-On Differences. When one style is based on another, XPress only keeps track of the *differences* between the base style and the new style. Let's say you have a style called "Head1" and it's 18-point Futura with the bold style applied, and a style called "Head2" that's based on "Head1," except that it's 12-point Futura and is not bold. The differences between the two are the point size and the bold attribute.

If you change the font of "Head1" to Franklin Gothic, then the font of "Head2" changes, too. But if you change the point size of "Head1" to 24 point,

Figure 7-14

Basing one style
sheet on another

then "Head2" does not change, because the point-size "link" is broken. However, there's one important exception: if you change the parent style to have attributes that are *the same* as the child style, the difference is broken. If you change "Head1" to "not bold," for example, then there's no difference in style between the two and the link is broken. Then, if you go back and change "Head1" to bold again, "Head2" follows suit and becomes bold. This is much the same as what happens when local formatting within a paragraph matches the formatting of the style (see "Local Formatting vs. Formatting with Styles," earlier in the chapter).

To summarize: As long as you don't change any formatting in the parent style to match the child style, you'll be fine. But as soon as you change an attribute in the parent style to match the child style's, that link is broken, the child style isn't different in that way anymore, and you're going to wish that you'd paid more attention to this paragraph.

▼ ▼

Next Style

If you're typing in QuarkXPress, and the paragraph you're on is tagged with the "Heading" style, you probably don't want the next paragraph to be tagged with "Heading" too, right? (Unless you want two headings in a row.) You can force XPress to automatically change the subsequent style sheet with the Next Style popup menu in the Edit Paragraph Style Sheet dialog box. If you want the subsequent paragraph to be "BodyText," then choose "BodyText" from the Next Style popup menu.

Note that this only works if the insertion point is at the very end of a paragraph when you press Return (turn on Show Invisibles to see where the current Return character is). If the insertion point is anywhere else when you press Return, you'll simply break that paragraph in two, and both new paragraphs will have the same style as the original one.

In other words, this feature is essentially intended to be used while you're typing, not while you're doing the simple kinds of editing or formatting you're likely to be doing in QuarkXPress. However, it certainly can come in handy once in a while.

When you're first creating a style sheet, the default choice on the Next Style popup menu is "Self," which simply means that the next style will be the same as the current style (no change at all).

▼ ▼

Character-Based Styles

If I had a dollar for every time someone said to me, "I wish I could apply a style sheet to a single word instead of to a whole paragraph," I would be writing this book on a beach in Tahiti (I'll leave my true "Winter in Seattle" surroundings to your own imagination). Fortunately, XPress has character styles, and I encourage you to use this feature to its fullest.

Almost everything that I said earlier about paragraph styles is also true of character styles. You create, edit, append, and delete them in almost exactly the same manner. There are, of course, some differences. For instance, to create a character style sheet, you should choose Character instead of Paragraph from the New popup menu in the Edit Style Sheets dialog box. Also, because these are character styles, you can only assign character formatting to them (the kind of formatting you can apply to a single character, such as font, size, color, shade, scale, type style, tracking, and baseline shift; see Figure 7-15).

As I said earlier, when you start typing in a new text box, the text automatically is set to the Normal paragraph style sheet. However, because the definition of the Normal paragraph style includes a reference to the Normal character style sheet, all your text is automatically set to that character style as well.

If you create a new character style (you can use the step-by-step "by example" approach outlined earlier) and apply it to some text that is already in the Normal style, it acts like local formatting on top of the Normal style.

There's no doubt that character style sheets can add to your general level of confusion, especially at first. However, there are several really good reasons to push through and keep using them until they become second nature.

▶ Using character style sheets throughout your document ensures consistency of formatting, and makes the process of formatting the text go

Figure 7-15

Editing or creating a character style sheet

faster. This is even more true if you have more than one document in a larger project (such as chapters in a book).

▶ By assigning character styles within paragraph styles, you can also ensure consistency among multiple paragraph style sheets. For instance, if your Heading1, Heading2, and Heading3 paragraph styles all use the same "Heading" character style sheet, you only have to change this one character style sheet to update all three paragraph styles.

▶ The most important reason to use character styles (or style sheets in general) is the inevitability that your art director or client will start laughing uncontrollably when they see your design and then make you change something. Because this change always happens just before a deadline, style sheets are your only good chance at salvation.

Of course, if the only character-based formatting you have in your project is bold and italic, character styles may not be that exciting. But where you are applying a collection of formatting to a single word or character, character styles are the way to go—for instance, to drop caps, run-in heads, fractions, or special types of emphasis. One real-world example is a project I worked on where I had to match the visual size of two different fonts that were placed side by side throughout a document. By assigning a character style sheet to each font, I could easily experiment with the look of the page by making little tweaks to the definition of one or both of the character styles, instead of selecting every instance of both fonts and changing them manually.

Note that there are times when Find/Change is just as fast at updating text formatting. However, I find that the character-styles feature is almost always faster and more powerful, especially once you get the hang of it.

Style Sheets palette. In order to accommodate character styles, the Style Sheets palette has been split into two halves; the top half displays paragraph styles and the bottom half displays character styles. To apply a character style, select the text you want to affect, then click on the character style sheet name in the palette. (Yes, if you're paid by the hour and want to do things the slow way, you could also choose the style name from the Style menu.) Even better, if you're using a character style sheet frequently, assign it a keyboard shortcut.

▼ ▼

Tip: The Balance of Style Power. Do you have more paragraph styles than character styles? You can change the palette's size by dragging the resize box in its lower-right corner. It turns out you can also drag the boundary marker between the paragraph styles and the character styles.

▼ ▼

Tip: Search and Replace Your Style Sheets. Back in Chapter 5, *Word Processing*, I discussed how you can use the Find/Change feature to search for and replace style sheets. However, here's one less-intuitive way to use Find/Change: search for particular character formatting and "replace" it with a character style. For example, let's say you have a document created in version 3.3 that is a perfect candidate for character styles because it has run-in heads throughout (like this book does).

Set up the Find side of the Find/Change palette to search for one or more of the particular character attributes of the run-in heads. On the Change side, turn off the checkboxes for everything except the Style Sheet popup menu, in which you should choose the character style you want to apply. Making this change is the same as manually applying the character style to each run-in head . . . but it's much faster.

One note, though: Make sure that the definition of the character style you're applying is the same as the formatting of the text you're searching for. If the formatting is different, then XPress will apply the style and leave some of the original attributes as local formatting, defeating the purpose entirely.

▼ ▼

Character styles in Based On paragraph styles. Earlier, I discussed the value of using the Based On feature in paragraph style sheets, but I mentioned that changing character formatting in a child style gets a little tricky. That was an understatement; in fact, the whole way that character styles and paragraph styles interact is probably the most confusing aspect of style sheets in XPress, and most likely to cause blood vessels to burst in your forehead. Fortunately, it's not without logic; it just takes some getting used to. Here are two rules to live by.

▶ If the Character Attributes Style popup menu within the parent style is set to Default, then you can easily edit the character formatting in the child style: just click the Edit button. (As the book goes to press, the Description field in the Edit Paragraph Style Sheet dialog box doesn't update accurately to display the change you've made—I think it's a bug, so it might be changed by the time you read this—so you just have to take the change on faith.)

▶ If the Character Attributes Style within the parent style is set to one of your character style sheets, then you have to be really careful when making a change (see Figure 7-16). Clicking the Edit button will edit the character style itself, which is rarely what you want. (If you edit the character style itself, it will affect both the parent and child styles, as well as any other text or style that uses that character style!)

Instead, you should create a new character style (by clicking the New button), and base this new character style on the same character

Figure 7-16
Editing character
formatting in
based-on styles
(Windows)

*Click New to create a
new character style sheet.*

*Click Edit to edit this
character style sheet.*

style that the parent style uses (use the Based On feature). Yes, this is annoying. Yes, this makes me want to kick someone. But that's the way it works (at least as I write this).

In the latter case (where you've assigned a character style to your parent style), here's a step-by-step method for how to proceed.

1. Create a new paragraph style sheet, and set the Based On popup menu to the desired parent style. At this point, everything about your new style is exactly the same as this parent style.

2. Note the name of the character style listed on the Character Attributes Style popup menu. If it's Default, you can stop here and go read the first bullet point again; if it's not Default, then commit the name to memory (or write it down, if it's at the end of the day).

3. Click the New button to create a new character style sheet.

4. In the Edit Character Style Sheet dialog box that pops up, choose the name of the character style from the Based On popup menu.

5. Finally, go ahead and make the changes you want to make to the character formatting (if you can still remember what you were trying to do by now).

6. Give this new character style a name (I usually use a name like "Style based on Such-and-such") and then press OK. This adds the new character style to your list, and also applies it to the child paragraph style you're working on.

7. Make any changes to the paragraph formatting you want applied to this child style, and then press OK.

This seems like it'd take longer than it really does, and after doing it a few times, you get the hang of it. I just wish that changing something as basic as character formatting in a child "based on" style were as easy as it used to be.

▼ ▼

Tip: Keeping Libraries of Styles. One of my favorite uses for libraries (see "Libraries" in Chapter 2, *QuarkXPress Basics*) is to save style sheets that I use in multiple documents. Here's what I do: In a small text box, I write out the name or the description of the style sheet, and whether it's a character style or a paragraph style (I've seen people use color codes so that all the character styles are in red, and all the paragraph styles are in blue). Then I add some text or a paragraph to the bottom of the text box, and apply the appropriate style sheet (if I'm saving a character style, I also apply the No Style paragraph style, or vice versa).

Finally, I drag this text box into my "style library" (which I've already saved on my hard disk). Because the text almost fills the small text box, it appears readable in the Library palette (as long as there isn't too much text; see Figure 7-17), so I can easily identify it later when I come looking for it. (You could also use the library labeling feature for this, if you've got a lot of styles.)

Figure 7-17
Keeping track of styles
in the Library palette

▼ ▼

What Word Processor to Use

Although QuarkXPress can import formatted text from several word processors, it can only interpret the styles of Microsoft Word files and styles saved in Rich Text Format (RTF) files. (If you have another word processor that uses styles and can save them as Microsoft Word or RTF files, you're in luck too.) In general, since styles are so important to the proper management of your copy, Word automatically becomes the best word processor for working with QuarkXPress. (Unless you decide to work exclusively with XPress Tags, which I cover in the next section. These can be used, albeit awkwardly, by any word processor that can import and export text-only ASCII files—that is to say, nearly all word processors).

By the way, while QuarkXPress does import pictures contained as anchored graphics in Word files, and can even export inline graphics to the correct location in a Word file, I really don't recommend that you do this because the imported images are always PICTs (see Chapter 9, *Pictures,* for information on why this is useless). Ultimately, the images would need to be manually replaced once they arrived in XPress.

Another option is to work with Quark CopyDesk SE (the "SE" special edition is the standalone version of CopyDesk, as opposed to the one that ships with the QPS workflow solution). CopyDesk SE is designed as a tool for editors or writers who need to edit stories to fit specific spaces in a layout. It's quite useful for some workgroup situations, especially those where editors don't have a copy of QuarkXPress on their machines. Because it uses all the same styles and typography as QuarkXPress (CopyDesk is actually a stripped down version of the XPress application, with some editorial features added), you don't have to worry about losing any styles or typography when moving back and forth between XPress and CopyDesk.

How QuarkXPress Style Sheets Work with Word

When you bring a Word document into QuarkXPress and you've checked Include Style Sheets in the Get Text dialog box, QuarkXPress imports every style from the Word file into its own style sheet, incorporating as much of Word's formatting as QuarkXPress can handle.

Character formatting. QuarkXPress can import a great deal of Word's own formatting. All the character attributes available in Word can be carried over into QuarkXPress, with a few exceptions (see Table 7-1).

Paragraph formatting. For paragraph formats, QuarkXPress brings in most available Word settings, except that it ignores the Page Break Before setting, and only the top and bottom rules set for boxed paragraphs will be imported (though QuarkXPress does a good job of interpreting the correct size and weight of rules). QuarkXPress ignores any values you've set for space between rules and their paragraphs.

Style formatting. Any of Word's attributes which can be applied to styles can be successfully imported as styles by QuarkXPress, with the exceptions noted above.

If your QuarkXPress document has style sheets with the same names as those in your Word file, you may be given the choice to import or override those Word styles (see Figure 7-18). This dialog box looks suspiciously like the conflicting style sheets dialog box we saw in "Append," earlier in this chapter, and in fact it gives you the same four options: Rename, Auto-rename, Use Existing, and Use New. About 99 percent of the time, you'll want to click Use Existing, so the style definition already within QuarkXPress will be applied (see "Tip: Don't Worry About Word Style Definitions," below).

Table 7-1

What QuarkXPress does with Word's formatting

Word's formatting	What QuarkXPress does with it
Double and dotted-line underlines	Turns them into normal underlines.
Super- and subscript settings	Applies whatever values you've specified for them within your QuarkXPress document (in Document Preferences).
Expanded and condensed type settings	Converts them to tracking values in XPress. Since you specify these values using points in Word, and QuarkXPress uses $\frac{1}{200}$ of an em, there is usually only a very rough correlation between how tightly type is set in Word, and what you get when you bring it into QuarkXPress.
Footnotes	Numbers are changed to superscript style; footnote text is added at end of story.

Whatever you do, the local formatting you've applied in the Word document is imported, too.

▼ ▼

Tip: Word Versions Spell Trouble. To be honest, even though Microsoft Word works better with QuarkXPress than any other word processor does, it's still not a perfect system. In fact, the success of an import (or export; see "Exporting Text," below) often depends on both the version of Word and the version of your Word import filter (the XTension that lets you import and export Word files). I have often had to return to earlier versions of the Word filter to get them to work properly, depending on the version of Microsoft Word I'm using. Often, exporting RTF from Word works best of all.

▼ ▼

Tip: Don't Worry About Word Style Definitions. Remember that QuarkXPress can override Microsoft Word's formatting for style sheets. Let's say that your Microsoft Word document's "Normal" style is 14-point Geneva with 24-point leading (for easy reading and editing on screen), and your QuarkXPress document's "Normal" style is 11-point Goudy with 15-point leading. When you import the file, QuarkXPress automatically uses the XPress version of the style sheet, and all the text that is tagged as "Normal" appears in 11/15 Goudy (like you'd want it to).

The implication of this is that you never really have to worry about what the styles look like in Word. In this book, for example, my Microsoft Word text was all in Helvetica and Georgia, but when I imported the text files into QuarkXPress, they came out in the fonts you're reading right now (Adobe Utopia and Stone Sans).

▼ ▼

Figure 7-18

Importing styles from
Microsoft Word

Tip: Don't Forget to Include Style Sheets. You should almost always turn on the Include Style Sheets option in the Get Text dialog box when importing text. If you don't, QuarkXPress may apply "No Style" to all the text. If you have any intention of applying other paragraph style sheets to these paragraphs, you're in for a surprise: all your local formatting—even italic—disappears as soon as you apply a paragraph style (see "Totally Overriding Local Formatting," above).

On the other hand, if you do turn on Include Style Sheets, XPress applies either the styles from the word processor (if there are any) or it just uses "Normal." In fact, one of the very few times I turn off Include Style Sheets is when I'm working with XPress Tags (which I discuss later in this chapter).

Tip: Text Reflow Between Versions. Each version of QuarkXPress flows text slightly differently, because Quark keeps changing features. Don't worry about how the text will change when you open an older-version document in a newer version of XPress. Each file is tagged with a version number, and XPress is smart enough to check that tag before starting to reflow the text. If you open a 3.3 file in 4.1 or 5.0, the program uses the 3.3 algorithms and feature set.

However, if you want to update the file to take advantage of the latest and greatest features and algorithms, hold down the Option/Alt key as you click Open in the Open dialog box. The old text flow is ignored, and XPress flows it the way it thinks it should. Often, there's no difference. But sometimes there's lots. It all depends on your document, how it's laid out, and what features you took advantage of (from justification to smart ligatures). The best thing to do is to peruse your file carefully after Option/Alt-opening it.

Tip: Database Publishing. Creating a telephone directory? Cataloging thousands of products? Formatting information taken from a database or spread-shoot? These all fall into the category of database publishing. Whether you're formatting 50 pieces of information or 50,000, a database-publishing tool can be of great help.

One method of manipulating lots of data is to program your database to export text in XPress Tags format (which I'll cover later). If your database can handle that and you know how to do it (or know someone who does), this can be very powerful. (For example, even relatively common database programs such as FileMaker Pro can be programmed to export in XPress Tags format without much hassle.)

A second method is to use the mail merge functionality in a program like Microsoft Word and then import the merged document into XPress. This works surprisingly well in some cases. I know of people who do whole catalogs using this method.

However, since I usually like to keep things simple, even when I'm doing complex jobs, I love the Xdata XTension from Em software (they can be found at www.emsoftware.com). That's not only because it is a Quark XTension and works well with QuarkXPress, but because it has made my life so much easier.

I once produced a 17,000-name directory using Xdata and XPress. Just when I thought I was stuck with manually applying paragraph styles to 17,000 names, I heard about Xdata. Each person's name, address, and telephone number was formatted precisely the way that I designed it, and, additionally, I could take advantage of almost every typographic feature in QuarkXPress.

Exporting Text

After you go through all the trouble of bringing copy into QuarkXPress and formatting it, then why would you want to export it? Aside from administrative reasons (backups, use in a database, archiving the text, and so on), there are three major situations in which exporting text can be important.

▶ If you have a *lot* of text in a story and XPress feels sluggish when you work with it, you might want to consider exporting your text to a word processor, editing it there, and then re-importing it back into QuarkXPress. In general, though, it's usually better to keep the text in XPress if you can, or else you may lose some of your formatting.

▶ You also might want to export text if you work in a busy workgroup-publishing environment. You may find it absolutely necessary to pull text out of QuarkXPress so that editors can work on it while you continue to refine a newsletter's or magazine's layout.

▶ The best reason to export text, however, is if you want to do something that can't be done easily (or at all) from within XPress. I'll give some examples of this when I discuss XPress Tags, later on in this chapter.

How to Export Text

Exporting text from your QuarkXPress document is pretty much the opposite of importing it.

1. With the Content tool, select a text box containing the story you want to export. Or if you want to export only a certain amount of text, select it first.

2. Choose Save Text from the File menu (or press Command-Option-E or Ctrl-Alt-E). The Save Text dialog box appears.

3. Give the exported file a name and tell XPress where to save it. Select either Entire Story or Selected Text button, depending on what you want saved.

4. Use the Format (or "Save as Type" in Windows) popup menu to choose the format for the file. The formats listed on the menu depend on which filters you have in your XTension folder.

5. Press Return or click OK.

Pitfalls

The most important consideration when bringing text out of QuarkXPress and then back in is how to do this without losing all the formatting you've applied within QuarkXPress. No current word processor (other than Quark's own CopyDesk SE) can handle horizontal scaling or kerning properly, for instance, and such formatting could easily be lost during the export/re-import process. The same thing goes for XPress's character style sheets. There are ways to keep this formatting intact no matter where your QuarkXPress text ends up, however, by using only paragraph style sheets or XPress Tags.

▼ ▼

Tip: Exporting Styles. I often use QuarkXPress's Export feature to export all my styles to Microsoft Word. This saves my having to re-create every style name on Microsoft Word's style sheet. For instance, I can design a whole book or magazine, then export the styles for writers and editors to use when creating copy, and be assured that the style names will match when I import the files. To export styles, create a little one-line paragraph for each style. Apply the style, then export that text in Word format. When you open the file in Word, all the styles will be there.

▼ ▼

Tip: Printing Your Style Sheet. The only way to print out a description of your style sheets is with a commercial XTension, such as PrintTools from Badia Software. However, if you export the styles as described in the last tip, you can print the styles from Microsoft Word. Open your Word document that contains all your styles, select Print from the File menu, choose Styles from the Print What popup menu (called Settings in some operating systems), and then click Print. A lot of the formatting in XPress styles doesn't get passed to Word, so the printout isn't complete. But it's better than nothing. (Thanks to Sandee Cohen for this one!)

▼ ▼

A Solution: XPress Tags

There is a solution to the problem of losing formatting when exporting and re-importing text, however: export the file in the special text-only ASCII format called XPress Tags. XPress Tags uses its own special—and complicated—coding that records every single one of QuarkXPress's text-formatting attributes, from style sheets to local formatting (see Figure 7-19). In fact, if you're familiar with the old code-based typesetters, you'll love XPress Tags.

You may find a text-only file with XPress Tags confusing to look at, with its multitude of arcane numbers and codes. However, there are many reasons why XPress Tags is the best format to use when you need to edit and then re-import copy.

▼ ▼

Tip: Learning XPress Tags. I've got a bunch of cool XPress Tags tips in this book, and there are truly hundreds (if not thousands) of other things you can do with this tagging language. However, the tags may be intimidating at first. The best way to learn the codes is to create some text in XPress, style it in various ways, and export the text in XPress Tags format (I discuss importing and exporting tags, below). You can then open this file in a word processor and decipher the codes by looking them up in the table in Appendix F, *XPress Tags*.

Note that when XPress exports text in XPress Tags format, it doesn't write that text in a particularly terse or smart fashion, and there are many more tags than actually necessary. (For example, sometimes the tags will specify that something should be in plain style, and then immediately specify that it should be in italic). This is not necessarily bad or wrong (after all, it's better to be redundant than to forget something); you just need to read XPress's codes with a grain of salt. But otherwise, you'll get a very good overview of tagging.

▼ ▼

Figure 7-19
XPress Tags

When you save this file in XPress Tags format . . .

. . . the text file looks like this.

```
@Normal=<*L*h"Standard"*kn0*kt0*ra0*rb0*d0*p(0,0,
0,0,0,0,g)*t(0,0," "):¶
Ps100t0h100z24k0b0c"Black"f"Gill Sans">¶
@Normal:<*L*h"Standard"*kn0*kt0*ra0*rb0*d0*p(0,0,
0,0,0,0,g)*t(0,0," "):¶
Ps100t0h100z36k0b0c"Black"f"Gill Sans">G<z24>rew
mean sunflowers that snapped at passing children¶
<z36>H<z24>is bicycle spat flames
<z36>A<z24>nd his four-stringed guitar moaned in
the kitchen¶
<z36>A<z24>s grover ran from near to far¶
```

Why Use XPress Tags?

Not only do XPress Tags files retain all of a story's QuarkXPress formatting, but because ASCII ("text only") is a universal file format, these files can be edited by virtually any word processor—Macintosh, Windows, MS-DOS, or UNIX. Although the coding may appear daunting if you're used to the WYSIWYG world of Windows or the Macintosh, professional typesetters have been working with code-based systems for years, and tagged files can be easily integrated into such an environment.

So if you find yourself regularly needing to export QuarkXPress stories with sophisticated text formatting, XPress Tags is clearly the way to go. While it may take a while to get used to editing an XPress Tags file, it's a lot less work than having to painstakingly reformat your copy every time you bring it back into your QuarkXPress document. Appendix F contains a comprehensive list of the codes used in XPress Tags.

How to Use XPress Tags

There are a small handful of issues you should keep in mind when you work with XPress Tags.

▶ To export a story from QuarkXPress in XPress Tags format, choose Save Text from the File menu (Command-Option-E or Ctrl-Alt-E) and select XPress Tags from the Format popup menu (or File Type popup menu in Windows). The file you get is a text-only file that can be opened in any word processor or re-imported into XPress.

▶ To import an XPress Tags file (or any text-only file that has XPress Tags in it) into XPress, use Get Text (Command/Ctrl-E), like you would for any other text file. However, if Include Style Sheets is turned on in the Get Text dialog box, XPress interprets the tags back into text formatting. If this option is turned off, XPress just reads the codes into a text box (this is useful if you don't have a word processor).

▶ If you import the tagged file into XPress with Include Style Sheets turned off, make sure you also turn off the Convert Quotes option in the Get Text dialog box. If Convert Quotes is turned on, XPress converts the straight quotes in the tagged file into curly quotes . . . and XPress Tags only understands straight quotes. If you're just looking at the file, it hardly matters; but if you're going to edit the codes, re-export them, and then re-import them with Include Style Sheets turned on, then those dang curly quotes will cause you no end of problems.

This also applies to editing the tags in a word processor that has a Smart Quotes feature. If something is going wrong when you're importing XPress Tags, checking for stray curly quotes is one of the first things you should do.

▼ ▼

Tip: Applying Styles in Text Editors. One of the most simple (yet powerful) uses of XPress Tags is to apply style sheets or formatting to text from within a word processor or text editor that doesn't support style sheets. For instance, if you use a simple text editor that doesn't even let you apply italic formatting, you can type <I> before and after a word. When you import the file into XPress, these simple tags are interpreted and the word is made italic (the first time the tag is applied, it turns italic on; the second time, it turns it off).

You can apply a paragraph style sheet by typing @stylesheet: at the beginning of a paragraph (yes, you need the colon at the end). The style sheet will be applied to all subsequent paragraphs until you specify a change to another style. Similarly, the code to apply a character style sheet as local formatting is <@stylesheet> (to apply the style) and <@$p> (to end the character style).

Once you're familiar with the coding format used by XPress Tags, you can easily set up a macro to apply formatting codes to an ASCII file in your word processor (you can use QuicKeys—for Mac or Windows—to do this in any text editor). If you're more ambitious, and handy with database programs, you can even design a report format that creates a file incorporating XPress Tags, so you can export data from your database and have it land on your QuarkXPress pages fully formatted and untouched by human hands.

▼ ▼

Tip: Overprinting Accents with Tags. Working in non-English languages can be a complicated proposition, especially when you're working with an American or English computer system. Some characters have to be "built" by overprinting two other characters, such as a letter and an accent. Kerning two characters, one superimposed on the other, ain't no big deal if you have to do one or two. But with a document full of them, it's time to switch to XPress Tags.

1. Somewhere in your document, create the overstrike character to look just like you want it, using baseline shift, kerning, sizing, or whatever. (You often need to *positively* kern *after* the accent character, because it's narrower and therefore the following character will be too tight without kerning. Try it; you'll see what I mean.)

2. Export the sample "character" and the text story that contains all the characters you want to overstrike in XPress Tags format.

3. Open the XPress Tags files in a word processor. The sample you made will look something like <k-90>s<k11b0.2>˘<k0b0>.

4. Perform a Find/Change between the overstrike pair and the XPress Tags version. For instance, replace all the examples of s˘ with the tags above to get š.

▼ ▼

Tip: Fake Fractions the XPress Tags Way. Here's an XPress Tags search-and-replace procedure that can save hours when you have to create a large number of well-set fractions. For example, you can search for all instances of "1/2" and replace them with <z7k-10b-3>1<z12k-8b0>⁄<z8k0>2<z$>. This set of codes makes the size 7 point, the kerning 10 units, and the baseline shift 3 points, then types "1". It then changes the type size to 12 point, the kerning to -8 units, and the baseline shift to zero before typing a fraction bar (Option-Shift-1 or Alt-0164 in the Symbol font in Windows). Finally, it makes the size 8 point, sets no kerning, and types "2" before resetting the type size back to its original value.

This may seem like a lot to you, but once you get the hang of it, it's extremely easy and can save you enormous amounts of time.

▼ ▼

▼ ▼

Tip: Expert Fractions with XPress Tags. The previous tip is useful for building "made" fractions: fractions that are created by resizing type and moving it around. What if you want "drawn" fractions—numerators and denominators predesigned just for this use? Expert Set fonts with this sort of character are available for many type families (Minion, Utopia, and Bembo, to name just a few). Using XPress Tags, you can automate their substitution, too.

This works for the fractions shown in Table 7-2. Export your text in XPress Tags format and open the file in a word processor. Let's say you want to convert all the "1/4" fractions. In the word processor, search for "1/4" and replace it with `<f"MinionExp-Regular">G<f"Minion-Regular">`.

The Expert Sets also contain the numerals zero through nine in the numerator and denominator positions so you can create any other fraction, too. Press Shift-Option-0 through Shift-Option-9 to get the raised numerators, and Option-0 through Option-9 to get the baseline denominators. The correct fraction bar is the slash in the Expert Sets. You can automate this process somewhat with XPress Tags, but you have to create each different fraction individually. For instance, to make the fraction $^{13}\!/_{16}$, you would search for "13/16" and replace with `<f"MinionExp-Regular">` followed by Option-Shift-1, Option-Shift-3, slash, Option-1, Option-6, and finally `<f"Minion-Regular">`. One step too complicated? Maybe—but it sure saves time if you've got oodles of text with fractions.

Table 7-2

Ready-made fractions in Expert Sets and their keystrokes (may be different in your fonts)

FRACTION	EXPERT KEYSTROKE
¼	G
½	H
¾	I
⅛	J
⅜	K
⅝	L
⅞	M
⅓	N
⅔	O

▼ ▼

Tip: Take Care with Tags. Using XPress Tags can be lifesaving—but coding them incorrectly can result in serious troubles. Fortunately, most illegal or improper coding won't kill XPress on import; instead, the program will stop at the error and tell you it found something wrong (see Figure 7-20).

Figure 7-20

When tags go wrong

However, some errors can cause all kinds of weirdness. For instance, if you use a character that begins a tag definition (like "@" or "<") and then neglect to close the definition properly (that is, by typing a colon, a definition, or a right angle bracket, depending on what you're coding), you may live to regret it (although QuarkXPress is now much better at finding these kinds of errors than previous versions).

The tip? First, be *very* careful not to do this in the first place. Second, use version control when editing XPress Tags files. For example, if you export an XPress Tags file called "mytags.xtg", after you edit it use Save As from the text editor to change the name to "mytags2.xtg" (don't write over the original—you might need it if you made a mistake the first time around).

▼ ▼

Tip: Converting Fractions with Torquemada. Every now and again you'll hear someone—usually the office techno-geek, who has spent too much time writing programming code and drinking Jolt cola—mutter something about "regular expressions," Perl, Python, grep, or sed. These are things that programmers live for: they're all ways to powerfully search and replace text. Well, XPress Tags code is just text, right?

Super XPress Tags demons make use of these tools to do very fast "text massage," transforming ordinary text into fully-formatted, ready to roll XPress Tags. There are a number of tools out there that let you search and replace with regular expressions, but none of them are particularly fun or easy to use. But a few days learning this stuff could mean weeks of time saved.

Note that Perl, grep, and sed are all built into OS X ("under the hood"), so you could use OS X's Terminal mode to do these sorts of manipulations. There are also many different shareware and commercial programs that can help, including BBedit on the Macintosh.

I have long relied upon a little Macintosh Classic utility written by Greg Swann called Torquemada the Inquisitor which performs these kinds of searches on text files such as XPress Tags. For example, you can use Torquemada to automate the fake fractions I mentioned in an earlier tip, *if* you're sure that all instances in your text of the form *00/xx* (where *00* represents any number of digits, and *xx* represents any number of characters before the next spaceband) is indeed a fraction.

Simply search for `^#^<^?/^&^<^@` plus a space ("one or more digits, a slash, and one or more alphanumeric characters, followed by a spaceband"), and replace it with the appropriate codes for the fraction (see "Tip: Fake Fractions the XPress Tags Way," earlier in the chapter) except replace the "1" in that tip with `^#^<` and the "2" in that tip with `^&^@`. Don't forget to include the spaceband in your replace string, too. For example, the replace string might be `<z7k-10b-3>^#^?<z12k8b0>⁄<z8k0>^&^@<z$>` plus a spaceband.

And if you study your Torq documentation, you'll see that you can even get around the lack of two numeric wildcards by constructing a Define-Your-Own wildcard . . . but I'll leave that to you.

▼ ▼

Tip: Commenting Torq Sets. One of the problems with Torquemada's search-and-replace sets is that they're often really hard to read and decipher on screen. One way to clear up the mess is by commenting the sets. That is, you can insert humanly readable comments to help you remember what each code (or set of codes) means.

To add a comment to a Torq set, type it in the Replace-string column (the right column in the search/replace set). As long as the Search-string column (the left one) is left blank, Torq ignores the right one entirely; but the comment remains there for you to read on screen. I heartily recommend you add extensive, thorough comments to your Torq sets; I can testify from sad experience that it's very easy to forget just what it was you were trying to accomplish, especially in your more complex search/replace strings.

▼ ▼

Tip: Those Silly Case-Sensitive Tags. Don't forget that all XPress Tags are case-sensitive. Typing `<H>` rather than `<h>` can mean the difference between small caps, horizontal scaling, and failure. Style, color, and H&J names are the same way. If you forget them, they're easy enough to search and replace in Word or a case-sensitive text editor.

▼ ▼

Tip: Getting XPress Tags Out of Word. What if you could get Microsoft Word to export XPress Tags directly? That's the goal of two excellent utilities you should look at if you're trying to streamline your workflow: QXPort (from www.bitmix.de) and QuarkConverter (from www.editorium.com). These are especially helpful when the files have a lot of local formatting applied to them or if you have used Word's character styles feature.

▼ ▼

Tip: Xtags is One Step Beyond. There is an alternative to the XPress Tags language and filter that ships with QuarkXPress. It's a third-party commercial XTension named Xtags, from Em Software. Xtags is a superset of XPress Tags, which means that all XPress Tags will work with the Xtags filter. However, Xtags adds much more functionality, such as powerful error checking, anchored boxes (text and picture), relative size changes (up a point, down two points, etc.), and much, much more. Another great feature is a translation table that replaces short codes with long tag strings (like those discussed in "Tip: Shorter Tags," earlier in this chapter).

There is simply not enough room here to even *begin* to describe some of Xtags's cooler features. Suffice it to say that once you start using Xtags for importing your text, you'll soon discover so many things you can automate with it that you'll wonder how you ever got along without it (see Appendix C, *XTensions and Resources,* for more information).

▼ ▼

BBEdit and Other Text Editors

The focus of this chapter (and of this whole book) is efficiency: how to take raw materials and quickly turn them into a finished product. The raw materials might be text from some DOS word processor, or it might be highly formatted text within a QuarkXPress document that needs even more formatting applied to it. Obviously, XPress Tags makes less sense when your document is a single-page ad. However, when you're preparing books or other long documents (even some magazines or newspapers), being able to make edits to XPress Tags is a powerful tool for massaging your text into the shape you want.

In general, I recommend using a text editor rather than a word processor for this kind of stuff—for two reasons. First, word processors have too many tools for formatting text and too few tools for editing it quickly (NisusWriter is one good exception). On the other hand, text editors, don't care much about formatting; they focus on the text itself.

Second, text editors typically allow you to view your text in either "wrapping" mode (where text wraps to the next line as soon as it hits the right edge of the screen) and nonwrapping, or "line" mode (where every paragraph is a line and every line is a paragraph, potentially extending far off the right side of your screen). I like to review XPress Tags files in nonwrapping mode because almost all the most important tags are at the beginning of paragraphs (paragraph style sheets, character styles for run-in heads, and so on). So if each line is a paragraph, it's very easy to check. Then, if you need to see what the rest of the paragraph looks like, you can always scroll or switch to wrapping mode temporarily.

One of the best text editors around is the BBEdit. There's a commercial version that's really powerful, but the free version is totally adequate for what I'm talking about here. BBEdit also has a very powerful search-and-replace capability, including being able to act on multiple files at once and giving you the choice of using grep, if you're into that advanced search-and-replace language.

▼ ▼

Tip: A Complex XPress Tags Example. I'll throw in one more XPress Tags example, just to show what a little extra work can do. Let's say you've just received some text files from someone who just LOVES to type LOTS of words in ALL CAPITAL LETTERS. If you're like me, you'd rather these words be in small caps.

You've got two choices: First, retype each of these words in lowercase and then apply a small-caps style to them. Like you've got nothing better to do, right? The much better choice is to use XPress Tags. This technique should not be tried by children without parental guidance; it's truly industrial strength, designed for processing a lot of text at once.

The trick is to use a program that can handle regular expressions, such as NisusWriter or Torquemada. In Torquemada, search for ^+^<^? and use <H>^L^+^?<H>^= as the replacement string. (Leave the period off the end, of course.) This horrible-looking thing means: Find all strings of two or more capital letters (this is the "Cast Wildstring Type" technique, where ^+ is a capital letter, ^< types the wildstring to what precedes it—in this case, capital letters— and ^? is the wildstring itself). Torquemada then replaces this with the small-caps tag (<H>), the command to convert to all lowercase (^L), the wildstring (which, on the replace side, is simply ^+^?), the small-caps tag again, and the command to turn off case conversion (^=).

If you use Perl (the inexpensive Nisus Writer can do this), then you could use this: s/[A-Z][A-Z]+/<H>\L$&\E<H>/g; to do the same thing.

Either way, if a line in the source file reads: "This is DEFINITELY a BIG pain in the NECK," then the output (after processing) will look like this: "This is <H>definitely<H> a <H>big<H> pain in the <H>neck<H>," and the final imported text will appear as "This is DEFINITELY a BIG pain in the NECK."

See? Nothing to it.

▼ ▼

Getting Your Stories Straight

Just because you've taken advantage of style sheets and XPress Tags doesn't mean you won't still find it necessary to burn the midnight oil making last-minute changes. But at least you'll have the full power of QuarkXPress on your side. Get to know styles, import and export filters, and especially XPress Tags, and you can go a long way toward being lazy: making your computer do the work, rather than having to do it yourself

8

LONG DOCUMENTS

One look at the size of this book and you know why the topic of long documents is so exciting to me. But everyone has a different opinion about what a long document is. Some die-hard technical writers insist that if it isn't over a thousand pages, it's not a long document. Others maintain that a document longer than five or 10 pages qualifies. Personally, I think that anyone building a book, a magazine, a newspaper, a journal, or a catalog—no matter how many pages—is dealing with long documents.

Unfortunately, while there are hundreds of thousands of people creating these sorts of things with XPress, it took 10 years for Quark to include even rudimentary long-document features into its flagship product. Today, XPress's long-document features aren't anywhere as powerful as Adobe FrameMaker, but they're pretty good nevertheless.

There are three features in QuarkXPress that relate directly to publishing long documents.

> ► **BOOKS.** You can tie multiple XPress projects together into a *book*, which appears in the form of a palette in QuarkXPress. (This only works if the project has just one print layout space.) From here, you can control page numbering, printing, and such document attributes as style sheets and colors.

> ▶ **LISTS.** If you use style sheets regularly, you're going to love the Lists feature, which lets you build a table of contents (or a list of figures, or a table of advertisers, or any number of other things) quickly and easily.

> ▶ **INDEXES.** Building an index is a hardship I wouldn't wish on anyone (I've done enough of them myself), but XPress's indexing features go a long way in helping make it bearable. I'll also discuss how indexing can be used in catalogs and other documents.

Again, even if you don't currently create what you'd consider to be "long documents," take a gander at these features; they're flexible enough to be used in documents as small as even a few pages.

Books

Even though you can make a document thousands of pages long, you should keep your XPress layouts small. This reduces the amount of strain on the program, and lessens the chance for document corruption. Working with smaller documents is generally faster and more efficient, especially when more than one person is working on the project at the same time. The question is: if you break up your larger project into small documents, how can you ensure style consistency and proper page numbering among them? The answer is QuarkXPress's Book feature.

You and I usually think of a book as a collection of chapters bound together to act like a single document. QuarkXPress takes this concept one step further. In QuarkXPress, a book is a collection of any XPress documents on your disk or network that are loosely connected with each other via the Book palette. In other words, just because it's called a "book" doesn't mean it's not relevant for magazines, catalogs, or any other set of documents (see "Tip: The Book Palette as Database," below).

There are four benefits to using the Book palette.

> ▶ It's a good way to organize your documents, and it's faster to open them from within XPress than using the Open dialog box.

> ▶ If you use automatic page numbering in your document (see "Sections and Page Numbering" in Chapter 4, *Building a Document*), XPress manages the page numbering throughout the entire book, so if the first document ends on page 20, the second document starts on page 21, and so on.

► You can print one or more documents from the Book palette using the same Print dialog box settings without even having the documents open.

► The Book palette's Synchronize feature lets you ensure that the style sheets, colors, H&J settings, List settings (which I cover later in this chapter), and Dashes & Stripes settings are consistent among the documents.

Obviously, the more documents in your book, and the more pages, style sheets, colors, and whatnot in each document, the more useful the Book feature will be to you. Even if you're juggling two or three documents, it may be worth the minor hassle it takes to build a book.

▼ ▼

Tip: The Book Palette as Database. Because there is only a very loose connection among the various documents in the Book palette, you could use this feature as an informal database of documents. For instance, let's say you've built 15 different product sheets and three small brochures for a client, and they're forever updating them.

Even though the documents may each use very different colors, style sheets, and so on, you could put them all on one Book palette and save this collection under the client's name. Next time the client calls for a quick fix, you don't have to go searching for a document; just open the Book palette, and double-click on the document name to open it.

Of course, this means you either cannot use automatic page numbering in your documents, or you have to be meticulous about using the Section feature (I discuss how you can use the Section feature to override a book's automatic page numbering in "Page Numbering and Sections," later in this chapter).

Note that in versions 5 and 6, the documents that make up the book must be on the same volume (as each other and as the book file itself).

▼ ▼

Building a Book

To build a new book, select Book from the New submenu (under the File menu; see Figure 8-1). At this point, you need to tell the program where to save your new book file (you can put it anywhere you want on your hard drive or network, but you should be able to find it easily because you'll be using it a lot).

Book files appear in QuarkXPress as palettes. You can save as many books as you want, though you can only open 25 of them at a time (I usually just stick to one or two open Book palettes, or else I get confused). When you've saved your new book, XPress displays a new, empty Book palette (see Figure 8-2).

Figure 8-1

Building a new book

(Note that QuarkXPress uses the term "chapter" to refer to single documents inside the book. In this discussion, I use both "chapter" and "document" interchangeably, though I prefer "document" because it reminds me that I can use the Book feature for catalogs or magazines or other sorts of projects.)

Adding documents. To add a document to your Book palette, click the Add Document button in the palette and choose a document from your disk or network. If no documents on the palette are selected when you add a new document, the chapter is added at the end of the list. If you select a document first, the new chapter is added before the selected document in the list.

You can have up to a thousand documents on your Book palette (personally, I wouldn't try to push this limit; I prefer to keep this number well below a hundred). By the way, if you add documents that were built in QuarkXPress version 3.x or 4.x, they are automatically resaved as version 6 files, and you won't be able to open them in the earlier version again.

While version 4 let you add any document to your book, beginning in version 5 the documents and the book file must be on the same hard drive (though that could be a drive elsewhere on your network). Also, note that XPress currently only lets you add projects to your book that have one (and only one) layout space. I hope this gets changed in a later version.

Removing documents. You can remove a document from a Book palette by selecting it and clicking the Remove Document button. If you want to remove more than one, you can select them with the Shift or Command key (Shift for contiguous selections, Command for discontiguous selections on the list). Note that deleting a document from the Book palette does *not* delete the file from disk; it simply removes it from the list.

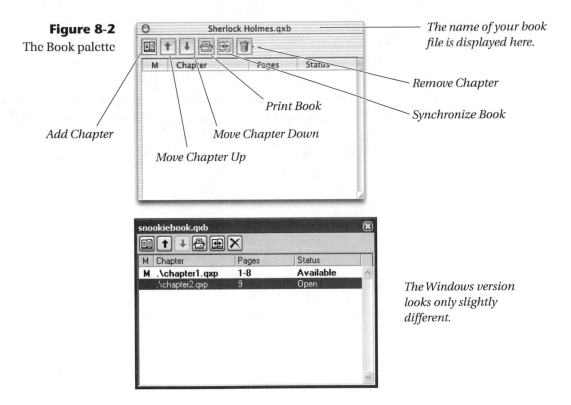

Figure 8-2
The Book palette

The name of your book file is displayed here.

Remove Chapter

Print Book

Synchronize Book

Add Chapter

Move Chapter Down

Move Chapter Up

The Windows version looks only slightly different.

▼ ▼

Tip: Reordering Documents. It seems like I always accidentally place one chapter in the the wrong order on the Book palette. You can move a document up and down on the list by selecting it and clicking the Move Chapter Up and Move Chapter Down buttons. But I think it's even faster to hold down the Option key and drag the chapter to where you want it.

▼ ▼

When you add a new document to your book, XPress actually opens the document behind the scenes (you don't see it, but you can hear your hard disk scratching away), writes some code into it so that the document knows it's part of a book now, and then closes it. (The same thing happens when you remove a document from a book.) This can take some time, especially with large documents, so be patient.

If you open a document from disk, there's almost no way to tell if it's part of a book or not. In general, though, you should not add a document to more than one book. You can do it, but if you do, XPress alerts you that the document's page numbering could get messed up. Other weirdness might ensue, as well . . . again, it's best to avoid it.

▼ ▼

Tip: Take Away That Book Setting. If you throw away or lose your book file on disk, the individual documents in the book don't know that—they still think they're part of a book.

You can, however, create a new dummy book, add your documents to it (just click OK when XPress tells you that this might mess up the page numbering), and then remove them all using the Remove Chapter button on the palette. This takes a little time to do, but it's the only way to tell a document that it's not part of a book anymore.

▼ ▼

Editing Your Book's Documents

Once you've added documents to your Book palette, you can go about your regular routine of editing and preparing the documents . . . with a few minor adjustments.

▶ Whenever possible, you should open your book's documents while the Book palette is open. (The fastest way to open a document is to double-click on it in the Book palette.) When you open and modify a document while the palette is not open, the palette isn't smart enough to update itself (see "File status," below). If XPress can't find your document, it'll ask you where it is.

▶ You can print documents the regular way, but if you want to print more than one document in a book at a time, you should use the Print button on the Book palette (see "Printing Books," later in this section).

▶ You should be careful about using the Section feature to renumber any of the documents in the book (see "Page Numbering and Sections," later in this section). In general, you should let the Book palette handle your page numbering for you.

▼ ▼

Tip: No Can Undo. QuarkXPress's books are like libraries in several ways. First of all, the changes you make to your Book palette, including adding, removing, and reordering documents, aren't saved until you close the palette or quit QuarkXPress (although libraries have the Auto Library Save feature, there is no such feature for books).

Also, you can't use the Undo or Revert to Saved features on books. This means you should be careful about what you do in a Book palette . . . there may be no turning back.

▼ ▼

File status. The Book palette monitors and displays the status of each document in the book. There are five possible messages in the Status column of the palette: Available, Open, Modified, Missing, or In Use (see Figure 8-3).

▶ AVAILABLE. The normal status of a document is Available. This means that no one has the document open for editing and that the document has not changed since the last time it was open on the computer you're using.

▶ OPEN. When you have a document open on your Macintosh or PC, the status of that file is listed as Open.

▶ MODIFIED. When you or anyone else who has access to the file opens and changes a document while the Book palette is not open, the status will be listed as Modified next time you open the palette. It's easy to change the status from Modified back to Available: just open the file while the Book palette is open, then close the document again.

▶ MISSING. If you move a document after adding it to the Book palette, XPress won't be able to find it, and the status is listed as Missing. (There's one exception to this rule: if you move the document into the same folder as the book file, the Book palette can find it.) To "find" a file again, double-click on the chapter name in the Book palette; XPress displays a dialog box in which you can tell it where the document now resides.

▶ IN USE. If someone else on your network opens one of the documents in your book via the Book palette, the Status field of the Book palette lists that chapter as in use. More precisely, it lists the name of that person's computer, so you know exactly who to call and yell at. However, if they open the file without having the Book palette open, QuarkXPress has no way of knowing that the document is open.

Figure 8-3
File status on
the Book palette

...	Chapter	Pages	Status
	.:Intro	i*–iv*	Available
M	.:Scandal in Bohemia.qxp	1*–25*	Available
	.:Red-Headed League.qxp	27–51	Available
	.:A Case of Identity.qxp	53–71	Available
	The Boscombe Valley Myste...	73–98	Available
	.:The Five Orange Pips.qxp	99–118	Available
	The Man With the Twisted Li...	119–...	Modified
	The Adventure of the Blue...	145–...	Modified

It's important to pay attention to the Status column readings, because documents must be either Available or Open in order to synchronize, print, or renumber properly.

▼ ▼

Tip: Update the Books Palette. The book palette could slow you down in version 4 because it was always checking to see the status of each file in the book. Now, XPress only updates the book status when you click in the Book palette; so, if you think someone else might be working on a file, just click somewhere in the palette (even a blank area) and the status column should update properly.

▼ ▼

Tip: Keep Those Books Open. Don't feel compelled to close your Book palette(s) before you quit QuarkXPress. Any books that are open when you quit will be open again (and in the same position on screen) when you relaunch the program.

▼ ▼

Tip: Network Booking. It seems like people are increasingly working on projects in groups rather than individually. Quark anticipated this, and if you put your book file and documents on a server, more than one person can open it at the same time. (Only one person can open a regular XPress document at a time, however.) While this isn't nearly as powerful as the full-blown Quark Publishing System (QPS), it's certainly useful if a group of people have to work on different documents in the book at the same time.

The thing is, I don't like working on documents when they're on a server. It just makes me nervous. (In older versions of XPress, you could permanently corrupt your documents if you did this; now it does seem to work fine, but I'm still superstitious.) Instead, I prefer to copy the file to my local hard drive, edit it at my leisure, and then return the file to the server after I'm done working with it.

There are two problems with this. First, the book palette doesn't update properly. Second, other people on your network might not realize that you've got the "live" file, so make it clear to them: hide the document on the server, or put it in another folder called "work in progress" or something like that.

▼ ▼

Tip: Restricting Network Access. QuarkXPress has no built-in features for restricting access to documents in a book. You can, however, set up access privileges on a person-by-person basis with most server software. For instance, you might give one person read-only access, so they could not make changes to your files, and then give read/write access to someone else who has good cause to edit the documents.

▼ ▼

▼ ▼

Tip: Careful With Save As. I use the Save As feature all the time as a way to track revisions of my documents. Each time I use Save As, I change the name slightly ("mydocument1," "mydocument2," and so on), so I can always go back to an earlier version if necessary. If you do this, however, note that the Book palette doesn't catch on to what you're doing; it just lists and keeps track of the original document. So every time you use Save As, you have to remove the old document name from the Book palette and use Add Chapter to add the new document in (very frustrating). I'm hoping that Quark will fix this, but it hasn't happened yet.

▼ ▼

Synchronizing Your Book

The more documents you're working with, the more likely it is that one or more of them contain settings inconsistent with the others in the book. Perhaps you decided to change a style sheet definition in one document out of 20, and then forgot to change it in the other 19. Or perhaps one person in your workgroup decided he didn't like the Standard H&J settings in the document he was editing, so he just changed them without telling anyone.

Fortunately, the Synchronize Book button on the Book palette lets you ensure that all style sheets, colors, H&J settings, List settings, and Dashes & Stripes settings are consistent throughout the documents in a book. Here's how it works.

The Master Chapter. One document on the Book palette is always marked as the *master chapter* (by default, it's the first chapter you add to the palette). The master chapter—which is listed in bold and with the letter M next to it—is the document to which all the other documents will be synchronized. That means if you add a new color to the master chapter and then click the Synchronize Book button, the color will be added to all the other documents in the book. If you add a new color to a document that is not a master chapter, it won't be added when you synchronize the documents.

You can always change which document is the master chapter: just double-click in the left column of the Book palette (next to the document you want to be the master chapter).

Synchronize. In version 4, synchronizing your chapters was about as simple as clicking the Synchronize Book button. It's not much harder now, but it does take a couple extra steps. First you must select *which* files you want to synchronize in the Book palette; remember that you can Shift-click to select contiguous chapters or Command/Ctrl-click to select discontiguous chapters. Or, if you want to synchronize *all* the files, just make sure *no* chapters are selected in the palette.

Then, when you click the Synchronize Book button, XPress asks you what document properties you want to synchronize (see Figure 8-4). Maybe I'm just lazy, but I usually just press the Synch All button. However, if you really want to synchronize some styles and not others, and so on . . . be my guest and tweak the dialog box as you wish. Note that after you click Synch All or OK, you may also get some style sheets that you didn't expect (for instance, if one style is based on another style). Here's the nitty gritty.

Figure 8-4

Synchronizing your book

▶ A style sheet, color, H&J setting, List setting, or Dashes & Stripes setting that is defined in the master chapter but not in another chapter gets added to that other document.

▶ If a setting is named the same in both the master chapter and another document, the definition for that setting in the master chapter overrides the one in the nonmaster chapter.

▶ If a setting is not defined in the master chapter but it is in some other document, it's left alone. (This means you can have "local" settings that exist in one document that don't have to be copied into all the others.)

▼ ▼

Tip: Save Your Eyes with Synchronize. It's always a hassle editing a document that contains colored text because it's often difficult to read. Let's say you've got 15 documents in a book that all use the same style sheets. You could change the style definitions in the master chapter so that the text appears in black (or whatever color is easy to read), and then synchronize the book so that the settings are changed in all the documents. Later, when you're done editing, you can reverse the process: change the style sheets back, and synchronize again.

▼ ▼

Note that synchronizing a document can be a time-consuming process—the more documents and the more settings there are, the longer it takes. You can watch XPress do its work in the Book palette: as XPress changes each document, you'll see its status change from Available to Open and then to Available again.

Page Numbering and Sections

Perhaps the most helpful aspect of the Book feature is that it keeps track of your page numbering for you and updates the page numbers when you add pages to or delete them from a document, or if you add a new document between two other documents in a book. Of course, this only works if you've used automatic page numbering in your documents. (The automatic page-number character is Command/Ctrl-3; see "Sections and Page Numbering" in Chapter 4, *Building a Document.*)

The page numbering feature works via the Section dialog box. When you add a document to the Book palette, XPress checks to see if the first page of the document has been defined as a section start. If it has been, XPress leaves the page alone. If it's not the start of a new section, then XPress turns on the checkbox labeled Book Chapter Start in the Section dialog box, and sets the first page number appropriately (see Figure 8-5).

Let's say you've got one 16-page document on your Book palette already. When you add another document, XPress automatically sets the first page number to 17 (as long as you hadn't already set up the first page as a section start in the Section dialog box). If you later open the first document and add two pages, XPress automatically renumbers the second document next time you open it so that it starts on page 19.

Manual sections. If you have manually specified a section start anywhere in your document, the automatic book-page numbering works slightly differently. Let's say you've used the Section dialog box to make a section start of any page in the second document of your book, and you've specified lower-case roman numerals for the page numbers. Now if you add a third document to the book, and this new document has no section-start settings, then XPress picks up on the roman numerals where they left off in the second document.

In other words, XPress keeps on numbering in the style of the previous document. If you wanted the third document to return to regular arabic numerals, you would have to manually add a section start to its first page, over-riding the Book Chapter Start setting. Of course, now when you add pages to the first or second document, the page numbers don't update properly in the third document because of the section start.

Figure 8-5

Page numbering in books

Odd versus even page numbers. To get even more picayune, I should men-tion that XPress always starts Facing Pages documents with an odd number. For instance, if the first chapter ends on page 23 and the second chapter is a Facing Pages document, XPress sets the first page of the second chapter as 25, skipping page 24. If you want to print a page numbered "24," you have to add it yourself to the first document.

Single-sided documents, on the other hand, can begin with either an odd- or even-numbered page.

▼ ▼

Tip: Spread-to-Spread Page Numbers. Some magazine publishers build their magazines one spread at a time—each spread is a separate document. (I think this is a very strange way to create a magazine, but those publishers insist they have their reasons.) If you're going to do this, set up your documents using single-sided pages rather than facing pages. You can still build a two-page spread with single-sided pages (just drag one page next to the other in the Page Layout palette), and this way the automatic page numbering works properly when the documents are all added to the Book palette.

▼ ▼

Printing Books

Even though I cover printing documents in Chapter 13, *Printing*, I should take this opportunity to mention a few things that are specific to printing books.

First, each chapter in a book must be listed as Open, Available, or Modified on the Book palette in order for the document to print. This is because XPress invisibly opens each document at print time (you don't see the document open on screen, but it does). XPress alerts you if a document is in use by someone else on the network or if it's missing, and if it can't immediately be found or made available you can cancel printing. (This only stops the print job for that one document; all the other documents print fine.)

Second, if you only want certain documents in a book to print, select them from the Book palette before clicking the Print Book button. Remember that you can select contiguous documents on the list by holding down the Shift key, and discontiguous documents with the Command key. If no documents are selected, then they'll all print.

Third, as this book goes to press, there is no way to print PostScript to disk (a "PostScript dump") for more than one document in a book on the Macintosh. The results are varied when you try to do this. Some people find that the first chapter is written to disk and that subsequent chapters get sent to a printer. Others find that every document is written to disk, but because the same file name is given to each PostScript dump, each file overwrites the last, until you have only one file—the last one—on disk. The workaround is simply to save PostScript dumps one document at a time. In Windows, this does work, but you still have to type a new file name in for each PostScript file that gets written to disk.

Lasly, there is also no way to automatically create an Acrobat PDF file of your entire book. You have to open each chapter, export it to PDF, and then put them together using Adobe Acrobat.

▼ ▼

Lists

If you've been searching through the menus for a "table of contents" feature, you can stop now. There is no such feature. Instead, Quark offers something much better: a Lists feature, which can not only generate a table of contents, but all kinds of lists, as well.

Technically, the Lists feature lets you build collections of text (words or paragraphs) that have been tagged with specific style sheets. For instance, if you use even two style sheets when you're formatting a book—one for the chapter name and another for your first-level headings—you can build a basic table of contents by collecting all the paragraphs tagged with these two styles. If you use paragraph style sheets to tag your figure titles, you can build a table of figures. If you apply a character style to the names of companies mentioned in your document, then you can collect them all with the Lists feature and build a list of them later. Anything you can tag with a paragraph or character style, you can build into a list. (In case you were wondering, the ability to use character styles was new in XPress 5.)

This all depends entirely on your using style sheets. Of course, you simply can't be efficient when you're building long documents if you don't use paragraph and character styles anyway. (If you don't currently use styles, go check out Chapter 7, *Copy Flow*, to see why you should.)

Setting Up a List

The great thing about Lists is that they're so easy to make and use. Here's the six-step procedure to define a list.

1. Select Lists from the Edit menu. Like style sheets and colors, making a list while a document is open means that the list appears only in that document; if no documents are open when you make the list, it'll appear in every document you create from then on.

   If the Lists palette is already open (select Show Lists from the Window menu), you can skip this first step by Control-clicking (Mac) or right-mouse-button-clicking (Windows) inside the palette and selecting New List from the context-sensitive menu.

2. Click the New button in the Lists dialog box to open the Edit List dialog box (see Figure 8-6), and type a name for your new list.

3. Choose which style sheets you want included in the list definition by double-clicking on them in the Available Styles list. (You can also Command/Ctrl-click to select discontiguous styles on the list and choose them all by clicking the right-arrow button in the dialog box.) The order in which you place the items on the list doesn't matter; at this point, it's just a list of style sheets.

4. Choose a level for each style sheet on the list by selecting the style and selecting 1 through 8 from the Level popup menu. These levels determine how the list appears on the Lists palette (which I'll discuss later in this section), and have nothing to do with how the list will appear on your printed page. For instance, you might apply level 1 to a style called Chapter Title, level 2 to a Heading style, and level 3 to a Subhead style.

5. You can control how the list will appear on your printed page with the Numbering and Format As popup menus. You've got three options for

Figure 8-6

Creating a new list

Choose the styles you want in your list definition here.

Moving styles here means the style will be included in your list definition.

Click here to remove a style sheet from the list definition.

Numbering: Text only, Text...Page #, and Page #...Text (see Figure 8-7). The first, Text only, tells XPress not to include the page number on which it finds the text tagged with this style. The other two options tell XPress to include the page number, separated from the text of the paragraph by a tab character. For instance, in the previous example, you might set the Chapter Title style sheet to Text only, and the Heading and Subhead styles to Text...Page #.

6. The Format As popup menu lets you apply a style sheet to the paragraph when it appears on the list. This is helpful because you'd rarely want a heading from your document to appear in your table of contents in the actual Heading style; instead, you'd probably create a new

Figure 8-7

Numbering

Preface

Chapter I: History of Pi
Early History 7
The Greeks .... .13
Pi in the East .... .19
A Millennium of Progress .... .29
Breakthroughs in Mathematics .... .41

Chapter II: The Personality of Pi
Irrational numbers .... .73
Patterns in Pi .... .101

Chapter III: The Circle Squarers
John Smith .... .113

Text...Page #

Text only

style sheet called "TOC-head" or something like that (see Figure 8-8). If you want certain paragraphs to be indented on your final list, you should apply style sheets here that include indentation.

That's it! However, here are a few things to keep in mind when you're defining a list.

▶ You can define thousands of different lists in a single document, but lists cannot span across multiple layout spaces in a project.

▶ You can have a maximum of 32 style sheets in a list definition.

▶ XPress only captures the first 256 characters of tagged text when it builds a list, so you should choose style sheets that correspond to text shorter than this (256 characters make about 40 words—more than enough for most headlines, bylines, and such).

▶ If you turn on the Alphabetical option in the Edit List dialog box, XPress sorts the list in alphabetical order when you build it (I discuss how to build a list below). Whether you want your final list alphabetized is up to you; you probably wouldn't want it when you build the table of contents for a book, but you might for a list of items in a catalog.

▶ If you want a list to work in multiple documents within a book, the list must be present in all the documents. You can use the Synchronize Book feature to ensure that the same list appears properly in them.

The Lists Palette

Once you've defined a list, it's time to open the Lists palette, which lets you get an overview for your list, navigate through your document based on the list,

Figure 8-8
Format As

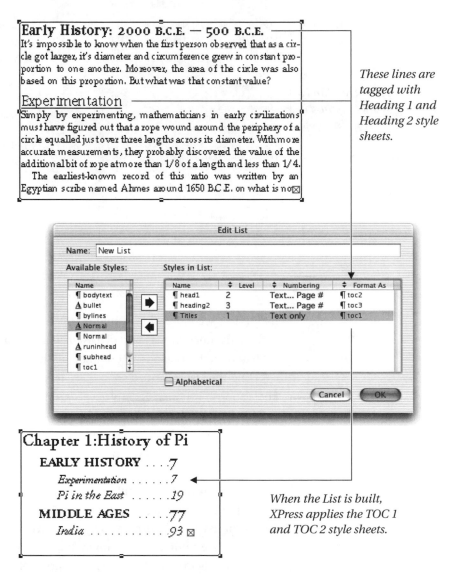

These lines are tagged with Heading 1 and Heading 2 style sheets.

When the List is built, XPress applies the TOC 1 and TOC 2 style sheets.

and ultimately build the final list on your document pages. You can open the Lists palette by selecting Show List from the Window menu or pressing Option-F11 (Mac) or Control-F11 (Windows).

As soon as you open the Lists palette, QuarkXPress goes and collects the text and paragraphs you've specified in the list definition (this might take a little while for a very large document). All that information is displayed in the lower section of the Lists palette (see Figure 8-9). The Lists palette doesn't contain the corresponding page numbers for these paragraphs; that information comes later, when you tell XPress to build the list on your document page.

The Lists palette offers you two options. First, if you have more than one list defined in a document, you can choose among them from the List popup

Figure 8-9
The Lists palette

Type here to find a word or phrase in the list below.

Choose either Current Document or the name of the book here.

If you have more than one list defined in a document, you can choose one of them here.

Click here to force XPress to update the list.

Double-click on a list entry to jump to that page.

menu. The second option, found on the Show List For popup menu, is only active if the document is part of a book; if it is, you can tell XPress to build the list based on this one document or on all the documents in the book.

I find the Lists palette a good place to get an overview of a document or a book, and—if I've specified my Levels properly—it's very helpful as a first step in figuring out if the final list is going to appear correctly on my pages (sometimes you don't realize that you left out a paragraph style sheet, or chose the wrong style sheet—until you peruse the Lists palette).

List navigation. If you double-click on any paragraph in the Lists palette, XPress jumps to the page where the text is. In fact, some people use the Lists palette for navigation purposes only, and never actually build the table of contents or whatever on their document pages.

The Find field of the Lists palette is very useful if you've got a very long list; just type the first few characters of a paragraph you think is on the list, and XPress selects it in the Lists palette. I find this most helpful in those long technical documents where every heading begins with a number.

Update. If QuarkXPress had to keep tabs on every little edit you make in your document and reflect it in the Lists palette, it'd be as slow as molasses on a cold January morning. No, if you make any changes to your document—add paragraphs, remove paragraphs, change the spelling of words—the Lists palette only updates when you click the Update button or when you close and reopen the palette.

Building and Rebuilding Lists

You've defined a list, you've browsed over it in the Lists palette, and now it's finally time to get that list onto your document page. This is potentially the most complex and hair-raising ordeal of the entire process. No, seriously—here's what you do: select a text box (preferably an empty one) and click the Build button on the Lists palette. That's it. If the list is supposed to include page numbers, now is when XPress goes out and finds them (see Figure 8-10).

Updating the list. There is nothing special about the text or page numbers on this list—they're just text and numbers. If you update the document on which the list is based (including changes to page numbers or to the list definition), you're going to have rebuild the list on your document page. I find that I build and rebuild a list at least several times for each document or book, due to various human errors (my own, generally). Here's how you do it.

1. First, make sure the Lists palette is up-to-date by clicking the Update button.

2. Select any text box in your document (it doesn't have to be the same box in which you originally built the list).

3. Click Build in the Lists palette. XPress is smart enough to know if you've already built a list in your file. If you have, it asks you if you want to replace the list that's already there (see Figure 8-11). Typically you'd want to choose to replace the already built list.

Figure 8-10

The final list

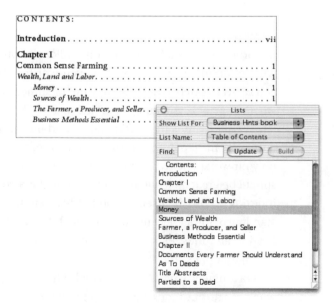

Figure 8-11

Rebuilding a list

▼ ▼

Tip: Use Dummy Text for Lists. One of my favorite aspects of lists is that they're document-wide rather than simply story-wide. That means that any text in any text box can be included on a list . . . even text in a text box that has Suppress Printout turned on. With this in mind, you can add "tags" to items on your page that don't appear in print, but do appear in your table of contents.

One of the best examples of this is an advertiser index. You can place a text box with an advertiser's name on top of that company's ad in your document. Set the text box's runaround to None and turn on Suppress Printout, and it's almost as though this were a "non-object" —the text box won't print, and it won't affect any text underneath. But if that advertiser's name is tagged with a style sheet, you can include it on a list of advertisers.

The same trick goes for building a list of pictures in a catalog, or for any other time when what you want on the list doesn't actually appear on the page.

▼ ▼

Indexes

It was Mr. Duncan, my elementary-school librarian, who first impressed the importance of a good index into my malleable young brain: A nonfiction book without an index, he said, wasn't even worth putting on the library shelf. If you've ever searched an index in vain for something that you're sure is some-where in a book, you know the value of a good index.

The problem is that sitting down and indexing a book is—in my experi-ence—the most painful, horrible, mind-numbing activity you could ever wish on your worst enemy. And yet, where this is the kind of task that a computer should be great at, it's actually impossible for a computer to do a good job of indexing a book by itself. A good index requires careful thought, an under-standing of the subject matter, and an ability to keep the whole project in your head at all times. Plus, until recently, it required a large stack of notecards, highlighter pens, and Post-It notes.

Fortunately, QuarkXPress has a built-in indexing feature which, while it won't make the index for you, does remove the notecard and highlighter requirements. Note that because a minority of XPress users actually ever index their documents, the folks at Quark put this feature into a separate XTension. The XTension is loaded (it's in the XTension folder) by default, but if you or someone else turned it off with the XTension manager, you may have to turn it back on and relaunch XPress.

▼ ▼

Tip: Concordance versus Index. Some people ask me, "Why can't a computer build an index? QuarkXPress should just give me a list of all the words in my document and what page they're on." Unfortunately, this is not an index; it's a concordance. The difference is that a concordance records the location of words, while an index records the location of ideas. There are times when a concordance is very useful, especially in catalogs. In those cases, you might want to use an XTension like Sonar Bookends, which can build concordances automatically and very quickly. But in general, if you're looking for an index, you're going to have to do it manually with the indexing features in XPress.

▼ ▼

Tip: Edit First, Index Last. You can index a document at any time in the production cycle, but it's almost always best to wait until the text has become fixed—until no text in the document will be deleted, copied, cut, pasted, and so on. The reason: as you edit the text, you may accidentally delete index markers without knowing it. In fact, as this book goes to press, even cutting and pasting text deletes index entries.

▼ ▼

The Index palette. Just as the List feature captures text that is tagged with specific style sheets, XPress's indexing captures specific words or phrases that you have manually tagged in the Index palette. The Index palette (choose Show Index from the Window menu) lets you add either single words or whole phrases to the index, and it displays a list of currently indexed words and phrases (see Figure 8-12).

First I'm going to discuss how to add, edit, and remove index entries with the Index palette. Then I'll explore how to collect all the tagged entries and build a finished index on your document pages.

Adding a New First-Level Index Entry

There's very little that is automatic about building an index. Again, it's not difficult, but you have to be methodical about it. Here are the steps you should go through for each new index entry. (Note that I always differentiate between a new index entry and a new reference to an index entry. For example, "Pigs" might be a new entry for page 34, but when it appears again on page 59, it

Figure 8-12

The Index palette

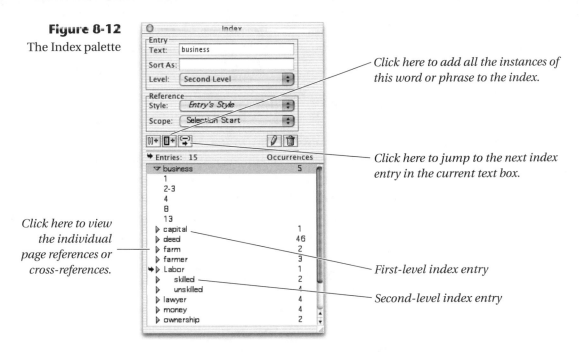

Click here to add all the instances of
this word or phrase to the index.

Click here to jump to the next index
entry in the current text box.

Click here to view
the individual
page references or
cross-references.

First-level index entry

Second-level index entry

would simply be a new reference to your already added index entry—see
"Adding a New Reference to an Entry," below.)

1. **TEXT.** Insert the index entry (the word or phrase that you want to
   appear in the index) into the Text field of the Index palette. If the entry
   actually appears in the text story, you can just select it with the cursor;
   when the Index palette is open, QuarkXPress automatically copies any
   text that is selected into the Text field. On the other hand, if the word or
   phrase doesn't appear, you will have to type it in yourself.

   For example, you may be discussing cows on your document page,
   but you want to index the word under the phrase "Farm animals." In
   this case, you would simply place the cursor somewhere in the text box
   and type "Farm animals" in the Index palette.

2. **SORT AS.** Index entries always appear in alphabetical order. However,
   occasionally you may not want your index entry to appear where it
   would normally be alphabetized. For instance, the famous "17-Mile
   Drive" would ordinarily be placed at the beginning of the index, before
   the "A"s. You can place it along with other words that begin with "S" by
   typing "Seventeen" in the Sort As field of the Index palette. You'll probably just leave this field blank for 98 percent of your index entries.

3. **LEVEL.** While some simple indexes have just one level of entry, most
   have two (some even have three or four; see Figure 8-13). For example,

"Cows," "Pigs," and "Ducks" might all be second-level entries found listed under the first level entry of "Farm animals." Since we're focusing on first-level entries right now, you can just skip over the Level pop-up menu. (I'll discuss the finer points of second-level entries in "Adding a New Second-level Index Entry," below).

Figure 8-13
A multilevel index

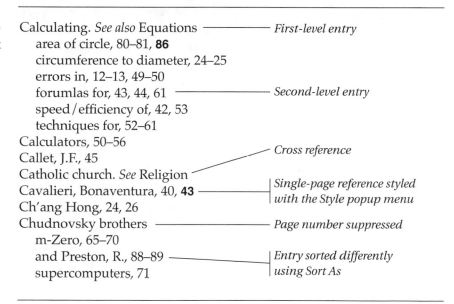

Calculating. *See also* Equations ——————— *First-level entry*
    area of circle, 80–81, **86**
    circumference to diameter, 24–25
    errors in, 12–13, 49–50
    forumlas for, 43, 44, 61 ——————— *Second-level entry*
    speed/efficiency of, 42, 53
    techniques for, 52–61
Calculators, 50–56
Callet, J.F., 45
Catholic church. *See* Religion ——— *Cross reference*
Cavalieri, Bonaventura, 40, **43** ——— *Single-page reference styled with the Style popup menu*
Ch'ang Hong, 24, 26
Chudnovsky brothers ——————— *Page number suppressed*
    m-Zero, 65–70
    and Preston, R., 88–89 ——— *Entry sorted differently using Sort As*
    supercomputers, 71

4. **STYLE.** The Style popup menu on the Index palette is yet one more control that you will ignore most of the time (though when you need it, it's great to have). Let's say you want the page numbers that refer to an illustration (rather than to just text on the page) to appear bold in the final index. You can build a character style sheet to define how you want the page numbers to appear and—when you're indexing that illustration—you can choose that character style from the Style popup menu. (See Chapter 7, *Copy Flow*, for more information on defining style sheets.)

5. **SCOPE.** If your treatise on pigs and goats spans six pages of your document, you don't want to have to make a separate index entry for each and every page. Instead, you can specify one index entry and choose a range of pages in the Scope popup menu. There are seven types of scopes.

   ▶ **SELECTION START.** When you choose Selection start (this is the default setting), XPress references the page on which the cursor is currently sitting. If you've selected a range of text that crosses from one page to the next, the first page (wherever the selection starts) is used.

▶ **SELECTION TEXT.** You can select any range of text (two words, two paragraphs, two hundred paragraphs . . . you get the idea) and index the whole range by choosing Selection Text. Personally, I find this option rather clunky to use (and even clunkier to edit later, if necessary), so I prefer using one of the other Scope settings instead.

▶ **TO STYLE.** If you use style sheets religiously, you'll love using the To Style option because you can specify a range based on paragraph styles. For instance, let's say you've got a book about farm animals where each animal's heading is tagged with a style sheet called "Heading-A." You could select the heading "Rabbit" and set the Scope to "To Style." Then you could choose Heading-A from the popup menu of styles (see Figure 8-14). If the "Horse" section starts three pages after the Rabbit section, the page range in the index will span three pages; if it starts 14 pages after, the page range will span 14 pages, and so on.

By the way, the default setting for To Style is Next, which means "from this paragraph onward until the style sheet changes to something else."

▶ **SPECIFIED # OF Ps.** If you want to index a long paragraph, one that may split onto two or more pages, you should probably

Figure 8-14
Indexing using To Style

select the scope called "Specified # of Ps." (Yes, "Ps" stands for "Paragraphs.") QuarkXPress's default setting of 1 means "include the pages that this paragraph falls on." Changing this setting to 2 means "include this paragraph plus the one after it," and so on.

▶ **TO END OF.** When you choose the scope called "To End Of," XPress offers you two options: to the end of the story or to the end of the document. If the current text story reaches to the last page of the document, then these options are the same, of course. In the example of the farm animals chapter, you could index the entire chapter by placing the cursor anywhere on the first page of the chapter, specifying an index entry labeled "Farm animals," and choosing To End Of Document.

▶ **SUPPRESS PAGE #.** Some first-level index entries don't include page numbers at all. For instance, in the book I've been discussing, "Animals" is too broad a topic to include page numbers (every page in the book would be indexed). So you might specify Suppress Page # for this one entry, and then follow it with 15 second-level entries, each with appropriate page numbers listed. (Again, I discuss second-level entries below.)

▶ **X-REF.** The last item on the Scope popup menu is X-Ref, which lets you add cross-references to your index. If you'll forgive me—because cross-references act a little bit differently than other index entries—I'm going to hold off on my discussion of this option for a moment.

6. **ADD.** If you've persevered through this procedure so far, the final step in adding an index entry is to click the Add button (the first of the three buttons in the palette). Sadly, after indexing for a long time, I sometimes forget this step and move on to the next entry, only to wonder later why I'm missing index entries that I *know* I made. Another *faux pas*: clicking Add before you change the various controls on the Index palette . . . that doesn't work, either.

Adding index entries is not hard at all, but it does take patience and attention to detail in each of these steps. As soon as you press the Add button, XPress inserts the entry into the Index palette and places an index marker in the text (see Figure 8-15). These index entries are actually hidden inside the text in the text box, though the index markers only show up when the Index palette is visible.

Figure 8-15

Index markers

*Index markers are
only visible when the Index
palette is open.*

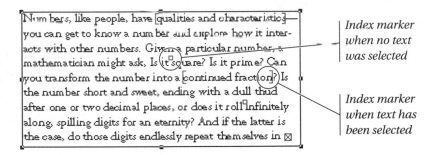

Index marker
when no text
was selected

Index marker
when text has
been selected

Tip: Be Careful With Add All. The second button in the Index palette is the Add All feature, which searches throughout your document for every instance of the index entry and adds it automatically to the index. For example, if you select the words "Bumble Bee" on your page and then click Add All, the entry will be added once, followed by the page number of each page that contains the words "Bumble Bee." This can be a great timesaver but it can also get you in trouble if you're not careful. When you press Add All, XPress uses the same Scope, Style, and Level settings for every instance of the entry text. In some cases this is fine, but in many indexes, each instance needs special attention— one only showing up on this page, one using a To Style scope, and so on.

Tip: Adding Names to the Index. Adding names to an index can be frustrating because you need to reverse the order of first and last names. In XPress 5 and 6, you can simply press the Option key before clicking the Add button. This changes the Add button to an Add Reversed feature, and phrases like "Michael Jackson" and "Quincy Jones" get added to the index as "Jackson, Michael" and "Jones, Quincy".

Tip: Index Keystrokes. There are two keystrokes you should keep in mind when you're indexing. First, Command-Option-I (Ctrl-Alt-I) jumps to the Text field in the Index palette (it even opens the palette first, if necessary). Second, pressing Command-Option-Shift-I (Ctrl-Alt-Shift-I) is the same as clicking the Add button in the Index palette. I find that both of these speed up indexing considerably.

Tip: Styling Indexes. Remember that however you type the word in the Text field of the Index palette is how it will appear in your final index. There is no single "correct" way to enter words into your index, though there are standard conventions, and it is best if you can keep your index consistent throughout.

For instance, you should decide on a capitalization scheme before beginning to index your document. Will all first-level entries be in initial caps, while second-level entries will be in lower case? Or should only proper names be capitalized, even in first-level entries? Before you answer these questions, it might behoove you to look over the section on indexes in a book on style conventions like *The Chicago Manual of Style*.

▼ ▼

Tip: Wrong Scope. As this book goes to press, QuarkXPress's Index XTension still contains an annoying bug. Let's say your text story starts on page 14 and then jumps to page 21. If you select and index a paragraph that spans the page break, the index entry appears as "14–21" rather than "14, 21." The former mistakenly appears to cover seven pages; the latter properly states that the entry is just on two pages. I hope they fix the bug by the time you read this, but if they don't, then just be aware that you might have some cleaning up to do later (see "Tip: Finessing Your Index," later in this chapter).

▼ ▼

Cross-References (X-refs)

One of the tricks to building a great index is to think of all the ways that your reader might look for a topic, and to include those words in your index. For instance, because you're familiar with your own book, you might include an index entry called "Llamas." However, another reader might look for "Cute wool-producing animals that spit." Fortunately, XPress lets you add cross-references in your index like "Spitting animals. *See* Llamas" and "Wool 34–46. *See also* Llamas."

To add a cross-reference to your index, you go through all the same steps as adding a normal index entry. The one difference is that when you set the Scope popup menu to X-Ref, XPress provides you with a text field in which you can type the cross-referenced word or phrase. If you want your index entry to be "Koi. *See* Carp" you would type "Koi" in the Text field of the Index palette, and type "Carp" in the X-Ref field.

Note that if you're cross-referencing to an index entry that you've already added to your Index palette, you can simply click on that index entry to copy it into the X-Ref field. That's certainly faster than typing the words in again.

Of course, because no page number is involved in a cross-reference, it doesn't matter where in your document you specify it (though it must be in a text box).

X-Ref options. QuarkXPress offers three types of cross-references which you can choose from the Index palette once you select X-Ref from the Scope popup menu: See, See also, and See herein.

▶ *See* is generally used when an index entry has no page number references, such as "Supermarket. *See* Grocery."

▶ *See also* is used when an index entry does have page references, but you also want to refer the reader to other topics, such as "Grocery 34–51. *See also* Farmer's Market."

▶ *See herein* is a special case in which you are cross-referencing to a second-level entry within the same entry as the cross-reference itself, and it's used more in legal indexes than anywhere else.

The Chicago Manual of Style recommends that you set these three phrases in italic in your index. XPress can automatically change this formatting for you (see "Index Preferences," later in this chapter).

Adding a New Reference to an Entry

Once you've got an entry on your Index palette, you can easily add more page references to it. Let's say you added the name "Farmer Jones" to your index back on page 13 of your document. Now, "Farmer Jones" appears again on page 51.

1. Place the cursor in the appropriate place in the text story. In this case, you'd probably put the cursor next to the word "Farmer" on page 51.

2. Click on the entry in the Index palette. Here, you'd click on "Farmer Jones." As soon as you click on an index entry, it appears in the Text field of the palette.

3. Make sure that the Level, Style, and Scope controls are set up properly in the Index palette, depending on how you want your new reference to appear.

4. Click the Add button.

Note that while you don't necessarily have to click on the entry in the Index palette in step 2 (you could just retype the entry in the Text field or select it on the page), I recommend the clicking method because it ensures consistency. For example, if you relied on your typing ability, you might create the index entry "Chickens" and then later—meaning to type the same thing—create a new entry, "Chicken," causing two different entries to be made when you only meant to make one.

Adding a New Second-Level Index Entry

Now that you've specified first-level index entries, you can—if you wish—add second-level entries. As I mentioned earlier, second-level entries are subcategories of the first-level entries. For example, under the first-level index entry "Wines," you might find the second-level entries "Merlot," "Chardonnay," and

"Côtes du Rhône." You can make a second-level index entry just like you make the first-level entry, but with two extra steps.

First, you must choose Second Level from the Level popup menu on the Index palette.

Second, you must tell XPress which first-level entry you want the new entry to fall under. You do this by clicking in the column to the left of the first-level entry (see Figure 8-16). When you click, XPress moves the Level marker (the little L-shaped arrow icon) to indicate that any second-level entries you create will be placed here.

The number-one mistake people make when adding a second-level entry is forgetting to move the Level marker, so the second-level entry shows up in the wrong place (see "Tip: Moving a Second-Level Entry," below). The second most common mistake is accidentally clicking on the first-level entry when you meant to click in the column to the left of it (to move the Level marker), which replaces whatever is in the Text field with whatever you click on . . . oops!

Again, patience and attention really do go a long way when you're making indexes.

Figure 8-16
Creating a
second-level entry

*Clicking in this
column moves the
Level marker here.*

Third and Fourth Levels. Once you've got a second-level entry, you can place a third-level entry under it—just change the Level popup menu to Third Level and place the Level marker appropriately. Similarly, you can put fourth-level entries under third-level entries. While it's nice that they give you this option, I find that third- and fourth-level entries are pretty confusing to readers, so restrain yourself unless it's really necessary.

▼ ▼

Tip: Where to Put the Cross-Reference. Some people like putting cross-references at the end of a list of second-level index entries rather than directly after the first-level entry. XPress won't do this for you automatically, but you can fake it by creating a dummy second-level entry and setting its Scope to X-Ref. The dummy second-level entry should just be named with a symbol like ^ or \ so that it automatically falls at the end of the alphabetized list of second-level entries. Later, once you build the index onto your document pages, you will have to perform a Find/Change to remove the symbols.

▼ ▼

Deleting an Entry

There are several ways to delete an entry from your index.

▶ If you want to delete an entire entry, including all its page references, select it in the Index palette and click the Delete button (the one that looks like a trash can on the Macintosh or a big "X" in Windows). Note that this also deletes all the subcategories under it and their page references, too.

▶ If you want to delete a single page reference, you can select it in the Index palette (click on the gray triangle next to the index entry to display its page references) and click the Delete button. Of course, if you only have one page reference under an index entry, deleting it will delete the whole entry, too.

▶ To get rid of a particular page reference in your index, you can also delete the index markers on the document page. If you selected text before adding the index entry, then this means deleting that whole range of text (deleting anything less leaves the index markers intact). If you did not select any text when adding the entry, you can still delete the little square marker by zooming in on it, clicking directly in its center, and pressing Delete. (You need to zoom in, because you generally can't select the tiny icon properly at Actual Size.)

▶ Last but not least, you can delete *every* index entry from the Index palette by Option-Shift-clicking (Alt-Shift-click) on the Delete button. This is drastic, so XPress always asks you if you really want to proceed.

Editing Index Entries

None of us is perfect, so it's a good thing that QuarkXPress has a way to edit the flubbed index entries that we make. When you're editing an index entry, you have to decide whether you want to edit the entry itself or a particular page reference of the entry.

Editing entries. Let's say that halfway through indexing your document, you realize that the index entry "Martha Washington" should have been indexed as "Washington, Martha." You can select the entry in the Index palette and click the Edit button (that's the button that looks like a little pencil)—or even faster, you can activate the Edit mode by double-clicking on the entry. Because you're editing an entry, XPress grays out everything but the Text, Sort As, and Level fields in the palette. In this case, you'd change the Text field to "Washington, Martha," and then click the Edit button again (or press Enter).

Editing references. You can also change the scope or style of a particular page reference. For instance, let's say the reference to Martha Washington on page 47 should have spanned nine paragraphs, but you accidentally set it to Selection start instead. To fix this, click on the gray triangle next to the index entry; this displays the page references for the entry. Double-click on the page reference that corresponds to the one you want to change (in this case, you'd double-click on the number 47). Because you're editing a page reference, XPress grays out the Text and Sort As fields and lets you change the Style and Scope popup menus. When done, press Enter, or click the Edit button to leave Edit mode.

Note that there's no way to move an index entry from one place in the text to another (for instance, if you actually wanted the above reference to begin on page 48 instead of page 47); you have to actually delete the entry and then re-enter it in the new location.

▼ ▼

Tip: Find the Next Index Entry. In order to edit either an index entry or an individual page reference, you need to have it selected on the Index palette. If the index entry is right in front of you on the page, sometimes it's faster to select it on the page than it is to select it in the palette (especially in really long indexes). The problem is that it's tough to select index markers on the page. The best solution is to place the cursor in the text box, a few characters or a few words before the index entry, then to click the Find Next button in the Index palette. This automatically selects the next index entry in the text box, and simultaneously selects it in the Index palette, too.

By the way, if you hold down the Option key, the Index palette's Find Next button changes to a Find First button; while this is a good way to jump to the first index entry in a story, I rarely find myself needing this.

▼ ▼

Tip: Moving a Second-Level Entry. As I said earlier, the most common mistake people make when adding second-level entries is to put them under the wrong first-level entry. If you do this, don't panic. Simply hold down the Option key and drag your new entry on top of the first-level you wanted it under. The

Option key (Alt on Windows) is the way you can re-arrange index entries in the list. But use this sparingly, XPress can get confused in long indexes.

▼ ▼

Index Preferences

Now that you've gone through the trouble of manually adding four thousand index entries to your document, can't you build the index yet? No, not yet. First you should take a quick glance at the Index panel of the Preferences dialog box (see Figure 8-17). This dialog box lets you change two things: the color of the index markers in your document, and the specific formatting characters that QuarkXPress will use when building the index.

Note that Index preferences are application-wide preferences, so they apply to all documents. (In earlier versions, they were only document-wide.)

Index Marker Color. There's nothing sacred about the color red . . . if you're color-blind to the color red, if your text is colored red, or if you just don't like seeing red, you can change the color of the index markers by clicking the color swatch labeled "Index Marker Color." Of course, this doesn't change anything about your document or your index; it only alters the on-screen display of the index markers when the Index palette is open.

Separation Characters. This might seem really trivial to you, but most art directors and professional indexers care a great deal about the formatting characters in their index (see Figure 8-18). For example, what kind of space

Figure 8-17
Index Preferences

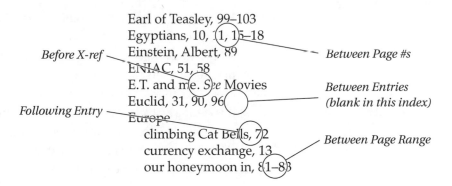

Figure 8-18

Separation characters

should separate an index entry and the page reference? The Index Preferences dialog box is the place to make this sort of decision.

▶ **FOLLOWING ENTRY.** This character sits between the index entry and the page reference numbers. The default character is a regular space, but I generally change this to a nonbreaking en space (Option-space on the Macintosh, or Control-Shift-6 in Windows) for better optical separation. You can put more than one character here—many people like to include a period, a comma, or a colon after an index entry, followed by a space, followed by the page reference numbers. In this case, type both the comma (or whatever) and the space in this field.

▶ **BETWEEN PAGE #S.** XPress places these characters between individual page-reference numbers. The important character is not the comma (which almost everyone uses), but the space after the comma. I typically leave this space alone, but some people like a larger or smaller space (like a punctuation space—Shift-space).

▶ **BETWEEN PAGE RANGE.** This character is used when the page reference spans multiple pages. The default character here is a regular hyphen, but I usually change this to an en dash (Option-hyphen on the Macintosh, or Control-Alt-Shift-hyphen in Windows). You could even change this to the word " to " if you want (don't forget to put spaces on either side), so that the page ranges look like this: "34 to 89".

▶ **BEFORE CROSS REFERENCE.** This character sits between the entry or a page reference number and a cross-reference. Like the Between Page #s character, the important character in the Before Cross Reference field is not the default period (which almost everyone uses), but the space after the period, which you might decide to make larger or smaller. Personally, I just leave this setting alone. (Note that if you want some special punctuation *after* a cross-reference, you generally have to type it yourself in the Index palette, though this is not usually the style.)

▶ **BETWEEN ENTRIES.** If you build a nested index (rather than a run-in index; I'll explain the difference in "Building the Index," below), XPress places the Between Entries character at the end of every line. While it may seem at first like you'd want a period or something at the end of every line, this is very rare in an index, so in general you should leave this setting blank (the default) for nested indexes.

In run-in indexes, however, you need to separate the entries from each other, so you should change this. The most common style is to use a semicolon and some kind of space character.

▼ ▼

Tip: Special Index Characters. You can type some special characters into the text fields in the Index Preferences dialog box by typing special codes. For example, if your index style calls for a tab character between the index entries and the page reference numbers, you could type "\t" in the Following Entry field (that's a backslash followed by a "t"). Similarly, you can get a flex space by typing "\f", and a line break by typing "\n". Why you'd want these characters in an index is beyond me; I just want to let you know that you can get them. Note that the codes are the same ones used in the Find/Change palette (see "Finding and Changing" in Chapter 5, *Word Processing*).

▼ ▼

Cross-Ref style. Quark snuck a little feature into the Index Preferences dialog box that lets you automatically apply a character style to the *See, See also,* and *See herein* text in cross-references. In most instances, you'll simply want to create a character style that is based on the regular index text style but is also in italic. (See Chapter 7, *Copy Flow*, for more information on defining character style sheets.)

Building the Index

Finally it's time to get that index onto a document page so you can see it in all its glory. This is the fun part, because you can just sit back, choose Build Index from the Utilities menu, and let XPress do the work of collecting the index entries and page numbers for you. (Build Index is only available when the Index palette is visible.) Unfortunately, there is still one more dialog box you need to pay attention to: the Build Index dialog box (see Figure 8-19).

The Build Index dialog box is a mish-mosh of choices you need to make in order to get the index of your dreams. While several of the options here might appear, at first, to fit better in the Index Preferences dialog box, who are we to question Quark's decisions? Fortunately, once you make your choices in this dialog box, XPress remembers them the next time you build an index for this document.

Figure 8-19

Build Index dialog box

Nested versus Run-In. There are two primary types of indexes in the world: nested and run-in (see Figure 8-20). In a nested index, each entry occupies its own paragraph; in a run-in index, the second-level entries merge with their first-level entry to form one big paragraph. Which you choose is entirely up to you, though it should depend in part on the content of the index. Run-in indexes make no sense when you have third- or fourth-level entries. On the other hand, run-in indexes typically conserve space better, especially when they're set in wide columns (because more than one entry fits on a single line).

The great thing about XPress's indexing is that you can build one type of index, then change your mind and replace it with the other type. Feel free to experiment!

Entire Book. If your document is part of a book (see "Books," earlier in this chapter), you can choose to build an index for the whole *megillah* by turning on the Entire Book option in the Build Index dialog box. I discuss this process in slightly more detail in "Indexing Books," below.

Replace Existing Index. QuarkXPress knows when you've already built an index in a document, and it automatically replaces that index with a new one unless you turn off the Replace Existing Index option. Probably the only time you'd turn this off would be if you wanted to compare two indexes to find differences between them.

By the way, note that when XPress replaces one index with another, it does not just replace the text. It actually deletes all the index pages and then rebuilds them from scratch. So if you've spent two hours adding extra formatting to the

Figure 8-20

Nested indexes versus
run-in indexes

Decimal notation 18, 27
Decimal point 30
Digits of pi
    calculating 18, 34, 41, 46
    memorizing 4, 111–112, 114, 118
    number of 2, 3, 34, 45, 51–53, 65,
        67, 87–91, 113
    random sequence of 68, 72–73
    search for 42–43, 51
Dinostratos 56, 90
Dudley, Underwood   93, 96
Duciad (Pope) 92

Decimal notation 18, 27
Decimal point 30
Digits of pi; calculating 18, 34, 41, 46;
    memorizing 4, 111–112, 114, 118;
    number of 2, 3, 34, 45, 51–53, 65,
    67, 87–91, 113; random sequence of
    68, 72–73; search for 42–43, 51
Dinostratos 56, 90
Dudley, Underwood   93, 96
Duciad (Pope) 92

index, or adding boxes or lines to the pages, all those additions are removed when you build the new index.

Add Letter Headings. If you want headings added to your index (like an "A" before all the entries that begin with an "A", and so on), turn on the Add Letter Headings option. When QuarkXPress builds the index, it adds the headings only as necessary (in other words, it won't add a "Q" heading if you don't have any entries that begin with that letter).

When this option is turned on, you can also choose a paragraph style sheet from the Style popup menu. This is the paragraph style that XPress uses to format the letter heading.

Master Page. When you click OK in the Build Index dialog box (don't do it yet), QuarkXPress adds new pages at the end of the current document and flows the index onto them. You can choose which master page you want the program to base the new pages on from the Master Page popup menu. Typically, you'll want to design a new master page specifically for the index, but you don't have to. Note that the master page you choose must have an automatic text box on it, or else XPress won't be able to flow the index onto the page.

Level Styles. The Level Styles section of the Build Index dialog box lets you apply paragraph style sheets to each entry in the index. In a run-in index, there's only one kind of paragraph: the first-level entry (all the second-level entries are merged into the same paragraph). In a nested index, however, each entry level is tagged with its own paragraph style. If you want all your second-level index entries to be slightly indented from the first-level entries (you probably do), make a new style sheet that includes indentation, and choose it from the Second Level popup menu.

Once again, designing a readable index is as much an art as a science. Take some time to peruse other people's indexes, checking for details like indentation (what does a first-level entry do when it's longer than one line, for example?) and punctuation.

If at first you don't succeed. Building an index can take a while if you have a very long document with a lot of entries, but you should plan on rebuilding it at least once. I find that there's almost always something I've forgotten or have messed up in the Index palette, Index Preferences, or the Build Index dialog box. Just go back and fix it, and then choose Build Index once again.

▼ ▼

Tip: Finessing Your Index. Just as it takes a human touch to build a great set of index entries, the index that XPress builds on your document pages requires some human intervention to become a final product. Here's a short (and certainly not exhaustive) list of fine-tuning suggestions you might consider.

▶ If you use letter headings, you might want to combine two or more of them into groups. For instance, if there are only one or two entries each under the last few headings in the index, you might want to merge them into one group and label them "X, Y, Z" or "X–Z."

▶ If any index entries are found on the Pasteboard or are overset from their text boxes when you build the index, QuarkXPress warns you and then places a dagger (†) next to those references in the built index. You can (and should) search your index for this character with Find/Change, just in case. If you find one, you can either remove it or fix the problem and rebuild the index.

▶ Indexes generally follow widow and orphan rules, as body text does (see "Widow and Orphan Control" in Chapter 6, *Type and Typography*). For instance, you should probably try to keep at least one or two second-level entries with their first-level entry in a column. And a single second-level entry sitting all by its lonesome at the top of a column is a terrible sight to see. Unfortunately, these problems typically have to be fixed by hand, as XPress's Keep with Next ¶ and Keep Lines Together features aren't designed to work very well with indexes.

▶ I find that when I use an en dash between page ranges in my indexes, the character typically appears to be too close to the numbers on either side. The only good solution is to add very thin spaces or kerning around the character, and the only good way to do this is with XPress Tags (see "A Solution: XPress Tags" in Chapter 7, *Copy Flow*, for more on building complex search-and-replace strings using tags).

Of course, the most important thing you can do with an index is to proofread it carefully for spelling and style consistency.

Remember that any changes you make once your index is built are wiped out if you rebuild the index.

▼ ▼

Indexing Books and Projects

There is a major problem lurking in the Index palette that applies directly to indexing multi-document books or multi-layout projects: The Index palette currently only displays index entries from one project or layout space at a time. There is no way to display entries from an entire book or across layouts. It may not seem like much, but in fact, the problem is so grave that many professional indexers simply give up and don't use XPress's indexing feature at all.

Given this limitation, you have two options when you're indexing multiple documents or layouts.

▶ You can merge all the documents, creating one enormous file, by dragging pages while you're in Thumbnails mode. If you do this, be sure to save the monster file under a different name than your original files, and keep plenty of backups—I trust big files about as far as I can throw them. (To merge layouts in a project, you have to drag thumbnails from your document into a dummy document, and then drag them back to the desired layout space.)

▶ You can just index your files one document at a time and hope that you can remember what you indexed in each document and how you indexed it. Going this route, it's helpful to build indexes every now and again and use printouts as a reference.

If you merge all your documents, you can build the index just the way I've described above. Or, if you are going to persist in indexing each document separately, here's what you need to do differently.

Test one chapter first. Before you go too far in indexing your book, try building an index from one chapter first. This way, you'll know if you've properly set up Index Preferences and specified the index entries.

Indexing the entire book. When you're building an index, you can tell QuarkXPress to include every document in your book by turning on the Entire Book option in the Build Index dialog box. You have to have your book's palette open at the time you open the document to do this.

Note that XPress doesn't necessarily put the index at the end of the book. Instead, the program builds the book's index at the end of the currently open document, using the style sheets and preferences of that document. Of course, after you build a four-page index at the end of Chapter 2, XPress has to renumber every document after Chapter 2, so most of the page numbers in the index will be wrong. Therefore, it behooves you to build your index *only* at the end of the last document in your book.

▼ ▼

Tip: Indexing in a New Document. Maybe it's just my tendency to segment each and every part of a long document, but I like having my index in a file all by itself. If you want this, too, here's how you get it.

1. Create a new document with the same specifications as the other documents in your book. Make sure you've got at least one master page that has an automatic text box on it in the document, and make sure the Auto Page Insertion option is turned on in Preferences (Command-Option-Shift-Y or Ctrl-Alt-Shift-Y).

2. Save this new document to disk along with your other files.

3. Add the new document to your book palette with the palette's Add Chapter button. (Make sure it's the last file listed on the book palette.)

4. If you haven't already built style sheets for the index entries (and letter headings, if you're using them), then build them now in this new document. If you have built them in your master chapter, then synchronize the book so they'll be available in your index document.

5. Build the book's index in the new document by choosing Build Index and turning on the Entire Book option.

6. Because XPress always adds index pages at the end of your document, you now have to manually delete the empty first page of your document.

Voilà! Now you've got a separate document that has an index for the entire book.

▼ ▼

Putting It Together

Long documents can be a drag to produce, but the Book, Lists, and Indexing features in QuarkXPress go a long way in helping make the process bearable. Whether you're building a magazine, a book, a journal, a catalog, or even a newsletter, I'm sure you'll be able to find good use for these features.

Remember that a little work up front—building style sheets, putting documents in a book palette, and so on—can go a long way and can save lots of time in the long run.

Now let's shift gears radically and start looking at how pictures can liven up your XPress pages, in any size document you create.

9

PICTURES

I've been talking a lot about text and rudimentary graphic elements such as arrows and ovals, but let's not forget that ultimately, QuarkXPress is designed to integrate not only text and lines, but also graphics from other programs, and it contains many powerful features to aid in this task. QuarkXPress handles line art and images such as four-color photographs with a degree of power and set of features previously only attainable by using several programs in conjunction.

In this chapter, I'll cover almost everything you can do with pictures other than running text around them (which I cover in Chapter 11, *Where Text Meets Graphics*).

- ▶ Importing images into QuarkXPress

- ▶ Rotating picture boxes and their contents

- ▶ Precision placement of images and picture boxes

- ▶ Horizontal skewing of graphic images

- ▶ Automatic re-importing of modified pictures

- ▶ Working with Publish and Subscribe and OLE

- ▶ Picture greeking

Here are the basic steps of importing pictures into your documents.

1. Create a picture box.

2. Select the box with the Content tool, and bring in a picture by either pasting from the Clipboard (not a good idea) or using the Get Picture command.

3. Size, skew, rotate, and crop the image until you like the way it looks on the page.

But what types of pictures are available for use? And how do you get them to look the way you want? In this chapter I explore the full range of possibilities for bringing graphics in from other applications and manipulating them on the page. In Chapter 10, *Fine-Tuning Images*, I'll talk about some of the effects you can create by modifying graphics once they're in QuarkXPress.

Let's first take a close look at the different types of pictures on the Macintosh and Windows that are applicable to QuarkXPress users.

Graphic File Formats

If there's a question I'm asked more often than "Why won't my file print?" it's "What's the difference between all those different graphic formats?" The question refers to a host of formats with names such as EPS, TIFF, GIF, PICT, LZW, TIFF, JPEG, Photo CD (PCD), and Windows Metafile (WMF). No one can be blamed for being confused when faced with such a list! Some of these are different names for the same thing, others are subtly different, and a few represent totally different concepts.

The fundamental question when considering a graphic file format is whether it is bitmapped or object-oriented.

Bitmapped Images

The most common file formats are based on bitmapped images. When you use a scanner and scanning software, you are generating a bitmapped image. When you use an image-editing and painting program such as Adobe Photoshop, you're working with and generating bitmapped images. However, no matter how ubiquitous bitmapped images are, you are still strictly limited as to how you can use them.

Bitmapped images are just that: images made of mapped bits. A *bit* is a small piece of information. To begin with, let's think of it as a single dot which can be turned on or off. When you look very closely at your computer screen, you can see that the screen image is made up of thousands of these tiny bits (also called *pixels*, which stands for "picture elements"). If your monitor is set to black and white, some of these bits are turned on (black), and some are turned off (white). The *map* is the computer's internal blueprint of what the image looks like: "bit number one is on, bit number two is off," and so on (see Figure 9-1).

Bitmapped images are complicated creatures. I cover them in much more depth in the book I wrote with Glenn Fleishman, Steve Roth, and Conrad Chavez called *Real World Scanning and Halftones*. You might want to check that out. However, in the meantime, here's a quick rundown. There are three primary pieces of information that are relevant to any bitmapped image: its dimensions, resolution, and pixel depth.

Figure 9-1
Each pixel sits
on the grid

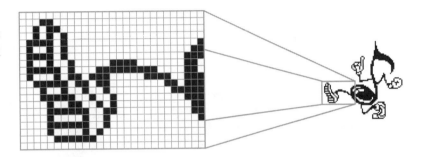

Dimensions. Every bitmapped image is rectangular and is broken down into a grid of many square pixels. Each pixel is whole and not fractured. You can describe the dimensions of the gridded area in several ways, but they are most often specified by the number of pixels or sample points per side (like 640 by 480 pixels), or by inches per side at a given resolution.

Resolution. The resolution of the bitmapped image is usually defined as the number of pixels, or sample points, per inch on the grid (of course, it's pixels per centimeter in countries using the metric system). A low-resolution bitmapped image may have 72 pixels per inch; however, this measurement is usually expressed as either dots per inch (dpi) or samples per inch (spi). A picture using only 72 dpi looks very rough. A higher-resolution bitmapped image may be 300 dpi or higher (many film scanners scan images at over 4,000 dpi). These images, when printed, are much crisper and cleaner, with fewer jaggies (see Figure 9-2).

Pixel depth. Each pixel is defined as a specific color. The range of colors available is determined by the type of bitmapped image it is (see "File Types," below). In the simplest bitmapped images, each pixel is defined as either black or white. These are called "bilevel," or "1-bit" images, because each pixel is described by 1 bit of information, and as I mentioned above, that 1 bit can be either on (1) or off (0).

Bilevel images are *flat;* they have little depth. More complex bitmapped images are *deep* because they contain pixels that are defined by multiple bits, enabling them to describe many levels of gray or levels of color. For example, an 8-bit image can describe up to 256 colors or shades of gray for each pixel (those of us in the Northwest, having to look at gray a great deal of the time, can identify and name most of those shades). A 24-bit image can describe more than 16 million colors (see Figure 9-3).

Manipulating bitmapped images. The limitations inherent in bitmapped images become most clear when you manipulate the picture in some way, such as enlarging it significantly. The key is that the picture's resolution is directly related to its size. If you double the size of a bitmap, you cut its reso-

Figure 9-2
Low resolution versus high resolution bitmapped line art

72 dpi

300 dpi

Figure 9-3
The number of bits determines the number of gray levels

One-bit (two shades)
Either zero or one

Four-bit (16 shades)
Each pixel defined by four bits: 0001, 0010, 0011, 0100, 0101, etc.

lution in half; if you reduce the picture to one-quarter of its original size, you multiply its resolution by four. For example, a 72-dpi, 1-bit graphic when enlarged 200 percent becomes a twice-as-rough 36-dpi image. However, when reduced to 50 percent, it becomes a finer 144-dpi image (see Figure 9-4).

A grayscale or color image becomes *pixelated*, rather than looking more jaggy, when it's enlarged. That is, you begin to see each pixel and its tonal value (see Figure 9-5).

Object-Oriented Graphics

Instead of describing a picture dot by dot, object-oriented files specify each object in a picture on a coordinate system. A bitmapped picture could take an

Figure 9-4
Scaling a bitmap affects its resolution

100 percent = 72 dpi

200 percent = 36 dpi

50 percent = 144 dpi

Figure 9-5
Pixelization from enlarging a grayscale image

72 dpi, four-bit grayscale TIFF at 100 percent

72 dpi, four-bit grayscale TIFF at 400 percent

enormous amount of space describing one circle (this dot on, this dot off, and so on), but an object-oriented file could describe it in one line: "Draw a circle of this size with a center at x,y." The computer knows what a circle is and how to create it. Different object-oriented formats can describe different things, but most can easily specify objects such as lines, curves, and type, as well as attributes such as shading and object rotation angle.

Most object-oriented graphics can also contain bitmapped graphics as objects in their own right, though you may or may not be able to edit those bitmaps with a paint program. These files are almost always created by an application such as Macromedia FreeHand or Adobe Illustrator.

The magic of object-oriented graphics is that you can stretch them, rotate them, twist them into pastry, and print them on various-resolution printers without worrying about how smoothly the lines will print. That is, when you print on a 300-dpi, plain-paper laser printer, you get a full 300 dpi; when you print to film with a 2,540-dpi imagesetter, you get beautifully smooth lines at 2,540 dots per inch. There is no inherent limit of information for the picture, as there is with bitmaps (see Figure 9-6). Theoretically, there is no inherent limit to the number of gray levels in an object-oriented picture. Realistically, however, each format has upper limits.

Figure 9-6
Object-oriented
graphics versus
bitmapped images

Object-oriented   *Outline*   *Bitmapped*

File Types

When I talk about *file types* in this book, I'm talking about two things: how the information is formatted within the file, and how the file is saved to disk. The common usage of the term—such as in "an Illustrator file" or "a QuarkXPress file"—refers to the way in which the information is formatted. Then there is the way the Macintosh and Windows operating systems name files when they save them to disk.

The Macintosh gives every file an actual, technical, four-letter file type. For instance, files generally referred to as "QuarkXPress files" are type XDOC;

Illustrator files are either EPSF or TEXT. These file types are hidden from the user, but you can examine a file's type using a utility such as File Buddy. For the sake of simplicity, I use the terms *file type* and *file format* interchangeably.

Windows, on the other hand, requires a particular three-letter file-name extension that indicates the file type. For example, an XPress project on Windows always has ".qxp" appended to its name (earlier versions of XPress used ".qxd"), and TIFF image files always have .tif extensions.

QuarkXPress writes its files to disk the same way on both Macintosh and Windows. TIFF files are also interchangeable from Mac to Windows. However, if you move a file from Mac to Windows without giving it the proper file-name extension, XPress may not be able to open it, or it may open incorrectly. Similarly, if you move a file from Windows to Macintosh without using some utility to assign the correct four-letter file type, the same thing can happen.

File types XPress understands. QuarkXPress can only import certain graphic file formats, and the formats it understands are different on the two platforms. However, no matter what type of machine you've got, I strongly suggest that you use either EPS, TIFF, or DCS images for the bulk of your print work and JPEG and GIF for your Web work (see "Tip: The Best Format to Use," at the end of this section). As I describe each of the following file types, you'll see that most of the other formats are just too unstable or limited.

TIFF. The Tagged Image File Format (TIFF) is a bitmapped image file format with lots of support for high-quality images. First off, a TIFF file can be created at any size and resolution, and include black-and-white, grayscale, or color information. Because of the flexibility of TIFF files, all scanning and image-editing programs can save and open the TIFF format.

As it turns out, there are several different TIFF formats, including compressed and uncompressed, and Macintosh versus Windows. Fortunately, QuarkXPress imports several different TIFF formats, including those written for either Mac or Windows, and even LZW-compressed TIFF files (though in XPress 4 or 5 you have to have the LZW Import XTension loaded to read these files).

Photoshop 6 and later can save TIFF files in several formats that may (or may not) confuse QuarkXPress. For instance, XPress does not currently read TIFFs with Zip or JPEG compression. You *can* import layered TIFF files into XPress (files that contain Photoshop layers), but they appear as flattened images. (Technically, layered TIFF files actually include both a flattened image and a layered image, and XPress just ignores the layers and reads the flattened version.) However, XPress does *not* recognize any transparency that your layered TIFF image might have—the image just appears opaque to XPress.

Encapsulated PostScript. Encapsulated PostScript (EPS) format is the most reliable format for putting images on paper or film, as long as your printer or imaging device can understand PostScript. PostScript is an object-oriented page-description language, though PostScript files may contain bitmaps as well. Although it has built-in font-handling features, it ultimately treats type as a graphic made of lines and curves. This makes working with fonts in a PostScript environment a joy, with many possibilities. It's easy to create a PostScript file, but to print it out you must have a PostScript-compatible printer (with non-PostScript printers, XPress just prints the low-resolution screen preview of the EPS graphic).

EPS images come in two basic varieties: EPS without a preview, and EPS with a preview. The preview-enclosed feature in most EPS files allows you to bring such a file into QuarkXPress and see a low-resolution representation of the image on the screen. When the file is printed to a PostScript printer, however, the bitmap is ignored and the underlying PostScript is used. If a preview image is not available, then you see a big gray box on the screen which may contain some basic information (such as the file's name).

On the Mac, the EPS preview may be saved as either a PICT or a TIFF. There's no trouble with using PICT previews, and if the graphic will stay on the Macintosh platform, PICT previews are probably preferable. However, if the file may at some point find its way to a Windows machine, a TIFF preview is the way to go (when you make an EPS on a Windows PC, you have to use TIFF). (The reason for this is somewhat technical: PICT previews are stored in a file's resource fork, which is stripped away when the file is moved to a PC; TIFF previews are stored in the data fork, which can survive moving back and forth between a Mac and Windows environment.)

Even though EPS files are robust and reliable, I don't use them as often as TIFF images when it comes to bitmapped graphics (see "Tip: The Best Format to Use").

▼ ▼

Tip: Great-Looking EPS Previews. Photoshop on the Macintosh lets you save EPS files with a JPEG preview. While I don't ordinarily use JPEG images (see "JPEG," below) and I *never* use the JPEG encoding in EPS files, I do like the JPEG preview option because it provides a much nicer on-screen representation of the image than the normal 8-bit color preview that Photoshop builds into EPS files. JPEG previews are actually high-quality compressed PICT previews, so they don't work on the PC. On the other hand, the big drawback to JPEG previews is display speed: EPS files with JPEG preview may display more slowly. Nonetheless, if your client is staring over your shoulder, you might get some benefit from a good-looking screen image in XPress.

▼ ▼

DCS. I'll talk about Desktop Color Separation (DCS) in Chapter 12, *Color*, but let's quickly go over it here. The DCS method is based on preseparating color images into five separate EPS files (which is why DCS is sometimes called "EPS-5" or "five-file EPS"). Four of the files contain high-resolution information for each of the process colors (cyan, magenta, yellow, and black). The fifth file contains a low-resolution composite image (for proofing), a screen representation of the picture, and pointers to the four higher-resolution files. This fifth file is the one that gets imported into QuarkXPress.

When you print your file, QuarkXPress replaces this representation file (sometimes called the "master file") with the four high-resolution files. This means that you can print the high-resolution separations directly from QuarkXPress to an imagesetter.

Some programs (including XPress) support the DCS 2.0 file format, which is basically a revised version of the DCS specification. In DCS 2.0 images, the four process plates and the preview "master" image can all be rolled into one big file. More important, DCS 2.0 lets you include spot-color plates, varnish plates—as many plates as you want. This means that you can create an image in Photoshop that includes spot colors, export it as a DCS 2.0 file, and separate the whole thing in QuarkXPress. (The one problem with this workflow is that Photoshop 4 doesn't let you save in the DCS 2.0 format, so you have to use a plug-in such as PlateMaker—from a lowly apprentice production.)

QuarkXPress not only understands DCS and DCS 2.0 documents, it can also create them when you save a page as EPS (see "Page as Picture," later in this chapter).

PDF. I discuss the Portable Document Format (PDF) in detail in Chapter 14, *Going Online with QuarkXPress*, but of course the PDF format is widely used for print publishing as well as the paperless office. QuarkXPress can import PDF 1.3 and 1.4 files (also called Acrobat 4 and Acrobat 5 files, respectively). At the time of this writing, XPress could not import PDF 1.5 (Acrobat 6) files, though that will likely change in time. It also cannot properly print PDF files that include transparency or files that have duotones in them. XPress lets you pick which page of a multi-page PDF file you want to import. However, if the PDF is locked in one way or another (no printing, no copying, and so on), XPress won't let you import it at all.

PICT. The PICT format (.pct in Windows), also a part of the original Mac system, can contain drawings that are object-oriented or that consist of a single bitmap ("bitmap-only PICT"). Unlike most programs, QuarkXPress can "see" when a PICT file is bitmap-only, and lets you manipulate it as such (you'll see later in this chapter that you can manipulate bitmapped images differently than object-oriented ones). PICT images can be any size, resolution, and color (like TIFFs or EPS files).

While PICT does sound quite useful, I don't like it for four reasons.

▶ The object-oriented PICT format is unreliable. For example, line widths can change when you move a picture from one program to another, and text spacing can change, sometimes drastically. Also, printing to imagesetters (1,200+ dpi) can be troublesome.

▶ Bitmap-only PICT images are RGB-only; you cannot preseparate them into CMYK (I'll talk about color separation in some depth in Chapter 12, *Color*). Fortunately, XPress can separate the RGB PICTs if you need to do this. Personally, I'd rather stick to TIFF images.

▶ PICT images are always fully embedded in your XPress document. That means if you import a 20 MB PICT image into a picture box, your XPress document gets 20 MB bigger. Add one or two more of these and you've got a file that is unmanageable and possibly unstable as well. I avoid embedding images like the plague (with one exception: when the image is really small).

▶ Last, XPress relies on the operating system, which is pretty slow, to display PICTs properly. The larger the image, the slower the display. Anything over a megabyte is painful.

Nonetheless, PICT is the primary format for printing from the Macintosh to non-PostScript devices, so if you're doing low-end printing with small object-oriented images you might consider using this format. For the sake of completeness, I should note that it is possible to import PICT images into XPress for Windows.

Windows Bitmap. Windows Bitmap (.BMP) is the bitmap format native to Windows Paint, but isn't usually encountered outside of Windows and OS/2 Presentation Manager. You can, however, bring .BMP files to the Macintosh and use them in QuarkXPress. I just don't think you should; I still prefer TIFF to this format.

Windows Metafile. Closely tied to graphics technology underlying Windows, Windows Metafile (.WMF) is a relatively reliable object-oriented format to use in Windows. However, when you take it out of that environment and onto the Macintosh, things get a little weird. Fonts that are embedded in the graphic really get messed up, and colors can get screwy, too. I suggest leaving this at home on the PC. Even better: use EPS for object-oriented graphics.

Scitex CT and LW files. QuarkXPress can import both Scitex CT (continuous-tone) and LW (line-work) files. However, it can only separate CT files. Note that when I say "CT files," I am actually referring to CT HandShake files. I know one guy who got burned because he asked a color house for CT files and got Scitex's proprietary format instead of the open-format CT HandShake files.

JPEG. JPEG is a bitmapped file format with built-in compression, so that these images can be a tenth of the size (or smaller) of a non-compressed image. However, the compression in JPEG is *lossy*, which means the more it's compressed, the worse the image looks.

Once you've imported the picture into QuarkXPress, the program decompresses it every time you print it (which can take a while) and sends it to the printer as though it were a TIFF image. Therefore, the only really good reason to use JPEG images instead of TIFFs is if you're scraping for hard drive space.

Note that a JPEG file is different from a JPEG EPS file or an EPS file with a JPEG preview (see "Tip: Great-Looking EPS Previews," earlier). JPEG EPS files are EPS files saved with JPEG encoding (this is an option in Photoshop). In theory, these should print correctly on PostScript Level 2 or 3 printers because the printer itself decompresses the file. In reality, they don't separate, so color images only appear on the black plate. JPEG DCS files (DCS files with JPEG encoding) do separate properly, however.

PCX. PCX is the granddaddy of bitmapped formats, and the current version supports 24-bit and 256-color palettes. Since a variety of color-model techniques have been applied to PCX over the ages, files from earlier programs can have some serious color-mismatch problems. If you absolutely need to use PCX images, then go for it. If not, see if your source can provide files in TIFF, which is an all-around better format.

GIF. The Graphics Interchange Format (commonly known as GIF, pronounced either "jiff" or "giff") is now the industry standard for graphics on the World Wide Web. GIF files are designed for on-screen viewing, especially for images where file size is more important than quality, picture which require transparency, and for screens that only display 8-bit color (256 colors). Photoshop GIFs are always 8-bit indexed-color images, making them reasonable for on-screen viewing, but certainly not for printing.

▼ ▼

Tip: The Best Format to Use. When my layout is destined for print, I rarely use a graphics file format other than TIFF, EPS, or DCS. (I would like to use PDF, but I'm still not convinced that QuarkXPress is robust enough at handling PDF files yet.) However, even with these three formats there are good reasons to choose one over the other, depending on the image and what you're using it for. Some people think that EPS is inherently better than TIFF, or vice versa. Not so. Don't choose one over the other because your service bureau or printer told you to; they often don't know any more about file formats than you do (they just think they do).

Here are a few of the many considerations you need to keep in mind when choosing a file format.

▶ **FILE SIZE.** Uncompressed TIFF files are about 20 percent smaller than EPS files. Plus, EPS files contain a preview, which can add even more to the file's size depending on its type and dimension.

▶ **PAGE PREVIEWS.** QuarkXPress creates a low-resolution screen preview when you import a TIFF image, which takes some time (the larger the image and the slower your computer, the more time it takes). EPS files, however, import very quickly because XPress simply grabs their built-in preview. The quality of a TIFF preview depends on how you set the Color TIFF preview option in the Preferences dialog box. The 32-bit setting provides a great preview, but your document's file size increases significantly, so I usually avoid it. The quality of an EPS preview is totally up to the software that creates it (see "Tip: Great-Looking EPS Previews," above). In general, the Photoshop-built preview in a CMYK EPS file is going to look better than the XPress-built preview in a CMYK TIFF image (unless you're using XPress's color management software correctly and use high-resolution preview).

▶ **IMAGE CONTROL.** In general, TIFF files are very flexible. If you import a grayscale TIFF image, you can apply a color to it, shade it, or even apply a custom halftone screen to it. Color TIFFs are only a little less flexible (you can't apply halftone screens to them). EPS files, on the other hand, are cast in stone (that's why they call them "encapsulated"). To make a change to an EPS file, you have to do it in some other program.

▶ **DUOTONES.** If you want to make a duotone in Photoshop, you must save it as an EPS file. Period.

▶ **CROPPING.** What happens if you import a 20 MB bitmapped image and crop it down to a little tiny square on your XPress page? If the file is saved in TIFF format, XPress only sends the necessary image data to the printer, which can speed up printing a lot. If it's an EPS file, however, XPress sends the entire 20 MB to the printer every time you print.

▶ **DOWNSAMPLING.** Proofing a 300-dpi bitmapped image on a desktop laser printer can take a long time if the image is saved as an EPS, because XPress sends all the image data to the printer every time you print. But the program can downsample TIFF files; in fact, XPress automatically downsamples the resolution of TIFF files to two times the current halftone screen frequency (lpi). So when you're printing a 60-lpi file on your laser printer, it reduces your high-resolution images to 120 dpi, saving a lot of time.

The same thing goes for reducing the size of your image. Remember, if you scale that 300-dpi bitmapped image to 50 percent, it is now effectively a 600-dpi image—way more than you need. XPress downsamples this, too. Of course, it's usually better to do your own downsampling in an image-editing program before you import the file into XPress.

▶ **CLIPPING PATHS.** Earlier versions of QuarkXPress couldn't read embedded clipping paths in TIFF files, so you had to use EPS files. No longer. In fact, XPress can even read multiple paths in TIFF files (see "Clipping Paths," in Chapter 10, *Fine-Tuning Images).*

▶ **SPOT COLORS.** If you create spot color channels in a Photoshop file, then you have to save it as a DCS 2.0 file in order to import it into QuarkXPress.

▶ **VECTORS.** XPress can only read vector data (like vector text or "shapes") in Photoshop files when the file is saved as an EPS or a PDF.

▶ **COMPRESSION.** You can compress TIFF images with LZW (non-lossy) compression. This type of compression works best on areas of flat color, and worst on images that have a lot of tiny details. Your only option for compression in EPS files is JPEG, which renders CMYK files mostly useless (QuarkXPress can't separate JPEG-compressed EPS files).

▶ **COLOR MANAGEMENT.** Because XPress can control the data in a TIFF file, it can color-manage the images (see Appendix A, *Color Management).* EPS files, however, are hopeless when it comes to color management because XPress can't really change any color values in them. This goes for separating RGB images into CMYK, too (TIFF images, no problem; EPS images, big problem).

▶ **CMYK SEPARATIONS.** When XPress prints color separations (see Chapter 12, *Color),* it has to send down the entire EPS file (the cyan, magenta, yellow, and black plates) each time it prints a plate. That means if you have a 20 MB EPS file, XPress sends 80 megabytes of information to the printer (20 MB per plate). That takes a long time. However, XPress treats CMYK EPS files from Photoshop differently.

With these files, it's smart enough to pull them apart and only send the cyan data with the cyan plate, the magenta data with the magenta plate, and so on. This is much (much!) faster.

TIFF files can also be pulled apart at print time. (I guess that means this isn't such a big difference between TIFF and EPS after all, as long as you're using Photoshop.)

All told, I tend to use TIFF images whenever I can because of their flexibility. Nonetheless, some jobs, like duotone images, images with spot colors, or those that require a special halftone screen, require EPS or DCS files. Also, occasionally I'll run into some high-end imagesetter that requires images to be in EPS format.

▼▼
Importing Pictures into QuarkXPress

Now that we know the types of pictures we'll be dealing with, let's look at how we'll deal with them. As I mentioned, the first step in importing a graphic from another application is to create a picture box within your QuarkXPress project. This is covered in Chapter 3, *Tools of the Trade*, in the discussion of rectangles, ovals, and polygons. When you have an empty picture box on your page, you can see an "X" in the middle of it. At this point you're ready to bring a picture into the box.

Note that I'm bringing a picture *into* the box, rather than replacing the box or even "merging" the two together. The picture box is one entity and the picture is another. You might think of the box as being a window frame through which you see the picture. You can manipulate the picture box, or the picture, or both.

The two primary ways to bring a picture in are to paste from the Clipboard or use Get Picture. In order for either of these methods to work, you must have the picture box selected. (In earlier versions of XPress you had to use the Content tool; now you can use either the Content tool or the Item tool.)

Pasting Pictures

There are at least four problems with pasting in pictures (selecting Paste from the Edit menu, or pressing Command/Ctrl-V) rather than using Get Picture, each one of which alone would be enough to convince me not to paste pictures into picture boxes in XPress.

▶ Because the image is pasted in, there is no accompanying disk file for it; if you want to edit the image, you have to copy it, paste it into a program that can edit it, make changes, copy it again, and paste it back into the picture box. If you've cropped or rotated the picture in XPress, all that information is lost when you re-paste it.

▶ The file format for an image typically changes when you move it from one application to another. For instance, if you use Copy and Paste on a Macintosh to move a picture from Photoshop to XPress, the image is converted to the PICT format. PICT images don't understand CMYK, so CMYK files are translated into RGB on the fly. On Windows, images are sometimes translated to WMF files. Whatever the case, these switches make me very nervous.

▶ XPress may not understand the file format for images that are on the Clipboard. For instance, you can copy a graphic from Adobe Illustrator, but XPress may not let you paste it into a picture box.

▶ If you paste in a big picture, your QuarkXPress project balloons in size because the document has to embed the entire image. With Get Picture, just a low-resolution image is imported with a pointer to the full file on disk (see "Picture Management," later in this chapter).

(I used to mention a fifth problem: that color images pasted into picture boxes could not be separated into CMYK. It's of dubious value to note that XPress can now separate these images, even when the color management XTension is turned off. The quality isn't exactly superb.)

Again, I recommend that you avoid the Clipboard approach to importing pictures (at least don't use it often, and certainly not for big important jobs).

Get Picture

With your picture box created, and either the Item tool or the Content tool selected, you can select Get Picture from the File menu (or act like the pros, and press Command/Ctrl-E). A directory dialog box appears, allowing you to find the file you wish to import. When a file of a type that QuarkXPress recognizes is selected (see "File Types," above), the file's type and size are displayed. If you're importing a multi-page PDF file, XPress also lets you choose which page you want.

You also have the option to turn on the Picture Preview checkbox, which lets you see a thumbnail view of most image files. This feature is, of course, a great help in finding a particular picture when you're not sure of the file's name. However, it does slow down the process, especially for files with complicated images, such as large color PICT or TIFF files. Similarly, if you're accessing images over a network it gets really, really slow. Clearly, judicious use of Picture Preview can save you time.

Once the file is selected in the dialog box, click the Open button or just double-click on the file's name, and the image appears in your picture frame. Some images import more slowly than others; when an image takes a while to import, QuarkXPress shows you its progress in the lower-left corner of the window. If you're importing a 50 MB file on your old Mac IIsi, you can see how quickly (slowly) it is processing (perhaps this is the best time of the day to make an espresso).

▼ ▼

Tip: Grab That Pencil. You will undoubtedly find yourself in a situation at some point where you want to manually re-import a picture or import a new picture into an already used picture box. Problem: you lose the specifications for the original picture box (scaling, offset, rotation, and so on)! This is a case where you can use the most technologically advanced tools available to humankind, but all you really need is a simple notepad and a pencil. Just jot down all the specs for the previous picture (nice of QuarkXPress to show them to you in the Measurements palette), then after you bring in the new picture, retype the original specs (remember, if you want to make multiple changes to the picture box, it's usually quicker to make them all at once in the Modify dialog box).

In earlier versions of XPress, you could also use the free PictAttributes XTension from Markzware (see Appendix C, *XTensions and Resources*) to retain all your specs when you're importing an image into a previously formatted picture box. However, as this book goes to press, they have not yet updated it to work with XPress 6.

▼ ▼

Tip: Drag-and-Drop Pictures. QuarkXPress for Windows lets you drag pictures into picture boxes from the Windows desktop or Explorer, as long as the picture box is already made.

▼ ▼

What Happened to My Picture?

When you import a picture, you may not see exactly what you were expecting or wanting in the picture box. It may be that you see only a gray box with some type, or that the image is misplaced, or even that you can't see it at all. If something unexpected happens, remember the First Rule of Computer Anomaly: Don't Panic.

Can't see the picture at all. The first thing to check for is whether or not the big "X" is still in the picture box; if it is, then Get Picture didn't work. Maybe you accidentally clicked Cancel instead of OK. (Don't laugh; this often happens around the same time you get what my friend Greg calls "pixel vision"—eyes that are glazed from looking at the screen too long.) If this happens, just try again.

If what you see is just a blank frame, then check to see if the guides are hidden (select Show Guides from the View menu). If the guides are on and you still don't see the "X," then the picture is probably somewhere in the box but you can't see it yet. The Get Picture feature automatically places the image in the upper-left corner of the bounding box of the frame. Note that I say the "bounding box" and not the box itself. The bounding box is the smallest rectangle that completely surrounds the frame. It's what you see when you are looking at your box with the Edit Shape option turned off (see Figure 9-7). If you have an oval or a polygonal box and the image is rather small, then you may have to move the object into the frame (see "Moving Your Pictures Around," later in this chapter).

Often, if you center the image in the box you'll be able to see it better (see "Centering," in the next section).

Figure 9-7
Polygons have rectangular bounding boxes

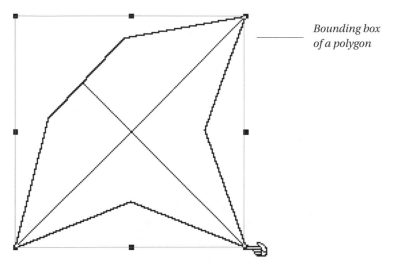

Bounding box of a polygon

There's no picture—just a gray box. If the image you import is an EPS file with no preview image attached for screen representation, then QuarkXPress represents the image as a gray box with the note "PostScript Picture" and the name of the file directly in the center of the gray box. This gray box shows the bounding box of the image, as defined in the header of the EPS document.

Another cause of the gray-box effect could be that you're looking at a complex picture from too far back. When you look at the page in Fit in Window view, it looks like a muddied gray box, but when you go to Actual Size, it looks like what you were hoping for.

The third cause of the gray-box effect might be that the picture you import is, in fact, a gray box. In this case, I can only suggest you think carefully about whether or not you really consider a gray box an exciting enough graphic for your publication.

Quality isn't very good. I'll discuss how XPress previews images on screen in "Preview Quality, Greeking, and Suppression," later in this chapter

Working with Pictures

Now that you have brought something (which may or may not look like the graphic you wanted) into the picture box, you can manipulate it in more ways than you ever thought you could, and certainly in more ways than you could in any other page-layout program.

Moving Your Picture Around

In Chapter 2, *QuarkXPress Basics*, you learned about moving your picture and text boxes around on the page. You can also move the picture itself around within the picture box. You may want to do this for two reasons: for picture placement, and for cropping out a portion of the image. In this section I discuss several methods for moving your image within (or even outside of) the box. Remember that the picture and the picture box are two different entities, and you can move and manipulate them using different tools: the content (picture) with the Content tool, and the box itself with the Item tool.

Centering. Often the first thing you'll want to do with a picture, whether or not you can see it on screen, is to center it within the picture box. Designers and computer hackers alike have muddled through various tricks to center graphics perfectly within boxes, with varying degrees of success. I suggest you just press Command-Shift-M (Ctrl-Shift-M) and let QuarkXPress do it for you. QuarkXPress centers the picture based on its bounding box (its lower-left and upper-right corners). Therefore, pictures which are oddly shaped (for example, an L-shaped picture) may not be centered as you'd expect them to be. If you forget the keyboard shortcut, don't fret: You can always select Center Picture from the Style menu.

Moving the picture. If you want the image to be somewhere other than in the upper-left corner or in the center, you can use the Content tool (which switches to a Grabber hand when it's placed over the picture box) to move the picture around. Anyone who has ever done this can tell you that if the image is a large one, it can take quite some time for the picture to respond to your hand movements. If you're thinking about zooming in for precision alignment, remember to turn on Full Resolution from the Preview Resolution submenu (under the Item menu; see "Preview Quality, Greeking, and Suppression," later in this chapter).

If you know how far you want to move the picture, you can type the offset values in either the Measurements palette or in the Modify dialog box (press Command/Ctrl-M, or Command/Ctrl-double-click on the picture). This method is a real godsend when precision is the key, but you can't always trust what you see on the screen. For instance, an EPS image might look like it's at the edge of the picture box, but in reality that could just be an artifact of its screen preview.

▼ ▼

Tip: Minimoves. When you have the Content tool selected and have selected a picture box, you can "nudge" the picture within the box in tiny increments by clicking the arrows on the Measurements palette. Each click moves the image 1 point in the direction of the arrow. Hold down Option/Alt while you click to move the picture in .1-point increments.

However, I typically find it even more useful to use the arrow keys on the keyboard. Again, each time you press a key, the picture moves 1 point; each time you press the key with Option/Alt held down, the picture moves .1 point.

Note that if you have the Item tool selected when you do this, you actually move the picture box itself.

▼ ▼

Cropping

If you only want a portion of the whole picture to be visible, then you can "cut out" the unwanted areas by cropping or clipping. Cropping is the way you change the size or shape of the picture box (see Figure 9-8); clipping is how you apply a clipping path (I discuss XPress's Clipping feature in Chapter 10, *Fine-Tuning Images*). Behind the scenes, both cropping and clipping are the same thing, but because XPress treats them separately, I will too.

A warning about cropping: there are people who crop out 90 percent of an image so they can use just one flower in a bouquet! Then they duplicate that image 12 times on the page and wonder why their file doesn't print. (Don't laugh too loudly; I've seen high-paid professionals do this!)

Fortunately, when you use TIFF and JPEG images, XPress is smart enough to send only the data it needs at print time, so the cropped-out information doesn't clog up your network and your printing times are faster. QuarkXPress cannot do this with EPS or PDF images, so the whole file must be sent at print

Figure 9-8
The edge of the picture
box crops the picture

Picture box

Cropped area

time, along with an instruction to the printer about what gets cropped and what doesn't.

No matter what file format you use, the program must save a preview image (the screen representation) for the entire graphic with the document, no matter how much you crop it. This way, you can always go back and change your cropping or picture specifications.

So remember to use cropping judiciously. If you only want a small portion of the file, then use an editing program to cut out what you don't want before you import the image.

▼ ▼

Tip: Shapely Cropping. You don't have to restrict your cropping to rectangular boxes, of course. Feel free to use the Shapes submenu (under the Item menu) to change the shape of the picture box in order to crop out unwanted parts of your picture.

▼ ▼

Tip: Cropping Multiple Pictures. As I mentioned back in Chapter 2, *QuarkXPress Basics*, you can crop several picture boxes at the same time by grouping them and either dragging the group's corner or side handles, or specifying a value in the Measurements palette. Either way, you must have the Item tool selected. For instance, if you know that you want every box to be half as wide as it is currently, you can select the boxes, group them, and then type "*.5" after the current width value in the Measurements palette.

▼ ▼

Tip: Fit Box to Picture. One of the most-requested features in early versions of QuarkXPress was the ability to fit the picture box to the size of the picture. I'm happy to report that this feature finally showed up in version 5, and lives in two places: You can select it from the Style menu or from the context-sensitive menu (Control-click or right-mouse-button click on the picture box).

▼ ▼

Resizing Your Picture

After placing the graphic image where you want it, you may want to scale it to some desired size. QuarkXPress allows you to resize the image within the picture box in the horizontal and/or vertical directions. Most often I find myself wanting to enlarge or reduce the picture the same amount in both directions in order to best fit the available space.

Keystrokes and menus. If the picture box you create is just the size you want your picture to be, you can quickly and automatically resize the picture to fit the box by selecting Fit Picture to Box from the Style menu (or press Command-Shift-F or Ctrl-Shift-F). However, because this usually stretches the picture disproportionately (adjusting the horizontal- and vertical-sizing measures differently in order to fill the box), you probably want to select Fit Picture to Box Proportionally (or press Command-Shift-Option-F or Ctrl-Shift-Alt-F— that's a handful!), which makes the picture as large as it can be within the box without distorting it. Note that if you've rotated or skewed the picture first (see "Rotating, Skewing, and Distorting" below), auto-resizing may not work exactly as you'd expect it to.

If you're not a keystroke kind of person, you can type the particular percentages you want into the Measurements palette or into the picture box's Modify dialog box (Command/Ctrl-M). Of course, you can use a combination of these two methods, too.

Dragging. Usually resizing the picture box has no effect on the image which is in it, other than possibly cropping out areas of the picture. However, if you hold down the Command key while you resize (clicking and dragging on one of the control handles), the image changes size along with the box (see Figure 9-9). As usual, holding down the Shift key constrains the picture box (and the image) to a square or circle; holding down the Option/Alt key along with the Command/Ctrl and Shift keys constrains the picture box (and the image) to their proper proportions.

▼ ▼

Tip: Watch 'Em Change. Back in Chapter 2, *QuarkXPress Basics*, I told you about how to watch the changes as you make them (see "Tip: Viewing Changes as You Make Them"). In case you don't remember, the important thing is to hold down the mouse button for about half a second (until you see the cursor change to the flashy Live Refresh cursor). Then when you scale or crop the

Figure 9-9
Resizing a picture
by dragging the picture
box handles

Original object   Scaled with a
                         Command-click and drag

image by dragging, you can actually see the image get scaled or cropped (otherwise, QuarkXPress just shows you a gray outline box).

▼ ▼

Tip: Scaling Groups of Objects. People have been clamoring to scale groups of objects for years, and now you can (sort of). To scale several objects at the same time, group them (Command/Ctrl-G) and then Command-Option-Shift-drag (Ctrl-Alt-Shift-drag) on one of the group's control handles. If you know exactly how large you want the group of objects, you can type those values into the Measurements palette instead of dragging the handles. If you want to scale the group by a specific percentage, use math in the height and width fields of the palette. For instance, if you want the height and width to both be 40 percent as large, type "*.4" after the values in both the H: and W: fields of the Measurements palette.

Personally, I'm still not that impressed with this scaling functionality, and until the folks at Quark get their act in gear and implement a real scaling tool, I can only suggest one of the inexpensive third-party scaling XTensions like those in Gluon's ProScale or alap's XPert Tools.

▼ ▼

Rotating, Skewing, and Distorting

Sure, you can crop and resize, but—as they say on television—that's not all! With this amazing program you get a set of free Japanese cutlery! And 32 ounces of French perfume! And . . . well, maybe not, but you do get to rotate and skew pictures, and that's not bad.

Rotation. QuarkXPress lets you easily rotate your imported pictures to a degree unheard of (and certainly rarely needed): $1/1{,}000$ of a degree. Once again, you are able to set the rotation of the image in several ways.

The first question you'll want to ask yourself is whether you want to rotate the frame, and the image along with it, or just rotate the image itself. You can do either of these things by typing the rotation angle in the appropriate place on the Measurements palette or in the Modify dialog box (see Figure 9-10).

While it's really great that you can rotate images in QuarkXPress, you should be careful with this power. When you use XPress to rotate large bitmapped images, your files can slow to a crawl when they print. Instead, try to rotate these images in Photoshop (or another image-manipulation program) first, and then import them (prerotated) into your picture boxes. This typically isn't a problem with illustrations from FreeHand or Illustrator, because they aren't usually bitmapped.

▼ ▼

Tip: Rotating Your Picture Boxes. Rotating the frame rotates the image, too! The quickest way to "straighten out" your image is to rotate it back by the same amount. That is, if you rotate your box 28 degrees but you want the picture to be straight, then rotate the image -28 degrees.

▼ ▼

Figure 9-10
The Modify dialog box and the Measurements palette

Skewing. Technically, skewing is the process of rotating the two axes differently, or rotating one and not the other. That is, if you rotate just the y-axis (the vertical axis) of the coordinate system to the right, everything you print out is "obliqued" (see Figure 9-11). QuarkXPress only allows you to skew in the horizontal direction (rotating the y-axis), which is not a hindrance since vertical skewing (or "shearing," as it is often called) is rarely required. Actually, horizontal skewing is rarely required, either, but it can be useful in certain situations, especially when you want to create interesting effects.

You usually use only one of these effects at a time, perhaps in conjunction with scaling (resizing), but using all three together can make a graphic look quite unusual (see Figure 9-12).

One of the great advantages of these features is that they're not incremental. In FreeHand and Illustrator, rotation is cumulative. If you rotate something to 60 degrees and later want to rotate it to 55 degrees, you have to enter "-5 degrees." QuarkXPress, on the other hand, keeps track of the current rotation, so you just enter the actual rotation you want. This makes it incredibly easy to get back to where you started with an image when you've distorted it beyond

Figure 9-11
Skewing rotates
the vertical axis

Normal object   *Skewed object*

Figure 9-12
Using all of the tools

Actual size

Scale across: 60%
Scale down: 100%

Across: 60%
Down: 90%
Rotate -30 degrees

Scale across: 224%
Scale down: 48%

Scale across and scale down: 60%
Rotate: -20 degrees, Skew: -50 degrees

recognition: just reset the scaling to 100 percent, and the rotation and skewing to zero degrees (if you really want to reset everything about a picture, try re-importing it).

▼ ▼

Tip: Faking Perspective. To make a picture look like it's lying on a flat surface, change the picture rotation to -15 degrees, the picture skew to 45 degrees, and the vertical scaling to 70 percent (see Figure 9-13).

Figure 9-13
Pseudo-perspective

▼ ▼

Tip: Making Multiple Changes to Your Picture. If you know you are going to make multiple changes to your graphic image—changing the skewing, rotation, scaling, and offset, for example—you can speed up your formatting by making those changes in the Modify dialog box (Command/Ctrl-M, or double-click on the object while you hold down the Command key) so that QuarkXPress processes all your changes at once rather than one at a time.

▼ ▼

Tip: Preformatting Picture Boxes. You can select an empty picture box and apply formatting to the picture that you're *going* to import into it. Select an empty picture box and change the picture attributes, such as rotation, skew, offset, and scaling, in the Measurements palette (or the Picture Specifications dialog box; Command/Ctrl-M or Command/Ctrl-double-click on the box). Then, when you import a picture into that box, XPress automatically applies those settings to it.

Why should you care? Well, if you need to apply the same attributes to a number of different images, you can create one picture box, apply the desired settings, then duplicate the picture box as many times as you have pictures (or store it away in a library for future use). Now, each time you import one of those pictures, it has the formatting you wanted already applied to it.

▼ ▼

Tip: Retaining Picture Box Specs. Here's a little knowledge that you should store in the back of your brain; it'll come in useful some day. When you cut or copy a picture out of a picture box, the specifications that the picture box had been set to (skew, scaling, offset, and so on), are "saved" with the copied image. When you paste the picture into another picture box, these specifications are transferred, too (even the link information—where the high-resolution image is on disk—is retained).

Picture Management

Possibly the worst nightmare of a desktop publisher is arriving at the local service bureau to pick up 300 pages of film-negative output, only to see that every illustration has come out as a low-resolution bitmap. Throwing away a thousand dollars is one way to learn some basics of picture management. Reading this section is another.

To Represent

The verb "to represent" means "to stand in place for" or "to act as a place-holder." It's important to note that QuarkXPress represents high-resolution images (including TIFF and EPS files) as low-resolution pictures on screen when you import them using Get Picture. When it's time to print, QuarkXPress searches for the original high-resolution images and uses them instead of the low-resolution images. It looks first in the folder where the document was originally imported from, then in the same folder as the document you're printing, and then, strangely enough, in the Macintosh System Folder. If QuarkXPress is successful in this search, your output will look beautiful. If it cannot find the original, it uses the bitmapped 36- or 72-dpi representation for printing. In this case, your output will look ugly.

Here are a few things to keep in mind about pictures.

▶ Don't trash your picture file after you import it, assuming that it's placed for all time.

▶ Don't move the picture file into another folder after you import it.

▶ Don't rename your picture files after you import them.

▶ Do be sure you know where your picture files are.

▶ Do keep your picture files together if possible, to avoid confusion if you need to move your document someplace (like to a service bureau).

▶ If you send your document to a service bureau (or anywhere else, for that matter), put the document and all the image files you imported using Get Picture together in the same folder. You may want to visually segregate the document from its pictures, but keep them in the same folder (see Figure 9-14, and also "Collect for Output" in the "Working with an Imaging Center" section of Chapter 13, *Printing*).

▼ ▼

Tip: Huge Files When Importing Graphics. It was kind and generous of Quark to offer us the ability to import images at higher bit depths (in the Display tab of the Preferences dialog box), but I urge you—plead with you: if you don't *need* to, then don't go above eight-bit color. The problem is that your document's size on disk balloons when you raise the color bit value (changing the Gray TIFFs value from 16 levels of gray to 256 levels of gray is fine, though). For instance, a document with 40 images in it may be 4 MB large when Color TIFF is set to 8-bit color, and 29 MB when it's set to 32-bit color. While there isn't anything inherently bad about larger file sizes, I tend to like to keep files as small as possible.

Of course, if you're building a Web layout (see Chapter 14, *Going Online with QuarkXPress*), then the higher bit-depth in the Preferences dialog box is almost always better.

▼ ▼

Picture Usage

Submitted for your approval: You've just completed a 600-page layout with FreeHand illustrations on every page. The day before sending it to the image-setter, you realize that you have to make changes to 200 pictures. Tearing your hair out in clumps, you stay up all night changing all the pictures and recreating new EPS documents to replace all the old ones. But now it's dawn, and you have to send it off or risk ruining the whole office's schedule. How will you re-import all those graphics in time? What about replacing and rotating and skewing them all to the correct positions? What will you do? What *will* you do?

Figure 9-14
Sending your disk to a
service bureau

Fortunately, QuarkXPress offers several features that help with picture management. I'm going to discuss the Usage dialog box first, and then I'll explore how XPress can update pictures automatically after you change them.

XPress keeps a running tally of all imported pictures in your layout, including when they were last modified. This information is on the Picture tab of the Usage dialog box (select Usage from the Utilities menu, or press Option-F13 on the Macintosh or Shift-F2 on Windows). The Picture Usage dialog box lists several important pieces of information about each image in the layout (see Figure 9-15).

▶ Where the image was originally imported from (its hierarchical disk path, starting from the disk name and moving folder-to-folder down to the file).

▶ The page number of the layout where the picture is located. A dagger (†) appearing next to the page number in the Picture Usage dialog box signifies that the picture is on the pasteboard, as opposed to on the page itself.

▶ The status of the picture: OK, Modified, Missing, or Wrong Type. Note that the more pictures you have in your layout, the longer it takes for XPress to check the status of each one (that's why it sometimes takes a while for the Usage dialog box to open).

▶ A column where you can tell XPress whether or not to print the image.

I'll cover picture suppression later in this chapter. Here's a quick rundown on the meaning of the various status messages.

OK. This is what you always hope for, especially before printing. QuarkXPress looks for the picture file first in the same place as the file was imported from, then in the same folder as the document, and finally in the System Folder (on the Macintosh). If it finds the picture file in any of these places, the Status column displays "OK."

Modified. If QuarkXPress finds the file but it's been changed in any way since you imported it (the modification date has changed), you see "Modified" in the Status column. You have two options at this point.

▶ IGNORE THE "PROBLEM." Remember that because QuarkXPress uses the external file for printing, the document prints with the updated version rather than with the original. However, if you've changed the image's resolution or proportions, you shouldn't ignore the Modified warning; the results are unpredictable.

Figure 9-15

Picture Usage dialog box

▶ **UPDATE THE IMAGE.** All this really means is that you get a new representation image in your layout. This approach may help you avoid the annoying dialog box "Some pictures have been modified or missing" at print time. To update the file, select its name from the Usage list and click the Update button. Note that if you've changed much about the image, you should make sure that all the rotation, scaling, and cropping attributes you've applied to it are still relevant.

▼ ▼

Tip: Update Multiple Images. More than one image in the Picture Usage dialog box needs to be updated? You can Shift- or Command/Ctrl-click to select more than one image in the Usage dialog box (Shift for images next to each other, and Command for discontinous images). However, if you press the Update button, XPress will ask you if you're *sure* you want to update each image. Instead, hold down the Option/Alt key while pressing Update, and the program updates them without asking you repeatedly.

▼ ▼

Tip: Synchronize Your Clocks. Many people have grumbled that the Usage dialog box mysteriously reports their images as Modified when they haven't even touched them. The problem almost always involves images that are stored on a network server where the clock settings for your computer and the server's are different. For instance, let's say you move a picture that you've used in a layout from your hard drive to a server. Then, daylight savings time comes, and the server administrator changes the clock on the server. All of a sudden, the image appears as modified.

This doesn't happen on all servers; typically only those that are able to change a file's "last modified" date (this might even happen when the security settings change on the server). The solution: just synchronize the clocks.

▼ ▼

Tip: Update Modified Images Fast. Need to update all the images in your project fast? No problem: Just hold down the Command/Ctrl key when you press the OK button in the Open dialog box. When the project opens, all the images should be updated.

▼ ▼

Missing. If QuarkXPress cannot find a file with the name it is expecting, it tells you that the file is missing. Again, you have two options.

▶ IGNORE IT. This method is appropriate if you are trying to get some wild artsy effect using low-resolution printing, but is inappropriate for anyone trying to get a normal, good-looking, high-resolution print. Remember that if the image is missing, QuarkXPress can only print what you see on the screen: a low-resolution representation.

▶ UPDATE THE IMAGE. If you have just moved the picture to another folder or renamed it, you can update the link by selecting the file and clicking Update. Here, you're both relinking the missing picture to the layout and bringing in a new representation. The picture preview used in Get Picture is also included in the Missing Picture dialog box.

The Usage dialog box is also valuable when you want to jump to a particular image, if you aren't sure where it is. For example, if you have many figures on many pages, and you want to go to the page which contains "Figure 28b," you can select that item on the Picture tab of the Usage dialog box and click the Show button. XPress jumps to the right page and highlights the picture box that contains the figure. This also works for graphics which have been anchored to text and have flowed to unknown places.

Wrong Type. Every now and again someone calls, complaining that their Picture Usage dialog box is listing the status of a picture as Wrong Type (usually it just says OK, Modified, or Missing). This cryptic message usually means that the file has been saved in a different format since it was originally imported into XPress. For instance, if you import a TIFF image into XPress, and then go back to Photoshop and save it as an EPS image with the same file name, you'll get this message.

The remedy is simple: click Update in the Picture Usage dialog box just as though the status read Modified.

More Information. The Pictures tab of the Usage dialog box also contains a checkbox labeled "More Information." I turn this option on and leave it on (I can't imagine why I wouldn't want more information about my pictures).

▼ ▼

Tip: Finding Picture Paths. If you're trying to find where a picture is on disk—you can select the picture on the page and open the Usage dialog box. That picture is highlighted on the list, so if you have a whole mess o' pictures in your layout, you don't have to go scrolling through the list to find the one you want (this also works if you have multiple picture boxes selected).

While the disk path name is displayed on the left side of the dialog box, if the picture is more than one or two folders deep, XPress will simply replace folder names with an ellipsis (. . .). Fortunately, if you turn on the More Information option in this dialog box, you can see the entire file path.

▼ ▼

Tip: Relinking with a New Picture. When you update an image in the Picture Usage dialog box, you don't have to relink with the same picture. You can relink with any other picture, and that image comes in using the same picture specifications as the original (scaling, skewing, and so on). Of course, like many other power tips in this book, this technique can really screw up your image if you don't pay attention. For example, as of this writing, the settings on the Clipping tab of the Modify dialog box don't change when you import the new image, which can cause all sorts of problems if you don't go back to this tab and reset the values.

▼ ▼

Tip: Finding a Bunch of Missing Files. If you move image files or rename the folders they reside in (or even rename the disk they're on), you can wind up with all your pictures missing. There are two easy ways to relink images.

The first method is the coarser solution, and only works if all your image files are in one folder. Move your QuarkXPress document inside that folder and open it. QuarkXPress looks for missing pictures first inside the folder where the document is located; it automatically relinks them. Save the document, and then move it wherever you like—the images stay linked.

The second method is more subtle, and works if you have clumps of missing files in one or more folders. When you find one missing file inside a folder, QuarkXPress "sees" the other missing files and prompts you to say whether or not you want to relink them all in one fell swoop (see Figure 9-16). You can then repeat this trick for other folders with missing images in them.

Figure 9-16
Updating missing files

Additional missing pictures are located in this folder.
OK to update these as well?

Cancel   OK

▼ ▼

Dynamically Updating Images

In the fast-paced production environment of most magazines, newspapers, and ad agencies (plus your business, of course), any technique to streamline the workflow is appreciated. If you work with a lot of images that are subject to change, you can use the Picture Usage dialog box to manually update images, or you can use QuarkXPress's built-in ability to dynamically update the graphics in your documents. Dynamic updating is not for everyone, but for some people it's a lifesaver.

In this section I'm going to discuss three methods you can use to keep pictures updated: Auto Picture Import, the Edit Original XTension, and Object Linking and Embedding (OLE).

Auto Picture Import

If you don't want to be bothered by checking Picture Usage all the time, you can use QuarkXPress's internal checking tool: Auto Picture Import. When you have Auto Picture Import turned on in the General panel of the Preferences dialog box, each time you open that project QuarkXPress checks to see if any of the linked pictures have been modified. If they have been, XPress brings in the new copy transparently and seamlessly. You won't even know that anything has changed.

Clearly, sometimes not knowing what QuarkXPress is doing behind the scenes is disconcerting or frustrating. There's another option here, which is to set your layout preference to "On (Verify)." When you select this option, QuarkXPress checks for modified or missing files when you open the document, and if it finds any, it asks you whether you want to re-import them. As with all QuarkXPress features, there is no one "right" way to set up your documents; in some situations you want verifiable auto-importing, and in some you want none at all. (Though to be honest, I'm more comfortable with the "On (Verify)" option; I like to keep a close eye on what images are changing in my document.)

▼ ▼

Tip: Update All Pictures. When Auto Picture Import is set to "On (Verify)," XPress can tell you that one or more pictures in your document have been changed. If you press OK in this warning dialog box, XPress opens the Usage dialog box, displaying only pictures that XPress thinks have been altered. Many people resign themselves to updating one picture at a time in this dialog box, but you shouldn't. You can select all the pictures on the list by clicking on the first one and then Shift-clicking on the last one. Or you can select discontiguous items on the list with the Command/Ctrl key. After you've selected the pictures you want to re-import, hold down the Option/Alt key and click the Update button, and XPress updated them all. (If you don't hold down the Option/Alt key, XPress asks you if you're *sure* you want to update them, one at a time.)

▼ ▼

Edit Original

Wouldn't it be nice if you could just double-click on a picture to update it? QuarkXPress 3, 4, and 5 were able to do this using the Publish and Subscribe features in the Macintosh operating system. However, Mac OS X doesn't have a Publish and Subscribe feature, so Quark was forced to write their own. The result is the free Edit Original XTension (you can download it from Quark's Web site). When this XTension is loaded, you can double-click on any image with the Content tool to open the Edit Original dialog box, which offers two options: Update and Edit Original (see Figure 9-17).

Figure 9-17

The Edit Original dialog box (Macintosh only)

▶ **UPDATE.** The Update button acts just like the Update button in the Usage dialog box: It automatically reimports and updates any modified file. However, I find it much faster to press Update here than to go through the rigmarole of the Usage dialog box (especially if there are a lot of pictures in my document, because the Usage dialog box takes so long to open).

▶ **EDIT ORIGINAL.** When you click the Edit Original button, QuarkXPress automatically launches the application that created the picture, and loads the picture file for you. Actually, technically, it opens the file with whatever application the Macintosh Finder thinks it should use, based on the Opens With item in the Finder's Get Info dialog box. The Edit Original feature is excellent when you have no idea where the original picture is located on your disk and you just can't be bothered to look for it in order to make a change.

There is some talk about Quark releasing this XTension for Windows users, too, but it was Macintosh-only as this book went to press. Also, note that this feature doesn't work if it can't find the original image on disk (images listed as "Missing" in the Usage dialog box).

Object Linking and Embedding (OLE)

Object Linking and Embedding, known commonly by its acronym OLE (pronounced *olé*, like the cheer people use at bullfights and those out-of-control tapas bars), is a glue with which you can seamlessly bind together various programs in Microsoft Windows. Anyway, that's the theory. Like Publish and Subscribe on the Macintosh, it's a function of the operating system rather than of XPress itself. However, it's typically not very useful in XPress.

Unlike the Publish and Subscribe features that could be used with any kind of picture in XPress, the OLE features don't work with anything but OLE objects and links, so I just ignore them.

▼ ▼

Tip: A Reason to Use OLE. One reader, Benji Smith, pointed out a workflow that makes OLE useful: If you use OLE's Copy Special, Paste Special, and Insert Object features (from the Edit menu), then plan on sending an Acrobat PDF file to your service bureau or printer rather than the XPress file itself. By making a PDF file, you no longer have to worry about whether or not the page is going to print properly.

▼ ▼

Preview Quality, Greeking, and Suppression

There are times when I'd really rather not see all those pictures. Maybe the screen redraw or printing time is taking too long. Or maybe I want to use the picture for placement only in the electronic document and don't want it to print out. Or maybe I just hate the pictures. Other times I like the pictures so much that I want to see them clearly, at their full resolution. Whatever the case, QuarkXPress has solutions: picture greeking, picture suppression, and high-resolution previews.

Picture Greeking

Back in Chapter 6, *Type and Typography*, I discussed replacing text with gray bars. I called that "greeking the text." Now with Greek Pictures, you can basically replace anything with a gray box. The primary benefit of doing this is to speed up screen redraw: it takes much longer to redraw a detailed picture than it does to just drop in a gray box where the picture should be. Another benefit is in designing your pages. Sometimes having greeked pictures allows you to see the page layout, including its balance and overall tone, better than if you are looking at the real thing.

To greek the pictures in your documents, check the Greek Pictures option in the Preferences dialog box. Note that when this box is checked, all picture boxes—except for empty and selected ones—are greeked. Selecting a picture box with either the Item tool or the Content tool ungreeks the picture while it's selected.

Suppress Printout

In the instances when you want the picture on the screen but not on your printouts, you can turn on Suppress Picture Printout in the Modify dialog box (press Command/Ctrl-M, double-click on the image using the Item tool, or select Modify from the Item menu). You can also select Suppress Printout, which suppresses both the picture content and the frame itself. Even easier yet, you can turn off the checkmark on the Pictures tab of the Usage dialog box. This is equivalent to turning on the Suppress Picture Printout option in the Modify dialog box.

Here's another option for suppressing images in your output: Set the Output popup menu to Rought in the Options tab of the Print dialog box (see Chapter 13, *Printing,* for more on the Output tab).

▼ ▼

Tip: Suppress Multiple Images. You can turn on (or off) the Suppress Picture Printout option for a bunch of pictures all at the same time in the Usage dialog box. Just select the pictures you want to change (holding down the Command key lets you choose discontiguous items from the list; holding down the Shift key lets you choose contiguous items), and select Yes or No from the popup menu at the top of the Print column (see Figure 9-18).

Figure 9-18
Suppress Printout for
multiple pictures

Full Resolution Preview

QuarkXPress users complained for years about the low-quality screen previews of images—whether EPS, PDF, DCS, TIFF, or JPEG—XPress displayed. Koyosha Graphics (KGA) created an XTension to help the problem, called Enhance Preview XT, and Quark even gave away a limited version of it for free. But in version 6, Quark has gone one further and built-in a feature which lets you see high-resolution versions of your images on screen.

Quark is currently using this feature to entice you into registering your copy of the program after installing it; you only obtain the two necessary XTensions after the registration process. The two XTensions—Full Res Preview and EPS Preview—place a Preview Resolution submenu in the Item menu and in the context menu (which you get by Control-clicking on the image on the Mac, or right-button clicking in Windows). The EPS Preview XTension ties into the Jaws PostScript interpreter software that Quark licensed from Global Graphics, letting you have high-quality previews of vector-based EPS and PDF files (see Figure 9-19).

Figure 9-19
Full Resolution preview provides a much better screen image, but it's slower

Low Res Preview   *High Res Preview*

To turn on the feature, select one or more images on your page and choose Full Resolution from the Preview Resolution submenu. The larger or more complex the image is, or the slower your computer, the longer it takes for XPress to display the high-quality version. To return the preview to its normal mediocre state, select Low Resolution from the Preview Resolution submenu.

There is unfortunately no way to turn Full Resolution on for all the images in your document at once. However, you might not want to anyway because when images are set to Full Resolution, it takes much longer to navigate around your document, zoom in and out, and so on.

However, after you turn on the Full Resolution setting for the images you want, you can hide all the high-quality previews at once by selecting Hide Full Res Previews from the View menu. (Select it again to show them all once more.) I suggest leaving images set to Low Resolution except for the few ones that you really need to see the image clearly, and even then doing most of your work with Hide Full Res Previews turned on (so XPress responds faster).

By the way, it's important to note that if you change Color TIFF from 32-bit to 8-bit in the Display panel of the Preferences dialog box (see "Tip: Huge Files When Importing Graphics," earlier in this chapter), the images that you import will only display using eight bits per channel (only 256 colors per image) rather than full "millions of colors." If you turn on the Full Resolution setting for an 8-bit image, you get the full resolution, but the bit depth is still poor. I hope that this is a bug in the program that will be fixed someday, as Full Resolution really should mean "make it look great!"

▼ ▼

Page as Picture

A few years ago, I worked on a book that required taking illustrations created in QuarkXPress and bringing them into PageMaker (horrors!). This is not an uncommon thing, of course; there are many times when you'd like to move text or graphics from XPress into other applications, or even bring a page of a QuarkXPress layout into another XPress document as a picture. QuarkXPress allows you to take care of these situations with the Save Page as EPS feature.

Selecting Save Page as EPS from the File menu (or pressing Command-Option-Shift-S or Ctrl-Alt-Shift-S) brings up a dialog box in which you can select a page of your layout and save it as a separate EPS file (see Figure 9-20). There are loads of ways to tweak this EPS image.

Page and Spread

The first two relevant items in the Save Page as EPS dialog box (besides where to save the file) are the Page field and the Spread checkbox. EPS files from XPress are only one page long; the Page field in this dialog box lets you specify which page in your layout you want to encapsulate. If you turn on the Spread option, XPress creates an EPS of whatever page spread includes the page you've specified. Note that Spread works with both facing-pages and single-sided documents; a spread is defined as any two (or more) pages sitting next to each other.

Scale

When you adjust the scaling of the page (for example, making the page 25 percent of full size), the page size is displayed in the dialog box so that you know how large the final bounding box of the EPS image is. You can adjust this by changing the scaling. Remember: because this is PostScript, you can scale your EPS page down to 10 percent, bring it into another program, scale it back up to original size, and you won't lose any quality in your output (though your screen preview image may look awful). Figure 9-21 shows a QuarkXPress spread that was saved and brought back into another QuarkXPress layout.

XPress lets you scale your page down to 10 percent of its original size, and it warns you if you try to enlarge it beyond 100 percent.

Bleed

If your page has items that bleed off the sides, don't expect the bleed to automatically appear in the EPS files. When you save a page as EPS, XPress cuts off the edges of the EPS at the edge of the page (the objects still jut out, but PostScript's clip command doesn't let the printer image them). Fortunately,

Figure 9-20
Save Page as EPS

Figure 9-21
QuarkXPress page
as EPS document

QuarkXPress lets you specify a Bleed value in the Save as EPS dialog box (you have to switch to the Bleed tab, and then choose either symmetric or asymmetric bleed first). If you set the Bleed value to .5 inch, XPress makes the EPS document wider and taller by an inch (half an inch on each side). Any page objects that sit within half an inch of the page get incorporated into the EPS, whether they're touching the page or not.

Unfortunately, this Bleed value doesn't help you if you're trying to prepare EPS files for processing with another prepress program, such as ScenicSoft's Preps or TrapWise. If you need to do this, you probably need the ScenicSoft Prepress XTension (known as PXT, which was once called LPX or APX), which you can get free from ScenicSoft (see Appendix C, *Resources and XTensions*).

Format

When you save a page as EPS, the dialog box gives you the option of saving the file in one of four different formats: Color, B&W (black and white), DCS, or DCS 2.0. In earlier versions of XPress, each of these was prefixed with either "Macintosh" or "PC," so there were eight options; now the Mac-versus-PC options have found their way into another popup menu—Preview (see "Preview," below).

Color versus B&W. If you choose Color or B&W, you get a normal EPS file. As it turns out, choosing between Color and B&W doesn't affect just the screen preview image. The choice also affects the way that QuarkXPress writes the PostScript code. If you choose the B&W option, color items are actually changed into black-and-white items (even gray values are dithered to black-and-white pixels).

DCS. Choosing DCS causes QuarkXPress to save five files to your disk: one master file that contains a preview image, and four files (one file per process color) that contain the actual image data (see "DCS," earlier in this chapter).

If the Quark Color Management System is turned on (see Appendix A, *Color Management*), you can set the target profiles for both the composite CMYK data and the high-resolution separation data. (Note that color management only works for DCS and DCS 2.0 images.) Whether or not the color management system is on, XPress converts RGB data into CMYK (the program just does a better job when the system is on).

Note that because the DCS file format only handles the four process colors, any spot colors you assign get separated into process colors and placed on the CMYK plates.

DCS 2.0. As I said earlier, DCS 2.0 handles cyan, magenta, yellow, black, and as many spot colors as you want. The cool part about this is that all your spot colors get put on their own plates. And as I also noted earlier, selecting DCS 2.0 results in only one file on your hard drive, rather than five or more.

Transparent Page

The folks at Quark made a change between version 3 and 4 in how XPress writes its EPS files: In version 3, XPress treated the white background of the page as atransparent in the EPS file. In version 4, it drew a big white box in the background so EPS files were always opaque. In version 5 and 6 they decided to offer users a choice with the Transparent Page checkbox. When you turn this on, XPress works like it did back in version 3. This is particularly helpful when you're going to open the EPS file in Photoshop, or composite it on top of some other image.

Space

XPress offers the choice of converting all your colors to RGB or CMYK in the Space popup menu of the Save as EPS dialog box. Generally, you'll want to leave this set to CMYK if you're going to be printing your EPS from some other program.

Preview

Earlier in this chapter, I mentioned that the primary difference between EPS files on the Macintosh and those on Windows had to do with the built-in screen preview. Macintosh EPS files typically have PICT previews; Windows

EPS files must use TIFF previews. When generating an EPS file from XPress, you have to choose one of these two preview formats from the Preview pop-up menu. If you're not sure which platform the EPS file will be used on, you should choose TIFF (it works on both).

Note that the Preview setting only affects the low-resolution screen representation of the image; once the image is imported into another program, the preview isn't really important. For instance, let's say you save an EPS file with a PICT preview, and then import that EPS file into a different XPress document on the Macintosh. You can move both the EPS file and the new XPress document to a Windows machine with no trouble. However, if you need to update or re-import the EPS file on the Windows side, you'll end up with just a gray box.

You have a third choice, too: you can choose None from the Preview pop-up menu. Probably the only time you'd use this is when you're using the EPS file as an intermediary format and are planning on immediately processing the EPS in some other program. For instance, you can save an EPS file from QuarkXPress and open it in Adobe Photoshop; Photoshop 4 (and later versions) generally rasterize the EPS data and ignore the preview, so there's no need to take up extra time and disk space by asking XPress to build a preview for you.

Data and OPI

There are two last features in the Save Page as EPS dialog box: the Data pop-up menu and the OPI tab. Both of these functions affect only bitmapped image data in TIFF and EPS file formats, so you can ignore them if you're not using one of the two.

Data. The first choice is whether to include TIFF images in ASCII or Binary format. What's the difference? Bitmapped images saved in Binary format are half the size of those saved in ASCII, so they print much more quickly. So why use ASCII? Some networks and print spoolers choke on binary image data, so people have had to use ASCII on these systems. Fortunately, QuarkXPress gives you a third choice: Clean 8-bit. This format is about as small as the Binary option, but usually prints more reliably on PC-based networks that can't handle the regular binary data. I recommend trying Binary first, and if you have trouble printing, switch to Clean 8-bit. (On the other hand, if you're creating EPS files but you don't know who's going to use or print them, you might opt for Clean 8-bit right off the bat.)

OPI. When you have the OPI XTension loaded, XPress displays the OPI tab in the Save as EPS dialog box. The OPI method is based on postseparating full-color pages that include color bitmapped images—especially scanned images. For example, you can import a low-resolution RGB TIFF file into a QuarkXPress layout, save that page as EPS, and separate it on your imagesetter using a program like Creo's Preps. Instead of Quark including the whole TIFF image in the PostScript file, it just throws in OPI comments that say what the name of the scanned image file is, and where the separation program can find it.

This is nice for a couple of reasons. First and foremost is file size. An EPS file with the image data included can be enormous. Sometimes it's nicer to leave the image data on disk somewhere else and just manipulate a minimal EPS file (one that just includes OPI comments about where to find the image data). Some workflows depend heavily on keeping the high-resolution data separate from the PostScript and EPS files using OPI.

The trick to building a PostScript file with OPI comments is the OPI tab in the Save Page as EPS and Print dialog boxes. The OPI Active checkbox simply determines whether XPress will include OPI comments in the PostScript; I just leave this turned on. You then have three choices: Include TIFF images, Low Resolution TIFF, and Include EPS images (see Figure 9-22). Leaving Include Images on is the way that XPress acts naturally: printing all the TIFF and EPS pictures (including the data in the EPS file). If you turn off either of the Include Images checkbox, XPress replaces the picture data with OPI comments. Note that this only applies to images for which OPI is turned on in the OPI tab of the Usage dialog box or for which the Use OPI option was on when you imported the file.

Apparently the OPI specs talk about OPI comments for EPS images as well as for TIFF images. At this time, however, no software pays any attention to those specs. So this selection (as far as I can tell) is useless for the time being.

Figure 9-22

Saving a page as an EPS with OPI comments

A Warning

A word of warning here about EPS files from QuarkXPress. Some people get overly optimistic about what's possible with PostScript. If you save a full-color QuarkXPress page as EPS, place it in Adobe Illustrator, save it, place that on a InDesign page, and then send it through some high-end program for final color separations—well, don't be shocked if it doesn't work.

Each of these programs was written by a different group of people and, consequently, handles color, type, and graphic elements differently. Even though, theoretically, the above process should work (PostScript is PostScript, right?), it might not. So be careful and prudent when you combine programs by nesting EPS files within EPS files; all this software isn't as integrated as it sometimes seems to be.

▼ ▼

Tip: Editing EPS Graphics. Exporting your file in EPS format doesn't mean you can never edit it again. Adobe Illustrator can open most EPS files, converting their elements back into editable objects again. After editing, you can save your file as EPS again. It's not a perfect solution, but it usually works pretty well if you don't have the original XPress document from which the EPS was created.

▼ ▼

Tip: Using EPS to Redimension a Job. Suppose you have a very complicated page layout in QuarkXPress, and your client suddenly decides on a slight change in page size that requires repositioning and resizing every element on the page. You could spend hours fixing the document, or do what an enterprising designer did in similar circumstances: save the page as EPS, import the EPS into a document with the new page size, and scale the EPS to fit. Slight changes to a page's proportions can sometimes be an acceptable tradeoff against getting a job done on time.

▼ ▼

Tip: Rasterizing EPS Files. Let's say you're creating a page that shows two year's worth of covers from your monthly magazine. That's 24 images. If the covers were created in XPress, you could save each one to disk as an EPS file, import the EPS on to your page, and then shrink it down to the right size. However, let's say each cover EPS was 20 MB large. That means you've got 480 MB of data on one page. Is that a good idea? I think not.

Instead, you could rasterize each EPS file in Photoshop. Remember that "rasterizing" is the act of converting vector art (like EPS files) into bitmap art (like most Photoshop files). You can rasterize almost any EPS file in Photoshop simply by opening it. Then you can downsample the file to the size and resolution you need. The result is a set of much smaller files which will be sure to print beautifully.

Image on the Half Shell

Now that your understanding of images has risen from the murky oceanic depths to the clear, naked light of day, it's time to take a step forward onto dry land, and—in the next chapter—fine-tune your images for brilliance on your page.

10

FINE-TUNING IMAGES

L et me be perfectly clear here: While QuarkXPress provides an astonishing array of controls over your page's text, the program is particularly poor at editing any images you may have imported. Nonetheless, XPress does contain a few image-editing features that you should know about, if only to keep yourself out of trouble.

In Chapter 9, *Pictures,* I discussed several graphic file formats, how to bring them into your QuarkXPress documents, and how to perform basic manipulations with them, such as rotating, skewing, and scaling. In this chapter, I look at how you can use QuarkXPress in place of other image-editing software to modify the imported image itself. Bear in mind that I'm not talking here about image *editing.* You can't actually change the content of imported graphics in QuarkXPress. You can, however, change some of their overall parameters such as contrast, color, clipping path, and halftone screen.

First, I'm going to examine the types of images you can modify, and then I discuss how to modify them. Much of this is potentially confusing, but bear with me, read carefully, and you'll be an inexorable image-modifier faster than you can say, "Ontogeny recapitulates phylogeny."

▼ ▼

The Picture File

In this chapter, I am concerned almost exclusively with bitmapped images. Bitmapped images, as far as QuarkXPress is concerned, are black and white, grayscale, or color, and are found in TIFF, JPEG, BMP, GIF, and bitmap-only PICT files. Bitmapped images can also be saved as EPS files, but because the image data is encapsulated, XPress won't let you change anything about them. Therefore, the only time I'll discuss EPS files here is when I explore clipping paths. The rest of the time, I'm just going to assume that you're using TIFF or JPEG files (see Chapter 9, *Pictures*, for why I don't like using the other bitmapped file formats).

Bitmapped Images

I want to take this opportunity to refresh your memory about bitmapped images and the TIFF and JPEG file types, which I discussed in Chapter 9, *Pictures*. Here are the highlights.

▶ Bitmapped images are simply rectangular grids of sample points (also called pixels or dots).

▶ The resolution of the image is the number of these sample points, specified in pixels per inch (ppi).

▶ Each sample point can be black, white, a level of gray, or a color. This color is represented by a number; for example, in a file with 256 gray levels, black would be zero and white would be 255.

▶ Scaling the image has a direct effect on its resolution. Enlarging the picture to 200 percent cuts the resolution in half (same number of samples in twice the space), which may result in pixelation ("jaggies"). Reducing the image to 50 percent doubles the resolution, which may improve image quality (see Figure 10-1).

Figure 10-1
Resolution and scaling for bitmaps (50 percent, 100 percent, and 300 percent)

▶ A TIFF or JPEG file can be a rectangle of any size with any number of dots per inch, and each pixel can have any level of gray or any color which is definable by the color models described in Chapter 12, *Color*. TIFF files are said to be *deep* if they have four or more gray levels (more than 2 bits per sample point), and they're *flat* or *bilevel* if they only have one bit (black or white) per sample point.

▶ JPEG files are compressed (made smaller on disk) by using a lossy scheme—some image data is lost, so the image degrades slightly.

▼ ▼

Modifying Images

Unless you're deliberately trying to achieve a muddied look, every image that you scan requires color correction (if it's a color image), tonal correction, and sharpening. Even synthetic pictures created with a painting program may require these adjustments. The place to do these things is in an image-editing program like Adobe Photoshop. Nonetheless, XPress gives you a few image-editing controls that may be useful, especially if you're looking for a special effect. Here's what you can do to a bitmapped image.

▶ Apply a color or tint to the picture.

▶ Add a clipping path to create a silhouette.

▶ Replace its contrast curve with preset posterized effects.

▶ Apply a custom contrast curve.

▶ Invert the image.

▶ Change the picture's on-screen or printed resolution.

▶ Change the picture's halftoning parameters.

Chances are that the feature from this list that you'll use most often is the ability to create a clipping path. However, I'm going to hold off on discussing clipping paths until I explore changing screen resolution, colorizing images, and adjusting image contrast.

Welcome to the world of image modification!

Importing High-Resolution TIFF Graphics

The first alteration you can make to your file is to upgrade or downgrade high-resolution TIFF or JPEG files. This control is available only when you first import the picture (see "Get Picture" in Chapter 9, *Pictures*).

Downgrading screen quality. QuarkXPress normally creates a screen representation of a high-resolution TIFF or JPEG file at 72 dpi. This low-resolution screen image provides for a relatively quick screen-refresh rate and keeps your document's file size low. However, if the image is really big or your computer is really slow, importing and displaying an image at even 72 dpi can be time-consuming. You can halve the screen resolution by holding down the Shift key while you click the Open button in the Get Picture dialog box. This doesn't have any effect on your printed output, but it may speed up your screen redraws (those of you who have a fast G5 workstation can stop chuckling).

Remember that you can always turn on Full Resolution preview (from the for these images when you want to see what the image really looks like (see "Preview Quality, Greeking, and Suppression" in Chapter 9, *Pictures*).

Changing TIFF types. If you are heavily into image editing and control, you will undoubtedly want to change the bit depth of a TIFF or JPEG image at some point. Here are two tricks for changing the bit depth as you import the image.

▶ Holding down the Option/Alt key when you click Open in the Get Picture dialog box changes a 1-bit TIFF line-art image into an 8-bit grayscale image. (I can't think of a single use for this feature, but I'll bet someone can.)

▶ Holding down the Command/Ctrl key when you click Open in the Get Picture dialog box changes TIFF or JPEG color images to grayscale, which I have found useful on several occasions. (Note, though, that you may get a better color-to-grayscale conversion in a program like Photoshop.) On the other hand, this Command/Ctrl-key trick also changes TIFF grayscale images to line-art (bitmap) images, which is rarely a change for the better.

▼ ▼

The Style Menu

Chapter 9, *Pictures,* describes how you can manipulate the "layout" of the picture in the picture box, including cropping, rotating, skewing, and moving the image. These effects are controlled from the Measurements palette or the Modify dialog box. Here I talk primarily about the image modification possibilities using features from the Style menu. Remember that you can combine both image manipulation techniques (rotating, changing the shape and size, and so on) and image modification techniques (changing the grayscale or color parameters, and so on) to create fascinating effects in your page layout.

▼ ▼

Tip: When the Style Menu Is Gray. If the items on the Style menu are grayed out, you have either imported an EPS (or some other file format that XPress cannot modify), or the Color TIFFs setting in the Display panel of the Preferences dialog box isn't set to 8-bit. Note that you have to change the Preference *before* you import the image—it has no effect on images you've already imported. If the menu is still grayed out, you may not have the Item tool or the Content tool selected, or you may not have the image's picture box selected. If still none of these things work, I can only suggest plugging in your computer.

▼ ▼

Color. I cover color fully in Chapter 12, *Color.* So at this point, suffice it to say that changing the color of a grayscale or black-and-white image using QuarkXPress's Color feature replaces all black (or gray) samples with ones of a particular color. (You cannot colorize a color image in XPress.) For example, if you have a black-and-white image and you change the color to red, you then have a red-and-white image.

This is not necessarily the same thing as colorizing an image in Photoshop, but it's usually pretty close. Note that you can create a "fake duotone" by colorizing an image with a multi-ink color (see Chapter 12, *Color*, for more on multi-ink colors).

Shade. In the same spirit as changing each pixel's color, you can change the gray value for each pixel in the image (this is also called "ghosting" or "screening back" an image). Again, this currently works only for grayscale and black-and-white images. To tint an image, select a percentage from the Shade submenu (under the Style menu) or change the tint value for the image on the Colors palette. What happens to the image when you do this depends on whether you're working with flat or deep bitmapped images.

▶ FLAT BITMAPS. With flat, bilevel, bitmapped images, changing the Shade alters the printed output; every black pixel in your graphic prints gray. Shading line art can sometimes give you a classier look than just black and white.

▶ DEEP BITMAPS. When you set a shade for a grayscale image in the Style menu XPress multiplies that shade for each sample point. A 50-percent shade of a 100-percent black sample point is 50 percent; 50 percent of a 60-percent sample is 30 percent, and so on. But you don't have to think about the math, because the result appears just like you'd expect.

Actually, it turns out that you can ghost back a color TIFF or JPEG image, too . . . you just have to be tricky about it (see "Tip: Ghosting Color Images," later in this chapter).

Negative. Selecting Negative from the Style menu (or typing Command-Shift-hyphen or Ctrl-Shift-hyphen) inverts all tone and color information in an image (see Chapter 12, *Color*, for more information on color models). What was 10-percent black becomes 90-percent black, what was 20-percent red becomes 80-percent red, and so on.

▼ ▼

Tip: More Negative Images. Here's another way to invert an image: color it white. This is often not only easier, but also more desirable. For example, if you want a white image on a blue background, you can select the picture box with the Content tool, change the shade of the picture to zero percent (or change the color to White in either the Color palette or the Style menu), then change the background color to some shade of Blue (such as 100 percent).

▼ ▼

Tip: Images and Blends Inside Images. Carlos Sosa turned me on to a very odd and potentially useful technique of putting images and blends inside images. Note that this tip only works with 1-bit (bitmap) images.

1. Import a one-bit (black-and-white) image into a picture box and set its color to White in either the Colors palette or the Style menu.

2. Set the image to Negative (Command/Ctrl-Shift-hyphen).

3. If you want to put a blend inside the image, give the picture box a blended background (see Chapter 12, *Color*, on how to do this). If you want to put another image inside this image, then set the Background of the bitmap image's picture box to None.

The trick here is that using Negative swaps the transparent and opaque pixels so you can see through what used to be black pixels (see Figure P on the color pages). Setting the color to White in step 1 matches the opaque area of the image to the color behind the picture box. If the picture box is on top of a 50-percent cyan background, you'd have to use 50-percent cyan in step 1.

Note that you can fake this effect for a grayscale image by first converting the image into a bitmap in Photoshop (change Mode to Bitmap, and select the Halftone Screen technique in the Bitmap dialog box).

▼ ▼

Tip: Making Your Grayscale Picture "Transparent." The simple answer to "How do I make my grayscale TIFFs transparent?" is "You can't." Grayscale TIFFs are not and cannot be transparent. On the other hand, in black-and-white, 1-bit TIFFs (the kind called "Bitmap" in Photoshop), the "white" pixels *are* transparent. (White pixels in black-and-white EPS bitmaps *can* be transparent—it's an option in Photoshop's Save As EPS dialog box—but bitmap TIFFs are more reliable for this.)

Of course, whenever I hear someone say "You can't," I immediately reply, "There must be a workaround somehow." And indeed, there are several. Note that these techniques are for letting you see through a grayscale image to whatever is below it; if you're trying to create a silhouette around the image, you should check out "Clipping Paths," later in this chapter.

▶ **INCLUDE BACKGROUND COLOR.** If you've placed the grayscale image over an area of flat color, you can set the background of the picture box to be the same as the flat color. For example, let's say you want a grayscale image to appear transparent over an area of 30-percent cyan. Just set the background color of the picture box to 30-percent cyan. In earlier versions of XPress, this technique looked right on screen but printed incorrectly because the grayscale image would knock out of the magenta plate. Fortunately, grayscale images now overprint the background color properly when you print color separations or to a composite color printer, even if the background color is a spot color or contains black.

Of course, this technique only works when the image is fully surrounded by an area of flat color. It won't work when you're trying to print over a scanned image or another page item.

▶ **SET TO OVERPRINT.** If your document is in color, you can change the Background value of the picture box to None and set the picture to Overprint in the Trap Information palette (see Chapter 12, *Color*, for more on the Trap Information palette). This lets you put the picture partially on top of a field of color, or even on top of a scanned image. There are three problems with this technique. First, because XPress doesn't display trapping on screen, you won't be able to see the overprinting effect until you print separations. Second, for the same reason, you won't be able to see the effect when you print to a color printer. Third, you cannot use this technique to overprint any color or object that has black in it (including a scanned image that has information in its black channel).

The reason there cannot be black in the background has to do with the nature of PostScript: when you print a light gray on top of a dark gray, the result is the light gray, not a combination of the two. The tint on top always wins, so there's no such thing as overprinting black on black. It's not just the color black; for instance, if you set the color of the grayscale image to cyan, then you can print it over a color that contains black, but not over anything that contains cyan.

▶ **SET TO "UNDERPRINT."** Another way to trick XPress into making a grayscale image look transparent is to put the picture box behind another box rather than in front of it. Then, in the Trap Information palette, set the foreground objects to overprint the picture. This has exactly the same restrictions as the last workaround, though in some instances you can make it look as if black is overprinting black.

For example, let's say you want a light grayscale image to appear transparent over some black text in a 30-percent magenta text box. You can put the image behind the text box and set the text box to overprint the image. The magenta box overprints the image, and the text knocks out the image; however, because the text is solid black, it looks like it's overprinting. (This is easier seen than explained; see See Figure O in the color plates for examples.)

▶ **CHANGE TO BITMAP.** As I said earlier, the white pixels in bilevel, bitmap TIFF images are inherently transparent. Therefore, if you convert a grayscale image to Bitmap mode in Photoshop, it can sit on top of anything you want in XPress and what's underneath will show through the white areas. The problem, of course, is that bitmap images have no gray in them, so gray values must be represented by dithering or by a halftone pattern (see "Halftones," later in this chapter, for a discussion of this topic).

When you convert to Bitmap mode in Photoshop, you can set the final resolution of the image. Typically, if you're printing to an image-setter for high-quality output, your final bitmap image needs to be between 600 and 1,000 ppi. If you're only printing to a desktop laser printer, you can typically get by with a lower value. However, when you import this bitmap image into QuarkXPress, the screen preview is usually pretty bad. So again, you can't trust what you see on screen; you have to print proofs.

Contrast

The Style menu also lets you change the contrast of grayscale and color images with the Contrast feature. If you are working with a one-bit (black-and-white) picture, this feature is inaccessible. It also doesn't currently work unless Color TIFF is set to 8-bit in the Display panel of the Preferences dialog box

Contrast refers to the relationships among the tonal values of a picture. A high-contrast picture divides up the gray shades or color saturation of an image into a few sharply distinct tones; a low-contrast picture has little differentiation between tones, and looks grayed out. You should try to strike some balance between these two, though you may want to create an unnatural-looking image by drastically altering the contrast controls.

The basic concept to remember with the contrast controls is "input/output." I like to think of the Contrast feature as a machine into which I'm inserting a JPEG or TIFF image, and out of which comes what is going to print on the page. Other people sometimes think of this process as a filter through which the image is poured each time the page gets printed. Remember, though, that neither you nor QuarkXPress actually alters the picture file on disk; you only alter the "machine" or the "filter" through which the image passes for display and printout.

(In early versions of QuarkXPress, there were several preset contrast controls, including Normal Contrast, High Contrast, and Posterized. These have been removed because they're completely redundant; there are identical features inside the Picture Contrast Specifications dialog box. Also, these features just weren't used very often.)

Picture Contrast Specifications

To change the contrast of an image, choose Contrast from the Style menu (or press Command-Shift-C or Ctrl-Shift-C). The Picture Contrast Specifications dialog box shows you the mechanism—or the filter—through which you are processing the picture. When you first open this dialog box, you see a 45-degree line on the graph (see Figure 10-2).

Looking carefully at the graph, you can see that the axes are labeled Input and Output, and each spans from zero to one (one means 100-percent). Tick marks are shown in increments of five and 10 percent.

The basic 45-degree normal contrast line defines a filter which makes no change to gray levels. For example, a gray level of 20 percent in the input picture is mapped (in output) to 20 percent, 40 percent to 40 percent, and so on. However, by changing this line, you can change the mapping of the gray levels, affecting the contrast and shading of the printed picture.

You can use the nine tools in this dialog box to change the contrast curve into either a straight line or a curve. By definition, any contrast curve which is not a straight line is a *gamma curve*. There's nothing mysterious about a gamma curve; it's simply a nonlinear curve with a fancy name. However, when it comes right down to it, Photoshop will always give you better quality; QuarkXPress's tools for making curves don't let you do much more than either very basic modifications or very weird ones (see Figure 10-3).

Figure 10-2
Adjusting the Contrast
Specifications for a
grayscale TIFF image

Normal contrast

*Contrast curve adjusted to create a
Posterized effect*

▼ ▼

Tip: Applying Your Changes. I've said this before, but it's worth repeating here: The Apply button is one of the all-time most helpful features that I've ever had the pleasure of using, especially on a screen larger than 9 inches. It's especially useful with the Picture Contrast Specifications dialog box.

You can move the Picture Contrast Specifications dialog box out of the way of the picture you're working with, then make changes to the curve and click the Apply button (or press Command/Alt-A) to see the change take place. If you don't like that effect, change the curve again or press Command/Ctrl-Z to undo that change. And don't forget Continuous Apply (Option/Alt-click Apply).

▼ ▼

Tip: Don't Use Other Contrast. I liken the Picture Contrast Specifications dialog box to fixing a delicate piece of electronic equipment with a hammer—it's just too blunt of an instrument to do much good. In fact, there are a dozen problems that make the contrast controls in QuarkXPress less than useful, the most essential of which is sharpening. Scanned images always need to be sharpened with a sharpening filter (preferably Photoshop's Unsharp Mask filter) before they're printed. Unfortunately, you need to apply sharpening *after* tonal correction. Since QuarkXPress doesn't have a sharpening filter, that's impossible.

Figure 10-3

Way-out contrast
correction

So if you need to perform tonal correction on a scanned image (you almost always do), don't use the controls in QuarkXPress. Do it in an image-editing program like Photoshop, which probably has better tonal-correction tools and where you can also sharpen the image. Then save the file and place it in QuarkXPress, fully corrected, sharpened, and ready to print.

Why discuss the Contrast feature at all? Because I'm the kind of guy who likes to have a tool and know how it works, even if I almost never use it. The one or two times per year that I use this feature for a special effect or a minor tweak make up for the short amount of time it took me to learn how to use this dialog box.

▼ ▼

Hand tool. You can use the Hand tool to move the curve (or straight line) around on the contrast graph by selecting the tool, positioning it over the graph, and dragging. You can constrain to either horizontal or vertical movements by holding down the Shift key while dragging. The Hand tool is the easiest way to make adjustments to the contrast curve as a whole. For an example, see "Tip: Adjusting the Break Point on a High-Contrast Image," below.

Pencil tool. If you've ever used a painting program, you're already familiar with the Pencil tool. By selecting this tool and dragging over the curve, you can make both large and small adjustments. You can draw curves with the Pencil tool which adjust for problems in the original scan (see Figure 10-4). Or you can draw wild and bizarre roller-coaster curves which map the gray levels in weird ways. You can also make small corrections in the curve by carefully drawing over areas. Remember, though, that you don't need to have a smooth curve all the time; slight bumps and dips have little effect on the final output.

Straight Line tool. If you haven't figured out that the Straight Line tool draws straight lines, I wish you the best of luck with the program. However, it's not so obvious what these straight lines are good for. Think of the slope of a line in the

Figure 10-4
Curve created with
the Pencil tool

The near-white background is pushed fully to white with this delicate curve made with the Pencil tool. However, parts of the image also become white.

same way as you think of the slope of a hill. A steep slope steepens very quickly; a shallow slope steepens slowly. You can draw steep and gentle slopes easily with the Straight Line tool.

The steeper the slope, the higher contrast the image has. The gentler the slope, the less contrast—the "grayer" the picture looks. However, remember that by using a straight line rather than a curved line, you are indiscriminately losing tonal values. A steep, contrasty line loses the highlights and the shadows; a flat, low-contrast line loses midtones (see Figure 10-5).

Posterizer tool. Posterization is the act of reducing or dividing an image's gray or color levels into a few basic tonal values. When you select the Posterizer tool, QuarkXPress adds handle points to your line or curve at 10-percent increments. By moving these handles, you flatten and move that entire 10-percent area. By lining up multiple handles, you can easily create posterized effects with any number of levels up to 10 (see Figure 10-6).

Spike tool. Whereas the Posterizer tool places handles between the 10-percent marks and levels out (flattens) that 10-percent area, the Spike tool places handles directly on the 10-percent marks and has no affect on the area between the handles other than to adjust the lines to keep them contiguous.

Figure 10-5
Linear adjustment

Figure 10-5
Linear adjustment

Figure 10-6
Using the Posterized tool

This is the best tool for creating smooth curves—much easier than the Pencil tool. Spiking a line is also pretty good for boosting particular tonal values. For example, if you want a 60-percent gray area to appear black, you can spike it up to 100 percent. Similarly, if you want to drop out all the dark areas of the cyan, you can use this tool.

Normal Contrast tool. Clicking on this icon reverts the contrast curve to its initial 45-degree straight line.

High Contrast tool. Clicking on this icon has the immediate effect of making your grayscale pictures look like they were badly scanned at a one-bit (black-and-white) setting, and it makes your color pictures look like poorly designed psychedelic flyers.

The literal effect of this filter is to change all values less than 30-percent gray to white, and all values greater than 30-percent gray to black. Color images are affected in the same way: the saturation levels are broken down so that all colors with over 30-percent saturation are transformed to 100 percent, and so on (see Chapter 12, *Color*, for a more in-depth discussion of color and its saturation levels). Why Quark chose the 30-percent mark is beyond me; it makes for some really ugly-looking images. I'll look at how to change this break point below.

Posterized tool. Whereas the High Contrast setting breaks down the image into only two gray or saturation levels—zero percent and 100 percent—Posterized divides the tonal values into six levels of gray or color saturation: zero, 20, 40, 60, 80, and 100 percent. Gray levels or color saturation in the original picture are mapped to these levels based on what they're closest to (for example, a 36-percent saturation of a color maps to the 40-percent level). Posterization is a common technique for special effects, though it should be used carefully.

Inversion tool and Negative checkbox. Contrary to popular belief, these two items in the Picture Contrast Specifications dialog box do not perform the same task, though in many instances you may achieve the same result. By using either of these, for example, you can invert grayscale files. That is, where there was white, there is black; where there was 20-percent black, there is 80-percent black, and so on. Switching to Negative and inverting the curve also creates the same effect while altering all three RGB values at once (see "Color," below, for more on the RGB contrast curve).

However, inverting color images while using other color models can give you varying effects. Simply put, clicking on the Inversion tool in the Tool palette flips the curve you are working on. Checking Negative has the same effect as selecting the Negative item from the Style menu.

▼ ▼

Tip: Adjusting the Break Point on a High-Contrast Image. As I described above, the cutoff point on a high-contrast image is 30 percent, which does hardly anyone any good. Using the Hand tool in the Other Contrast dialog box, you can adjust this point horizontally to anywhere on the scale. Try moving the vertical line over to around 60 percent. This cuts out most of the lower gray values and gives you a clean and recognizable image for many grayscale or color pictures (see Figure 10-7).

This technique is also of great help when you're working with line art scanned as a grayscale image. By adjusting the cutoff point, you can alter the line thicknesses in the artwork (see Figure 10-8). Remember that holding down the Shift key while you're using the Hand tool constrains the movements to horizontal or vertical.

Of course, to get a really good-looking image, you'd have to start with an 800-dpi grayscale image (because you want to end up with a minimum of 800

Figure 10-7

Adjusting the high-contrast break point for a grayscale image

Normal contrast

High contrast (30 percent)

High contrast (60 percent)

Figure 10-8

Line art scanned as a grayscale image

High contrast (30 percent)   *High contrast (60 percent)*

dpi for line art). This would be a really enormous file! So once again, the caveat is that this grayscale-to-bilevel bitmap conversion is better done in Photoshop or another image-editing program.

▼ ▼

Color

If you aren't familiar with working with color and the various color models that QuarkXPress supports, you may want to skip over this section until you've read Chapter 12, *Color*. In this section, I discuss contrast modification of color images using the various color models and their components.

QuarkXPress allows you to modify color TIFF and JPEG images using the same tools you use for grayscale images, except that you can alter one color at a time. This clearly allows significantly greater control over the way your images print.

As I've said before, there are few reasons to use these controls in QuarkXPress other than to create really weird-looking images—especially given the lack of a sharpening filter in QuarkXPress (see Figure N in the color pages). Instead, Photoshop is the tool of choice for making color correction and adjustments. Nonetheless, let's look at the steps you can take to modify these pictures in QuarkXPress.

Model. The Modify popup menu in the Picture Contrast Specifications dialog box appears when you are modifying a color bitmapped image. You can work with four different color models: HSB, RGB, CMY, and CMYK. When you change from one model to another, the image resets to Normal. Thus, you cannot make changes to an image in more than one color model.

Color. When you select one of the color models, QuarkXPress brings up the appropriate color-selection checkboxes; that is, when you click HSB, Hue, Saturation, and Brightness checkboxes appear. Clicking CMY gives you Cyan, Magenta, and Yellow checkboxes, and so on. Each checkbox can be on or off, and you can have any number of checkboxes turned on at one time.

The theory is simple: the checkboxes you turn on control which items change when you alter the contrast control curve. In the RGB, CMY, and CMYK models, QuarkXPress gives you color checkboxes. If you check Magenta and Yellow, for example, and change the contrast curve using the tools described above, you change the curve for only those two colors. Everything else remains the same.

The HSB model's checkboxes have slightly different functions. Changing the contrast curve with only Hue turned on maps various colors to other colors. This can be seen on a color screen by examining the color spectrum on the horizontal and vertical axes as well as the curve itself. In theory, this means you could make all the red in an image become yellow . . . in practice, this is easier said than done.

The Saturation checkbox lets you map various saturations from zero to 100 percent, and the Brightness checkbox lets you map the brightness levels (levels of black) to other brightness levels. Once again, you can adjust each of these settings with any, some, or all of the checkboxes turned on.

▼ ▼

Tip: Ghosting Color Images. The Shade feature is grayed out (unusable) for color TIFFs. However, if you need to tint—or ghost, or screen back, or whatever you want to call it—a color image, you can adjust shading with the Picture Contrast Specifications dialog box. You will get different effects depending on the model you use. One option is to set the Model popup menu to RGB and then use the Hand tool to move all three contrast curves vertically. Moving the curves up makes the image lighter, and moving them down makes it darker.

In HSB mode, you can turn off the Hue and Saturation checkboxes and simply increase the Brightness curve to lighten the image.

Note, however, that when you move these curves up or down, you're likely to cut out possible gray levels. If you make the image darker, for instance, dark areas go black; make it lighter, and light areas go white. In either case, you lose detail. Because of this, you may want to adjust the curve using the Pencil tool or the Spike tool instead (or use an image-manipulation program), as described above.

▼ ▼

Tip: Clone and Ghost. All the tools I've discussed so far apply to the entire image. How can you ghost back or colorize just a portion of an image? As usual, there's a trick (see Figure 10-9).

Figure 10-9
Changing one part of an image by cloning and adjusting contrast

The original image   *A clone of the picture box, cropped differently and with a different contrast*

1. Select the picture box and use Step and Repeat (from the Item menu) to make one duplicate with both Horizontal and Vertical offsets set to zero. (I call this "cloning" the box.)

2. Crop the duplicate image down by changing the size or shape of the picture box. You can do this by dragging its corner or side handles, changing its shape from the Shape submenu (under the Item menu), or—if it's a Bézier box—altering the points on the edge of the box. Note that when you do this you don't move the picture within the box at all, so the two pictures stay in registration.

Instead of (or in addition to) cropping, you can change the duplicate box's clipping path (see "Clipping Paths," on the next page, for more on how to do this).

3. Apply the effect you want either to the duplicate or to the original image.

There are all kinds of variations on this tip. For instance, let's say you have a color TIFF in the picture box. After cloning the box in step 1, you can re-import the picture into the cloned picture box, but this time as grayscale (hold down the Command/Ctrl key when you click Open in the Get Picture dialog box). Now when you change the cropping of the box or change the image's clipping, one portion of the picture is grayscale.

▼ ▼

Clipping Paths

A clipping path is a mathematically based PostScript path, much like other Bézier lines in QuarkXPress, Illustrator, or FreeHand. However, a clipping path acts like a pair of scissors, cutting out an image in any shape you want. Clipping an image is actually the same as cropping it, but because QuarkXPress makes a distinction, I will, too: the shape of a picture box crops the picture, but the Clipping feature clips it. You can use clipping and cropping together or alone. Let's see how.

Applying a Clipping Path

If you've used QuarkXPress for a while, you're sure to have heard someone say, "Never put a TIFF in a picture box that has a background of None." The reason is simple: in version 3.x, if you set the background to None, XPress would assume that you wanted a silhouette of the picture and it would build a clipping path for you. The problem was that it built this clipping path with straight line segments based on the 72-dpi screen preview of your image, and it did it in a pretty brain-dead fashion. The result was a very jaggy edge around the image, which looked really ugly.

However, I'm happy to announce that you can throw that outdated rule out the window. Now you have the option of applying a smooth clipping path based on the high-resolution image data (choose Clipping from the Item menu, or press Command-Option-T or Ctrl-Alt-T). This works whether the Background of the box is set to None or to an opaque color. (If Background is set to None, the clipped image appears against whatever is behind the picture box; if the background is opaque, the clipped image appears in front of whatever background color you've specified.)

The Clipping tab of the Modify dialog box looks confusing at first, but it's really pretty basic once you get the hang of it (see Figure 10-10). The most important feature in this dialog box is the Type popup menu, which lets you choose one of five clipping path options: Item, Embedded Path, Alpha Channel, Non-White Areas, and Picture Bounds.

Item. When you select Item from the Type popup menu (this is the default setting for most pictures), QuarkXPress sets the clipping path to be the same as the cropping path. In other words, this is just like turning off the Clipping feature so that XPress just crops the picture the way it always has.

Embedded Path. Adobe Photoshop lets you draw and save Bézier paths with its images. XPress is smart enough to see and read those paths in TIFF, EPS, and JPEG images, and lets you choose one of them as your clipping path. This turns out to be incredibly useful. Let's say you have a picture of four books fanned out on a table. You can create several paths in Photoshop, each of which "cuts out" one book, two books, the first and third book, and so on. When you get the image into XPress, you can choose which silhouette looks best in your design (see Figure 10-11).

Alpha Channel. It's a strange phenomenon, but whenever someone says "alpha channel," half the people in the room avert their eyes. The popular belief is that alpha channels are really difficult to understand, so we'd better

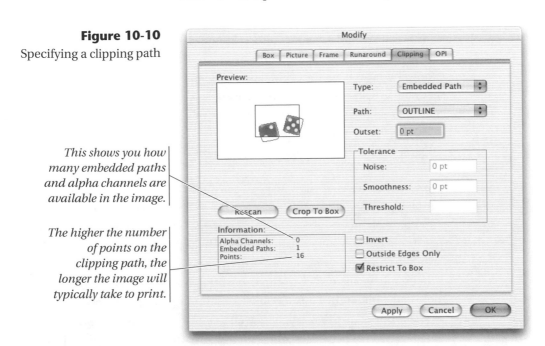

Figure 10-10
Specifying a clipping path

This shows you how many embedded paths and alpha channels are available in the image.

The higher the number of points on the clipping path, the longer the image will typically take to print.

Figure 10-11

Choosing an
embedded path

not even try. However, alpha channels are really easy to understand: an alpha channel is just a way to visually represent a selection as a grayscale picture. In Adobe Photoshop, you can select an area of an image and save it as an additional channel on the Channels palette. (As far as I can tell, people use the term "alpha" just to sound important; it's just the same as a plain ol' additional channel—see Figure 10-12.)

Then when the Type popup menu is set to Alpha Channel, XPress lets you convert one of these channels into a clipping path. It's almost as though XPress is reading your original Photoshop selection. The problem is that selections in Photoshop can have soft anti-aliased or feathered edges, and clipping paths cannot, so QuarkXPress has to convert soft edges into hard-edged Bézier paths. (See "Tolerance," below, for a description of how it does this.)

Note that if you want to include alpha channels in images bound for XPress, you have to use the TIFF file format.

Non-White Areas. If your image doesn't have either an alpha channel or an embedded path, XPress still lets you build a clipping path on the fly based on the non-white areas of the image. If you choose Non-White Areas from the Type popup menu, XPress searches through the picture for white or near-white pixels to clip out, leaving the pixels that are not near-white (see Figure 10-13). You even have the choice to clip out white pixels inside the image—like the hole in the middle of a hula hoop (see "Clipping Options," below).

This option works reasonably well in a few instances, notably where the image has very crisp edges and is on a clean, white background. If the edges

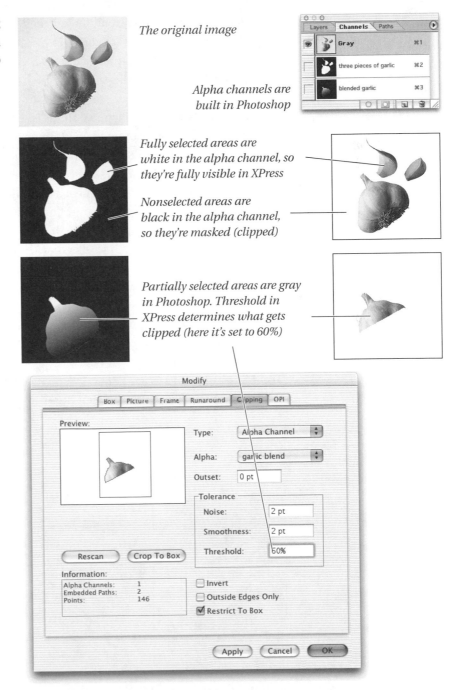

Figure 10-12
Alpha channels in
Adobe Photoshop

The original image

*Alpha channels are
built in Photoshop*

*Fully selected areas are
white in the alpha channel, so
they're fully visible in XPress*

*Nonselected areas are
black in the alpha channel,
so they're masked (clipped)*

*Partially selected areas are gray
in Photoshop. Threshold in
XPress determines what gets
clipped (here it's set to 60%)*

of the foreground image have a lot of detail or if the image is colored similar to the background, Non-White Areas can't figure out which details are important and which are not (like a human eye can), and the clipping path suffers for it. Of course, if your image is not on a white (or near-white) background, this option doesn't help much at all.

In fact, to be really honest about it, I tend to shy away from this option unless I'm trying to build a quick comp for a client or if I'm planning on spending some time editing the clipping path (see "Clipping Caveats" and "Editing the Clipping Path," later in this section).

Picture Bounds. Selecting Picture Bounds is second in simplicity only to the Item option on the Type popup menu. Bitmapped images are always rectangular, so selecting Picture Bounds sets the picture's clipping path to the four sides of the picture. If the picture box is the same size as the picture, then this option has pretty much the same effect as selecting Item. The primary difference is that you have the option to inset or outset the clipping path from the picture's edge. Use negative numbers in the Top, Left, Bottom, and Right fields to inset the path (make the path smaller than the image); use positive numbers to outset the path (make it larger than the image).

I find Picture Bounds most useful when I need to crop off a portion of one or more sides of the image with great precision. For instance, if you know that you want to shave off 1.5 points from the bottom of a picture, you can set the clipping type to Picture Bounds and type "-1.5pt" into the Bottom field.

▼ ▼

Tip: Clipping TIFFs versus EPSes. I've made my preference for the TIFF file format abundantly clear already, but here's just one more reason why I use

Figure 10-13
Clipping out
the white pixels

These near-white pixels get clipped out.

These white pixels are retained because they're surrounded by nonwhite pixels (you have the option to clip these or not).

The final clipping path in QuarkXPress (you can make the clipping path visible in the Edit submenu under the Item menu).

TIFF images whenever I can: XPress has more control over clipping TIFFs than EPS files. If you need to use an EPS file for some reason, and you've built paths in Photoshop, don't tell Photoshop to use one of those paths as a clipping path; if you later change your mind and choose a different clipping path in XPress (using the Embedded Path option), XPress won't be able to replace the built-in clipping path with your choice.

▼ ▼

Clipping Caveats

Before I go any further in my discussion of clipping paths, I need to point out a major problem: You can't make good decisions about clipping by looking at a 72-dpi representation of your high-resolution image. It's like a doctor doing brain surgery on the day she forgot to wear her glasses.

Fortunately, XPress 6 lets you increase an image's screen preview resolution by turning on Full Resolution from the Preview Resolution submenu (under the Item menu or in the context menu). This works up to 800 pixels per inch, so if you have a very high-resolution image (or an image that has been shrunk down, resulting in higher effective resolution), you might still get some fuzziness. However, Full Resolution lets you edit and view clipping paths while you're zoomed way in so you can see which pixels are going to be clipped out.

The upshot is that in the next two sections, I'm going to discuss how you can change the various clipping paths XPress offers you, and even how to draw your own. But you had better take these controls with a grain of salt unless you're sure that you're looking at your image's real pixels. To be honest, I still *much* prefer to create and edit clipping paths in Photoshop.

Clipping Options

Now that I've gotten that caveat out of the way, I can tell you about the various ways in which you can change how XPress builds your clipping paths. Each of these controls (in the form of buttons, text fields, and checkboxes) sits on the Clipping tab of the Modify dialog box. Note that the changes you make to these options affect only this particular picture in this particular picture box; when you edit a clipping path in XPress, the edits aren't saved in the image's disk file.

Outset. The Outset field lets you spread or choke—enlarge or reduce—the clipping path. It's available when the Type popup menu is set to Embedded Path, Alpha Channel, or Non-White Areas. Positive values increase its size; negative values decrease it (see Figure 10-14).

Typically you want to adjust this by only a very small amount, or else strange things start happening to your clipping path. For instance, if it's clear that the background color of the image is showing up as a halo around the clipped image, you might set the Outset value to -.5 point to reduce the size of the path by about one pixel (the exact measurement-to-pixel amount depends entirely on the image's resolution, of course). Similarly, setting Outset to about 1 point or so might be just enough to save some edge detail which has been cut out by a hard-edged path.

Tolerance. The Tolerance settings help XPress figure out which pixels should be included in a path and how smooth the path should be. Though these settings are available for clipping types of Embedded Path, Alpha Channel, and Non-White Areas, they're primarily important when you ask for a path based on an alpha channel or a nonwhite area.

▶ NOISE. Many people assume that Noise refers to how gritty or dirty the bitmapped image is, and it does, in an indirect way. If there is a lot of "grit" in the image or the alpha channel, XPress may capture it in the

Figure 10-14

Outset

Outset of 4 points (Much larger than you'd typically use)

Outset of -4 points

form of tiny, independent clipping paths (see Figure 10-15). The Noise setting looks for these stray clipping paths. If you set this to 10 points, then the program deletes any clipping path smaller than 10 points in diameter. While most images don't contain enough tiny stray pixels to generate tiny clipping paths like this, some do, especially those that have lots of edge detail (like wispy hair or a fuzzy sweater). In these cases, judicious use of the Noise setting becomes indispensable.

▶ **SMOOTHNESS.** The Smoothness setting lets you tell XPress how much care to take when it makes your clipping path for you (this setting only applies if you choose Alpha Channel or Non-White Areas). The lower the Smoothness value, the more precisely XPress matches the clipping path to the high-resolution data. The problem is that to get greater precision, XPress must place more points on the clipping path. A setting of zero tells Photoshop to match the pixel boundaries of the image as closely as it can, but you may get thousands of points on your clipping path. Typically, the more points on the path, the harder it is for the printer to process the image and the slower the page prints (in some cases, the page may not print at all).

It's tempting to always use low Smoothness values, because it feels like you're being more true to the image, but you often get worse results than if you use a value of five or 10 or even higher (see Figure 10-16). Each image is different and must be evaluated independently.

Figure 10-15
The Noise setting

By changing the Noise setting from 4 points to 10 points,
many of the small, independent clipping paths are removed.

Note that some people (including Quark's documentation team) liken Smoothness to the concept of flatness in PostScript (if you don't know what that is, don't worry about it). It's really not the same thing at all, though it does have some similarities.

▶ **THRESHOLD.** The Threshold setting is perhaps the most important control in the Tolerance area of the Clipping tab. Threshold is like a volume knob for what is and is not included when XPress builds a clipping path (this is only applicable for the Alpha Channel and Non-White Areas clipping types). When you have Non-White Areas selected, XPress clips out every pixel that is fully white plus any nonwhite pixel that is shaded up to the Threshold value (it actually uses a luminance value based on the RGB data, but that's not worth worrying about most of the time). For instance, the default setting of 10 percent tells XPress that an eight-percent-gray pixel should get clipped out, but a 15-percent-gray pixel should not.

When you have Alpha Channel selected, Threshold acts in the opposite manner: XPress clips out the black pixels, plus any pixel within the Threshold value from black—so with a 10-percent Threshold, a 95-percent-gray pixel drops out, but an 85-percent gray pixel does not. With alpha channels, I usually set Threshold to between 40 and 60 percent.

It appears that XPress takes the three Tolerance settings into consideration like this: first it applies the Threshold value to the alpha channel or the image, then it finds a Bézier clipping path based on the Smoothness value, and final-

Figure 10-16
The Smoothness setting

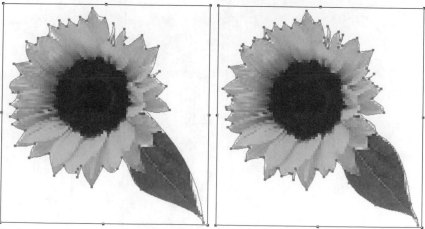

As the Smoothness value decreases, XPress adds more points to the path and the clipping path more successfully traces the image.

ly it drops out stray paths based on the Noise setting. And by no accident, this is the best way for you to control the clipping path as well.

1. Given that the default Tolerance settings will rarely create a clipping path that's perfect for your needs, first adjust the Threshold value until the path is approximately the shape you want in the Preview area of the Modify dialog box. Note that you don't have to click OK or Apply between each change; you can simply press Tab or click in another dialog-box field (though you have to wait one or two seconds for XPress to realize that you aren't making further changes before it rebuilds the path).

2. Next, set the Smoothness value, watching the number of points in the Information section of the dialog box. At this point, you'll probably need to click OK or Apply to see the clipping effect on the actual image. This is the hardest part to do if you only have the low-resolution screen preview to work from (see "Clipping Caveats," earlier in this section).

3. If you see that there are tiny stray clipping paths still extant, kill them off by increasing the Noise setting.

4. Finally, if the clipping path is still not "just right," you can edit it by hand (see "Editing the Clipping Path," later in this section).

Invert. The Invert checkbox performs a very simple trick: it switches what is and what is not clipped out. While it's great that QuarkXPress lets you do this, you probably won't use it for anything other than creating special effects (see Figure 10-17).

Outside Edges Only. The hole in a doughnut, the spaces between the wires in a whisk, the keyhole in a door . . . you must make a decision as to whether or not these should be transparent (and clipped out). Once you've made that decision, the tool to make the change is the Outside Edges Only checkbox (see Figure 10-18). When this checkbox is turned on, XPress removes any clipping paths that are surrounded by other clipping paths. (If you remember back to the Merge features in Chapter 3, *Tools of the Trade*, XPress is using Union to merge all the paths when you turn on this option.)

Restrict To Box. So your art director says, "Crop this picture of a man inside a box with a 3-point black border so he's only visible down to the waist, but make sure his elbow sticks out on top of the frame." You blink, nod your head, and wander off in a daze, wondering how to get this effect. In earlier versions of XPress, you'd have to create duplicate boxes, change multiple clipping paths

Figure 10-17
Inverting a clipping path

in Photoshop, and generally give yourself heartburn. But now pictures don't have to be confined to the edges of their picture boxes anymore.

When you turn off the Restrict To Box checkbox, XPress lets you move the picture outside the boundaries of its picture box (see Figure 10-19). In fact, you can move a picture entirely out of its picture box (though you can't delete the box). In the example I mentioned earlier, you would choose a clipping path that included the man's elbow but cut him off at the waist (see "Tip: Cropping and Unrestricting," below). In an "unrestricted box," the elbow could poke out over the box's frame.

Here's another way to think of this: when you turn off the Restrict To Box option, you're turning off the box's cropping feature. All you're left with is the clipping.

Crop To Box. The Crop To Box button also performs a very simple operation: it pares down any portion of your clipping path that extends beyond the borders of the picture box. The result is a clipping path that extends only as far as the edges of the picture box. When Restrict To Box is turned on, this has no effect at all. But when this option is off, pressing Crop To Box can help you create all kinds of cool effects (see "Tip: Cropping and Unrestricting," below).

Note that if you later go back and change the size of your picture box, the clipping path does not update automatically. You may need to click the Rescan button, which tells XPress to reset the clipping path to the current settings on the Clipping tab of the Modify dialog box. Then you can use Crop To Box again.

▼ ▼

Tip: Cropping and Unrestricting. If you're still awake this late in the chapter, you may have noticed that I glossed over the steps involved in clipping out part of an image but not other parts (the example I used was the man who is cropped to the waist but whose elbow extends past the edge of the box). There are a number of ways to achieve this effect, but here's one of my favorites (see Figure 10-20).

Figure 10-18
Outside Edges Only

*Outside Edges
Only turned off*

*Outside Edges
Only turned on*

Figure 10-19
Restrict To Box

Restrict To Box on   *Restrict To Box off*

1. Choose a clipping path that includes all the parts of the image you want to be visible, even if it contains more of the foreground image than you need. For instance, the clipping path might include the entire man (or, in the figure below, the bread).

2. Set the size of the picture box so that it crops out the parts of the image you want to crop out, but leaves the other parts visible. In this example, the man's legs and waist would be cropped out, but his arms would be visible.

3. In the Modify dialog box, click the Crop To Box button and turn off Restrict To Box. Press OK to leave this dialog box.

4. Now change the size of the picture box to achieve the final effect.

Figure 10-20
Cropping and
unrestricting

Crop the image so that the parts you want visible are inside the box.

Here is the same image, but with the clipping path made visible.

After you click Crop To Box and turn off Restrict To Box you can change the picture box's size so that it crops in some places and clips in others.

The final image

Note that step 2 might require more than just resizing the picture box. You may actually have to edit the shape of the picture box (select Shape from the Edit submenu, under the Item menu; press Shift-F4 on the Macintosh, or press F10 in Windows) so that the parts of the image you want to be visible are showing (see Figure 10-21).

▼ ▼

Editing the Clipping Path

Okay: so you've cajoled the perfect clipping path out of XPress's (or Photoshop's) clipping tools . . . and then you print the image and realize that it's not perfect after all. Fortunately, you can manually edit the Bézier curves and points on a clipping path. Note that you have to start with a clipping path that is already there; XPress still doesn't let you draw a path from scratch.

The first step in editing a clipping path is to make it visible, which you can do by selecting Clipping Path from the Edit submenu (under the Item menu), or by pressing Shift-Option-F4 (Macintosh) or Control-Shift-F10 (Windows). Now you can edit it to your heart's content, using the same techniques that work on regular Bézier boxes and lines (see Chapter 3, *Tools of the Trade*).

- ▶ You can drag a point or a segment between points.

- ▶ You can add or remove points by holding down the Option/Alt key.

- ▶ You can use keystrokes or the Measurements palette to adjust the position of points or control handles.

Unfortunately, you'll run into a lot of things you wish you could do, but can't. For example, you can't use the Merge or Split features. You can't draw a new section of a clipping path from scratch or even "pinch off" a portion of a clipping path. I'm hoping that the folks at Quark will give us more functionality someday, but for now, we're limited to simple editing.

User-Edited Path. It's important to remember that editing an image's clipping path does not change the image on disk at all. Even though XPress lets you edit an embedded clipping path that was built in Photoshop, when you go back to Photoshop, the path hasn't changed. Instead, as soon as you edit the path, the Type popup menu on the Clipping tab changes to User-Edited Path. You can still change the path's Outset value and use the Crop To Box feature (see "Clipping Options," earlier in this section), but that's about it.

▼ ▼

Tip: Watch When You Drag. One of the most frustrating parts of editing clipping paths (or Bézier boxes, for that matter) is dragging a point or a segment on the path when you meant to use the Grabber Hand. Or clicking on a point when you were just trying to zoom in or out. There's really nothing you can do about this except to be vigilant about where you're clicking, and to keep one hand on the Command/Ctrl-Z (Undo) keys.

▼ ▼

Tip: Changing Clipping Colors. When you edit a clipping path, its default on-screen color is green (it's also green in the Preview area of the Modify dialog box). Is it by chance that guides are also green? Nope. If you change the

Figure 10-21
Advanced cropping

The original image

Turn off Restrict To Box.

Reshape the box so that the parts of the image you want are inside the box.

Now click Crop To Box on the Clipping tab and remove the extra points you added to the box.

Ruler color (in Application Preferences), the clipping path color changes, too. When the edges of your image are also green, then changing the clipping path to hot pink makes the path stand out.

By the way, Quark's documentation says you can change the blue boundary in the Preview area—the one that signals the edge of the picture's box by changing the Margin color in Application Preferences. Doesn't work for me at the time of this writing. But it doesn't matter; I can't think of any good reason to change this anyway.

Halftones

Let's face it. Every high-resolution imagesetter on the market prints only in black and white. And almost every laser printer prints only in black and white. There's clearly a lot to be said for black and white. What you need to realize, however, is that black and white is not gray. Real laser printers don't print gray (at least not the ones I'm going to talk about).

So how do I get a picture with grays in it into the computer and out onto paper? The answer is halftones. The magic of halftoning is that different levels of gray are represented by different-sized spots, which, when printed closely together, fool the eye into seeing the tint I want.

Take a look at any photograph in a newspaper, and it's easy to see the halftoning. Notice that the spacing of the spots doesn't change; only their size changes—large spots in dark areas and small spots in light areas.

Glenn Fleishman, Steve Roth, and I talk about halftones in great detail in our book, *Real World Scanning and Halftones*. However, let's take a quick overview here of the elements that make up digital halftones, just in case you don't have that book yet.

Dots. A laser printer prints pages by placing square black dots on a white page. Each and every dot on a 300-dpi printer is $1/300$ inch in diameter (or thereabouts). That's pretty small, but it's enormous compared with what you can achieve on a high-resolution imagesetter, where each dot is about $1/3,000$ inch (almost too small for the human eye to see). The primary factor with the size of the dot is the *resolution* of the printer (how many dots per inch it can print).

Spots. As I said before, a halftone is made up of spots of varying sizes. On a black-and-white laser printer or imagesetter, these spots are created by bunching together anywhere between one and 65,000 printer dots. They can be of different shapes and, to be redundant over and over again, different sizes. I discuss several different types of spots later in the chapter.

Screen frequency. In the traditional halftoning process, a mesh screen is placed in front of the photograph to create the desired effect of spots all in rows. Keeping that process in mind can help you understand this concept. The *screen frequency* of a halftone is set by the mesh of the screen, and is defined as the number of these rows per inch (or per centimeter, if you think in metric). The lower the screen frequency, the coarser the image looks. The higher the screen frequency, the finer the image looks (see Figure 10-22).

To complicate issues a bit, the screen frequency of a halftone is often called its "line screen." Whatever you call it, it's still calculated in the number of lines per inch (lpi). See Table 10-1 for information about when to use a particular screen frequency.

▼ ▼

Tip: Gray Levels in Your Halftones. Each halftone spot is made up of tiny dots, and different gray levels are produced by turning dots on and off (in a 10-percent tint, 10 percent of the dots within a spot's cell are turned on). Okay, now remember that the lower the screen frequency, the bigger the spot, and more dots are used per spot. The higher the frequency, the fewer dots used. Thus, the higher the screen frequency, the fewer possibilities for levels of gray there are.

This is why you may get posterization when an image is printed on a desktop laser printer (where there may only be 100 printer dots per halftone cell) but not on an imagesetter (where there may be many more dots per cell).

To find out how many levels of gray you can get, divide the resolution by the screen frequency, square it, and add one. For example, you can get 92 levels of gray when you print a 133-line screen at 1,270 dpi ($(^{1,270}/_{133})^2+1$), but only six levels of gray when you print a 133-line screen at 300 dpi ($(^{300}/_{133})^2+1$). The output is clearly posterized. To get 92 levels of gray on a 300-dpi laser printer, you would need to print at 30 lines per inch! It's an unfortunate fact, but this is one of the inherent tradeoffs in digital halftoning.

▼ ▼

Angle. The halftone screen doesn't have to be horizontal or vertical—in fact, it rarely is. It's normally rotated to different angles (see Figure 10-23), which are used in both special-effects halftoning and color separation (see Chapter 13, *Printing*). Zero and 180 degrees are horizontal, 90 and 270 degrees are vertical (some types of spots look the same at all four of these angles, and others look different when rotated). A 45-degree angle is most common because it is the least distracting to the eye. Remember that changing the angle of the halftone screen doesn't change the angle of the picture itself!

Making Halftones Work for You

Once again, just to be clear: Anything that contains gray requires halftoning. Even a simple box or block of text with a 10-percent tint comes out as a halftone. There's no other way to render grays on a black-and-white output device.

Figure 10-22
Various screen
frequencies

20 lpi   *70 lpi*   *120 lpi*

Table 10-1
Screen frequencies
to use for different
printing conditions

OUTPUT	LINES PER INCH (LPI)
Photocopier	50–90 lpi
Newspaper quality	60–85 lpi
Quick-print printer	85–110 lpi
Direct-mail pieces	110–150 lpi
Magazine quality	133–175 lpi
Art book	175–300 lpi

You don't have to do anything special to a bitmapped image to make it print as a halftone; XPress has built-in defaults for halftone screen, angle, and spot shape. However, if you want to override those values for a single *grayscale* bitmapped image, you can select the picture box and choose Halftone from the Style menu (or press Command-Shift-H or Ctrl-Shift-H; see Figure 10-24).

Following is an in-depth description of these settings.

Frequency. My dream is to print out a halftone image with a screen frequency of one, with each spot having a diameter of 1 inch. I don't have a particular reason for this; I just think it would be neat. Unfortunately, QuarkXPress won't accept any value under 15. The upper range of 400 lpi is less of an inconvenience, though you may never have the urge to approach either of these limits. Select the screen frequency you want by typing it in, or just choose a preset value from the popup menu. Choose Default to defer to the setting assigned in the Page Setup dialog box.

Angle. I discussed angles several sections ago, and I'll discuss them again in Chapter 13, *Printing,* when I talk about color separations, so I won't discuss them here. Just type in a number from zero to 360 (or zero to -360, if you think backwards).

Figure 10-23
Rotating the halftone
screen to zero-, 30-,
and -45-degree angles

Zero degrees

30 degrees

-45 degrees

Dot screen   *Line screen*

Function. Function refers to the spot shape. You have five shapes to choose from (see Figure 10-25).

- ► **DOT PATTERN.** This is the round spot that you see in almost all output. At low tint values, it's a round black spot. As the tint value increases, it gets larger. At 50 percent, it changes to a square. At higher values, it inverts to a progressively smaller white spot.

- ► **LINE PATTERN.** Straight-line screens seem to go in and out of fashion, but they're always good for waking up your audience and, if you use too low a line screen, for making eyeballs fall out. The line is thick at high tint values and thin at low values.

- ► **ELLIPSE PATTERN.** No, this is not a traditional elliptical spot. Printers have used elliptical spots for years and customers have grown accustomed to asking for them by this name, even though the shape of the spot is more of a rounded-corner diamond. QuarkXPress creates an oval spot. I haven't found any use for this.

- ► **SQUARE PATTERN.** Here's another funky special-effect spot which may come in handy some day. Each spot is square: lower tint values are little squares, higher values are big squares. Try really coarse screen frequencies for this one.

Figure 10-24
Picture Halftone
Specifications
dialog box

> ▶ **ORDERED DITHER PATTERN.** This spot shape is a dither pattern optimized for printing on laser printers. Because the pattern adjusts to the resolution of the laser printer, you shouldn't use this if you're planning on printing to an imagesetter (you'd get a dither at over 1,000 dots per inch, which could not be reproduced). The Ordered Dither pattern is also not optimal for offset printing.
>
> When should you use this? Quark maintains that you should use it when you are printing to a QuickDraw (non-PostScript) laser printer for making multiple copies on a photocopier. Don't even bother if you have a PostScript printer; it looks terrible. Well, I guess it's nice to have the option.

Display Halftoning option. While XPress 3.x gave you the option of displaying your custom halftone on screen, you can no longer do this. Therefore, you just have to remember that your image has custom halftoning information. Why did they take it out? I wish I knew.

▼ ▼

Tip: Beware of Screen Swapping. Note that specifying custom halftones in XPress may not work when you're printing to an imagesetter that automatically replaces halftone screens (most do these days). For instance, Balanced Screens technology may automatically swap your custom screen with one that it thinks you should use. If this is the case, ask how your service bureau can shut off the screen swapping.

▼ ▼

Tip: Areas of Halftone Patterns. Halftone patterns are great for special effects, but sometimes it's nice to apply them to a box with no picture. You can't use the Halftone feature in XPress unless there is a picture in the box. But here's what you can do.

1. Import any grayscale TIFF image—the smaller the better (it could even just be a tiny gray box).

2. Set the background color of the picture box to a solid color or a tint of black.

Figure 10-25
Various halftone spot
shapes (patterns)

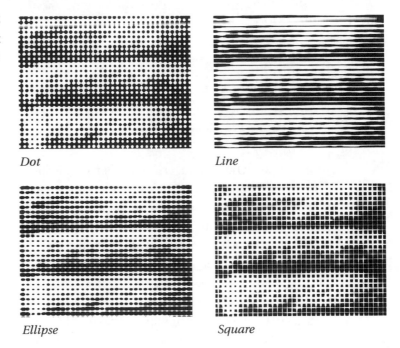

Dot   *Line*

Ellipse   *Square*

3. Choose Halftone from the Style menu, and select a very coarse halftone screen (under 40 lpi works best for special effects).

4. Finally, use the Content tool to move the picture beyond the edges of the box so that it can't be seen.

When you print, the halftone values you specified apply to both the picture and the box . . . however, the picture doesn't appear because it's cropped out, so all you see is the flat coarse-screened halftone area. (Note that this tip—as well as others that rely on QuarkXPress's image halftoning—may not work when printing direct to plate or on some types of imagesetters.)

Many Colorful Shades of Gray

In this chapter, we've taken a pretty good look at the options you have for working with images in your QuarkXPress documents, from rotating them to changing their halftone spot shape. Next, I'll move on to the world of placing graphics and text together on your page, and then I'll discuss how to bring color onto your pages. Finally, I'll cover what is perhaps the culmination of all we've learned in this book: printing out your documents.

11

WHERE TEXT MEETS GRAPHICS

I t's a curious place, the wild frontier. Whether it's the border between Mexico and the United States, or the border between our tiny planet and the great unknown of space, we humans strive to conquer and control. This book takes a slightly more microcosmic stance: we're only trying to conquer and control the text and graphics on a page. Nonetheless, it's a task that has been known to make designers shudder. This chapter will show you how this seemingly hostile frontier can be easily subdued.

In QuarkXPress, text and graphics on a page can interact in four ways.

▶ They can be positioned so that they don't interact at all.

▶ They can intrude on each another, with either the picture or the text prevailing (the text flows on top of the graphic, or the graphic sits on top of the text).

▶ They can bump into one another, with the text keeping its distance (the term for this is *text runaround*).

▶ One can become embedded in the other and move wherever the other goes.

QuarkXPress allows for each of these possibilities with features like transparent boxes, text runaround, and anchored boxes. In this chapter I look at each of these features and how they affect your pages. So let's take one giant step forward to that vast frontier where text meets graphics.

▼▼

Transparency

It's easy to make a text or picture box transparent: just give it a background color of None in the Modify dialog box (double-click on the box with the Item tool, or select it with the Item tool or Content tool and press Command/Ctrl-M). If you want transparency around a picture (like a silhouette of the image), you have to use a clipping path, which I discuss in Chapter 10, *Fine-Tuning Images*.

Unfortunately, XPress still offers no way to make the contents of a box or the box itself semi-transparent so that it blends into the page or other objects, like you can do in Adobe InDesign.

Note that just because you put a transparent box on top of a text box doesn't mean that you'll be able to see the text under it. The reason: The top-most object might be causing the text in the text box below to wrap, or runaround. So before we go any further, I'd better explain how text runaround works.

▼▼

Text Runaround

Text can flow around any kind of object on a page: text boxes, picture boxes, tables, contentless boxes, and lines. Each object can have its own runaround specification, controlled on the Runaround tab of the Modify dialog box (select the text box or the picture box and choose Runaround from the Item menu, or press Command/Ctrl-T). For example, if you want to wrap text around a picture box, you should apply a runaround setting to the picture box. Note that the text box has to sit *behind* whatever it's running around.

If you jumped from XPress 3.x to version 6, the Runaround tab may appear quite daunting, as it has changed a lot since that version (see Figure 11-1). Fear not; it's quite painless if you tackle one section of the dialog box at a time. The primary settings you need to pay attention to are the Type popup menu and the Outset field.

Runaround Type

Each item on the page has its own text runaround specification, but different types of objects can have different types of runaround. The runaround options are listed on the Type popup menu on the Runaround tab of the Modify dialog box. (Unfortunately, you cannot apply a runaround to a group of objects, or even to more than one selected object at a time.)

▶ You can set the runaround for text boxes and contentless boxes to either None or Item.

▶ Lines (including text paths) have three options: None, Item, and Manual.

▶ The options for picture boxes are None, Item, Auto Image, Embedded Path, Alpha Channel, Non-White Areas, Same As Clipping, and Picture Bounds. If some of these sound eerily similar to those listed on the Clipping tab of the Modify dialog box, it's because they're almost identical in nature. In fact, if you haven't yet read the section on clipping paths in Chapter 10, *Fine-Tuning Images*, I suggest you go back and check that out before continuing here, as I skim over several features in this section that I discussed back then.

Let's look at each one of these options in detail.

None. When you specify None as the Runaround mode, text that is "behind" a runaround box flows normally. No text is offset; nothing is different. You may not be able to see much of the text behind the item, but hey, that may be your design choice (see Figure 11-2). This option is available for all types of objects (except for anchored boxes and lines, which I'll discuss later in this chapter).

Figure 11-1
Runaround tab of
the Modify dialog box

Figure 11-2

Text Runaround
Mode: None

The night was uncommonly dark, and a pestilential blast blew from the plain of Catoul, that would have deterred any other traveller however urgent the call: but Carathis enjoyed most whatever filled others with dread. Nerkes concurred in opinion with her; and cafour had a particular predilection for a pestilence. In the morning this accomplished caravan the woodfellers, who directed their route, halted marsh, from whence so noxious a vapour arose, as animal but Alboufaki, who naturally inhaled these The night was uncommonly dark, and a of Catoul, that would have deterred any ther how gent all: but Carathis enjoyed most whatever filled concurred in opinion with her; and cafour had a parti pestilence. In the morning this accomplished caravan, with the woodfellers, who directed their route, halted on the edge of an extensive marsh, from whence so noxious a vapour arose, as would have destroyed many animal but Alboufaki, who naturally inhaled these malignant fogs with delight.

Item. The Item runaround specification is also available for every kind of object. The key here is to remember that Item refers to the box or line itself. That is, it doesn't matter what's in the box. Any text that bumps into the box or line flows around its edges (see Figure 11-3).

When you have Item specified on the Type popup menu, you can change how far away from the item the text should flow. This distance is called the *text outset*. If your object is a rectangular box, you can set the text outset value for each of its four sides. However, if it's a line or a nonrectangular box, XPress only provides one text outset setting, and it uses this value for all sides of the item.

Auto Image. The Auto Image text-runaround mode is available only for picture boxes (as are the next five runaround settings listed here). As far as I can tell, the folks at Quark included Auto Image simply because it existed in earlier versions of XPress (see Figure 11-4). The result is quite similar to the Non-White Areas setting (which I discuss below), and I have found no good reason to actually apply this setting to images. On the other hand, if you're opening old version-3 documents, you may not want to switch to some other setting—changing the setting drastically alters the runaround.

One of the problems with the Auto Image runaround setting is that you cannot control the clipping path of the image; the path is simply drawn for you and you have no control over the points or even the Outset value. In fact, if you've already specified a clipping path for an image when you switch to Auto Image runaround, XPress will remove the clipping path and replace it with a new (usually inferior) one.

I think it's better to avoid Auto Image. If you're trying to simplify your life and use only a runaround or a clipping path, I suggest setting your clipping path and then changing your runaround to Same As Clipping.

Figure 11-3
Text Runaround
Mode: Item

The night was uncommonly dark, and a pestilential blast blew from the plain of Catoul, that would have deterred any other traveller however urgent the call: but Carathis enjoyed most whatever filled others with dread. Nerkes concurred in opinion with her; and cafour had a particular predilection for a pestilence. In the morning this accomplished caravan, with the woodfellers, who directed their route, halted on the edge of an extensive marsh, from whence so noxious a vapour arose, as would have destroyed many animal but Alboufaki, who naturally inhaled these malignant fogs with delight.

The night was uncommonly dark, and a pestilential blast blew from the plain of Catoul, that would have deterred any other traveller however urgent the call: but Carathis enjoyed most whatever filled others with dread. Nerkes concurred

Figure 11-4
Auto Image
(I never use this)

Strangely, although all these settings work the same as they do with Non-White Areas selected, the Invert option is grayed out here.

By the way, while you can open an old version-3 document and be sure the runaround won't change, applying Auto Image in this version won't give you the same results as if you'd done it in version 3. As they say, you can't look back.

Embedded Path. The Embedded Path option on the Type popup menu is identical to that on the Clipping tab of the Modify dialog box: XPress can read paths saved in Photoshop's TIFF, JPEG, and EPS images and lets you apply them as text runarounds. It's a rare day when I use this feature, but it's nice to have the option, especially if you want to draw your runarounds in Photoshop.

Figure 11-5 shows an image that uses one embedded path as a clipping path and a different embedded path as a text runaround.

Alpha Channel. Like Embedded Path, the Alpha Channel runaround setting is identical to the feature with the same name on the Clipping tab. While I like the option of having XPress convert my TIFF's extra channels into text-runaround paths, I really can't think of any reason to use this feature. (Remember that alpha channels in TIFF files can increase the size of the file on disk considerably, while embedded paths add almost nothing to a file's size.)

Non-White Areas. When you choose Non-White Areas, XPress draws a text-wrap path around pixels in the image that are anything other than white or near white (exactly how white depends on the Threshold value, typically set to

Figure 11-5

Using an embedded
path as a runaround

*The image contains
two paths in Adobe
Photoshop (only one
is visible here).*

*In XPress, one path is
used on the Clipping
tab and the second one
is used for text
runaround.*

10 percent; see Figure 11-6). The Non-White Areas setting is basically identical to the feature of the same name on the Clipping tab.

Same As Clipping. If you choose Same As Clipping from the Type popup menu, XPress uses whatever clipping path is applied to the image as your text runaround as well. I find this very convenient because I don't have to worry about two different paths. However, there's one exception: currently, you cannot edit this kind of runaround (see "Editing the Runaround," below). If you need to edit the runaround path, you'll have to use one of the other settings.

Also, remember that you can enter different Outset values for the runaround and the clipping paths. This is fortunate, because you almost always have to set these values differently—the outset for Clipping is typically zero, while a zero outset for Runaround would let the text get too close to the image (I will often use anywhere between 6 and 10 points of text runaround).

Figure 11-6
Non-White Areas
runaround

*QuarkXPress builds a runaround
path with lines and curves
around the image, based on
non-white pixels*

Picture Bounds. The Picture Bounds runaround setting is really simple: when you select it, XPress simply sets the text runaround to the edges of the picture (which is always a rectangle). Remember that the picture's edges are not the same as the edges of the picture box. I bet there's an awesome reason for someone to choose this setting . . . I just can't think of one right now.

▼ ▼

Tip: Watch the Box's Edges. QuarkXPress won't extend your image's text runaround past the edges of the picture box unless you turn off the Restrict To Box option on the Runaround tab of the Modify dialog box. You need to be careful with this checkbox, though. Generally, you'll want to turn this option off when the checkbox of the same name is turned off on the Clipping tab. On the other hand, if your image is close to the box's edge—even if it's not turned off—you may want to turn off Restrict To Box (or just make the picture box bigger; see Figure 11-7).

▼ ▼

Figure 11-7
Extending the box to
make the wrap work

*Problem: This text isn't
affected because the
runaround doesn't expand
past the edges of the box.*

*Turning off Restrict To Box
fixes the problem . . .*

*. . . so does simply
expanding the box.*

Editing the Runaround

QuarkXPress usually does a pretty good job of creating runarounds for you, but sooner or later you'll want to customize those paths by editing them manually. You can edit a runaround path if the Type popup menu on the Runaround tab is set to Embedded Path, Alpha Channel, Non-White Areas, Picture Bounds, or Manual. (Manual is only available for lines and text paths.)

To edit a path, select Runaround from the Edit submenu (under the Item menu, or press Option-F4 on the Macintosh or Control-F10 in Windows). All the same rules for editing paths in XPress apply here, including dragging points, adding and removing points with the Option/Alt key, and holding down the Control key (or Control and Shift on Windows) to convert a corner point to a curved one. (Again, you may want to review these features in Chapter 3, *Tools of the Trade,* as well as some of the tips on editing paths in "Clipping" in Chapter 10, *Fine-Tuning Images.*)

As soon as you edit a runaround path, XPress lists the item's runaround type as User Edited Path on the Runaround tab of the Modify dialog box. You can still change the path's Outset value on the Runaround tab, though, which is convenient (see Figure 11-8).

▼ ▼

Tip: Moving the Runaround Path. When you move a picture, its text-runaround path moves with it, of course. But you can also move the runaround path independently of the picture. First, select all the points on the runaround path by double-clicking on one point. (If the runaround path consists of more than one subpath, you can select all the points on all the subpaths by triple-clicking on a point.) Now, when you drag a point, you move the entire runaround path.

▼ ▼

Tip: Speed Up Polygon Editing. Every time you change a corner point or a line segment of a text-runaround polygon, QuarkXPress redraws the polygon and recomposes the text to go around it. This quickly becomes tedious. You can make the program hold off on reflowing the text until you've finished editing by holding down the spacebar. When you're finished, let go of the spacebar, and QuarkXPress reflows the text.

▼ ▼

Tip: Picture Wrap with No Picture. Generally, when you delete a picture from a picture box, the text runaround goes, too. However, XPress lets you save the runaround with the picture box, even if the picture is gone. All you have to do is choose Runaround from the Edit submenu (under the Item menu) and then move one of the runaround path's corner points (you can even just move it a tiny amount). Now that this path has been edited manually, when you

Figure 11-8

Editing a
text-runaround path

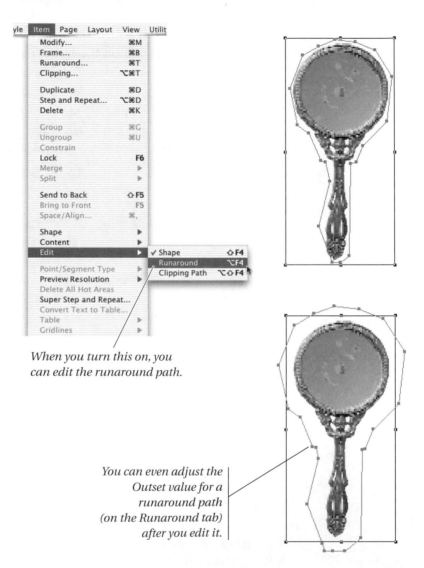

*When you turn this on, you
can edit the runaround path.*

*You can even adjust the
Outset value for a
runaround path
(on the Runaround tab)
after you edit it.*

delete the picture with the Content tool, the program asks you if you want to delete the runaround, too. Say "No," and the path remains.

This is useful when you're trying to force text into fancy shapes. Import a picture in the shape you're looking for, set up the runaround, and then delete the picture, leaving the runaround and the text just the way you want (see Figure 11-9).

▼ ▼

Tip: Wrapping around Text Paths. Trying to wrap text around a text path can be tricky (see Figure 11-10). The most important thing is to set the path's Text Alignment popup menu set to Center in the Modify dialog box. Then, try to get the text and the path shape as close to final as you can because it's a has-

Figure 11-9

Wrapping without
a picture

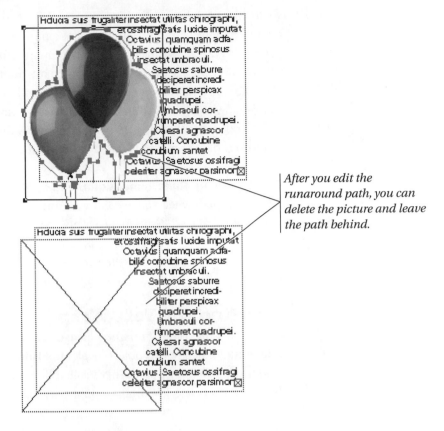

*After you edit the
runaround path, you can
delete the picture and leave
the path behind.*

Figure 11-10

Wrapping around
a text path

*Wrapping text around a
text path can be tricky.*

*Set the text to run along the center of
the path and the Runaround to
Manual (Outset to ½ the type size).*

*Now you can turn on Edit Runaround
and fine-tune the path.*

*Caution: If you reshape the text path,
the manual runaround stays behind.*

sle to change it later. I find it's often easiest to set the runaround Type to Manual and the Outset to about half the type size.

At this point, you can always edit the runaround path. But remember that you cannot change the shape of the path after you manually edit the runaround . . . well you can, but the runaround generally won't follow your change, so you'll have to dramatically adjust the runaround.

The only time that the runaround *does* follow the path change is when the text path is based on a straight line rather than a Bézier line.

▼ ▼

Tip: Changing Runaround Color. Unhappy with the color of the text-runaround path when you're editing it? You can change it by clicking on the color swatch labeled "Grid" in the Display panel of the Preferences dialog box (press Command-Option-Shift-Y or Ctrl-Alt-Shift-Y). Of course, this also changes the color of your baseline grid lines.

▼ ▼

Inverting the Text Wrap

Each of the types of text runaround I've discussed is based on wrapping text around the outside of an object or picture. However, you can also flow text *inside* a text runaround path. This is called "inverting the text wrap." Inverting the text wrap is less important than it used to be when you couldn't make Bézier-shaped text boxes; however, it still comes in handy sometimes.

The trick to inverting the text runaround is the Invert checkbox on the Runaround tab of the Modify dialog box. When you turn this on, XPress flips the runaround path so that text flows where the image is, and doesn't flow where the image is not. Of course, this isn't very useful at first because the image obscures the text. However, remember that if you then manually edit the runaround path (even a little), you can delete the image with the Content tool and keep the runaround path, achieving the inverted-runaround look.

▼ ▼

Tip: Disappearing Runaround Text. Remember that text runaround is based entirely on box layering. A runaround box must be on top of a text box in order for the runaround to have any effect on the text. If you assign a text runaround and find that you can't see the text behind the picture box, make sure that your box has a background color of None and that the image in the picture box has an appropriate clipping path applied to it.

▼ ▼

Running Text On Both Sides of an Object

For 10 years, people complained to Quark that they wanted to be able to wrap a column of text around both sides of an object rather than just around one side (see Figure 11-11). And for 10 years, the folks at Quark said "No, that would encourage you to make ugly designs that are difficult to read." However, they finally gave in, and now we can create as many unreadable designs as we want!

By default, text still only flows around one side of an object, and where it flows is entirely determined by which side is wider and fits more text. You can get text to flow around both sides of an object by turning on the Run Text Around All Sides option on the Text tab of the Modify dialog box. Note that you set this option for the text box itself, *not* the box that is causing the runaround.

You're not alone in thinking this is a strange place for this particular checkbox. However, there is a benefit here: if you want the text to flow around multiple objects on your page, you only have to turn on this option once, rather than for each individual runaround object.

Figure 11-11
Text wrap on all sides

Please keep in mind that the new and improved KvetchPaint 2000, with panoramic 3-D virtual reality halftone support, psychic toolbox, master enslavement for extended thought control, weather control, and blather control, is not yet Y2K compatible. On January 1st, your version of

Before:
The text wraps on the side of the graphic that offers more space.

Please keep in mind that the new and improved KvetchPaint 2000, with panoramic 3-D virtual reality halftone support, psychic toolbox, master enslavement for extended thought control, weather control, and blather control, is not yet Y2K compatible. On January 1st, your version of KvetchPaint 2000 will grind to a halt, along with much of the world economy.

After:
The text wraps right past the graphics.

▼ ▼

Anchored Boxes

When Samuel Clemens said, "Pictures are in picture boxes and text is in text boxes and never the twain shall meet," he just didn't know about anchored boxes. (What? He didn't say that? Never mind.) In fact, many programs let you paste graphic images directly into text so that as you type, the images flow along with the text in the same position. These are usually called *inline graphics*.

QuarkXPress takes this concept one step further, however, by letting you anchor either a picture or a text box directly into the flow of text. You can even anchor a line or a text path into text. (For the sake of simplicity, I'm going to stick with the phrase "anchored box" instead of "anchored boxes and lines and text paths and . . . .")

Anchored boxes can be used in many situations: placing small pictures in text as icons, creating drop caps with pictures, or allowing tables and figures to keep their place in text. Let's look at how these anchored boxes are created and how to work with them.

Turning a Box into a Character

I like to think of anchored boxes as a way of turning a picture or a text box into a character that can be manipulated in a text block. This proves to be a useful model for working with anchored boxes. There are two steps involved with anchoring a picture box or a text box as a "character."

1. **Cut or Copy.** The first step in creating an anchored box is to cut or copy the picture or text box using the Item tool. Click on the picture or text box, and select Cut or Copy from the Edit menu (or press Command/Ctrl-X or Command/Ctrl-C). Because you're using the Item tool rather than the Content tool, the box itself is being cut or copied, along with its contents.

2. **Paste.** The second step is to paste the box into the text using the Content tool. Select the text box and place the cursor where you want your anchored text box to sit, then select Paste from the Edit menu (or press Command/Ctrl-V). Because you're using the Content tool, the box is pasted in as a character in the text block rather than as a separate box.

▼ ▼

Tip: Item Cutting with Content Tool. The Content tool is selected in the Tool palette, but you want to cut or copy with the Item tool? Don't go fussing around with palettes; just Command-Option-X or Command-Option-C (or

Ctrl-Alt-X or Ctrl-Alt-C). Adding the Option/Alt key tells XPress to cut or copy the item rather than the contents of the box.

▼ ▼

What you can't do. You can't anchor everything. In XPress 3, you could only anchor rectangular boxes. Then, in version 4, there were only two prohibitions: you couldn't anchor a group of objects, and you couldn't anchor a box inside an anchored box. In version 5, they added the ability to anchor groups. So now in version 6 everything is fair game—even Bézier curves and text on a path— except you can't anchor a box that has an anchored box in it.

Modifying Anchored Boxes

Those friendly engineers at Quark removed some other restrictions on anchored boxes, too—for example, what you can and can't do to an anchored item after it's been pasted into text. You couldn't rotate boxes in version 3; now you can. You had limited resizing and cropping abilities; now you can crop and resize at will. In fact, I can find only three limitations to what you can do to anchored boxes.

▶ You can't select and drag an anchored box to a new location on the page (see "Tip: Dragging Anchored Boxes," below).

▶ You can't use the Rotate tool (you have to use the Measurements palette or the Modify dialog box).

▶ You can't use text linking to connect an anchored box to another text box (or vice versa).

Otherwise, you can modify an anchored box in the same ways you modify regular boxes.

Remember that an anchored box acts like a character in your paragraph, and it follows all the same rules as normal text (though the only character-level attributes that really have any effect on anchored boxes are baseline shift and kerning).

▼ ▼

Tip: Adjusting Runarounds for Anchored Boxes. Early versions of XPress offered almost no control over the runaround specifications for anchored boxes; you had to set the runaround before anchoring the box, and even then, XPress only paid attention to the Top field of the Runaround dialog box. Fortunately, those days are over, and you can specify any kind of runaround you want. In fact, I was surprised to find that you can even specify a negative runaround for an anchored item. This turns out to be really useful and lets you create all kinds of special effects.

One reader, Christopher Deignan, points out that you can use this to overlap two anchored boxes or even to remove space between rotated boxes (see Figure 11-12).

Figure 11-12

Negative runaround
for anchored boxes

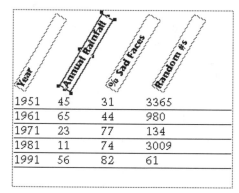

By changing the Left and Right runaround setting to a negative number, these anchored boxes are placed more closely together. (Kerning would also work, but you couldn't get them as close.)

▼ ▼

Tip: Backgrounds in Anchored Boxes. Note that the background color for an anchored box is not necessarily the same as that of the text box in which it is located. For example, if your text box is set to 10-percent gray and you anchor a white picture box in it, the anchored picture box won't match its surroundings (you'll get a white box on a gray background). If you can think of a better word than "tacky" to describe this, let me know. Instead, be sure to specify None for the background color in all anchored boxes.

▼ ▼

Alignment. You can vertically align an anchored box in two ways: by specifying Ascent or Baseline (see Figure 11-13).

▶ ASCENT. When you specify an anchored box to align by Ascent, the top of the box aligns with the tallest ascender in that text line. The rest of the figure drops down and text wraps around it. Ascent is most commonly used for creating initial caps and heads.

Figure 11-13

Baseline alignment versus
Ascent alignment for
anchored boxes

Align with Text settings (when you select an anchored box)

Align on Baseline   *Align on Ascent*

▶ **BASELINE.** When you specify an anchored box to align by Baseline, the bottom of the box aligns with the baseline of the line it's on. This is very helpful if the anchored box is attached within a line of text and is acting as if it were a special text character.

How the text in previous lines accommodates this baseline alignment depends on the leading in the paragraph. If you specify absolute leading, the anchored box may overlap the text above it (see Figure 11-14). If you are using automatic or relative leading, the space between lines is increased to accommodate a larger anchored box. Again, the model of the anchored box as text character is particularly fitting, as these are exactly the effects you would achieve by using an oversize character in a text block (see "Initial Caps" in Chapter 6, *Type and Typography*).

Figure 11-14

Anchored box alignment

F ⁀ ⁀ ⁀ ⁀ /e thy father lies;
C   are coral made;
T   arls that were his eyes:
                    Nothing in him that doth fade,
But doth suffer a sea-change
Into something rich and strange.

Box is aligned by baseline; text has absolute leading.

Full fathom five thy father lies;
Of his bones are coral made:
Those are pearls that were his eyes:

                    Nothing in him that doth fade,
But doth suffer a sea-change

Also aligned by baseline, but text has automatic leading.

When you're using a baseline-aligned anchored box that acts as a character within a line, I recommend that you use absolute leading for your paragraph. Otherwise, all hell can break loose and text is shoved all over the place (see "Tip: Anchored Figures on Their Own Line," below).

You can choose the alignment of the anchored box in two places: on the Box tab of the Modify dialog box or on the Measurements palette.

▼ ▼

Tip: Anchored Figures on Their Own Line. You might use anchored boxes for symbols, complex dingbats, or company logos within a line of text, but more frequently you'll use them as single "characters" within their own paragraph.

I know I said that I hated automatic leading and that you should never use it, but here's an exception. Setting the paragraph that contains the anchored box to Auto leading ensures that there is enough space above the image that it doesn't overlap any text. The alignment of the anchored box should be set to Baseline, too (see Figure 11-15).

▼ ▼

Tip: Aligning Anchored Text Boxes. If you're trying to align the baselines of text in an anchored text box with text that surrounds the box, you need to make sure of four things (see Figure 11-16).

▶ The leading and font size of the text in the anchored text box and in the surrounding text box must be equal.

▶ The runaround for the anchored text box must be set to zero on all sides.

Figure 11-15

Putting anchored
boxes on their own line

*Absolute
leading
(yuck!)*

*Automatic
leading
(just for the
paragraphs
with anchored
boxes)*

*This anchored
text box is a
caption that
will always
stay with the
graphic.*

▶ The anchored text box must have a Text Inset value of zero. You enter this value in the Text Inset field of the Modify dialog box.

▶ The anchored text box must be set to Ascent alignment.

▼ ▼

Working with Anchored Boxes

What happens if you don't place the anchored box exactly where it should be? Or if you decide to change your mind and delete the anchored box? Don't worry, I've got answers for those questions, too.

Moving anchored boxes. As I said earlier, you cannot move an anchored box by just dragging it around like you would any other box. There are two ways to

Figure 11-16
Aligning anchored text

Squares have become symbolic of our human ability to measure, to solve, and to partition. Where circles denote the infinite, squares indicate the finite. Where circles reflect the mystery of the natural world, squares enabled early civilizations to segment the land for farming and for ownership. We no longer live in circula

This text is shaded and has a border around it. The trick? It's an anchored box. Note that the baselines are aligned perfectly.

Squares have become symbolic of our human ability to measure, to solve, and to partition. Where circles denote the infinite, squares indicate the finite. Where circles reflect the mystery of the natural world, squares enabled early civilizations to segment the land for farming and for ownership. We no longer live in circular

move an anchored box: the way that the documentation says you can, and the way that makes the most sense.

Quark's documentation says that you must select the anchored box with the Item tool, select Cut from the Edit menu, and then switch to the Content tool to position the cursor and paste the box. This is consistent with the way that anchored boxes are placed in text anyway. However, using the concept that once an anchored box is placed in a text block it behaves like a text character, I prefer to move this anchored box "character" by cutting and pasting it with the Content tool alone. This just seems more intuitive to me, and it works just fine.

▼ ▼

Tip: Selecting Anchored Boxes. If you want to select an anchored box as a text character, try placing the cursor just before or after it and then pressing the Left or Right Arrow key while holding down the Shift key. This is often easier than trying to drag the cursor over the anchored box.

▼ ▼

Tip: Dragging Anchored Boxes. Actually, it turns out that you *can* drag anchored boxes. The key is the program's Drag and Drop text-editing feature, plus a little ingenuity. When Drag and Drop is turned on in the Preferences dialog box, you can select a range of text and drag it to where you want it to be. If an anchored box is part of that text, it goes, too. If you select *just* the anchored box, you must strategically place the cursor directly over the left side of the item before dragging. Be sure to have the text-insertion cursor rather than the arrow cursor, or else it won't work.

▼ ▼

Deleting anchored boxes. I'll say it just one more time: anchored boxes are just like text characters. Do you delete text characters with the Delete function from the Item menu (or press Command/Ctrl-K)? No. A character is not an item; it's a character, and should be treated as such. If you want to stamp out the measly existence of an anchored box, place the cursor after it and press the Delete key—or place the cursor before it and press Shift-Delete.

▼ ▼

Tip: Getting an Anchored Box Out Again. At first it seems like there's no way to turn an anchored box into a regular box again. But I like to say, "There's always a workaround." As it happens, there are actually two ways to get an anchored box out as a standalone item. The first way is to select it with either the Content tool or the Item tool (click on the box rather than dragging over it as if it were a character) and select Duplicate from the Item menu (Command/Ctrl-D). This makes a copy of the box, but in a standard (nonanchored) form.

The second method is to select the anchored box with the Item tool (just click on it), copy it, and then select Paste, still using the Item tool.

▼ ▼

Tip: Too-Wide Anchored Boxes. It's easy to make an anchored box wider or taller than the text box it's in. Don't do it! XPress automatically pushes the anchored box (and all the text after it) out of the text box. If no other boxes in the text chain are large enough to fit the anchored box, the story hangs indefinitely in "overset" limbo until you figure out a way to delete or resize the anchored box again.

This happens most frequently when people try to paste an anchored box that is the same width as the surrounding text box. What they're forgetting is that the text box usually has a Text Inset value of 1 point and that the anchored box often has a runaround value as well. Set both the Text Inset of the text box and the Runaround value of the to-be anchored box to zero, and one will fit in the other.

▼ ▼

Tip: Vertical Rules. Placing a vertical rule to the left of a paragraph has always posed a tricky problem in XPress, but no longer. With anchored lines, it's a snap. Just draw a line of the proper height and format it the way you want it to look (width, style, color, and so on), cut it out, and paste it in (with the Content tool) as the first character in the paragraph. Make sure the anchored line is set to Ascent rather than Baseline on the Line tab of the Modify dialog box.

In order to get it out into the margin, you'll have to use the hanging-indent trick: give the paragraph a positive Left indent, and then a negative First Line indent. Finally, place a tab between the anchored line and the first character of text in the paragraph (see Figure 11-17).

▼ ▼

Tip: Return of Vertical Rules. The technique in the last tip built vertical rules to the left of a column. Getting a vertical rule along the right side of a paragraph is tougher (see Figure 11-18).

1. Create and format the vertical line as before, but this time, paste it as the only character in its own paragraph, *after* the paragraph you're trying to mark.

2. Set the horizontal alignment for this paragraph to Right.

3. Set the leading for this paragraph to .001 (as near as you can get to zero). This ensures that the baseline of the anchored line is at the baseline of the last line of the preceding paragraph.

Figure 11-17
Anchored vertical rule

Figure 11-18
Vertical rules to the right
of the paragraph

This rule is anchored by itself on a flush-right paragraph with leading set to .001 points.

You'll have to adjust the Right indent for the paragraph so that the vertical rule doesn't overlap the text. And don't forget that you can always stretch the line after it's anchored, if you didn't get its height just right.

▼ ▼

Paragraph Rules

While you can now anchor rules (lines) into text, you can produce anchored rules using a different method as well: the Rules feature. This kind of rule is actually a paragraph attribute and is found in the Paragraph Attributes dialog box (see Chapter 6, *Type and Typography*). There are several benefits to using paragraph rules, including the ability to build them into style sheets. In this section I'll explore how to make these anchored paragraph rules. Unfortunately, these rules can only be horizontal (see "Tip: Vertical Rules," earlier in this chapter).

Rule Above/Rule Below

The one way to set anchored paragraph rules is via the Rules tab in the Paragraph Attributes dialog box. While your text cursor is in a paragraph or highlighting it, you can select Rules from the Style menu (or press Command-Shift-N or Ctrl-Shift-N). You then have the choice to place a rule above the paragraph, below it, or both (see Figure 11-19).

You have many options for the placement, size, and style of your horizontal rules. Let's look at each element of the dialog box.

Style. The right side of the Rules tab contains the style specifications for the rule. You can choose the line style, width (thickness), color, and shade for the rule using the popup menus. You can also type in your own value for the Width and Shade fields, to the thousandth of a point or tenth of a percent.

The line styles available are the same styles available for all lines (see "Lines" in Chapter 2, *QuarkXPress Basics*).

Length. You can specify the length of the rule and its horizontal position using the Length popup menu and the From Left and From Right fields. The initial decision you need to make is whether you want the rule to stretch from the left indent of the paragraph to the right indent (select Indents from the Length popup menu) or to stretch only as far as the text (select Text from the same menu). Figure 11-20 shows examples of these two settings.

Horizontal offsets. The next considerations in determining the length of the rule are its offsets from left and right. You can specify how far from the left or

Figure 11-19
Rules tab of the
Paragraph Attributes
dialog box

right the rule should start (or end) by typing a measurement into the From Left and/or the From Right fields. Your only limitation in offsetting the rule is that it cannot go outside the text box. For instance, if your paragraph is set to a left indent of "1p6", the minimum left offset you can specify is "-1p6" (anything more than that would extend the rule out of the box).

Vertical position. The third specification you can make for an anchored paragraph rule is its vertical position relative to the paragraph to which it is attached. This concept is a little tricky, and Quark's documentation doesn't do a lot to help clarify the idea. Let's break it down into pieces.

The vertical positioning of the rule is set in the Offset field. I don't like the word "offset," as it confuses the issue. I prefer the term *positioning*, so that's what I'll use. Just remember that these values go in the Offset field. You can specify positioning with either an absolute measurement or a percentage. QuarkXPress handles each of these very differently.

▶ **ABSOLUTE.** An absolute measurement for a rule above is measured from the bottom of the rule to the baseline of the first line in the paragraph. An absolute measurement for a rule below is measured from the baseline of the last line in the paragraph to the top of the rule (see Figure 11-21).

▶ **PERCENTAGE.** Specifying the vertical position of a rule by percentage is slightly more complex. The first thing to remember is that the percentage you are specifying is a percentage of the space between paragraphs. This space is measured from the descenders of the last line of the paragraph to the ascenders of the first line of the next paragraph.

Let's look at an example. If you set Rule Below for a paragraph with an offset of 60 percent, QuarkXPress measures the distance between the two paragraphs (descender to ascender) and places the top of the rule 60 percent of that distance down. The rule grows *down* from that position as you increase its weight. Rule Above is placed with its bottom, rather than its top, in the appropriate position, and the rule grows *up* from there. A rule above and a rule below, when both are set to 50 percent, fall at exactly the same place (halfway between the paragraphs).

To me, percentage-based positioning is equivalent to automatic leading: I don't like it. I don't think it should be run out of town, because there's always

Figure 11-20

The Length setting in Rules Above/Below

Rule Above: Length set to Text

The night was uncommonly dark, and a pestilential blast blew from the plain of Catoul, that would have deterred any other traveller however urgent the call: but Carathis enjoyed most whatever filled others with dread. Nerkes concurred in opinion with her; and cafour had a particular predilection for a pestilence. In the morning this accomplished caravan, with the woodfellers, who directed their route, halted on the edge of an extensive marsh, from whence so noxious a vapour arose, as would have destroyed many animal but Alboufaki, who naturally inhaled these malignant fogs with delight.

Rule Below: Length set to Indents

Figure 11-21

Vertical positioning of rules

How many psychiatrists does it take to change a lightbulb?

Absolute positioning measures from the baseline to the top of the rule below.

Only one. But the lightbulb has to want to change.

How many graduate students does it take to change a lightbulb?

Percentage positioning measures the space between the paragraphs.

Only one. But it takes nine years.

a place for that kind of feature, but in general, I don't like to use it. Why? There are some problems with percentage-based rules. For example, if you give a rule above a percentage Offset value, the rule doesn't show up if that paragraph sits at the top of a text box. (The reason is obvious, when you think about it: at the top of a column, you can't take the percentage of space between two paragraphs.) Similarly, a rule below with a percentage Offset doesn't show up if that paragraph is the last one in the text box.

It is nice that positioning a rule based on a percentage ensures that the rule doesn't overlap any text (if it needs to, it pushes the paragraphs away from each other). But all in all, I would rather have complete control over the rule's position and feel sure that the rule is there, no matter what happens to the paragraph.

On the other hand, if you want a rule halfway between two paragraphs, setting Offset to 50 percent is much faster than trying to figure out what absolute value you should enter.

▼ ▼

Tip: Reversed Type in Rules. This is one of the oldest tricks in the book. You can reverse type that is anchored to text by putting a thick rule above a paragraph and setting the type in the paragraph to White. You need to specify a vertical position for the rule so that it "overlaps" its own line. Out of habit, I always use a rule above, sized about 4 or 5 points larger than the text, and I specify a -2-point or -3-point Offset (vertical position). You can use this same technique to create multiple-tinted tables (see Figure 11-22).

Figure 11-22				
Type in a rule				

Figure 11-22
Type in a rule

SPRING—1624			
Spread	750	1000	——— *Rule Above with an Offset of -2 points*
Full page	600	800	
Half page	400	500	*These are rules, too!*
Quarter page	275	375	
Spot	175	250	

You can specify a negative Offset up to half the thickness of the rule. This is why negative values work when you're making big rules like this, but not when you're making dainty fine lines.

▼ ▼

Tip: Changing Underscore Position. There are very few ways to change the position or size of the underscore style (the line that runs under text). Most people don't care about this because it's often considered a typographic abomination. Nonetheless, some people need to use it (or at least *think* they need to use it), so here's a tip for how to adjust the position, size, color, and so on.

1. Select the text to be underlined, cut it, and paste it in a separate text box. Now cut that text box and paste it (as an anchored box) where the original word was. Make sure that the baselines of the anchored text match the baselines of the text around it (see "Tip: Aligning Anchored Text Boxes," earlier in this chapter).

2. Give the text inside the anchored text box a rule below. Set the rule below to whatever size, offset, shade, style, and color you want (see Figure 11-23).

Figure 11-23
Creating a custom underline by using anchored boxes

Custom underline built in an anchored box

His mother was a witch, and one so strong
That could <u>control the moon,</u> make flows and ebbs,
And deal in her command without her power.

Here's one more way to do this: Use the Custom Underline feature from Quark's Type Tricks XTension (it ships free with XPress). This feature lets you apply any color, shade, thickness, and vertical offset from the baseline (see Figure 11-24). You can create a custom underline by selecting some text and then choosing Custom from the Underline Styles submenu (under the Style menu). Unfortunately, although the feature name implies you can save them as "styles" to be used elsewhere, you cannot—you have to apply the formatting manually each time you want to use it.

Figure 11-24
Custom Underlines
(with Type Tricks)

Later, if you want to remove the underline, choose Remove Custom Underlines from the Type Style submenu (under the Style menu)

▼ ▼

Tip: Anchored Rule Below. You can create all kinds of interesting effects by anchoring boxes inside other text boxes. Figure 11-25 shows an example of how a multi-line text box can be added. Remember that all aspects of this can be tagged with paragraph and character style sheets, so you can change the formatting later at will.

Figure 11-25
More anchored
underscores

Once upon a time, there was a _____ (noun) that couldn't _____ (bodily function) except when s/he _____ (verb). Then, one day, a beautiful _____ (type of royalty) came out of the nearby forest and proclaimed _____ (cliché).

Once upon a time, there was a _____ that couldn't _____ except when s/he _____.
(noun)   (bodily function)   (verb)
Then, one day, a beautiful _____ came out of the
(type of royalty)
nearby forest and proclaimed _____.
(cliché)

▼ ▼

Poking and Prodding

Where text meets graphics: like I said, it's a wild, woolly frontier just waiting to be mastered. We've explored how different boxes and page elements can interact, but these are mysterious regions where there is no substitute for poking and prodding on your own.

The next chapter deals with an aspect of working with XPress that is critical to most of us: color. After reading that chapter, you'll be able to create any kind of page known to humanity (and a few that aren't).

12

COLOR

L ook around you. Unless you're fully color-blind, everything around you has color. It's not really surprising that folks have wanted to work with color in their documents since . . . well, since they've been creating documents! What *is* surprising is how complicated working with color can be, especially with all this computer equipment that's supposed to make life easy for us.

There's a range of complicated issues in desktop color: specifying the color you want, getting that color to print on a color or (more likely) a black-and-white laser printer, and producing separated films ready for offset printing. Getting color off the desktop was once a joke among the few people who had actually tried. However, as the '90s rolled in, people's success stories outnumbered their failures and it became clear that desktop color was here to stay. Of course, achieving quality color on your Macintosh or PC is still not as easy as turning on the computer; we still have our work cut out for us. But at least now we know it's possible.

I begin this chapter with an overview of some basic theories of color, including the various color models (ways in which you specify color on the computer). This next leads me into the color components of the QuarkXPress features set, including building and applying colors, and generating traps for better print quality. Although I discuss the fundamentals of color separation here, I'll cover the area of generating color separations of your documents in Chapter 13, *Printing*. Also, note that I won't cover XPress's color management system (CMS) much here; I discuss that in Appendix A, *Color Management*.

▼ ▼

What You See and What You Get

Before I even begin talking desktop color, it's important for you to know that the color you see on the screen is almost never what you'll get from your color printer or slide recorder, much less what you can expect to see come off a printing press.

The medium is the message. The primary reason for this color differential is the difference in the medium. Colors are displayed on the screen by lighting up phosphors which emit colored light. This is significantly different from printed color, which depends on other light sources to reflect off it into your eyes. If you use a different method of showing colors, you will always see different colors.

Pantone colors are a great example of this: take a Pantone swatch book and pick a color. Hold that color up to the screen next to QuarkXPress's Pantone color simulation. Chances are it'll look like a totally different color.

Even similar devices can generate wildly differing color. If you've ever walked into a television store and seen the same image on thirty different screens, you know that different monitors display color differently (that's why your document looks different on your officemate's screen than it does on yours). The same thing goes for printing presses and color printers: even though they may claim to print with cyan, yellow, magenta, and black, those four colors may well be different depending on where in the world you're printing, which company's inks you're using, what sort of press your job is printing on, and even what the weather is like that day.

Calibration and color management. There's only so much you can do about the color discrepancies you'll encounter. Some monitors are better than others at displaying certain colors. And if you don't already have a 24-bit color video card ("millions of colors" or "true color"), you should definitely get one. You can buy a monitor-calibration system from companies like Radius or Colorific to adjust your screen's colors so that they'll more closely match your printed output.

Another solution is color management, using a system like ColorSync (see Appendix A, *Color Management*). These systems adjust the colors that show up on the screen to more closely match the final output colors. However, even these are limited and often can't manage everything on your page.

Whatever you end up using, remember that what you see is *rarely* what you get.

Use swatch books. Because of all this uncertainty, it's important to specify your colors from a swatch book. Look at the book, see what color you want, and specify it. If possible, create your own swatch book, and print it on your final output device—offset press, color printer, slide recorder, whatever. If you're printing with process inks, spec your colors from a process swatch book such as TruMatch. If you're printing with PMS inks, use a PMS spot-color swatch book. (If these terms don't mean much to you, I'll explain them all in the next section.)

Describing Color

In a perfect world you would be able to say, "I want this object to be burnt sienna," and your computer, service bureau, and lithographer would know exactly the color you mean. Outside of picking Crayola colors, however, this just can't be done. Everyone from scientists to artists to computer programmers has been trying for centuries to come up with a general model for specifying and re-creating colors. In the past 50 years alone, these color models have been created: HSB, NTSC, CMYK, YIQ, CIE, PAL, HSL, RGB, CCIR, RS-170, and HSI, among others. (And you thought that graphic file-format names were far out!)

QuarkXPress presently handles four color models (RGB, CMYK, HSB, and Lab), plus several color-matching systems, or libraries: Focoltone, TruMatch, Toyo, DIC, Pantone Coated, Pantone Uncoated, Pantone Process, Pantone Solid to Process, and Pantone Hexachrome. These color models are intimately connected with printing and other reproduction methods, so I'll first discuss the particulars of printing color, then move into each color model in turn.

Spot Versus Process Color

When dealing with color, either on the desktop or off, you'll need to understand the differences between process and spot color. Both are commonly used in the printing process. Both can give you a wide variety of colors. But they aren't interchangeable. Depending on your final output device, you may also be dealing with composite colors. Let's look at each of these, one at a time.

Process color. Look at any color magazine or junk mail you've received lately. If you look closely at a color photograph or a tinted color box, you'll probably see lots of little dots that make up the color. These are color halftones consisting of one to four colors: cyan, magenta, yellow, and black (see Chapter 10, *Fine-Tuning Images,* for more information on halftones). I'll talk about this color model, CMYK, a little later on; what's important here is that many, many colors are being represented by overlaying tints of the four basic colors. Our eyes blend all these colors together so that ultimately we see the color we're intended to see.

Cyan, magenta, yellow, and black are the process colors. The method—or process—of separating the millions of colors into only four colors is referred to as creating *process-color separations*. Each separation, or plate, is a piece of film or paper that contains artwork for only one of the colors. Your lithographer can take the four pieces of film, expose a plate from each of the four pieces, and use those four plates on a press.

Don't get me wrong: process color is not just for full-color photographs or images. If you're printing a four-color job, you can use each of the process colors individually or in combination to create colored type, rules, or tint blocks on your document page. These items generally appear as solid colors to the untrained eye, but are actually made from "tint builds" of the process colors.

Spot color. If you are printing only a small number of colors (three or fewer), you probably want to use spot colors. The idea behind spot colors is that the printing ink is just the color you want, which makes it unnecessary to build a color using the four process colors. With spot color, for example, if you want some type to be colored teal blue, you print it on a plate (often called an overlay) which is separate from the black plate. Your lithographer prints that type using a teal-blue ink—probably a PMS ink (see "Pantone and Pantone Uncoated," below) like PMS 3135 or 211—and then uses black to print the rest of the job.

Let me recap: The difference between process and spot colors is that process colors are built by overlaying tints of four separate inks, while spot colors are printed using just one colored ink (the color you specify). In either case, your lithographer runs the page through the press once for each color's plate, or uses a multicolor press that prints the colors successively in a single pass.

Mixing process and spot colors. There is no reason why you can't use both spot and process colors together in a document, if you've got the budget for a five- or six-color print job. Some lithographers have six- or eight-color presses, which can print the four process colors along with two or more spot colors. In fact, one book I know of—Edward Tufte's *Envisioning Information*—was printed with 12 solid spot colors.

Composite color. If your final output is created on a film recorder (slides or transparencies) or on a color printer, you may well encounter what I call "composite color." Composite color falls between spot color and process color. For example, most film recorders print using RGB format (more on this format a little later on), whether your color is specified as CMYK or RGB or anything else QuarkXPress allows you to do. Similarly, some color printers represent both spot and process colors alike by mixing colored waxes or dyes on the paper.

The key here is that the colors you specify are being represented using some color model which you may not have intended. If you know that you are printing on such a device, you should refer to the service bureau and/or your owner's manual for tips on how to work best with that device.

▼ ▼

Tip: Spot-Color Pinch Hitters. You don't *have* to create your own spot colors in your documents. If your job contains only black and one to three spot colors, you can use a process color (cyan, magenta, or yellow) to pinch-hit for each spot color. When you take your film to the printers, give them written instructions such as "Print all film labeled 'Cyan' as Pantone 234 and all film labeled 'Magenta' as Pantone 567." If you do this, though—to avoid confusion down the line—clearly label each piece of film with a piece of white tape with the correct color written on it (such as "PMS 567"). If you're extra cautious, use a black permanent marker to black out the original color name on the film.

This trick makes it easy for periodicals who use a new set of spot colors each month. You don't have to painfully respec your imported graphics that use the spot colors; spec them once as the same process color as you're using in XPress, and it gets mapped automatically.

▼ ▼

Tip: Put Black Type on a Fifth Plate. While process color is printed in four colors, that doesn't mean you have to only have four pieces of film for each page. Especially if you're running the type of operation where last-minute type changes are frequent, you might find it helpful to make your black type a spot color, instead of normal black. You can spec this fifth color to look black (or near black), and set it to overprint. When you print separations, all the type ends up on a fifth plate all by itself. Then, when you take the film to the printer, tell them to burn that extra piece of film on the black plate.

While you increase your film costs at first (five plates instead of four), you'll find that last-minute changes are much less expensive (you only have to reprint that one plate instead of four). It's up to you to determine which method will be the more cost-effective for you.

▼ ▼

Color Models

Before I jump into how to create and use colors in XPress, let's talk a bit about each of the color models that QuarkXPress handles and what each model is good for.

RGB. Color models are generally broken down into two classes: additive and subtractive systems. An *additive* color system is counter-intuitive to most people: the more color you add to an object, the closer to white you get. In the RGB model, adding 100 percent of red, green, and blue to an area results in pure white. If you have a color television or a color monitor on your computer, you already have had a great deal of experience with RGB. These pieces of equipment describe colors by "turning on" red, green, and blue phosphors on the screen. Various colors are created by mixing these three colors together.

▶ Black = zero percent of all three colors

▶ Yellow = red + green

▶ Magenta = red + blue

▶ Cyan = green + blue

All slide recorders image using RGB because they're projecting light at film. Color scanners always scan in RGB mode (even for those big, expensive drum scans) because light is always measured in RGB. If the image is destined for print, some software (perhaps the software that runs the scanner) must convert it to CMYK.

CMYK. *Subtractive* colors, on the other hand, become more white as you subtract color from them, and get darker as you add more color. This is analogous to painting on a white piece of paper. CMY (let's leave the K aside for a moment) is called a subtractive color model: the more cyan, magenta, and yellow you add together, the closer to black you get.

The connection between RGB and CMY is interesting: they are exact opposites of each other. You can take an RGB color and mathematically invert each of the RGB values and get the same color in the CMY model (see Figure 12-1). If this doesn't come intuitively to you (it doesn't to me), don't worry. The theory behind this is much less important than what it implies.

The implication of RGB and CMY having an inverse relation is that colors in either model should be easy to convert. This is true. They are easy to convert. The problem is that the CMY model has few practical applications. Cyan, magenta, and yellow inks don't really add up to black in the real world because ink pigments are never pure cyan, magenta, or yellow. Adding CMY together makes a muddy brown. Thus, lithographers over the years have learned that they must add a black element to the printing process, and that's where the K comes in. (K stands for "key," and signifies black because B might be confused for blue.)

While you can describe many colors using these four, you can't generate as many colors as RGB can (or the number of colors we can see). In fact, many different combinations of CMYK actually describe the same color. (Later in this chapter, I'll discuss an offshoot of CMYK, called Hexachrome, which uses six colors to represent even more colors.)

It's important to remember that knowing the percentages of cyan, yellow, magenta, and black does not actually tell you what a color looks like. CMYK is like a cooking recipe, and just as different chefs or different ingredients will generate very different tastes, different printers, presses, or brands of ink will produce different colors.

Because of these factors, the conversion from RGB to CMYK (again, this is called "color separation") is nowhere near as precise as one could hope. In fact, different programs use different conversion algorithms, so an RGB color from QuarkXPress prints differently from how it would from Photoshop or some other application.

Figure 12-1

Complementary colors

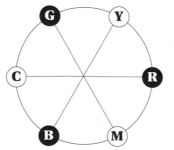

Emitted and reflected (additive and subtractive) colors complement one another. Red is complemented by cyan, green by magenta, and blue by yellow.

HSB. Rather than breaking a color down into subparts, the HSB model describes a color by its hue, saturation, and brightness. The *hue* is basically the color's position in a color spectrum which starts at red, moves through magenta to blue, through green to yellow, and then through orange back to red. The *saturation* of the color can be described as the amount of color in it. Or, conversely, the amount of white in it. A light pink, for example, has a lower saturation than a bright red. The color's *brightness* reflects the amount of black in it. Thus, that same bright red would, with a lower brightness, change from a vibrant red to a dark, dull, reddish-black.

You could say that mixing a color (a hue) with white produces a *tint* (a degree of saturation). Mix it with black to produce a *tone* (a degree of brightness).

HSB is not easy to understand intuitively, especially when it comes to specifying colors. For example, here are the hue values for the three spot colors in XPress's default color list.

- ▶ Red = zero

- ▶ Green = 21,845 (QuarkXPress calls this 33.3 percent)

- ▶ Blue = 43,690 (QuarkXPress calls this 66.7 percent)

You may find HSB useful if you're creating slides on a film recorder or doing multimedia, but it's not of much use for print publishing. I tend to simply forget that it's there.

Lab. CIE Lab (which appears in XPress simply as "Lab") is designed to describe what colors look like, regardless of what device they're displayed on. Because of this, Lab colors are called "device-independent." Where HSB represents colors positioned around a color wheel, Lab uses a more accurate but significantly less intuitive arrangement. L stands for luminance, describing how bright the color appears to the human eye. (Unlike brightness in HSB, luminance takes into account the fact that we see green as brighter than blue.)

The "a" and "b" channels in CIE Lab represent spectrums from green to red, and from blue to yellow, respectively. Don't feel dumb if you find it hard to get your head around Lab color. It *is* difficult, because it's an abstract mathematical construct—it doesn't correspond to anything we can actually experience.

The fact that Lab is device-independent should mean that it's a great way to transfer colors from one application or machine to another. Unfortunately, XPress's implementation of Lab is so limited that it's not really worth using. But who knows? Maybe I'll see improvements in future versions that will change my mind.

Color-Matching Systems

In addition to the four color models in QuarkXPress that you use to define colors, there are also ten color-matching systems—essentially libraries of predefined colors that are based on actual, printed color swatch books. Four of these systems—Pantone, Pantone Uncoated, Toyo, and DIC—are for use with spot-color printing. The others—TruMatch, Focoltone, Pantone Process, Pantone Solid to Process, and uncoated and coated versions of Pantone Hexachrome—are for process-color work.

While software companies love to top the feature lists on how many color libraries they offer, these libraries are really little more than conveniences. You can specify process colors by simply typing in the values, for instance, without ever going near the color libraries. And with spot colors, you can use any names and any color specifications you want; the spot-color plates still print out as black. There are advantages to using these libraries, however, aside from their paint-by-number simplicity.

▶ **SPOT-COLOR LIBRARIES.** With spot-color systems like Pantone Coated and Uncoated, using the library ensures that the right color name prints on each overlay, and makes it more likely that the color name in your document will match the one in imported EPS graphics (see "Color from Outside Sources," later in this chapter). Also, the colors are set up with color specifications designed to give you the best output that's reasonably possible on screen and on color printers; you don't have to figure it out yourself.

▶ **PROCESS-COLOR LIBRARIES.** With process-color work, the only two advantages to using the color libraries are that you don't have to type in the color name and color specification by hand, and that you can easily communicate a color to someone else who also has your kind of swatch book.

Again, these color libraries are merely conveniences. No matter what method you use for specifying colors, you should be looking at printed swatch books to decide what color you want.

Given those caveats, here's a rundown of the color libraries available in QuarkXPress.

TruMatch. TruMatch is a system for specifying process colors that was built by people who know and use color from the desktop (especially color from QuarkXPress, as it turns out). This is more important than it might seem. Creating tint builds from the desktop has a particular advantage over having a printer build tints traditionally: I can specify (and a properly calibrated imagesetter can provide me with) a tint value of any percentage, not just in 5- or 10-percent increments. The folks at TruMatch took advantage of this and created a very slick, very easy-to-use system with over 2,000 evenly gradated colors (see the sample swatch in Figure C in the color plates).

The folks at TruMatch built the system around the intuitive HSB model. The colors in the swatch book (and, as we'll see later in this chapter, in XPress's TruMatch color selector) are arranged in the colors of the spectrum: from red through yellow to green through blue to violet and back to red. The first number in a TruMatch code indicates a color's hue (its place on the spectrum). These numbers range from 1 to 50.

The second item in a color's TruMatch code indicates its tint or value strength, which ranges from "a" (saturated, 100-percent value strength) to "h" (faded, unsaturated, 5-percent value strength). The third item, a number, indicates the color's brightness (the amount of black). Black is always added in 6-percent increments. The brightness code ranges from 1 (6 percent black) to 7 (42-percent black). If there's no black in a color, this third code is left off.

Why is this so great? Well, first of all, you can quickly make decisions on the relativity of two colors. For example, you can say, "No, I want this color to be a little darker, and a little more green." When you go back to the Edit Color dialog box, you can quickly find a color that suits your desires. Compare this to the jumbled colors in the Pantone or FocolTone matching systems and you'll understand. TruMatch gives me hope that there really is a positive evolution in electronic publishing.

Pantone and Pantone Uncoated. Pantone, Inc.'s sole purpose in life (and business) is to continue to develop, maintain, and protect the sanctity of the spot-color Pantone Color Matching System (PMS for short).

Printers and designers alike love the PMS system for its great simplicity in communicating color. As a designer, you can look at a Pantone-approved color swatch book, pick a color, then communicate that color's number to your printer. He or she, in turn, can pull out the Pantone color-mixing guidelines, find that color's "recipe," and dutifully create that exact ink for you. Almost all spot-color printing in the United States is done with PMS inks. (See "Pantone Solid to Process," below, if you're tempted to simulate a Pantone color using process-color inks.)

Pantone, knowing a good thing when it sees it, has licensed its color libraries for coated and uncoated stocks to Quark so that you can specify PMS colors from within QuarkXPress. However, the color you see on the screen may have little correlation with what the actual PMS color is on paper. A computer screen is no substitute for a swatch book, especially when you're dealing with custom-mixed spot-color inks (I'll talk more about this later).

There are three problems with PMS color.

▶ Only certain colors are defined and numbered. If you want a color which is slightly lighter than one described, but not as light as the next lightest color in the Pantone book, you have to tell your lithographer to tweak it.

▶ Color fidelity of the specification books decreases over time. The books are printed under tight press, paper, and ink conditions, but the colors change as the ink and paper age, and entropy increases in the universe. (This happens with every kind of swatch book, of course.) For this reason, Pantone recommends buying a new book every year. Of course, they have a bias: they make a lot of money from selling the books. Just make sure at the beginning of a job that your book and the printer's book are fairly close—or plan to leave a cut-out swatch from your book for the printer to match the color.

▶ I've never met anyone who actually understood the PMS color-numbering scheme. For example, PMS 485 and PMS 1795 are very similar, though every number in between is totally different.

The only good reason to use Pantone books is if you're printing with Pantone inks. In that case, go ahead and use the Pantone color pickers in QuarkXPress; that way, the right color name will print on each piece of overlay film, and your printer won't get confused.

Pantone inks are great for two- and three-color jobs, of course, but they're also worth considering if you have the budget for four or more colors— especially when you consider that you can create tint builds in between the various PMS ink colors (see "Multi-Ink Colors," later in this chapter). For example, some road maps are designed and printed using from one to five different Pantone colors in various carefully chosen tints and combinations. This way, tiny details—like type or cartographic symbols—can be accurately printed with a solid spot color (the halftoning used with process colors can wreak havoc on these small elements).

Pantone Solid to Process. When Pantone realized that they were being left behind (by TruMatch) in the process-color game, they shifted into first gear and released two process-color libraries. The first, Solid to Process (this is also called ProSim), is designed to simulate the PMS spot colors with the four process colors. It's based on the Pantone Process Color Simulator swatch book, which shows Pantone spot colors printed side-by-side with their best-match process simulations.

The main problem with the Solid to Process library is that it's really hard to simulate spot colors with the four process colors. Some simulations are better than others. A pale blue is fairly easy to simulate with process inks, for instance; a rich, creamy, slate blue is almost impossible; and you'll never get anything approaching metallic copper or gold with CMYK inks.

It's very tempting to choose a color from Pantone's spot-color swatch books (or worse, by picking a color on screen) and then decide to print it with process colors. Perhaps your client wants to use their corporate color in a process-color print job, or maybe the PMS swatch book is the first thing you grab when you're looking for a color . . . . Whatever the case, stop yourself and remember: chances are that the spot color you choose won't be faithfully reproduced with process colors. Always look up the color in Pantone's ProSim swatch book, or just use a process-color swatch book to begin with. You may even discover a better CMYK match for your color than the one Pantone suggests.

Pantone Process. Pantone Process is a process-color matching system much like TruMatch's, and has no relationship to the Pantone spot colors; it's just a CMYK swatch book (actually, there are two versions—one based on the SWOP inks, and another based on Euroscale inks). Fortunately, it uses a different numbering scheme than the spot colors do. Unfortunately, Pantone Process is hardly worth describing because it doesn't appear to make any sense; on the other hand, it does have a few things going for it. First, it's generally easier to find colors in it than in the Pantone spot-color swatch books. Second, there are more colors to choose from than in any previous process-color matching system. Third, because Pantone is so well established, it's sometimes easier to find Pantone's swatch books.

I personally feel that the TruMatch system is the best process-color system for designers; it's more intuitive and easier to use than Pantone's. However, both work in more or less equivalent ways. They're just process-color swatch books, though both are produced with rigorous quality-control standards.

Hexachrome. Printers have known for years that printing with cyan, magenta, yellow, and black inks restricted them to a limited color palette that didn't include many of the rich, vibrant colors that designers want to use. They sometimes resorted (and still do resort) to printing process-color images with extra spot colors to achieve these effects. To make this process easier, Pantone has developed the Hexachrome system, which uses the four process colors plus particular orange and green inks. (If they had added a third color, you'd be able to reproduce even more vibrant colors, but there are a significant number of six-color printing presses in the world, so Pantone stopped with six colors.)

The folks at Pantone are convinced that there are a lot of people who want or need the Hexachrome system. I'm not. It's not that I don't like Hexachrome. Actually, I think it's great. I just don't think that it's always worth the extra expense of printing six colors to achieve those lovely rich greens and reds. As one friend quipped, "Hexachrome is like quadraphonic hi-fi sound . . . it's awesome when you get it right, but most people aren't going to bother."

Some of you are wondering about what halftone screen angles to use when you're printing six colors instead of four (see "Color Separations" in Chapter 13, *Printing*). The cool thing about Hexachrome is that the orange ink never prints over cyan, and green doesn't print over magenta, so you can double up the halftone settings for those inks.

Not to flog a dead rutabaga, but once again: if you're choosing Hexachrome colors in XPress, make sure you're picking them first from a printed swatch book. I discuss Hexachrome at greater length in Appendix A, *Color Management*, because you can't really do anything with Hexachrome colors without Quark's color management system.

Focoltone. Developed in Wales, Focoltone is a process-color matching system used widely in Europe, and used very little in North America. After buying Focoltone's rather expensive cross-referenced swatch books, you have to wade through their disarrayed pages to find the color you want (you have a choice of 763 colors based on combinations of CMYK inks at 5-percent increments from zero to 85 percent). While newspaper publishers may find Focoltone marginally useful, it's a less appropriate system for designers.

Toyo and DIC. Toyo and DIC are both spot-color matching systems from Japan, created by the Toyo Ink Manufacturing Co. and DIC (Dainippon Ink and Chemicals, Inc.), respectively. These spot-color inks have a built-in feature which is helpful: their names reflect how closely you can simulate them in process color. If the name (number, really) is followed by one asterisk, it means that the spot color cannot be closely matched in process color. If the number is followed by two asterisks, it means that the spot color won't even be close to the color you see on screen. For instance, metallic colors can never be represented on screen, so they're followed by two asterisks.

If you're creating documents that will be printed in Japan, then you may want to specify spot colors in either one of these systems rather than with an American system like Pantone (so that the proper spot-color name prints on each overlay). Otherwise, you can probably relax and keep reading.

Specifying Color

In previous chapters I've discussed applying colors to objects using the Style menu and the Modify dialog box, and I've alluded to the Colors palette. Here I'll discuss how to create colors in QuarkXPress over and above the nine which come as default settings. Then I'll get into the nitty-gritty of the Colors palette before covering the important issues of trapping and importing color from other programs.

The Color List

Before you can use a color in QuarkXPress, you have to create it, so that it appears on your document's color list. XPress allows thousands of different colors on this list, including the six colors which must be present: Cyan, Magenta, Yellow, Black, White, and Registration (I'll talk about this last "color" later in this chapter). You can access this list—and thereby add, delete, and modify colors—by selecting Color from the Edit menu.

The Colors dialog box (see Figure 12-2) contains the color list, along with several buttons to manipulate the colors on the list.

Figure 12-2
The Colors dialog box

▼ ▼

Tip: Making Your Colors Stick Around. Changing the color list while a document is open only changes that document's list; it doesn't change any future documents you may create. However, you can alter the default color list—the list with which all new documents open—by adding, deleting, and modifying colors while no document is open. These changes stick around forever, or at least until you either change them again, reinstall QuarkXPress, or delete your XPress Preferences file.

I recommend that you remove Red, Green, and Blue from your default color list unless you're using XPress for multimedia or if your final output is from a color printer. These colors aren't appropriate for prepress because they're neither process colors nor true spot colors. If you apply Red to text in XPress, that text comes out on its own color plate (labeled "Red") when you print separations, but this doesn't tell your printer which spot color you're really referring to.

▼ ▼

Show

It's easy to accumulate so many colors on your color list that you don't know what is what anymore. Fortunately, XPress includes the Show popup menu which lets you display subsets of particular colors on the color list. We've seen this popup menu before in the Style Sheets and the H&Js dialog boxes, though this one has its own properties. The six options on the Show popup menu are All Colors, Spot Colors, Process Colors, Multi-Ink Colors, Colors in Use, and Colors Not Used. Here are a few ways you might use this feature.

▶ If you're printing a CMYK job, choose Spot Colors to make sure that you don't accidentally have any spot colors in the document.

> ► If you've got dozens of colors in your document, you can see which ones are really being used by selecting Colors in Use.

> ► Conversely, if you want to delete a lot of colors from your color list, choose Colors Not Used to make sure you're not removing any important ones.

New

Now we get to the good stuff: making your own colors. Click the New button in the Colors dialog box to open the Edit Color dialog box (see Figure 12-3, and Figure E in the color plates). Here's a rundown of the choices offered in this dialog box.

Color name. The name that you type in the Name field appears on the Color scroll list and on the color lists in other menus throughout the program. You can call your color anything you want. When I'm working with a process color, for example, I usually define my color using CMYK, and then I name it something like "10c80m0y20k." It's a bit cryptic at first, but I like it. On the other hand, you can just call the color by some name; for example, you might have a palette full of "Fuchsia" or "Royal Blue."

If you use the latter method for spot color, you'll want to be sure you know what the corresponding color in your color swatch book is. If you use the name "Copper," for example, it's crucial that you remember that it represents PMS 876 so that you can communicate this color identifier to your lithographer. If you use the name "PMS 876," on the other hand, that's what prints out on the edge of the sheet when you print separations. "Copper" would print out otherwise.

Figure 12-3
The Edit Color dialog box

Spot Color. Probably the most important choice in this dialog box is whether the color is a spot color or will be separated into process colors at print time. You use the Spot Color checkbox to determine whether a color is process or spot (this was called "Process Separation" in earlier versions). When this option is turned on, the color is a spot color (that is, it won't separate into CMYK). When it's turned off, the color is never a spot color (it always separates).

Note that you can create a Pantone color—which usually would be specified as a spot color—as a process color by turning off this checkbox, thereby forcing the color to separate into four plates at print time. What results is a process simulation of the Pantone color. Similarly, you could create a CMYK color which would print as a spot color on its own plate. The first example has some usefulness; the second has almost none.

Halftone. When you're creating a spot color (and the Spot Color checkbox is turned on), the Halftone popup menu becomes active. This has been a mystery to a lot of people, so let me explain it carefully. Spot colors aren't always solids, of course; it's easy to make a tint of a spot color. For instance, you could have a blend from White to Red (see "Blending Colors," later in this chapter), and the spot color Red would be tinted from zero to 100 percent. The Halftone popup menu lets you adjust the halftone screen angle and frequency of these tints. If you leave the menu set to Black, tints of that spot color are always the same as Black (usually 45 degrees, and the screen frequency set in the Page Setup dialog box). If you set it to Magenta, then the spot color has the same angle/frequency combination as Magenta.

The Halftone setting is only important when the spot color is involved in a blend, a multi-ink color, or an overprint situation (I cover all three of these later in this chapter). In other words, unless a tint of your spot color is going to print on top of a tint of some other color, you can ignore this setting.

Model. Once you've named a color and decided whether it's process or spot, you have to tell XPress how you want to spec the color—as CMYK, Pantone, TruMatch, or whatever—by choosing a system or library from the Model popup menu. Depending on which model you pick, XPress displays different choices on the right side of the dialog box.

For instance, if you choose RGB, HSB, or CMYK, the program shows you a color wheel along with fields that you can type in. You must fight the temptation to click on an area on the color wheel. Sure, it's easy to choose colors this way—but remember that what you see on the screen probably has no relation to what you'll actually get on paper or film. It's much more reliable to choose a color from a CMYK swatch book and then just type the values into the C, M, Y, and K fields.

When you have a color-matching system—like Pantone, TruMatch, or Hexachrome—selected as the color model, you can select a color by either clicking on it in the Selector box (see Figure 12-4) or by typing the desired number into the field in the lower-right corner of the dialog box. Type in the number, and XPress jumps to that color. If you're working in Pantone and type "312", it jumps to color 300, then 310, then 312.

The Multi-Ink option on the Model popup menu is sort of a blend between spot and process colors, and I'll discuss it in more detail later in this chapter.

Figure 12-4

Pantone selection in the Edit Color dialog box

▼ ▼

Tip: Grab Any Color. There's one time that I condone using the color wheel in the Edit Color dialog box: if you're looking for a color, but you just don't know which one yet. For example, if you know that you want a greenish PMS color, but you're not sure exactly which green you want, you could just pick one from the color wheel and name it "Kelly Green" or whatever. If you later decide to change the look of your page, you could go back, adjust the brightness gauge next to the color wheel, and then change the name to "Forest Green."

When it comes time to print the piece, you can sit down with your printer and decide on a PMS color that will—you hope—match what you see on screen. Even then, you don't have to go back and change the color in the Edit Color dialog box . . . just tell your printer that your Forest Green plate should be printed with the PMS color you decide on. Again, as long as the final decision is based on a swatch book, it hardly matters what you specify in this dialog box or what you call the color.

▼ ▼

▼ ▼

Tip: Clean Out Your Color Models. QuarkXPress lets you clean up the Model popup menu, removing the color models that you don't use by taking them out of the Color folder (which sits inside the same folder as QuarkXPress). This modular approach is more than just a convenience, however. It enables Quark to easily release future color models (or updates to a model) as small files, too.

▼ ▼

Tip: Importing Colors from Other Programs. It turns out that you don't have to create the colors from within QuarkXPress. You can just as easily import an entire color library from an illustration program such as Illustrator or FreeHand. QuarkXPress imports the colors and places them on the color list when you import an EPS file that uses them. The key is that the colors must be named in those programs. In Illustrator, you need to create the colors with the Custom Color item, or they don't appear on the color list as named colors. Likewise, in FreeHand, only named spot colors (Custom or PMS) come across into QuarkXPress.

Only colors that are actually used in an EPS file are imported (see "Color from Outside Sources," later in this chapter). If you just want to import the colors, but don't need the picture itself, you can make a few rectangles and apply the colors you want to those objects. Then save the page as an EPS file (with or without a preview). When you import the EPS into XPress, those colors are added to the color list. You can then delete the picture from the document, and the colors remain.

▼ ▼

New/Original preview. The final element in the Edit Color dialog box is the New/Original preview, which is really only relevant when you're editing colors (see "Edit," below). When you are creating a new color, the lower half of this rectangle remains white (blank), as there was no "original" color to show. When you specify a color using one of the methods described above, the upper rectangle shows what that color looks like. You can specify a color, look at this preview window, then change the specifications and actually see the change in the way the color looks.

When you have the color the way you like it, clicking OK closes this dialog box and adds your color to the palette.

▼ ▼

Tip: Tinted Colors. Do you have a document in which you often use 60-percent magenta? Instead of forever appying the color and then setting a tint, just make a new color swatch that is defined as a tint of the color and then apply it at 100-percent strength. What's the difference? No difference, really. Just another way to go about your business.

It's easy to make a tint of a process color in the Edit Color dialog box. Making a tint of a spot color is a little more tricky: You have to use a Multi-Ink color (see "Tip: Permanent Tints," later in this chapter.)

▼ ▼

Edit

Once you've built a color, you can edit it by clicking on that color's name in the Color scroll list, then clicking Edit (or just double-clicking on the color's name). In the default color list (the one that's there when you first open QuarkXPress) you can edit four of the colors: Red, Green, Blue, and Registration. The other five colors, which include the four process colors plus White, cannot be edited or deleted. When you edit a color, you see the same Edit Color dialog box as described above, except that the color is mapped out, just as you originally specified it.

You can change any of the color's specifications using the same methods described above. When you like the new color, click OK to save these changes to the color palette.

▼ ▼

Tip: Multiple Models. You may be interested to note that you can switch among the various color systems on the Model popup menu to make adjustments to a color. For instance, you might choose a Pantone color but decide that what you see on screen doesn't match your swatch book very well. Go ahead and switch to RGB or HSB mode and adjust the color. As long as the Spot Color checkbox is turned on and you don't change the name of the color, then adjusting the Pantone color this way simply affects its screen representation.

On the other hand, let's say you use a process-color simulation of a Pantone color, but when you print a proof, you find that the color is too dark. Assuming that your proof is accurate, you can switch the color to CMYK mode to see what CMYK values are being used, and then you can adjust them (reduce the black value, perhaps, or raise the Brightness gauge slightly). Of course (as if you haven't heard me say it enough), you can't trust what you see on screen, so this technique is only useful for minor tweaks.

▼ ▼

Tip: Color Tricks the Eye. Placing a colored object next to a different-colored object makes both colors look different from how each would if you just had one color alone (see Color Plate F in the color plates). Similarly, a color can look totally different if you place it on a black background rather than on a white one. These facts should influence how you work, in two ways. First, when you're selecting colors from a swatch book, isolate the colors from their neighbors. I like to do this by placing a piece of paper with a hole cut out of it in front of a color I'm considering. Second, after you've created the colors you're going to work with in your document, try them out with each other. You may find that you'll want to go back and edit them in order to create the effect you're really trying to achieve.

▼ ▼

Duplicate

Let's say you love the color blue. I do. You want a new blue color that's really close to the one that's on the color palette, but you don't want to change the one already there. Click on "Blue," then click Duplicate. This opens the Edit Color dialog box, just as if you were editing the color, but the name of the color will be changed to "Copy of Blue." As long as you don't change the name of your new color back to its original (or to the name of any other color already specified), you can change the specifications, and save it onto the Color scroll list without replacing the original color.

QuarkXPress won't allow you to replace a color on the Color scroll list with another of the same name, but it does allow you to merge colors with a workaround, as I discuss next in "Delete."

Delete

Is this button self-explanatory enough? Click on the color you hate most, then click Delete. If you've assigned this color to any object in your document, QuarkXPress prompts you with a dialog box asking if you want to replace all instances of the color you're deleting with another color.

Note that you cannot delete the four process colors, White, or Registration. And if you delete a color that's not used anywhere in the document, it's removed without a prompt, so make sure you really don't need it before clicking Delete.

▼ ▼

Tip: Search and Replace Colors. Let's say you've got a two-color monthly newsletter, and you always print with black and one other spot color. It's a pain to create a new color and then apply it to each element in the newsletter each month, but XPress doesn't have a "search and replace" for colors. Or does it?

You can replace one color with another using one of two quick workarounds. Let's say you want to replace every instance of PMS 286 in your document with PMS 570. Here's how you should do it if you haven't already defined your new Pantone color.

1. Select Pantone 286 in the Colors dialog box and press Duplicate. Don't make any changes to the duplicate "Copy of Pantone 286"; just click OK.

2. Double-click on the original Pantone 286 to edit it.

3. Choose Pantone 570 by typing the number into the field in the lower-right corner of the Edit Color dialog box. (Note that at this point, you could even change to some other color mode, like TruMatch, if you wanted to.)

4. Click OK, and then click Save to leave the Colors dialog box.

Unfortunately, this technique won't work if you already have that particular Pantone color on your color list because XPress isn't very smart about color naming (it doesn't realize that two colors on your color list that are named the same should be the same). So here's another workaround you can use if you've already built the new color.

1. Duplicate the color you're trying to replace. Don't make any changes to the copy; just click OK.

2. Select the color (in this case, the Pantone 286) and click the Delete button.

3. When XPress asks you what color you want to replace it with, choose the new Pantone color (or whatever color you're replacing it with) from the popup menu.

4. Click OK, and then click Save to leave the Colors dialog box.

Of course, these methods don't let you search and replace the colors on selected objects; it's an all-or-nothing change. Note that the only reason you duplicated the Pantone color in step 1 (of both techniques) was in case you wanted to use that color again somewhere. If you know you'll never use it again in this document, then just omit that step.

▼ ▼

Append

When you click the Append button, QuarkXPress lets you find another QuarkXPress file. Then when you click Open, the program gives you a choice as to which colors from that document you want to import. Note that when you select a color, its specification appears in the Description field (see Figure 12-5), which can be useful, particularly if the colors have been named "My favorite yellow," "IBM Blue," and so on.

This feature acts just like the Append feature in the Style Sheets and H&Js dialog boxes. If you pick a multi-ink color that is based on other spot colors, those spot colors are imported automatically as well. And if you import a color with the same name as one you already have in your document (but with a different specification), XPress gives you the chance to rename it upon import,

Figure 12-5

Appending colors

If you append a color that has the same name as one in your document, you'll see this dialog box.

to use the color definition of the imported color, or to use the existing color (which is the same as not bringing in the new color at all).

▼ ▼

Tip: One More Way to Append a Color. Here's one more way to import one or more colors from another document. You can either copy and paste, or drag an object filled with that color from one document to another. As long as the color's name isn't already used in the new document, the color and its specifications come across too, and are added to the color list. Delete the object, and the color remains on the list. (If the color is already specified, then this method doesn't work; instead, the object's color is stripped away and replaced with the existing color.)

▼ ▼

Tip: Libraries of Colors. Here's one more way to save your colors so that you can bring them into a new document. Place an object (even just a picture box with a colored background) in a Library. Let's say you're working with a designer across the country, and you want to send her various sets of colors you think would be appropriate for the job. You could apply three different colors to three different boxes, then put all three into a library (select all of them and drag them in all at once). Now change the colors in the boxes, drag the "new" set into the library, and so on. You could e-mail this library to your colleague, and when she drags out a library item, those colors are added to her document's color list.

Within the Library, of course, you can even group your colors into types such as "Warm Colors," "Cool Colors," or "Newsletter Colors," using the Library's labeling feature.

▼ ▼

Edit Trap

Selecting the Edit Trap option in the Colors dialog box brings up the Trap Specifications dialog box. Trapping is a whole other *mishegoss* (Yiddish for "craziness"), so I'll put it off for now and discuss it at some length later in this chapter.

Save

When you are finished adding, deleting, or editing your colors, you can click Save to save those changes to your document's color palette. Remember that even when you save the changes, you can still come back and edit them later. If you made these color changes while a document was open, the changes only apply to the document's color palette. If no documents were open, then they're added to the default color list.

Cancel

Almost every dialog box in QuarkXPress has a Cancel button. This one works the same as all the rest: it cancels your entries without saving any changes. (I find this most useful when I've accidentally deleted or changed one or more colors.)

▼ ▼

Multi-Ink Colors

If you can overlay two tints of process colors to create a third color, it stands to reason that you can do the same thing with spot colors. QuarkXpress's Multi-Ink feature helps considerably, because it lets you build "process colors" based on spot colors. That is, you can make a single color based on varying percentages of other colors on your color list. While at first this feature seems mundane, it turns out to be very powerful, and it's shocking that so few people make use of this incredible feature.

Nonetheless, the road to "process spot colors" isn't entirely clear.

▶ Most spot colors are made with inks that have a different consistency than process-color inks; the more opaque the inks, the harder it is to mix varying tints of them at the same place on a page.

▶ Some inks don't tint well; for instance, metallic and fluorescent inks lose much of their special appearance unless you use a very coarse halftone.

▶ There's only one spot-color swatch book that shows what happens when you mix colors together (the Pantone Two-Color Selector), and while it's extensive, it certainly doesn't show every combination of every spot color on the market. Therefore, there's often a lot more guessing involved when you mix spot colors.

It's important that you discuss multi-ink colors with your printer before jumping in and using them. Ask them if it'll be okay to mix two particular spot colors on press. Perhaps they will make a "draw-down" for you so that you can see how the colors will look when they're mixed together (this only shows you what the colors will look like when they're overprinted at 100 percent).

Building a Multi-Ink Color

It was always painful to mix two spot colors together in XPress 3.x because you had to duplicate objects, apply a different color and tint to each object, and then make sure one properly overprinted the other. It was always hit or miss, and you could never see a simulation of the final color on screen or on a color printer. Now, mixing colors is as easy as one, two, three.

1. Create a new color by opening the Colors dialog box and pressing New.

2. Set the Model popup menu to Multi-Ink.

3. Select a color from the list on the right of the Edit Color dialog box and choose a tint from the Shade popup menu (see Figure 12-6). Repeat this step for each color you want to include.

You can even mix process colors with spot colors in this dialog box. However, I still can't think of a particularly good reason why you'd want to do this, other than perhaps mixing a color with some tint of black.

After applying your multi-ink colors to objects on your page, you can print color separations, and each color appears on its proper plate, just as you'd expect. Remember what I said about specifying the Halftone settings for spot

Figure 12-6

Multi-Ink colors

colors that overprint: each spot color within your multi-ink color needs a correct halftone angle, or else you'll get dot-doubling (halftone spots that overprint each other, creating muddy colors) or moiré patterns when your pages come off press.

▼ ▼

Tip: Multiple Selections. You can select more than one color at a time when you specify a color in the Multi-Ink model by Command/Ctrl-clicking on each color you want on the color list. This is only helpful if you're going to apply the same tint to all the colors you select.

▼ ▼

Tip: Multi-Ink Hexachrome Colors. If you want to get really fancy, take a look at the Process Inks popup menu that appears in the Edit Color dialog box when you select the Multi-Ink model. When you select Hexachrome from this popup menu, you can build a multi-ink color with Pantone's Hexachrome inks. This way, if you don't like the preset Hexachrome colors that are built into QuarkXPress, you can build your own. You can even mix Hexachrome with your spot colors, and while I can't imagine what you'd end up with, it sure is fun to speculate.

Note that Orange and Cyan are meant to be complementary, so you shouldn't mix them together in the same multi-ink color. Same thing goes with Green and Magenta. And remember that you can only separate Hexachrome colors when XPress's color management system is active (see Appendix A, *Color Management*).

▼ ▼

Tip: Build a Swatch Book. While XPress tries to simulate multi-ink colors on screen (and on color printers), it's far from a perfect system (I find you often get much darker colors on screen than you would in real life). Ultimately, it's still a guessing game unless you're using a swatch book. If the two colors you're using don't appear in Pantone's Two-Color Selector swatch book, and you're going to use mixes of these colors a lot in your print jobs, then you might consider building your own swatches. Build a set of multi-ink colors in every combination you can think of, apply them to small square boxes on a page, and print them (perhaps you can place them outside the trim marks on some job you're already printing with these inks).

▼ ▼

Tip: Permanent Tints. You don't have to mix two or more colors together in a multi-ink color. You can build a color in the Multi-Ink model that is simply 30 percent of one PMS color. This is useful if you're going to apply that same color tint to several items in your document; it's certainly much faster than applying the color and then changing the tint for each object individually (and it's often more consistent, too).

Special Colors

QuarkXPress has two special colors that aren't really colors. They are Registration, which I have mentioned above, and Indeterminate, which I'll talk about soon in "Trapping," below.

Registration

This "noncolor" appears on the Colors scroll list and on all color selection lists throughout the menus. When you apply this color to an object or to text, that object or text prints on every color separation plate you print. It's especially nice for job-identification marks, and for registration or crop marks (if you are creating your own rather than letting the program do it for you; see Chapter 13, *Printing,* for more information on these special marks).

For example, I sometimes like to bypass QuarkXPress's regular crop-mark feature and draw my own crop marks in the border around my page. Then I color these Registration, and they print out on every piece of film that comes out for that job.

▼ ▼

Tip: Editing the Registration Color. If you use the Registration color regularly, you might want to change its color so that you can tell it apart from normal Black. You can use the Edit feature described earlier to change the on-screen color of Registration to anything you like. Also, because the Registration color is originally black, the Edit Color dialog box appears with the brightness scroll bar set to zero. Just raise the brightness to the level you want, and then change the color.

No matter what color you specify, objects with the color Registration always print on every plate. Changing the color changes nothing but the screen representation for that color. Use a color that is distinctly different from anything else in the document you're creating. That way you always know at a glance what's normal black stuff and what is colored Registration.

▼ ▼

Tip: Four-Color Black. Most people still think that printing black ink over something else on their page completely covers it. Not so. Black ink is almost never completely opaque, so you can actually see through to what's below it on the printed page. This isn't a concern in black-and-white printing, but when you print multiple colors on a page, it can mean the success or failure of your design. (I once saw a magazine ad that showed a shirtless male jogger running along the road. A wide black box printed over his midriff was supposed to make the jogger appear naked, but the joke was on the ad's designer: the black ink, being somewhat translucent, clearly showed that he was wearing jogging shorts, defeating the purpose of the advertisement.)

The solution is to build a *rich black*—a separate black in your color palette that contains a bit of other process color in it. The standard rich black that color strippers use is 100-percent black along with 40-percent cyan. I prefer to add 20 percent each of magenta and yellow, too. When a plain black (100-percent K) object overlaps colored objects, it can look mottled over different colors (see Figure K in the color plates). Adding color to your blacks solves the problem.

This trick not only achieves a richer black on a printing press, but usually also better blacks from a color printer.

Note, though, that you should think carefully about how you apply this rich black. A potential problem lurks behind this technique: the cyan can show up from behind the black if (or when) the printing press misregisters (see "Tip: Knocking Out Rich Black," later in this chapter).

▼ ▼

Indeterminate

When QuarkXPress looks at a selection and finds that either several colors are specified within that selection or that it's a color picture, it calls this an "Indeterminate" color. This is not something you can change in any way. It's just a definition that the program uses to tell you there are several colors in the selection. In "Trapping," below, we'll see the great benefits of the Indeterminate "color."

▼ ▼

Colors Palette

Just like style sheets, you can apply and edit colors with a click using the Colors palette (see Figure 12-7). This floating palette contains a list of every available color, along with a tint-percentage control popup menu, and three icons. These icons gray out depending on what object you have selected. When you select a text box, the icons represent frame color, text color, and background color for that box. When you select a line, two icons gray out, and only the line-color icon remains. Each color in the palette also displays an icon that shows whether it's a spot color or process color.

To apply a color to an object, first click the correct icon for what you want to change, then click on the desired color in the color list. If you want a tint of that color, first change the percentage in the upper-right corner, then press Return or Enter to apply the change. You can also just click somewhere else than on the palette. For example, let's say you want to change one word in a text box to 30-percent cyan.

1. Select the word in the text box.

2. Click the center icon on the Colors palette, which represents text (it looks like an "A" in a box).

3. Click on Cyan on the colors list.

4. Select "30%" from the popup menu on the palette, or type "30" in the field and press Enter.

It's funny, but those four steps are often much faster than selecting a color and tint from the Style menu. Note that you can change the color of a box's frame, even if the box doesn't have a frame. If you later add a frame, it will be the color you designated.

Figure 12-7
The Colors palette

The center icon changes depending on what item you have selected.

Spot color

Process color

▼ ▼

Tip: Jump to Edit Colors. The Colors palette is more like the Style Sheet palette than meets the eye. On both palettes, Command/Ctrl-clicking on an item quickly brings you to a dialog box. In this case, Command/Ctrl-clicking on any color brings up the Colors dialog box, in which you can edit, duplicate, append, delete, or create new colors. This is also the fastest way to the Edit Trap dialog box.

▼ ▼

Tip: Drag-and-Drop Color Application. Sometimes I think the folks at Quark like to toss in features just because they're cool—for example, drag-and-drop color application. Try it: hold your mouse down on one of the tiny color squares on the Colors palette, and drag it over your page. Notice that as you drag, the image of that color square stays attached to your pointer. As you move the pointer over objects, their color changes to the color you're dragging. Move the pointer past an object, and its color reverts to whatever it was before.

To apply a color to an object, just let go of the mouse button. Note that you can apply a color in this way to backgrounds and borders, but not to text, even if you have the text icon selected on the Color palette. And since the palette is grayed out until you select an object, you can't drag anything until you've selected at least one object.

▼ ▼

Tip: Drag-and-Drop Color, Part Two. The engineers at Quark sneaked a feature into XPress and forgot to tell anyone about it. Let's say you've got three boxes on your page. If you drag a color swatch over the first box, it changes color; but as soon as you leave the box, dragging the swatch over to the second box, the first box's color reverts back to its original state. Now, if you're holding down the Command/Ctrl key when you drag the swatch out of the box, XPress actually applies the color to the box, so that it doesn't change after your swatch leaves the box.

If you want all the boxes on your page to be colored yellow, drag the Yellow swatch over each of them with the Command/Ctrl key held down. If you want all but one to be colored yellow, just don't hold down the Command/Ctrl key while the swatch leaves that box.

▼ ▼

Blending Colors

You can call them fountains, dégradés, gradations, or blends, but the concept is always the same: the background of a text or picture box can make a gradual transition from one color to another (see Figure 12-8). Unlike other pro-

Figure 12-8
Color blends

grams that create graduated fills, in XPress you can blend any combination of spot colors and process colors (even white).

QuarkXPress has a dizzying array of blends: Linear (straight blend), Mid-Linear (goes from one color to another, then back again), Rectangular, Diamond, Circular, and Full Circular. (If you find you only have the Linear blend, then you're missing the Cool Blends XTension that ships with QuarkXPress; you might want to check the XTension Manager to see if it has been inadvertently turned off.) See Figure 12-9 for examples of these.

Colors palette. QuarkXPress lets you create blends in either the palette or the Modify dialog box. Here's how to apply a blend to a selected object from the Colors palette.

1. Click the background icon on the Colors palette, if it's not already selected.

2. Select the blend you want from the popup menu on the Colors palette.

3. Click button #1, then click on the beginning color of the blend (you can adjust the tint level, too).

4. Click button #2, and select the ending color of the blend (and adjust the tint, if necessary).

5. Specify the angle of the blend. For Linear and Mid-Linear blends, zero degrees (the default value) puts color #1 on the left and color #2 on the right. Increasing the value rotates the blend counterclockwise (so that at 75 degrees, color #1 is almost at the bottom of your box).

If you later want to change one of the colors in the blend, click button #1 or #2; then you can select the color, change its tint, or adjust the angle. You don't have to blend between two colors, of course—you can also blend between two tints of a single color.

Figure 12-9
The cool blends

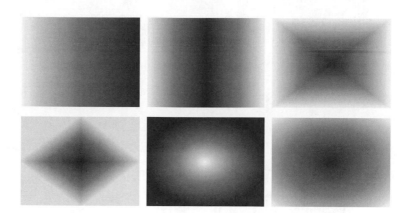

Modify dialog box. I find making blends in the Colors palette to be preferable unless I already happen to be in the Modify dialog box making other changes. You can apply a blend to an object on the Box tab of the Modify dialog box (see Figure 12-10). Note that there's no "color #1" and "color #2" here. Instead, the first color is always the color you've chosen in the section of the , dialog box labeled "Box." The second color is always the color you've chosen in the section labeled "Blends."

▼ ▼

Tip: Don't Mix Blends and Grayscale TIFFs. A warning for those placing blends behind grayscale TIFFs: my experience has shown that this usually results in something that looks as pleasant as a baboon's behind. The problem is that color #1 gets mixed in with the TIFF itself. Quark thinks it should work this way; I think it's crazy. Proceed at your own risk.

▼ ▼

Tip: Rotation Changes Blends. Surprisingly, the angle value you specify has a curious effect on certain kinds of blends. While it simply rotates Linear and Mid-Linear blends, it actually changes the look of the other blends. For instance, a Circular blend at zero degrees generally appears smaller than one at 45 degrees (see Figure 12-11). It's worth playing with the angle in order to achieve the effect you're looking for.

▼ ▼

Tip: Banding in Blends. The number-one problem people have with blends in QuarkXPress is banding (visible bands of tint or color within the supposedly smooth blend). Unfortunately, this is almost always a problem with digital halftoning technology and not just with XPress, so there's not much you can do about it from within the program.

Banding usually occurs because PostScript can only image 256 levels of gray. If you've got a black-to-white blend that's 256 points (about 3.5 inches) long, then XPress builds the blend by creating 256 1-point-wide boxes, each

Figure 12·10

Building blends

with a different tint in it. If the blend is 7 inches long, then each of those boxes has to be about 2 points wide, which typically creates visible bands.

There are two lessons to be learned here.

▶ The larger the blend, the worse the banding. If you stick to 1- or 2-inch-long blends in XPress, you shouldn't get banding.

▶ You can get better blends if you make them in Adobe Photoshop. When you make a blend in Photoshop, the program automatically dithers the colors within the blend to reduce banding. If you're making process-color blends in Photoshop, make them in CMYK mode (making a blend in RGB mode and then converting to CMYK can cause color shifts). Of course, you can't easily make spot-color blends in Photoshop yet.

I discuss dithering, blends, and other banding issues in more detail in *Real World Scanning and Halftones*, which I wrote with Glenn Fleishman and Steve Roth, and in *Real World Photoshop*, which I wrote with Bruce Fraser.

▼ ▼

Tip: Blending to Black. If you've worked with blends before, you've found that they don't always appear in print as they do on screen. For instance, if you make a blend from 100-percent magenta to 100-percent black, you would think you'd get a nice, even blend between the two colors. Unfortunately, when you print separations and throw them on a printing press, you may find a big grayish band in the middle of the blend (see Figure G in the color plates).

Figure 12-11
A blend's angle
affects its look.

Zero degrees   *45 degrees*

Instead, try blending from 100 percent of magenta to a rich black (in this case, 100-percent black plus 100-percent magenta). This way, the magenta simply appears to become darker throughout the blend.

▼ ▼

Tip: A New Dimension. Maybe I'm just easily amused, but I think this trick for creating three-dimensional buttons in XPress is pretty keen.

1. Draw a rectangle or oval (I think it looks best with a square or a circle).

2. Give it a straight Linear blend. I like to set the angle at 45 degrees, but it's up to you.

3. Duplicate the object, and make it smaller. The amount you make it smaller is up to you. Remember that if you want to reduce it to 80 percent, you can simply type "*.8" after the measurement in the Width and Height fields.

4. To figure out the second object's blend angle, subtract the first object's blend angle from 270. So if the first object had a 45-degree blend, the second object should have a 225-degree blend (270 – 45 = 225). You don't have to do the math if you don't want to; just type "270 – 45" in the angle box of the Colors palette.

5. Space/Align the two objects so that their centers are equal (set Vertical and Horizontal alignment to zero offset from the objects' centers in the Space/Align dialog box).

You can really see the effect best when the page guides are turned off (see Figure 12-12). It's even nicer when you add a .25-point white frame around the inside object (sort of a highlight to the button's ridge).

▼ ▼

Tip: 3-D Boxes. While you *can* create rectangular 3-D boxes using the last tip, it's not the only way to create them. Here's one more method.

1. Make a rectangular picture box (the closer to a square it is, the better) with a background shaded to 40-percent of some color.

2. Clone it (Step and Repeat with zero offsets), and change the shade of the new top box to 80 percent.

3. While the top box is still selected, change it into a polygon (by selecting the last item in the Box Shape submenu under the Item menu). Turn Reshape Polygon on so you can modify its shape.

4. Delete the upper left corner point of this rectangular polygon (Command/Ctrl-click on the corner point).

5. Now draw a new rectangular picture box, shaded at 60-percent of that same color. Make sure that the corners of the box align with the diagonal line of the triangular picture box.

Once again, this may be a process more easily performed in an illustration program. But for a quick-and-dirty, this technique can come in handy.

Figure 12-12
Two kinds of
three-dimensional
buttons

The process   *The result*

Trapping

Nothing is perfect, not even obscenely expensive printing presses. When your print job is flying through those presses, each color being added one at a time, the paper may shift slightly. Depending on the press, this could be an offset of anywhere between .003 and .0625 inches (.2 to 4.5 points). If two colors abut each other on your artwork and this shift occurs, then the two colors may be moved apart slightly, resulting in a white "unprinted" space. It may seem like a $^3/_{1,000}$-of-an-inch space would look like a small crack in a large sidewalk, but I assure you, it could easily appear to be a chasm. What can you do? Fill in these potential chasms with traps and overprints.

The concept and practice of trapping and overprinting contain several potential pitfalls for the inexperienced. Up until now, most designers just let their lithographers and strippers handle this stuff. There is a school of thought that says we should still let them handle it. But you know these desktop publishers—they always want to be in control of everything. The problem is that designers weren't trained to do trapping! Let's look carefully at what it's all about.

Tip: Just (Don't) Do It. Trapping is as much art as science—in fact, if you look up "difficult" in the dictionary, it offers the synonym "trapping." I often don't have time to mess around making sure my traps are proper throughout a document, and sometimes even if I have time, it'd just be too much of a hassle.

QuarkXPress's trapping is usually pretty good, all in all, but it's lacking in some important areas, such as blends, choking type, and partially overlapping objects. Ultimately, QuarkXPress isn't designed to be a great trapper. If you want to spare yourself a lot of hassle, you can turn auto trapping off (see "Trapping Preferences," below), and use a program like ScenicSoft's TrapWise (from Creo), which can trap XPress documents infinitely better than you can with XPress alone.

You probably won't want to own TrapWise yourself (it costs about five thousand dollars), but your service bureau or printer should have a copy of it (or some other trapping solution). Find out how much it will cost you for them to trap the page, and then compare that with how much it's worth to you not to worry about it anymore.

Overprinting. Picture the letter "Q" colored magenta on a cyan background. Normally, when you make these color separations, the cyan plate has a white Q *knocked out* of it, exactly where the magenta Q prints (I talk more about color separations and plates in Chapter 13, *Printing*). This way, the cyan and the magenta don't mix (see Figure 12-13). You can, however, set the magenta to overprint the cyan. This results in the Q not being knocked out of the cyan; the two colors *overprint* in that area—resulting in a purple Q on a cyan background.

There are a few very important times when you'll want to overprint colors. The most important of these times may be when you're printing fine black lines or type on a colored background. In fact, almost any time you have a black foreground object, it should overprint the background (it does in XPress by default).

Trapping. A trap is created by very slightly overprinting two colors right along their borders. Then when the paper shifts on the printing press, the space between the colors is filled with the additional trap color (see Figure 12-14). The trap can be created using two methods: choking and spreading. *Choking* refers to the background area getting smaller. *Spreading* refers to the foreground object (the Q in the example above) getting slightly larger.

Figure 12-13
Knocking out and
overprinting

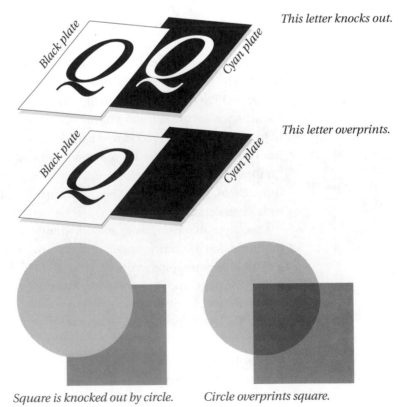

This letter knocks out.

This letter overprints.

Square is knocked out by circle.   *Circle overprints square.*

Figure 12-14
Trapping two
colored objects

Untrapped

Trapped

Simple idea, right? But not necessarily a simple process when you're just beginning. How much to spread or choke an object is determined by the printing press, the colors you're using, and even the paper you're printing on. With some color combinations, you don't even have to trap at all (see "Tip: Who Needs Trapping?" later in this chapter). When you build a color document, you should always talk to your printer about trapping.

In the sections that follow, I'll look at the various ways to trap objects in QuarkXPress. Note that there are two ways to specify trapping in XPress: automatic trapping (which you control on a color-by-color basis) and object-level trapping (which you can apply to a particular item on your page). Even if you don't do anything in XPress, the program still applies some trapping, based on the values on the Trapping tab of the Document Preferences dialog box.

Trapping Preferences

In a valiant effort to save you from unsightly gaps between colors, QuarkXPress always applies a little bit of trapping to your page objects (unless you tell it not to). You can control the way that XPress handles trapping on the Trapping tab of the Preferences dialog box. The changes you make—like most other preferences—are specific to only the document that you have open at the time; if you want them to apply to all future documents, change them while no other documents are open.

The Trapping tab contains seven controls: Trapping Method, Process Trapping, Auto Amount, Indeterminate, Knockout Limit, Overprint Limit, and Ignore White (see Figure 12-15). These controls let you get pretty specific about

Figure 12 15

Trapping tab of the
Preferences dialog box

how you want QuarkXPress's trapping to act. Don't worry, they're not nearly as
confusing as they sound.

Trapping Method. The first popup menu on the Trapping tab, Trapping
Method, lets you turn QuarkXPress's trapping controls on and off. The default
value, Absolute, tells XPress to always use the same-sized trap (the width in the
Auto Amount field). The second setting, Proportional, tells the program to
adjust the size of the trap according to how different the two abutting colors
are. As far as I'm concerned, there's rarely a reason to use Proportional trapping, so when I want trapping I always leave the Trapping Method set to
Absolute.

The third choice, Knockout All, is the same as turning trapping off. When
this is set, every color knocks out colors beneath it, with no trap at all. It's rare
that you'd want to use this setting unless you were using a postprocess trapping solution like TrapWise (where you don't want XPress to interfere with
TrapWise's superior trapping).

(I don't like the Proportional method because it can make certain abutting
colors not trap when they really should. If you insist on using it, however, you
should know how it works. Because Proportional trapping tells QuarkXPress to
look at the "darkness" of a color—which is difficult to quantify—it's a little hard
for me to describe the exact mathematics here on paper without getting really technical. Basically, though, QuarkXPress takes the difference between the

two darkness values and multiplies that by the number in the Auto Amount field. For example, let's say the background color were 80-percent dark, the foreground object were 20-percent dark, and the Auto Amount setting were 0.5 point. Then the background would choke by 0.3 point. (That's $0.8 - 0.2 = 0.6 \times 0.5$ point = 0.3 point. Fun, huh?)

Process Trapping. Before I tell you exactly what the Process Trapping feature is all about, let me just say one thing: If this preference is not turned on (it usually is by default), then turn it on and leave it on. Now if you want to really understand Process Trapping, read on. Or, if you couldn't care less, then jump ahead a few paragraphs to the next section.

Take a look at the two process colors (foreground and background) listed in Table 12-1. If you spread this foreground color (a yellow) into the background color (a muddy brown) with Process Trapping turned off, the trap area doesn't mesh the two colors the way you'd want. That is, the slight sliver of trap (where the colors overlap) is made up of magenta, yellow, and black (the foreground color spreads). However, since there's no cyan in the foreground color, the cyan from the background shows through, making a really ugly puke-green trap area. Now you might say: For a 0.25-point trap, who cares? No one will see it anyway. Think again. That green line stands out clearly around the edge of the yellow object. (See Figure H on the color plates.)

However, when Process Trap is turned on, some process colors get spread while others are choked. Here's how it works. Any process color in the foreground object that is darker than the same color in the background object is spread by half the trapping value (typically, half the value in the Auto Amount field). Any process color that's lighter is choked by half the trapping value.

In the example above, the cyan plate is choked by half the trapping value because there is less cyan in the foreground box than in the background box. Magenta also chokes. However, the yellow and black plates are spread by the same amount.

The result is a trap area as wide as the specified trapping value (in the example above, 0.25 point), centered on the edge of the foreground object, and with the darkest process colors of each of the objects.

	COLOR	FOREGROUND BOX	BACKGROUND BOX
Table 12-1 Color breakdown for trapping example	Cyan	0	30
	Magenta	20	50
	Yellow	100	90
	Black	5	0

If you don't understand this, read the last few paragraphs over several times. If you still don't understand it, then give up and believe me when I tell you that it's a really good thing. Leave Process Trapping turned on.

A couple of notes on this feature. When all the process colors in the foreground object are darker or when they're all lighter than in the background object, then QuarkXPress doesn't trap at all. This is because it doesn't need to. Also, Process Trap doesn't do anything for spot colors, again because it doesn't need to.

Auto Amount. The value that you set in the Auto Amount field tells XPress the maximum value that Proportional trapping can use, and the specific value that Absolute trapping should use. The default value of 0.144 point (about $2/1,000$ of an inch) seems a little small to me, so I usually change this to 0.3 point. As I said earlier, however, the proper value depends a great deal on your printing process; if you're printing a newspaper, the trap value might be significantly higher! Remember to check with your printer first.

One fine point: if you are familiar with trapping using illustration programs such as FreeHand or Illustrator, you know that when you apply a trapping stroke to an object, your trap is really only one half that thickness (the stroke falls equally inside and outside the path). If you're in the habit of using 1 point when you want a 0.5-point trap, break it when you use QuarkXPress. This program handles the conversion for you.

Indeterminate. If QuarkXPress can't figure out what the background color is, it labels the background "Indeterminate." There are three cases in which this happens: a color picture in the background, a background where several different colors are present, or an item only partially covering a background color when Ignore White is turned off (see "Ignore White," below). Note that XPress can only spread a foreground color over an Indeterminate color (for instance, it can only spread text over an image; it cannot choke the image under the text).

Knockout Limit. Remember that the main idea behind trapping is to avoid white paper showing through between two abutting colors, also sometimes called "light leaks." Very light-tinted type, boxes, or lines may be close enough to white so that whether you trap them or just let them knock out isn't very important. The Knockout Limit tells XPress when it can get away without trapping and can instead just knock an object out of the background. The default value is zero percent, which means that every object traps as it did in earlier versions of the program. If you raise this value to 10 percent, then any black object tinted to 10 percent or lighter knocks out, and no trap value is applied.

Figure A
Process-color
separations

Process-color image (four colors)

Cyan

Magenta

Yellow

Black

Figure B
The elegant solution
for shadow type with
process colors

*Normal shadow style applied
(background color is
80-percent magenta)*

*Shadow is in separate text box
(text color set to 30-percent
black and 80-percent magenta)*

Figure C

A color swatch page
from the TruMatch
color selection book

*You can type this number directly in the Edit
Color dialog box with TruMatch selected.
(Or you can type in the CMYK values.)*

Figure D

Linear color blend between two process
colors with an EPS image over it

Figure E

The Edit Color
dialog box

Figure F
Color tricks
the eye

*This color looks
different over
different-colored
backgrounds*

Figure G
Blending tip

*(Note: these
two blends look
the same on screen)*

Blend from 100-percent magenta to 100-percent black

Blend from 100-percent magenta to 100-percent black and magenta

Figure H
Process Trapping

*The bottom object has
a large trap applied so
you can see the effect
more easily*

Process Trapping on   *Process Trapping off*

Figure I

Some colors don't need trapping. Here, the process colors in the foreground colors are all lower values than the background color.

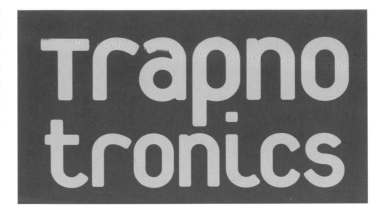

Figure J

Trapping large type

Normal text, trapped with Process Trap on

This text has been converted to outlines and trapped with a frame (see page 682).

Figure K

Rich black versus 100-percent black

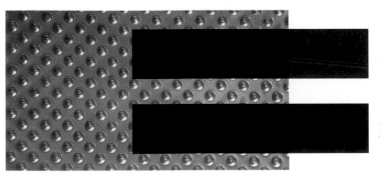

100-percent black

Rich black (includes cyan and magenta)

Figure L
Knocking out
from rich black

*If QuarkXPress didn't
use a special algorithm
for rich blacks (black
mixed with other colors),
misregistration on press
would be a mess!*

*Here is the actual text
knocked out from a rich
black in QuarkXPress.
Note that only the colored
plate(s) are spread so the
type retains its weight.*

Figure M
Using Color Contrast
to ghost back a
portion of an image

Figure N

Using Color Contrast
to adjust the colors
within an image

*This is a silly thing to do
in QuarkXPress unless
you're just making a
quick mockup. You'd get
much better quality
using Adobe Photoshop.*

Figure O

Overprinting images
to simulate
transparency

*Shadow is a separate
grayscale image set
to overprint the
background. It works
fine as long
as there is no black
in the background
color.*

*Shadow is a 600-ppi
bilevel Bitmap that
appears to overprint
all colors.*

C
O
L
O
R

P
A
G
E
S

Figure P
Blend and an image
inside a one-bit image

Figure Q
Sometimes
overprinting
colors has
unexpected
results

*A 20-percent magenta
circle—set to overprint—
sits on top of this square*

40-percent cyan

25-percent yellow

*When the page is separated,
the 20-percent magenta
knocks out of the darker
magenta background*

80-percent magenta

10-percent black

Figure R
Halftone screen
frequencies

60 lpi   *120 lpi*   *150 lpi*

Figure S
Duotones from Photoshop

Figure T
Faking duotones in QuarkXPress

*Image placed in a box
colored 40-percent cyan*

*Two TIFFs: each has a custom
contrast applied, and the top
one is set to Overprint.*

*Three cloned TIFFs, each with
a custom contrast applied
(the top one overprints)*

Actually, that's oversimplifying it a bit because the percentage is based on the luminance of the color, not the tint value, so the limit is different for each color. For instance, a Knockout Limit of 5 percent sets the knockout cutoff at 5 percent for Black, 10 percent for Cyan, and 45 percent for Yellow. In CMYK colors, the luminance of the combination of colors is what counts, not the individual channels. (I like setting the Knockout Limit to about 5 percent, but most people seem to get along just fine without setting it above zero.)

Overprint Limit. Black always overprints any color below it, right? Wrong. Automatic overprinting is controlled by the Overprint Limit setting. The default setting of 95 percent means that black—or any other color that is set to overprint in the Trap Specifications dialog box (which I'll discuss in just a moment)—only overprints when its tint level is above 95 percent. As it turns out, dot gain on press will almost certainly change any 95-percent tint into a solid color, so this is no big deal.

On the other hand, let's say you have the color Green set to overprint by default. If you screen it back to 50 percent, QuarkXPress knocks the color out rather than overprinting it, because the tint falls below the Overprint Limit.

By the way, if you set an object to overprint in the Trap Information palette (which I'll cover later in this section), it will overprint no matter what the tint— object-level trapping ignores the Overprint Limit.

Ignore White. Let's say that a red picture box lies partially on top of another page item, and partially on the white page background (see Figure 12-16). The Trapping tab of the Document Preferences dialog box gives you the choice as to whether it should consider the background color "Indeterminate" or not. When Ignore White is turned on, QuarkXPress won't call a partial overlap "Indeterminate" because it just ignores the white page background; it traps

Figure 12-16
Ignore White

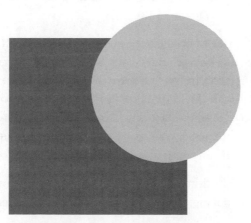

When Ignore White is turned on, the trap value for this circle is determined by its relationship to the box, rather than "Indeterminate".

based on the color of the overlapped object. If you turn this option off, however, it "sees" the white background page, and considers the mix of background colors to be Indeterminate. I don't see any reason why you should turn this option off.

Custom Color-Pair Trap Settings

Remember, there's no such thing as two objects truly being next to each other on an XPress page; one is always on a higher "layer" than the other. QuarkXPress takes advantage of this and always traps based on *pairs* of colors: the foreground color and the background color. For example, picture some red type on top of a blue rectangle. The blue is the background color; the red is the foreground color.

QuarkXPress's default trapping system uses the following built-in trapping algorithm.

▶ Note the darkness (luminosity) of each color.

▶ If the foreground color is lighter, then spread it so that it slightly overlaps the background color.

▶ If the background color is lighter, then choke it so that it slightly "underlaps" the foreground color.

This algorithm is based on the rule that in trapping, lighter colors should encroach on darker ones. That way the darker element defines the edge, and the lighter color overlapping doesn't affect that definition (see Figure 12-17).

In general, XPress does a pretty good job of figuring out what should be trapped and how. However, you can always override XPress and assign your own default trapping behavior for a pair of colors.

1. Select a color (typically the foreground color) in the Colors dialog box.

2. Click the Edit Trap button to open the Trap Specifications dialog box (see Figure 12-18).

3. The list of colors down the left side of the dialog box displays the potential background colors. Select one or more (you can select contiguous colors by holding down the Shift key, or discontiguous colors on the list with the Command/Ctrl key). Note that the first "color" on the list is Indeterminate, which lets you control how your foreground color will trap when it sits on top of an indeterminate background (I discussed the meaning of Indeterminate earlier in this section).

4. The third column in the dialog box—the one filled with those strange-looking, co-mingling arrows—lets you specify whether the color pair's

Figure 12-17
Traps should go
from light colors
into dark colors

Darker color

Lighter color

*This border of lighter
color overprints the
darker background.*

Figure 12-18
The Trap Specifications
dialog box

trapping should be reversible; that is, if you want the same trap settings for the two colors when the foreground color is the same as the background color, and vice versa. When the arrows are intertwined (they are by default), the color-pair trapping is reversible. If you'd rather the settings not be constrained, you can choose Independent from the popup menu at the top of the column (which is unfortunately just labeled "?"). Or, faster, just click the arrow icon once to toggle it from one state to the other.

5. Select the proper setting from the Trap popup menu, which offers you six options: Default, Knockout, Overprint, Auto Amount (+), Auto Amount (–), and Custom (I describe each of these in more detail when I discuss object-level trapping, later in this chapter). If I'm going to change the trap settings from the default value, I typically use Knockout, Overprint, or Custom (depending on what I'm trying to do). Note that as soon as you make a change, XPress displays an asterisk next to the trapping values to indicate they're not the default settings.

If you select Custom, you can type any value between -36 and 36 points, in 0.001-point increments (why anyone would want a trap larger than 1 or 2 points is beyond me). A positive value spreads the foreground object (making it slightly larger by drawing a line around it). A negative value leaves the foreground object alone and chokes the background object.

6. If the color-pair trapping is Dependent (what I call "reversible"), then XPress figures out the reverse of the trap for you. If you change the pair to Independent, you can now set the reverse trapping value in the Reverse column.

Again, you probably won't spend a lot of time figuring out your color-pair traps in this dialog box because XPress does a good job of it already.

▼ ▼

Tip: Who Needs Trapping? You don't need to use any trapping at all in your documents. Does that sound crazy? Well, it's true in two cases. First, you never need trapping if your press operator is obsessed with perfect registration on press. It is possible to control press registration; it's just rare that any press operator has the luxury of time and money to have such a perfect run.

Another way you can entirely avoid trapping is to use process-color combinations that don't need trapping in your documents (remember that only colors that touch require trapping). Here are two rules that can help you build and arrange color on your page so that you won't need trapping.

▶ **ALL LIGHTER, ALL DARKER.** If the cyan, magenta, yellow, and black tints in your foreground color are all darker or all lighter than the corresponding tints in the background color, you don't need to trap. When the Process Trap option is turned on—which it should be—XPress simply doesn't trap color combinations like this, so you don't have to do any extra work to stop QuarkXPress from trapping (see Table 12-2).

▶ **COMMON COLORS.** If two colors share a process-color element (cyan, magenta, yellow, or black), and the common element is within 30 percent, you probably don't need a trap. Let's say you color some text deep purple—made of 80-percent cyan, 70-percent magenta, and 20-percent black. If you put that text on a bright yellow background, you'll probably need to trap it because there are no common color elements. On the other hand, you don't have to trap it if you put the purple text on top of a light blue background—made of 50-percent cyan and 10-percent black. Why? Because both cyan and black are shared elements in the foreground and background colors, and their respective tints are both within 30 percent of each other. (The 30-percent rule is a some-

Table 12-2

Examples of colors that
don't need trapping
(see also Figure I
on the color plates)

	CYAN	MAGENTA	YELLOW	BLACK
ALL LIGHTER, ALL DARKER				
Color #1 (dark green)	100	20	80	15
Color #2 (yellow)	10	10	70	0
COMMON COLORS				
Color #1 (orange)	0	60	90	10
Color #2 (tan)	25	40	75	0

what arbitrary, middle-of-the-road choice; in some cases, you may want to be more or less conservative.)

QuarkXPress does not recognize common colors by itself. If you don't want these color pairs to trap, you should set them to Knockout in the Trap Specifications dialog box or in the Trap Information palette (see "Object-Level Trapping," below).

▼ ▼

Tip: Trapping Small Type. You can run into trouble when you're using small type, especially serif type, in a color document. Since the type is so fine—especially the serifs—even a small amount of trapping can clog it up. The counters can fill in, and the serifs can become really clunky (see Figure 12-19). Bear this in mind when you're setting up your trapping preferences, and when you're specifying colors for type.

Figure 12-19

Trapping serif type

Monsieur de Bergerac
Untrapped

Monsieur de Bergerac
Trapped

Serif type can clog up, and the serifs can get clunky when trapped.

However, the folks at Quark have made some hidden allowances for small text (under 24 points) and small objects (less than 10 points in height or width). When XPress encounters one of these, it won't allow spreads or chokes that might compromise the object's shape. This is both good and bad. On the one hand, it's nice because your small objects look better. On the other hand, it's bad because you can only rarely trap small objects even if you want to. This includes thin lines (under 10 points)!

You usually don't have to think about what XPress is really doing here, but if you want to know, here's what happens. The program spreads the object on a color plate only if the object's tint is less than or equal to half the corresponding color tint on its background; choking will occur only when the background-plate component is less than or equal to half the darkness of the object.

The upshot is that there won't be a trap unless the foreground and background colors are pretty similar.

▼ ▼

Tip: Trapping Large Type. Even the untrained reader can quickly spot type (especially thin, serif type) that has been "bulked up" by QuarkXPress's trapping. For example, if you put a dark-green 48-point headline over a light-blue background, you may find the text appears slightly heavier in print than the same text would look over no background color at all. The problem is that it's difficult to get XPress to choke a background behind some text without spreading the text, too.

Here's another use for the Text to Box feature.

1. Create a new color that is a combination of each darkest process-color tint in the foreground and background. For instance, let's say the foreground has 40-percent cyan plus 20-percent yellow, and the background object is set to 20-percent cyan and 40-percent yellow. The new color would have 40-percent cyan and 40-percent yellow.

2. Convert the headline text to a Bézier box using Text to Box on the Style menu.

3. Give this box a frame (Command/Ctrl-B) the width of the desired trap (.3 points or so) and apply the new color.

4. In the Trap Information palette, set the Frame Outside and Frame Inside popup menus to Overprint (see "Object-Level Trapping," below).

This actually looks far worse on screen, because XPress can't simulate the overprinting. However, when you print color separations, you'll see that the background has choked in under the "text," and it often looks cleaner (see Figure J in the color plates). Of course, this is a lot of work, so you'll only want to do this when you find that XPress's built-in trapping won't work for you.

▼ ▼

Tip: Knockout Black. If you find yourself wishing that black would overprint sometimes and knockout at other times, you might want to duplicate Black (in the Colors dialog box) and change the dupe's name to "Knockout Black." You can then edit the trapping specifications for your new color to either knock out or trap to some custom value. Now you've got a choice: apply Black to the items you want to overprint, and Knockout Black to those you don't.

▼ ▼

Tip: Knocking Out Rich Black. The biggest problem with rich black is that when you have text or an object knocking out the black, any misregistration on press results in the cyan peeking out horribly from behind the black. The engineers at Quark have built a very cool internal solution to this problem.

QuarkXPress checks to see if an object is knocking out a rich black. If it is, XPress only spreads the cyan, magenta, and yellow plates of that rich-black color by the trapping amount, leaving the black plate alone. You need this kind of help most when you're placing a white object (such as white, reversed text) over a rich black. (See Figure 12-20 and Figure L on the color plates.)

Figure 12-20
Knockout from rich black

*White type knocking
out from the black
plate of a rich black*

*The cyan plate:
Note the type is spread and
the background is choked.*

XPress also chokes the additive colors (leaving the black plate alone) around the edges of a rich black object that is sitting on a white or colored background. This ensures that the colored inks won't appear as a fringe around the black object.

▼ ▼

Tip: To Overprint or Not To Overprint. Sometimes people get confused when a color they've specifically set up to overprint in the Trap Specifications dialog box doesn't overprint at all. Even when they check the Trap Information palette (always the first place to look for your trapping questions), they see that it's not overprinting.

Often, they've simply forgotten that XPress only overprints a color when it's above the overprint limit (in the Trapping Preferences dialog box). Usually the overprint limit is set to 95 percent, so any color tinted below 95 percent won't overprint automatically. You can change this limit's value, or select the object and tell it to overprint (override the Default setting) in the Trap Information palette.

▼ ▼

Tip: Thicker Reversed Text. One of the problems with reversing text (like white text on a colored background) is that it often gets clogged up by the background ink spreading slightly. And even if it doesn't get literally choked, our eye perceives it as being choked.

One way around this is to spread the type's color slightly (see Figure 12-21). First, create a CMYK color that is set to one percent black and in the Edit Trap dialog box set the color to spread .125 points over black. Then turn off Process Trap in the Preferences dialog box and apply this new color to your type. When you print, turn Separations on, even if you're only going to print the black plate. Because your new color is set to spread, the one-percent black (which is almost white, and will probably not show up on press) spreads over the background black.

Figure 12-21
Thicker reversed text

A man planted a vineyard, encircled it with a hedge, excavated a wine press, built a tower and leased it to tenant farmers, then went away.

A man planted a vineyard, encircled it with a hedge, excavated a wine press, built a tower and leased it to tenant farmers, then went away.

This text has a spreading trap value applied to it.

▼ ▼

Object-Level Trapping

Instead of just specifying trapping-color pairs (all reds over all blues, all blacks over all yellows, and so on), you can specify trapping on an object-by-object basis. For example, if you want one green line to overprint a yellow area, and another similar line to knock out, you can specify that. You do this in the Trap Information palette. Again, you don't *have* to use this; the default trapping is often good enough (and using your service bureau's trapping software is even better). But when you need to tweak your trapping in XPress, here's the place to do it.

Unlike most palettes in QuarkXPress, where you can either use them or use menu items, the Trap Information palette is the only place you can use object-by-object trapping. Let's go ahead and take a gander at this palette's anatomy (see Figure 12-22).

The Trap Information palette shows you the current trap information for a selected page object, gives you "reasons" for why it's trapping the object that way, and lets you change that object's trap value. The trap values that you can change depend on the type of object you've selected.

For example, for a text box with no frame, you can adjust the trap for the background color of the box and the text in the box. If the text box has no background color, then the Background setting is grayed out.

Figure 12-22

The Trap Information
palette and its popup
information window

▶ **BACKGROUND.** You can set the Background trap value for boxes that
have a background color (anything but None) and do not have a frame.

▶ **FRAME INSIDE/FRAME OUTSIDE.** As soon as you put a border
(Command/Ctrl-B) around a box, the Background trap setting grays
out and the Frame Inside and Frame Outside settings become available. The inside and outside portions of a frame are exactly half the
frame width; in a 4-point frame, the Frame Inside (which abuts the
background color of the box, or the image inside a picture box) and
Frame Outside (which abuts whatever is behind the box) are each 2
points wide.

▶ **FRAME MIDDLE.** If you choose a border style that has gaps in it (in other words, any style other than the solid frame, such as the dotted or
double-line frame), XPress activates the Frame Middle popup menu.
The Frame Middle lets you control the trap between the frame and the
gap area. If the gap area is blank (if the Gap color is None), then this
should typically be the same as the Frame Outside setting.

The Frame Middle setting is also the only setting available when
you have a fancy bitmapped frame around a box (which I don't like

doing). In this case, the only options are Knockout and Overprint. On the palette, it may seem that the default setting is to spread or choke by the Auto Amount, but that doesn't reflect the reality (unless the frame is black, it will probably just knock out of its background).

▶ **GAP INSIDE/ GAP OUTSIDE.** As soon as you set a frame's gap color (in the Modify dialog box), you can set that gap's trapping with Gap Inside and Gap Outside. Like the frame trapping controls, Gap Inside refers to where the gap color touches the image or the background color of the box, and Gap Outside refers to where it touches the color behind the box.

▶ **LINE.** Lines trap to their background, of course, and if you don't like the default trapping, you can change it here. The problem is that because lines under 10 points thick are "small objects" (see "Tip: Trapping Small Type," earlier in this chapter), XPress currently won't trap a thin line at all unless its color is very similar to the background (I'm lobbying Quark to change this . . . maybe they will by the time you read this).

▶ **LINE MIDDLE.** Like Frame Middle, the Line Middle setting lets you set the trap between a line and the gaps in nonsolid line styles (whether the gap is transparent or colored). Again, unless the line is thick, the settings here won't make any difference. (Personally, I think we should be able to force XPress to trap thin lines in this palette . . . maybe a later version of XPress will allow it.)

▶ **GAP.** If you've gone hog-wild and added a gap color to your styled line, the Gap setting lets you trap that color to the background.

▶ **TEXT.** Where XPress 3.x would either trap every character in a text box or none at all, XPress is now a little smarter: it decides on trapping line by line. If only the first three lines of a text box are over a colored background, it will trap them and leave the other lines alone. If, however, the left side of a text box is over a colored background and the right side is not, XPress isn't smart enough to only trap the characters on the left side of the box, so every character gets trapped by default. This is a job for the Text setting on the Trap Information palette, which lets you change trapping character by character. If only half a character is overlapping text, XPress can't trap just half of it—that's a job for postprocess trapping software, like TrapWise.

▶ **PICTURE.** The Picture trap setting does not let you trap objects to a background in XPress. Instead, it simply gives you the choice of overprinting or knocking out the background. The only use I can think of for this is overprinting grayscale images, which was particularly diffi-cult in earlier versions of XPress, but which is now quite easy with this feature.

By the way, don't get confused if the Trap Information palette displays a positive trap value (spread) when you know it should be negative (choke). Remember that when the Process Trap option is turned on, some plates will spread and others will choke, so the positive and negative numbers don't mean much.

Default trap. Unless you've changed the trap value, the Trap Information palette displays all objects at their Default trap. This means that the objects trap at whatever value is set in the Trap Specifications dialog box and on the Trapping tab of the Document Preferences dialog box. QuarkXPress displays the trap value to the right of the word "Default," and then displays a gray button labeled with a question mark. If you click this button and hold it down, QuarkXPress displays the Default Trap window, which explains why it's trapping the object this way. For example, if you have a black line selected, the window might tell you that it's overprinting the black line because of the relationship between black and the background color.

If there are any special reasons why XPress is trapping the object the way it does, they're highlighted in the Properties section of the Default Trap window. Unfortunately, it doesn't usually provide much detail. For instance, if you've selected some white text that is knocking out of a rich black, "Rich Black" is highlighted, but nowhere does it mention that the additive colors in the rich black will be spread or choked by the Auto Amount. It just happens. Similarly, the only way you'd know that small type isn't getting a trap ("Tip: Trapping Small Type," above) is the phrase "Small Object" highlighted on the Properties list.

Nonetheless, it's better than just leaving you up in the air.

Custom trapping. To change the trap value for part of an object (for example, the inside frame of a picture box), you use the mini-popup menu on the Trap Information palette. The menu is usually set to Default, but you can change this to Overprint, Knockout, Auto Amount (+), Auto Amount (–), or Custom. Overprint and Knockout are pretty self-explanatory. The two Auto Amount values use the value in the Auto Amount field of the Trapping Preferences dialog box (the value is either positive or negative, denoting a spread or a choke). Personally, I don't find much use for the two Auto Amount settings.

The last item, Custom, is where the power is. QuarkXPress gives you a field in which to type any trap value you want (from -36 to 36 points, though you probably will never use more than 1 or 2 points).

Note that text can be trapped a character at a time (see Figure 12-23), and that one black object can be overprinted where another black object knocks out (this kills the need for my "Knockout Black" tip, above).

Trapping to Multiple Colors

I said earlier that when QuarkXPress sees one colored object only partially covering another colored object, the program thinks of this as Indeterminate trapping. I then went further and said that when Ignore White is turned on in Trapping Preferences, the program ignores the white background entirely, making it *not* Indeterminate. Now I have the final word on the subject.

If the foreground object partially overlaps two colored objects, XPress still doesn't always think of this as Indeterminate. First it looks at the trapping relationships among all the colors. If the foreground color chokes to both background colors, then the foreground object gets choked. If the Edit Trap specifications are set to spread to both background colors, then QuarkXPress spreads the trap. If it's supposed to spread to one and choke to the other, *then* the program defaults to the Indeterminate trap.

Also, just for the sake of completeness, if you set the Edit Trap specifications so that the foreground color spreads one value (let's say 1 point) to one background color, and a different value (let's say 2 points) to the other background color, QuarkXPress uses the lesser of the values (in this case, 1 point).

None of this may apply to you, but it's still good information to tuck into the back of your brain . . . just in case.

▼ ▼

Tip: Use Big Traps. An easy way to make sure your traps are working correctly is to temporarily set extremely large values for your color and object traps: anywhere from 1 to 6 points. Print your separations on transparencies or thin paper, align each plate, and you can quickly determine how well XPress is handling your trapping requests. Don't forget to reset the traps to their normal values before your final imagesetting, though! (When I do this, I save the document, then change the traps, print separations, and then use Revert to Saved to get back to the original settings.)

Another good way to check trapping is to use the enlargement feature in the Print dialog box to magnify the trap area (see "Tip: Printer as a Magnifying Glass," in Chapter 13, *Printing*).

▼ ▼

Tip: Overprinting Duotones. I really like the way Adobe Photoshop handles duotones (or tritones or quadtones). They're simple to make, they separate beautifully from QuarkXPress as EPS files (as long as you have the spot colors' names the same in both programs), and you can see what they look like in color. However, there's more than one way to spin a cat. Here's a way to make duo-

Figure 12-23

Trapping type
character
by character

tones right in XPress. The method relies on overprinting one TIFF image on another. I generally import a grayscale TIFF into a picture box, size it, and position it where I want it. Then I clone it (use Step and Repeat with the Offsets set to zero), change the color and the contrast curve for this second image, and make sure the background color of the overprinting image is set to "None." Last, I set the trap for the topmost picture box background to overprint in the Trap Information palette. (See Figure T in the color plates.)

Color from Outside Sources

Up until now in this chapter I have concentrated my discussion on color items—text, boxes, rules, and so on—which are built entirely in QuarkXPress. But what about bringing color graphics in from other programs? And although I discussed modifying color bitmapped images in Chapter 10, *Fine-Tuning Images,* what about being prepared for creating color separations? I'll address these points now.

One area you won't read about here is working with object-oriented color PICT or WMF images, because I think they're kludgey (that's pronounced "cloodgy"), and so unreliable that I wouldn't use them for my own documents (see Chapter 9, *Pictures,* for a slightly longer discussion of this format). The only formats that I find really reliable for prepress work are TIFF, JPEG, PDF, and EPS (and DCS, which is an offshoot of EPS).

Object-Oriented EPS Files

I've avoided the subject of object-oriented graphic files for several chapters, but now it's time to dive back in. Designers frequently generate color artwork using programs such as Adobe Illustrator or Macromedia Freehand, saving them as Encapsulated PostScript (EPS) files. XPress can not only import files from these programs, but can also generate color separations of these files.

Once again, the details of generating color separations (or "seps," as they're often called) is covered in Chapter 13, *Printing,* and Appendix A, *Color Management.* But while I'm on the subject of color on the desktop, I need to cover some general information about using these programs with QuarkXPress. I'll tackle this discussion one color method at a time: process first, and then spot (I include Pantone colors in the spot-color discussion, though you can create process simulations of Pantone inks).

Process color. QuarkXPress can create color separations of illustrations built in FreeHand or Illustrator which contain process colors. Period. All you have to do is specify your process colors in either application, save them as EPS or PDF, and import them into your QuarkXPress document using Get Picture. Nice and easy. As I noted earlier in this chapter, if the colors are named (process colors in Illustrator or spot colors in FreeHand), the colors are added to the QuarkXPress document color list.

Note that I say you must use Get Picture. If you use Copy and Paste to paste a graphic into a picture box, QuarkXPress won't separate it. In fact, while I'm on the subject, I should note that QuarkXPress may not be able to separate color EPS or PDF files from applications other than Illustrator or FreeHand. It depends entirely on whether those applications create the files according to Adobe's document-structuring specifications.

Spot color. The key to working with spot colors brought in from either FreeHand or Illustrator is being careful with your naming. In order for QuarkXPress to separate the spot colors properly, you have to have a color in your QuarkXPress document named *exactly* the same as the color in the illustration. Fortunately, XPress automatically adds named colors from illustrations to your color list when you import the picture. Also, note that when working with spot colors, you must save them in an EPS or DCS format; PDF files with spot colors do not currently work in XPress.

If you don't have a same-named color in QuarkXPress (perhaps you deleted it accidentally), the spot color separates into a process color in XPress. Remember that with spot colors, the colors' actual specifications make no difference except for screen display and color-printer output.

The same goes for the Pantone colors. If you use a Pantone color in your Illustrator file, just make sure it has the same name in your QuarkXPress file, and it'll print fine (although it'll probably look wrong on screen). Fortunately, Illustrator, FreeHand, and QuarkXPress name their Pantone colors the same, so if you're using the color libraries included in each program, the names will probably match.

What You Can and Cannot Change

QuarkXPress prints exactly what is specified in every EPS file. In fact, XPress has no way to change them: encapsulated PostScript files and PDF files are totally self-contained and cannot easily be modified from outside sources. All the halftoning information for objects and bitmapped images (if it's included in the EPS), all the trapping and tinting information, and all the color specifications are set in hard-packed mud (I like to think that you at least have a chance with hard-packed mud; "stone" is a bit too final).

All this means that you must take a little more control into your own hands. You must specify your own trapping from within FreeHand or Illustrator, and make sure that these images contain traps for their surroundings in XPress documents.

Luckily, all overprinting specified in Illustrator or FreeHand (or any other program that handles its color PostScript properly) is handled correctly when you generate color separations from QuarkXPress. An object that's set to overprint in a FreeHand EPS file not only overprints objects within that EPS, but also QuarkXPress objects. Conversely, if an object is not set to Overprint, it knocks out any background colors or objects within QuarkXPress.

You cannot adjust any trapping for EPS files from within QuarkXPress. For example, if your EPS picture contains a spot color (let's say PMS 345), and you have set up the equivalent spot color in QuarkXPress as described above, any trapping or overprinting assignments you make to PMS 345 in the Trap Specifications dialog box do not (and actually cannot) make any difference to the EPS file. They do, however, make all the difference to any objects created within QuarkXPress that are colored PMS 345.

The same is true with Quark's Color Management System: it has absolutely no effect on the colors in your EPS graphics (see Appendix A, *Color Management*).

Bitmapped Images

Let's cut to the chase: process colors are CMYK (cyan, magenta, yellow, and black). A picture saved in any other color model (most TIFF images are, especially scans) has to be translated into CMYK mode before it can be imageset. QuarkXPress can create separations of these RGB images by itself, but it won't necessarily do a good job of it.

Version 4 of XPress had a problem wherein RGB TIFF and JPEG images were always converted to CMYK at print time, even when printing to a composite color printer. This typically made vibrant images look washed out because XPress doesn't know how to separate the colors as well as the printer can by itself. Fortunately, you can now send RGB images to composite printers directly in the RGB model, and the images look much better.

If you're working with scanned RGB images and want to print color separations, you have two options for the RGB-to-CMYK conversion.

▶ Preseparate the image using Photoshop or the like, and import it into QuarkXPress as a CMYK TIFF, PDF, EPS, or DCS file.

▶ Place the image as an RGB TIFF or JPEG in QuarkXPress, and let the Quark CMS XTension do the process-separation work (see Appendix A, *Color Management*).

Although I'll really be talking about color separation in detail in Chapter 13, *Printing*, and Appendix A, *Color Management*, let's explore these three methods briefly here.

Preseparating. Adobe Photoshop allows you to translate RGB images into CMYK using the Mode submenu, under the Item menu. This is a simple process, but to get good-quality CMYK images, you need to spend some time learning about and tweaking the various color-separation preference dialog boxes; I cover this in great depth in the book I wrote with Bruce Fraser, *Real World Adobe Photoshop*.

Once you've separated a file in Photoshop (or some other capable program), you can save it in one of four formats—EPS, DCS, PDF, or TIFF—and import it into QuarkXPress, fully separated and ready for output. I discussed these formats in detail in Chapter 9, *Pictures*.

Saving as CMYK EPS. Note that you don't have to save EPS files in DCS format in order for your images to separate from XPress. However, there are differences in the way the two formats function.

▶ The biggest drawback to CMYK EPS files is that they consist of one gigantic file. DCS 1.0 files have the added benefit of letting you work with a small master file while the large CMYK files can be sitting someplace else. (On the other hand, this means you have to keep track of five files rather than just one.)

▶ DCS files print faster from XPress than do EPS or TIFF files. It used to be the case that EPS files were much slower than DCS, because XPress had to send the entire EPS file to the printer for each plate (imagine a 40 MB file getting sent four times, once each for cyan, magenta, yellow, and black). Now XPress is smart enough to recognize Photoshop EPS files, and it knows how to pull these apart so that it only sends the cyan information for the cyan plate, and so on (this is only true with Photoshop EPS files). The result is that DCS is still faster, but not much faster.

Of course, I've already said that color separation is not as easy as clicking a button. If you're looking for quality color, you had better know Photoshop well enough to work with its undercolor-removal and color-correction settings. Remember: QuarkXPress cannot apply any image modification to the EPS files that you import. All that must be done before you import the picture.

Saving as CMYK TIFF. Once you've switched to CMYK mode in Photoshop, you can also save files as CMYK TIFF images. I find CMYK TIFFs to be a bit easier than DCS files for several reasons. First, you only have one file to work with. Second, QuarkXPress can do more with TIFF files than it can with EPS or DCS images. For example, QuarkXPress can downsample the TIFF image at print time if necessary, which can save you time. Also, you can make tonal and screening adjustments to TIFF images from within the program. Finally, if you're working with an OPI system (see "OPI" in Chapter 13, *Printing*), you can use TIFF images as for-position-only (FPO) images and let another program strip them in at print time.

Separating with an XTension. If you want to postseparate your RGB images, you can import them directly into QuarkXPress and then separate them with the color management system, Quark CMS, that ships with the program. Color management is a way to map colors from one space to another (for instance, mapping RGB on a 17-inch Apple Trinitron monitor to CMYK on a Web press with 22-percent dot gain using SWOP inks), but it takes some work to produce quality images efficiently (see Appendix A, *Color Management*).

Which to use. Do I suggest using preseparation (typically with Adobe Photoshop) or postseparation (with Quark CMS)? The most important consideration is your workflow. The biggest argument for preseparation is the translation time: preseparating your bitmapped images requires translating them from RGB to CMYK only once. Postseparating them with an XTension requires that same translation time whenever you print. This translation can be incredibly time-consuming. Given a choice, I'd rather just have to deal with it once.

However, which of these methods results in the superior separation? Here I get to the aesthetics of color separation, and I wouldn't want to sway your opinion (which is a nice way of saying that—just this once—I'm not going to preach my own opinions).

▼ ▼

Tip: Duotones from Photoshop. Many people create duotones (or tritones or quadtones) in Photoshop and then save them as EPS files (you have to save them as EPS files) before importing them into QuarkXPress. If the duotone uses spot (such as Pantone) colors, you have to make sure you've got the same-named color in your QuarkXPress document. People have had difficulty with this in the past because the two programs sometimes named their Pantone colors differently.

Fortunately, QuarkXPress now automatically imports the color names into your document, so you're sure to get a match. On the other hand, if you're already using Pantone Uncoated colors in your XPress document, you may need to rename the colors (in either Photoshop or QuarkXPress) so that they match.

Also note that if your duotones are set to a spot color and a process color (like black), you have to adjust the halftone screen for the spot color so that you don't end up with moiré patterns or dot-doubling (see "Halftone" in the "Specifying Colors" section, earlier in this chapter).

▼ ▼

Deciding to Work in Color

While this chapter should get you up and running with color in XPress, I think it's only fair to end with a suggestion about the logical steps toward successful color desktop publishing.

1. Complete a black-and-white project with text only.

2. Complete a black-and-white project with text and graphics.

3. Complete a project with several spot colors.

4. Complete a project with process-color tints.

5. Finally, attempt the use of color photography.

The computer, no matter how powerful a tool, is still no substitute for experience. Work slowly and carefully, and in time you will become a raging color pro.

13

PRINTING

O nce upon a time, probably somewhere at some university, someone had an idea and named it "the paperless office." People wouldn't be bothered anymore with having to store the thousands (or millions) of pieces of paper that come through their offices every year. Instead, the information would all be placed on some sort of storage medium, easily referenced by computer. It was a magic concept; everyone agreed that it would make life easier, more efficient, and certainly more fun.

Go ahead and ask people who have been involved with electronic publishing for a while if they have seen any sign of the paperless office. As an example, in my office, the ratio of expended paper to normal refuse is such that I empty my small garbage can every couple of weeks and the voluminous paper-recycling boxes weekly. When it comes right down to it, unless you use QuarkXPress exclusively for building Web pages or Acrobat PDF files, almost every document that you create is probably based, ultimately, on a printed page or an imaged piece of film (which will probably be used later to print on paper).

How can you extract the digitized information from disk to print on paper? Many people mistake the process as being as easy as simply choosing the Print command. In this chapter I'll discuss what's behind the act of printing, and go into some depth on how to get the most efficient and best-quality output you can for your document. I'll also touch on tips for working with service bureaus and printers—both the mechanical and the human varieties.

Before I get into anything too complex, though, let's deal with two simple yet critical issues in most people's print jobs: PostScript and fonts.

▼ ▼

PostScript

To put it simply, PostScript is what makes desktop publishing with QuarkXPress possible. PostScript is a page-description language—a collection of commands that PostScript laser printers understand. When you tell QuarkXPress to print a page, it writes a computer program in PostScript describing the page, and sends that program to the printer. The printer (or imagesetter), which has a PostScript interpreter inside it, interprets the PostScript describing the page, and puts marks on the paper (or film) according to that description.

For instance, the PostScript command *lineto* tells the printer to draw a line from one point to another; *curveto* draws curves, and *setlinewidth* changes the thickness of the line the printer is about to image. You don't really need to know much about PostScript in order to get your job done, but it's important to know that it's there, working behind the scenes.

This chapter is dedicated, in part, to Chuck Geschke, John Warnock, and the other people who created PostScript. And I need to say one thing up front: I'm not talking PCL or CORA here. Those languages were also designed for putting marks on paper or film. In this chapter, however, I'm going to assume you're working with a PostScript printer because that's what QuarkXPress assumes.

You can output to a non-PostScript printer, but as they say: "Your mileage may vary." A large percentage of printing problems that people encounter are related to using printers that don't understand PostScript. For instance, you can typically print on one of those inexpensive color ink-jet printers, but some page elements print better than others. EPS files, in particular, print horribly unless you turn on Full Resolution from the Preview Quality submenu (under the Item menu) for each image, because the printer can't parse them, so it only prints the low-resolution screen previews you see in XPress.

(By the way, because Adobe makes the interpreter that lives inside most printers, people talk about "Adobe PostScript" as being the standard. Nonetheless, many other companies offer PostScript clones, which usually work just as well. Every now and again, people find that a page won't print on a clone interpreter but will print on a true Adobe PostScript interpreter.

Because of this, my personal bias is toward using printers, whenever possible, that use Adobe PostScript.)

▼ ▼

Tip: Printing to Inkjet Printers. It seems like almost everyone has a desktop inkjet printer these days—they're inexpensive and they produce beautiful output. However, XPress really expects to be printing to a PostScript printer, and these inkjets rarely support PostScript. Some have software add-ons that will interpret PostScript, but I have never heard anyone say that they were happy with these solutions. QuarkXPress can print most page elements decently, but EPS files are a disaster. Version 5 added the ability to scale pages and print TIFF images better than earlier versions, but the results are still often yucky. So what's the best way to print your QuarkXPress document to an inkjet printer? Export the file as a PDF file and print it from Acrobat or Acrobat Reader. (I cover Acrobat and PDF files in Chapter 14, *Going Online with QuarkXPress*.)

▼ ▼

Deciphering the Print Dialog Box

We all demanded more features in QuarkXPress, and Quark gave them to us. Unfortunately, sometimes having more features means more complexity. The Print dialog box is a perfect example of this. The folks at Quark have tried their hardest to squeeze over 40 features into this one dialog box in a way that is still reasonably usable, and they've mostly succeeded. However, the result is something that appears, at first, to be like one of those 1950s computer consoles with hundreds of dials and knobs and flashing lights (see Figure 13-1). Don't worry, it's much easier than it looks.

If you're familiar with earlier versions of XPress, you'll soon figure out that the folks at Quark folded the Page Setup dialog box into the Print dialog box, stuck in several features from the long-defunct QuarkPrint XTension, and topped it off with a few great new features. Note that you can make changes to the various tabs in the Print dialog box in any order you like. In general, however, I make choices in this dialog box in the order that I discuss them in this chapter.

Choosing a Printer: Macintosh versus Windows

My discussion of the Print dialog box is made slightly more complicated by the fact that Macintosh and Windows operating systems handle printing slightly differently. The key distinction is in how you specify which printer (the digital kind, not the lithographer type) you want to use. No matter which platform

Figure 13-1

The Print dialog box on the Macintosh

you use, it's imperative that you choose a printer before you take any further steps toward printing.

Macintosh. On the Macintosh, you can specify which kind of printer you want to use—as well as which particular printer, if you have more than one on a network—by clicking the Printer button in the Print dialog box, which tells XPress to display the operating system's printer driver dialog box (see Figure 13-2). To choose a printer, select it from the Printer popup menu, which lists every printer you've set up on this machine. Unlike the old Classic Mac Chooser, you do have to set up printers before you use them; if your printer doesn't appear in this list, select Edit Printer List at the bottom of that popup menu.

If you are working with just a single PostScript laser printer, you hardly need to worry about the Printer dialog box. Just set it once and forget it, except when you want to switch between PostScript printers on the network. I'll discuss the other features you see in the print driver dialog box later in this chapter, in "Page Setup, Printer, and Properties."

Windows. In Windows, you must choose a printer from the Print dialog box itself (see Figure 13-3). The only printers that appear listed here are those that you have already set up in Windows. (You can add a new printer with Windows' Add Printer utility. I'll step you through one example of this process later in this chapter when I discuss how to print PostScript files to disk.)

Once you've chosen a device, it behooves you to click the Properties button to ensure that the printer settings conform to your wishes. The Properties dialog box controls the way the printer driver works. Note that there are several fea-

Figure 13-2
The Mac OS X printer
driver dialog box

tures that appear both in the Properties dialog box and QuarkXPress's Print dialog box; in these cases, ignore the settings in the Properties dialog box and use XPress's instead. (I discuss these settings in more depth in "Page Setup, Printer, and Properties," later in this chapter.)

The Pages You Want

There are three other settings in the Print dialog box that stick around no matter what tab you choose: Print Style, Copies, and Pages. I'm going to hold off on the Print Style popup menu until later in this chapter—for now, suffice it to say that it's a way to save various Print dialog box settings so you can choose them quickly later. Here's the run-down on the other two controls.

Copies. I might as well start with the simplest choice of all. How many copies of your document do you want printed? Let's say you choose to print a multiple-page document, specifying four copies. The first page prints four times, then the second page prints four times, and so on. In other words, you may have a good deal of collating to do later (see "Collate" in "The Layout Tab," below).

Pages. You can tell XPress to print all the pages in your document, or just a selection of pages. In the past, you had to have an XTension to print discontiguous pages in your document. Now it's easy: just type commas or hyphens between the page numbers. For instance, typing 1, 4-6, 9 prints the first page, the fourth through sixth pages, and the ninth page.

The values you type in the Pages field must either be exactly the same as those in your document or must be specified as absolutes. If your document starts on page 23, you can't type "1" in the From field; it must be either "23" (or whatever page you want to start from) or "+1" (the plus character specifies an absolute page number—in other words, "the first page"). Similarly, if you are

Figure 13-3

Choosing a printer in Windows

You can change various printer-level settings by clicking Properties.

Choose the device you want to print to from this popup menu.

using page numbering in an alphabetical system (such as "a," "b," "c," etc.) or using a prefix (see "Sections and Page Numbering" in Chapter 4, *Building a Document*), you have to type these sorts of numbers into the slots. It's annoying, but if you don't type the page number exactly the way it's used in the program (or use absolute numbers), the program tells you that "no such page exists."

There's one more potential problem with typing page numbers into the Pages field: if you have used prefixes such as "A-" then your page numbers appear as A-1, A-2, A-3, and so on. This means you can't type a range of page numbers. (If you type A-1-A-6, XPress will just get confused.) Fortunately, you can change the separation characters that XPress pays attention to in the Preferences dialog box (see Figure 13-4). You can change the hyphen and the comma characters to just about any other symbol you want, except letters and numbers.

▼ ▼

Tip: From Beginning or End. You can print all the pages in a document by typing "All" into the Pages field (or choosing it from the popup menu to the right of the field). On the other hand, if you only want to print the first four pages, you can type the cryptic "+1-+4" (remember that the plus sign means "absolute page number," no matter what page-numbering scheme you're using). To print from page 15 to the end of the document, type "15-end".

▼ ▼

Tip: Capture Settings. It seems to happen to me at least once a day: I go to the Print dialog box, I spend time setting up the options in the various tabs, and then I remember a change I forgot to make on the document pages. In this situation in the past, you'd have to press Cancel and lose all the work you did

Figure 13-4
Range Separators

in the Print dialog box. Fortunately, now you can click the Capture Settings button. This closes the dialog box but remembers the values and options you have chosen.

Unfortunately, this feature doesn't remember all the settings. For instance, it won't remember values you type in Page Range or Copies, and it won't remember which color plates you *don't* want to print (see "The Output Tab," later in this chapter).

▼ ▼

Print Status

As soon as you click Print, XPress displays the Print Status dialog box, which not only tells you what page it's printing, but also what color plate, tile, and EPS/TIFF images it's working on (see Figure 13-5). Remember that no program can know how long a page will take to print on a PostScript printer, so there's no way to show how much longer the print job will take. Instead, the status bar in the Print Status dialog box only displays the percentage of pages that have been printed (for example, if you have two pages in your document, the status bar is 50-percent full after the first page, even if the second page takes 10 times longer than the first one to print). Nonetheless, this is a nice intermediate step, and often makes me feel better when I'm waiting for those long jobs to print.

Figure 13-5
Print Status dialog box

Currently Processing:

Page: 1
Plate: Cyan

Picture: Amrita OS X:...:Desktop:Testing:ID Testing:Amma.tif

To cancel printing,
hold down the ⌘ key and type a period (.)

▼ ▼

The Layout Tab

The Layout tab of the Print dialog box provides overall controls for how your document appears on printed pages. As you've heard me say many times before, looking at the whole shebang is too overwhelming, so it's best to take the various checkboxes and popup menus one at a time (see Figure 13-6).

Separations. I'm going to discuss separating color documents into single, black-and-white plates in "Color Separations," later in this chapter. For now, let's just say that if you want your color documents to separate, turn on the Separations checkbox. Of course, unless you've applied color to elements in your document, this option has no effect.

Include Blank Plates. As I write, my white-paper recycling bin overfloweth. I go through so much paper that I feel guilty every time I drive through a forest (which is difficult to avoid in the Pacific Northwest). Therefore, whenever I have the chance to save a tree here and there, I jump at it. QuarkXPress is giv-

Figure 13-6
The Layout Tab

Print Layout 1

Print Style: Default

Copies: 1   Pages: All

Layout Setup Output Options Layers Bleed OPI Preview

☑ Separations   ☐ Spreads   ☐ Collate
☐ Print Blank Plates   ☐ Thumbnails   ☐ Back to Front

Page Sequence: All
Registration: Center...   Offset: 6 pt
Tiling: Off   Overlap: ☐ Absolute Overlap

Page Setup...   Printer...   Capture Settings   Cancel   Print ing me just this chance with the Include Blank Plates control on the Layout tab of the Print dialog box. When you turn on Include Blank Plates (it's on by default), QuarkXPress prints as it always has: every page, no matter what is (or isn't) on it. When you turn off Include Blank Plates, QuarkXPress won't print a page if there isn't anything printable on it. This includes pages whose only objects are colored white, or are set to Suppress Printout. I've gotten in the habit of always turning this off when I print.

Spreads. This is a powerful but potentially dangerous feature, so it should be used with some care. Checking Spreads in the Print dialog box tells QuarkXPress to print spreads as one full page rather than as two or three pages. For example, printing a two-page, facing-pages spread with registration marks normally results in one page printing with its set of crop marks, then the next page, and so on. When Spreads is turned on, both pages abut each other and sit between the same crop marks (see Figure 13-7).

Figure 13-7
Printing spreads
versus printing
individual pages

Two pages printed as a spread; this only works for center spreads, or when you've set up panels of a brochure or poster as individual pages.

A reader spread printed as two pages. This is what your printer generally wants. Note the bleed for images that cross the page break.

I think there are two good uses for the Spreads feature.

▶ If you're building a folding brochure (like a tri-fold) and you lay out each panel on a separate page, you need to turn on the Spreads option in order for the panels to print out next to each other. (Note that the primary problem with doing this is that the third panel in a tri-fold brochure typically needs to be slightly more narrow so that it folds inside the other panels—and XPress won't let you have different-sized pages within a document.)

▶ Turning on the Spreads feature is a good way to proof a document on a desktop printer so you can see what two pages will look like next to each other in the final bound document.

The Spreads feature is not an imposition feature. That is, it won't create printer spreads, which are required when the document will be bound (however, see the next tip).

▼ ▼

Tip: Roll Your Own Printer Spreads. Page imposition is a tricky business, and there's lots of software out there to help you do it. QuarkXPress itself does not perform any kind of imposition, including basic printer spreads (where pages 1 and 16 print together, then pages 2 and 15, and so on). Fortunately, there are some great page imposition tools out there. On the high-end, there's Creo's Preps and Dynagram's InPosition XTension. More appropriate for the smaller design shop is A Lowly Apprentice Production's Imposer or Imposer Pro (see Appendix C, *XTensions and Resources*).

However, sometimes you just want to do a quick little booklet at just as little cost. You can use the Spreads feature in conjunction with the Document Layout palette to "strip" together pages which will be double-sided and saddle-stitched. Just follow these steps.

1. Create your document as usual, but don't use facing pages or automatic page numbers (see Chapter 4, *Building a Document*). Make sure you have an even number of pages.

2. When you're finished, use the Document Layout palette to move the last page to the *left* of the first page. Then move the second-to-last page (which has now become the last page) up to the *right* of the second page (which is now the third page). Then, move the next last page to the *left* of the next single page, and so on.

3. When you're done, every page should be paired with another page, and the last pages in the document should be the middle pages. For example, in an 8-page booklet, the final pages would end up being the spread between pages 4 and 5.

4. Make sure the Spreads feature is selected in the Print dialog box when you print the document page.

▼ ▼

Tip: Printing Spreads in a Document. Don't waste paper or film when you print contiguous spreads from a single document; if for no other reason, it's expensive. If you have a multiple-page spread crossing pages 45 through 47, have your service bureau print the pages from 1 through 44 and 48 through the end as single pages, and then print the three-page spread on a separate pass.

▼ ▼

Thumbnails. Selecting Thumbnails shrinks each page of your document down to about 12 percent of its size and lines up each page next to the other. It then fits as many as it can onto each printed page. This is great for an overview of your file, though the output you get is usually too small to really give you much of an idea of anything except general page geometry (see "Tip: Faster, Larger Thumbnails," below). Note that on PostScript printers, it takes just as long to print this one sheet of many pages as it does to print every page individually, so plan your time accordingly. If you just want to look over the pages, it would probably be faster to see them on screen in Thumbnails view. Remember that you don't have to print all your pages when you select Thumbnails. I often find it helpful to just print one or two pages at a time to see how they're looking.

▼ ▼

Tip: Faster, Larger Thumbnails. I find the size that Thumbnails usually gives me pretty useless; it's just too small! And if I have pictures on the pages, the job takes too long to print. So I use this feature in conjunction with two others: Rough, and Reduce or Enlarge. Rough is nearby on the Output popup menu, on the Options tab. Just make sure this is selected, and your thumbnails print with "X"s through the pictures and with simplified frames. You can find the Reduce or Enlarge feature on the Setup tab (see "The Output Tab" and "The Page Setup Tab," later in this chapter). Change Reduce or Enlarge to 200 percent, and your thumbnails are printed at 24 percent instead of a little over 12 percent. This is just about the right size for most letter-size pages.

▼ ▼

Tip: Two Thumbnails per Page. If you want your thumbnails much larger, you can up the scaling factor to 375 percent and turn the page orientation to Landscape on the Setup tab of the Print dialog box. With this value, you can get two letter- or legal-size pages on one page. You can get two tabloid-size pages on one letter-size landscape page with an enlargement of 300 percent. If your document is made of two-page spreads, then you can print letter- and legal-size pages up to 400 percent (the maximum allowed for enlargement), and tabloid-size pages up to 350 percent.

Note that both the Macintosh and Windows printer drivers offer the ability to print more than one document page per printed page. However, XPress seems to conflict with the drivers on both platforms, causing either strange printing or PostScript errors most of the time. It's too bad, but I just stick with XPress's own Thumbnails feature.

▼ ▼

Collate. I said earlier that when you printed multiple copies of your document you would receive *x* copies of the first page, then *x* copies of the second page, and so on, leaving you to manually collate all the copies. You can have QuarkXPress collate the pages for you instead, so that the full document prints out once, then again, and again, and so on.

The problem with Collate is that it takes much longer to print your complete job. This is because the printer cannot "remember" what each page looks like after it goes on to the next page, and so it has to reprocess the entire document for each new set of copies. How long this takes depends on the number of fonts and pictures you use, among other things. On a long document, the time difference becomes a toss-up: do you take the time to collate the pages yourself, or have the printer take the time to process them?

Back to Front. The problem with talking about printing from QuarkXPress is that each PostScript printer model is slightly (or not-so-slightly) different from the next. For example, when you print a multiple-page document on your laser printer, does the first page come out face up or face down? Some printers do one, some the other, and some give you a choice. If the pages come out face up, you'll love the Back to Front feature. Selecting Back to Front prints the last page of your page selection first, then prints "backwards" to the first page. The stack of pages that ends up in the output tray will be in proper order.

Note that you can't select this feature when you are printing spreads or thumbnails (if you want a good brain twister, try to think of how pages would print if you could select these together).

Bleed. Are you looking for the Bleed control in this tab of the Print dialog box? Those friendly folks at Quark enhanced the Bleed feature so much that it now requires a whole tab of its own. See "Setting Bleeds," later in this chapter.

Page sequence. The first popup menu on the Layout tab is Page Sequence, which gives you slightly more control over which pages in your document get printed. You have three choices: All, Odd, or Even.

▶ **ALL.** This is the default position for printing pages from QuarkXPress. It means "all pages that you have selected above." In other words, if you have selected a page range from 23 to 28, having All Pages selected won't counteract your desires; it'll just print all those pages.

▶ ODD/EVEN. These two choices are mutually exclusive. I sometimes joke about this feature when I'm working on jobs with several strangely designed pages: "Just print the odd ones, and leave the rest." The only real value I've ever gotten out of this feature lies in the following tip, "Printing Double-Sided Documents."

▼ ▼

Tip: Printing Double-Sided Documents. You can print double-sided pages with the following technique.

1. Print all the odd-numbered pages (select Odd).

2. Place these pages back into the printer, face down (or face up, depending on how your printer feeds the paper).

3. Select Back to Front.

4. Print all the even-numbered pages (select Even).

If everything is set up right, and if your document has an even number of pages, the second page should print on the back of the first, and so on.

You can use this same technique to print documents when photocopying onto two sides of a page (if your photocopier handles automatic two-sided copying, ignore this). Print the odd-numbered pages first, then the even-numbered pages, then ask your local Kinko's person what to do next.

▼ ▼

Registration and Trim Marks. In addition to the text and graphics of the pages themselves, your printer (I'm talking about the human lithographer here) needs several pieces of information about your camera-ready work. One is where the sides of the printed page are. If you're printing multiple colors, another piece of information your printer needs is how each color plate aligns with the others. Additional job and page information may be helpful also. Selecting the Registration feature answers all of these needs—QuarkXPress places *crop marks* (or *trim marks*), *registration marks*, and page information around your document (see Figure 13-8).

▶ CROP MARKS. Crop marks specify the page boundaries of your document. They are placed slightly outside each of the four corners so that when the page is printed and cut to size, they will be cut away. These are also called "trim marks" or "cut marks."

▶ REGISTRATION MARKS. Registration marks are used primarily for color-separation work, but you get them even if you just need crop marks

Figure 13-8

The Registration feature places items around your page

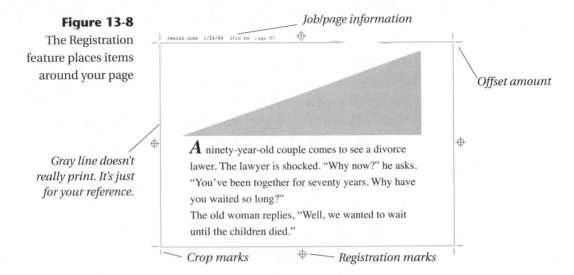

Job/page information

Jewish Joke 1/24/84 3:20 PM Page 87

Offset amount

Gray line doesn't really print. It's just for your reference.

A ninety-year-old couple comes to see a divorce lawer. The lawyer is shocked. "Why now?" he asks. "You've been together for seventy years. Why have you waited so long?"
The old woman replies, "Well, we wanted to wait until the children died."

Crop marks   *Registration marks*

on a one-color job. These are used by your printer's stripper to perfectly align each color plate to the next (see "Tip: Better Registration Marks").

▶ **PAGE AND JOB INFORMATION.** The page and job information that is printed in the upper-left corner of the page includes the file name, a page number, and a date and time stamp. If you want more job information than is listed here, see "Tip: Additional Job Information," below.

▶ **COLOR BARS AND STEP WEDGE.** When you print color separations (again, more on that in "Color Separations," later in this chapter) along with registration marks, QuarkXPress also adds a color bar and a grayscale step wedge to your output. This lets your lithographer take densitometer readings from the film and final output, as well as ensure that colors are registering well.

To make QuarkXPress add all these marks to your printed page, you need to select either Centered or Off Center from the Registration popup menu in the Print dialog box. These features refer to the placement of registration marks. If you select Centered, each registration mark is placed exactly in the center of each side of the printed page. This is where most strippers need it. Others, because of their pin-register systems, need the registration marks slightly off center. Ask your printer.

▼ ▼

Tip: Better Registration Marks. The registration marks that QuarkXPress creates for you are okay, but not great, and certainly not optimal from a stripper's point of view. This is how you can make a better registration mark directly in QuarkXPress (you can also make one in FreeHand or Illustrator, and bring it in as an EPS; see Figure 13-9).

1. Draw a line about ¼ inch long. Set its width to .25 points, with Midpoints selected on the Measurements palette.

2. Use the Step and Repeat feature from the Item menu to create one copy with no horizontal or vertical offset.

3. Make this second line perpendicular to the first by adding or subtracting 90 degrees from the line angle on the Measurements palette. Color the lines "Registration" (see Chapter 12, *Color*).

4. Draw a square picture box about ⅛ inch large (hold down the Shift key to maintain a square, or just type ".125"" in both the Height and Width fields of the Measurements palette) and center it over the lines. You could center it by either using the Space/Align feature (see Chapter 2, *QuarkXPress Basics*) or by just aligning the box's handles directly over the lines.

5. Set the box's background to 100-percent Registration.

Figure 13-9

A more versatile registration mark

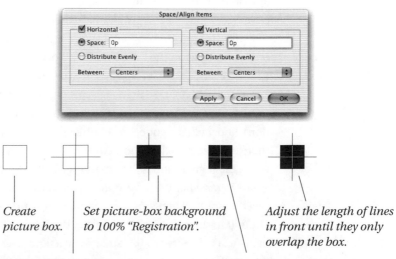

Begin with a .25-point line, .5 inch long.

Step and repeat as shown; rotate second line to 90 degrees.

Create picture box.

Set picture-box background to 100% "Registration".

Adjust the length of lines in front until they only overlap the box.

Use Space/Align as shown to position the center of the box directly over the lines' intersection.

Duplicate (step and repeat) lines; bring duplicates to front; color them "White".

6. Select the two lines, and step-and-repeat both of them once with no off-sets. Bring these lines to the front, if they're not already there.

7. Color the second set of lines White, and shorten them so that they only overlap the box.

The great benefit of this registration mark is that when you print negatives, your printer can still align black crosshairs on a white background. (If you print film positives rather than negatives, QuarkXPress's marks are probably easier to work with.) After you create one of these, you can duplicate it as needed. Also, you can save it in a library or make an EPS out of it so that you can import it quickly onto other pages.

You can use your registration marks alongside the standard ones by putting them on the Pasteboard just outside the page boundary (though try a test print to make sure XPress isn't printing its marks on top of yours). Also remember to increase the Bleed value in the Print dialog box, or else they won't print.

Even better than going this route is using an XTension such as XPert ItemMarks (part of the XPert Tools Volume 2 bundle from a lowly apprentice production), which gives you even more control over registration marks and job information (but of course costs more, too).

▼ ▼

Tip: Additional Job Information. Custom registration marks aren't the only thing you can place in the margins, outside the trim marks. This is an ideal place for additional job information, such as your contact information or even a small logo. Be careful with anything that is larger than a thin line: objects that appear on every plate (anything colored Registration) cause 400-percent ink coverage, which can be problematic on press. Check with your printer if you're not sure about this. And, once again, remember to increase your Bleed value or else nothing on the Pasteboard will print.

▼ ▼

Offset. You just have to understand that sometimes the engineers at Quark don't know what's good for us unless we tell them. Case in point: someone there decided that they should remove the setting in QuarkXPress that lets you move the registration and trim marks farther away from the page. Instead, in QuarkXPress 4.0, the trim marks would only move when you increased the Bleed amount. Even stranger than this was that no one seemed to complain about it in the software's beta cycle. But when XPress 4 shipped, people went ballistic. Fortunately, 4.02 (and now versions 5 and 6) handles this properly by adding the Offset field to the Layout tab of the Print dialog box.

The default value of 6 points seems a little tight to me. I don't operate a two-ton paper cutter at a bindery, but if I did, I'd sure wish people would increase the space between page and trim marks (and registration marks) to at least 12, perhaps 18 points. It's just the courteous thing to do. Again, you can set this up as the default value by changing the print style (see "Print Styles," later).

Tiling

What's a person to do with a 36-by-36-inch document? Printing to paper or film is . . . well, almost impossible without a large-format printer. You can break each page down into smaller chunks that will fit onto letter-size pages. Then you can assemble all the pages (keep your Scotch tape nearby). This process is called *tiling*, and is controlled on the Layout tab of the Print dialog box. The three options for tiling are Off, Auto, and Manual.

Off. Off is off. No shirt, no shoes, no tiling. QuarkXPress just prints as much of the page as it can on the output page, starting from the upper-left corner.

Auto. Selecting the Auto tiling feature instructs QuarkXPress to decide how much of your document to fit onto each printed page. You do have some semblance of control here; you can decide how much overlap between pages you would like. Remember that you have a minimum of ¼-inch border around each page (at least on most laser printers), so you'll probably want to set your overlap to at least ½ inch to get a good fit. I generally use a value of 4 picas, just to be safe.

Note that QuarkXPress does not make an intelligent decision as to whether it would be more efficient to print the pages in Landscape or Portrait orientation, so you'll want to be careful to set this appropriately on the Setup tab of the Print dialog box.

Note that the Overlap amount might vary slightly when the Absolute Overlap checkbox is off (it's off by default). This is because XPress tries to center the tiled document on the printed pages (see Figure 13-10). When you turn on Absolute Overlap, XPress just gives up and places the upper-left corner of the document in the upper-left corner of the first page.

Manual. Most people seem to overlook the value of Manual tiling, skipping over it to Auto tiling. But there are times to trust a computer and times not to, and when it comes to breaking up my pages into manageable sizes, I generally prefer to make the choices myself.

When Manual tiling is selected, QuarkXPress prints only as much of the page as fits on the page selected, starting at the ruler coordinate "0,0." You can then move the "0,0" coordinate to some other place on the page (see "Rulers" in Chapter 2, *QuarkXPress Basics*, for more on this) and print the page again. In this way you can manually perform the same task as Auto tiling does, or you

Figure 13-10
Tiling documents

*Note that the
overlap is not shown
in this illustration.*

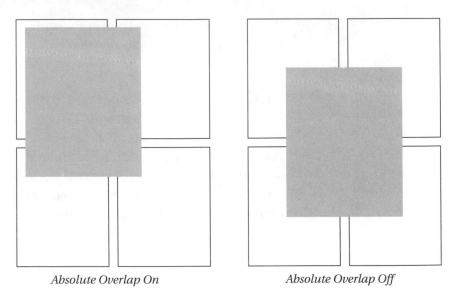

Absolute Overlap On   *Absolute Overlap Off*

can be specific about what areas of the page you want to print. Note that if you have a six-page document and print using Manual tiling, you get (for example) the upper-left corner of each of the six pages before the printer stops. If you only want one page or a smaller range of pages, use the From and To specifications at the top of the Print dialog box.

I should point out that where you place the "0,0" point is usually not where QuarkXPress starts printing. It actually tries to give you a little extra room so that the area you selected prints on the imaged area of the printer. For example, if you're printing to a desktop laser printer, QuarkXPress actually moves your starting point a couple of picas up and to the left. This is another area where QuarkXPress tries to be helpful, but ends up just being confusing and difficult to predict.

▼ ▼

Tip: Printer as Magnifying Glass. You can use the Manual Tiling and Enlarge features to blow up a particular area of the page for inspection (when 800-percent magnification on the screen still doesn't suit you). Change the enlargement factor on the Setup tab to 400 percent (or whatever enlargement you desire), then move the "0,0" point of the rulers to the area you want to inspect. Now print that page with Manual Tiling on, and—*mirabile dictu!* A super-size sectional.

▼ ▼

Tip: Assembling Your Tiled Pages. This really has nothing to do with the use of QuarkXPress, but when it comes to assembling tiled pages, I find it invaluable. The idea is simple: when fitting two tiled pages together, use a straight-edge to cut one, then use the other blank border area as a tab.

▼ ▼

The Page Setup Tab

The second tab in the Print dialog box is the Setup tab, which lets you tell QuarkXPress about the device you're printing to, as well as how you want your document pages to land on the film or paper. Several of the features on the Setup tab were located in the Page Setup dialog box in earlier versions of XPress. In fact, choosing Page Setup from the File menu takes you to this tab (or press Command-Option-P or Ctrl-Alt-P; see Figure 13-11). On the Macintosh, there is still a "real" Page Setup dialog box, found by clicking the Page Setup button in the Print dialog box. (I'll discuss this second Page Setup dialog box later, in "Page Setup, Printer, and Properties.")

There are nine settings on the Setup tab, the most important of which is certainly the Printer Description popup menu.

Printer Description

Specifying the type of PostScript printer you'll be printing to with this popup menu lets QuarkXPress optimize the way it prints your document. It also determines several other aspects of the print job, including activating or deactivating the roll-fed printer specifications features (see below). I wish I had a dollar for every time I solved someone's printing problem simply by getting them to pick the correct printer from this popup menu. Believe me: the choice you make here is crucial to success in printing. However, if you choose a non-PostScript printer in the Print driver, this popup menu will likely be grayed out.

To explain what changes are made to each printer would probably not be productive; just pick one and take a leap of faith that it's really doing some-

Figure 13-11
The Setup tab

Print Layout 1
Print Style: Default
Copies: 1   Pages: All
Layout / Setup / Output / Options / Layers / Bleed / OPI / Preview
Printer Description: Apple LaserWriter Select 360
Paper Size: US Letter
Paper Width: 51p   Paper Offset:
Paper Height: 66p   Page Gap:
Reduce or Enlarge: 100%   ☐ Fit in Print Area
Page Positioning: Left Edge   Orientation:
Page Setup... Printer...   Capture Settings Cancel Print

thing. Do note, though, that changing the printer type here does not change the Print driver or the Printer selection—those are both operating system-level controls, while this is an XPress control. Nonetheless, the type of driver you selected in the Print driver or on the Printer popup menu should properly reflect the printer selected here.

Printer Description Files. If the type of printer you're using is not listed on the menu, you probably don't have a PPD (PostScript Printer Description) file for it. In XPress 3.x, you could use either a PPD or a PDF file (that's Quark's Printer Description File, *not* the Acrobat file type of the same acronym). However, PDFs are now a thing of the past, and XPress only reads PPDs.

The proper PPD file for your device probably came with the printer, but you can often find updated PPD files at the Web site of your printer's manufacturer. If you're printing PostScript dumps that will be output at a service bureau, ask them for the proper PPD file for their printers (see "Working with an Imaging Center," later in this chapter).

If you can't find a PPD specifically designed for your printer, you can usually select a printer that is similar to the one you have from the Printer Description popup menu. For example, I print to my Ricoh PC 6000/PS using the LaserWriter II selection since both printers are old 300-dpi desktop laser printers of comparable speed, and so on. On the other hand, an Epson Stylus color ink-jet printer is not the same as an Agfa SelectSet 9000.

▼ ▼

Tip: Managing Your PPDs. Some programs come bundled with dozens of PPDs, and they install them all on your hard drive. Then, next time you launch XPress, you've got a Printer Description popup menu a half-mile long! If you're never going to use a particular printer, you can delete its PPD file from your hard drive. (On both the Macintosh and Windows, PPDs are scattered over a number of different folders; try doing a system-wide search for ".ppd" to find the ones you're looking for.)

If you don't use a PPD now, but you might in the future, you can "hide" it using QuarkXPress's PPD Manager (under the Utility menu; see Figure 13-12). To hide a PPD, click the checkmark in the Include column. To make it active again, click in the column again. Note that this doesn't actually move or change the PPD file at all—it still appears normally in other programs—it just tells XPress not to include the PPD on the Printer Description popup menu in the Print dialog box.

Here are a couple more PPD-management tricks.

▶ If you have a lot of PPDs, you could break them down into separate folders or directories on your hard disk. When you want to switch from one folder's PPDs to another, you can click the Select button.

Figure 13-12
PPD Manager

▶ If you add, remove, or change a PPD while XPress is running, you can update the PPD list by clicking the Update button. Note that XPress automatically updates the list each time you launch the program (if there's anything to update).

▼ ▼

Tip: Editing Your PPDs. One of the best things about PPDs is that they're editable. In fact, they're just text files that you can edit with any word proccssor. Because XPress gathers so much information about your printer from the PPD, customizing it is sort of like setting print preferences in QuarkXPress. For instance, you can change the name of your printer (how it appears on the Printer Description popup menu), the default halftone settings, or even the printer's default paper size. Be careful when messing with PPDs, however; little errors can cause jobs not to print. Always work on a copy of the file, and don't edit it unless you feel comfortable with this kind of thing.

▼ ▼

Paper Specifications

The next four settings—Paper Size, Reduce or Enlarge, Orientation, and Page Positioning—apply to every printer type (except the printer types with the word "Generic" in their names, since these are built into XPress and aren't based on PPD files).

Paper Size. PPDs contain information about the paper sizes that a printer can handle. For instance, a PPD can tell QuarkXPress that a particular printer can or cannot handle A4 pages. It's a good idea to match the Paper Size popup menu to the setting in the printer's driver (found by clicking Page Setup on the Macintosh, or Properties in Windows).

If the Paper Size popup menu is grayed out, then QuarkXPress knows that the printer either only prints on one size of paper or is a roll-fed device that can print any size you want. If it's not grayed out, the available choices are determined by information in the PPD or in the printer driver. Once again, you don't need to select a paper size that is consistent with your document's size (though the paper size must be larger than your page size, or else your page will be cropped down to the paper size). This only determines the image (printable) area. Note that selecting a page size does not determine where the automatic crop marks are placed (see "Registration and Trim Marks," earlier).

Reduce or Enlarge. Changing the Reduce or Enlarge field value affects the scaling of the document when you print. You can enter any whole number (no decimal points) between 25 and 400 percent. This is especially nice when printing proofs of a larger-format document, or when trying to create enormous posters by tiling them. You could create a 4-by-4-foot poster in QuarkXPress and then enlarge it to 400 percent, so that when that last sheet printed out of your printer and you'd tiled all 439 sheets together, you'd have a 16-foot-square poster.

Note that changing the Reduce or Enlarge field here is exactly the same thing as changing it in the printer driver's dialog box (see "Page Setup, Printer, and Properties," later in this chapter, for more information on printer drivers).

Fit in Print Area. When you turn on the Fit in Print Area checkbox, XPress calculates the Reduce or Enlarge setting for you, so that your document fits snugly on whatever paper size you're using at the orientation you specify (see "Orientation," next). This is much faster than trying to figure out the proper percentages to get a tabloid page onto a letter-sized page, or vice versa.

By the way, Fit in Print Area is grayed out whenever you've turned on the Spreads, Thumbnails, or Tiling options. The last two are understandable, but I still can't figure out why the feature doesn't work with Spreads. Oh well.

Orientation. Remember back to college when they had Orientation Day? The idea was to make sure you knew which way you were going while walking around the school grounds. Well, this Orientation is sort of the same, but different. The idea is to make sure QuarkXPress knows which way you want your document to go while it's walking through the printer. You have two choices: Portrait and Landscape. I've included some samples in Figure 13-13 so you can see what each one does.

▼ ▼

Tip: Save the RC Trees. When you're printing onto a roll-fed imagesetter (more on these later), you can often save film or paper by printing your letter-

Figure 13-13
Page orientation

*The left column is "portrait"
or "tall"; the right column is
"landscape" or "wide."*

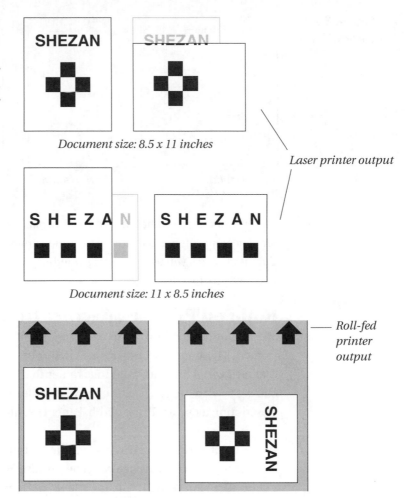

Document size: 8.5 x 11 inches

Laser printer output

Document size: 11 x 8.5 inches

Roll-fed
printer
output

Document size: 8.5 x 11 inches

size pages in landscape rather than portrait orientation. That way you only use around 8.5 inches on the roll rather than 11. It may not seem like a great difference, but those 3.5 inches really add up when you're printing a long document. For example, a 100-page file will save more than 300 inches of film or paper. Printing the pages landscape also makes it easy to cut them apart and stack them. Check with your service bureau to see if they'll give you a discount for the time and energy you've saved them.

▼ ▼

Page Positioning. When you select a paper size that is larger than your document, XPress lets you specify where on the page you want your document to sit. You've got four choices: Left Edge, Center, Center Horizontal, and Center Vertical (see Figure 13-14). Left Edge is the default (it's the way QuarkXPress has

Figure 13-14
Page Positioning

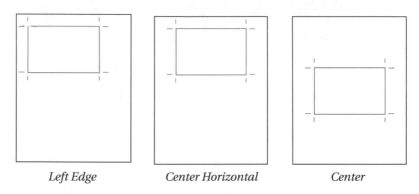

Left Edge   *Center Horizontal*   *Center*

always worked); the other three are self-explanatory. I find this control a matter of personal preference most of the time, though using one of the Center settings is critical if you want to print something on both sides of a piece of paper and have the two sides align.

Roll-Fed Printer Specifications

The last four features on the Setup tab apply only to—you guessed it—roll-fed printers. These are imagesetters, such as those in the Linotronic and Agfa lines, that feed paper and film from rolls rather than one sheet at a time. The four choices available to you when you have a roll-fed printer selected in the Printer Description menu are Paper Width, Paper Height, Paper Offset, and Page Gap.

Paper Width. The Paper Width specification is not an actual control so much as a description of the device you'll be printing to. An old Linotronic 300, for example, can image to 11.7 inches ("70p2" in QuarkXPress's pica notation). An Agfa CG9400 images to 14 inches, and a Linotronic 530 images to 17.5 inches. Whatever the case, and whatever the measurement style, just replace the default number with the proper paper width.

(Note that you can only type a value into the Paper Width field when the Paper Size popup menu is set to Custom. If you have some reason to choose a specific paper size, know what you're doing, go ahead, and choose one. In this case, XPress fills in the Paper Width and Paper Height settings for you and grays them out.)

I so fondly recall the time when I printed several pages on a Linotronic 330 with Paper Width set to "11p7" (11 picas, 7 points—or 139 points), instead of 11.7 inches. Everything on each page was cut off at exactly "11p7" from the left edge. The rest of the page was blank. I was not a happy camper, and I've been studiously monitoring this feature ever since.

Paper Height. When QuarkXPress prints to a roll-fed printer, it has to tell the printer exactly how long each page will be. That is, while the Paper Width field tells XPress how wide the paper is, the Paper Height field tells XPress how much paper has to roll in order to image a page correctly. When the Paper Size popup menu is set to Custom (it is by default for roll-fed imagesetters), the Paper Height setting is changed to Automatic. I generally leave this as is, since XPress is usually better at calculating measurements than I am. Again, if you know what you're doing and you think you need to tweak this, go ahead, but go carefully.

Paper Offset. This feature controls the placement of your document on the paper or film. The printer's default paper offset, even when set to zero, is almost always large enough so that you don't have to worry about changing the value of Paper Offset here. For example, on a Linotronic imagesetter, when Paper Offset is set to zero inches the file is printed ¼ inch from the edge. If you want it farther from the edge for some reason, change this value.

However, the Paper Offset setting shouldn't exceed the document height subtracted from the paper width (that is, if you have a 10-inch-tall document printing on 14-inch paper, your offset certainly should not be more than 4 inches, or else you'll chop off the other end of the page).

Page Gap. The last roll-fed printer specification determines the amount of blank space between each page of the document as it prints out on the roll. Initially, this value is zero. I recommend changing this to at least ¼ inch ("1p6") so you can cut the pages apart easily. If you're printing with the Spreads option turned on, this gap between pages is placed between the spreads, not between the pages within the spread (again, there's rarely any reason to turn on the Spreads option when printing to an imagesetter). Some imagesetters suppress this value, however, and rely on lower-level settings that an operator has to change via proprietary software or front-panel settings. Check with your service bureau before output—they may have advice on the correct setting.

The Output Tab

The third tab in the Print dialog box, the Output tab, is focused primarily on controlling color and halftone output (see Figure 13-15). If you're printing a black-and-white document, the only setting you probably need to think about here is Frequency, which determines the lpi setting—in fact, if there aren't any grays in your document, you don't even have to pay attention to this. On the other hand, for those of us who work in color, this tab is incredibly powerful when printing both proofs and final film.

Figure 13-15

The Output tab

Print Colors. Earlier versions of QuarkXPress offered a checkbox labeled "Print Colors as Grays." When on, XPress would convert every color in your document into a value of gray at print time—darker colors appeared as darker grays, lighter colors were lighter gray. This feature has evolved into the much-more-powerful Print Colors popup menu, which gives you lots of options for how to handle the colors in your layout. Note that when the Separations checkbox is on in the Layout tab of the Print dialog box, Print Colors turns into the Plates popup menu (see "Color Plates," later in this section, and "Color Separations," later in this chapter for more information).

When you print to a black-and-white printer like a desktop laser printer, you can pick either Grayscale or Black & White. When you choose a PostScript color printer (or a simulation, like Acrobat PDF) in the Printer Description popup menu on the Setup tab, the Print Colors popup menu lets you tell XPress how to send color information to the printer. The choices are Black & White, Grayscale, Composite CMYK, Composite RGB, As Is, and DeviceN.

Which of these you choose depends on your workflow, your printer, and the output you're trying to achive.

▶ **GRAYSCALE VERSUS BLACK & WHITE.** Choosing Grayscale is the same as turning on Print Colors as Grays in the old version of the program. Unfortunately, you don't have too much control over which shades of gray go with which color, so subtle differences in colors (such as between a pink and a light green) may blend together as one shade of gray. But it's still better than printing the file out as a page of solid black, which is what you get when you set the Print Colors popup menu to Black & White (see Figure 13-16).

▶ **COMPOSITE CMYK/RGB.** Desktop color printers should generally be considered RGB devices, so you should send composite RGB data to them. In this case, even CMYK data gets translated to RGB before the page is printed. If you choose Composite CMYK, then XPress will separate all your RGB data (including any RGB TIFF files) into CMYK mode before sending them, causing some images to appear washed out.

▶ **As Is.** When you choose As Is, XPress doesn't bother with any color transformations; RGB images and colors are sent as RGB, CMYK images and colors are sent as CMYK—XPress just leaves it to the printer to sort it all out.

▶ **DEVICEN.** You should use the DeviceN option when you want to create composite color PostScript, but have applied spot colors to images (like TIFF or JPEG), used spot colors or multi-inks (including hexachrome colors), or imported duotones into your document. Where RGB defines three "inks" and CMYK defines four inks, DeviceN lets XPress define any number of inks. Then, the PostScript RIP can later determine whether the inks should be separated onto separate plates or combined to create a composite color.

In general, you're more likely to use the DeviceN color space when exporting PDF files (the Print Colors dialog box appears in the Export Layout as PDF dialog box, too; see Chapter 14, *Going Online with QuarkXPress*). Note that output of DeviceN requires a PostScript 3 RIP to process.

When printing to a non-PostScript device (like a desktop inkjet printer), the popup menu simply reads "Defined by Driver," indicating that you must

Figure 13-16
Print Colors as Grayscale versus Black & White

Print Colors set to Black and White

Print Colors set to Grayscale

use the printer driver dialog box to adjust the settings (see "Page Setup, Printer, and Properties," later in this chapter).

Halftoning. XPress offers you two choices on the Output tab's Halftoning pop-up menu: Conventional and Printer. The difference is simple: Conventional means that QuarkXPress includes halftone settings (angle, frequency, and spot function) when sending PostScript to the printer. Choosing Printer means that XPress won't send halftone information at all. Why should you care? Some devices—like color ink-jet printers—don't print with normal halftones, so there's no reason to specify values like halftone frequency and so on.

Note that the Halftoning control is not an option when you're printing color separations. There's really no reason it should be, as the feature was mostly designed for color printers.

Resolution. Don't change this number with the expectation that it has any major significance to how your job prints. It doesn't determine the resolution at which your job prints. However, it does determine some important issues when printing bitmapped images. Low-resolution, 72-dpi black-and-white images can be smoothed with Quark's proprietary bitmap-smoothing algorithms, which depend on knowing the resolution of the printer. Also, bitmapped images that have a very high resolution may print significantly faster when you include the right printer resolution. For example, QuarkXPress internally reduces the resolution of a 600-dpi line-art image when it knows it's printing to a 300-dpi printer. The printer doesn't need any more than that anyway, and you save time because QuarkXPress only has to download half as much information (and the PostScript interpreter has to wade through only half as much).

Frequency. I talked at some length about halftones and halftone screens back in Chapter 10, *Fine-Tuning Images*. The Frequency setting on the Output tab of the Print dialog box is where you get to specify the halftone screen frequency of every tint in your document (except for those graphic images which you have set using the Halftone feature on the Style menu, and EPS graphics that have their screen specified internally). This includes gray boxes, tinted type, screened colors, and so on.

The default value for the halftone screen (the one that QuarkXPress uses unless you specify something else) is determined by the PPD you've chosen in the Printer Description popup menu. On most laser printers, the value is 60 lpi (lines per inch). You can type your own setting from 15 to 400 lines per inch. Raising the screen frequency nets you "smoother" grays, but you'll find you have fewer gray levels to work with (I talk about this trade-off in the book *Real World Scanning and Halftones*).

▼ ▼

Tip: A Colorful Shade of Gray. A couple of caveats to this tip, before I get to it: this is helpful primarily if you're printing proofs which won't be reproduced, and if you don't need a wide spectrum of gray values in your output. That said, I think a great screen frequency to use for printing to a 300- or 600-dpi printer is 106 lpi. Go ahead and try it. I think you'll like the tone of the gray.

▼ ▼

Color plates. The last option on the Output tab is the color plates list, which identifies which colors can or will print. The color list has three states, reflecting your printing options.

► When you're printing to a black-and-white printer and the Separations checkbox is turned off on the Layout tab of the Print dialog box, the color plates list displays only the black plate. After all, the printer can only print black.

► When you're printing to a color printer, the Separations checkbox is turned off, and you've selected a composite color setting from the Print Colors pop-up menu, the color plates list displays the process colors (cyan, magenta, yellow, and black) plus other spot colors you've used.

► When the Separations checkbox is turned on, the color plates list displays either just the process colors or the process colors plus all your spot colors, depending on the status of the Plates popup menu (see Figure 13-17).

Figure 13-17
Color plates when
Separations is turned on

When Separations is turned on, the Plates popup menu appears. If you set this to Convert to Process, all spot colors will print in CMYK.

I'm going to hold off describing the various controls on the color plates list until "Color Separations," later in this chapter. For now, suffice it to say that this is where you can suppress printing of colors, as well as set color-specific halftone information.

▼ ▼

The Options Tab

As far as I can tell, the Options tab in the Print dialog box is simply a catch-all for items that either don't belong on the other tabs or simply couldn't fit there (see Figure 13-18). There are eight controls on this tab, ranging from PostScript error handling to whether or not TIFF images should be down-sampled at print time. Let's take them one at a time.

PostScript Error Handler. As I said earlier, when you print to a PostScript printer, your computer writes a little program in PostScript language and sends it down the network to the printer. If there are any errors in the PostScript, or if the PostScript file contains an instruction that the printer can't fulfill, you get a PostScript error. I discuss some of the more common errors in "Troubleshooting," later in this chapter.

The problem is that sometimes your page won't print and you'll have no idea why. Fortunately, the PostScript Error Handler (on the Options tab of the Print dialog box) can come to the rescue.

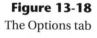

Figure 13-18

The Options tab

Print Layout 1

Print Style: Default

Copies: 1   Pages: All

| Layout | Setup | Output | Options | Layers | Bleed | OPI | Preview |

☐ Quark PostScript Error Handler

Page Flip: None   ☐ Negative Print

Pictures

Output: Normal   ☐ Full Res of Rotated Objects

Data: Binary   ☐ Overprint EPS Black

OPI: Include Images   ☐ Full Resolution TIFF Output

(Page Setup...) (Printer...)   (Capture Settings) (Cancel) (Print)

If you think you're getting a PostScript error, switch on this feature. QuarkXPress adds some extra code to the PostScript file that is sent to the printer. As soon as anything goes wrong, this code catches the error and prints out the page up to the point of the error. Then it prints a second page with a little PostScript information (if you don't know PostScript programming, this probably won't help you much) and a gray box; the box specifies where on the page the error occurred. With this in hand, you can often quickly figure out if the PostScript error is based on a corrupt graphic or font or on some other page element.

Most PostScript printer drivers also include an error handler. For instance, on the Macintosh, you can turn on the driver's error handler by clicking the Printer button in the Print dialog box. In Windows, you can turn it on by clicking Properties in the Print dialog box. I find that Quark's built-in error handler is usually more useful in identifying problems, so I use it instead of these.

Page Flip. QuarkXPress can mirror pages at print time if you choose Horizontal, Vertical, or Horizontal & Vertical from the Page Flip popup menu. Flipping an image is used mainly for creating either wrong- or right-reading film from image-setters, or film with emulsion side up or down. The differences? Let's look at what happens when you print onto film.

As the film moves through the imagesetter, the side of the film that is coated with a photographically sensitive emulsion is exposed to a laser beam. If Page Flip is set to None (it is by default), the film is imaged right-reading, emulsion up (or wrong-reading, emulsion down, if you prefer). This means that when you are holding the film so that the type reads from left to right and graphics are oriented correctly ("right-reading"), the emulsion of the film is facing you. If you select either Horizontal or Vertical from the Page Flip pop-up menu, the film emerges right-reading, emulsion down (which is how most printers want it, especially in North America). To look at it a different way, this means that when you hold the film with the emulsion away from you, the text and graphics look correct ("right-reading").

If you want to know why you'd ever care whether the emulsion is up or down, check with your lithographer (and then talk to a screen printer; you'll see they need different film output for similar but different reasons). Providing film in the right format could reduce the reproduction generations at the printer—saving time and money, and improving quality.

Note that setting the Page Flip popup menu is exactly the same as turning on "Flip Horizontal" or "Flip Vertical" in the Macintosh printer driver (see "Page Setup, Printer, and Properties," below, for more information on setting values in the printer driver).

Negative Print. Clicking this checkbox inverts the entire page so that everything that is set to 100-percent black becomes zero-percent black (effectively, white). It is the same as selecting the Inversion tool from within the Contrast Specifications dialog box, except that it affects the entire page. In some countries—most notably Italy, Switzerland, Hong Kong, and Singapore—lithographic plates are typically made from positive film (rather than film negatives, used in North America). The end result is the same, but they use different techniques to get there. Always check on this specification if you're printing outside of North America.

The Negative Print option is really just a shortcut to the Invert Image setting that is found in the Macintosh printer-driver dialog box (see "Page Setup, Printer, and Properties," below, for more information on setting up the driver).

Picture Output

The six controls in the Pictures section of the Options tab all relate to how QuarkXPress downloads pictures to the printer. Of course, each of these is a global setting, affecting all the pictures in the document rather than just specific images.

Output. The Output popup menu gives you the opportunity to speed up your printing significantly . . . but at the cost of the pictures in your document. Pictures are often the single most time-consuming part of printing a page; but if you're only printing rough proofs, you may be able to cut corners.

▶ **NORMAL.** What can I say about Normal? It's normally how you'd want your normal documents to print out. This is the default setting in the Print dialog box, and the only times you change it are when you want special printing effects like those listed below. You get just what you created—no better, no worse.

▶ **LOW-RESOLUTION OUTPUT.** If you select Low Resolution from the Output popup menu, QuarkXPress prints your document using the picture-preview image built into the document, rather than the source picture file. If you've imported a huge high-resolution TIFF or EPS, Low Resolution mode prints the document using the low-resolution (36- or 72-dpi) screen image that QuarkXPress creates when you import the picture.

This is a godsend if you have to make many proofs to a low-resolution desktop printer. I can't tell you how much time I've wasted either sending documents with high-resolution pictures to low-resolution devices (it takes forever for them to print), or manually hiding the pictures somewhere on my hard disk so QuarkXPress can't find them, then telling it to print anyway (that was the old trick for making QuarkXPress use the internal low-res image).

▶ **ROUGH.** If your document has many illustrations or special frames in it, you may want to print your proof copies with Rough selected. This feature automatically replaces each picture in your document with a big "X," and every complex frame with a double line of the same width (see Figure 13-19). Clearly, the pages print significantly faster than with Normal or Low Resolution.

Data Format. I discussed binary versus ASCII data formats back in Chapter 9, *Pictures*, when I talked about QuarkXPress's Save as EPS feature; here the choice appears again. To recap, this only pertains to how bitmapped images (like TIFF and JPEG) are sent to the printer. While sending the information in ASCII format is more reliable over some networks, binary is almost always fine and has the benefit of creating a much smaller PostScript file (the images are half the size of ASCII).

The third choice, Clean 8-bit, is a good compromise. It is as small as binary, but it strips out the particular binary characters that cause some networks to go into conniptions. I generally use the Clean 8-bit setting unless I'm on a strictly Macintosh-based network, in which case I use Binary. On the other hand, you may want to use ASCII if you're making PostScript files for your service bureau and they're going to transfer the files to a PC- or UNIX-based system for output.

OPI. The OPI popup menu that appears in the Print dialog box is grayed out when you have the OPI XTension loaded (which most people do, as it's installed by default). See "The OPI Tab" later in this chapter.

Figure 13-19
Page printed with
Rough selected

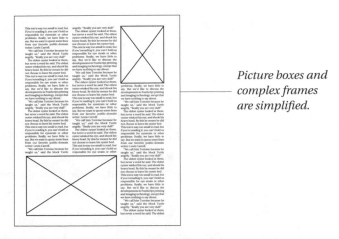

Picture boxes and complex frames are simplified.

Full Res of Rotated Objects. When you print to a non-PostScript printer, rotated images often look jaggy and icky. Here, XPress gives you the choice of downloading your rotated images at full resolution. The problem is that this takes longer to print and uses much more system memory to process. I rarely use this because I'd rather rotate images in Photoshop before importing them.

Overprint EPS Black. I explored overprinting and trapping back in Chapter 12, *Color*, but there is one overprinting control that you can only set in the Print dialog box: Overprint EPS Black. When you turn this checkbox on, every object colored black in EPS images overprints its background, regardless of whether you set it to overprint in the original illustration program. Note that this control ignores the Overprint Limit on the Trapping tab of the Document Preferences dialog box, so even an EPS object that is only 10-percent black will overprint.

I find this feature most useful when working with EPS files built in programs that don't let you specify overprinting. For instance, my friend and colleague Phil Gaskill recently laid out a textbook that contained hundreds of molecular diagrams built in a scientific illustration application. The people who wrote this program didn't expect anyone to place these graphics over colored backgrounds, so there was no control for overprinting at all. All those thin lines would have been a trapping nightmare if it weren't for the Overprint EPS Black feature.

Full Resolution TIFF Output. When you print a document that includes TIFF or JPEG images, QuarkXPress may downsample the image data behind the scenes. The program figures that you'll never need more resolution in your images than two times the halftone screen frequency, so it cuts off the data at that point. If you have a 200-dpi image reduced to 50 percent on your page (which makes it a 400-dpi image; see Chapter 9, *Pictures*), and you've specified an 80-lpi screen in the Frequency field on the Output tab, QuarkXPress chops off the image resolution at 160 dpi (two times the frequency). Typically, that's okay. In fact, it's great if you're proofing high-resolution images on a laser printer. However, every now and again, this feature can jump up and bite you.

For example, if you reduce an image considerably in a picture box, you can sometimes get mottling or jaggy artifacts from the downsampling. Or, if you're purposely printing at a very low screen frequency because your color printer requires it (some do), your images may look really weird because QuarkXPress has downsampled them so much.

Fortunately, you can turn on the Full Resolution TIFF Output checkbox and none of your bitmapped images will get downsampled at print time. Note that this feature (and solution) only affects TIFF images. EPS pictures don't get downsampled because QuarkXPress can't touch the data that's encapsulated in them. Also, XPress always turns this option on when you set the Halftoning popup menu to Printer on the Setup tab (because there's no halftone screen to use as a reference).

▼ ▼

The Layers Tab

I don't mean to be crass, but I just don't see the need for the Layers tab in the Print dialog box (see Figure 13-20). This tab lets you specify which layers will print and which will not. A noble feature, indeed, but you can control the same thing by setting the visibility of each layer in the Layers palette (see "The Layers Palette," in Chapter 3, *Tools of the Trade*). I'd much rather turn on and off layers in the Layers palette because I get immediate visual feedback of what my document will look like when printed. It's just too easy to make a mistake in the Layers tab of the Print dialog box.

By the way, if you make a change to the printing status of one or more layers in the Print dialog box, you can turn on the Apply to Layout checkbox. This tells XPress to update the Layers palette to match what you've set in the Print dialog box (non-printing layers get their Suppress Output option turned on; you can tell because the layer name appears italic in the palette). Again, I have to stretch my imagination for a use for this.

▼ ▼

Tip: Find the Mysterious Color. Here's one use for the Layers tab of the Print dialog box: Let's say the Output tab tells you that you're using a spot color

Figure 13-20
The Layers tab

somewhere in your document, but you can't figure out where. You can click on each of the layers listed in the Layers tab to see what ink plates are being used there. By narrowing down on which layer the spot color appears, you might find it easier to discover the offending object.

▼ ▼

Setting Bleeds

The Bleed control is a good example of how a little feature can sneak into a product and cause havoc when people don't take the time to understand it. I know people who just ignored the Bleed control and lost a *lot* of money throwing away their film output. Fortunately, the control isn't difficult to understand; you just need to remember to use it.

The term "bleed" refers to an object that prints all the way to the edge of your page. In prepress, it's very important for bleeding objects to print past the page boundaries by at least ⅛ inch (often more like ¼ inch; check with your printer) because paper trimmers aren't perfect. If the object only extends to the edge of the page boundary and the paper cutter slips by a few points, the object won't sit at the edge of the paper anymore (ugly). Extending the object past the boundary is kind of like setting a trapping value for the bleed (see "Trapping," in Chapter 12, *Color*).

Back in XPress 3.x, to make something bleed off a page, you simply placed it so that it was partially on the Pasteboard. As long as it touched the page, the object would print (see Figure 13-21). I'm not sure why they changed this, but now, by default, XPress crops out everything beyond 1 point past the edge of the page. In other words, you can extend a picture box ½ inch past the page

Figure 13-21
Bleeding objects

This object bleeds off the page.

Keyline represents the side of the page

How the page looks when Bleed is set to zero

After increasing the Bleed setting

boundary, but when you print the page, the bleed only extends by about a point.

Fortunately, the Bleed tab of the Print dialog box lets you extend this puny bleed to whatever you want (see Figure 13-22). Note that this tab only appears when you have the Custom Bleeds XTension installed in XPress's XTension folder (it should be there unless someone has turned it off with the XTensions Manager). The Bleed Type popup menu offers three choices for extending your bleeds: Page Items, Symmetric, and Asymmetric.

▶ **PAGE ITEMS.** When you choose Page Items, XPress acts like it did back in those heady XPress 3.x days: anything touching the page gets printed. That is, the bleed amount is automatically extended to include the bounding box of any object on the page.

▶ **SYMMETRIC.** Choosing Symmetric lets you specify a single bleed setting, which XPress uses on all four sides of every page. This is the setting I use most often. In fact, I've gotten into the habit of setting this to at least "1p6" even when I'm not bleeding objects. Later in the chapter, you'll see how to set this as your default value.

▶ **ASYMMETRIC.** The Asymmetric setting lets you choose a different bleed amount for each of the four sides of the page. The only time I find myself using this is when I'm putting job slug information outside the print area (see "Tip: Job Slugs," below).

When you choose either Symmetric or Asymmetric from the Bleed Type popup menu, XPress offers one additional choice: the Clip at Bleed Edge

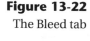

Figure 13-22

The Bleed tab

checkbox. This feature acts like the Page Items setting: When you turn it off, XPress automatically extends the bleed amount to include all objects that are inside the bleed area. For instance, if you specify a half-inch symmetric bleed, and you happen to have a 5-inch wide text box on the pasteboard that is within a half-inch of the page, then the *whole* text box prints out. Again, this might be useful for job slugs, but I tend to leave this checkbox turned on so I'm not surprised at print time.

There's one other aspect of the Bleed feature you should know about. When you set the Bleed value, any object on the Pasteboard that falls within that distance of the page gets printed, whether it's touching the page or not. This is especially useful if you want to create your own registration marks or job information slugs (see "Color Separations," later in this chapter).

▼ ▼

Tip: Job Slugs. Bleeds are typically objects that print mostly on the page, but bleed slightly off it. But you can also create items that are mostly off the page, or even entirely off the page. This is ideal for adding additional job information on your documents, often called "job slugs." (Of course, those of us in the moist Pacific Northwest know our slugs well, and these page items rarely look like slugs at all.) In order for your job slug to print properly, you need to make sure the bleed setting is large enough to include the text or picture boxes.

The OPI Tab

The features in the OPI tab in the Print dialog box are exactly the same as those in the Save Page as EPS dialog box, so I'll save my breath here by referring you to "Page as Picture," in Chapter 9, *Pictures*. In general, if you're not using an OPI server software, you can leave the OPI Active checkbox turned off.

The Preview Tab

The Preview tab in the Print dialog box doesn't offer any controls at all, but that doesn't mean you shouldn't look at it. In fact, I find that it's worthwhile to take at least a quick peek at this tab every time you print because the Preview tab provides information that can tell you in advance whether what comes out of your printer will match your expectations (see Figure 13-23).

On the left side of the Preview tab, XPress lists several of the most important details of your print job.

Figure 13-23

The Preview tab

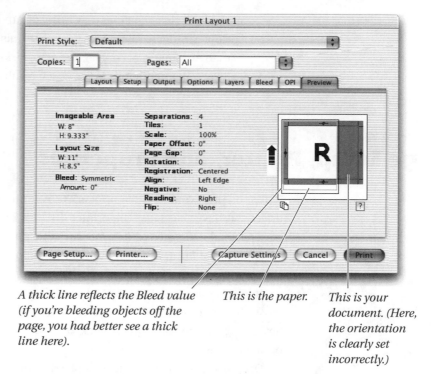

A thick line reflects the Bleed value (if you're bleeding objects off the page, you had better see a thick line here).

This is the paper.

This is your document. (Here, the orientation is clearly set incorrectly.)

▶ **PAPER SIZE VERSUS DOCUMENT SIZE.** Imageable Area reflects the Paper Width and Paper Height fields on the Setup tab, minus the paper margins (see below). Layout Size shows the dimensions of the document itself (the measurements in the Layout Setup dialog box). By comparing these two, you can quickly gauge whether your document page will fit on the paper size you've specified.

▶ **PAPER MARGINS.** Where the margin settings in QuarkXPress are merely guides that you can ignore when necessary, the paper margins are absolutes—anything outside these margins simply won't print. XPress doesn't actually show you the paper margins (they used to, but don't anymore for some reason). Instead, you have to infer them by subtracting the Paper Width and Paper Height fields on the Setup tab with the Imageable Area values. The paper margins are meant to reflect the physical limitations of the device. That is, most laser printers simply can't image closer than .1 or .2 inch from the edge of the page.

▶ **PRINT OPTIONS.** The last section of the Preview tab displays values for Paper Offset, Page Gap, Bleed, Tiles, Scale, Separations, Rotation, Registration, Align, Negative, Reading, and Flip. These are simply copies of information that appears on other tabs in the dialog box, but it's handy to see it all together here. I find the Tiles information quite useful, as it clearly defines how many printed pages XPress will have to spit out in order to fully image your page (this only applies when you set Tiles to Automatic, of course). You can quickly compare the Landscape and Portrait orientations to see which results in fewer printed pages

▼ ▼

Page Setup, Printer, and Properties

When you print your document, QuarkXPress interacts with whatever printer driver you have selected. (The printer driver is based on which printer you have selected. As I noted earlier, you can choose a printer on the Macintosh by clicking on the Printer button in the Print dialog box. In Windows, you just choose one from the Printer popup menu in the Print dialog box.) The driver controls some aspects of the print job and XPress controls others. I've been discussing in some detail the settings you can make to QuarkXPress's Print dialog box. Now I want to take a quick break to discuss some options you have in the printer driver itself.

Of course, printer drivers are completely different on the Macintosh and in Windows, so I need to cover them one at a time. Also, note that there are many different versions of these drivers, and the one you use may well appear differently than the ones I show here. Don't fret about it too much; with a little exploration, you'll find that many of the features are the same.

Macintosh: Page Setup and Printer

In QuarkXPress for Macintosh, you can access the printer-driver settings by clicking on the Page Setup and Printer buttons in the Print dialog box (see Figure 13-24). In most cases, the settings you make in these two dialog boxes apply to this one print job only, and you'll have to change them again next time you print.

After making changes to either the Page Setup or the Printer dialog box, when you leave the dialog box (by clicking OK, Cancel, Print, or Save, depending on what you're doing), XPress returns to the normal Print dialog box.

Page Setup. The Page Setup dialog box is split into three or more "pages," each found in the Settings popup menu. However, all the features here—including settings for Scale, Orientation, and Paper Size—are duplicates of settings in QuarkXPress's Print dialog box. As XPress either ignores the settings you make here or overrides them, I just don't pay any attention to this dialog box.

Figure 13-24

The Macintosh printer
driver settings and Page
Setup dialog box

Click these buttons to access the printer-driver dialog boxes.

Printer. If the dialog box you get when you click the Printer button looks familiar, that's because it's the same dialog box you get when you choose Print from almost any other Macintosh application (see Figure 13-25). However, in this case, after you click Print or Cancel, you're dropped back into QuarkXPress's Print dialog box.

The Printer dialog box lets you control a number of aspects of the print job, including which printer to use, how many document pages per printer page you want to be laid out, and which printer tray to pull paper from (if the printer has more than one). This print driver dialog box lets you print the PostScript file to disk instead of to a printer, too. I'll explore printing PostScript "dumps"

Figure 13-25

The print driver's Printer
dialog box

There are seven different "pages" of controls.

to disk later, in "Working with an Imaging Center." Many of these driver features are also ignored over overriden by XPress's own print features.

Windows: Properties

You can adjust printer-driver settings in Windows by clicking the Properties button in the Print dialog box (see Figure 13-26). There are a number of different settings here, spread out over four or five different tabs (depending on the version of the PostScript driver you're using), but there's one theme that runs through them all: almost none of them apply to working with QuarkXPress. (On the other hand, if you're working with a non-PostScript driver, many of the controls will affect your output; but again, I'm not talking about non-PostScript devices here.)

The controls fall into three categories.

▶ Most are duplicates of settings in QuarkXPress's Print dialog box. These get overridden by XPress, so you should ignore them.

▶ Some cause PostScript errors or strange things to occur.

▶ Some just don't do anything at all, even though they look like they should.

Okay, I am being a little harsh here. There are two items that I do use in the Properties dialog box. The first, Paper Source, lets you choose among various paper trays in your printer. The second, PostScript Output Option, lets you choose among different PostScript formatting attributes. The default setting, Optimize for Speed, usually works well enough for me. However, if the PostScript file will be postprocessed by some other prepress utility, you probably want to change this to Optimize for Portability (this uses more of the Adobe Document Structuring Conventions, or ADSC).

Figure 13-26
The Properties dialog box
in Windows

Print Styles

One of my favorite features in the old QuarkPrint XTension was the Print Styles feature, which let you save collections of Print and Page Setup dialog-box settings under one name. Fortunately, the folks at Quark built this feature right into QuarkXPress, so no additional XTension is necessary. There are two great benefits to print styles. First, you can easily change the default settings for XPress's Print dialog box. If you have one printer and you're tired of selecting the same PPD from the Printer Description popup menu or turning off the Include Blank Pages option every time you print, this is the feature for you.

Print Styles is also great for service bureaus or anyone else who prints to a number of different devices from one copy of XPress, because you can build dozens (hundreds? Sorry, I've never tried) of different print styles.

Building a print style. You can make a new print style by choosing Print Styles from the Edit menu (see Figure 13-27). Print styles are like application Preferences in one way: changes you make here apply to the program as a whole, not just to documents you may have open. Once the Print Styles dialog box is open, you can either click New or select a style and click Edit or Duplicate. At this point XPress displays the Edit Print Style dialog box, which looks awfully similar to the Print dialog box. It's not an exact duplicate; for instance, there is no Preview tab. (If you think about it, how could there be?)

Go ahead and make changes to the Edit Print Style dialog box, then give the collection of settings a name. I tend to make the name as descriptive of my settings as possible. Finally, click OK to leave the Edit Print Style dialog box, then click Save to leave the Print Styles dialog box, saving your work. That's it!

There are a few things you cannot change in the Edit Print Style dialog box. For instance, you can't turn off particular process-color plates on the Output tab. You also can't specify a page range, the number of copies, or the settings in the Page Setup, Printer, or Properties dialog boxes. This is unfortunate, because these often need to be changed every time you print.

Selecting a print style. Once you have built a print style, you can select it from the Print Style popup menu in the Print dialog box. It's as easy as that (see Figure 13-28).

Moving print styles around. Print styles are application-wide and are stored in the XPress Preferences file. If you lose this file or if you need to delete it because it has become corrupted, your print styles are lost. (It's a good idea to keep a regular backup of the XPress Preferences file.) If you use the same print style from more than one computer, you can move it in one of two ways.

▶ You can copy your XPress Preferences file from one computer to the next. This copies all your preferences, even including Hyphenation Exceptions and kerning table edits, which may be more than you hoped for. This doesn't work cross-platform.

▶ You can select one or more print styles in the Print Styles dialog box and click Export to save the print style(s) to disk. Then, in a different copy of QuarkXPress, you can click Import in the same dialog box to append the style(s). This does work when moving the file from Mac to PC (or vice versa), as long as the file name includes the three-letter ".qpj" file-name extension.

▼ ▼

Tip: Comparing Print Styles. If you have two print styles that are similar, you might find it useful to ask XPress to compare them for you. Just select them both in the Print Styles dialog box (you can use the Command/Ctrl key to select discontiguous styles on the list), and hold down the Option/Alt key while clicking the Import button (the Import button changes to read "Compare" when you hold down the modifier key). As this book goes to press, the Compare Print Styles dialog box doesn't list every item in the style; for instance, all the features on the Options tab plus many features on the Layout tab (like Thumbnails) don't appear, so the comparison is pretty limited. Perhaps if we all prod the folks at Quark, a later version will provide more information.

▼ ▼

Figure 13-27
Building a print style

Figure 13-28
Selecting a print style

▼ ▼

Color Separations

I come now to the last area of the Print dialog box, which as a subject deserves a whole section of the book to itself: color separation. The concept behind color separation is simple, and QuarkXPress does a pretty good job of making the practice just as easy, but the truth is that this is a very complicated matter which, in the space of this book, I can only touch on briefly.

The Basics of Color Separation

A printing press can only print one color at a time. Even five- and six-color presses really only print one color at a time, attempting to give the ink a chance to dry between coats. As I discussed in Chapter 12, *Color*, those colors are almost always process colors (cyan, magenta, yellow, and black), or they may be spot colors, such as Pantone inks.

Colors that you specify in your QuarkXPress documents may look solid on the screen, but they need to be separated and printed onto individual plates for printing. Each of the four process colors is printed as a tint or a halftone (if you don't understand the fundamentals of halftoning, I *really* recommend that you look at Chapter 10, *Fine-Tuning Images*). By overlapping the screened tints, you can create a multitude of colors.

If you print color separations for a job with only process colors, you output four pieces of film for every page of the document. Each spot color requires adding another plate to the lineup.

Printing Color Separations

To print color separations, turn on the Separations checkbox on the Layout tab in the Print dialog box. This activates the color plates list on the Output tab, giving you a choice of which color plates you want to print and at what halftone settings. As long as the printer type is a black-and-white printer (like a laser printer or an imagesetter), by default the color plate list is set to print all the color, which includes the four process colors plus any spot colors you have defined (see Figure 13-29).

Even if all the color plates are set to print, QuarkXPress only prints plates for the colors that are actually used in your document. If you create custom spot colors, but don't actually use them in your document, they still appear on the color plates list. But don't worry: they won't print.

▼ ▼

Tip: Convert to Process. It's driven service bureau owners stark raving mad . . . . It's caused thousands of dollars in wasted film output . . . . It's one of the greatest problems affecting humankind today . . . . (Well, okay, maybe that last one was a little extreme.) I'm talking, of course, about people leaving the Spot Color checkbox turned on in the Edit Colors dialog box when they really meant to build process colors. The result: every color they create is a spot color, and therefore prints out on its own plate.

But fear no more! When you print separations, XPress changes the Print Colors popup menu (on the Output tab of the Print dialog box) to Plates, and offers you two choices: Process & Spot or Convert to Process. If you want all your spot colors to separate into CMYK, select Convert to Process. Note that this only changes your spot colors to process colors at print time; the colors in the document are actually still specified as spot colors.

▼ ▼

The Rosette

When the process-color plates are laid down on top of each other, the halftones of each color mesh with each other in a subtle way. Each plate's halftone image is printed at a slightly different angle, and possibly at a different screen frequency as well. The result is thousands of tiny rosette patterns (see Figure 13-30). If this process is done correctly, our eyes blend the separate colors together to form one smooth, clean color. However, if the angles or screen frequencies are slightly off, or if the registration (alignment) of the plates is wrong, then all sorts of chaos can ensue. Both of these problems can

Figure 13-29

Making separations

The checkmark indicates that the plate will print. Click on it once to turn it off.

If you have more than one color selected on the list, you can turn them all off (or on) with this popup menu.

Figure 13-30
A simulated
process-color rosette

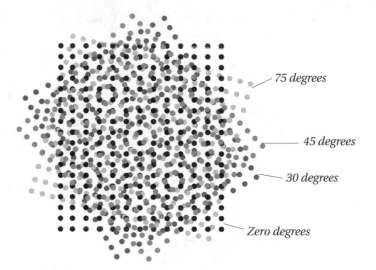

75 degrees

45 degrees

30 degrees

Zero degrees

come about from error on the lithographer's part, but more likely they indicate problems with your imagesetting process.

The most common effect of the above problems is a patterning in the color called a *moiré pattern* (that's pronouced "mwah-ray"). There's almost no good way to describe a moiré pattern; it's best to just see a few of them. They might be pretty subtle, but it would behoove you to learn to identify them and learn how to make them go away. Figure 13-31 shows an outlandish example of this patterning caused by the screen frequency and angles being set completely wrong.

Making sure you don't get moirés was a major undertaking in the color prepress industry during the 1990s, and resulted in screening technologies that are often built right into the imagesetters. Balanced Screens and High Quality Screening (HQS) are two examples of this, available from major imagesetter vendors Agfa and Heidelberg. For these technologies to work, you need to make sure that QuarkXPress is using its default screening angles (black at 45 degrees; cyan at 75; magenta at 105; and yellow at 90). Once again, it's critical that you choose the correct printer (and therefore the correct PPD) from the Printer Description popup menu in order to receive the proper screen angles for that device.

Screening and moiré problems are discussed in much more depth in a book that I co-wrote with Steve Roth, Conrad Chavez, and Glenn Fleishman, *Real World Scanning and Halftones.*

The Color Halftone Settings

QuarkXPress lets you change the halftone settings for each color in your document on the Output tab of the Print dialog box (see Figure 13-32). If you're

Figure 13-31
Moiré patterning

working with the right PPD file, you rarely need to do this, but when you need this flexibility, it's great to have the opportunity.

There are four halftone settings you can control on the color plates list: Halftone, Frequency, Angle, and Function. To make a change, select a color (or select more than one color with the Shift or Command/Ctrl key), and choose from one of the popup menus at the top of the list.

▶ **HALFTONE.** As I mentioned back in Chapter 12, *Color,* each spot color you create is assigned a matching process color—whatever halftone settings are applied to the process color are also applied to the spot color. The Halftone column on the color plates list lets you change the associated color at print time. For instance, if you see an "M" next to a Pantone color, you know that this Pantone color will use the halftone settings for Magenta. If you want, you can then change this to C, Y, or K. Personally, I think if you're going to make this kind of change, you should do it in the Edit Color dialog box instead.

▶ **FREQUENCY.** The values in the Frequency column are pulled from your printer's PPD file. They may not always match the Frequency field at the top of the dialog box. In fact, it's not uncommon to find different frequency values for each process color. There's a level of faith here . . . you've got to trust that whoever built the PPD knew what they were doing.

▶ **ANGLE.** The angle column lists the halftone angle at which each color will print. As I said earlier, the angles are usually 0, 15, 45, and 75 degrees, but they may be radically different (again, depending on the PPD file). Note that just because you specify a particular angle doesn't mean you're going to get it. Due to some technical issues, some angles

Figure 13-32

Changing color
halftone settings

are actually impossible to set on digital printers. (Unfortunately, 15 degrees is one such angle; screening systems such as Balanced Screens actually catch the call for 15 degrees and change it to an appropriate number on the fly.)

▶ **FUNCTION.** The last column on the color plates list is labeled Function, which refers to PostScript's spot function. This controls the shape of the halftone spot for each color. It's quite rare that you need to change this unless you're building low-lpi special effects. I discussed the various spot shapes that XPress can build back in Chapter 10, *Fine-Tuning Images.*

Working with an Imaging Center

Whether you're sending your XPress documents to a service bureau or to a commercial printer that has their own imagesetter or platesetter equipment, it's important to include the right information and files. Imaging centers have developed standard etiquette and rules spoken only in hushed voices (and usually after the customer has left the shop). In this section I bring these rules out into the open and take you through, step by step, how to best send files to your service bureau, and how to ensure that you'll receive the best-quality output from them.

The first thing to remember when dealing with service bureaus is that they don't necessarily know their equipment or what's best for your file any better than you do. That's not to say that they are ignorant louts, but I am of the opinion that really good imaging centers are few and far between, and you (the customer) have to be careful and know what you're doing. The principal relationship I talk about in this section is that of you, the customer, sending your QuarkXPress files to a service bureau to be imageset. I'll talk first about sending the actual XPress document, and then about sending either a PostScript or a PDF file. Many of my suggestions may be totally wrong for the way your particular service bureau functions, so take what works and leave the rest. Some prefer PDF files, for instance, while others opt for the XPress files.

▼ ▼

Tip: Some Questions for Your Service Bureau. Here is a list of questions which you may want to ask when shopping for an imaging center.

▶ What imagesetters or platesetters do they have available, and what resolutions do they support?

▶ Do they have dedicated equipment just for film or platesetting, and do they calibrate it using imagesetter linearization or other software? If they're using other software, do you need a component on your system when making files to output with them?

▶ Do they have an in-house color-proofing system? Is it a laminate system (like Press Match) or digital composite (like the 3M Rainbow)?

▶ Do they have a customer agreement that lists what they're responsible for and what the customer is responsible for?

▶ Do they have a job ticket for output that lets you fill in all the details of your particular project?

There are no right or wrong answers to any of these questions. However, asking them not only tells you a lot about the company, but also teaches you a lot about the process they're going through to output your files.

▼ ▼

How to Send Your File

You have three basic choices in transporting your document to a service bureau to be imageset: sending the file itself, sending a PostScript dump, or sending an Acrobat PDF version of the document. While my preference has always been to send a PostScript dump, many service bureaus want the file itself. It's a question of who is in control of the final output: me or them.

When I send the file off to be printed using someone else's system, I don't know whether their fonts are different, whether the text will reflow, whether they'll forget to set up registration marks, or whether they'll print the file at the wrong screen frequency. By sending them a PostScript dump, you put yourself in the driver's seat: you can control almost every aspect of the print job. An Acrobat PDF file is even better; it lets you have a lot of control, but leaves the ultimate printing controls in their hands.

Sending QuarkXPress Files

These days, I prefer to send PDF files to imaging centers. However, I know that most places still prefer to receive the actual QuarkXPress file, which gives them the control to fix certain aspects of the job if something goes wrong. And the truth is that many QuarkXPress users don't want to be responsible for checking all the buttons and specifications necessary to print PostScript or PDF to disk. If you find yourself in either of these situations, you'll need to know what to do in order to optimize your chances of success. Let's look at the steps you need to take.

Check your fonts. I can't tell you how important it is to keep track of which fonts you've used and where they are on your disk. Make sure that your service bureau has the same screen fonts that you do, and has the printer fonts (downloadable) that correspond to each and every font you've used in your document. I generally send my own fonts along with my job to the service bureau because I believe that sometimes screen fonts that are supposed to be the same simply aren't. Either they've gotten corrupted, or it was a different release, or something. But I'd rather be overly careful than have film come back totally wrong.

Print Driver and Page Setup. On the Macintosh, I've always found it helpful to make sure I've got a LaserWriter driver selected, and that I've at least checked the Page Setup dialog box once before proceeding to the next step. You don't need to specify which printer you're using in the Setup tab of the Print dialog box if you're not sending PostScript dumps (the service bureau has to select theirs on their machine).

Look over your document. Take the extra time to carefully peruse your entire document. If you need to, zoom in to 200 percent and scroll over the page methodically. Also, look over the Usage dialog box to see what fonts and pictures you used. Many problems with printing occur not with the printing at all, but with that one extra word that slipped onto its own line, or the one image that was "temporarily" set to Suppress Printout and then was never switched back.

Print a proof. If you can print the document on a desktop laser printer, chances are the file will print at your service bureau. That's not a guarantee, but it's usually a pretty good bet. When you print this proof, go over it, too, with a fine-tooth comb. You might have missed something in the on-screen search. If you're printing color separations, try printing proofs of them, too. Are objects overprinting when you want them to knock out? Does the type look correct in separations?

Include your illustrations. If you have imported pictures into your document using Get Picture, you need to include the original files on the disk with your document. Remember that QuarkXPress only brings in a representation image for the screen, and then goes to look for the original at print time. You can use the Usage dialog box to see which graphic images you imported, whether they're set to Suppress Printout, and whether they are missing, modified, or present.

The idea is to send your service bureau a folder rather than just a file. Give them everything they could ever think of needing, just in case. The Collect for Output feature can really help this process along (see "Collect for Output," below).

Checklists for Sending QuarkXPress Files

I find checklists invaluable. Not only do they improve your method by encouraging you to do the appropriate task in the right order, they're satisfaction-guaranteed every time you can check an item off the list, which in itself is a boon to flagging spirits as a deadline looms. Below are examples of checklists I use before sending files to a service bureau.

FONTS

▶ What fonts did you use in your document? Are you sure they are PostScript or OpenType fonts rather than TrueType fonts?

▶ Does your service bureau have your fonts? (If not, send them.)

DOCUMENT CHECK

▶ Check for boxes and lines set to Suppress Printout.

▶ Check for text-box overflows.

▶ Check for missing or modified pictures in the Usage dialog box.

▶ Check for widows, orphans, loose lines, bad hyphens, and other typographic problems.

PROOF

▶ Print a proof on a laser printer or use Acrobat Distiller to distill the file (if that can handle it, then the service bureau probably can).

▶ Check it carefully to make sure it's what you want. If you're working with a client, have them look over the proofs and sign off on them.

RELEVANT FILES

▶ Did you include EPS, TIFF, PDF, and JPEG files?

▶ Did you include the document itself? (Don't laugh; sometimes this is the one thing people *do* forget after a long day.)

Collect for Output

To make the above process significantly easier for y'all, Quark has included a cool feature called Collect for Output. Selecting this command from the File menu copies your document and all the picture files necessary for its output to a folder of your choice—it doesn't move or remove the original files. New in version 5 was the ability to also copy your document's fonts, which was a great step forward. XPress also creates a report containing detailed information about your document, including fonts and pictures you used, and trapping information. Then all you have to do is get the folder to your service bureau or color prepress house by modem, messenger, or carrier pigeon.

Using Collect for Output is simplicity itself. When you choose it from the File menu, it prompts you to find a folder, and asks you to specify a name for the report (see Figure 13-33). I typically just use QuarkXPress's default name; it's simply the name of your document with "report" stuck on the end. Then, when you click Save, QuarkXPress copies your document and extra files, wherever they might reside, to that target folder. If you haven't saved your file before selecting Collect for Output, QuarkXPress asks you if you want to save first.

Note that to avoid potential copyright problems, QuarkXPress won't copy fonts to the folder unless you specifically ask it to. The legal ramifications of sending these files are between you, your service bureau, and your font vendor. I don't blame Quark for wanting to stay out of this one!

Collecting files for output often takes longer than manually copying each file, as QuarkXPress does a very thorough search for each file it needs. This may take a bit longer, but the process does give you the satisfaction of knowing you haven't forgotten to copy that little bitty logo illustration hidden at the bottom of page 32.

Also note that you may need lots of space on your hard drive to do this. I recently worked on a job in which the combined size of the document and all the pictures in it was over 500 MB. When I went to Collect for Output, not only did it take almost forever to do, but I ran out of hard-drive space halfway through the procedure. If you're working with big files like this, it may be easier and less painful for you to simply copy files yourself.

Figure 13-33
Collect For Output

You won't see this little side tab unless you have the cool Mac OS X utility DefaultFolder.

▼ ▼

Tip: Catching All the Fonts and Pictures. You can find out what fonts and pictures you used in the Font Usage and Picture Usage dialog boxes. Unfortunately, you can't print these lists out. However, all this information is in the report that QuarkXPress builds when you use Collect for Output. Better yet, XPress offers a checkbox called Report Only in the Collect for Output dialog box, which lets you get the report even if you don't have enough space on your hard drive (or time on your hands) to do a full Collect for Output.

After saving the report to disk, you can open it in a word processor or import it into a new QuarkXPress document and find the names of the fonts and the graphics (as well as a lot of other information).

▼ ▼

Tip: Formatting the Report. If you open the report that Collect for Output builds in a word processor, the first thing you'll notice is that it's full of weird codes. Those are XPress Tag codes (see Chapter 7, *Copy Flow*, for more information on XPress Tags) and they're included so that you can quickly format the report. In fact, QuarkXPress ships with a document called Output Request Template (it's in the Templates folder, inside the QuarkXPress folder), which has style sheets pre-defined for this report. You can import the report from disk using Get Text, and each paragraph, including headings, is formatted for you.

▼ ▼

Sending a PostScript Dump

It's probably clear that I not only don't trust many service bureaus to do the right thing, but I also don't trust myself to always remember everything I need to while standing at the service bureau counter. Because of this, I like to use PostScript dumps. A PostScript dump (also known as a "print-to-disk"), when performed correctly, ensures that you get what you ask for, and is sometimes even preferred by low-maintenance service bureaus. Instead of having to open your file, make sure all the correct fonts are loaded, check all your settings, and then print it, they can simply download the PostScript file.

The biggest difference is that with PostScript dumps you have the responsibility for making sure your file is perfect for printing. However, this isn't as difficult as it may seem. Let's go through the steps you need to go through to create the perfect PostScript dump. At the end I include a checklist that you can copy or re-create for your own use.

▼ ▼

Tip: Writing PostScript for Acrobat PDF Files. People are increasingly using Acrobat PDF files in their workflow, and although XPress can now write PDF files directly to disk, many people still want to process a PostScript dump with Adobe Distiller instead. I discuss this process and why you might want to use PDF files in Chapter 14, *Going Online with QuarkXPress*, but I should note here up front that almost everything I say about writing PostScript files to disk for print also applies to writing them to disk for the Distiller.

▼ ▼

System setup. Make sure you have enough memory on your disk to save the PostScript file—twice. PostScript dumps are often large. To figure out how large a print-to-disk file will be, you can usually add up the size of all the pictures and fonts, add the size of the file itself, then tack on another 10 percent. If you've got a 100 MB image in your file, your PostScript dump has to include that, too (unless you're using an OPI system), and will be accordingly enormous. Plus, you need twice as much space because the LaserWriter driver spools the information to disk first, then writes the PostScript file afterward.

Fonts. You must have the screen font loaded for every font you use in your document. One way to check which fonts are in your document is with the Usage feature on the Utilities menu. If you don't have the screen font for a document, try to get it; without it, you run the risk of having your document print in Courier. In addition, all your line spacing will be messed up due to a difference in character widths. Note that this means you have to have the fonts loaded for typefaces used in EPS files, too.

Most people have both a screen font and an outline printer font on their machine so that the type looks smooth on screen. However, as long as the printer font is already in the printer—either in RAM or on the printer's hard disk—it's not necessary to have the printer font yourself when making a PostScript dump. Check with your service bureau to find out if your fonts are available on their printer.

Pictures. The next step in making a PostScript dump is to check the Picture tab of the Usage dialog box to see if all the image files you used in your document are available. This is a suggested step but is not crucial, because if you don't do this, QuarkXPress checks for you at print time and then gives you the opportunity to find any missing image files (see Chapter 9, *Pictures*, for more information on this dialog box).

Print. The most common mistakes in creating PostScript dumps are made on the many tabs of the Print dialog box. Be careful with the buttons and menus here. You must have the proper PPD file, and select it in the Setup tab of the Print dialog box. If you want registration marks (along with trim marks and job information), you must turn them on here. If you want multiple copies (not likely, for high-resolution output), choose your value here. But if you only want one copy of each page, make sure that you specify "1" here! I've had friends who've gotten 10 copies back from their service bureau simply because they didn't check this. Expensive mistake.

Remember, if you don't set these controls correctly now, no one else can later on down the line.

Printing to Disk: Macintosh

After taking the above steps to ensure that you'll get a good PostScript file, the actual process of getting the PostScript saved to disk is determined by your operating system and printer driver. Let's take a look first at how to do it on a Macintosh.

Print driver setup. Because you're printing to a PostScript device, you need to have a LaserWriter device selected in the printer driver. It doesn't matter whether you actually have a PostScript printer hooked up or not. Click Printer in the Print dialog box and then choose a PostScript printer in the Printer pop-up menu.

▼ ▼

Tip: PostScript Printerless. In Mac OS 9, you could select a LaserWriter driver without actually having a PostScript printer on your network. In Mac OS X, however, it's more tricky. If you don't have a PostScript printer, but you want to make PostScript files, try this.

1. Click Printer from XPress's Print dialog box and select Edit List from the Printer popup menu; this launches the Print Center utility.

2. Click the Add button in Print Center.

3. Choose "IP printing" from the top popup menu, and type "localhost" (without the quotation marks) in the Printer's Address field. I suggest turning off the "Use default queue on server" checkbox, which lets you type in your own name for the "printer" (like "MyPostScriptDriver").

4. Pick a printer from the Printer Model popup menu (if you don't know what type of printer you're targeting, try Generic), then click Add. You now have a PostScript "device" on your system.

Note that you may also need to do this if you want to write PDF files to disk using Export Layout as PDF (because XPress needs to write PostScript file before converting them to PDF; see Chapter 14, *Going Online with Quark-XPress* for more on PDF files).

▼ ▼

Of course, if the device you're printing to requires a driver other than the standard LaserWriter driver, you'll have to have that loaded and selected.

Destination. Remember that whether you're outputting your file to a printer or to disk, QuarkXPress and the Macintosh's printer driver are doing the same thing: building a PostScript file and sending it somewhere. You get to choose where that file should be sent (to a printer or to disk) in the Output Options section of the printer driver dialog box (click the Printer button in Quark-XPress's Print dialog box, then select Output Options from the popup menu; see Figure 13-34).

Figure 13-34
PostScript file options
in the print driver's
dialog box

When you turn on the Save as File option, the Print button changes to Save. You can choose whether you want the driver to write PostScript or PDF files to disk (in this case, I recommend PostScript). Then, when you click the Save button, the Macintosh gives you the option of where you want the file to go and what you want to name it. Remember that when you click Save again, XPress returns to the Print dialog box and waits for you to click Print. If this sounds like a really roundabout process just to get a file, it's only because it is; but once you get in the habit, it's not too annoying.

Note that the PostScript written to disk includes everything you need to print, including all fonts and images.

Printing to Disk: Windows

I've heard it both ways: some people think the way Windows prints PostScript to disk is more confusing than the Macintosh method; others think it's easier and more intuitive. No matter what you think, it's certainly different. Basically, you don't tell QuarkXPress to write to disk; you tell the particular driver you're using to print to disk. And you can't do that from within XPress; you have to do it in the Printers folder (select Printers from the Settings popout menu, under the Start menu in Windows). What you do in the Printers folder depends on whether or not you already have a printer driver that matches the device you're printing to. If you don't have an appropriate printer driver, you have to add one. If you do have a driver, you can set its port to FILE. Let's look at each of these scenarios.

Adding a print-to-disk printer. Here's a quick step-by-step describing how to add a new printer type that always prints PostScript to disk.

1. Open your Printers folder and launch the Add Printer wizard (double-click on its icon in this folder). The wizard asks you whether the device is local or on the network. Choose Local, and click the Next button. (Of course, this doesn't happen if you're not connected to a network.)

2. The wizard asks what kind of printer it is. It's important to pick the proper printer—the one that the PostScript file will later be printed on—from this list, or else the driver and the PPD file will be incorrect and you'll get unexpected results (that's just a nice way to say that your document may not print). If the printer you're looking for doesn't appear on the list, you'll need to get the PPDs and installation files (the .INF files that the wizard is looking for) from somewhere. Printer manufacturers often have these available on their Web sites.

3. Next, the wizard asks you what port you want to use. This is the crucial step for making a print-to-disk "printer": Choose FILE from the list of ports (see Figure 13-35).

4. When the Add Printer wizard asks you to name the printer, I suggest giving the "printer" a descriptive name, such as "BrisquePrintToDisk".

5. Finally, when the wizard asks you if you'd like to print a test page, politely decline.

Changing the printer port. If you already have a printer driver installed in your Printers folder, you can make it print to disk even more easily. Just follow these steps:

Figure 13-35
Adding a printer that
prints to disk

1. Select the printer driver in the Printers folder and choose Properties from the File menu.

2. Select the Details tab of the Properties dialog box.

3. Choose FILE from the popup menu labeled "Print to the following port."

4. Click OK.

That's it! When you print a document with this printer driver, the PostScript file will be directed to your hard drive instead of to the port. Of course, when you're finished printing to disk, you must change the port setting back to wherever the driver was pointing originally.

Printing to disk. Once you've told your printer driver to print PostScript to disk, you can choose it from the Printer popup menu in the Print dialog box and proceed to choose other Print dialog-box settings as usual. As soon as you click Print, however, Windows displays a dialog box asking you where you want to save the file and what you want to name it. I suggest giving your PostScript file the extension ".ps" (if you don't specify anything, Windows automatically changes it to ".prn").

Checklist for Sending PostScript Dumps

Your service bureau will appreciate you for checking these items.

System and Font Setup

▶   Do you have enough memory on your disk to save the PostScript dump?

▶ Do you have the proper fonts loaded for the fonts that are in your layout? EPS files?

PAGE SETUP, PRINTER, AND PROPERTIES

▶ Do you have the LaserWriter or other appropriate driver selected in the print driver (Macintosh) or Printer popup menu (Windows)?

▶ Have you made necessary changes to the Page Setup and Printer dialog boxes (Macintosh) or Properties dialog box (Windows)?

PICTURES

▶ Do you have all the EPS, TIFF, and other image files available? Check the Usage dialog box.

PRINT DIALOG BOX

▶ Have you made all the proper settings? Registration marks? Page range? Color separations? Do you need to specify Page Flip and Negative Print, or does your service bureau handle that with imagesetter-direct controls?

▶ Have you selected File in the Destination area of the Printer dialog box (Macintosh) or specified a FILE: "printer" on the Printer popup menu (Windows)?

SENDING THE FILE

▶ Rename the file to something appropriate.

▶ Make sure that your service bureau has the same kind of removable media that you're going to send.

▼ ▼

Troubleshooting

After all of this, printing should be a breeze, right? Well, I wish it were. Too often, I get phone calls from my service bureau saying, "Your job wouldn't print." Back in the good old days, a service bureau would offer to fix it for you. Now life has gotten busy for them, and they usually expect you to do the fixing. Here are some tips that I've found, over the years, to work.

Graphics Look Awful

One of the most common problems with print jobs from QuarkXPress has never had anything to do with QuarkXPress itself. The problem is with the people sending their files. Remember that QuarkXPress does not actually embed any EPS, PDF, DCS, JPEG, or TIFF files that you have imported. It only brings in a low-resolution representation of the screen image, and maintains a link with the original file. If that file changes or is missing when QuarkXPress tries to print it, the graphic will look different from what you expected.

Two notes to write on your forehead follow.

▶ If you're going to send your QuarkXPress document, then send a folder, not a file. The folder should include the document, all linked images that you used, and possibly the fonts, too. Use the Collect for Output feature that I discussed earlier in this chapter.

▶ PostScript print-to-disk files (PS dumps) contain the images, as well as all the information QuarkXPress needs from the preferences file, fonts, and so on. PDF files might even be better.

Because QuarkXPress downsamples TIFF images to two times the halftone screen frequency, sometimes you can get strange mottling or jaggy images, especially if you've scaled down an image considerably (see "Picture Output," earlier in this chapter).

General Fixes

QuarkXPress sometimes causes PostScript errors at print time. Almost all these errors are the result of printer-memory problems (called VMerror), and almost all of them can be avoided with a few tricks.

Reset the printer. My favorite technique for avoiding memory problems is simply to turn the printer off, wait a few seconds, and turn it back on again. This flushes out any extraneous fonts or PostScript functions that are hogging memory. It's sort of like waking up after a good night's sleep, but different.

Rotate your own graphics. If you've scanned in big bitmapped graphics, and need to rotate them, you should use Photoshop or another image-manipulation program rather than doing it in QuarkXPress. Rotating large bitmapped images in QuarkXPress may or may not choke the printer, but it certainly slows it down a lot—an important point if you're paying a per-minute surcharge at a service bureau. (Note that I'm not talking about object-oriented, vector artwork here, such as those from Illustrator or FreeHand.)

Take care in selecting your fonts. If you play with a lot of different fonts trying to find one you like, you may inadvertently leave remnants of old fonts lying around. For example, a space character may be set to some font that you don't use anywhere else. Nonetheless, QuarkXPress must download that font along with every other font you use. This takes up memory that could be used for something else. Try using the Usage dialog box to see which fonts are sitting around in your document. Then purge the ones you don't need.

Print fewer pages at a time. I have successfully coached long documents out of an imagesetter by printing two to 10 pages at a time, rather than all 500 pages at once. This is obviously a hassle, but it's better than not getting the job printed at all. Much of the work can be done early by creating multiple PostScript dumps, then queuing them up on a spooler at the service bureau.

Remove enormous graphics. One of the great promises of desktop publishing was that I could print an entire page with every graphic and text block perfectly placed. Remember that promises are often broken. Case in point: large graphics (and even small graphics) sometimes choke old printers. These files often print all by themselves, but when placed on a page they become the chicken bone that kills the giant. Yes, using every trick possible, you might get the page out, but is it worth the time? Perhaps it's more efficient to let your printer or stripper handle that graphic. Or, god forbid, hot-wax that puppy and paste it down yourself.

Make sure you're current. Someone recently called and asked me why her file wouldn't print (this question is, by the way, almost impossible for anyone to answer over the telephone). I suggested a few things, and then asked what version of QuarkXPress she was using. It turned out she was using an older version of the program, and as soon as she updated, the printing problem went away. This is not uncommon. They don't talk about it much, but the engineers at Quark are constantly trying to make their program print better. For instance, QuarkXPress 4.0 was a disaster in some respects, but Quark quickly released free patches for 4.01 and then 4.02, which fixed most of the really egregious printing errors.

What's amazing to me is that there are people who say, "QuarkXPress has a lot of trouble printing," but when pressed they admit that they only heard that someone else had trouble with XPress 4.0 when it first came out. Those first impressions sure do die hard.

Save As. Logically, it makes no sense that resaving your document under a different name should help a file print, but it has been known to work.

Selective printing. You can try to pinpoint what page element is causing the error by printing only certain parts of the page. For example, select Rough in the Print dialog box to avoid printing any pictures or complex frames. If the page prints, chances are that one of the graphic images is at fault. You can also use Suppress Printout to keep a single image from printing.

If the page still doesn't print after you print a rough copy, try turning off one layer at a time, or suppress the printing of one text box at a time, or changing the fonts you used. If you are printing color separations, try printing a single plate at a time. And so on.

Re-import. If the problem turns out to be a graphic you've imported, you might try re-importing it. If the image is a PICT, you might have better luck using Get Picture than Paste. Even better, convert the PICT into a TIFF (for bitmaps) or EPS (for object-oriented graphics) file. Then re-import it.

Check printer type. Make sure you have the correct printer type selected on the Setup tab of the Print dialog box. Picking the wrong PPD is the single most common problem people have when printing.

Big Ugly White Gaps Appear Between Colors

You've output your four-color separations and sent the file off to your lithographer. A few days later you show up for the press check and you see, much to your surprise, big ugly white gaps appearing between each of the colors. What happened? You forgot about traps. It's easy to do, believe me. The remedy? Go read the section on trapping in Chapter 12, *Color,* and redo your negatives.

Wrong Screen Frequency

QuarkXPress can neither read your mind nor the mind of your lithographer. If you print your file out with the default halftone-screen frequency setting of 60 lpi, that's just what you'll get. This is coarse, but fine if you're just going to photocopy your page. However, it looks pretty awful compared to the 120 or 133 lpi (or higher) used in most print jobs. Check with your lithographer for what screen frequency to use, then check your Print dialog box settings before you print your job. Note that this is usually not something that your service bureau can change if you provide a PostScript dump.

Document Settings

If you use custom kerning or tracking tables, hyphenation exceptions, or custom frames, QuarkXPress will bark at your service bureau as soon as they open your file. "The preferences are different," XPress says, and asks if you want to use the document's preferences or just the ones in the current copy of the program. The appropriate answer is almost always "Document Preferences." If your service bureau tells XPress to use XPress Preferences instead, then your painstaking work may be screwed up and your page won't print as it's supposed to.

One problem: in version 3.x, the keystroke for Keep Document Settings was Command-period or Esc. In every later version, this same keystroke "clicks" Use XPress Preferences instead. That could be an "oops" if you're not paying attention.

Fonts Come Out Wrong

Don't forget that you have to have the fonts loaded for every font in the document when you print. "Every font" means the fonts you selected, those that were imported, and those that are stuck somewhere in an EPS document. Also, watch out for EPS files nested inside of EPS files nested inside of EPS files. Depending on which application created each EPS file, QuarkXPress may or may not be able to dig deep enough to find every font you used.

Registration Problems

Imagine the Rockettes, kicking their legs to chorus-line stardom in perfect synchronization. Then imagine the woman at one end having no sense of rhythm, kicking totally out of sync with the others. This is what happens when one color plate is misregistered to the others. When a sheet of paper is rushed through a printing press and four colors are speedily applied to it, there's bound to be some misregistration—somctimes up to 1 or 2 points. However, you can help matters considerably by making sure that your film and plates are always as consistent as possible.

Whenever I am told that a job printed great "except for one plate that was off-register," I immediately ask if that plate was run at a different time than the others. The answer is almost always yes. I realize it's expensive and time-consuming to print four new plates every time you want to make a change to a page, but it is a fact of desktop life that you can almost never get proper registration when you reprint a single plate. One service bureau I know of also had this problem when they ran two or three plates at the end of a roll of film, and the rest of the job at the start of the next roll. Why? The weather, roll stretch, alignment of the stars . . . all sorts of reasons contribute to this massive hassle.

▼ ▼

"Job Finished"

As I said way back at the beginning of the book, don't give up until you get it to work. If you run into difficulty, there is almost always a workaround. Working through to that solution almost always teaches a valuable lesson (as

Grandma used to say, "It builds character."). However, remember that the solution is sometimes to just print the job in pieces and strip them together traditionally. It feels awful when you have to clean off your drafting table and dust off your waxer, but efficiency is often the name of the game.

And when the last page comes out of the imagesetter, don't forget to thank your computer, QuarkXPress, the service bureau, and yourself for a job well done.

14

GOING ONLINE WITH QUARKXPRESS

Since you're a QuarkXPress user, you probably create, or will create, your share of print documents. Today, however, most companies also want to use the Web as an additional advertising or information distribution medium. Using the Internet has become an integral part of our lives. Checking the weather or keeping informed with up-to-date news items can be accomplished with a few clicks of the mouse. Want new product information? Check the company's Web site. Lost your manual for that new digital camera? Download a PDF of the manual.

With faster connections now available to more people, not only can you publish your content, but you can add more graphics to your designs to make your pages more appealing. Of course, there are limitations to publishing on the Web (and to multimedia in general).

- ▶ Few people want to read a lot of text on screen.

- ▶ You can't take a computer with you in the bathtub.

- ▶ Availability of electricity, much less a good connection to the Internet, is limited around the world.

- ▶ It's difficult to protect the copyright of your work because it's so easy to copy the digital files of anything published on the Web.

Nonetheless, people have been clamoring to build Web pages for the past several years, and there's no reason to think this trend will stop. And because there are more than a million people around the world who already publish with QuarkXPress, the question has inevitably arisen: How can I get content out of XPress and onto other people's screens?

The Web versus Multimedia. Most of what I'm talking about in this chapter revolves around publishing for the World Wide Web. However, anything you can put on the Web can be put on a CD-ROM or a kiosk or a disk. The differences are primarily distribution (how many people will be able to access your work?) and file size (larger files may be inappropriate for the Web, depending on your audience). So, when I talk about getting stuff online, don't think I'm just talking about the Internet.

Repurposing content. As you'll soon see, QuarkXPress is not the world's best Web-page generator, although it is greatly improved from version 5. So why did Quark put all that time and energy into adding so many Web tools? For a simple reason: They saw too many of their customers mocking up Web page designs using QuarkXPress, Illustrator, and Photoshop, then printing the designs out and telling the Web folks to recreate the whole thing using other tools. It's a sadly common workflow, and it's incredibly inefficient.

The Web tools in QuarkXPress let you cut out a major step in the process because you can quickly build a mock-up of a Web page or Web site using the XPress tools you already know how to use, and the Web folks can use your work as a first draft. Sure, you can build a finished Web page or a Web site in XPress, but in most cases you'll want to tweak your results in a more sophisticated program, like Macromedia Dreamweaver or Adobe GoLive.

HTML and PDF. There are two primary methods of putting interactive XPress pages onto the Web: creating HTML and creating PDF files. Each of these has its limitations and strengths, and you might find yourself using different methods for different situations (I discuss each of them fully in this chapter). There's one thing that they both have in common, though: they all require a radically different approach to laying out pages and presenting material than print-based publications do. You can't just plop a for-print brochure into one of these formats and call it quits. As I've said before, *how* to design is outside the purview of this book, but what you can and cannot achieve with each method is essential to making the switch to online publishing.

Note that while XML is also often considered a "Web format," it's really more of a way to encode your content so that it can be formatted in a number of different ways, including print. I'll discuss QuarkXPress's XML tools in more detail in Appendix E, *XML Tools.*

▼ ▼

Tip: Getting Online. There are more than a thousand Internet books on the market, so I'm just going to defer to them to cover many of the basics—like how to get an Internet account, use a Web browser, build a Web page from scratch, place your Web pages on a Web server so that people can see them, optimize your graphics for the Web, and so on. For instance, Elizabeth Castro's *HTML for the World Wide Web: Visual QuickStart Guide,* also from Peachpit Press, is a good reference for HTML codes. Instead, this chapter will focus on getting your XPress pages into an interactive screen-ready form.

▼ ▼

HTML and Web Browsers

Almost everyone who "surfs" the Web is looking at pages built with HTML (HyperText Markup Language). HTML is like QuarkXPress's XPress Tags language (see Chapter 7, *Copy Flow*); it is code-based (formatting is handled using special codes like <b> and </b> in the text) and it's generally linear—it describes the first paragraph, then it describes the second paragraph, and so on (see Figure 14-1).

Originally, HTML was based on the idea that the viewer, rather than the publisher of the information, should determine the look of the page. In this model, you just add codes specifying where the headings are, what words should be emphasized, and so on; then your audience configures their browsers to display your headings and emphasized words in certain ways. One person will see headings in Helvetica, another person sees them in Times Roman. Over the past few years, however, HTML has grown to include additional formatting that lets you—the author/publisher—control how you want the page to look.

In order to view an HTML file properly, you need a Web browser—basically just a program that interprets the HTML codes ("make this <i>italic</i>") into WYSIWYG text ("make this *italic*"). The two primary Web browsers are Microsoft's Internet Explorer and Netscape's Navigator. If you are using Macintosh OS X, Apple's Safari browser is also a serious contender in the browser wars.

However, it turns out that HTML has some severe design limitations.

▶ Different Web browsers interpret the codes differently, so line spacing, fonts, font sizes, and column widths (and more!) may be completely

Figure 14-1

HTML pages

A basic HTML page viewed in a Web browser

A slightly more complicated HTML page

```
<TABLE border=0 WIDTH=475 cellpadding=3 cellspacing=3>
<tr><TD WIDTH=315 valign=top align=left>
<h2>Sample Chapter</h2><P>
<I>Zap!</I>'s chapter on eyestrain is one of two chapters
specifically on the topic of eyes and computer use. Additional
chapters in  <I>Zap!</I> relating to this subject include
<b>Monitors</b>, <b>Lighting</b>, and <b>Finding a Doctor</b>,
among others.<P> You can read the sample chapter below, or, if
```

HTML source code. Note the similarity to XPress Tags.

different from what you expect. While it's not hopelessly impossible to control typography on the Web, it does take some work. But you can forget about kerning or tracking your type!

▶ You might think that Futura displays well and matches your design, but if that font is not available on a user's computer, then another font is substituted and may change the look of the page.

▶ Color consistency is impossible, so what you see on one screen may be quite different from what you see on another.

There are a host of other problems, too, but given a proper understanding of the limitations, you can begin to gain mastery over the medium. The key is to remember that you just can't design and produce pages the way you've become accustomed to over the years.

Exporting Your Content

If you're reading this chapter, chances are that you want one of two things from QuarkXPress: you either want to export final Web pages that look just like what you see in XPress, or you want to export your content (text and perhaps graphics, too) so you can use it in another Web design program. XPress gives you some of the tools you want, but not all.

It comes down to page geometry (*geometry* is the part of the HTML code which says *where* something should be on a page). The basic Export HTML feature (which I'll cover later in this chapter), exports your page with geometry, so that your final HTML looks almost exactly like what you see in XPress. There is no way to export your whole document (text and graphics) without the accompanying geometry—a major oversight in my opinion.

Save Text as HTML. You can, however, export a single text story as HTML without page geometry by selecting the Content tool, clicking in the story, and then choosing Save Text from the File menu (or press Command-Option-E or Ctrl-Alt-E; see "Exporting Text" in Chapter 7, *Copy Flow* for more on this procedure). From here, you can select HTML from the Format popup menu. The result is a text file with HTML codes that you can import into another program.

Note that the HTML created using Save Text is styled using Cascading Style Sheets (CSS), which are much fancier ways of styling text. While most Web programs (Dreamweaver and so on) support CSS, some older programs do not. I haven't found any way to get simple, non-CSS tags out of XPress.

Note that you can use this Save Text method from both Web and regular print layouts. (I cover the difference between these two formats soon.)

Use an XTension. Before version 5, everyone who wanted to export HTML from QuarkXPress used a commercial XTension such as Extensis BeyondPress or Gluon's WebXPress. As it turns out, many people will still want to continue using these XTension because they let you do things that QuarkXPress can't do by itself. For instance, both can export all your text and graphics from a regular XPress document, without reformatting it as a Web document.

More importantly, they can export all your stories and graphics as linear HTML, without page geometry. Unfortunately, at the time of this writing, BeyondPress doesn't work with QuarkXPress 5 or 6 and it's pretty unlikely that Extensis will update it.

Fortunately, Gluon's WebXPress (see Figure 14-2) does work in QuarkXPress 6, and it offers a number of other cool features, like XML, eBook format, and Palm HTML export. It can also create a Web page with a table of contents page. This is a very cool XTension for converting your XPress documents (you don't have to convert your file to a Web layout first).

Figure 14-2
Gluon's WebXPress

Web Documents and File Structure

While people have been writing HTML code by hand for years, the trend is increasingly toward using WYSIWYG ("What You See Is What You Get") editors that write the HTML for you, such as Macromedia Dreamweaver, Adobe GoLive, or Microsoft FrontPage. These programs make it easy to add JavaScript and advanced features of HTML, which XPress does not. If you plan to do extensive Web development and site management, you might want to use one of these programs in conjunction with QuarkXPress. For example, you would design the page in XPress, adding the text and graphics, export as HTML, and then modify and manage the page in Dreamweaver or GoLive.

So, what is the advantage of even using QuarkXPress? First, you can design your Web page using the familiar Text Box and Picture Box tools, and moving the boxes around to your liking. You can even preview the page in a browser before exporting to make sure that your design displays properly. Second, you can easily convert existing XPress content to a Web document.

Setting up Folders

Before you begin building your site, you need to develop an outline of the site. The outline is similar to a storyboard for a multimedia project or a movie, giving you an idea of the scope of the project and a start for setting up the file structure you need for the site. At a minimum, each site should have a single folder containing your HTML files and images. Depending on the complexity of your site, you may also have subfolders to help you organize the files (see Figure 14-3). Don't put your QuarkXPress documents inside the same folder as the HTML files—it makes it harder to manage them later.

It's a good practice to keep all your graphics in one or more folders within your site. For example, within your site folder you would create a subfolder with a name such as "images". You might also want to create separate folders for different areas within the site. For example, you might have a product section, or a series of press releases. Creating separate folders for each of these areas makes it easier to manage the files. Once you create a Web site, the number of pages within that site seems to grow exponentially in time, so organizing

Figure 14-3
Site folder containing
HTML pages and folders

your site before you begin building your pages makes your file maintenance job much easier, When you complete all the pages, you transfer the site folder to the Web server, and then you are ready to go!

▼ ▼

Tip: Naming Files and Folders. Naming your files for use on a Web server is different from naming your files for print. Some Web servers are case-sensitive; some require that you use only lowercase file names. Your best bet is to use lowercase characters for all your files. Here are some other rules to follow:

▶ HTML pages need either the .htm or .html extension at the end of the file name. Generally it doesn't matter which extension you use; just be consistent. There are exceptions based on your Web server. Check with your Web Administrator if you are unsure.

▶ Don't use spaces within your file names. Use the underscore or dash character to simulate a space to separate words. For example, use *info_page.htm* instead of *info page.htm*. The space character is translated to "%20" and some Web browsers have trouble with this sort of thing.

▶ Use letters and numbers, but not characters such as %, *, or /.

▶ Use the same rules for naming folders within the site—use lowercase and don't use spaces. (But don't use a file name extension like .htm or .html in folder names.) If you can, keep your folder and file names as short as possible. The folder name becomes part of the URL (the address of the page). For example, the address of a page might be: *http://www.moo.com/foldername/info.htm*

▼ ▼

Creating Web Pages

As I said earlier, Web layouts are totally different than regular print files. To create a new Web document, choose Project from the New submenu (under the File menu; or press Command/Ctrl-N) and choose Web from the Layout Type popup menu. Or, if you already have a project open, you can add a Web layout by selecting New from the Layout menu and picking Web from the Layout Type popup menu. The New Project and New Layout dialog boxes let you define the basic parameters of your Web page (see Figure 14-4). Remember that you can always change these settings later if you want to change your page design. Let's take a look at these settings.

Figure 14-4

The New Web
Layout dialog box

Tip: Converting to a Web Layout. If you have an existing XPress print document, you can use the Layout Properties dialog box (in the Layout menu) to
turn it into a Web layout space. I suggest first using the Layout menu to duplicate the print layout, then converting the duplicate into a Web layout. That
way, you still have the original print layout space, just in case.

Because of the differences between Web and print layouts, you need to pay
special attention to what happens to your text boxes. Print layouts can contain
more text styling options than HTML documents—for example, drop caps,
tracking, and kerning. To solve this problem, XPress turns on the Convert to
Graphic on Export on all text boxes when you change a print layout into a Web
layout. (I cover this feature in "Building the Web Page," later in this chapter.)

This conversion ensures that the resulting Web page resembles your print
page as closely as possible, but it means the entire page is a series of graphics.
This may or may not be what you want. Remember, graphics take longer to
download than text, so people with slow connections may have to wait to see
your pages. If you don't want your text to be converted to a graphic, you will
later need to turn off this option in the Modify dialog box for each of the text
boxes.

Of course, some features (particularly those that are marked with an asterisk in the Edit Style Sheet dialog box) simply have no equivalent in HTML. For
example, tabs are not supported in HTML. Any tabs you have in your document are converted to spaces.

Page Width. In the print world, you could create documents as small as a postcard or as large as a poster (four feet square). Your Web pages can be any size, too, but realistically, you're limited to the width of the computer monitor that displays your page. Common screen sizes include 640 × 480, 800 × 600, 1,024 × 768, and 1,600 × 1,200 pixels. People don't usually mind scrolling up and down, but few people like scrolling to the left and right, so your pages need to fit the width of their screens. Your best bet is to pick a size that appeals aesthetically and contributes to onscreen readability. I usually use 800 pixels as the starting point for the page width, though sometimes I go for the lowest common denominator: 600 pixels.

You can also choose Variable Width Page, which means your page can expand or contract as the browser window changes. When you use Variable Width Page, your Web page width is based on a percentage of the width of the browser window—usually between 90 and 100 percent. This may sound appealing, but I find that it usually just gets you in trouble. XPress just doesn't give you enough tools for managing how images and other page elements should flow when the browser window changes. If you're laying out Web pages in XPress, I recommend leaving Page Width set to an absolute value.

Page Colors. You can control the background color of the page, the color of the text, and the color of the links on the page. The default colors are based on standard browser defaults—a white page with black text, blue text hyperlinks, and so on. You can override any of these colors using the popup menus. There are the normal XPress colors, plus ten common Web colors (see the next tip) in the list (see Figure 14-5). However, if you don't like these colors, you can choose "New" from the list to choose any color you want from XPress's standard Edit Color dialog box (see Chapter 12, *Color*, for more on choosing colors). Any color you create using this "Other" method, shows up in your document's Colors palette, so you can use it there, too.

▼ ▼

Tip: Web-Safe Colors in XPress. In the "bad old days," most people had 8-bit color monitors which could only display 256 colors at any one time, and colors would often get dithered (which looked kind of mottled and ugly). In order to counteract this, people tried to pick colors from a palette of 216 "Web-safe" colors, which wouldn't dither on screen. Today, every computer is sold with a 24-bit color card, few colors are ever dithered on screen, and many designers simply choose whatever RGB color they want. However, if you really care about using Web-safe colors, XPress can give 'em to you.

When you have a Web document open, XPress automatically displays a bunch of Web colors in the Colors palette, like Web Navy and Web Maroon. However, these are not necessarily Web-safe colors. If you want to add a Web-

Figure 14-5
Web-safe color
popup menu

safe color to your document, you can select Web Safe Colors from the Model popup menu in the Edit Color dialog box (see Chapter 12, *Color*) for more on how to create and edit colors. Or, use my favorite method.

1. Pick any RGB color in the Edit Color dialog box.

2. Change the percentage values in each of the Red, Green, and Blue fields to the nearest 20-percent mark—0, 20, 40, 60, 80, or 100 percent. For instance, if the Red field reads 24 percent, change it to 20 percent. If the Blue field reads 71 percent, change it to 80 percent.

3. Save the color (you might include "Web safe" in its name to remind you).

That's all there is to it.

▼ ▼

Background Image. A background image is generally a small graphic that "tiles" behind the contents of your page by repeating itself to the width and height of the browser window. To add a background image, turn on the Background Image checkbox, and then use the Select or Browse button to direct XPress to your image on the hard disk.

By default, the Repeat popup menu is set to None, which means the image will not be repeated (tiled). This only makes sense when you have a single large image you want behind your Web page. That's pretty rare. Instead, select "Tile" from the Repeat popup menu to repeat the image on the page horizontally and vertically (like the tiles on a bathroom floor). Or you can choose "Horizontal" to repeat the image across only the top of the page, or "Vertical" to repeat the image down the left side of the page.

Setting Up File Paths

Once you have a Web document open, you need to tell QuarkXPress where you're going to be putting your HTML files. The reason has to do with file paths. If XPress doesn't knows where your HTML files will be saved, it cannot correctly create links to graphics or write proper HTML codes for your hyperlinks—the path names would work as you are testing your pages on your local hard drive, but would break when you transfer your HTML files to the Web server. Therefore, it's essential that you take this site management step.

QuarkXPress has pretty limited site management tools, so you have to pay attention to where you put your files. While some other Web programs have sophisticated features to manage HTML and graphic files), XPress offers just two features: Image Export Directory and Site Root Directory. These both live in the General tab of the Preferences dialog box—but only for Web layouts (they're not relevant for regular print layouts; see Figure 14-6).

Choose Preferences from the Edit menu (or press Command-Option-Shift-Y or Ctrl-Alt-Shift-Y), and select the General category under Web document. First, set the Site Root Directory by clicking Select (Macintosh) or Browse (Windows), and locate the site folder you made on disk. Next, if you have already created a folder (in your site folder) in which you want your graphic files saved, then type this name of the folder for your images in the Image Export Directory field. The default name is "image", but you can change it to whatever you want. If the folder you enter does not yet exist, then XPress creates it when you export your HTML.

Figure 14-6

Web Layout preferences

If you will be creating a number of XPress Web documents for a single Web site, you can set up the Image Export Directory and the Site Root Directory while no documents are open. This way, the preferences are picked up by all subsequent new Web documents.

▼ ▼

Tip: Single Document Sites. While some folks create a different Web document for each Web page, I find that it makes more sense to keep all or most of a site's pages together in the same document. Each page in the Web document gets saved as a separate HTML file. This way, you can maintain consistency in the look and feel of your pages by using the document's master pages, style sheets, and colors.

▼ ▼

Page Properties

Once you have set up the Web document's file paths, and before you start building the elements on your page, you should take a moment to visit the Page Properties dialog box (choose Page Properties from the Page menu or press Command-Option-Shift-A or Ctrl-Alt-Shift-A; see Figure 14-7). Note that this menu item only appears when you have a Web document open. All the settings you made when you first created the document are displayed in this dialog box (you can change them, too), along with three more options: Page Title, Export File Name, and Meta Tag Set.

If you have a multi-page Web document, each page will get exported as a separate HTML document, so you need to open and change the Page Properties dialog box for each and every page.

Page Title. Every HTML page must have a title, which appears in the Web browser window's title bar (see Figure 14-8), and often is listed in Web search

Figure 14-7
The Page Properties
dialog box

Page Properties	
Page Title:	Down the Rabbit Hole
Export File Name:	rabbithole
Meta Tag Set:	None

Colors
Background:	White
Link:	Blue
Visited Link:	Web Purple
Active Link:	Red

Layout
Page Width:	800 px
☐ Variable Width Page	
Width:	100%
Minimum:	300 px

☑ Background Image: | Fatty:Jobs:Peachpit:RWQX6 screens | Select...
Repeat: | Tile |

Cancel | OK

Figure 14-8
The page title appears
in the browser window

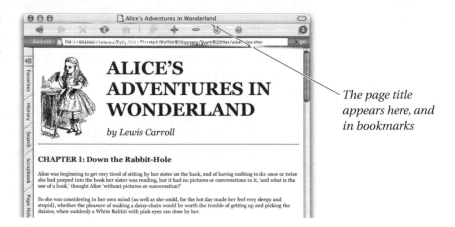

*The page title
appears here, and
in bookmarks*

engines. If someone bookmarks your Web page in their browser, the title is what appears in their list of bookmarks, so it's important that you type a descriptive word or phrase into the Page Title field of the Page Properties dialog box. If you forget to title the page, it is left blank, which—to be blunt—looks dumb and unprofessional.

Export File Name. The Export File Name option is where you set the file name for the HTML file that XPress creates when you export to HTML. (See "Tip: Naming Files and Folders," earlier in this chapter for more on how to name HTML files.) If you don't enter a name, XPress creates file names such as Export1.htm, Export2.htm, and so on. Trust me, these are not good names for your HTML pages!

By the way, if you enter a file name without a three-letter extension, XPress adds ".htm" to file name. If you want the ".html" extension or some other extension instead, enter the full name in the Export File Name field.

If you have a multi-page Web document, make sure that the Export File Name is different for each page.

▼ ▼

Tip: Quick Name Changes. You can change the export file name of the page in the Page Layout palette. Just select the name and then type the name you want.

▼ ▼

Meta tags. Many search engines use meta tags for keywords and descriptions of the page. If you want to increase the probability of users finding your page, you should always include some meta tags. Meta tags are one of those things that can't hurt and may help a user find your page, so it is worth the time to set them up.

Applying meta tags to your document is a two-step process: first you have to create a meta tag set, and then you use Page Properties to apply them to the Web page.

1. Choose Meta Tags from the Edit menu. Here, you can either edit the default "Set 1" or define a new one (see Figure 14-9). Unless you are very familiar with the meta tag format, I think it is easier just to edit that set. Later, if you want to create more sets (perhaps for different pages in your site), you can duplicate this set or create a new one. Go ahead and name the sets anything you want.

2. After selecting a set and clicking Edit, select the first line in the Edit Meta Tag Set dialog box (the one called "keywords"; see Figure 14-10), and then click Edit. Type a series of words or phrases, separated by commas, in the Content text area. Enter all the words or combination of words that a user might enter in a search engine to locate your page. Try to think outside the box. For example, if you offered services using QuarkXPress you might enter something like: Quark, QuarkXPress, XPress, Quark Xpress, Quark Express, and any other variations of the spelling of the name that someone might use.

3. Click OK, then select the second line ("description") and click Edit (or just double-click on the line). Enter a short (a sentence or so) description about the contents of the page in the Content field. Then click OK.

4. If you want, you can add more meta tags by clicking the New button, selecting an option from the Meta Tag popup menu, selecting a type of meta tag from the Name popup menu, and then typing the value of the meta tag in the Content field. For instance, you might select "name" from the Meta Tag popup menu, "author" from the Name popup menu, and then type your name in the Content field. When you export the

Figure 14-9
The Meta Tags dialog box

Figure 14-10

The Edit Meta Tag Set
dialog box

HTML, this information is saved at the beginning of the HTML file, so people looking at the HTML code will see your name (see Figure 14-11).

5. When you're done setting up the meta tag set, click OK and Save to save the set in your document. Then open the Page Properties dialog box and choose your set from the Meta Tag Set popup menu.

Meta tag sets act just like style sheets or colors: If you want to use a particular set of meta tags in a bunch of documents, you can create them while no documents are open. Then they'll be available in every new Web document you create.

▼ ▼

Tip: Learning More About Meta Tags. There are over a dozen cool meta tags that Web browsers understand. Most of these are listed in the Name popup menu when you click Add in the Edit Meta Tag Set dialog box. For instance, you can choose "name" from the Meta Tag popup menu, "copyright" from the Name popup menu, and in the Content field, type something like: "© 2002 Eddie Poole" (without the quotation marks). The © is HTML code for "display the copyright symbol," though because it's a meta tag, nothing is displayed anyway.

Similarly, you can use the ROBOTS meta tag to stop the little programs called robots or spiders that many search engines use to find new Web pages

Figure 14-11

Adding custom meta tags

they can add to the database. If you don't want your page added (perhaps it contains private information, or is simply a listing of products), you can use meta tags to tell the robots to go away. Create a new meta tag in your meta tag set; choose "name" from the Meta Tag popup menu, "ROBOTS" from the Name popup menu, and then type "noindex" in the Content field (don't include the quotation marks, of course). If you create a similar meta tag but with "nofollow" in the Content field, then robots and spiders won't follow any of the links that are listed on that Web page.

To find out more about meta tags and what sort of values you can use, look at *www.webreference.com* or some other online HTML guide.

▼ ▼

Building the Web Page

Once you define the properties for your Web page, you are ready to start drawing text and picture boxes and importing your content. The Web layout looks similar to a print layout within XPress, though the ruler is set to pixels and you'll see the Web Tools palette under the regular Tool palette. (If you don't see this palette, select Show Web Tools from the Tools submenu, under the

Window menu.) These tools are for creating forms and drawing image maps, which are covered later in this chapter.

You can use almost every feature in XPress to build your Web page, though some features are grayed out because HTML doesn't support them. For instance, you cannot rotate a text box because there's no such thing as rotated text in HTML. However, if you choose to convert the text box to a graphic (see "Converting Text to a Graphic," below) then suddenly you can rotate it. Similarly, you can put text on a Bézier line, but XPress will automatically convert the object to a graphic upon export.

Text Boxes

Here are some other restrictions to creating text boxes in Web documents.

▶ The box must be rectangular. If you create any other shape, XPress converts the box (and the text inside it) to a graphic.

▶ You cannot apply fractional point sizes to text. If you enter a fractional size, XPress rounds the point size to the nearest whole size. For example, 12.5 points becomes 13 points.

▶ Text runaround is turned off for all text boxes unless you convert them to a graphic (see the next section).

▶ You cannot link text boxes across pages. In fact, when you are in a Web document, you can only view one page at a time, and the Pasteboard is not available. This is an icky limitation, and I'm hoping that they'll let you do this in future versions of the program.

If you set up your documents to have a variable page width, you also need to turn on the Make Variable Width checkbox (on the Text tab of the Modify dialog box; see Figure 14-12) for each text box that you want to stretch when the Web browser window changes width.

Converting Text to a Graphic

As I said earlier, character formatting and text box attributes that are not supported in HTML—such as kerning, tracking, baseline shift, and so on—are disabled in Web documents. If you want to include any of those features, you first need to convert the text box to a graphic. Select the text box and then choose Modify from the Item menu (or press Command-M or Ctrl-M). Then, turn on the Convert to Graphic on Export checkbox in the Modify dialog box (see Figure 14-13).

Once that option is checked, then all typographic controls are enabled for that text box. As the feature's name indicates, this doesn't convert your text box

Figure 14-12
Make Variable Width
option in the
Modify dialog box

Figure 14-13
Modify dialog box with
Convert to Graphic on
Export turned on

*Features such as
First Baseline
become active
when Convert to
Graphic is on.*

to a graphic until you export the HTML. After you turn on this option, you can tell XPress how you want to export the graphic: what file format, color palette, alternate text, and so on.

GIF or JPEG. By default, when you turn on the Convert to Graphic on Export checkbox, QuarkXPress converts the text box as a GIF image. This is almost always a better choice for text than JPEG. GIF is suited for text and line art with solid colors, and JPEG is best for photos and continuous tone graphics. However, you can change the file format in the Export tab of the Modify dialog box (see Figure 14-14), if you really want to. A third option, PNG, is not fully supported by all browsers (especially in earlier versions), so I usually avoid it. (If you want to know more about these file formats, check out one of the many other books on the market that discuss Web graphic file formats, including a book I coauthored, *Real World Photoshop*.)

Figure 14-14

Export tab

Color Palettes. When you select GIF as the export format, you can choose among the Web-safe palette, a system palette, or the Adaptive palette in the Export tab of the Modify dialog box. As I mentioned earlier, the Web-safe colors will not dither on 8-bit color monitors, but there are very few of those types of screens around anymore. While in the "old" days I would have recommended always using Web-safe colors, today I almost always use the Adaptive palette, which creates a custom palette containing the majority of the colors in your text, whether or not they are Web-safe colors.

The two other color palettes in the Palette popup menu—Windows and Mac OS—limit your colors to the one operating system. These are dumb; pretend they're not even there.

By the way, because GIFs can only contain 256 different colors, XPress needs to know what to do with colors that don't exactly fit into the image's color palette. If you turn on the Dithering checkbox, XPress will use a diffusion dither for colors that don't fit the palette exactly. If you leave this turned off (which is what I almost always do), all colors in the exported graphic snap to the nearest color that is in the palette.

Use Interlacing. You have the choice to make your GIF images interlace or not. When you turn on Interlacing, the graphic will appear in the Web browser in stages, almost like a venetian blind opening. You first see a very-low-resolution version, then it becomes increasingly more detailed. The only time you want to turn this on is when you have a relatively large image which is used for navigation. That is, turn it on if it would really help the viewer to see a low-resolution version as quickly as possible. I leave it off for most images. It makes your file size a tiny bit larger.

Alternate Text. Alternate Text displays in the Web browser in three cases: when the user rolls over an image, if the browser can't find the image for some reason, or if the user has disabled the viewing of graphics in the browser. Alternate text is also an accessibility feature: The alternate text you enter for an image is spoken in systems for the visually impaired. Not all images need alternate text, but you should always include this text for graphics that are important for understanding the purpose of the page, and for any navigation buttons on the page. For most images, just one or two words will suffice.

Export To. The default folder for saving your images is the folder name you created in the General panel of the Preferences dialog box. If you did not change the name, XPress uses the name "image" for the folder. You'll see that name listed in the Export To fields of the Export Modify dialog box. You can enter a new folder name for the selected image by typing a new name in the field. When you export your page as HTML, XPress creates the folder in the root directory. If you have specified multiple folders already, you'll see all the folder names (up to seven) in the popup menu.

▼ ▼

Tip: Use Photoshop Instead. Now that you know how to convert text to a graphic in XPress, I am going to recommend that you use a graphics program such as Adobe Photoshop or Macromedia Fireworks to create your graphics instead. Even though XPress gives you tremendous control over your type, it has limitations for exporting text as an image. First, you can't create anti-aliased text. For graphic headings, the smooth edges that anti-aliasing produces makes for better looking text on the screen. Also, you can't add special effects such as a drop shadow with soft fuzzy edges or beveled edges. In Photoshop, you can wrap the text to give the appearance of text on a path. In Fireworks, you can attach text directly to a path.

▼ ▼

Defining CSS Font Families

Of course, you probably don't want to convert all your text boxes to graphics. If you don't make the text boxes into images, when choosing fonts for your Web layout, you'll need to pick a font that is available to your users. You might love your specially designed typeface for your print job, but you need to stick to common fonts for your Web projects. To control the font usage in your document, you can define a set of fonts that will be used if the original font is not available on the user's machine. For example, you might use Futura as the font for a heading, but if the person looking at your Web page doesn't have Futura, then you should specify a second (maybe Helvetica) or third (maybe Ariel) choice. This is called making a CSS font family. It's easy (see Figure 14-15).

1. Choose CSS Font Families from the Edit menu, then click New.

2. Choose the font you want to use as the primary font from the Available Font list and then click the right arrow to move it to the Font Family list.

3. Add alternate fonts to the list in the same manner.

4. Finally, choose a generic font from the Generic Font popup menu (like Serif or Sans Serif). That "font" will be used if none of the other fonts in your list are available.

You can use the up or down arrows to change the order of the fonts in the list. Use the left arrow to remove a font from the list.

Figure 14-15

Setting up CSS font families

Picture Boxes

When you create pages for print, you typically import either TIFF or EPS graphics. You can import those file types into a Web layout, too, and XPress converts those files to either GIF or JPEG when you export the page. Unfortunately, you don't get as much control over the conversion process as you do in Photoshop or Fireworks. For instance, you can't optimize the image to reduce its file size, and you're limited to QuarkXPress's default optimization settings.

The only settings you can change are in the Export tab of the Modify dialog box (select the picture box and press Command-M or Ctrl-M). If you choose JPEG, you can select the image quality, but you have no way to preview the final results until you view the page in the browser. In comparison, Photoshop and Fireworks let you preview the results of your optimization choices, tweaking the settings to get the best combination of both file size and image quality.

As with text boxes, you can choose the folder for exporting the image in the picture box. Choose an existing folder name from the Export To popup menu, or type a new folder name in the Export To field.

▼ ▼

Tip: Use Full Resolution on your EPS Files. Sure, XPress can automatically convert your document's TIFF and EPS pictures into GIF or JPEG files upon export. However, because EPS graphics contain "encapsulated" data, XPress can't really get in and convert them properly, so you end up with GIF or JPEG versions of the low-resolution screen previews you see in XPress. Yuck! If you're going to repurpose your XPress pages, make sure you change the Preview Resolution on each EPS graphic to Full Resolution (see "Full Resolution Preview" in Chapter 2, *QuarkXPress Basics*) or stick with TIFF files. (Though to be painfully honest, you'll often get a better result if you convert images yourself in Photoshop and import them into XPress as GIF or JPEG.)

▼ ▼

Tip: Don't Crop GIFs and JPEGs. If you use another program such as Photoshop or Fireworks to create your GIF or JPEG images, make sure the picture box you draw for the image is the exact size as the image (or larger than the image). That way, XPress just uses the original GIF or JPEG image. However, if you rotate, scale, or crop the image in any way, XPress has to re-export the image with the settings in the Export tab of the Modify dialog box. That means further image degradation, and often larger image sizes (XPress doesn't do as good a job at compressing as Photoshop and Fireworks do). You can ensure the picture box is the same size as the picture by using the Fit Box to Picture feature in the Style menu.

▼ ▼

▼ ▼

Tip: Careful with Transparency. You can import a TIFF image with an embedded clipping path into a Web document and use the Clipping feature to make the background appear transparent (see Chapter 10, *Fine-Tuning Images*, for more on clipping paths). However, when you export your page as HTML, you need to be careful. The GIF format handles transparency like this just fine, but JPEG does not (there's no such thing as transparent pixels in a JPEG image). So, if your TIFF is being exported as a JPEG (which it is by default), XPress has to fake the effect by merging whatever is behind the image into the image itself. If the image is on top of a flat colored background, it usually works okay (though there may be some color shift). If it's on top of a pattern or text or another image, then watch out! In some cases, the result is pretty icky (see Figure 14-16).

Figure 14-16

Transparency problems

When it comes to HTML, you should never trust that what you see in XPress will be what you get in a Web browser!

Note that what was transparent is now opaque, obscuring some of the text.

▼ ▼

Tables and Lines

While lines are always automatically converted into graphics when you export HTML, tables made with the Table tool can be a graphic or a regular HTML table. The difference, like text boxes, determines what you can do with the tables. For example, you cannot use dashes or dotted lines for the table grid unless you turn on the Convert Table to Graphic on Export checkbox in the Modify dialog box.

▼▼▼

Previewing Your Pages

As you build your Web pages, you'll want to preview them in a Web browser because what you see in your XPress document is not necessarily the way it'll look in the browser. Plus, not all browsers display the page the same way, so you might want to see the page in several different browsers.

First, you need to let XPress know what browsers you have and which one you want to use as the default. Choose Preferences from the QuarkXPress application menu (Mac OS X) or the Edit menu (Windows), or press Command-Option-Shift-Y (Ctrl-Alt-Shift-Y) and then select the Browsers panel (see Figure 14-17). You may see a browser listed in the Available Browsers list if XPress located your default browser when you installed the application. If

Figure 14-17
Adding browsers to
the preferences

not, click the Add button, then locate a Web browser on your hard drive. Add all your Web browsers to this list, and then select the Default checkbox next to the browser you want as the primary browser (the one you use most often).

Then, to preview your document in a Web browser before you actually export it, click the HTML Preview button near the bottom corner of the document window. You may see a brief message explaining the page is being exported as HTML, and then your default browser is opened and the page is displayed. If you want to preview the page in one of your other browsers, press and hold down the HTML Preview button, and then choose another browser from the popup menu (see Figure 14-18). This Preview HTML menu is also available in the context-sensitive menu (Control-click on Macintosh, right-button click on Windows).

Note that when you preview your page in the browser, your local links (links to other Web pages on your hard drive) won't work. You'll have to wait until you export your page to check the links. Links to other pages in this document will work.

Figure 14-18
Popup menu from
HTML Preview button

▼ ▼

Tip: Refresh the Page. If you make changes to a graphic on the page, such as cropping or changing the box size, the new image may not appear properly the next time you preview the page in the Web browser. Generally, pressing the Refresh button loads the new graphic properly. If not, quit the browser and try to preview again.

▼ ▼

Hyperlinks

What is a Web page without links? Links let your users explore your site, jumping from Web page to Web page. You can also add links to files that your users can download, or you can add links to send an email. Links can also be added to take your users to another site all together.

About URLs

A hyperlink uses a URL to link you to somewhere. (URL stands for Uniform Resource Locator, an awkward name but descriptive of what it stands for.) The URL provides a standard method of locating something on the Internet. You can think of it as the linked item's address. The URL contains the method to access the item, the name of the server or domain, the directory path to the item, and the file name of the item. (It can also include a named anchor in the HTML document, but I'm not going to talk about that quite yet.) These items are separated in the URL by a delimiter such as a comma, a slash, a colon, or a number sign.

▶ The *method* is the way you access the item. On a Web page, that method is the HyperText Transport Protocol, or HTTP. Some of the other methods are FTP, HTTPS, and mailto.

▶ The name of the server could be an IP address such as 129.30.104.4 and the domain name could be of the form such as mycompany.com, mygovernment.gov, or myorganization.org. The domain name is normally preceded by "www.", but it can be left off depending on how the Web server is configured.

▶ The directory is the path name on the Web server of the resource. If an item is located several directories deep, the path name might look like: products/images/.

An example of a URL using all the elements might look like: *http://www.mycompany.com/products/home.htm*

▼ ▼

Tip: Use Relative Links. Not all the URL components need to be included when you specify a hyperlink. For example, if you are linking to a page that resides in the same directory as the page you're linking from, you can simply type the name of the linked file. For example, instead of typing the super-long URL *http://www.moo.com/products/cows/prices.htm*, you could just type *prices.htm* (as long as the two Web pages are in the same directory). This is called using a *relative URL*—a Web address that is specified relative to the current document.

Anytime you leave out the method (the *http://* part, for instance), the Web browser assumes that you're using a relative URL. So, if you type */fish/index.html* the Web browser looks for a file called *index.html* inside a directory called *fish* inside the same directory that the current Web page is in.

When specifying relative URLs, you can also use the "../" (period period slash) format to indicate "the directory that contains the directory this document is currently in." For example, *../dogs/prices.htm* means "the file called

prices.htm that is inside the folder *dogs* which is inside the *products* folder"
(which contains both *cows* and *dogs*). This seems really complex at first, but
once you use it a few times it's really logical; and it's good to get in the habit of
using relative URLs like this instead of absolute URLs, whenever possible.

▼ ▼

The Hyperlinks Palette

The Hyperlinks palette (see Figure 14-19) is where you create the links for your
page, and also apply them to text and pictures. Choose Show Hyperlinks from
the Window menu to access the palette. One the palette is open, making a
hyperlink is easy.

Figure 14-19

The Hyperlinks palette

1. Click the New Hyperlink button (at the top left, it looks like a chain link)
   in the Hyperlinks palette.

2. Type a name for your link. This name is internal to your XPress document only and displays in the Hyperlinks palette.

3. Choose the type of link from the Type popup. Your choices here are:
   URL, Page, and Anchor. The dialog box changes based on which option
   you choose from the list. I cover the Anchor type later in this chapter.

   ▶ If you choose URL, then type the URL for the link. There's a pop-
     up menu to the right of the URL field that lists several common
     methods for the URL (see Figure 14-20). You can either use
     those or type them yourself (they're just there to save you some
     typing). This popup menu also lists the other hyperlinks in the
     palette; this is useful if you want to make a new link similar to
     an earlier one you made.

   ▶ If you have multiple pages in your document, you can easily
     link to other pages in your document. Choose Page from the

Figure 14-20

Making a
new hyperlink

*Hyperlinks you have already made
show up at the bottom of the list.*

Type popup menu, and then choose the page you want for the link from the Page popup menu.

4. Optionally, you can add a target for your link in the Target field or select one of the preset targets from the popup menu to the right of the field. The target is the window you want the link to open in. Your options here are: none, _blank, _self, _parent, and _top. Blank opens a new browser window, self and none replace the current page with the new page. Top and parent are used when your page contains frames. If you type any other word in the Target field, the Web browser will open a new window and name it whatever you typed; the name doesn't appear on screen anywhere, but if you later use that target again, the Web browser knows which window you're talking about.

5. Click OK.

If text, a picture box, or a line was selected when you made your new hyperlink, the link is automatically applied to that text or object. Otherwise you have to apply it manually. If you want to create a hyperlink that you'll use later and don't want to apply it to anything right now, then make sure nothing is selected on your page.

▼ ▼

Tip: Show Your Links. When viewing the Hyperlink palette you can choose to see either the name of the link or the actual link. Use the Show popup menu to choose either Name or Link. You can also isolate the type of links you want to display in the palette. Click each icon (URL, Anchor, or Pages) to show or hide those types of links.

▼ ▼

Applying hyperlinks. Once you add your links to the Hyperlinks palette you can begin creating links on the page. Links can be added to text, images, or lines. To apply a hyperlink, select the word, phrase or image on the page, and then click the link in the Hyperlinks palette. If you selected an image for the link, a small link icon is added to the top right part of the picture box. If you selected text for the link, it is underlined and changed to the link color. (The link color was defined when you created your Web document or was set with Page Properties.)

Editing and deleting hyperlinks. If you need to edit the hyperlink, select the link in the Hyperlinks palette (make sure nothing is selected, or this will apply the hyperlink) and then click the Edit button (it looks like a pencil). You can also Command/Ctrl-click on the hyperlink to edit it.

If you want to delete a link from the palette, select it, then click the Delete Hyperlink button. If you're just trying to remove the link from some text or an object, you need to select that text or object name in the Hyperlinks palette first (you can just select the text or object on the page, too), and then click the Delete Hyperlink button. That removes the hyperlink from that object.

▼ ▼

Tip: Contextual Hyperlinks. You can also add, edit, and remove hyperlinks in the Hyperlink submenu in the context-sensitive menu (Control-click on the text on the Mac; right-button click on Windows). This is often much faster than managing links in the Hyperlinks palette.

▼ ▼

Tip: Reapplying Hyperlinks. When you select an object or some text on your page that has a hyperlink, it gets highlighted in the Hyperlinks palette. To remove the hyperlink, just press the Delete Hyperlink button in the palette. To apply a different hyperlink, just click on a different link in the palette. Or, alternately, Command/Ctrl-click on the object's name in the palette (the part that is already highlighted) and choose a different URL (either type a new one in or select one from the popup menu).

▼ ▼

Creating Named Anchors

Creating a link to a new page is easy: you just link to the URL of the page. When the user clicks the link, the top of the new page is displayed. But what if there is much more information on the Web page than can fit on one screen? How do you jump to a specific section within a long page? The trick is using named anchors. A named anchor is invisible HTML code that can be inserted on a page. Once there's an anchor in place, you can link to that page *and* that anchor. When the user clicks the link, the browser jumps to the page and then jumps down to the anchor.

You can have as many anchors on your page as you want. And you can link to the anchor from within the same page, or you can link to the anchor from another page.

Using named anchors is a two-step process. First, you create the anchor, and then you create the link to the anchor. To create the anchor, place the cursor in some text (preferably at the beginning of a paragraph) or select a picture box or line. Then, click the New Anchor button in the Hyperlinks palette (it looks like an anchor or—if you squint—a smiling cyclops). A pink arrow covers the first letter if you were in a text box; an anchor icon is added to the image or line if you had one of those selected. The Hyperlinks palette adds the anchor to the list (see Figure 14-21).

Once the anchor is created, you can add the link: Select some text, a picture box, or a line and then click the anchor name in the Hyperlinks palette.

This works as long as the named anchor is on the same page or in the same document as the link. If you're linking to a named anchor in some HTML file that isn't being generated from this document, then you'll need to write out the URL and add the name of the anchor preceded by a number sign. For example, if the named anchor was on a page named *info.htm*, and the anchor name was *staff*, then the link would be: *info.htm#staff*.

Figure 14-21
A named anchor in the
Hyperlinks palette

Rollover Images

Web page designers love rollovers. A *rollover* is an image on a Web page that changes in some way when the user moves the cursor over it. For example, it may appear to change color or shape; maybe it lights up to indicate that it's a hotspot. Then, when the cursor is moved away, the image returns to its original form. A rollover indicates interactivity to the user, usually signifying a link to another page. XPress 6 includes both single-position, "basic" rollovers and two-position rollovers. I cover the latter in the next section.

Before adding a rollover to your XPress document, you need to create the graphics for each state of the rollover: the original image on the page (the "off" state), and the image you see when the cursor is over the image (the "on" state). You can use programs like Photoshop or Fireworks to create the two rollover images. Actually, in those programs, you can even create a four-state rollover (the other two states involve what happens when you actually click on the image), but XPress only supports a simple rollover with two images.

You should probably put these images in whatever folder you're keeping your Web graphics (like your images folder). You can save these images in any normal file format XPress can read (TIFF, JPEG, GIF, EPS, and so on)—XPress will convert non-Web formats to GIF or JPEG upon export—but if you know these images are going to be used for rollovers, I suggest saving them as GIF or JPEG in the first place.

Creating the rollover. Once you have both images on disk, you're ready to create the rollover in XPress. First, draw a picture box and import your graphic. I suggest you use the Fit Box to Picture feature in the Style menu (or in the context-sensitive menu) to ensure the box size is exactly the same as the picture. (This was imperative in XPress 5, but is only suggested in version 6.)

Next, choose Create Rollover from the Basic Rollover submenu (under the Item menu) to open the Rollover dialog box (see Figure 14-22). Here, you have a choice as to how to import the two rollover images.

▶ You can use the Select (Macintosh) or Browse (Windows) buttons to locate the on state images on disk (what XPress calls the Rollover state). You can also set the off ("default") state in this dialog box if you got excited and jumped into this dialog box before using Get Picture.

▶ You can also just click OK without setting the Default and Rollover state images in the dialog box. In this case, to set the rollover image, select

Figure 14-22
The Rollover dialog box

Rollover Image from the Basic Rollover submenu (in the Item menu). The default image should be replaced by an empty picture box, which you can fill using Get Picture, just like any other picture box. To switch back to the default image, choose Default Image from the same submenu.

Finally, if the rollover is to be a hyperlink, you can type the link in the Create Rollover dialog box, or tell XPress where to find the HTML file (if it's already on disk). If you forget this step you can just use the Hyperlinks palette to apply a hyperlink later. (As usual, there are several ways to do the same thing in XPress.)

If you later want to change your rollover image back to a regular picture, you can select Remove Rollover from the Basic Rollover submenu (in the Item menu). Similarly, you can edit the rollover by choosing Edit Rollover.

▼ ▼

Tip: Rollover with Context. The Create Rollover, Edit Rollover, and Remove Rollover commands also live in the context-sensitive menu. If you Control-click (Macintosh) or right-click (Windows) on a rollover picture box, XPress gives you the option to edit or remove the rollover. Otherwise, it lets you turn the box into a rollover. This also lets you switch your view from Default Image to Rollover Image, so you can see them. (You couldn't do this in version 5, which was a real pain in the behind.)

▼ ▼

Two-Position Rollovers

Now that you understand basic rollovers, you can move on to what XPress calls a two-position rollover. Everyone calls these things something different, but here is what happens. In a basic rollover, a new image replaces the original image when a user moves the mouse pointer over the original image. In a two-position rollover, a separate image elsewhere on the page is replaced when the user rolls over the original image. Let's say you have navigation buttons on your page for linking to product pages in your site. When the user rolls over each button, you want a picture to appear *below* the button that represents the linked page. For example, a button for the shoes page would display a picture of some shoes; the button for watches would display a picture of a watch, and so on.

As with basic rollovers, you need to create the two images you want to use as the rollover images. Again, both images need to be the exact size. Let's say you have a grayscale and a color version of the same image. Here is how you can create the two-position rollover that swaps them.

1. Draw a text box and type "Show Color Photo" into it. Format the text and the text box to your liking. (Of course, you could also create a button in Photoshop that says the same thing and import the button into a picture box. If you do that, skip step 2.)

2. Check Convert to Graphic in the Modify dialog box for this text box.

3. Draw a picture box elsewhere on the page and import the grayscale image into it. This picture is the one that displays as the page loads.

4. With the picture box still selected, choose Create 2-Position Target from the 2-Position Rollovers submenu (under the Item menu). Don't panic. Your original image disappears and you see a target icon in the top right corner of the box.

5. Import the second picture (the color one, in this example) into the picture box. You now have two pictures contained in the same picture box (though you can only see one at a time).

6. From the Web Tools palette, select the Rollover Linking tool. Click the text box with the Rollover Linking tool, and then click the picture box. This action links the two boxes together.

Finally, preview the page in a browser to test the rollovers: You should see your text button and the grayscale image. When you move the cursor over the text button, the image in the picture box switches to the color image. Cool, eh?

Viewing the rollover images. XPress displays the first image in your picture box. If you want to see the rollover image instead, choose it from the Show submenu (in the 2-Position Rollovers submenu under the Item menu or the context-sensitive menu).

Removing the target image. If you decide you want to remove the rollover action, select the target image, and then choose Remove Target from the 2-Position Rollovers submenu (under the Item menu or in the context-sensitive menu). Select the image name that appears when you select the submenu. Once you remove the target image, the rollover no longer works.

▼ ▼

Tip: Appearing and Disappearing. You don't have to have an image in the picture box in either the default or the rollover state when creating basic or two-position rollovers. For example, you could leave the default position blank (no picture imported) and just put a picture in the rollover state. In this case, when the cursor rolls over the trigger (either the rollover itself or the link to the two-position rollover), the image suddenly appears out of nowhere!

▼ ▼

Cascading Menus

Cascading menus are menus that pop up when the user moves the mouse pointer over them. The advantage to using them is that you can squeeze a lot of links into a small amount of space. If you are not sure as to how they work, check out the *www.quark.com* page. As you move over the Products button, for example, a menu "cascades" down, listing all of the Quark products.

Once you create the cascading menus, you then attach them to either a text or picture box. (Though if you use a text box, you must turn on the option to export the contents as a graphic.)

Creating the Menus

Before you can place a cascading menu on your Web page, you have to create the menus. Choose Cascading Menus from the Edit menu and then click New to create the first menu.

Formatting the menu. The Menu Properties tab of the Edit Cascading Menu dialog box lets you specify what the cascading menu will look like and how it will act. Type a name for your menu and choose from the options in the Menu Properties tab of the dialog box to format your menu (see Figure 14-23).

▶ **BACKGROUND COLOR.** Choose a color from the popup menu to define the color of the menus. This menu is just like the popup menu for choosing the background color of your page.

Figure 14-23

Creating a cascading menu, part 1

▶ **STYLE SHEET.** To control the look of the text in the menu, you can define a character style sheet for the text. All character style sheets you have previously defined display in the popup menu.

▶ **TEXT INSET.** Just like text inset for a text box, the Text Inset option moves the text the amount you specify from the left side of the menu.

▶ **MENU ORIENTATION.** Choose Vertical to drop the menu down from the bottom of the box, choose Horizontal to push the menu from the right side of the box.

▶ **BOX SIZE.** The default setting for Box Size is Auto, which uses the contents of the largest menu item to control the size of the menu. If you are not happy with the menu size, you can enter your own values.

▶ **BORDER.** Choose the outside border size and color for the menu. Set the value to zero if you don't want a border around your menu.

▶ **SEPARATOR.** Choose the size and color for the separator line between the items in the menu.

▶ **OPENING ANIMATION.** You can choose the animation direction for the menu (which direction it moves) from the popup menu: Top to Bottom, Bottom to Top, Left to Right, or Right to Left.

▶ **SPEED.** If you choose an option other than None from the Opening Animation direction, you can then choose the speed (in milliseconds) of the menu animation. If you enter zero, there is no time delay between the time the user moves over the menu and when it displays. (Don't make this number too large or else your users will think the menu isn't responding.)

▶ **OFFSET.** By default, the cascading menu appears at the same position as the box where it is attached. This means that the first item in the menu covers the text or picture box. Generally, you will want your menus to appear either below (for vertical menus) or to the left or right (for horizontal menus) of the attached box. Use the Measurements palette to determine the height of the box (for vertical menus) and type that value in the Y field. If you are using horizontal menus, type the width of the box in the X field. Then, your menus appear either below or to the side of the box.

Adding menu items. Once you've told XPress how you want the cascading menu to look and behave, select the Menu Items tab in the Edit Cascading Menus dialog box to add the menu items (see Figure 14-24). First, choose

Menu Item from the New popup button to create a new item in your menu. Type the text you want to appear in the Menu Item Name field and then enter a link in the Hyperlink field. If you want to add a submenu to one of your menu items, select the item and then choose Submenu Item from the New popup button. Add the name and link for that item as you did for the menu item.

Note that there is no good way to change the order of the items in your menus other than deleting them and adding them again in the right order, so plan out your menus before you start adding the items.

Figure 14-24

Creating a cascading menu, part 2

The other options in the Menu Items tab of the Edit Cascading Menu dialog box are options to change the background color and font color of the menus and submenus as the users move the cursor over them. Generally, you'll want to change the background color of the menus to give your users visual feedback as to which menu item is selected. Of course, you would want to choose a contrasting color to the background for the font color. Again, the color popup menus are the same as other color menus.

Attaching the Menus

Once you create the cascading menus, then you can attach them to either a picture box or a text box. However, as I noted earlier, if you use a text box, you must first turn on the Convert to Graphic on Export option (in the Modify dialog box). Select the box, choose Cascasding Menu from the Item menu (or the context-sensitive menu), then select the menu you want to use from the sub-menu list.

Cascading menus, like the other Web interactive elements, don't work in XPress. To test your menus, click the Preview in HTML button at the bottom of the document window or export the HTML to disk (see "Exporting Your Page as HTML," later in this chapter). Your links on the menus may not work until you export your document, but you should be able to see the menus and sub-menus appear as you move the mouse pointer over them. By the way, there appears to be some bug in XPress's code that leaves the cascading menus visible if you scroll on and then off them without clicking in the Web browser.

▼ ▼

Tip: Hide Visuals. When you add a cascading menu to a text box, a small icon (looks like a submenu) appears in the box. If you have a small text box, the icon for the cascading menu plus the icon for converting the text box to a graphic may cover your text. To see your text, choose Hide Visual Indicators from the View menu to hide those pesky icons.

▼ ▼

Image Maps

An image map is a graphic that contains multiple hotspots that add user inter-activity, usually as hyperlinks to other pages. For example, you might have a simple map of the world, and want to direct people to different Web pages depending on where they click on the map. In order to make an image map in QuarkXPress, you must have the ImageMap XTension active in the XTensions folder. When it's active (it should be, unless someone has turned it off with XTension Manager), you'll see the Image Map tool at the top of the Web Tools palette.

Actually, there are three Image Map tools, each of which let you draw a dif-ferent shape: a rectangle, a circle, and a Bézier box. To get a different tool, press and hold on the tool in the palette (see Figure 14-25).

Applying an image map to a picture is easy: Select the picture box, and then use one of the Image Map tools to draw the shape of each hotspot area over the picture. Remember that holding the Shift key as you drag with the Oval or Rectangle tool creates circles or squares. By the way, when you export your HTML, XPress always converts your nice ovals and Bézier shapes into polygons with straight edges, so don't get too particular about how perfectly you draw these shapes.

Once you have the hotspots drawn on the image, you can then apply your hyperlinks for those areas. Adding hyperlinks to these hotspots is exactly the

Figure 14-25
The Image Map tools

same as adding them to pictures; just select the hotspot before clicking on the link in the Hyperlinks palette.

▼ ▼

Tip: Draw Inside the Box. While you can draw hotspots that extend outside the boundaries of the picture box, you shouldn't. It won't do any good anyway; XPress always crops your hotspots down to fit within the picture box when you export the file.

▼ ▼

Deleting image maps. To remove one hotspot in an image, select it and then press Delete or Backspace. To delete all of the hotspots in an image, choose Delete All Hot Areas from the Item menu.

▼ ▼

HTML Forms

Go to almost any large site, or even a small site, and you'll see a page with a form. It could be as simple as a text entry field to enter your email address or search the site, or as complex as a survey or a form to place an order. Unfortunately, it's sort of a pain to make forms in most programs. But not QuarkXPress! It's positively easy to make a form in this program, and it's one of the best reasons to use XPress for authoring your pages.

How forms work. Here's how forms work: Once the user fills in the form fields (checkboxes, menus, text entry fields, and so on), they press a button that submits the data to the Web server. Sitting on the server is a program that can be run using the CGI (Common Gateway Interface), and this program processes the data, does something with it (such as send an email with the posted information or create a new record in a database), and then passes a result page back to the user.

The key to making all this work is the program sitting on the server (often called a "cgi script"), which is usually written in a programming language like Perl, C, or AppleScript. You'll need to ask your Web Administrator how to access the appropriate CGI script on your server before putting a form on a Web page. Usually, it's a URL address, like *../cgi-bin/processdata*.

You also need to know exactly what data the CGI script is expecting. For instance, if the script is going to put the form data into a database, you probably need to know the exact names of each field in the database. Once you have that information, you can use XPress to create the page and the fields of the form.

Just to be clear, QuarkXPress cannot make CGI scripts that will run on your Web server. Those have to be made separately; XPress just gives you the tools to create the Web page that can send data to those little programs.

Define the Form

The first step in creating a form on your page is to draw a form box with the Form Box tool—all the form items on your page must fit inside that form box. The Form Box tool is the second tool in the Web Tools palette (see Figure 14-26). A small icon at the top right of the box indicates that the box is a form box.

▼ ▼

Tip: Fast Forming. You actually don't need to use the Form Box tool to make a form box. If you use any of the form tools on your page, XPress automatically makes a form box for you. The size of this form box is determined by the pixel dimensions in the Preferences dialog box (double-click on the Form Box tool and then click the Modify button to change these dimensions). You can also make any box into a form box by selecting Form from the Content submenu (under the Item menu, or in the context-sensitive menu).

Figure 14-26
Making a form box

By the way, you can have more than one form box on your page, with each one acting as a separate form, with different Submit buttons, and so on.

▼ ▼

After making a form box, you need to give XPress some details about the form, like where and how to send the data on the form. This is all handled on the Form tab of the Modify dialog box. With the form box selected, choose Modify from Item menu (or press Command-M or Ctrl-M), and then select the Form tab (see Figure 14-27). Here you must specify six settings: Name, Method, Target, Encoding, Action, and Form Validation. Some of these—like Method and Encoding—are technical and depend on the settings in your CGI program, so you'll need to discuss them with your Web server administrator.

Name. The first field on the Form tab is where you can enter a name for your form. The default value for this field is FormBox1. The name of a form is important if you are going to add some JavaScript (in some other program) that references or validates the form. If you have multiple forms on the page, each form must have a unique name. Don't use spaces or special characters when naming your forms.

Method. The Method popup menu tells the CGI how the form is processed. The default value—Post—is generally what you will use. The Post option specifies that the Web browser should send the form data to the CGI as a separate HTTP transaction. The Get option specifies that the Web browser should append the form data to the URL.

Figure 14-27
Form tab of the Modify
dialog box

Target. Server scripts usually reply to a form being submitted with a response in the form of a URL. You can set a target window for that response. If you don't set a target, the form page is replaced by the reply page. However, you can use any target window (see "Hyperlinks," earlier in this chapter for more on target windows).

Encoding. When data is passed from a form to a Web server, the data is passed as a string of characters. The Encoding popup menu lets you specify how to pass that string: urlencoded (the default), form-data, or plain. With the urlen-coded option, spaces are replaced by the + symbol and nonnumeric characters are replaced with the % symbol followed by the hexadecimal value of the character. Plain leaves the text as it was typed. Form-data is used if you are sending attached files to the server (see "The File Select Tool," later in this chapter). Generally, if you are using a CGI to process the form, you'll want to use the urlencoding option. The CGI parses the encoded data string before processing.

Action. In the Action field, you enter the location of the CGI program that will be used to process the form. This is usually a URL like *../cgi-bin/myscript.cgi*, but check with your Web server administrator.

Form Validation. As you'll soon see, you can make certain items in your form "required," meaning that the viewer must fill them out before submitting the form. When you do this, XPress adds some JavaScript to the HTML to perform some simple validation. If a required field is left empty, an error message is displayed, and the form is not submitted. The Form tab of the Modify dialog box lets you specify how that error message appears.

The default setting, Dialog Message, means that in case of an error, the Web browser will display an alert dialog box. You can use the default message ("The required field <missing field> is missing") or enter your own message (see Figure 14-28). If you select Error Page, you'll also need to type the page name or click Select (Macintosh) or Browse (Windows) and navigate to the page on

Figure 14-28
Error message in browser

Internet Explorer Script Alert

The required field Address, Name is missing.

OK

your hard disk. Of course, you need to make sure that this URL actually exists on your Web site, too!

The File Select Tool

Hiding behind the Form Box tool (if you click and hold on that tool) is the File Select tool, which lets you add a file selection feature to your form. Very few forms actually require this feature, which lets a user upload a file from their hard drive to the Web server (but only when the CGI script is set up to accept it). However, it's nice that XPress lets you do it, just in case.

To add a file selection field in your form, drag out a box with the File Select tool (it should be wide enough to display the file name once the user selects one, plus the width of the Browse button itself). Then, while this form item is selected, choose Modify from the Item menu (see Figure 14-29). In the Form tab of the Modify dialog box, give the item a unique name and turn on the Required checkbox if the user must select a file before submitting the form.

The Accept field is supposed to let you determine what kinds of files the Web browser will accept, but very few (if any) browsers actually pay attention to this information yet. Just in case you still want to try, you have to type the file type in a MIME format. For instance, if you only want to let the user select JPEG files, you could type "image/jpeg" here. For more than one MIME type, separate them with commas. Or, to accept all file types, leave this field blank. But as I said, I haven't seen this actually work yet, so I leave it blank.

By the way, if you're making a form that lets you upload a file, you'll need to change the form method to "Post" and the encoding to "form-data".

Figure 14-29
File Selection
tool options

Text Fields

If you are gathering text information in your form, you need to create a text field for each piece of information. For example, you might have a name field and an email field. To add a text field inside your form box, select the Text Field tool and drag out a box. By default, the height of the box is preset for you (one line high), but you can make the field any width you want. Next, you should make a text box next to the text field box and type in a label for the field (or else no one will know what to type in the field; see Figure 14-30).

After making a text field, select it, open the Modify dialog box (press Command-M/Ctrl-M or Command/Ctrl-double-click on it; see Figure 14-31), choose the Form tab, and fill out a few options for that field. The options are Name, Type, Max Chars, Wrap Text, Read Only, and Required.

Name. You need to choose a unique name for your text field. This name is passed along with the information in the form in order for the CGI script to know what to do with it. If the script is going to put this in a database, then the Name field should probably match the database field name.

Figure 14-30
Text boxes with labels
next to text fields

Figure 14-31
Text field options

Type. You can choose among four types of text fields in the Type popup menu: Text – Single Line, Text – Multi Line, Password, and Hidden Field. If you're asking for something like a name or an email address, choose Text – Single Line. However, if you're asking for a bunch of text (like for comments or descriptions), you should choose Text – Multi Line. If you chose Password, then the Web browser will automatically replace whatever the user types with asterisks. Note that this type of field only hides what is entered on the screen; the data that is passed to the form is not secure or encrypted.

You can use hidden text fields for entering data that needs to be sent to the Web server, but which shouldn't be displayed in the browser. For example, if you created a form that sends an email to you, you might add a hidden field that contains your email address. Of course, the information in an hidden field can still be seen if you view the source in the browser (so it's invisible on the Web page, but not secure).

By the way, form items cannot typically overlap each other; XPress just won't allow it. However, hidden text fields *are* allowed to overlap if space is tight, since they won't actually be visible on the Web page.

Max Char. To limit the number of characters the user can enter into the field, type a number in the Max Char field. If the width size of the field is smaller than the Max Char size, then the data scrolls as the user types in the field. Unfortunately, when you turn this on, QuarkXPress automatically overrides the width setting of your text entry field; the program has some magic formula for setting the size, which is sort of annoying.

Wrap Text. When you set the Type popup menu to Text – Multi Line, XPress offers you the option of wrapping text in the text entry field. When the Wrap Text checkbox is turned off, the result is a text entry field that has horizontal and vertical scroll bars. You need the horizontal scroll bars because the text that the user enters can extend past the boundaries of the frame. When you turn on the Wrap Text option, however, you only get a vertical scroll bar. In most cases you'll want to turn Wrap Text on.

Read Only. If you turn on the Read Only option, the Web browser won't let the user change the text in the field. Why would you want to do this? Trying to come up with a good reason strains my brain.

Required. As I noted earlier, if you turn on the Required checkbox for a text entry field, the Web browser won't allow the form to be submitted with that field left blank. There's no way to do any kind of special checking that the data is the correct type (like saying "make sure it's a valid credit card number")—just that the user has typed something.

▼ ▼

Tip: Start with Default Text. If you want some default text in the text entry field, you can simply type it in the field. Whatever is in the field when the HTML is exported, becomes default text. As long as the Read Only checkbox is not turned on, the user can select that text and change or delete it.

▼ ▼

Lists and Popup Menus

A list or popup menu provides a way to offer choices to the user in a compact form. For example, you could place a popup menu in your form that lists all the states or countries. Or you might display a list of ten software applications and ask the user to select one or more items from that list. The opportunities are infinite! (Well, maybe not infinite. Maybe just "a lot.")

Making menus. QuarkXPress thinks of both popup menus and lists as menus, and requires that you create a menu "set" before making a popup menu or a list. Fortunately, making a menu set is easy.

1. Select Menus from the Edit menu. The Menus dialog box (see Figure 14-32) looks a lot like the Style Sheet dialog box, and works much the same. Click New to create a new menu, or select an existing menu, and then click Edit. If you have a similar menu in another Web document, you can click Append and import that list into the current document.

2. Type a name for your menu. The name is internal to XPress and not used in the exported HTML, so you can give it a descriptive name—you can use spaces in this name.

3. Your menu can be set up so that each menu item has a hyperlink to a different Web page. For example, a popup menu might help the user navigate around your Web site. In this case, turn on the Navigation Menu checkbox in the Edit Menu dialog box.

4. Click Add to add a menu item. In the Menu Item dialog box (see Figure 14-33), type the value you want to appear in the menu in the Name field. This information is what the user sees in the list. If you turned on the Navigation Menu option in the previous step, then you should type the URL associated with this menu item in the URL field. Otherwise, in the Value field, type what you want the form to send to the Web server if the user selects this option. For example, you might type "Washington" in the Name field and the two-letter abbreviation "WA"

Figure 14-32
Menus and
Edit Menu dialog box

Click in this column to make this menu item the default item in the list.

Figure 14-33
The Menu Item
dialog box

For non-navigation menus

For navigation menus

in the Value field. If the user selects Washington from the menu, then the value WA will be sent to the server.

5. If you want this menu item to be the default selection (the one that shows up selected when the Web page first appears), click Use as Default. You can also set the Default menu item in the Edit Menu dialog box by clicking in the Default column.

6. Repeat this process until you have added all the items you want to your menu, then press OK, and then Save.

▼ ▼

Tip: Rearrange Menu Items. As you build your menu, you might decide to change the order the items appear in the Edit Menu dialog box (which, in turn, determines how the items appear in the popup menu or list in your browser). To rearrange a menu item, hold down the Option (Macintosh) or Alt (Windows) key, and then drag the item in the list either up or down. When you click the item with the modifier key held down, a dotted line appears, indicating you are moving it.

▼ ▼

Drawing out menus. To add a popup menu or list to your form, select the Popup Menu tool or the List Box tool from the Web Tools palette and click inside the form box. At this point, you cannot control how large the list or popup menu will be, so just position it so that it has room to grow to the right. Once you add one of these items to your form box, you need to visit the Form tab of the Modify dialog box (press Command-M or Ctrl-M; see Figure 14-34).

▶ **NAME.** The first item in the Form tab of the Modify dialog box is always Name. Get in the habit of always naming your items instead of using the default names that XPress generates. The name is used when you reference the field using JavaScript, and it appears in the data that is sent to the CGI script. Even if you are not going to use scripting now, you may in the future and the names will already be in place. When you pick a name, don't use spaces or special characters.

▶ **TYPE.** If you used the List Box tool to draw the box, then List appears in the Type popup menu. If you used the Popup Menu tool, then Popup Menu appears in the list. However, you can always change the type of list here if you picked the wrong tool. (I tend to do that a lot.)

▶ **MENU.** Here, pick the name of the menu you created in the Edit Menu dialog box. However, remember I said you had to build the menu set first? Well, I sort of lied. If you want to create a new menu set, you can

Figure 14-34
Changing options for
popup menus and lists

click New in this dialog box. The Edit Menu dialog box appears, and you can follow the instructions for making a menu set that I discussed earlier.

► **LIST OPTIONS.** When the Type popup menu is set to List, XPress gives you two more options to think about: Allow Multiple Selections and Required. As I've said before, Required means that the user has to select something from the list before the form is submitted. Allow Multiple Selections tells XPress whether you want people to be able to choose more than one item in the list. Unless you have a good reason for the user not to select more than one item in the list, just turn on the Allow Multiple Selections checkbox. In fact, if you only want them to choose one, then a popup menu might be a better way to go anyway.

▼ ▼

Tip: Multiple Selections. For the user to select multiple items in a list on a Web page, they need to hold a modifier key. Holding the Shift key selects multiple items in a row, the Command key (Macintosh) or the Ctrl key (Windows), selects discontinuous items in the list. You might want to provide this information next to your lists to remind folks.

▼ ▼

Checkboxes and Radio Buttons

Another method of providing selection options for your users is to use either checkboxes or radio buttons. The advantage to these is that the user sees all the options on the Web page. Checkboxes allow the user to choose multiple items; radio buttons allow only one choice.

To add a checkbox or radio button, select either the Radio Button tool or the Check Box tool from the Web Tools palette. Both these tools work the same: Draw a box on the page wide enough to include the checkbox or radio button, plus a label. The box looks and acts just like a text box, except that there's either a radio button or checkbox on the left side. Now, with the Content tool selected, type a label in the box (see Figure 14-35). You can format this label using XPress's normal text formatting tools.

You'll need to modify these buttons using the Form tab of the Modify dialog box to make them operational.

Radio buttons. Radio buttons are social creatures; they only make sense in groups because the idea of radio buttons is that when you click on one, the other radio buttons automatically deselect. So the first thing you need to do after drawing out two or more radio buttons is open the Modify dialog box and type in their group name (see Figure 14-36). Here is a potential "gotcha." Each radio button in your group must have *exactly* the same group name. If you rename the group, make sure you enter that same name for each radio button. If one radio button has a different group name than the rest, it won't work with the group.

▼ ▼

Tip: Apply Group in a Group. The best way to ensure that all the radio buttons in a group have exactly the same Group name is to select them all when you apply the Group name in the Modify dialog box.

▼ ▼

Note that each radio button in your group needs a unique value that describes the button. That value is what is sent to the CGI script on the Web server—the user doesn't see it. For example, in a form asking what operating system you're using, you might see four radio buttons labeled Macintosh, Windows, Unix, and Linux. However, behind the scenes (in the Modify dialog box), the values might be set to 1, 2, 3, and 4. If you click the Unix button, the number 3 would get sent to the CGI script, along with the name of the group.

If you want one of your radio buttons to be pre-selected when the user first sees the form, turn on the Use as Default option in the Modify dialog box.

Figure 14-35
Radio buttons and
checkboxes on the page

Figure 14-36
Radio button options

Checkboxes. Checkboxes don't require a group name. Instead, each item must be named uniquely in the Form tab of the Modify dialog box. As with radio buttons, the data you type in the Value field is what is sent to the CGI on the Web server, along with the checkbox's name. Note that if the user does not turn on the checkbox, then that information is not sent to the CGI script.

Checkboxes have two other options: Initially Checked (which tells the browser to turn the checkbox on by default) and Required (which means the checkbox must be turned on before the form is submitted. Required checkboxes are good for agreement forms (like "Click here to acknowledge that you have read this contract").

Buttons

Perhaps the most important element in a form is the button that actually sends the form information to the Web server, called a submit button. You can create two kinds of buttons in QuarkXPress: text buttons and image buttons.

Text buttons. True to their name, text buttons have text in them—usually something like "Find," "Submit," or "Send." To make a text button, select the

Button tool and click once within the form box. The button always starts off small and scraggly; it expands as you type in it. (Just like a text box, you have to use the Content tool to type in a text button.) The name you type doesn't matter, as long as it conveys the message to click this button to send the form.

As it turns out, your button can do one of two things: It can submit the file, or it can reset the form back to its original default state. By default, the button is a submit button. If you want a reset button, then choose Modify from the Item menu (or press Command-M or Ctrl-M) and change the Type popup menu to Reset. Of course, it's a good idea to change the Name field in the Modify dialog box, no matter what kind of button you've got (see Figure 14-37).

Image buttons. While text buttons are like text boxes, image buttons are like picture boxes. You can use the Image Button tool to drag out an image button box to any size you choose, and then use Get Picture to import a picture into it. Image buttons are always submit buttons (that is, when the user clicks on it, the Web browser immediately submits the form to the CGI script). But they have another interesting side effect: Along with any other data in the form, the image button includes the X and Y coordinates of where the user clicked.

For example, you could make an image button that fills an entire form box (so that it's the only item in the form), and import a picture of a city street map. When the user clicks on the picture, the X and Y coordinates of the click would be sent to a custom CGI script, which could (perhaps with the help of a database) return the nearest restaurants to that place on the map.

Figure 14-37
Button options

▼ ▼

Exporting Your Page as HTML

When you have completed your Web page, and have previewed it in the browser, you are then ready to export the document to disk as an HTML page.

▶ If you haven't done it already, create a folder on disk to store your HTML files.

▶ Verify that you've defined the Site Root Directory in the General panel of the Preferences dialog box.

▶ Check the Page Properties dialog box for each page of your document to verify that you have set the Title and export file name.

Finally, choose HTML from the Export submenu (under the File menu) or from the context-sensitive menu (Control-click on the Macintosh, or right-button click on Windows). In the Export HTML dialog box (see Figure 14-38), navigate to (and open) the folder you defined as the Site Root. This is where you want your HTML files to be saved. You can save the HTML files anywhere, but if they're not inside your Site Root directory, then some links may be messed up.

Before you actually click the Export button, take a look at three options here: Pages, Launch in Browser, and External CSS File.

Pages. If you have more than one page in your Web document, then XPress lets you choose which pages you want to export as HTML files. Remember,

Figure 14-38
Export HTML
dialog box

each page in the document becomes a different HTML file. To choose specific pages, separate the page numbers by commas or hyphens. For instance, "3, 6, 9-10" will export four HTML pages.

Launch Browser. I almost always want to see how the HTML file turned out after exporting it, so I turn on the Launch Browser checkbox. When this is on, XPress immediately launches the default Web browser and opens the HTML file. However, if you export more than one HTML file, the Web browser only opens the first one.

External CSS File. QuarkXPress uses an HTML feature called Cascading Style Sheets (CSS) to format your text. CSS styles are very much like style sheets in QuarkXPress: they're named groups of typographic formatting. When you export your document as HTML, XPress automatically turns your document style sheets into CSS styles with the same names. Any text that has no specific style sheet is given a default CSS style name, like Text1 or Text2. Note that every text character in your document must be given both a paragraph style sheet and a character style sheet to make CSS work cleanly. All local formatting shows up as separate CSS styles like "Text1." (See Chapter 7, *Copy Flow*, for more information on style sheets in your QuarkXPress documents.)

If you leave the External CSS File checkbox turned off, QuarkXPress saves your CSS style definitions in your HTML files. That is, each file has its own CSS definitions. However, if you turn on this option, XPress saves the CSS definitions in a separate file (in the same folder as your HTML files). The benefit of external CSS files is that you can quickly use a text editor to change the definitions of that single file (or replace the file with another one that has the same names but different definitions). When you do this, *all* the HTML files that reference that external CSS file are updated immediately. It's very slick.

Turning this feature on is also good when you're going to send the HTML file off to a Web geek in another department. That way, he or she can quickly apply the proper corporate formatting to the text instead of being bogged down with whatever styles you thought looked cool.

PlaceHolders. When the XML Import Filter XTension is active, XPress adds one more option to the Export HTML dialog box: PlaceHolders (no, I have no idea why the "H" is capitalized). However, unless you have added placeholders to your document using the Placeholder palette, this feature is grayed out. If there are placeholders in the document, and you turn this option on, then XPress exports an XSL (Extensible Style Language) document instead of an HTML document. XSL is much like XML, but it is only used by XSL servers to format documents on the fly. That is, the XSL document is like a template into which the XSL server drops content. I explore XML in more depth in Appendix E, *XML Tools*.

Tables in HTML

One of the trickiest problems in HTML is positioning text or graphics precisely around a page. There are two methods for specifying page geometry: complex tables and absolute positioning in Cascading Style Sheets. You don't have to think about this much because it's all handled behind the scenes when you export the HTML; but the more you know about how this works, the more efficient you can be.

Tables in HTML were originally meant to be a means of presenting information in an organized manner. For example, tables were used to display financial data or statistics in rows and columns. However, tables can be used to position things on your page. For example, in a Web document, XPress creates a table the size of the page. When you draw a text or picture box, XPress converts it to a cell within the table. These tables have nothing to do with the Table tool in the Tool palette; these HTML tables are just for positioning things on your page.

The complex tables technique breaks down when you place one object on top of another on your page because cells of a table can't overlap each other. In this case, XPress uses the absolute positioning feature of Cascading Style Sheets (CSS), which tells the Web browser exactly where on the page to place the object. The problem with this is that some older Web browsers can't deal with these tags and the page ends up looking wrong. Fortunately, this is pretty rare these days, as most people have more modern browsers.

▼ ▼

Tip: Seeing the Table. If you want to see the complex table that XPress generates in HTML files, you can open the HTML file in an HTML editing program like Adobe GoLive or Macromedia Dreamweaver. Another option is to open the HTML in a text editor (like BBEdit on the Macintosh), search for any text that says "BORDER=0" and replace it with "BORDER=1". Then you can save the file and open it in a Web browser, which will show you the table lines. This won't look pretty; it's just for educational purposes.

▼ ▼

Tip: Make Tables Simpler. Knowing what is happening "behind the scene" helps you create pages that display properly in all browsers. Let's say you are creating a page containing two columns of text and you want to use two separate text boxes instead of one text box with two columns. You should make sure the two boxes begin at exactly the same position down on the page. Of course that is true even for print, but on a Web page, uneven text boxes cause unnecessary code to be inserted. XPress inserts small transparent spacer images into empty cells to make the table cells match the boxes in your document. Take the time to align your boxes with the Space/Align command from the Item menu (see Chapter 3, *Tools of the Trade*) or use the Measurement palette to verify that the Y values of the boxes are the same.

▼ ▼

Tip: Printing Your Web Document. Unfortunately, you cannot print your Web document to a printer from within QuarkXPress. Instead, when you select Print from the File menu, XPress exports the current page as a temporary HTML file, launches your default Web browser, opens the HTML file there, and then prints from that program. That means you can't print more than one Web page in your document at a time, and it means you can't use any of QuarkXPress's regular Print dialog box features. Is this annoying to you? It should be.

▼ ▼

Importing HTML

QuarkXPress not only exports HTML codes to disk, but it can also import HTML into a text box. You must have the HTML Text Import XTension active in order to do this (which it should be, unless someone turned it off in the XTensions Manager dialog box).

Importing an HTML file works exactly the same as importing a Microsoft Word document: you select a text box with the Content tool and then choose Get Text from the File menu. Note that if you're using QuarkXPress for Windows and the HTML file has a .html file name extension (instead of .htm), you will probably have to select Display All Files from the File of Type popup menu (in the Get Text dialog box).

Unfortunately, XPress isn't very smart at importing HTML files and there is a *lot* that it just ignores. For starters, the HTML Text Import XTension currently doesn't understand Cascading Style Sheet (CSS) tags. That's sort of a problem, because XPress exports all its HTML with CSS tags. That means XPress cannot import the HTML that it exports. Well, it can, but all the formatting is stripped away. Similarly, it ignores all images and turns HTML tables into tab-separated text.

What *can* it import properly? It understands very basic HTML codes, such as <B> (bold text), <HR> (a horizontal rule, which becomes a Rule Below in XPress), and
 (a soft return). Codes to make ordered and unordered lists work pretty well. The best part is that the headings are mapped to style sheets in your document. For example, if you have a paragraph style called H1 in your document, the import filter will automatically apply that style sheet to paragraphs that have the <H1> code in the HTML.

Clearly, Quark has a way to go with this import filter. But, nevertheless, it is nice that you can import basic HTML files.

▼ ▼

Tip: Importing HTML Codes. If you want to import the actual HTML codes instead of XPress interpreting them into formatted text, turn off the Convert Quotes and Include Style Sheets checkboxes in the Get Text dialog box, and then hold down the Command key (Macintosh) or Control key (Windows) when you click the Open button. I'm not sure why you'd want to do this, but ain't it good to know that you can?

▼ ▼

XPress Page as Picture

Trying to replicate in HTML exactly what you see on your XPress page is tricky. However, I find that I've often got an element of an XPress page that I want to duplicate exactly on the Web (like a logo built in XPress, or a particularly well-designed headline). One of my favorite methods of converting QuarkXPress pages into a form that Web browsers can understand is one of the simplest and yet least used: simply transform the whole page—text, pictures, and all—into a picture (see Figure 14-39).

1. Reduce the size of your document so that it's just bigger than the objects on the page (select Document Setup from the File menu). You may want to copy the page items to a new document before doing this.

2. Save the QuarkXPress page as an EPS (select Save as EPS from the File menu; see "Page as Picture," in Chapter 9, *Pictures*). Note that there are XTensions available that let you save just a portion of your XPress page as an EPS; if you have one of these, you can skip the first step and just save the area you're interested in using the XTension.

3. Open this EPS file in Photoshop. When Photoshop displays the Open Generic EPS dialog box, you should probably choose a resolution of 72 ppi and the RGB color mode. The size of the page/image is up to you (I usually just leave it the same size). Turning on the Anti-aliased option typically provides a better-looking result, but your final image size may be slightly larger.

4. Once the image is rasterized (turned into a bitmapped image) in Photoshop, you can crop it and save it as a GIF or JPEG image, depending on the content of the page. Typically, the JPEG format is better for natural, scanned images, while GIF is good for images with solid colors.

Figure 14-39
Converting pages
to pictures (part 1)

Save your XPress document as an EPS file...

... and open it in Photoshop.

(If you don't know how to save in these two file formats or why you'd want to, check out one of the many other books on the market that discuss Web graphic file formats, including *Real World Photoshop*.)

5. You can place this file on the Web as is, but it won't be interactive in any way. However, you can easily add links to the page by importing the graphic back into XPress and giving the page/picture an image map. You can then save this image as an HTML file, and XPress will write the appropriate image-map codes for you.

By turning your XPress page into a bitmapped graphic, you make sure your audience will see everything that you see on your page—including fonts, lines, and page geometry. But there are a number of problems with this technique.

▶   If you're not careful, you can end up with a very large graphic that will take so long to download that no one will bother.

Figure 14-39
Converting pages
to pictures (part 2)

Export the rasterized Photoshop image as a GIF file using Save for Web . . .

. . . and place it in your HTML Web document.

▶ Small text sizes are unreadable when rasterized at such low resolution, even if they're anti-aliased.

▶ Your audience cannot zoom in or out, change the fonts, or even print the page very well (what they see on screen is exactly what they'll get on paper).

Nonetheless, if you're trying to re-create a masthead that you've built in XPress, or even just a simple page without a lot of text or graphics on it, this technique can work surprisingly well (I've made full-page pictures like this that are only 20 K in size).

▼ ▼

Acrobat PDF Files

The idea of a paperless office has long been a sort of Shangri-La, where no one would have to be burdened with paper cuts and filing cabinets. Instead, all documents would be electronic, easily read on any computer platform, easily stored on disk or somewhere on the Internet. Adobe has done its part in bringing us closer to this utopia with its Acrobat format, which lets you build and edit Portable Document Format (PDF) files from almost any program. These PDF files, in turn, can be viewed on any computer that has a reader program (which is free from *www.adobe.com* and available for Macintosh, Windows, Linux, and even Palm operating systems).

While the PDF format was originally designed for archiving or viewing documents that were meant for paper output, it has grown to incorporate features suitable for Web or multimedia publishing, too (see Figure 14-40). Plus, PDF files are now widely used to send files to output providers, such as when advertisements are sent to magazines and newspapers (because PDF is more flexible and often more robust than the EPS format).

There are many reasons why you would create a PDF file of your XPress document. Perhaps you want to send a draft or final version to a client for approval. Instead of sending your actual QuarkXPress document to a client or a publication for printing, you can simply email the more-compact and less-volatile PDF file. Most printing companies accept print jobs as PDF files. (If you

Figure 14-40
Acrobat features

Acrobat's tools let you navigate through the document quickly.

Bookmarks act like a table of contents.

Anything you can design on your page can be included in the Acrobat PDF file.

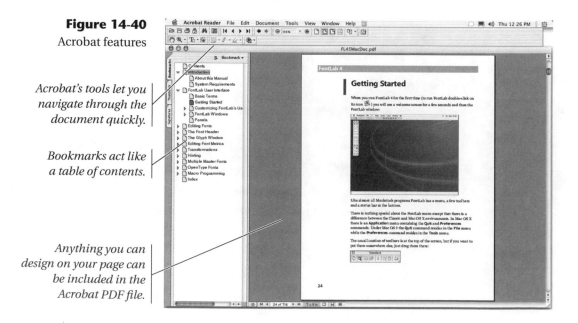

are printing colors—especially spot colors—make sure the printer has experience with printing color separations from PDF files.) If the PDF file will be viewed primarily on screen, you can create a more robust experience by adding hyperlinks so that the user can navigate to different sections in the document.

Note that this section includes information about creating Acrobat PDF files for either the Web or print.

Viewing PDF on the Web. There is a browser plug-in (PDFViewer) that lets you view PDF files within your Web browser window, but it still requires that you have the Reader program somewhere on your hard disk. Plus, this plug-in is notoriously buggy and slow, so many people (like me) configure their Web browser to view their PDFs directly in Acrobat Reader. In this case, the Web browser downloads the whole PDF file to disk and then opens it with the Reader application.

Creating a PDF File

There are three ways to make an Acrobat PDF file from a QuarkXPress file: using the Mac OS X print driver, exporting directly using the built-in Jaws software, or using Acrobat Distiller.

Mac OS X print driver. Mac OS X can write Acrobat PDF files to disk from any OS X application, including QuarkXPress 6. The process is simple: First, click the Printer button at the bottom of the Print dialog box to open the print driver's dialog box. Click the Save as PDF button and then tell the operating system where to save the file. Finally, after you click OK (which returns you to the XPress Print dialog box) click Print to create the PDF file on disk.

"Printing" a PDF does a reasonable job on text and simple page items such as lines. However, it doesn't do well with graphics, especially EPS files. The reason: the PDF print driver can't translate the PostScript commands in an EPS, so you get the low-resolution screen preview that you see in XPress. Also, there's currently no way to control font embedding, image compression, or any of the other important features you get with the other methods. Ultimately, hardly anyone uses the PDF print driver; it's much better to use the other two methods.

Note that at the time of this writing, OS X 10.3 ("Panther") was not shipping. However, Panther should be able to make robust PDF files even more easily, and produce better results from image files. Nevertheless, it will likely still be better to use the next two methods I describe.

The Jaws solution. If you really want a good-quality PDF file, you'll be much better off using the Export Layout as PDF feature (in the File menu). This forces XPress to write a PostScript file to disk and then turn it into a PDF using the Jaws PDF engine. (Jaws is PostScript and PDF technology that Quark licensed from Global Graphics—it is not a true Adobe technology, like Acrobat Distiller, but it works well most of the time.) I discuss this feature in more depth in "Export Layout as PDF," below.

Acrobat Distiller. Although QuarkXPress can write PDF files directly to disk (via the Jaws engine), I still often use Acrobat Distiller (part of the Adobe Acrobat Professional product) because it offers much more control and some features which are missing from XPress's implementation. For example, XPress cannot save files in the PDF/X format, which many ad agencies and magazines now insist on receiving. Also, Acrobat Distiller lets you save your PDF settings (Print, Screen, and so on), while you have to set these each time you create a PDF from XPress.

If you want to use Distiller rather than the Jaws engine, select Create PostScript File for Later Distilling in the PDF panel of the Preferences dialog box (see Figure 14-41). Now, when you select Export Layout as PDF from the File menu, XPress only writes the PostScript to disk and lets you process it with Distiller later. If you have set up a "hot folder" in Distiller (a folder that Distiller

PDF Preferences

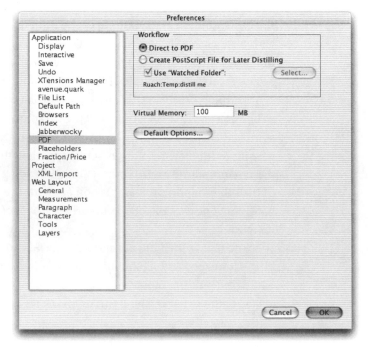

watches for incoming files), you can choose this same folder in XPress's Preferences dialog box and skip the step of telling XPress where to write the PostScript file.

Note that it's a good idea to visit the PDF Export Options dialog box before saving the PostScript to disk. This lets you control what does and doesn't get into the PDF file (for example, whether you want hyperlinks or not). I cover PDF Export Options in the next section.

Export Layout as PDF

In order for Jaws or Acrobat Distiller to generate a PDF file, QuarkXPress needs to write PostScript to disk. There are two ways to do this: you can use the Print dialog box to print to a file, or you can use the Export Layout as PDF feature. I discuss how to write PostScript to disk in Chapter 13, *Printing*. Suffice it to say that using Export Layout as PDF is easier and gives you more control. Plus, you can't take advantage of any of QuarkXPress's interactive features—like hyperlinks—unless you use Export Layout as PDF, so we'd better focus on that here.

As I mentiond earlier, you can create a PDF in this way by choosing Export Layout as PDF from the Export submenu (under the File menu). After a short stop in the Export as PDF dialog box (see Figure 14-42), where you tell the program where to save the PDF file, XPress writes a PostScript file to disk. By default, XPress then uses Jaws to "distill" this file into a PDF file. If you have turned on the Create PostScript File for Later Distilling option in the PDF panel of the Preferences dialog box, then XPress leaves the PostScript file where it is and lets you process it with Acrobat Distiller.

But wait: let's take another look at that Export Layout as PDF dialog box. To get the most of XPress's PDF features, click the Options button to open the PDF Export Options dialog box. Here you're presented with five tabs of preferences: Layout Info, Hyperlinks, Job Options, Output, and OPI.

Layout Info. In the Layout Info tab (see Figure 14-43) you can supply a title, a subject, an author, and a list of keywords separated by commas. This information is embedded in the PDF file and available from within the Acrobat Reader by viewing the document properties.

▼ ▼

Tip: Set up PDF Preferences. If you find yourself often visiting the PDF Export Options dialog box and making the same or similar changes each time, you should consider changing the default settings for this dialog box in the PDF tab of the Preferences dialog box. I discuss these Preferences more in "Default Settings," in Chapter 2, *QuarkXPress Basics*.

▼ ▼

Figure 14-42

The Export as PDF dialog box

Hyperlinks. In the Hyperlinks tab (see Figure 14-44) you can choose to include interactive features in your PDF—hyperlinks that let the viewer bounce from place to place within (and without) your document. If you're creating a document that you're sending off to be printed, you might as well turn off the Include Hyperlinks checkbox because no one will need them. However, if someone will be viewing the PDF file on screen, these hyperlinks can be very helpful.

You can also make several other choices in the Hyperlinks tab of this dialog box, including whether your indexes will turn into hyperlinks and what hyperlinks will look like on screen in the Acrobat Reader.

▶ **EXPORT LISTS AS HYPERLINKS.** If you have used the Lists feature to create a list (like a table of contents) in your layout, you can turn those list items into hyperlinks automatically by turning on Export Lists as

Figure 14-43

The Layout Info tab
of the PDF Export
Options dialog box

Figure 14-44

The Hyperlinks tab

Hyperlinks. For instance, when this is on, a viewer looking at your table of contents could click on a page number and be transported to that page. (I discuss lists and indexes in Chapter 8, *Long Documents*.)

▶ **EXPORT INDEXES AS HYPERLINKS.** Page numbers in your layout's index can also be exported as hyperlinks, which is very helpful and appreciated by users. Of course, you have to have used the Index feature to make your index first!

▶ **EXPORT LISTS AS BOOKMARKS.** One of my favorite interactive tools in PDF documents is the Bookmarks feature—sort of a table of contents that can be visible all the time in the Acrobat Reader application. QuarkXPress can create bookmarks for you automatically based on any or all lists in your document. Again, you have to use the Lists feature for this to work. You have two choices here: Use All Lists or Use List. If you only have one list specified in your layout, then these are the same, of course.

▼ ▼

Tip: Hidden Lists and Bookmarks. Unfortunately, at the time of this writing, the bookmarks only appear in your PDF file if you actually build the list in your document *and* you export that page (the page with the list on it) to PDF. This is pretty annoying, because sometimes you want bookmarks in your PDF document, but you don't actually want to display the list as one of your pages. The only way around this, as far as I can tell, is to build the list as the last page of your document, export the whole document as PDF, and then use the Acrobat application to delete that last page.

▼ ▼

► **APPEARANCE.** When the Include Hyperlinks checkbox is turned on, XPress automatically includes all the links you have added using the Hyperlinks palette (see "Hyperlinks," earlier in this chapter). However, while hyperlinks appear underlined and in a different color on screen in QuarkXPress, they are often invisible in PDF files—that is, there is no visual indication that text or pictures are hot links. If you want your PDF file's hyperlinks to be visible, you need to set the Frame popup menu to Visible and then set the Width, Color, and Style popup menus to indicate how the hyperlinks should appear.

The Appearance section of the PDF Export Options dialog box offers one other setting: the Highlight popup menu, which tells XPress how you want the link to appear when you click on it. You have four options: None, Invert, Outline, and Inset (which looks like a button that gets pressed in).

► **DISPLAY.** The last setting here, the Display popup menu, lets you tell XPress what view percentage you want Acrobat Reader to use when it jumps to the new page (this only affects hyperlinks to other pages within your document, like those from an index or bookmark). The options are Zoom, Fit Window, Fit Width, and Fit Length. You're on your own on this one; it depends entirely on your document and your audience's needs.

Job Options. The Job Options tab (See Figure 14-45) lets you determine whether and how much XPress should compress images and embed fonts. You may be familiar with these from the Acrobat Distiller's job options. There are so many options here that I can't cover them well enough; instead, I encourage you to get a copy of *Real World PDF with Acrobat* or the *PDF with Acrobat 5 Visual QuickStart Guide* (both from Peachpit Press) in order to learn about them. However, I will say this much: While it's nice that XPress gives us these settings, when I'm using Acrobat Distiller I much prefer to leave these checkboxes turned off and control all the job options in Distiller itself.

Output. The Output tab of the PDF Export Options dialog box is like the Print dialog box for PDF files (see Figure 14-46). This is where you can set the bleed amount (how much of the pasteboard is included with the document page) and specify whether registration marks are added to the page.

Figure 14-45
The Job Options tab

Figure 14-46
The Output tab

The Color Output section of the dialog box is very important, as it can drastically affect your document's colors. If you want QuarkXPress to generate color separations, then choose Separations from the Type popup menu. If you have a one-page document with black, cyan, and a spot color, you'll get three black-and-white pages. However, if you turn on the Produce Blank Pages checkbox, you'll get five pages: cyan, magenta, yellow, black, and the spot color—but the second and third pages will be blank.

Unless your printing company specifically asks for separations, however, it's probably best to choose Composite from the Type popup menu, and then choose CMYK (or DeviceN; see Chapter 13, *Printing*) from the Print Colors popup menu. In this case, they will actually do the color separations from this file. If the PDF file is destined for the Web, you should also use Composite, but you can use RGB colors or Grayscale instead.

If you don't have the OPI XTension loaded, the Output tab gives you the chance to use OPI anyway. However, if you're going to use an OPI workflow, you'll want the OPI XTension loaded, so you can just ignore this checkbox.

OPI. When the OPI XTension is active, XPress displays the OPI tab of the PDF Export Options dialog box, which lets you specify whether to include your TIFF and EPS images. I cover OPI workflows in Chapter 13, *Printing*.

▼ ▼

Tip: PDFs of Books and Multiple Layouts. Please note that there is no way to make a single PDF of multiple documents (like books in a Book palette) or multiple layouts at the same time. Instead, if you need this, you'll have to save each of them individually and then combine them into a single PDF using Acrobat Professional.

▼ ▼

The Future of Publishing

One of the basic elements of democracy has long been "freedom of the press," but freedom of the press has always been reserved for those who own one. Now for the first time in history, almost anyone can publish their own work on the Internet and the World Wide Web. And because QuarkXPress has been the tool of choice for most publishing professionals, it makes sense that people would look to this program to take them into the brave new world.

In this chapter, I've briefly summarized the various tools that ease the transition from print to screen. Of course, the future of publishing depends less on which tools you use than on *what* you create. Happy XPressing!

A

COLOR MANAGEMENT

For years, "What You See Is What You Get," or WYSIWYG (pronounced "wizzywig"), was one of the key buzzwords of desktop publishing. It meant that the page layout you saw on your computer screen was, more or less, what you'd get out of your printer. WYSIWYG works fine for a page with any color of ink—so long as it's black (to paraphrase Henry Ford). But it's significant that nobody felt the need to come up with a similarly cute acronym to describe color fidelity between computer and printer. My editors and I considered "Color You See Is Color You Get," but we wouldn't want to be responsible for unleashing "kissykig" on the world. My colleague, Steve Roth, says he prefers WYGIWYG: "What You Get Is What You Get."

Silliness aside, the main reason nobody's come up with such an acronym is that until recently, it would have described a condition that didn't exist. If you've ever created color pages, you've learned—probably with no little pain—that the colors you see on your screen have little more than a passing resemblance to what comes out of your color printer or off a printing press. In fact, a major part of working with color on desktop computers has been learning through trial and error that when you see color A on your screen, you'll actually get color B out of your color-proofing printer, and color C off of a four-color press run. Your only guides were process-color swatch books, test prints, and experience.

▼ ▼

Managing Color

Well, the times they are a-changing. Color management systems (CMS) promise to provide fidelity between the colors on your computer screen and those of your printed output. Apple, Eastman Kodak, Pantone, and Agfa, among others, have systems that sometimes actually cooperate with each other. However, color management is still far from a push-button experience, and without some knowledge of what's going on behind the scenes it's very possible to make your color output worse rather than better.

If you own QuarkXPress, you already have a color management system, or at least major components of it: the QuarkCMS XTension, supported by Apple's ColorSync and Kodak's KICC.

▼ ▼

Tip: Color Management in the Real World. I want to throw in a short commercial plug here for two books. First, *Real World Photoshop*, which I wrote with Bruce Fraser. Much of the overview material in this appendix is distilled from that book. However, because *Real World Photoshop* contains much more information about color management, and because Photoshop is such an integral part of most people's color management work flow, it's worth taking a look at that book as well. The other book is *Real World Color Management*, by Bruce Fraser, Chris Murphy, and Fred Bunting. This book covers it all, from "a to zed." Okay, the commercial break is over.

▼ ▼

What QuarkCMS Attempts

While learning about color management is not easy, it's often worth the trouble in the end because a CMS can help us in a number of ways.

▶ MATCHING THE ORIGINAL. Color management systems are designed to make the colors on your document's page consistent—from your original scan to your screen to a color proof to your final output device. It's this consistency that lets you trust what we see on the monitor, letting you work visually rather than by the numbers.

▶ COLOR-SPACE CONVERSION. CMSes really should be called "color conversion systems," as that's what they're doing: converting colors from one system into another. This means that QuarkCMS is very good at converting RGB to CMYK and vice versa.

▶ SOFT PROOFING AND PREPROOFING. Soft proofing is the ability to proof your images and document pages on screen. Preproofing is the ability to proof your images and document pages on a color printer—

like a good quality inkjet printer. A well-implemented CMS can save you a lot of money by letting you trust your monitor and composite color proofs instead of relying on multiple Match Prints.

Why Color Management "Can't" Work

Don't get me wrong: QuarkCMS is not performing any magic. If there's one thing I want you to get out of reading this appendix, it's that it's just plain not possible for computer monitors, dye-sublimation color printers, color copier/printers and four-color lithographic presses to exactly match each other, color for color. Each device uses different technology to create color, and each uses differing methods of specifying its colors. The red, green, and blue colors emitted from a monitor are additive: the more color you add, the closer to white the screen gets. On the other hand, printers that apply ink, wax, powders, or toner to paper generally create colors by combining values of cyan, magenta, yellow, and black. This color model is subtractive: the more of each component you add, the darker your final color becomes. When you try to create the same color using two different methods, there's really no way that the two can look exactly the same.

Plus, the same RGB values on two different monitors might not look like each other at all, because the screen phosphors and technology might be slightly different. You have probably seen a wall of televisions at a department store: each set displays the same image, yet has a different color cast. Similarly, the same CMYK values printed on a color inkjet printer look very different from "identical" values printed on a four-color press on coated stock, and those colors also look different than colors printed on newsprint.

Each of these color systems are called *device dependent* because the color is specific to only one device—a brand of monitor, color printer, or whatever. QuarkCMS tries its best to create consistency among various devices, but you need to understand that it's not entirely possible.

What color management does enhance is the predictability of colors among these disparate systems and preserve the overall appearance of your page. You can learn to visualize how an image on your screen will appear when it's printed to various output devices.

"I Only Paint What I See"

Matching colors might be a hopeless comparison of apples, oranges, and grapefruits, except that there's one constant shared by every method of creating colors: the human eye. The fact is that your eyes don't care what technology a monitor or printer uses to create a color; they just see colors. Just as monitors and printers are device *dependent*, your eyes are device *independent*.

They're the one constant in this whole *mishegoss*, and not surprisingly, they're the key to color management systems such as QuarkCMS.

No, QuarkCMS doesn't try to calibrate your eyes with some sort of cybernetic gizmo. Rather, it uses a color-space model based on a statistical analysis of how most people perceive differences between colors. This model was designed by the Commission Internationale de l'Eclairage (that's the International Commission on Illumination, or CIE, to you and me) in the 1930s. The CIE color space describes every different color the human eye can see, using a mathematical model that isn't dependent on fickle things like the density of phosphor coatings or the amount of ink spread on paper stocks.

Unlike RGB or CMYK values, which don't really describe a color (the same values might look quite different on different devices), CIE values actually describe a color's appearance, not just the values that make it up on a specific device.

Color Management Concepts

Before I go further into this discussion, I have to take a break and define a couple of important words: *gamut* and *profile*. I'll use these words a lot throughout this appendix.

Gamuts. A device's color *gamut* describes the range of colors which that device can create or sense. Since the CIE color space describes every perceivable color, by default it has the largest gamut. No device—monitor, scanner, or printer—can come close to reproducing this range of colors, and so the gamut of any specific device is smaller than the CIE gamut. Plus, different devices are able to image different sets of colors (the available colors are spread out differently). So one device may be able to reproduce many hues of red, while another may be weak in reds, but especially competent in producing a wide range of blues.

Profiles. QuarkCMS uses files called *device profiles* to keep track of not only the color gamuts of particular devices, but also other information about their capabilities and limitations. Most of the profiles you use with QuarkCMS are actually generic descriptions of Apple 13-inch monitors, or printing presses that use SWOP (Standard Web Offset Press) coated inks, not specific descriptions of your personal device or your lithographer's press (see "Canned versus Custom Profiles," later in this chapter).

From Device to Device

Here's how color management systems work: First, you hand the CMS an RGB or CMYK color along with a profile. As I've said, by itself the color is meaningless; it's just a recipe (this much red, that much green, and so on). The profile—called the "source" profile—gives meaning to the color by saying it's this color *on such-and-such device.* For instance, 100-percent red means less than "100-percent red on my Trinitron monitor that displays red like this . . . ."

Second, you tell the CMS where the color is going by specifying another profile—this one is called the "target profile." The CMS then has an engine (sometimes called a CMM, for color matching method) that translates the original color into its native CIE color space format, and then from this format into the appropriate target color.

Here's another way to think about this: let's say that CMSes work with words instead of colors, and the purpose of our hypothetical word-CMS is to translate words from one language to another. If you just feed it a bunch of words, it can't do anything. But if you give it the words and tell it that they were written by a Polish person (the source), it all of a sudden can understand what the words are saying. If you then tell it that you speak Japanese (the target), it can translate the meaning for you.

Note that a color monitor can display a different set of colors than a desktop color printer, which, in turn, has a much greater gamut than a four-color press. QuarkCMS's color transformations work best when they reduce one device's gamut to match another; it's just not possible to *increase* a device's gamut to match another's, although there are ways of faking it. That is, a color monitor is good at displaying the limited gamut of a four-color press, but a four-color press is hard-pressed (no pun intended) to simulate a display.

Who does the separation? Perhaps the most important aspect of this technology is the conversion between RGB and CMYK color models. Once QuarkCMS transforms a color into its internal CIE color space, it can transform it to any other color model it knows about. And while the RGB-to-CMY conversion is relatively simple (see "Color Models" in Chapter 12, *Color*), converting to CMYK has traditionally been quite difficult. QuarkCMS does this for you behind the scenes.

Whether or not you want QuarkXPress's color management software to be handling your color separations is another matter. I discuss some of the pros and cons of using QuarkCMS as your color separation tool in "Color from Outside Sources," in Chapter 12, *Color*, but the debate is primarily one of time and quality. When you convert an image from one color space to another—like RGB to CMYK—it takes time, and I generally don't have a lot of that on my hands. If you import an RGB image into XPress, it has to convert it each time you print. Therefore, I often prefer to separate my bitmapped images in a program like Photoshop before importing them into XPress.

As for quality, well you'll forgive me if I just stay out of the argument over which pieces of software—Adobe Photoshop, Apple's ColorSync, or Kodak's KICC—offers the superior separation.

Canned versus Custom Profiles

Getting good color with a color management system depends almost entirely on three things: the quality of your image, the quality of the color management system's engine, and the quality of the profiles you use. As for the first two: The color engines that QuarkCMS uses are quite good, and I'd rather not comment on the quality of your images (that's for your audience to decide). However, I do want to discuss profiles for a moment.

QuarkXPress ships with a set of 12 or so profiles (see Table A-1) that you can use. You can obtain additional profiles from your device's manufacturer (one may have come on disk when you bought it), commercially from companies like Praxisoft or Chromix, or even download them from sites on the Internet (like *www.colorsync.com*). These are usually referred to as "canned profiles," and they vary dramatically in their usefulness because they describe only how the device is supposed to work, or perhaps how it worked once in the factory.

You can (and in some cases should) also create your own profiles for the devices you use—monitors, scanners, color printers, and presses. It's become much easier to build custom profiles in recent years using software such as Candela ColorSynergy. However, unless you really want to get deep into this stuff, I typically recommend just hiring a profiling service, such as Chromix (*www.chromix.com*) or the Imaging Revue (*www.imagingrevue.com/profile/*).

Custom profiles characterize the behavior and gamut of your monitor, your color printer, and so on. Custom profiles always give you a better result in a color management system, but it's not always worth the considerable hassle involved with building one (much less the sometimes even greater challenge of keeping the device in the same state as it was when you built the profile). It usually depends on the type of device you're using.

Monitors. Canned monitor profiles are almost always useless; even a little turn of the brightness or contrast knobs renders the profile obsolete because the screen is displaying color differently. Also, as I've said, even monitors from the same company can act very differently, especially over time. In order to trust your screen, you *must* either have a custom profile or calibrate your screen as closely as you can so that it matches the canned profile you're using. You can quickly and easily make monitor profiles with hardware (suction-cup) devices such as the Colorvision ColorSpyder.

Note that some color experts believe that it's hardly worth doing color management on an LCD monitor because just looking at the screen at two dif-

Table A-1 ICC Profiles that are installed along with the QuarkCMS XTension	**CANNED PROFILES***
	Generic Monitor (GENDISP7.ICM)
	Pantone Hexachrome Normal SID (HEXNSID2.ICM)
	KODAK SWOP Proofer CMYK — Uncoated Stock (SWUL28A7.ICM)
	KODAK SWOP Proofer CMYK — Coated Stock (SWCL32A7.ICM)
	KODAK SWOP Proofer CMYK — Newsprint (SWNM26A7.ICM)
	SWOP Press (SWOPM18.ICM)
	Tektronix Phaser III Pxi (TPIIIPX7.ICM)
	Canon CLC500/EFI Printer (CLC500A7.ICM)
	150-Line (Pantone) and 150-Line (Pantone) (ncp) — Macintosh only
	KODAK Generic DCS Camera Input (GENKDCS1.ICM)
	Nikon LS-3510 AF (LS3510A7.ICM)
	Microtek 600ZS (MT600ZA7.ICM)

*On the Macintosh, these are placed in Library/ColorSync/Profiles. In Windows, they're placed in Windows/System32/Color/.

ferent angles can cause significant shifts in tone and color. The ColorSpyder does have an attachment that lets you create a profile for a flatscreen LCD monitor (you shouldn't use the regular suction cup device because it can damage your screen), but you may still want to use regular phosophor-based monitors for your crucial color work or work out a system so that you can rely on your LCD.

Scanners. Scanners are significantly more stable than monitors, so canned settings often work, especially in the better scanners on the market. Nonetheless, if you're trying to capture exact color in a scan (perhaps you don't trust what you see on screen and you're just trying to reproduce the original), you can build a custom profile by scanning an IT8.7 or a Q-60 target and using a CMS utility like MonacoProfiler to compare your scan with readings taken when the target was created. This effectively builds a profile that characterizes your particular scanner. Note that scanner profiles are usually also media-specific, so you may have a Fuji film profile, a Kodak film profile, an Agfa film profile, and so on.

Color printers. Like scanners, the canned profiles for composite color printers are usually pretty good, though they're dependent on the correct colored ink or ribbon, paper stock, and so on. If you have a particular set up that you always use, you can optimize your color by building your own profile using the software mentioned above. This can be a time-consuming process, requiring using a spectrophotometer (like the X-Rite DTP41 or the Gretag Spectrolino) to sample dozens or even hundreds of printed swatches on a printed page. Again, hiring a company to do this makes much more sense.

Presses. It's a naïve assumption in the desktop publishing world that all printing presses are more or less the same. In fact, web presses are different than sheetfed presses, inks in one part of the world (or even the continent) that are labeled cyan, yellow, magenta, and black are actually different hues, different paper stocks make a drastic difference on color fidelity, as can humidity and the mood of the press operator on the day of your press run. However, while it's optimal to have a custom profile for your press, it's probably not necessary. Instead, you can use the profile for your particular proofing system as your target. For instance, you could use a canned profile for a Match Print or an AgfaProof system—both of these are quite stable. Then it's up to your press operator to match the proof you provide.

Of course, having a custom press profile becomes significantly more important if you're one of the many people who are printing CTP (computer-to-plate), where no film is burned, and no proof is made. In this case, you should try to obtain a custom profile from your printer or have one made by a professional.

Rendering Style

Here's one more potentially confusing concept you need to understand: rendering intents. It's easy to pick an RGB color that cannot be printed in CMYK on a press. The question is: what should the color management system do about it? It needs to somehow transform the color into the CMYK space, based on what it knows about the destination device. The ColorSync and KICC engines provide several options, called *rendering styles*, each with their own scary-sounding name: Perceptual, Colorimetric, and Saturation.

▶ **PERCEPTUAL.** Perceptual (also called photographic) rendering compresses the entire color range of your picture to fit into your printer's gamut, maintaining the balance of color throughout the picture. All the colors in the picture change, but they maintain their relationships to each other, resulting in a more true-to-life rendition of color photographs. Balance, it turns out, is often more important to maintain in photographic images than the colors themselves. For example, the colors in a picture of a face can be pretty far off, but as long as the colors maintain a relative balance—among the skin, the eyes, the hair, for instance—our eyes adjust to it fine.

▶ **COLORIMETRIC.** Colorimetric (also called solid color) rendering only changes colors that fall outside the target device's gamut, snapping them to their nearest equivalent in the gamut. Colors that are already in gamut are left alone. This rendering style is best for areas of solid colors—like if you apply a Pantone color to a block of text or if you save a Freehand or Illustrator image as a TIFF—because you're generally more interested in getting as close to the original specified color than in keeping some sort of color balance throughout an image.

There are actually two kinds of colorimetric intents: Relative and Absolute. The different is minor, having to do with how those out-of-gamut colors are mapped (clipped).

▶ **SATURATION.** The Saturation rendering intent pays more attention to the saturation of an image's colors rather than its hues. The only time this intent makes sense is when you're trying to reproduce really bright charts from a program like Microsoft Excel or Powerpoint (images in which you need the result to be similarly bright, but not necessarily the closest color).

QuarkXPress 4 didn't let you control an image's rendering intent, but XPress 5 and 6 do. I'll cover how that works in a little while.

▼ ▼

Before You Use QuarkCMS

If QuarkCMS is so great and wonderful, why would you ever *not* want to use it? There are lots of reasons, from speed to consistency. Before I dive headlong into how to use Quark's color management system, I want to discuss a few things that you should consider about the process.

Performance

When QuarkCMS transforms a color to look right on your screen or your proofing printer or your final output device, the color gets *processed*. That takes time. Sometimes a lot of time. Imagine converting a 30 MB image from RGB mode to CMYK mode in Adobe Photoshop. It takes a while, doesn't it? QuarkCMS can't do it any faster than those programs can, and that's just what it's doing when you print an RGB TIFF from QuarkXPress with QuarkCMS turned on. And it has to make that conversion every time you print.

Similarly, when you import any sort of TIFF or PICT image, QuarkCMS has to convert the screen preview to look correct on the screen. That can easily make importing pictures take four or five times as long as without QuarkCMS. When you turn on Full Resolution from the Preview Quality submenu (in the Item menu), your images may take even longer to display.

(Of course, your processor speed has a lot to do with your performance results; on really fast machines, the slow-down may not be a hindrance to your workflow at all.)

Dollars and Sense

Time, we all know, is money. And if QuarkCMS is a hit to my performance at output time, then money may be at stake. Back when QuarkXPress version 3.3 first shipped, many service bureaus were bewildered as they started receiving documents that suddenly took five or 10 times longer to output than they expected. The culprit? The EfiColor color management XTension. Service bureau operators weren't prepared for the amount of time it could take to convert even moderately sized RGB images to CMYK separations. Their clients weren't prepared for the kinds of per-minute charges the service bureaus started charging them.

So for those of you who operate a service bureau: warn your clients in advance about using RGB TIFFs (or against it, if you aren't willing to support QuarkCMS). You might suggest they make PostScript dumps or Acrobat PDF files, so it's *their* machine time that's being eaten. If you use a service bureau, find out if you're being charged extra for time charges.

Incompatible File Formats

The QuarkCMS XTension really only works with images that QuarkXPress itself can change. If you remember Chapter 10, *Fine-Tuning Images*, QuarkXPress can only modify TIFF, JPEG, and bitmap-only PICTs. That means that QuarkCMS won't even attempt to transform any EPS or DCS files.

What happens when you import a color EPS image from Macromedia FreeHand or Adobe Illustrator onto your page, and surround it with colors that you've matched exactly within QuarkXPress? You can throw the words "matched exactly" out of your vocabulary. The colors you assign in QuarkXPress are transformed according to the profiles you choose. The colors in the EPS image are not transformed at all, either on screen or in output.

You have to understand the philosophy of EPS images. The whole idea of Encapsulated PostScript, originally, was that a program should never need to look "inside" them, and should certainly never change anything inside them. Therefore, according to this school of thought, QuarkCMS should never adjust the color inside an EPS or DCS image.

The problem is that people use these file formats all the time—especially for duotones and object-oriented, vector images—and they go nuts when the colors don't match what comes out of QuarkXPress. Unfortunately, I don't really have a good answer for how to handle this situation right now. Praxisoft's CompassProXT color manages EPS images (like those from Illustrator) as well as everything else on the page, but it has other limitations and can't change your screen display.

Until Quark can implement a complete color management solution which can interpret and manipulate EPS files, we'll all just have to hold our breath and wait for a whole, cross-application integrated color management system that includes QuarkXPress.

The Problem with OPI

Trying to manage color with OPI images (see "OPI" in Chapter 13, *Printing*) is even more difficult than with EPS, because QuarkXPress never even touches the final image. Remember that with OPI, you export PostScript from QuarkXPress without image data; only little tags are inserted in the PostScript saying what the name of the image is and how it should be adjusted (rotation, cropping, and so on). That's why QuarkXPress is called an *OPI writer*.

The PostScript that comes from QuarkXPress gets passed on to another program—an *OPI reader*—that interprets the PostScript and substitutes high-resolution images where appropriate. OPI workflows that involve color management do exist, like the one made by Helios. But if the OPI server you're using doesn't do this already, you may be out of luck. The solution, again, is to adjust for the target printer when the image is scanned or saved from an image-manipulation program.

▼ ▼

Using QuarkCMS

OK, so now that you have an idea of what QuarkCMS is supposed to do (and what it can't do), let's talk about how it works with QuarkXPress, and how you tell it what you want.

Installing QuarkCMS. There are three parts to the QuarkCMS color management system for QuarkXPress: the color engine, the device profiles, and the QuarkCMS XTension itself. The QuarkCMS XTension doesn't do anything by itself; rather, it depends on system-level engines (.DLLs in Windows) to actually process the color data. On the Macintosh, QuarkCMS uses Apple's ColorSync (which is built into the system). In Windows, you get Kodak's ICM (which is installed when you install QuarkXPress). As I noted earlier, XPress also installs a bunch of profiles for you.

Turning it on. Quark got yelled at badly back in version 3.2 for shipping the EfiColor color management system with a default setting turning it on for all new documents. They learned their lesson. Now, if you want color management, you need to turn it on yourself. First, make sure the QuarkCMS XTension is loaded properly (see "XTensions" in Chapter 2, *QuarkXPress Basics*). Next, open the Preferences dialog box (press Command-Option-Shift-Y or Ctrl-Alt-Shift-Y) and select the QuarkCMS panel. Finally, turn on the checkbox labeled "Color Management Active."

Note that this preference acts like many other preferences: If you turn it on when a document is open, the change is to this document only. If no documents are open, then the change is to every document you create from now on. Of course, you can always turn off the checkbox to disable the color management system for a document.

▼ ▼

Tip: QuarkCMS Ain't the Only Game in Town. There's no doubt that the QuarkCMS XTension is a step in the right direction, but as one Quark employee noted, "let's just say it's a work in progress." There are a number of limitations, though I'm sure that the folks at Quark are working on updates. Meanwhile, if you want to get heavy into color management, you might consider another XTension on the market, Praxisoft's CompassProXT, which removes several of the most heinous restrictions of QuarkCMS, including color managing vector images. However, it has it's own limitations, too. Helios also offers the ColorSyncXT, which is a powerful color management system but doesn't handle vector images.

▼ ▼

The QuarkCMS XTension

The QuarkCMS XTension adds several dialog boxes and commands to QuarkXPress. Rather than tackle them on an item-by-item basis, I want to take you on a tour of how I think you may use the XTension's features.

Although the range of choices you can specify with QuarkCMS seems daunting, you can break the system's choices into three broad categories: telling it about your devices, telling it about your pictures and document colors, and then telling it how to print. When the QuarkCMS XTension knows all these variables, then it can correctly transform color between color spaces and gamuts, resulting in closer color matching between all the devices.

Color Management Preferences

The heart of QuarkCMS is the Color Management panel of the Preferences dialog box. The first step after turning color management on is to choose your settings from among the controls in this dialog box (see Figure A-1).

Destination Profiles. The three popup menus in the Destination Profiles section let you specify the three important targets you'll send your page: your monitor, your color printer, and the device you're separating for (usually the printing press). The Composite Output and Separation Output settings are just defaults, and you can override them in the Print dialog box if you decide to print to a different device (see "Color Management at Print Time," later in this appendix). Note that you can only choose CMYK profiles from the Separation Output popup menu, but you can pick CMYK or RGB output profiles for the Composite Output (low-cost inkjet printers are usually RGB devices).

The Monitor setting, however, is fixed: this is where you tell QuarkCMS what you're looking at. As I said earlier, the canned RGB profiles are rarely worth messing with; without a custom profile that describes the behavior of *your* monitor, you'll be hard-pressed to really trust what you see on screen.

Default Source Profiles. There are three tabs in the Default Source Profiles—RGB, CMYK, and Hexachrome—and on each tab there are two sections: Solid Colors and Images. The Profile and Rendering Intent popup menus in the Solid Colors section let you determine the source profile and rendering intent for colors you create in QuarkXPress. The two popup menus in the Images section set the default profile and intent that XPress applies to images when you

Figure A-1
Color Management
Preferences

import them. You can always override the Image profile (I'll discuss how in the next section), but once you choose a profile and intent for Solid Colors, XPress applies them to all colors throughout your document.

▶ **RGB.** Let's say you specify a color in RGB mode. The Profile popup menu in the Solid Colors section of the RGB tab tells the CMS that you mean *this* particular RGB color on *this* particular monitor (the profile you choose here). Generally, you should set the Color popup menu on the RGB tab to your monitor profile. However, if somebody else built the document and specified the RGB colors on their screen, you might want to pick their monitor profile instead.

The Images section refers to images that are in RGB mode. If you're just scanning pictures and trying to match the colors from the original image, you should probably choose your scanner's profile in the Image popup menu. However, if you typically import pictures that have been corrected in Photoshop, then you should probably select the Adobe RGB profile (or whatever other RGB working space profile you use in Photoshop). Ultimately, however, most RGB images from Photoshop have embedded profiles, so this default setting isn't as important.

▶ **CMYK.** If you're creating CMYK colors in QuarkXPress (including named colors based on CMYK, like Trumatch and Pantone Process), you need to similarly tell QuarkCMS what device those CMYK colors are based on. If you're using a swatch book that was printed based on an uncoated web press, you might want to pick a SWOP-Uncoated profile (or a proofing device of the same type). Note that the profile you pick in the Solid Colors section also determines how RGB images are converted to CMYK, either when you change color modes in the Edit Color dialog box or when you print separations of your document.

One of the great myths in color publishing is that all CMYK images are the same. Not so: when you convert an image from RGB to CMYK, you're separating it for a very specific press condition. Change the press, change the inks, change the paper stock, and you need to reseparate the image. The Images popup menu on the CMYK tab lets you tell QuarkCMS for what device an image was separated. XPress uses this information to simulate the image on your RGB screen, on a composite color printer, or when cross-rendering to a different CMYK device. (Cross-rendering means transforming a CMYK image to a different CMYK color space than it was originally intended.) Again, these are the default settings, so they're not necessarily relevant if your imported image has an embedded profile.

▶ **HEXACHROME.** The last tab in the Default Source Profiles section is Hexachrome. You can just ignore these settings, even if you're creating Hexachrome colors (see "Using Hexachrome Color," later in this appendix), as there are currently no Hexachrome source profiles available.

RGB to RGB, CMYK to CMYK. The last feature in the Default Source Profiles section is a checkbox in each of the tabs, labeled Color Manage RGB Sources to RGB Destinations (or CMYK, on that tab). These control whether colors that you create in QuarkXPress are transformed when the target profile's color space is the same as the source profile's.

Here's an example: Let's say you build a CMYK color and apply it to some text. If the checkbox is turned off in the CMYK tab (it is by default), then the color is managed when displayed on screen (because that's a CMYK to RGB transformation), but it is not changed when printed to a CMYK device. The idea is that if you specify a particular blend of CMYK, you probably know what you're doing and QuarkCMS won't mess with it. However, if you're printing CMYK colors to a composite printer or cross-rendering them to a different device than they were originally specced for, you need to turn the CMYK Correction checkmark on.

Similarly, by default RGB colors are corrected (the checkmark is on). If you turn this off, then QuarkCMS won't transform your RGB colors on screen, no matter what profiles you have specified because the monitor is always an RGB space. On the other hand, this doesn't affect the RGB to CMYK translation at print time (because the color spaces are different).

Again, the correction list only refers to colors you build in XPress; not to imported images.

Display Simulation. The Display Simulation popup menu lets you control your screen display. The default setting, Off, tells QuarkCMS to go ahead and manage color behind the scenes at print time, but to leave the screen alone. If you haven't set a Monitor profile or if your screen only displays 8-bit color (256 colors), this is your only option. This isn't as bad as it sounds; you can't trust what you see on screen, but you also don't experience the slow-downs that you get when XPress does try to manage what you see on screen.

If you are working on a calibrated monitor with a good monitor profile, you can choose Monitor Color Space, Composite Output Color Space, or Separation Output Color Space. People sometimes ask, "Which one displays the most accurate color?" The answer is that they all do, depending on what you're trying to match accurately.

▶ **MONITOR COLOR SPACE.** The Monitor Color space option tells QuarkCMS to transform all colors to match your particular screen (based on your monitor profile). In other words, you see what the RGB and CMYK colors throughout your document really look like. For instance, if you and the guy down the hall both have set up your monitor profiles and you specify an RGB or a CMYK color, when this is turned on, you'll both see the same color. This might be good while you're working on a document, but it won't help you figure out what your colors will look like when they're printed.

▶ **COMPOSITE OUTPUT COLOR SPACE.** Choosing Composite Output Color Space tells the CMS to make your screen colors appear how they will print on your Composite Printer (based on it's default profile). Unless your composite printer is your final output this isn't very useful.

▶ **SEPARATION OUTPUT COLOR SPACE.** If you want to know what your document will look like when it comes off press (or whatever your target separation device is), you can select Separation Output Color Space from the Display Simulation popup menu. Here, all your colors are transformed into the separated CMYK color space, and then converted back to RGB in order to be displayed on screen.

I find that I tend to work with Display Simulation turned off most of the time so I can save time. When I want to match colors on screen to either what someone else is seeing or to my final separation device, I switch to the appropriate Display Simulation setting . . . and then I go make a cup of tea. It takes a while for XPress to reset all the colors, especially on large imported images, because it has to find the data on disk, read it, and create a new screen preview.

Telling QuarkCMS About Pictures

Once you've told QuarkCMS about your monitor and printer, and you've set up your default profiles for colors, you need to tell it a little about the pictures you're importing. When you first import a picture, XPress applies the default source profile to it unless you override that in the Get Picture dialog box. Or, you can also change an image's source profile in the Profile Information palette. Let's look at each of these options.

Selecting a Profile

The QuarkCMS XTension adds a popup menu and a checkbox to the Get Picture dialog box (see Figure A-2). If a picture didn't have a profile assigned to it, then QuarkCMS couldn't transform its colors because it wouldn't know what to transform *from* (it doesn't know what the colors are *supposed* to look like). Therefore, no color matching would be possible. Again, the point is that when you tell QuarkCMS where the image came from, here in the Get Picture dialog box or elsewhere, you're telling it how the colors should really look.

For instance, my default source profile for images is generally set to AdobeRGB, because that's my working space for RGB images in Photoshop. However, if I import an image directly after scanning (without embedding a profile), I can assign my scanner profile in the Get Picture dialog box, overriding the default profile. QuarkCMS then knows not only the RGB values in the image but also what device created those values—hence, what the colors really look like.

In general, you should select a profile that corresponds to how the picture was saved. QuarkCMS is smart enough to examine the format of a file and only display acceptable profiles. That is, it lets you choose process-color profiles such as SWOP-Coated only when you're importing a CMYK image, and RGB color profiles when the image is stored in an RGB mode. In QuarkXPress for Macintosh the Profile popup menu is only available when you have the Preview checkbox turned on in the Get Picture dialog box.

Figure A-2

Overriding the default profile in Get Picture

Note that if your picture has a color profile embedded in it (most Photoshop documents do), the profiles popup menu appears as "Embedded." You can change to a different profile if you want to, but I wouldn't advise it.

The Get Picture dialog box also lets you apply a rendering intent to an image when you import it. While there might be a reason to override the Profile Default setting, I can't think of one.

To Correct or Not to Correct

The third item in the Get Picture dialog box is the Color Manage to RGB Destinations checkbox (or "CMYK Destinations" for CMYK images). When this option is turned off, XPress will not transform the image's colors when the source profile and the target profile both have the same color space. For example, if you import an RGB image with the Color Correction checkbox turn off, QuarkCMS will not transform the image's color on screen (because both the image and the monitor are in RGB), but it will transform it when you print CMYK.

Similarly, if you import a CMYK TIFF image when this option is turned off, QuarkCMS won't color correct the image when you print color seps or to a CMYK composite printer, because both of these are CMYK spaces, too. But it will manage the colors when printed to an RGB device.

The default setting for this checkbox is determined by how you've set up the Correction List in the Color Management Preferences dialog box. By default, the Color Correction checkbox is turned on for RGB images and off for CMYK images, but you can always override it if you want.

▼ ▼

Tip: Set the Same Profiles. If you set the source profile for a CMYK image to the same setting as your target separation profile, QuarkCMS will not touch your image data when it prints separations, even if the Color Correction option is turned on.

▼ ▼

Changing the Profiles for a Picture

What happens if you've imported a picture, and then realize you've chosen the wrong profile for it? You could spend a lot of time reimporting the picture, or you could simply select the picture and change the Profile popup menu in the Profile Information palette (choose Show Profile Information from the Window menu; see Figure A-3). The palette has the same popup menus and checkbox as the Get Picture dialog box. Simply change the values to whatever you want.

If you want to change a lot of pictures at the same time, you can use the Profiles tab of the Usage dialog box (see Figure A-4), found under the Utilities menu. You can find where a profile is used in your document by selecting the profiles from the Profile popup menu. Note that this displays the profiles applied both to images and within popup menus in the Color Management Preferences dialog box, but I suggest only changing profiles applied to images from here. You can change an image's profile by selecting the image and clicking Replace. (You can select more than one image at a time—as long as they all have the same profile—by Command/Ctrl-clicking on each item in the list.)

Show. The Show button is active only when you've selected an image within the Profile Usage list. Clicking it takes you to that picture.

More Information. Underneath the list of objects in the Usage dialog box is the More Information checkbox. When on (I always have these "More Information" checkboxes turned on because I like knowing what's going on), XPress displays three details about each profile you select: the Preferred CMM, the Class, and the Device Manufacturer.

Figure A-3
Profile
Information
palette

Figure A-4
Profile Usage

The Preferred CMM tells you which color engine will probably perform the color transformations with this profile (on the Macintosh, it's usually just ColorSync; in Windows, there is usually just KICC). Generally, you'll see either "KCMS" (this is another name for KICC . . . it seems that those folks at Kodak can never stick to a naming decision) or "appl", which means that ColorSync is the preferred engine. Ultimately, who is doing what hardly matters because the difference in final output is so subtle.

Class refers to the type of profile you've selected. You can usually interpret the four-letter abbreviations pretty easily: "mntr" means it's a monitor profile, "scnr" is a scanner profile, "prtr" is a printer profile. As for who the device manufacturer is, I just don't care much.

▼ ▼

Using Hexachrome Color

Back in Chapter 12, *Color*, I discussed Pantone's Hexachrome six-color system, which uses cyan, yellow, magenta, black, green, and orange to simulate many more colors than the normal four-color process system. However, color management is key to working in Hexachrome. In fact, you can only separate Hexachrome colors that you define in QuarkXPress under two conditions:

▶ The QuarkCMS XTension must be activated.

▶ You must have a Hexachrome profile selected as your target profile (see Figure A-5). You can select it either in the Color Management Preferences dialog box or on the Profiles tab of the Print dialog box (see "Color Management at Print Time," below).

If either of these conditions are not met, your Hexachrome colors are separated into CMYK, which sort of defeats the purpose. (By the way, QuarkXPress cannot currently include Hexachrome colors when you use Save as EPS, even if you use the DCS 2.0 format; see "Saving Files as EPS," below.)

▼ ▼

Tip: Hexachrome Images. You can use Pantone's HexWrench software to preseparate RGB images into the Hexachrome color space and then save them in the DCS 2.0 format. When you import them into QuarkXPress, the program separates them properly because XPress just sees the orange and green plates as regular spot color in the file. (Of course, because QuarkCMS doesn't manage DCS files, these images can't be transformed into other color spaces.) Note that there's no reason to convert CMYK images to the Hexachrome space because colors outside of the CMYK gamut will have already been clipped or

Figure A-5
Selecting a
Hexachrome profile

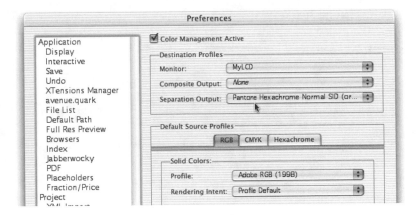

compressed; rather it only makes sense to convert RGB images with a large color gamut that cannot be represented by CMYK alone.

Color Management at Print Time

I suppose the Print dialog box is inevitable at the end of our color management process; after all, it's getting consistent color at print time that is ultimately most important to most of us. When the QuarkCMS is active, you get a sixth tab in the Print dialog box called Profiles (see Figure A-6). This tab lets you override the default Separation and Composite profiles that you earlier chose in the Color Management Preferences dialog box. It also allows you to force your composite color printer to display colors as though it were your final separation device.

Separation versus Composite. Which profile QuarkCMS uses when you click Print depends entirely on the Separation checkbox on the Layout tab of the Print dialog box. When the Separation option is on, QuarkCMS uses the Separation profile selected on the Profile tab; when off, it uses the Composite profile. Of course, you should also choose the proper printer type from the Printer Description popup menu on the Setup tab; for instance when printing separations, you want a black-and-white printer; when printing a color proof, you'd better have a color printer selected (see Chapter 13, *Printing*, for more on these settings).

Proofing on a Color Printer

Hard-copy proofing—often known as preproofing—lets you use an output device with a wide gamut, such as a dye-sublimation or ink-jet printer, to simulate the gamut of a press or (more commonly) of a proofing system such as

Figure A-6
The Print dialog box
when QuarkCMS is active

3M Match Print. Preproofing on a composite color printer may be more accurate than a soft proof on the monitor, but I've seen many instances when it was not. The advantage of a hard-copy proof is that it provides a tangible record of your intentions and expectations—you aren't likely to find a printer who will sign your monitor, but a growing number are willing to let an Epson inkjet proof form the basis of the contract.

The problem is that if you simply send a CMYK image that's been targeted for a printing press to a dye-sub printer, the results will quite likely look strange because the dye-sublimation printer's inks are nothing like four-color process inks. The trick is the Composite Simulates Separation checkbox on the Profiles tab in the Print dialog box. When on, QuarkCMS asks ColorSync or KICC to render your colors in the final separation device's color space, and then cross-render this CMYK data into the color space of your composite color proofer. Of course, in order for this to work, you really need accurate profiles all around. Also, note that this only works when your composite printer is a PostScript printer (which rules out most inkjet printers).

If you're using RGB images, you can still use the Composite Simulates Separation checkbox. In fact, you should, or else your color proof will probably appear better than it possibly could on press. (Of course, ignore this if the composite color printer is your final output.)

Missing Profiles

Progress is never without a price. When you use a new typeface, you have the burden of making sure your service bureau and other people who receive your documents have that typeface as well. It turns out that ICC profiles are the same way. When you send a file to another QuarkXPress user, you must make certain that your recipient has legal copies of all the QuarkCMS profiles you've used in your document (see "Tip: Moving Profiles," below). Fortunately, just as with fonts, the Collect for Output feature (see "Collect for Output" in Chapter 13, *Printing*) will automatically assemble all the profiles used in a document.

However, let's say you've received a document without all the needed profiles. How will you know? What can you do about it? If you're familiar with the ways QuarkXPress handles missing fonts and pictures, you should have no trouble coping with missing profiles.

When you open a document that uses one or more profiles that are not on your system, an error message appears. If you can obtain the proper profile from someone—perhaps from the person who sent you the QuarkXPress document, or from the manufacturers of the device—then do it (See "Tip: The Profile Manager," below).

However, if you can't obtain the profile, you can either go ahead and do nothing about it, or replace it with a profile that is active in your system. If you're only interested in a fast and dirty proof—let's say you're proofing page geometry or type—then there's no need to replace profiles. But if you need color matching, you must replace the missing profiles (see "Changing the Profiles for a Picture," earlier in this chapter).

Printing anyway. If you attempt to print a file which uses profiles that are missing from your system, you'll get the same alert as when you opened the document (it's virtually identical to the one you get when you try to print a document with missing or modified pictures). You've got two options in this dialog box: click OK to proceed with printing despite the missing profiles, or click List Profiles to display the missing profiles. If you choose the second option, you get the Missing Profiles dialog box, which is almost identical in appearance and function to the Profile Usage dialog box, with a few changes.

First of all, it only displays missing profiles and the items associated with them. There's also a Done button, which lets you proceed with printing the file regardless of the number of profiles you've replaced. Unfortunately, there's no Cancel button to stop replacing profiles or to stop your print job.

▼ ▼

Tip: The Profile Manager. The QuarkCMS XTension offers a Profile Manager, which is very similar to the PPD Manager (see Chapter 13, *Printing*). One notable difference is that the Profile Manager lets you choose an Auxiliary Profile Folder (see Figure A-7). If a client sends you a folder full of profiles that they used, you don't have to mix them among your own profiles in your System folder. Instead, you can just select Profile Manager from the Utilities menu, click on Auxiliary Profile Folder (the button is called Browse in Windows), and choose their folder on your hard drive.

If you add or remove a profile from your system while QuarkXPress is running, it won't register the change until you click the Update button in the Profile manager. (It automatically updates the list whenever you launch XPress, however.)

Of course, the Profile Manager also lets you turn profiles on and off, making them available or not available to you within the program. Unless you have four bazillion profiles and know that you will only be using a handful of them, you can probably ignore this function.

▼ ▼

Tip: Moving Profiles. ICC profiles are little pieces of software. And, like most pieces of software, they're copyrighted. While many profiles are free and can be copied from one user to the next, others are proprietary and, like fonts, you're not really supposed to copy them from one machine to another; rather, the developers want you to buy a profile for each machine you use. The key is to read the license agreement that comes with the profile. Of course, if you're only sending a profile to a service bureau in order to print your document, I don't think anyone is going to start breathing down your neck . . . .

▼ ▼

Tip: Missing Monitor Profiles. If your custom monitor profile is missing from the Monitor popup menu in the QuarkCMS panel of the Preferences dialog box, XPress probably can't find it. For instance, if you make a profile in Mac OS X, it's hidden deep inside the Users folder. Search for it using Sherlock, then use Profile Manager to activate it.

▼ ▼

Saving Files as EPS

The Profiles tab appears in one other place than the Print dialog box: the Save Page As EPS dialog box (see Figure A-8). However, your options here change depending on what you choose in the Format popup menu. If you select Color, your EPS is by default a composite color file, so you can only choose a profile from the Composite popup menu. On the other hand, if you chose DCS or DCS 2.0 from the Format popup menu, QuarkCMS lets you choose both a composite and a separation profile. The reason: As I mentioned back in Chapter 9, *Pictures*, a DCS file contains both separated CMYK data (and spot color, for DCS 2.0) and a composite color rendition.

If you know where this EPS file is going, setting these popup menus can be quite useful. Otherwise, you should probably leave them set to None so that QuarkCMS doesn't change the data at all.

Also, note that the Composite Simulates Separation checkbox appears here, too. I tend to leave this on so that the composite image accurately reflects the high-resolution data in the DCS file, though if the EPS file were going to be used for two purposes (printing high-res separations to an imagesetter and printing lower-resolution composite color to a short-run printer perhaps), you might want to turn it off.

Figure A-8

Color management in the Save Page as EPS dialog box

Pros and Cons

When it comes right down to it, I think that the QuarkCMS XTension is not only really cool, but it can be incredibly useful. However, it obviously has limits and isn't for everyone all the time. In fact, as it turns out, I very rarely use it; instead,

I focus on color-managing my images in Photoshop and then I just try to ignore the solid colors I create in XPress. One of the most important things to note is that color management works best when you're comparing apples to oranges rather than to salmons or coffee beans. You'll get a better idea of a final color by looking at a printed color proof than at the screen. You can calibrate all you want, and you'll still always get a more reliable image from a printer than from the screen. It still won't be a perfect match to your final output, of course, but it's that much closer. Clearly, as with just about every other aspect of desktop publishing, WYSIWYG color is a relative thing.

B

MACINTOSH VS. WINDOWS

I know many hard-core Mac users who prefer to wear cloves of garlic (or rubber gloves) when working with computers based on Microsoft Windows. I also know Windows users who still think the Macintosh is just a toy. No matter what you think, two facts simply can't be denied: First, there are lots more Windows boxes out there than Macs (though as I write this, there are still many more people doing electronic publishing on Macintoshes than on PCs). Second, increasingly, people have to use both platforms, sometimes at the same time.

Fortunately, QuarkXPress works almost identically on both computer platforms (if it weren't for the different look and feel of dialog boxes and menus, most of the time you couldn't tell the difference between the two versions). Plus, QuarkXPress for Windows can open QuarkXPress for Macintosh files, and vice versa, providing pretty decent two-way transferability of files between the two programs.

But while bringing files from one platform to the other and back again is possible, it's certainly not a no-brainer. The problem is rarely XPress; rather it's the underlying operating system infrastructure that you have to worry about: fonts, graphic file formats, file naming, and so on. In this appendix, I want to take a quick tour of the obstacles in your way when transferring files.

▼ ▼

Tip: Translations vs. Universal File Formats. While you can move QuarkXPress files between Macs and PCs, there's still no such thing as a "universal" QuarkXPress document format that's identical on both platforms. Each time QuarkXPress opens a document saved on the opposite platform, it must translate the file. The file name doesn't change, but—as one Quark tech-support person puts it—"the dirty bit is on," so you should immediately save the file. And since some information gets lost (as I'll describe) or needs to be fixed when you translate files, I'd recommend you keep your cross-platform transfers to the minimum necessary to finish a job. Remember: fewer translations equals less clean-up.

▼ ▼

File Names, Types, and Creators

The first hassle (though minor) in moving files from one platform to another is that PCs and Macintoshes save files differently. On the Macintosh, most files have several attributes attached to it, including file type and creator. These are four-letter keys that tell the Macintosh what sort of file it is and what program generated it. For example, when you double-click on a file, the Mac looks at the file's creator to see what application to start up. (In Mac OS X, not all files have a type and creator. Apple has muddied the waters by mixing these four-letter keys with file name extensions.)

In the PC world, it's simpler: no file types, no file creators—only file names. PC files all have names that include a three-letter suffix called a "file extension." In the early days of Windows, files had to be "eight-dot-three" (the name could be no longer than eight letters, followed by a period, and ending with a three-letter extension; for example, "8LTRBLUS.TXT"). Now you can use up to 255 characters in a file name, but the file must still end with a period followed by the file extension. This extension provides all the information (and it ain't much) about the file's type and creator.

Moving from PC to Mac

When you're trying to open a QuarkXPress for Windows document on a Macintosh, you must be sure that the document has either the correct three-letter extension (it almost certainly will by default) or the right file type and creator. The document icon may look like a blank page on the Macintosh, but as long as the file has the proper DOS extension (".QXD" in XPress 5 and ".QXP" in XPress 6) QuarkXPress can still "see" and open the file.

These are the only kinds of documents on your Mac that will ever show up in QuarkXPress's file-opening dialog box; you'll never see a Microsoft Word or FileMaker Pro file in there, because QuarkXPress filters out all files except those which have these four specific file types.

One way to ensure that a file is associated with QuarkXPress is to select the file and choose Get Info from the File menu (on the Finder desktop, not in XPress). Click on the triangle button to the left of the Open With option in the Get Info dialog box, and then choose QuarkXPress from the application menu (see Figure B-1).

Note that when you open a QuarkXPress for Windows file on the Macintosh, the Open dialog box tells you that it's a PC file; when you click Open, it displays a message saying it's converting the file.

Figure B-1

Forcing a file to open in QuarkXPress in Mac OS X

Mac to PC: Filenames and Extensions

It's really easy to change the file type and creator for a PC file while on either a Macintosh or a PC: just change the three-letter extension. You can name the file anything you want, but the relevant extensions are ".QXD" or ".QXP" for documents, ".QXL" for libraries, ".QXT" for templates, ".QWD" for Web documents, and ".QXB" for books. If you assign a legal name to a document using these extensions, it should be easily opened by QuarkXPress for Windows, either by double-clicking in the Windows desktop, or from within QuarkXPress for Windows.

Another option: Instead of changing the name of the file, you can select "All Files *.*" in the popup menu in the Open dialog box, and it shows even files with the wrong extensions.

In my opinion, you should simply always make a habit of adding the three-letter file extensions on your files.

▼ ▼

Tip: Careful with Your Naming. Just because Mac OS X and Windows XP let you use up to 255 characters in a file name doesn't mean you should. The Macintosh version of XPress, in particular, still can't deal with long file names. I recommend keeping file names under 31 characters on both platforms.

But there is one other trap that you can fall into when naming your files: the characters you can and cannot use. DOS-based systems like Windows and UNIX-based systems like Mac OS X use lots of these "internal" characters for all sorts of stuff. That means you shouldn't use colons, straight quotes, question marks, asterisks, slashes, backslashes, or angle brackets in filenames. (For those of you who like pictures, that is: ?, *, /, \, ", :, <, or >.) Because of this, if you work in a cross-platform environment, you should avoid any of these prohibited characters, and stick to letters (A through Z), numbers (0 through 9), underscore (_), tilde (~), exclamation point (!), dollar sign ($), the number sign (#), hyphen (-), parenthesis, and apostrophe (').

▼ ▼

What Does (and Doesn't) Transfer

Physically moving your QuarkXPress files from one platform to the next and successfully opening them is only half the job of transferring files. In general, all page-layout, text, and picture information comes across just fine in either direction, as do any changes you've made to the Document preferences. Also, any colors, style sheets, and H&J settings you've defined in the document generally transfer without a hitch. However, you'd better be aware of what doesn't get transferred. QuarkXPress documents on each platform are almost identical, but that "almost" can trip you up if you're not careful.

XPress Preferences. There is no way to move the XPress Preferences file from one platform to the other, but fortunately, that's not something that many people need to do. All the document-level preferences are saved within the document itself, and almost all of them translate perfectly (Auto Ligatures is one notable exception). When you open a Macintosh file in QuarkXPress for Windows, you're often prompted with the "XPress Preferences does not match" dialog box. I just click the Use Document Preferences button (or press Enter).

Character-set remapping. Probably the biggest hassle in transferring files between platforms is character-set remapping. The problem here is that

Macintosh and Windows font character sets don't match completely. All the basic "low-ASCII" characters (letters, numbers, punctuation) map just fine, but special characters (characters with ASCII codes above 127) can sometimes get messed up.

If a special character shows up in both Mac and Windows typefaces, QuarkXPress does its best to map it correctly. But there's only so far it can go. Table B-1 shows a list of characters that are commonly found in Windows and Macintosh fonts that have no equivalent on the opposite platform (unless you switch to a special typeface). You can also use this table to select special characters if you know you'll be printing from the other platform.

Note that the mathematical symbols that seem to appear in every PostScript font on the Macintosh are often just mapped from the Symbol font. So unless the font you're using has the math symbols built in—unfortunately, there's no good way to find this out without FontLab or another font-editing program—several characters won't transfer correctly. In Table B-2, I've listed where each math character is found in the Symbol font, so you can search and replace before transferring a file to Windows (or just use those characters to begin with).

Ligatures. The "fi" and "fl" ligature characters on the Macintosh are not to be found on the PC. That's right: ligatures used in your Mac document will go bye-bye when they're opened by QuarkXPress for Windows. This is an annoying oversight not by Quark, but by Microsoft, which just never thought that ligatures were an important part of a character set.

Table B-1
Special characters that map differently in Windows and on the Macintosh

WINDOWS	ANSI CODE ▸ MAPS TO ▸	MACINTOSH	ASCII CODE
Š	138	˘	255
š	154	π	185
¦	166	ı	245
²	178	≈	197
³	179	Δ	198
¹	185	◊	215
¼	188	⁄	218
½	189	fi	222
¾	190	fl	223
Đ	208		240
×	215	˘	249
Ý	221	·	250
ý	253	″	253

NAME	LOOKS LIKE	IN MOST FONTS	SYMBOL FONT
Division	÷	Option-/	Option-Shift-P
Plus or minus	±	Option-Shift-=	Option-Shift-=
Greater or equal	≥	Option-period	Option-period
Lesser or equal	≤	Option-comma	Option-3
Approximate equal	≈	Option-X	Option-9
Not equal	≠	Option-=	Option-P
Infinity	∞	Option-5	Option-8
Partial differential	∂	Option-D	Option-D
Integral	∫	Option-B	Option-Shift-;
Florin	ƒ	Option-F	Option-7
Capital omega	Ω	Option-Z	Shift-W
Capital delta	Δ	Option-J	Shift-D
Product	∏	Option-Shift-P	Shift-P
Summation	∑	Option-W	Shift-S
Pi	π	Option-P	P
Radical	√	Option-V	Option-/

If you used actual ligature characters on the Macintosh (Option-Shift-5 and -6), you had better use Find/Change to change them back to normal "fi" and "fl" pairs before transferring the file. On the other hand, there is little reason to type those characters anymore, as QuarkXPress for Macintosh has automatic ligature support (see "Punctuation and Symbols" in Chapter 6, *Type and Typography*).

QuarkXPress for Windows doesn't have the automatic ligatures feature, so when you move a Mac file with automatic ligatures turned on over to Windows, your ligatures go away (and because of that, you may get some minor text reflow). But at least you have fi and fl, rather than the ½ and ¾ characters Windows substitutes, which you have to search for and replace.

The second solution is to use a program like Fontographer to either mess around with the ASCII numbers assigned to ligatures in Windows fonts, or to create new fonts on the PC that include the ligatures. I only recommend the latter if you're particularly brave, and aren't working on a deadline. (This still doesn't work with auto ligatures, however, because QuarkXPress wouldn't know where to find them in the character set.) Or you can resort to Expert Set fonts from Adobe and other font vendors, and use the Find/Change dialog box to replace fi's and fl's with Expert Set characters. The Expert Set characters are typically the same in both Macintosh and Windows versions of the fonts.

Font metrics. Font metrics describe the width of each character in a font, and the kerning pairs for those characters. On the Macintosh, PostScript fonts store their character widths and kerning pair values in the screen font files. Macintosh TrueType fonts store metrics entirely in the printer font (the screen fonts contain just bitmaps). On the PC, the font metrics for PostScript fonts are located in ".PFM" files; metrics for TrueType fonts are found in ".TTF" files.

However, no matter where the metrics of a font may reside, you need to be aware that the metrics of a PC font may differ from those of a Macintosh font, even if they're from the same company. I don't know why this is, but it's certainly a major problem when moving files back and forth between the two platforms. If the metrics change, then the text in a document reflows. Sometimes this is hardly a problem, and other times it can spell hours of work.

It's a good idea to have a printed proof of a Macintosh document handy after you've imported it into your Windows version of QuarkXPress (or vice versa). That way you can check to see if the layout got altered in the transfer. When proofing the document, look for any widows or orphans that may result from the minute differences in font metrics. If you notice a problem, you can sometimes adjust the spacing parameters through kerning or tracking to compensate for the differences in font metrics.

This is much less of a problem when you use OpenType fonts, which are completely cross-platform.

Forbidden fonts. There are certain typefaces that exist only on Macs or only on Windows machines. You should never use them on documents that you intend to shuffle between platforms, unless you enjoy spending a lot of time staring at the Font Usage dialog box. On the Macintosh, avoid using system fonts such as Chicago, Geneva, Monaco, and New York (a good rule, with some exceptions, is never to use a font named after a city). In Windows, avoid fonts such as MS San Serif, Modern, Helv, System, or Tms Rmn, or any other font listed in the Windows Fonts control panel with an "A" in its icon, instead of "TT", and an .FON extension to their filename listing. These are bitmapped fonts of fixed size, meant only for the Windows interface.

If you open a file and its document fonts are missing, QuarkXPress gives you a chance to immediately change them (see "Missing Fonts," in Chapter 6, *Type and Typography*). QuarkXPress catches missing fonts if you've used them anywhere in your document, including in style sheets and on master pages. In other words, even if you don't use a particular style sheet or master page anywhere in your document, you get notified.

Kerning information. If you've spent a lot of time making kerning tables within QuarkXPress's Kern/Track Editor, you might want to save the hassle of doing them over on another platform. I'm happy to note that you can move the kerning information from the PC to the Macintosh (or vice versa) by exporting the information as a text file (click the Export button in the Edit Kerning dialog box) and importing into the other program (use the Import button in the same dialog box in the Windows version).

The only problem with this technique is that the fonts on each platform are often different, even if they're the same font from the same company—just like with the metrics (unless you're using OpenType fonts). Therefore, the kerning used on the Macintosh might not always apply precisely to the Windows font of the same name.

Transferring libraries. You can't transfer libraries from the Mac to Windows or from Windows to the Mac. That's just the way it goes. I used to tell people about a great tip that let you work around this limitation, but it turns out that it only worked in earlier versions of QuarkXPress. Let me know if you find any good solution for this painful restriction.

Transferring Graphics

The last (but certainly not the least) of your problems when transferring files between platforms is graphics. In fact, this is one of the least understood issues in cross-platform compatibility. The basic problem is that graphics, like fonts, are described in different formats on each of the two computer platforms.

The good news is that QuarkXPress is smart enough to do most of the translation work for you. No matter which platform you're working on, QuarkXPress can import files in either IBM or Macintosh format. It simply doesn't care whether you're on a Macintosh importing a PC format file, or on a Windows machine importing a Macintosh TIFF file. This is great, but if you're using pictures in your documents, you still might have some work ahead of you.

Graphic links. The first and most basic problem is that links to EPS and TIFF images can get messed up in the transfer—the Picture Usage dialog box shows the image as either missing or modified. You can usually remove the chance of this happening by keeping the images in the same folder as the QuarkXPress document you're opening, but even this gets a little screwy when the file resides on a file server and you access it from both Macintoshes and Windows machines.

If you send a document to the PC to work on it temporarily, the picture links to the files on the Macintosh are retained (as long as they aren't changed on the PC by clicking Update in the Usage dialog box). Similarly, links within Windows documents are retained when you move a file to the Mac and back, as long as you don't change them on the Mac. The trick is to update a picture in the Usage dialog box only if you're certain you won't be sending the QuarkXPress file back to its original location, or if you absolutely must print with current versions of artwork, regardless of the platform.

EPS screen previews. The next thing you need to be careful of is how images are transferred between the Macintosh and PC. Screen previews are handled differently on each platform. When you create an EPS on a Macintosh and you specify a Macintosh PICT preview, the screen preview is stored in what's called the file's resource fork. The problem is that resource forks don't exist on the PC, so if you move the graphic over and try to import it into QuarkXPress for Windows, you can't see the preview. In fact, without a screen preview, all you see on the screen is a gray box where the picture should be. Note that the picture still prints properly, even if you can't see it on screen.

There are two solutions to this problem: importing into Mac XPress and then transferring the document to the PC, or saving the picture as a PC EPS.

> ▶ **QuarkXPress for Macintosh.** Because QuarkXPress saves a preview image of each picture within your documents, you can bring those documents to the PC and still see the preview image on screen. The images are linked to the EPS files, so even if you move the image *and* the QuarkXPress document to the PC, you can still print properly. Even runarounds are transferred okay.

> ▶ **PC EPS files.** The second solution for the EPS screen preview problem is to give your EPS files PC previews. Adobe Illustrator, Macromedia FreeHand, Adobe Photoshop, the LaserWriter 8 driver, and a slew of other programs let you save or export a file as a PC EPS—with a TIFF preview that's saved in the data fork rather than the resource fork. Therefore, when you move it over to the PC, you can import it, screen preview and all.

File names and extensions. Just as QuarkXPress documents need the right file extensions when transferred to the PC, graphics that get transferred also need the right file names, or else XPress won't be able to recognize them as graphics. That means they'll often need to be renamed with a three-letter ".TIF", ".EPS", or ".PCT" extension (see "File Types" in Chapter 9, *Pictures*, for more information on this).

File types to avoid. Some formats to avoid: PICTs contained in Mac documents and transferred to PCs sometimes print poorly or not at all (just like on Macs!), and WMF pictures in PC documents may (similarly) not print correctly on the Mac. Sometimes EPS images from the Mac look wrong on screen after they're transferred to a PC. Often if you simply re import the picture, it'll clear up any problems (as long as the EPS file has a TIFF preview rather than a PICT preview).

And when it comes to edition files (with Publish and Subscribe), forget it. If you've subscribed to an edition file on your Mac, that link gets lost for all time as soon as the file is opened and saved by QuarkXPress for Windows. Similarly, if a Windows user has made OLE links (the Windows version of Publish and Subscribe) within a Windows document, that information will be lost when the document's opened on a Macintosh (see Chapter 9, *Pictures*).

▼ ▼

Modern Myths

I have very mixed feelings about cross-platform compatibility. On the one hand, moving documents and graphics between Macintoshes and PCs sometimes works like a charm. On the other hand, sometimes the strangest things happen and it can cause horrible nightmare scenarios (of course, right on the eve of a deadline). Although QuarkXPress is very similar on the two platforms, and tries its hardest to make cross-platform issues irrelevant, there are clearly issues that are beyond its control.

Nonetheless, because more and more people are finding themselves in that "third-culture" arena—where they are literate on two or more platforms—transferring files is becoming almost commonplace. No doubt, with a dose of experience and a patient hand, you may soon find yourself making the process more or less painless.

C

XTensions and Resources

When you set up that grill you bought for barbecuing your chicken and vegetables, it's unlikely that you're going to find all the best grilling instruments in the box. So what do you do? You drive back to the store and fill up your shopping cart with a big fork, a spatula, a baster, cleaning equipment, and so on. If you're into carpentry and you buy a table saw, you know you're also going to buy a cross-cut blade separately.

And, after you pull your copy of QuarkXPress out of its packaging, one of the first questions you should ask yourself is: "What other tools do I need to get my job done?"

As any QuarkXPress Demon knows—and as I've tried to make clear throughout the book—QuarkXPress is not an island. I don't use QuarkXPress for everything, and I don't expect you to, either. And even if you do, there are many add-on XTensions from Quark and other developers that increase your power and efficiency in making pages.

In this appendix, I briefly discuss some of the third-party tools and resources you might want to think about exploiting in order to make your life a happier place to be.

Real World QuarkXPress Web Site. In past editions of this book, I've included long lists of XTension developers, software developers, magazine publishers, users groups, and so on. I've gotten great feedback on this practice because it's often hard to know where to find these companies or their products. However, my efforts are quickly frustrated when a company moves its office, changes its phone number, or discontinues a product line.

In this edition, I'm not including this information in printed form. Rather, it's all on the book's Web site: *www.peachpit.com/blatner/*

If you want to find an XTension or product that I've mentioned in this book, you can find it at the Web site. If you're looking for an XTension that jiggles your whatchamacallit, follow the links on the Web site. If you need more information about how to expand your QuarkXPress world, you can find that on the Web site.

Utilities and software. Part of being efficient in electronic publishing, I believe, is using the right tool for the job. Don't use a pair of pliers on a hex nut; don't use a pair of scissors to prune your roses; don't use QuarkXPress when other programs do something better. I rely on dozens of utilities and other software programs to get my work done, including Adobe Photoshop, Microsoft Word, CE Software's QuicKeys, FileBuddy, Macromedia FreeHand, Adobe Illustrator, Design Science's MathType, Adobe GoLive, FontLab, BBEdit, Greg Swann's Torquemada . . . the list goes on and on.

In this appendix, I primarily talk about XTensions and information resources, but I'm not trying to minimize the importance of these other tools. You can find more information, what they are and where to get them, on my Web site, too.

XTensions

I first covered XTensions and how they can add functionally to QuarkXPress back in Chapter 2, *QuarkXPress Basics*. Throughout the book, I have mentioned several commercial vendors and their products, but there's no way I could cover them all (there are more than 300 XTension developers alone). More importantly, I haven't told you where you can get them.

Remember that Quark XTensions that worked in any previous edition of QuarkXPress do not work with version 6—they must be updated for the new version. Unfortunately, some XTension developers have shown little interest in updating some of their XTensions. Check with the developer to see if an XTension you rely on has been updated.

Quark's Freebies

There's no reason not to get—and use—the free XTensions that Quark publishes. The best way to find them is to download them from their Web site (*www.quark.com*).

Where these XTensions used to be called Bob, Son of Bob, and other Bobish names, Quark now uses slightly more conservative names, such as TypeTricks (which includes many type-related features like Make Fraction, Make Price, Word Space Tracking, and so on) and Jabberwocky (my personal favorite: it lets you fill any text box with random text). Both of these now ship with QuarkXPress 6—Quark often releases a feature as an XTension first, then builds the XTension into the next version of the software. As this book goes to press, the only free XTension for version 6 is Edit Original for the Macintosh, but I expect more to be posted on the Quark Web site soon.

More Freebies

Many XTension developers have also released free XTensions. This is great for the developer because it helps build awareness of their other products and it's great for the rest of us because we get cool tools. For example, the SortText XTension (you can dowlonad it from Durrant Software's Web site: *www.durrant.co.uk*) lets you alphabetize paragraphs. It's simple, but very helpful when you need that sort of thing. Badia Software (*www.badiaxt.com*) has several cool XTensions for free, including Vistas XTension, which gives you a palette to navigate in your document, and OpenNow XT, which is even better than Quark's own Edit Original XTension.

Go Buy a Package

You don't have to purchase XTensions in order to be happy working with QuarkXPress, but I think you may be even happier if you do. For instance, I'm a big fan of XTension bundles like A Lowly Apprentice Production's XPert Tools (*www.alap.com*). Production bundles typically offer ten or fifteen general-purpose, efficiency-oriented XTensions for a pretty reasonable price, often the kind of features that you think should be in QuarkXPress in the first place. But until these features—like the ability to link two filled text frames together, for example—appear in QuarkXPress, you might as well get them elsewhere.

Most XTensions have to be purchased one at a time. Many have very broad appeal, such as Gluon's (*www.gluon.com*) ProScale or DocuSlim. Similarly, just about every QuarkXPress user on the planet could benefit from adding Badia's FullMeasureXT to their XTensions folder.

There are hundreds of other XTensions that have a more focused appeal, too. KyTek's AutoPage (*www.kytek.com*) is brilliant at laying out whole books based on rules like you'd find in the textbook industry; A Lowly Apprentice

Production's ImagePort lets you import layered Photoshop format images directly into XPress and their ShadowCaster is tops for making drop shadows on the fly; Em Software's Xdata (*www.emsoftware.com*) makes it easy to get information from a database or spreadsheet into QuarkXPress, formatted and ready to fly. Some XTensions are only available for Macintosh or the Windows platform, others are available on both.

Where to Find and Buy XTensions

Now you know there are XTensions out there . . . but how do you find them? While you can often buy XTensions directly from the developer, it's usually easier to use one of several companies that specialize in distributing XTensions. Here are two of the larger distributors.

▶ **THE POWER XCHANGE.** The Power XChange sells plug-ins and XTensions for all kinds of programs, including XPress and Acrobat. The Power XChange is a combination of two compaies: The XChange and The World Wide Power Company. You can find them in the USA at 800-940-0600 or at 303-940-0600, or on the Web at *www.thepowerxchange.com* or *www.thepowerco.com*

▶ **XCITE AND XCHANGE.** If you live in Europe, check out XCite, which also sells XTensions and plug-ins for various program. You can find them at *www.xcite-international.com*. Similarly, you should check out the XChange UK (*www.xchangeuk.com*) and the XChange in France (*www.xchangefr.com*).

There are many other distributors in other countries, as well as mail-order companies and so on. (More links and contact information for all these companies is at the *Real World QuarkXPress* Web site.)

If you're looking for a demo version of an XTension, you can try the above distributors, but you might also search Web repositories such as Verstion Tracker (*www.versiontracker.com*).

▼ ▼

Published Resources

I have a love-hate relationship with computer magazines. On the one hand, I love getting magazines such as *Step-By-Step Electronic Design*, *Publish*, *Macworld*, and *Design Graphics*. On the other hand, the stacks of publications in my office are becoming life-threateningly high. Nonetheless, there is a lot of information about publishing in QuarkXPress (and publishing in general) in these magazines.

One solution to the paper problem is Jay Nelson's *Design Tools Monthly*. Each month he combs all the rags for great publishing-related news and tips, and then presents it to you in a short newsletter. It's much more expensive than the magazine subscriptions themselves, but it sure is cheaper than the time it takes to read those magazines (plus, you get a cool disk of goodies each month). You can find DTM in the USA at 303-543-8400, or on the Web at *www.design-tools.com*.

World Wide Web. As much information as there is in print, there's exponentially more on the Web. While I provide a number of links on the *Real World QuarkXPress* Web site, there are a couple of places you should know about immediately.

▶ Quark's site at *www.quark.com* is full of great information. Every XPress user should check in here at least once a month to see what's new.

▶ One of the better QuarkXPress-related sites on the Internet is *www.xpressobar.com*. It's certainly worth exploring, and as I said earlier, it has a great compendium of software you can download.

Get it While it's Hot

It's so easy to just launch QuarkXPress and start using it that I find it's hard to stop and think about how life could be made easier with the addition of some other tools or information. Of course, if you work by the hour, then it's a benefit to your bank account for you just to keep your blinders on and be as inefficient as possible. For the rest of us, it's worth it to take the time now to save much more time down the road.

Enjoy!

D

SCRIPTING

I don't know why, but some people just like doing things the hard way. Like those people who insist on doing long division on the back of an envelope rather than using a calculator. Or like folks who scroll around their documents using the scroll bars instead of using the grabber hand. Yes, it's weird, but they seem happy enough; so why bother them by telling them there's an easier way to do it?

Well, I don't know about you, but it drives me crazy doing repetitive tasks in QuarkXPress. Stepping through a document to make a tiny formatting change to one little character on each page . . . searching for all the paragraphs in my 100-page story that start with a numeral and applying the proper style sheet to them . . . changing the border around every picture in my document one at a time . . . Each of these just seemed like another one of those monotonous, robotic tasks that I do every day when working on my computer.

I'm here to tell you that the days of repetitive monotony, the weeks of dull mechanical routines, the months of dreary, unchanging keystrokes are over! There are two things that can alleviate all these woes: macros and scripting.

Macintosh only. Before I get started, there's one other thing you need to know: Scripting in QuarkXPress is Macintosh-only. I feel pretty confident that Quark will update XPress for Windows to be scriptable as quickly as they can. Until then, if you only use Windows, you won't be able to script. However, you will be able to use macros if you buy a separate macro utility.

Macros Versus Scripting

While some folks use the terms "macro" and "script" interchangeably, they're very different critters. Let's take a quick look at how macros and scripting are similar and different.

Macros. Let's just get one thing perfectly clear: If you don't own and use a copy of CE Software's QuicKeys, you're just not being efficient in your work. QuicKeys (there are versions for both the Macintosh and Windows) lets you create macros to tell QuarkXPress—and any other program or utility you use, including the Finder—what to do. A macro can be an action or sequence of actions. It can be triggered by a keystroke, by the time of day, or by selecting it from a menu.

I have lots of QuicKey macros on my computer. To start QuarkXPress, I just press Control-Shift-Q. To create a new text box, put it six picas from the top of the page, and automatically jump into the measurement palette, I can press Control-Option-N. To clone an object (Step and Repeat with zero offsets), I like Command/Ctrl-=. All of these work on my machine because I've made QuicKeys macros.

Any menu item you can select, any key you can press, any printer or server you can choose on the network, any event you can cause to happen can be assigned a macro keystroke or be built in to a sequence macro. They're incredibly helpful and can speed up work enormously because they're easy to create and use.

While I like QuicKeys, there are several other utilities that do the same or similar things, including Westcode's OneClick for the Macintosh and Wilson WindowWare's WinBatch for Windows.

Scripting. There are two basic differences between macros and scripts. First, macros are entirely dependent on the user interface—the menus, dialog boxes, keyboard shortcuts, and so on. Scripts, however, let you sneak in the back door of the program and control it from behind the scenes, almost like a puppeteer pulling the strings of a marionette—and there are things you can do behind the scenes for which there is no interface in XPress (like locking guides). Second, scripts have flow control. Flow control is a programming term that means you can set up decision trees and loops, like "keep doing this until such-and-such happens"; plus, scripts often contain variables. You can do much more complex and interesting things with scripting than you can with simple macros.

When people talk about scripting, they're usually talking about either program-specific scripting, or AppleEvents. AppleEvents is a Macintosh feature that lets programs communicate with and control one another.

The rest of this appendix is going to focus on AppleEvents-based scripts and scripting, including a description of a bunch of scripts that come with QuarkXPress and from the *Real World QuarkXPress* Web site.

Editing and Running AppleScripts

The Macintosh version of QuarkXPress 6 ships with an XTension called Script (it's in the XTensions folder) that not only allows XPress to be scriptable, but also adds a Scripts menu to the menu bar (see Figure D-1). You can add or remove the scripts listed in this menu by moving files in and out of the Script folder, which you should be able to find in the QuarkXPress folder on your hard drive.

The Scripts menu lets you run scripts, but it won't let you write or edit them. For that, you need to use an application such as Script Editor (for AppleScript scripts), UserLand Frontier (for UserTalk or Frontier scripts), or CE Software's QuicKeys. I think the best place to start is Apple's free Script Editor that ships on all Macintosh systems. In OS X, it's in the AppleScript folder, inside the Applications folder.

Note that scripts that are in the Scripts menu should be *compiled*, but not self-running applications. The difference has to do with how they're saved in Script Editor's Save As dialog box.

▼ ▼

Tip: Hard-core Scripting. If you really get into scripting, you will find yourself spending a lot of time writing or debugging scripts and you will want to take a look at some of the other scripting applications on the market. For instance, Late Night Software's Script Debugger and Main Event's Scripter are full-featured tools that help you write and debug scripts, and are better than

Figure D-1
The Scripts menu

the rather spartan (but free) Script Editor. UserLand Frontier is also a very powerful script editor, though it primarily uses its own scripting language rather than AppleScript.

Also, the more complicated a script, the more it requires a way for the user to interact with it—buttons, text fields, dialog boxes, popup menus, and so on. If you're interested in building user interfaces for your scripts, take a look at Apple's own AppleScript Studio or DTI's FaceSpan.

▼ ▼

Tip: Hiring a Scripter. Even though scripting is extremely powerful, it's just a fact of life that most people don't want to learn the ins and outs of scripting. Fortunately, there are a number of scripters for hire. In case you're looking for such a beast, I've compiled a small list of freelance scripting consultants—including Ray Robertson of Scripting Matters and the inimitable Shane Stanley—on the *Real World QuarkXPress* Web site.

▼ ▼

Getting Scripting Information

It's nearly impossible to learn how to script QuarkXPress without extra documentation. Fortunately, Quark ships some information about AppleEvent scripting along with the Macintosh version of QuarkXPress, but it's not immediately obvious. It's an Acrobat PDF file called Apple Events Scripting, hidden inside the Apple Events folder, which is hidden inside the Document folder which is, in turn, inside the QuarkXPress folder. (Do these lists ever remind you of Leviticus, in which Izzy begat Herbie, and Herbie begat Pearl, and Pearl begat . . . ?)

Books. Fortunately, since the last edition of this book, several good books have been published on AppleScripting. Most are somewhat general, such as *Danny Goodman's Guide to AppleScript* and the *AppleScript for Applications Visual QuickStart Guide*. Those are great, but if you're going to script QuarkXPress, you owe it to yourself to get a copy of *AppleScripting QuarkXPress* by Shirley Hopkins; it's very good and comes with a CD-ROM with lots of example scripts.

Examples. The best way to learn how to script QuarkXPress is by first looking at and deconstructing other people's scripts. If you can find a script that already does what you want, then use it. If the script isn't quite right, then edit it to make it work for you. Quark has provided a number of scripts in the Scripts folder, inside the QuarkXPress folder. You can open these in Script Editor to see how they work or edit them to suit you.

Scripting Dictionary. All scriptable applications have a built-in scripting dictionary that outlines the various things that can be scripted in that program. One way to see this information is by choosing Open Dictionary in the File menu of the Script Editor utility. The dictionary is often most helpful as a quick reference when your books or documentation isn't around.

The Web. The World Wide Web is, of course, one of the best sources for AppleScript information. There are a number of great sites out there that offer both tutorials on scripting and scripts that you can download, use, and learn from. The best place to start, of course, is Apple's own scripting site: *http://www.apple.com/applescript*. I have also included scripting links on the *Real World QuarkXPress* Web site.

Training. Several organizations also provide training in automating your workflow using AppleScript. Once again, see the Web page for links.

Writing a Script

Although scripting is programming, it's much easier to pick up than most other programming languages because it uses "natural language" commands. Nevertheless, it still may take you a while to start to understand the concepts. I know it's a cop-out, but there's neither time nor space truly to teach you how to program here.

What I *can* do here is give you a pretty solid foundation on which to build your scripting knowledge. Then you can go off, look through the scripts I've included in this appendix and on the Web, and try your own.

The main concepts you've got to understand are the object model, hierarchies, properties, and events.

The Object Model

Let's get one thing clear: The object model is not a feminist theory regarding the objectification of fashion models in magazines. Rather, the object model describes the way AppleEvent scripting works. That is, in order to "get" scripting, you have to think in terms of the object model.

The object model says that everything is an object that you can "talk to." For example, an object might be a text box, or a word, or a picture, or a whole document. Objects can (and usually do) contain other objects; for instance, a page can contain text boxes, which can contain paragraphs, which can contain words.

There are currently over four dozen kinds of objects in QuarkXPress. Each of these can be controlled or queried through basic scripting commands. Although some objects are intuitively similar to items you know in the program, others are a little more obscure. For example, while text boxes and words are clear and you can easily get a handle on what they are, Master Document and Delimit Table may be confusing at first (see "Difficult Objects," below).

▼ ▼

Tip: Naming Objects. One of the coolest things about scripting XPress is that you can name most objects. You can always identify *text box 1* (the top-most text box on the page) or *line box 3*, but it's much easier to choose and manipulate a text box named "Lead story" or a line box called "VerticalLine." For example, you can type `set the name of text box 1 to "My Text Box"`. The more complicated your script, the more important it is to name your objects.

▼ ▼

Hierarchies, Elements, and Containers

You can't understand the object model and scripting without understanding hierarchies, elements, and containers. As I said earlier, most objects in QuarkXPress contain other objects; for example, a paragraph contains words, which contain characters.

Hierarchies only get complicated when you can't remember what contains what (see Figure D-2). That's when you really need to rely on the documentation and the dictionary.

In working with hierarchies, two terms are helpful to keep in mind: elements and containers. An element is an object that is contained inside another object. A text box is an element of a page, for instance. A container is simply an object that has elements. The QuarkXPress application is a container for windows, documents, and so on.

Properties

Every object in QuarkXPress has properties that you can look at and—usually—change. A property is a characteristic of an object. For example, picture boxes have the properties of background color, rotation, placement on the page (called *bounds*), and many more.

Difficult Objects

As I noted earlier, some objects in QuarkXPress are pretty confusing if you haven't seen them before. Objects such as document and picture box are pretty simple, so I'm just going to focus on the objects in QuarkXPress that may raise your eyebrow.

Application. The highest object in the hierarchy is Application. You can think of the QuarkXPress application as being the program with or without a document open; changes made here are application-wide and affect any document that is open or is created from then on. Note that if you've renamed your copy of QuarkXPress, then the application's name might be different for you.

Window. When I first saw the Window object, I thought it was the same as Document. However, that's not the case. Documents are only open documents, but you can control all the windows in QuarkXPress. That includes the palettes and dialog boxes. You can't do a lot to them, but you might want to write a script that brings all the palettes up and then sets their sizes and positions on the screen.

Default document. The default document contains all the preferences and settings for the New dialog box, the H&Js, colors, and style sheets—whether a document is open or closed. For example, with no document open, you can set

Figure D-2

Much of the AppleScript
hierarchy in QuarkXPress

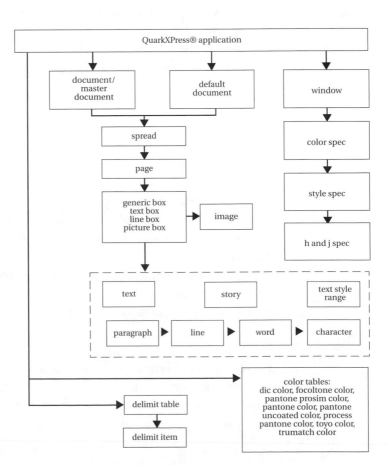

the default document's settings; when you create a new document, it will be configured in that way.

Spread. Spreads are pretty obvious, but here's an important point you should know: Items on the pasteboard fall in the domain of the spread, but not the page. So if you change all the text boxes in a spread to red, then the text boxes on the pasteboard get changed, too. If you do it to all the objects on a page, only the ones that are touching the page get changed.

Also note that a spread includes all the pages that are next to each other. So you can have a one-, two-, three-, or more page spread.

Master document. The master document is the object that contains the master pages. What does that mean? Dave Shaver, one of the engineers at Quark who worked on scripting, describes the master document as being a "shadow" of the document. You can talk to its light side (the actual document pages), or you can talk to its dark side (the master pages).

For example, if you want to change something on a master page, you need to address a page or spread in the master document. You can't change a master page from within the document itself. Of course, `master document 1` and `document 1` are just different parts of the same document. Note that if you're going to change something throughout a document, it's best to change it on the master document pages first, then, if necessary, on the document pages.

Color spec. There are no color objects in QuarkXPress, only color specs (or color spec objects, to be precise). Color specs don't contain anything, but have various properties. Just to confuse you, the property of an object is called color, but the color itself is a color spec. For instance, you can say `set color of text box 1 to "Red"` because you're setting a property of a box. However, if you want to change the values of "Red" then you'll need to address it as a color spec of the document, like: `set the color type of color spec "Red" to CMYK type`.

There are several other "specs" like this in XPress. For instance, to edit or create a style sheet, you have to talk to a style spec (like `make new style spec at end`) and to edit an H&J setting you have to talk to an object called an h and j spec.

Horizontal and vertical guide. You can create and manipulate ruler guides through scripts by working with horizontal and vertical guides. In fact, you can even do things to guides that you can't do in the program itself, such as make them undeletable or immobile.

Line. Don't get fooled: a line is not a rule. That is, the line object is a line of text, not a graphic on the page. The line extends from one margin to another in a column of text.

Line box. For some obscure reason which I haven't figured out yet, lines (graphic rules) are considered "line boxes." I suppose that makes it all consistent under the hood, but it can kind of screw you up if you're not careful.

Image. Even though each picture box can contain only one image, you still have to type `image 1`. For instance, you can import a picture into a picture box by setting the image to a file on disk. For example: `set image 1 to alias "myharddisk:picture1"`.

Generic box. A generic box is any page item in QuarkXPress, whether a picture box, a text box, or a rule (see "Line box," above). This can be helpful, especially when you're telling a whole bunch of items to do the same thing. Note that generic boxes take the lowest common denominator properties of all objects. For instance, line boxes don't have a bounds property, so neither do generic boxes.

Story. A story is, as you may have guessed, all the text in a chain of boxes. Each text box has only one story (but, of course, a story can go through many text boxes). The nice thing about stories is that you can find and change things in them really quickly (much faster than if you specify changes by word), for instance `set the font of every word of story 1 of text box 1 where it is "Moose" to "Helvetica"`.

Text style range. Most people who use QuarkXPress don't think in terms of ranges of text. However, there are times when you want to select a block of text that contains all the characters with the same text formatting. This block is called a text style range. Note that the "same formatting" includes color, font, style, kerning, tracking, and so on. As soon as the style changes in any way, QuarkXPress breaks the text down into another style range.

For example, if you set the color of every word whose color is "Red" to "Blue," it won't catch the words whose first three characters happen to be green (because QuarkXPress only looks at the first character of a word when assessing color). However, if you set all the text style ranges whose color is "Red" to "Blue" then, all the red characters change.

Events

The way you alter an object is by sending QuarkXPress an "event," which is AppleEvents-ese for a command. If you want to set the tint of a line on page four, you need to send an event. In AppleScript format, the event would be a "set" command (such as `set shade of line box 1 of page 4 to 30`). Events are relatively simple, and there aren't that many of them, but there are enough so that I can't really discuss them here. My suggestion is that you pick them up as you go along by looking at other scripts and seeing how they work.

▼ ▼

Tip: Scripting Web Documents. I've been searching high and low and I've come to the sad conclusion that—at least at the time of this writing—not one of QuarkXPress's Web features is scriptable. No hyperlinks, no rollovers, no menus, no exporting HTML. It's like the engineers just plain forgot about those features. So until Quark gets their act together, you'll have to just focus on print layouts.

▼ ▼

Looking at a Script

The next step in learning how to script with QuarkXPress is to look at a few actual, real, live AppleScripts and see how they work.

Add a Dingbat

Many magazines and newsletters end every story with a little dingbat character. However it can take a lot of time going through every story in a document just to add a single character. This script does it for you.

```
tell document 1 of application "QuarkXPress"
  --this script adds a dingbat character
  make character at end of every story with properties ¬
    {contents:"n",font:"Zapf Dingbats", size:11}
end tell
```

If you've never programmed before, looking at that script is probably somewhat unnerving. But I assure you that scripting is not as difficult as it looks, especially in the AppleScript language.

There are two conventions that you should be aware of. First, all comments in this script have two hyphens before them. AppleScript just ignores those lines (they're included to help scripters remember what is being done). Second, the character that looks like a sideways "L" is a line-break character (its printable character is made by pressing Option-L in most PostScript fonts, or by pressing Option-Return in the Script Editor). You only have to use one of these if you break a single line of code into two or more lines (it's especially helpful in a book format like this).

Opening and closing. You always need to specify in the script what application you're talking to with the `tell application` command. In this case, "QuarkXPress" is the way that my copy of QuarkXPress is named. If you change the name of the program without changing the name in the code, AppleScript won't be able to find it.

When you're done talking to an object (in this case the application itself), you have to use an `end tell` command. Every `tell` must be followed by an `end tell`, just like a closing parenthesis or a closing quotation mark in a sentence.

In this script, I'm actually being more specific, and the tell command says that I'm talking to the front-most document that is currently open in XPress.

Make character. The meat of the script is the make character command, which simply tells XPress to add an 11-point "n" character in the Zapf Dingbats font as the last character of every story in the document. Every story means *every* story, even empty text boxes! You have to be careful with the "every" command, because it is very powerful.

Change to Superior

What if one of your esteemed colleagues decides to create superscript characters using a 3-point baseline shift rather than the proper Superior or Superscript styles? This would be a hassle to change because you can't search for characters with baseline shift. Here's a quick script that does the search for you.

```
tell application "QuarkXPress"
   activate
   if not (exists document 1) then return
   tell document 1
      try
         tell every story
         set the properties of (every character ¬
            whose base shift is "3 pt") to ¬
            {base shift:"0 pt", style:{on styles:superior}}
         end tell
      on error
         beep
         display dialog ¬
         "There are no letters with a Baseline Shift of 3." ¬
         buttons {"Cancel"} default button 1
      end try
   end tell
end tell
```

There are several weird things going on here. First, the activate command at the beginning of the script tells QuarkXPress to come to the front of all other applications. Also, note the error-handling using *try* and *if/then*. The first `if` statement checks to make sure there is at least one document open. If there is no "document 1" then it stops the script. Otherwise, you'd get an error when you tried to "talk" to document 1. The try statement says "try to do the following and if there's an error at any time, then jump to the `on error` statement."

When applying text styles, there are "on styles" and "off styles". In this case, I'm turning on the Superior style.

If there is an error, the script makes a dialog box appear with an error message. You can make the error say anything you want. In this case, there is only one button in the dialog box: Cancel. You can make more complex dialog boxes, too, with a little extra code.

Stuff You Should Know About

Now, before you go off half-cocked with scripting ideas, let me throw a few "things you should know about" at you. This list is going to get bigger and bigger as we all learn more about scripting.

Not completed yet. Unfortunately, not everything in XPress is scriptable. As I said earlier, you can't script the Web features yet. Also, you can't yet script libraries, groups of objects, auxiliary dictionaries, hyphenation exceptions, box creation defaults, color pair trapping, blends, anchored boxes, and sections.

More annoying, many of the features that are scriptable don't work properly yet—things that worked in earlier versions are broken in this version. Granted, XPress 6's scripting is in better shape than XPress 5, but I believe that Quark will really only clean up their act and make everything scriptable again if enough of us yell at them and tell them that this is important.

Interrupting and canceling. You can always interrupt a script while it's running by pressing Command-period. Note that moving the mouse or typing on the keyboard usually won't do anything, so don't get paranoid about it. Also, remember that you can't Undo a script after it's run, so be careful and make backups.

Page names. Pages are named so you can quickly access them even if you've set sections with different pages numbers. If you want to do something to the fourth page, you can script page 4; however, if your numbering system is in roman numerals, you can also call it page "iv". The name of the page (in quotation marks) is whatever is in the lower-left corner of the document window in QuarkXPress. This goes for master pages within the master document, too.

Variables. Watch out for what variables you specify within your scripts. Many of the words are already taken by QuarkXPress itself. In fact, when using AppleScript, I like to set the formatting for different identifiers so that when I compile or run the script, I can quickly see what is a variable, what is an object, what is an event, and so on. You do this by selecting AppleScript Formatting from the Edit menu in the Script Editor.

Hidden text. You may notice while browsing through the scripting docs that you can make text "hidden." Even though it's tempting, resist it. First of all, it doesn't really do anything to the text. Secondly, hidden text is complicated enough so that it should be kept out of scripting and left to XTension developers (who do use it occasionally).

One more thing about hidden text. There are times that you might search and replace text throughout a story and you might accidentally change some text that was hidden by QuarkXPress or an XTension. For example, anchored picture boxes have hidden text around them, and if you screw it up accidentally, weird things can happen. I can't say what you should and shouldn't do, but it's something to watch out for.

The Future of Scripts

Clearly, AppleEvent scripting gives you extremely powerful control over your environment in QuarkXPress (and other programs). As more people learn about it, I'm expecting that I'll hear of some amazing applications online and in the press. I recently sat next to a publisher of a magazine who wanted to start putting stuff online. His problem was that he had no good way of automating the process from a database to QuarkXPress to output (like Acrobat). As soon as I started talking about scripting, his eyes lit up. That's one man out of thousands who wants to hire a scripter. Any takers?

E

XML Tools

Take this test to determine whether you should read this appendix. Rate your true feelings about style sheets between one ("I don't even know what they are") and ten ("I am totally in love with style sheets and I scream epithets at my colleagues when they don't use them properly"). If you score five or less, go back and read Chapter 7, *Copy Flow*, until you appreciate style sheets more. If you rate above five, you're on the right track. If your feelings tend toward 11, then read this chapter.

Before I get into the details of what XML is, let me explain why your feelings about style sheets will determine your success with XML. First, it's almost impossible to be efficient with XML if you haven't been somewhat religious about using style sheets in your documents. In fact, documents that don't really require style sheets (like ads and one-page flyers) are totally inappropriate for XML anyway. XML is all about magazines, newspapers, books, and other documents that have the same kinds of elements week after week, month after month, or file after file.

Second, it takes a certain kind of person to make both style sheets and XML work properly. Someone who enjoys intricate details, problem-solving, and precision. Someone who prefers databases over design and production over prettiness.

I'm not saying that designers shouldn't pay attention to this stuff; they are an important part of the process. But they're going to have to work with a production person who really understands XML and who can lay the groundwork for these kinds of documents. The more designers can speak the language of XML, the better the communication will be, and the more successful the undertaking will prove.

Theory and practice. While I will discuss the basics of making and handling XML files in this appendix, I won't get into the nitty-gritty details of how the software works for two reasons. First, the XML XTensions that shipped with QuarkXPress 6.0 are still somewhat crude at the time of this writing, and some things that should work simply don't.

Second, and perhaps more important, many (perhaps most) people who want to get into an XML workflow with XPress won't be using the XML tools that ship with the program. For instance, today most companies that are creating XML from their QuarkXPress documents use a third-party system, such as Apropos's RoustaboutXT (*www.attd.com*), Noonetime's Xtract and Constellation (*www.noonetime.com*), Easypress's Atomik (*www.easypress.com*), or North Atlantic Publishing Systems's NTS (*www.napsys.com*).

These systems typically offer more (or different) control than the technology that comes with XPress. For instance, Quark's avenue.quark XTension can export XML files, but it can't currently handle some special characters in your text (like dingbats, math symbols, and so on), which RoustaboutXT can. On the other hand, where avenue.quark is designed to export a number of stories from a document at the same time (even if they're not linked together), RoustaboutXT can only export a single story at a time.

However, programs like Atomik, NTS, and Xtract are designed for automating the XML export process significantly more than avenue.quark allows. If you're trying to export the past five years of your magazine articles in XML format, you're going to want as much automation and batch processing as possible.

So, while some folks will be using XPress's tools, it doesn't make sense to really focus on them. Instead, it's more important to look at why XML is important and what sorts of things you need to know in order to start using XML workflows.

▼ ▼

Tip: Check Out the Docs. Whether or not you're using the XTensions that come with QuarkXPress, if you're interested in learning more about XML, you should read through the "Guide to avenue.quark" that comes with

QuarkXPress (it's an Acrobat PDF file and it was installed in a folder called Documents, inside your QuarkXPress folder). While much of what it talks about overlaps what I discuss here in this appendix, it's a good "next step" after reading this.

▼ ▼

Separating Content and Form

The basic concept of XML (eXtensible Markup Language) is that your content (the words and pictures that make up your documents) and the form that content takes should be two separate things.

For example, let's say you have a magazine article written in Microsoft Word and four different QuarkXPress documents. You could use Get Text to pour the article into all four templates to get four very different looks (perhaps one in color, one in black and white, one Web document, and one for print). If you were careful in your use of style sheets (again, see Chapter 7, *Copy Flow*), then the text would automatically be formatted properly (and differently) for each template.

In this simple example, the Word document is the content and each XPress template is a form the article can take. XML takes this idea even further, letting you do things that you can't do with proprietary formats like Microsoft Word. If your article were in XML format, you could not only flow it into several different layouts (in XPress and even in other programs, like Adobe InDesign), you could even create an "abstract" version for display on a cell-phone screen. Or you could archive it in a database, transform it automatically into HTML and put it on the Web, or convert it to Braille for the blind.

If you had a thousand articles in XML format, you could quickly process them to pull out just the titles and bylines. In fact, XML makes no sense for a single short article, but makes lots of sense when dealing with a large amount of data, many different documents, or many different looks for the same document.

XML is simply a way to describe your content so that it can do all these things relatively quickly. No wonder so many companies around the world want to start using XML.

The call from above. So what do you do when your boss storms in and says, "The vice-president of executive whims has declared that we're going to an all-XML workflow"? First, take a deep breath. Then think about the following issues.

▶ Using XML is a long-term, major decision. It requires a *lot* of planning. I highly recommend that you work with a company that specializes in XML in order to choose or create a DTD and workflow (I'll explain DTDs later in this appendix).

▶ It is possible for people who don't know anything about XML to import and export XML from QuarkXPress, but not without a sophisticated third-party system and careful planning behind the scenes. The primary XML XTension that ships with XPress, avenue.quark, doesn't give you all the tools you need to create XML files, so there's no way to just jump in.

▶ The underlying concepts of QuarkXPress and XML are at odds in many ways. While XPress is all about formatting content (text and graphics) and putting it anywhere you want on a page, XML is all about sticking to a strictly-defined linear structure. QuarkXPress is like techno-grunge music; XML is like a Bach cantata. Where making a page in QuarkXPress is like drawing with crayons, XML is the equivalent of filling out your tax forms—one lets you draw outside the lines of the coloring book, the other forces you to do it right, or else.

▶ There are lots of things you can do in XPress that are hard (or impossible) to export into XML. Notoriously difficult are exporting tables, special characters (math symbols, dingbats, bullets, and so on), lists, and anything that you might consider content but isn't (like dividing lines or text converted to outlines).

▶ XML is all about breaking down your documents into logical components, but the logic is often complex. In an XPress document, the "title" style sheet will always look the same. However, it's not unreasonable for "title" to mean very different things within the same XML document, depending on whether it falls after a tag called <book>, one called <heading1> or one called <real_estate_insurance>. (I'll cover tags and other XML terminology in the next section.)

▶ If you can't get your production folks to use style sheets, you might as well give up now.

▶ A lot of systems on the market focus more on getting XML out of XPress than getting it back in again. If you're going to use a third-party program, make sure you ask the vendors about XML Import.

If your boss still wants to work with XML after you discuss these issues (and you've waited a week to see if the V.P. will have spontaneously changed his or her mind), then you'd better keep reading and see how all this XML stuff works.

▼ ▼

XML Basics

In HTML (HyperText Markup Language), you can make a paragraph look like a heading by putting <H1> at the beginning and </H1> after it. Adding this label is called *tagging* the paragraph with the <H1> ("heading 1") tag. Similarly, you can make a word bold by tagging it with <B> (and </B>, which ends the tag). Most HTML tags or codes tell a Web browser what your content should look like.

XML (Extensible Markup Language, which is a descendent of SGML, the Standard Generalized Markup Language) is a way of applying *any* kind of tag to your content—you can even make up your own bizarre tags. Most XML documents focus entirely on what your content is—what it means—rather than what it should look like. For instance, your XML might include tags like <author>, <title>, and <publisher> (yes, tags are always surrounded by angle brackets). Later, you can use an XML processing program to convert these tags into something else by *mapping* tags to HTML tags, or XPress Tags, or some other kind of formatting. (No, this kind of processor utility isn't included.)

It's important to emphasize that XML tags may have nothing to do with how something will get formatted. For instance, you might tag all the names of companies in your document with an <inc> tag, whether they show up in a heading or the middle of a paragraph. This way you could later use an XML-aware database to search for all the companies mentioned in your document.

Note that XML, also like HTML, is always written as plain text files, so you can open and edit them in any text editor like BBEdit or Windows Notepad.

Syntax and Structure

XML is extremely flexible, but it also requires a strict syntax. For instance, every tag must have a closing tag (that's the one with the slash in it), and multiple tags must be fully nested. For instance, you might find this in an XML file: <software><layoutapps>QuarkXPress</layoutapps></software>. In this case, the <layoutapps> tag is *nested* inside the <software> tag, and you must close it before you close the <software> tag.

As you can see, it's pretty easy to write XML. What's difficult is writing XML in a form that can later be read and understood by an XML processor (software that can read the XML and do something with it, like map the tags to HTML properly). In order for this to happen, your XML must conform to a set of rules, called a DTD (Document Type Definition).

A DTD (please don't call it a DDT; that's an insecticide) defines both the names of the tags and how the file will be structured. For instance, the DTD for this book might define the following tags and structure.

- ▶ <paragraph>

- ▶ <heading1>

- ▶ <heading2>

- ▶ <heading3>

- ▶ <chapter_title>

- ▶ <chapter>, which must include a <chapter_title> followed by a collection of one or more chunks of text tagged with <paragraph>, <heading1>, <heading2>, and <heading3> (not necessarily in that order)

- ▶ <book>, which must include one or more <chapter> tags

Of course, the actual structure of this book is more complex than that (it also includes illustrations, lists, tips, and so on), but it's good to start simple. If you were trying to export XML from a book that was already laid out in XPress, you might use the already-defined style sheets to determine the XML tags for paragraphs, headings, and so on. More on that later in this appendix.

Choosing a DTD. The DTD is an extremely important part of the XML workflow, but it's a complex document that takes time and planning to create. While you can use a custom DTD for your documents, there are a number of industry-standard DTDs which might work for you. The best reason to use an already-defined DTD (besides not having to pay someone to write a new one) is that if two companies write to the same DTD, they can exchange data.

For instance, if two scientific journals use the same DTD, they can be assured that their content will be transportable. If a database company wants to pay you for your journal's content, it'll be much easier (and cheaper) for everyone if the content is already in a form that the database company can understand. You can find a number of industry-standard DTDs at *www.xml.org* (this, and other links, are available on the *Real World QuarkXPress* Web site, too).

Well-formed versus valid XML. Any properly-tagged XML document can be called *well-formed*. However, only XML documents that conform to the strict rules of a given DTD can be called *valid*. There are utilities that can confirm whether an XML file is well-formed, and others that can compare an XML file with a DTD to see if it's truly valid.

By the way, a DTD only defines the form of an XML file, not the meaning of the tags. That means you could have a valid XML file that has the wrong kinds of data in it—like putting someone's name inside a tag that is reserved for a credit card number. Describing and confirming *meaning* is a much more difficult challenge. XML *schemas* can help some by providing information about what kind of data should be allowed for a piece of tagged data (see *www.schema.net*).

How to Read a DTD

In order to really understand XML, it helps to be able to read a DTD. The DTD may be in its own separate file, but it's often included at the top of an XML file (especially XML files exported from QuarkXPress). Again, this information is all plain text, so you can see it in any text editor. (Special thanks to Deborah Lapeyre of Mulberry Technologies for her help with this appendix.)

DTDs have four basic parts (called declarations): document type, comments, elements, and attributes. There are others (like entities, notations, and processing instructions), but I don't need to get into those details here.

Document type. The DOCTYPE declaration is always at the top of the DTD and it tells you the name of the top level element. It then either points to an external DTD file or includes the definition of the DTD inside square brackets: [and].

Element. Each tag you can use must be defined by an element declaration which first gives the name of the element and then (in parentheses) describes what makes up this element. For example:

```
<!ELEMENT  firstname (#PCDATA) >
```

This declares a tag called <firstname> which must consist of "Parsed Character DATA," which is basically text (anything that can be typed). Here's another example:

```
<!ELEMENT  author (surname, firstname?) >
```

This declares a tag called <author> which consists of two other elements: surname and firstname.

In an Element declaration, every little symbol means something. Here, the question mark after *firstname* means that this element is optional, and the comma between the "child" element names means that if there is a <firstname> tag, it must follow the surname.

If you replace the comma with a vertical bar (surname|firstname), it would mean the author tag could include either <firstname> *or* <surname>. See Table E-1 for information on what the various codes mean. These codes can also be placed outside parentheses, too, like this:

```
<!ELEMENT  authors (firstname, surname)+ >
```

In this example, the <authors> tag may include one or more groups of text that is tagged with <firstname> and followed by <surname>.

▼ ▼

Tip: Everything is Case-Sensitive. Note that the names of tags and attributes are case-sensitive, so a <video> tag is different than a <Video> tag. Similarly, the ELEMENT, #PCDATA, and other items that you see in all capital letters here must be typed that way. That detail has gotten more than one person in hot water.

Just to make the process even tougher, remember that in general every element and attribute name must begin with either a letter or an underscore. That means A123 is a valid name, but 123A is not. Names may then contain upper- or lower-case letters, numbers, the colon, underscore, hyphen, and period. Nothing else. No asterisks, no commas, no percent signs. Hey, I told you that XML was strict.

▼ ▼

Attribute. An attribute lists additional information that is associated with an element. For example, you might want a <book> element to have a "pub_date" attribute which never shows up in print (or on the Web, or whatever), but is useful to parse or search in a database. You will see attributes declared like this:

```
<!ATTLIST book pub_date CDATA #IMPLIED >
```

Attribute declarations are always lists that have four parts: the element name, the attribute name, the attribute type, and whether or not it's required. In the example above, the *pub_date* attribute is declared to be associated with the <book> element, the attribute is CDATA (which is sort of like #PCDATA; it just means any kind of text), and it's optional.

You can see any XML reference guide for the various sorts of attribute types. Here are the four options for the fourth "column."

▶ #REQUIRED means this attribute must be present whenever the tag appears in the XML file.

▶ #IMPLIED means the attribute is optional.

▶ #FIXED is always followed by some value (a "fifth column"); if the attribute is missing, then it's assumed to be this value, but if it is present then it must be set to this value.

▶ Some default value. If the attribute is present, it can specify any value, but if the attribute is missing, then this value is assumed.

For example, here's an element and two attributes in a list:

```
<ELEMENT clothing (#PCDATA) >
<ATTLIST clothing size    (large | small) "small"
                  model   CDATA           #REQUIRED>
```

Here, the XML tag <clothing> can specify an attribute called "size" and that attribute can equal either "large" or "small." However, if the attribute is miss-

Table E-1
DTD codes

SYMBOL	WHAT IT MEANS
+	Required, and may repeat (one or more)
?	Optional, but can't repeat (zero or one)
*	Optional, and may repeat (zero or more)
no mark	Required, and cannot repeat (exactly one)
,	"Followed by"
|	"Or"

ing from the XML document, then "small" is assumed. The second attribute, "model", can be any text and must be present.

You can specify attributes inside an XML document like this:

```
<clothing size="large"  model="FunkyChicken">
        T-shirt</clothing>
```

Comments. As you can tell, DTDs can be dense, so when people write them they add comments that are ignored by XML parsers (software that can read and process XML tags) but will remind them of what things mean when they later want to read or edit the DTD. Comments are always surrounded by these tags: <!-- and -->. Note that you cannot use double hyphens within a comment. For example, you may see a comment like this:

```
<!-- This section declares the various
elements within chapters. -->
```

In general, if a comment doesn't mean anything to you, you can ignore it.

An Example of DTD and XML

Now that you know a bit about DTDs and XML, read through the following file, which inclues a DTD followed by XML. The first line simply describes what version of XML we're using, what character set encoding we're using, and says this file is "standalone"—that is, it contains the DTD and doesn't depend on any external files.

Of course, this is a very simple example. Real world situations require more complexity, but, again, we've all got to start somewhere.

```
<?xml version="1.0" encoding="UTF-8" standalone="yes" ?>
<!DOCTYPE report [
<!ELEMENT  report    (meta, title, body)        >
<!ATTLIST  report  xmlns:HTML CDATA #FIXED
        "http://www.w3.org/TR/REC-html40"       >
<!ELEMENT  meta         (author, subject) >
<!ELEMENT  author       (surname, firstname?)>
<!ELEMENT  surname      (#PCDATA)>
<!ELEMENT  firstname    (#PCDATA)>
```

```
<!ELEMENT  subject      (#PCDATA)>
<!ELEMENT  title        (#PCDATA | inc)*>
<!ELEMENT  body         ((para | figure | blockquote)*,
                          section*)>
<!ELEMENT  para         (#PCDATA | inc)*>
<!ELEMENT  figure       (HTML:img, caption)>
<!ELEMENT  HTML:img     EMPTY>
<!ATTLIST  HTML:img  src  CDATA    #REQUIRED>
<!ELEMENT  caption      (para+)>
<!ELEMENT  blockquote   (para+, caption?)>
<!ELEMENT  section      (title, (para | figure |
                          blockquote)*)>
<!ELEMENT  inc          (#PCDATA)>
]>
<report>
<meta>
<author>
<surname>Schultz</surname>
<firstname>Howard</firstname>
</author>
<subject>Global Domination</subject>
</meta>
<title>Our Great and Grand Test</title>
<body>
<para>First body paragraph, which tells all about our plans
to take over the world by selling coffee.</para>
<para>Second body paragraph, which discusses
<inc>Superbucks</inc> and other stores. </para>
<figure><HTML:img src="beans.gif"></HTML:img>
<caption>
<para>The caption to the illustration goes here.</para>
</caption></figure>
<para>Here is the first paragraph that follows the
conclusion of a figure.  It will be followed
by a second, blank paragraph</para>
<para></para>
<blockquote>
<para>First para in a block quote </para>
<para>Second para in a block quote</para>
</blockquote>
<section>
<title>This is a section</title>
<para>1st section para</para>
<para>2nd para of this section.</para>
</section>
</body>
</report>
```

SVG: A Special Kind of XML

I need to tell you about one particular flavor of XML, called SVG (Scalable Vector Graphics). This is actually a graphic file format which is written in XML, with an industry standard DTD. The SVG format describes vector artwork—like Adobe Illustrator or Macromedia Flash files—but because it is written in XML, it is very versatile. For instance, you can put an SVG file into an XML-aware database, search for it (like "find all the color charts that include the text '1998 GNP' "), and then build a Web page dynamically based on the search.

Of course, in this case, your content is *not* separate from its form, but it's still a proper use of XML.

Because SVG also relies on CSS (Cascading Style Sheets), you can define styles that can be reused or easily changed throughout a number of graphic elements. For instance, imagine changing a single style definition in a .css file which changes the color of every red logo on your entire Web site to green or makes those logos 10 percent smaller.

SVG isn't only for the Web. And it's not just for graphics. In theory, you could export a whole QuarkXPress page in SVG, including boxes, graphics, text, and geometry (where things sit on the page). However, I say "in theory" because while the folks at Quark have built and demonstrated an XTension that exports XPress pages as SVG files, at the time of this writing they haven't released it yet. However, it wouldn't surprise me if Quark put it on their Web site before too long.

There are all kinds of amazing things you can do in SVG, but until Quark really fully supports this format, it's not worth going into too much depth here. Note, however, that Adobe Illustrator, Adobe InDesign, and a number of other programs currently do support SVG.

Quark's XML Tools

I strongly applaud Quark's movement toward supporting industry-standard file formats like XML. For many publishers, XML is like a miracle that lets them repurpose their data in a myriad of ways. In the future, this kind of repurposing will become increasingly important, as people begin to shift their ideas of page-layout programs away from "here's where it all ends up" to "this is one end out of many."

However, the XML tools that QuarkXPress 6 ships with are currently a bit problematic. In fact, given that the software has various bugs and oddities, and given that only a small percentage of QuarkXPress users will really want to take advantage of these tools, I find it somewhat mysterious that Quark's three XML XTensions are installed and activated by default. I think about 90-percent of XPress users should use the XTensions Manager to turn these off.

Nevertheless, even though these tools are in flux (as is the whole industry), it's worth taking a quick look at what these XTensions do and how they're cool in spite of their problems.

Before You Start

Although some programs let you export XML even without a DTD, QuarkXPress won't let you import or export XML without one. If you just want to start playing with these tools, you can use a DTD that is installed in the Templates folder, inside the QuarkXPress folder. This DTD is part of the XML tutorial that Quark ships. XPress can also infer a DTD from any valid XML file.

Another problem with Quark's tools is that they simply cannot be approached without a reasonable amount of training (both in XML and in the tools themselves). This is very different than any other aspect of XPress. I've long said that the best way to learn any aspect of XPress is just to play around with it—even color management can be learned this way. However, Quark's XML XTensions will drive you insane before you figure them out on your own.

A third problem is that these XTensions don't give you much room for error—when you make a mistake, you can rarely undo it. Therefore, train your fingers to save (or better, Save As) often, so you can always revert to an earlier version when something goes wrong.

avenue.quark and Other XTensions

QuarkXPress ships with three XTensions that handle XML tasks: avenue.quark, XML Import, and Item Sequence. When avenue.quark first shipped, it was extremely limited in functionality and sold separately. It quickly gained a less-than-stellar reputation and the third-party market for XML XTensions grew quickly. However, even though these XTensions are still flawed, they're much better than they were originally, and you shouldn't totally write them off.

avenue.quark. XPress's primary XML tool is avenue.quark (an XTension that editors hate to see at the beginning of a sentence because it's written in all lower-case characters). This XTension lets you tag the content in your document relatively quickly through a combination of dragging text boxes around and automatically matching your document's style sheet names to the tags specified in a DTD.

avenue.quark's basic workflow is straightforward.

1. While your document is open, select XML from the New submenu (under the File menu).

2. In the New XML dialog box, choose a file that has an embedded DTD (see Figure E-1). The files that show up here are in the Templates folder, inside the QuarkXPress folder.

3. After the XML Workspace palette opens (see Figure E-2), you can set up tagging rules that map your document's style sheets to the tags in the DTD. You do this by selecting Tagging Rules from the Edit menu (see Figure E-3).

4. Hold down the Command/Ctrl key and drag a text box on top of an element in the XML Workspace palette. XPress applies the tags to the story according to the tagging rules and shows you the result in the palette (see Figure E-4).

Figure E-1

The New XML dialog box

Figure E-2

The XML Workspace palette

Figure E-3

Tagging Rules

Figure E-4

A tagged story

5. You can preview the XML document by clicking on the XML Preview button (the one that has an icon of a little set of eyeglasses), or save the XML document to disk by clicking the Save button (the button in the corner of the palette; see Figure E-5).

That's basically it. There is a host of other features that lets you insert various XML elements, which are accessed primarily by Control-clicking (Macintosh) or right-button clicking (Windows) on the XML tree in the palette. If you need more information about these, check out the avenue.quark documentation.

Figure E-5

Saving XML to disk

Turn this on to include the DTD in the XML file.

XML Import. While most QuarkXPress users focus on how to get XML out of their documents, most XML people look at the problem from the opposite perspective: They expect that people's content will *start* as XML and that the main problem is how to import it into various templates. Quark's XML Import XTension does a pretty good job of getting XML into an XPress document, based on "placeholders" that you add to the document. Here's how you do it.

1. While a QuarkXPress document is open, open the Placeholders palette (select Show Placeholders from the Window menu).

2. Click on the first button in the Placeholders palette. This lets you select an XML or XMT (XML template) file with an embedded DTD. The DTD's tree shows up in the palette (see Figure E-6).

3. Drag various elements from the Placeholders palette into text boxes in your document. Parent elements automatically bring their child elements with them.

4. Apply formatting to the placeholders in the text box. You can double-click on a placeholder to select it and then apply whatever regular text formatting you wish. Save your file!

5. Click on the Select XML File button in the Placeholders palette to choose an XML file to import. If you have a folder full of XML files with the same DTD, click the Select XML Folder button instead and choose that folder.

6. Click the Toggle Placeholders/Content button (that's the one with the little magnifying glass icon). The placeholders are automatically replaced by the content in the XML file (see Figure E-7). If you chose a folder full of XML files, you can step through them by pressing Next and

Figure E-6

Adding placeholders
to text boxes

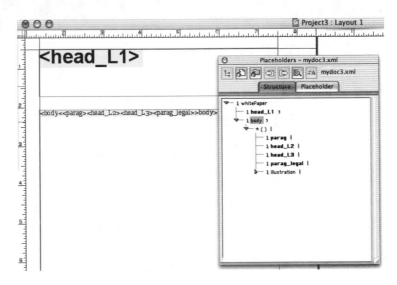

Previous XML File buttons (the ones with arrows). You can turn this button on and off to switch between the placeholders and the imported content.

7. When you're ready to import an XML file, click the last button in the palette, the Convert Placeholders to Text button. This action can't be undone; that's why you saved your file after formatting the placeholders!

At this point, the document is just like any other QuarkXPress file. Note that the imported XML doesn't retain any of its tags, so you can't easily turn around and export it to XML again.

I have to be honest and say that I've had a lot of problems with the XML Import XTension, primarily when it comes to formatting the placeholders. The steps for applying styles to placeholders that Quark insists will work simply don't for me, making this procedure less than useful. Sigh. With luck, this will get worked out soon.

Item Sequence. It's a hassle to drag one text box into the XML Workspace palette at a time, and often people don't have all the parts of a story in a single text box anyway. Enter the Sequences palette! You can open this palette by selecting Show Sequences from the Window menu (see Figure E-8).

1. To create a new sequence, click on the New Sequence button (that's the first one on the left).

2. Now select a text or picture box and click the Add Item button (that's the second button). This box is added to the current sequence in the palette. Repeat this until the sequence includes all the boxes you want to be tagged with XML.

Figure E-7

Importing XML in place of the placeholders

3. You can change the name of any item in the sequence (or the sequence itself) by selecting it and clicking the Edit Name button (that's the third one). If you want to change the order of items in the sequence, just select it and use the Up and Down buttons in the palette.

4. When you're ready to tag the content with XML, hold down the Command/Ctrl key and drag the sequence name on top of the top element in the XML Workspace palette. This doesn't seem to be working in the currently-shipping version.

Of course, if you had to create a sequence for each new document, it would drive you batty. Fortunately, you can make a sequence once and then save the XPress document as a template—the sequence is saved with the file. Then, when you flow text or graphics into this template, the sequences are already built and ready to tag.

As I said earlier, there are some items that are difficult to convert to XML, such as tables. Sadly, there is no way to add a whole table to the Sequences palette. You can, however, add a single cell of a table; if you have enough patience, you could add all the cells, one at a time.

Figure E-8
The Sequences palette

▼ ▼

Tip: Exporting XSLT. Something really interesting happens when you export HTML from a Web document in which you have inserted placeholders (with the Placeholders palette): You get an XSLT file instead of HTML. XSLT is a way to transform XML data into HTML to serve Web pages on the fly. For instance, let's say you have 100 magazine articles saved in XML, and you want to display them on your Web site using the same layout. You could build the template in XSLT and then use an XML/XSL-aware processor to create the HTML whenever the user requests one of the articles.

This can work beautifully, but whether the XSLT files that QuarkXPress generates would function in this workflow is unclear. At the time of this writing, I have not heard of anyone making use of these files, and some XML experts think it's unlikely that most Web browsers could use them. If you prove them wrong and can serve up HTML based on one of the XSLTs, please let me know!

▼ ▼

The Open Street

For folks who create structured documents that they need to repurpose with different formatting or for different media, there is little doubt that XML is the best thing since that little slicer thing that cuts up hard boiled eggs. On the other hand, folks who like to draw outside the lines and make shorter documents, like ads, will likely find XML almost completely useless.

A QuarkXPress document has always been like a dead-end road for your content—once your text and graphics hit the page, it's been hard to get them out again. XML changes that, turning XPress into just one stop on a through street. XML lets your data flow in and flow out. In a perfect world, your data would begin as XML before it even gets close to QuarkXPress. It's not always as easy as it sounds, but XML is certainly a powerful workflow when you use it correctly.

F

XPRESS TAGS

I t's impossible to remember every XPress Tag code, so I wanted to print this table on laminated cardstock that you could tear out and put next to your computer. Unfortunately, the publisher didn't go for that one. Second-best solution: put a Post-It note on the side of this page so you can find it easily next time you need it!

By the way, note that all codes that are set in angle brackets can be combined within one set of angle brackets. For example, <BI*d(1,3)> changes the formatting to bold, italic, and with a drop cap.

Character Formats

STYLE	CODE[1]
Plain	<P>
Bold	<B>
Italic	<I>
Outline	<O>
Shadow	<S>
Underline	<U>
Word underline	<W>

Style (continued)	Code[1]
Strikethrough	</>
All caps	\<K>
Small caps	\<H>
Superscript	\<+>
Subscript	<->
Superior	\<V>
Apply type style of current paragraph style sheet	\<$>
Apply type style of current character style sheet	<$$>
Reapply type style of paragraph's character style sheet	\<a$>
Reapply type style of the current character style sheet	\<a$$>

[1] *These codes act as toggle switches; the first time they're encountered, the format is activated. The second time, the format is deactivated. Note the similarity to formatting keystrokes.*

Style/Attribute	Code[2]	Value type or units
Typeface	\<f"name">	Name of font, exactly as it appears in QuarkXPress's font menu
Size	\<z#>	Points
Color	\<c"name">	Name of color (you can specify with C, M, Y, K, and W, without quotes, as in \<cY>). Color must already be created in document.
Shade	\<s#>	Percentage
Horizontal scale	\<h#>	Percentage
Vertical scale	\<y#>	Percentage
Kern	\<k#>	1/200 em
Track	\<t#>	1/200 em
Baseline shift	\<b#>	Points

Paragraph Formats

Attribute	Code[3]	Value type or units
Left-align	<*L>	None
Center-align	<*C>	None

Right-align	<*R>	None
Justify	<*J>	None
Force-justify	<*F>	None
Paragraph attributes	<*p(#,#,#,#,#,#,G *or* g)>	Left Indent, First Line, Right Indent, Leading, Space Before, Space After, Lock to Baseline Grid (G = lock, g = don't lock)
Drop cap Count	<*d(chars,lines)>	Character Count and Line
Keep With Next ¶	<*kn1> *or* <*kn0>	1=keep with next, 0=don't keep with next
Keep Lines Together	<*kt(A)> *or* <*kt(start,end)>	"A"=all; start and end are number of lines
Set Tab Stops	<*t(#,#,"character")>	Position, Alignment (0=left, 1=center, 2=right, 4=decimal, 5= comma), Fill character or characters [4]
H&J	<*h"name">	Name of H&J specification
Rule Above	<*ra(#,#,"name",#,#,#,#)>	See "Rule Below"
Rule Below	<*rb(#,#,"name",#,#,#)>	Width, Style (from 1–11), Name of color, Shade (percent), From Left, From Right, Offset (if Offset is a percentage, add a percent sign). Enter T in front of Left Indent value to base rule length on length of text.

[2] *In these codes, "#" should be replaced with a number. This number can be set to the same precision as QuarkXPress's measurements (tenths, hundredths, or thousandths of a unit). The measurement units used are shown. If you replace "#" or any other code value with a dollar sign ($), QuarkXPress uses the formatting of the current style sheet. For Kern, Track, and Baseline Shift, the numbers can be either positive (no sign) or negative (use hyphen for negative sign). Positive Kern and Track values make the type looser; negative Kern and Track values make the type tighter. Positive Baseline Shift values shift up; negative Baseline Shift values shift down.*

[3] *In these codes, "#" should be replaced with a measurement in points. If you replace "#" or any other code value with a dollar sign ($), XPress uses the formatting of the current style sheet. If the code requires multiple values, every value must be present and delineated by a comma up until the last code you wish to specify (i.e., if you only wanted to specify Left Indent, you could just type <*p(2p)>; you wouldn't have to type <*p(2p,$,$,$,$)>.)*

[4] *Align on is specified by replacing the alignment number by the one or two characters contained within quotation marks.*

Special Characters

CHARACTER	CODE
Soft return ("new line")	<\n>
Discretionary return	<\d>
Normal hyphen	<\->[5]
Discretionary hyphen	<\h>
Indent Here	<\i>
Previous text box page #	<\2>
Current text box page #	<\3>
Next text box page #	<\4>
New column	<\c>
New box	<\b>
@	<\@>
<	<\<>
\	<\\>
Standard space	<\s>[5]
En space (figure space)	<\f>[5]
Em space	<\f><\f>[5]
Flex space[6]	<\q>[5]
Punctuation space	<\p>[5]
ASCII character	<\#decimal value>[5,7]
En dash	<\#208>[5,7,8]
Em dash	<\#209>[5,7,8]
Open double quotes	<\#210>[5,7,8]
Close double quotes	<\#211>[5,7,8]
Open single quote	<\#212>[5,7,8]
Close single quote or apostrophe	<\#213>[5,7,8]
Return (new paragraph)	<\#13>[5,7,8]
Tab character	<\#9>[5,7,8]
Right-align tab character	<\t>

[5]*Precede these codes with an exclamation point to make them nonbreaking. For example, <\!-> for a non-breaking hyphen.*

[6]*The QuarkXPress documentation continues to insist on incorrectly calling this a "1/4-em space." It can conceivably be defined as such, of course, but it's totally user-configurable.*

[7]*Note that the number sign (#) must precede the ASCII value. See Appendix G for codes on Windows.*

[8]*You can also type the character itself on the Macintosh.*

Paragraph Style Sheets

DESCRIPTION	CODE	VALUES
Define style sheet	@name=	Name of style sheet[9]; follow the equal sign with definition, just as if you were inserting "manual" or "local" formatting in the text stream
Based on/next style	@name=[S"based-on_name","next style name"]	Name of based-on style sheet, followed by definition
Apply style sheet	@name:	Name of style sheet
Apply "Normal"	@$:	
Apply "No Style"	@:	

[9] *You cannot use these symbols in the name: @, ", :, or =*

Character Style Sheets

DESCRIPTION	CODE	VALUES
Define style sheet	@name=	Just like defining a paragraph style sheet, except (of course) don't specify any paragraph attributes
Apply style sheet	<@name>	Name of style sheet
Apply Normal character style	<@$>	
Apply "No style"	<@>	
Return to character style sheet that "belongs" to current ¶ style sheet	<@$p>	

General Codes

CODE	MEANS...
<v#>	XPress Tags filter version number. XPress 3.2's filter is version 1.6; XPress 3.3's is version 1.7; XPress 4.0's is version 2.0; XPress 4.1 is 2.05. QuarkXPress 5.0 is version 3.0. You can typically ignore this tag.
<e#>	Platform number: 0=Mac, 1=Windows; 2=ISO Latin 1. These control the character sets for special characters; you can ignore these unless you're moving XPress Tags files from one computer platform to another.

Indexing

ATTRIBUTE	CODE
Entry marker[10]	`<XI,"first level index entry","second level entry","sort as", "character style",scope code, additional info code,"x-ref">`
Entry start range	`<XO>`
Entry end range[10]	`<XC,"first level index entry","second level entry","sort as", "character style",scope code, additional info code,"x-ref">`

[10]*You can leave any of the strings blank, except for the first level index entry. For instance, `<XI,"Fish","","","",0,0,"">` means place an index entry called "Fish" here without any sort as, special character style, or x-ref.*

Scope code: 0 = Selection Start; 1 = Selection Text; 2 = To Style; 3 = Number of paragraphs; 4 = To End Of; 5 = Suppress Page Number; 6 = X-Ref.

Additional info code is based on the Scope code: If Scope equals zero or one, then the additional info code would be the same; if Scope = 2, then the additional info code should be "stylesheetname"; if Scope = 3, then the additional info code should be the number of paragraphs; if Scope = 4, then type 0 for Story and 1 for Document; if Scope = 5, then type 0 for the additional info code; if Scope = 6, then type 0 for "See", 1 for "See also," and 2 for "See herein".

G

ANSI CODES

ANSI CODE	TIMES	SYMBOL	ZAPF DINGBATS
1–45 No characters			
46	.	.	✎
47	/	/	✏
48	0	0	✐
49	1	1	☜
50	2	2	☞
51	3	3	✓
52	4	4	✔
53	5	5	✕
54	6	6	✖
55	7	7	✗
56	8	8	✘
57	9	9	✚
58	:	:	✜
59	;	;	✛
60	<	<	✤
61	=	=	†
62	>	>	✞
63	?	?	✝
64	@	≅	✠

ANSI CODE	TIMES	SYMBOL	ZAPF DINGBATS
65	A	A	✿
66	B	B	✜
67	C	X	✣
68	D	Δ	♣
69	E	E	✤
70	F	Φ	◆
71	G	Γ	◇
72	H	H	★
73	I	I	☆
74	J	ϑ	✪
75	K	K	☆
76	L	Λ	✬
77	M	M	★
78	N	N	✩
79	O	O	✫
80	P	Π	☆
81	Q	Θ	✻
82	R	P	✺
83	S	Σ	✳
84	T	T	✵
85	U	Y	✶
86	V	ς	✷
87	W	Ω	✸
88	X	Ξ	✹
89	Y	Ψ	✺
90	Z	Z	✻
91	[	[	✼
92	\	∴	✽
93	]	]	✾
94	^	⊥	✿
95	_	_	❀
96	`	‾	❁
97	a	α	❂
98	b	β	❃
99	c	χ	❄
100	d	δ	❅
101	e	ε	❆

Ansi Code	Times	Symbol	Zapf Dingbats
102	f	φ	�֍
103	g	γ	✳
104	h	η	✳
105	i	ι	✳
106	j	φ	✳
107	k	κ	✳
108	l	λ	●
109	m	μ	○
110	n	ν	■
111	o	o	❑
112	p	π	❐
113	q	θ	❑
114	r	ρ	❐
115	s	σ	▲
116	t	τ	▼
117	u	υ	◆
118	v	ϖ	❖
119	w	ω	◗
120	x	ξ	❘
121	y	ψ	❙
122	z	ζ	❚
123	{	{	❛
124	|	|	❜
125	}	}	❝
126	~	~	❞
127–129 No characters			
130	‚		
131	ƒ		
132	„		
133	…		
134	†		
135	‡		
136	ˆ		
137	‰		
138	Š		
139	‹		
140	Œ		

Ansi Code	Times	Symbol	Zapf Dingbats
141–144 No characters			
145	'		
146	'		
147	"		
148	"		
149	•		
150	–		
151	—		
152	~		
153	™		
154	š		
155	›		
156	œ		
157–158 No characters			
159	Ÿ		
160 No character			
161	¡	ϒ	✁
162	¢	′	✂
163	£	≤	✃
164		⁄	♥
165	¥	∞	✆
166	¦	ƒ	✇
167	§	♣	✈
168	¨	♦	♣
169	©	♥	♦
170	ª	♠	♥
171	«	↔	♠
172	¬	←	①
173		↑	②
174	®	→	③
175	¯	↓	④
176	°	°	⑤
177	±	±	⑥
178	²	″	⑦
179	³	≥	⑧
180	´	×	⑨
181	µ	∝	⑩

ANSI CODE	TIMES	SYMBOL	ZAPF DINGBATS
182	¶	∂	❶
183	·	•	❷
184	‚	÷	❸
185	¦	≠	❹
186	º	≡	❺
187	»	≈	❻
188	¼	…	❼
189	½	⏐	❽
190	¾	—	❾
191	¿	↵	❿
192	À	ℵ	①
193	Á	ℑ	②
194	Â	ℜ	③
195	Ã	℘	④
196	Ä	⊗	⑤
197	Å	⊕	⑥
198	Æ	∅	⑦
199	Ç	∩	⑧
200	È	∪	⑨
201	É	⊃	⑩
202	Ê		
203	Ë	⊄	❷
204	Ì	⊂	❸
205	Í	⊆	❹
206	Î	∈	❺
207	Ï	∉	❻
208	Ð	∠	❼
209	Ñ	∇	❽
210	Ò	®	❾
211	Ó	©	❿
212	Ô	™	→
213	Õ	∏	→
214	Ö	√	↔
215	×	·	↕
216	Ø	¬	↘
217	Ù	∧	→
218	Ú	∨	↗

Ansi Code	Times	Symbol	Zapf Dingbats
219	Û	⇔	→
220	Ü	⇐	➜
221	Ý	⇑	→
222	Þ	⇒	→
223	ß	⇓	➡
224	à	◊	➔
225	á	⟨	➡
226	â	®	➢
227	ã	©	➣
228	ä	™	➤
229	å	∑	➥
230	æ	⎛	➦
231	ç	⎜	➧
232	è	⎝	➨
233	é	⎡	⇨
234	ê	⎢	⇨
235	ë	⎣	⇦
236	ì	⎧	⇦
237	í	⎨	⇨
238	î	⎩	⇨
239	ï	⎪	⇨
240	∂		
241	ñ	⟩	⇨
242	ò	∫	⊃
243	ó	⎡	➤➤
244	ô	⎢	➘
245	õ	⎦	➤➤
246	ö	⎞	➚
247	÷	⎟	➘
248	ø	⎠	➤➤
249	ù	⎤	➚
250	ú	⎥	→
251	û	⎦	↔
252	ü	⎫	➤➤
253	ý	⎬	➤➤
254	þ	⎭	⇒
255	ÿ		

Colophon

If anything shows that I practice what I preach, it's this book. *Real World QuarkXPress 6* was created using almost every technique and many of the tips that I divulge throughout the chapters.

Text

Because the pages for the previous edition of the book were in QuarkXPress format, all the text was exported as Microsoft Word files (fortunately, the style sheets were exported with the text). Chapters were edited and written in Microsoft Word v.X, and then reimported into QuarkXPress to be laid out. The bulk of the work was done on an Apple PowerBook G4.

Artwork

I created all the artwork in QuarkXPress, Adobe Photoshop, Adobe Illustrator, and Macromedia FreeHand. The screen captures were created with Ambrosia Software's SnapzPro. Photographs and line art images were scanned on various scanners, including a Lintotype-Hell Saphir. Stock art was graciously provided by PhotoDisc and ImageFarm. All images were edited and saved as either TIFF or EPS files using Adobe Photoshop. Then, each figure was imported, cropped, and sized within QuarkXPress, and saved in a library along with its caption and callouts (one library per chapter). For fast access to each figure, I labelled them using the library's labelling feature.

Design

The book design was based on an original design by Olav Martin Kvern. For this revised edition, the body copy was set in Adobe Utopia and Utopia Expert (for fractions, footnotes, etc.); the heads are in Adobe's Stone Sans Bold. Adobe's Universal News with Commercial Pi was used throughout the book for the bullet symbol (▶), math symbols, and other dingbats.

Output

The book was printed and bound by Edwards Brothers in Ann Arbor, Michigan on 50# Husky Offset paper. The color pages were printed on 70# Sterling Litho Satin.

Where to Reach Me

Information is never a one-way street. I want to hear about your favorite QuarkXPress techniques, tips, and tricks! The best way to reach me is through the *Real World QuarkXPress Book* Web site:

http://www.peachpit.com/blatner/

Remember that you will need to have this book nearby to get access to the private pages (the password is hidden in the pages of this book). Or, you can try e-mailing me at *qxbook@moo.com*. I can't always answer right away, but I'll do my best.

And whatever you do, don't forget to enjoy this stuff! If you're not having fun, you're not doing it right.

INDEX

▼ ▼

2-Position Rollovers 770
32-bit TIFF display 96, 529

A

A4 Letter 245
About QuarkXPress 47
Absolute trapping 650
Accents 353, 381, 403, 457
Acrobat Distiller 7, 798–799
Acrobat PDF 511, 796–804
    as PostScript interpreter 673
    bookmarks 801–802
    color in 666–667
    color separations 804
    hyperlinks in 800–802
    job options 802
    OS X print driver 797
    PDF/X 798
    preferences 104–105, 798, 799
    sending to imaging center 721, 726
    versus HTML 738–739
    viewing on Web 797
Add Printer 674–675, 729
Adding pages 267, 272
Additive color 618

Adobe
    FrameMaker 404
    GoLive 742
    Illustrator 133, 508, 665
    InDesign 122, 168
    PageMaker 122, 168
    Photoshop 545, 549, 556, 668–670, 757, 793–795
Adobe Type Manager (ATM) 309
a lowly apprentice production 843
Aliens 178–179
Aligning objects 185–190
Aligning text
    anchored boxes 600–601
    horizontal 333–335
    on path 130
All Caps 290
Allocating RAM 46
Alpha channels 565–566, 567, 590
Anchored boxes 598–607
    alignment 600–603
    deleting 605
    restrictions 599
    rule below 612
    text boxes 604
    unanchoring 605

Anchor hyperlinks 766–767. *See also* Web documents
ANSI Codes 402, 885–890
Append 240
   colors 633–635
   conflicts 439
   H&Js 367–369
   style sheets 437–440
AppleScript. *See* Scripting
Application Preferences. *See* Preferences
Apply 76
Arabic numerals 280
Arrow keys 167
Arrows. *See* Lines
As Is color 697
ASCII data 543, 703
Asymmetric bleed 707
Auto Backup 62–63
Auto Constraint 184
Auto leading 346–347
Auto Library Save 239
Auto Page Insertion 276
Auto Picture Import 534–535
Auto Save 61–62
Automatic Text Box 248–250, 259–262
Auxiliary dictionaries 303–305
avenue.quark 52, 872–874

B

Background color 115, 122, 600
Backing up 50
Bad File Format 58
Badia Software 454, 843
Bagels 160, 161
Balanced Screens 583, 718
Banding 643
Banister, Tim xi, 51
Baseline grid 375–378
Baseline shift 331–332
Baseline to baseline space. *See* Leading
Basic rollovers 768
BBEdit 58
Beveled Corner boxes 123
Bézier boxes and lines 132–166
   adding and deleting points 149
   changing point type 149–150
   Edit Shape 145–146
   flipping shapes 152–153
   Scissors 153
   Shape menu 160–164
   symmetrical 159
   text shapes 164–166
Binary EPS 543
Bitmapped images 504–507, 548–584
   colors in 667–670
   frames 222

Black & White printing 696
Black, four-color 639, 659
Blatner, David 892
Bleed 706–708
   in spreads 274
   Save as EPS 540–541
Blends 641–646
   inside images 552
Bloating frames 213
BMP files 512
Bob XTension 843
Bold text 317–318
Bookmarks in PDF 801
Books 464–475
   as database 465
   file status 469
   indexing 482–501
   lists 475–482
   making new 465–468
   on network 470
   page numbering 473–474
   palette 74, 467
   printing 475
   sections 473–474
   synchronizing 471–473
   Undo 468
Borders. *See* Frames
Bounding box 120–122
Bounding boxes 519
Boxes. *See* Text boxes *and* Picture boxes
Bozek, Sandy xi
Bring to Front 180, 197
Browsers 761–762
Build Index 496–500
Bullets 290
Burnt sienna 615
Buttons 787–788

C

Cancel 82
Captions 188
Carlson, Debbie xii
Cascading menus 771–774
Cascading Style Sheets (CSS) 790
Castro, Elizabeth 739
CD-ROMs 738
CE Software's QuicKeys 9
Cells. *See* Tables
Centered text 334, 336, 338
Centering pictures 520
Centering on the page 189–190
CGI scripts 776
Chaining. *See* Linking: text boxes
Character formatting 27–28, 313–332
   all caps 290

baseline shift 331–332
color and shade 321–322, 617
find/change 296–297
kerning 325–328, 382–385
scaling 322–324
size 315–316
styles 316–321
tracking 328–330, 385–387
typeface 313–314
versus style sheets 424
Web documents 754
wordspacing 330–331
Character Map 401
Character spacing. *See* Letterspacing
Character styles 443–448. *See also* Style sheets
Characters. *See* Special characters
Chavez, Conrad 718
Check spelling 299–305
Checkboxes 786–787
Choking with frames 213–214
Chooser 674
Ciceros/Cm 108
CIE Lab color 620, 808
Clean 8-bit data 703
Clicking. *See* Selecting
Clipping paths 564–579
applying 564–569
editing 577–579
problems with 569
Restrict To Box 573–574
TIFF vs. EPS 568–569
Clone item 177
Close 58
CMYK. *See* Process color
Cohen, Sandee xi, 358
Collate 682
Collect for Output 724–725
Colophon 891–892
Color 613–670
appending 633–635
As Is 697
blends 641–646
composite 617
default document 626
deleting 632–633
DeviceN 697
DIC 625
discrepencies in 614–615, 631
drag-and-drop 641
editing 631–632, 641
Focoltone 625
four-color black 639, 659
Hexachrome 624, 637, 819, 824–825
HSB color 619–620
importing 630, 633–635, 665–670

Indeterminate 639, 652, 664
Lab color 620
libraries 634–635
management 614, 805–830
models 615–625, 630
Multi-Ink 635–638
new 627–631
on screen 614
overprinting 647–648, 659
Pantone 622–623
printing 696, 717
Registration 638–639
RGB 618
separations 616, 668–670, 699–700, 716–720
Show menu 626–627
Spot Color checkbox 628
spot versus process 615–617
swatch books 615, 620–625
text 321, 617
TIFF and JPEG images 551, 561–563
tints 630–631
Toyo 625
trapping 635, 647–665
TruMatch 615, 621–622
typographic 348, 349
Web documents 746–747
wheel 619
Color management (CMS) 614, 805–830
basics 808
color printers 811
Display Simulation 819–820
EfiColor 4
gamuts 808
Get Picture 820–822
installing 815–816
monitors 810–811
OPI 815
preferences 816–820
Print dialog box 825–829
problems with 807
Profile Information palette 73, 822–824
profiles 808–813, 826–828
rendering style 812–813
Save as EPS 829
scanners 811
Usage dialog box 822–824
XTensions 814
Color TIFFs preference 96
Colorimetric rendering 812
Colors palette 73, 640–641, 642
ColorSync 815
Column guides 247–248
Columns 25, 123, 354–355. *See also* Tables
Combine 157
Combine Cells 227–228

Combs 231–232
Comparing
    dashes and stripes 222
    print styles 714
    style sheets 440
Composite color printing 697
Compound objects 158–159, 160
Compressed Image Import XTension 52
Compressed text 322
Concentric frames 213
Concordance 483
Constraining 183–185
Contacting author 892
Content menu 124, 127
Content tool 21, 114–117, 313
Contentless boxes 124
Context-sensitive menus 78, 77–79, 433
Continued on... 281–283
Continuous Apply 76
Contrast 554–564
Control Key Activates 101
Convert Quotes 291, 400–401
Convert Table to Group 232–233
Convert Table to Text 232–233
Convert Text to Table 224–225
Convert to Graphic on Export 754–757
Cool Blends 642
Copy and Paste 176–178, 196
    anchored boxes 598
    linked boxes 204
    pictures 516–517, 527
CopyDesk 449, 453
Copyright symbol 401
Corner Radius 122–123
Corrupt documents 58
Crashing 62
Create 2-Position Target 770
Create Outlines 164–166
Create Rollover 768
Cropping 521–523, 574, 759
Cross-platform compatibility 831–840
Cross-references. See Indexing
CSS Font Families 758
Curves. See Bézier boxes and lines
Custom Bleeds 52

D

Damaged documents 58
Dashes and Stripes 214–222
Database publishing 451–452
Daylight savings time 531
DCS. See Desktop Color Separation (DCS)
Deco frames 210
Default layer 194
Default pages. See Master pages

Default Path 103–104
Defaults. See Preferences
Dégradés. See Blends
Deja Vu XTension 52, 103–104
Delayed Item Dragging 100, 168
Delete
    colors 632–633
    items 178–179
    pages 89, 91
    text 288
Delimiters. See Tables
Design Tools Monthly 845
Desktop Color Separation (DCS) 511, 542, 668–669
DeviceN color 697
Diacritical marks. See Accents
Dialog boxes 74–76
DIC color 625
Dictionaries 299, 303–305
Didot system 108
Difference 155, 156
Dingbats 405–408
Discretionary hyphen 393
Display DPI 98
Display Halftoning 583
Display Simulation 819–820
Distributing evenly 185–190
Document Layout palette. See Page Layout palette
Document Preferences. See Preferences
Documents 12–14
    adding pages 17, 269, 272–274, 276
    adding to book 466
    closing 58
    corruption 58
    facing pages 276
    file names 832–834
    long 463–502
    making new 12–14, 244–250
    master pages 254–258
    multipage spreads 277
    opening 58
    projects and layouts 250–254
    save position 102
    saving 18, 59–63
    single-sided pages 248
    size of 273, 275
    start on left 280
    templates 63–64
    Web versus print 742–744
    window management 64–65
Dot leaders 360
Dot patterns 582
Drag and drop
    text 101, 288
    color 641
Dragging objects 167–168, 169, 178

Drop Caps 412–416
Drop shadows 418–419
DTD file 865–871
Duotones 664, 669–670
Duplicating items 175–178, 196

E

Easter eggs 50–51, 179
Ebrahimi, Fred xi
Edit menu 66
Edit Original XTension 535, 843
Edit Printer List 674, 727
Edit Shape 145–146, 153, 170
Edit Trap. *See* Trapping
EfiColor 4
Einstein, Albert 506
Em and en dashes 397
Em Software 452, 460, 844
Em units 324–325, 395
Encapsulated PostScript (EPS) 510, 513–516, 539–545
    color in 665–666
    color management 814
    opening in Photoshop 793
    overprinting 704
    Web documents 759
Endcaps 126, 219
Endpoints of lines 170–171
Environment dialog box 47, 50–51
EPS Preview XTension 52, 538
Epson. *See* Inkjet printers
Erasing. *See* Deleting items
Error Reporting XTension 52
Excel 225
Exceptions, hyphenation 389–390
Exclusive Or 155, 157
Expert set fonts 411
Explorer 761–762
Export
    HTML 789–792
    PDF 799–804
    text 452–454, 456, 741–742
    XML 872–874

F

Facing pages 248, 276
Fast Save 292
Features
    new in version 5 5–7
    new in version 6 7–8
Fields. *See* Tables
"f i" and "f l" ligatures 399, 835–836
File Buddy 509
File menu 66
File naming 744, 832–834
File Select tool 779

File type 508–516
Files. *See* Documents
Find/Change 292–299
    colors 632–633
    fonts 311, 312, 314
    ligatures 400
    style sheets 445
First Baseline 352–353
First Line indent 341–342
Fisher, Harry 556
Fit Box to Picture 522
Fit in Print Area 692
Fit in Window 85, 86
Flags. *See* Visual indicators
Fleishman, Glenn 505, 878
Flex space 396
Flip
    printing 701
    shapes 152–153, 173
    text 131
Flush left 333
Flush Zone 366
Focoltone 625
Fold-outs 277
Font Reserve 309
FontBook 309
Fonts 308–313
    choosing 313–314
    cross-platform issues 835, 837–838
    families 320, 758
    forbidden 837
    management 309
    missing 310
    printing 726, 732–734
    sending to service bureau 722, 724–725
    size 315–316
    styles 316–321
    Usage dialog box 311–313
Footnotes 450
Forced justification 366–367
Form combs 231–232
Form items 775–788. *See also* Web documents
Fountains. *See* Blends
Fractions 77, 408–411, 457–458
Frame Editor 222
Frames 36, 210–222. *See also* Text boxes and Picture boxes
    gap color 211–212
    indside/outside 213–214
    Inside versus Outside 166
    trapping 661
    typographic 212–213
Fraser, Bruce xi
Freehand tool 136–138
Freezing up 62
Friedman, Susie xi

Frison, Zach xl
Full Res of Rotated Objects 704
Full-resolution preview 8, 53, 104, 537–539, 759
Full-Resolution TIFF Output 704–705
FullMeasureXT 843

G

Gamma curves 555
Gap color 211–212
Gaskill, Phil xi
Geschke, Chuck 672
Get Document 92
Get Picture 517–518, 528
Get Text 291, 451, 792–793
Ghosting images 551, 562–564
GIF files 513
Gluon 183, 742, 843
Go To page 88
Grabber Hand 84
Gradients. *See* Blends
Graphic formats 504–516. *See also* Pictures
Gray TIFFs preference 96
Grayscale printing 696
Greeking 106, 420, 536
Grid, baseline 375–378
Gridlines. *See* Tables
Grouping objects 180–183, 184, 188–189, 197
    radio buttons 786
    scaling 524
Guides 17–18, 206–209
    color 94
    Guide Manager 53
    margins 246–247, 259–260
    preferences 106
Guillemet 404
Gutter width 123

H

H&Js. *See* Hyphenation and justification
Hairlines 125
Halftones 579–584
    popup menu in Edit Color 628
    Print dialog box 698, 718–720
    rosettes 717–718
Hand tool
    Content tool 114
    grabber hand 84
Hanging indents 342, 356
Hard formatting. *See* Local formatting
Hardware requirements 8–10
Helios 816
Hexachrome color 624, 637, 819, 824–825
Hiding objects 200
High Quality Screening (HQS) 718
High resolution previews. *See* Full-resolution preview

Horizontal Measure 205
Horizontal scaling 322–324, 375
HSB color 619–620
HTML. *See* Web documents
Hyperlinks
    default color 107
    in PDF files 800–802
    image maps 774
    palette 74, 762–767
Hyphenation and justification (H&Js) 361–367, 367–372, 388–391
Hyphenation Exceptions 389–390, 394
Hyphenation Method 388
Hyphens, discretionary 393

I, J

Ignore White 653–654
Image Export Directory 748
Image maps 774–775
ImagePort XTension 844
Imaging centers 720–731
Importing
    colors 665–670
    HTML 792–793
    Item versus Content tool 115
    Photoshop files 844
    pictures 32–33, 516–520, 549–550
    text 23, 449–452
    XML 875–876
    XPress Tags 456, 879–884
Importing text 290–292
Imposition 680
Include Style Sheets 291, 451
Indents 340–344
    indent here character 392
InDesign. *See* Adobe InDesign
Indeterminate color 639, 652, 664
Index palette 73, 483–484
Indexing 482–501
Initial caps 354, 411–416
Inkjet printers 673
Inline graphics. *See* Anchored boxes
InPosition XTension 680
Insert pages 269, 272–274, 276
Insert space 371
Insets 123–124
Installing 44
Inter ¶ Max 338, 339
Internet 737–804. *See also* Web documents
Internet Explorer 761–762
Interruptible redraw 82
Intersection 155, 156
IP printing 727
Italic text 317–318
Item Coordinates 205

Item menu 66
Item Sequence palette 876–878
Item tool 21, 114–117
Jabberwocky 53, 104, 843
Jaws PostScript interpreter 538, 798
Job Slugs 708
Johns, Kass xi
Join Endpoints 158
Jolt Cola 7
Joy of π, The 148
JPEG files 510, 513
Jump lines 281–283
Justified paragraphs 333–335, 338, 364–367

K

Keep Attributes 227
Keep Lines Together 373–375
Keep With Next ¶ 372–373
Kerning 324–325, 325–328, 382–385
    cross-platform issues 837
    drop caps 413
    text on path 132
Key Caps 401
Keyboard shortcuts 57
    dialog boxes 14, 75–76
    environment dialog box 48
    font size 315–316
    indexing 488
    kerning 328
    leading 346
    macros 848
    Measurements palette 72
    navigating pages 87
    pictures 520–521, 523
    quote marks 400
    style sheets 431
    switch windows 64
    tables 225
    text editing 287
    type styles 318
    wordspacing 331
    Zapf Dingbats and Symbol font 885–890
    zooming 86
Kiwis 760
Knockout Limit 652–653
Kurz, Juergen xi
KyTek 843

L

Lab color 620
Launching XPress 56
Layers
    assigning 195–197
    Bring to Front 180
    deleting 197–199

    groups 197
    hiding/showing 200, 201
    Layers palette 74, 193–202
    Locked 200
    master pages 194
    merging 197–198
    preferences 201
    Print dialog box 705–706
    runaround 200–201
    selecting through 116
    Send to Back 180
    stacking order 179–180
    Suppress Printout 200
    visual indicators 195
Layout Properties 253, 745
Layout spaces 7, 250–254
    synchronized text 190–193
    Web 744–753
Leaders 359–360
Leading 28–29, 344–351, 354, 378, 602
Left Indent 341
Left Point 170–171
Left-hand start 280
Letterspacing 324–332, 365
Libraries 74, 235–239
    auto save 101–102, 239
    colors 634–635
    cross-platform issues 838
    labeling 237
    style sheets 447
Ligatures 398–400, 835–836
Line break character 30
Line Check 390
Lines 37–38, 124–132
    anchored 605–606
    Bézier curves 132–134
    changing shape 160–164
    constrain to angle 171
    converting to boxes 163–164
    custom dashes/stripes 214–222
    defining endpoints 170–171
    frames 210–214
    in Web documents 761
    miter 218, 221
    Rule Above/Below 607–612
    snap to guides 209
    text on 127–132, 162–163
Linespacing. *See* Leading
Link to Current Text Chain 273
Linking
    text boxes 24–25, 202–204
    text cells 225–226
List tool 782–786
Lists 475–482
    dot leaders 360

exporting as bookmarks 802
Lists palette 478–480
Live Refresh 100
Live Scroll 84, 99
Local formatting 424–426, 435
Localhost printer 727
Lock to Baseline Grid 375–378
Locking items 174, 200
Logan, Dan xi, 51
Long documents 463–502
    books 464–475
    indexing 482–501
    lists 475–482

M

Mac OS X 7, 9, 797
Macintosh versus Windows 831–840
Macromedia
    Dreamweaver 742
    Fireworks 757
    FreeHand 133, 508, 665
Macros 57, 848
Magnification 15, 84–87
    thumbnails 90–91
Maintain Geometry 229
Maintain Leading 378
Make Fraction 410
Margin guides 246–247, 259–260, 276
Margins, paragraph. *See* Indents
Markzware 58, 97
Marquee 116
Martians 178–179
Master pages 254–271
    applying to document pages 266–267, 271
    changing items on document pages 262–265
    copying 271
    deleting 269
    graphics on 256
    layers 194
    margin guides 259–260, 276
    naming 270
    page numbers 255–256
    printing 258
    spell checking 302–303
    synchronized text 193
    viewing 257
    when adding/removing pages 266–267
MasterJuggler 309
Math in palettes and dialog boxes 76–77, 168, 170, 358
Math symbols 403–405
Maximum page size 245
Measurement systems 77, 107–108
Measurements palette 70–72
    alignment 335
    fonts 314

Memory management 46
Memory requirements 9
Menus 66–67
    cascading 771–774
    context-sensitive 78, 77–79
    in Web layouts 782–786
Merge 153–159
Merging layers 197–198
Meta tags 750–753
Metafile 512, 839
Microsoft Excel 225
Microsoft FrontPage 742
Microsoft Windows 831–840
    choosing printer 674–675
    Display DPI 85, 98
    file naming 832–834
    printing to disk 729–730
Microsoft Word 292, 449–452
    XPress Tags 460
Midpoint on lines 171
MIME types 779
Mirrored text. *See* Synchronized text
Mirroring shapes 152–153, 173
Missing
    in book palette 469
    fonts 311
    pictures 532
Miter 218, 221
Mock Turtle 703
Modified pictures 530–531
Modify dialog box 120, 121
    groups 181–182
    tables 229–230
Moiré patterns 718
Monitor redraw 82
Moving
    items on page 167–168
    objects between documents 92
    pages 89–90, 91
    pages between documents 92
    pictures 520–521
    points on curve 146–147
    windows 92
Moving through document. *See* Navigation
MS-Word 6-2000 Filter 53
Multi-ink colors 635–638
Multi-user packs 45
Multilingual publishing 193
Multiple Insets 124
Multiple Undo 80–82

N

Navigation 82–89, 480
Negative 552
Nelson, Jay xi, 845

Netscape 761–762
Networked versions 45
New
    documents 244–250
    layouts 251–252
    pages 272–274, 276
    projects 244
    Web layout 744–753
    XML workspace 872
New column/box character 395
New features in this version 5–8
New-line character 30
No Style 434–435
Noise 570
Non-White Areas 566, 590–591
None content boxes 124
Noonetime 862
Normal style 434–435
Notes 175, 200
Nudging objects 167
Numbering. *See* Page numbers

O

Object Linking and Embedding (OLE) 536
Object oriented images 507–508
Off-screen Draw 95
Offset
    first baseline 352–353
    indents 340–344
    Rule Above/Below 607–608
Opaque Text Box Editing 96, 115
Open 58, 103–104
OpenType fonts 308–309
OPI 543–544, 708, 815
Ornamental fonts 213
Orphans 372–375, 390
Other Contrast 554–564
Outline style 317
Outlined text 214
Output Request Template 725
Overprinting 553–554, 647–648, 653, 659, 664, 704

P

Page breaks 352, 395
Page guides 207
Page Layout palette 72, 91–92, 267–271, 273–274
Page menu 66
Page numbers
    automatic 255–256, 278–281
    books 473–474
    continued on 281–283
    last page 90
    range separators 100, 676
    typing 396
    typing absolute 88, 675–676

Page Properties 749–753
Page Setup 710–712
Page sizes 245–246, 275
Palettes overview 68–74
Pantone (PMS). *See* Spot colors
Paragraph formatting 28–29, 332–351
    copy between paragraphs 428
    H&Js 369–372
    horizontal alignment 333–335
    indents 340–344
    Keep Lines Together 373–375
    leading 344–351
    page break 352, 395
    Rule Above/Below 607–612
    space before/after 351–352
    tabs 353–360
    text box ruler 343
    versus style sheets 424
Paragraph styles. *See* Style sheets
Parent-and-child boxes 183–185
Passport 403
Paste. *See* Copy and Paste
Paste in place 8, 176
Pasteboard guides 207
Pasteboard Width 96
PasteboardXT 97
Pathfinder commands. *See* Merge
Paths. *See* Lines
PCX files 513
PDF. *See* Acrobat PDF
Peachpit.com 842, 892
Pen tools 136–138
Perceptual rendering 812
Perspective 527
Pi fonts 405–408
PICT files 511–512
Picture boxes 31–38
    Bézier curves 138–139
    changing shape 160–164
    changing to text box 124
    image maps 774–775
    in Web layouts 759–760
    making 119–124
    origin 120, 122
    pre-formatting 527
Pictures 503–546
    auto import 107
    Auto Picture Import 534–535
    best format to use 514–516
    bitmapped images 504–507, 548–584
    BMP 512
    clipping paths 564–579
    color management of 820–824
    colorizing 551, 562–563
    contrast curves 554–564

cropping 521–523
cross-platform issues 838–840
data type 543
DCS 511, 542
display on screen 529, 550
encapsulated postScript (EPS) 510, 539–545
fit box 522
ghosting 562–564
GIF 513
greeking 106, 536
halftones 579–584
importing 32–33, 516–520, 549–550
JPEG files 513
JPEG previews 510
linking 528–533
metafile 512
moving in box 520–521
object-oriented images 507–508
OLE 536
PCX 513
printing 702–704, 731–732
relinking 533
resize 523–524
rotating 524
Save as EPS 539–545
Scitex CT 513
sending to service bureau 723, 724–725
skewing 526–527
TIFF 509
tinting 551
troubleshooting 518–520
usage 529–533
vector artwork in 515
Pixel sizes 746
Pixels 504
Placeholders 875–876
PNG files 53
Pointer tool 114
Points/Inch 108
Popup Menu tool 782–786
Post-it notes 175
Posterizing images 560
PostScript Error Handler 700–701
PostScript fonts 308–309, 312
The Power XChange 844
PPD Manager 690
Praxisoft 814, 816
Preferences 93–112
    application 94–103
    auto save 61–62
    color 626
    color management 816–820
    Display 94–98
    Display DPI 85, 98
    document 105–112

folder 49
Framing 213
General 105–107
indexing 494–496
Interactive 98–101
Layers 111, 201
Measurements 107–108, 205
Paragraph and Character 109
PDF 798–799
Save 101–102
Tables 233–234
Tool 109–111
trapping 111, 649–654
undo 80
Web layouts 748, 761–762
XPress Preferences 48–51
Prefixes 280. *See also* Page numbers
Preps 541, 680
Preview Resolution 538
Previewing HTML 761–762
Prices 419
Printer Spreads 680
Printing 671–736
    As Is color 697
    back to front 682
    basics 38
    binary data 703
    black and white 696
    bleeds 706–708
    books 475
    Capture Settings 676–677
    choosing a printer 673–675
    Collate 682
    Collect for Output 724–725
    color management 825–829
    colors as 696
    composite color 697
    DeviceN 697
    double-sided pages 683
    driver settings 710–712
    flipping 701
    full resolution 704
    grayscale 696
    halftones 698, 719–720
    Include Blank Plates 678–679
    inkjet printers 673
    job slugs 708
    Layers tab 705–706
    Layout tab 678–688
    master pages 258
    missing fonts 310
    negatives 702
    offset 686–687, 695
    Options tab 700–705
    orientation 692

Output tab 695–700
overprinting 704
page gap 695
page selection 675–677
paper size 691–692
paper width/height 694
pictures 702–704
PostScript 672–673, 700, 725–731
Preview tab 708–710
Print dialog box 673–677
Print Styles 713–714
Printer Description (PPD) 689–691
reduce/enlarge 681, 688, 692
registration and trim marks 683–686
resolution 698, 702, 704
rosettes 717–718
Rough 703
separations 699–700, 716–720
service bureaus 40, 720–731
Setup tab 689–695
spreads 679–681
status 677, 678
style sheets 454
thumbnails 681–682
tiling 687–688
to disk 725–731
troubleshooting 731–735
Web layouts 792
Problem solving 49, 731–735
Process color
    basics 615–616, 618–619
    in bitmapped images 668–670
    in EPS files 666
    in place of spot 617
    swatch books 621
    versus spot 615–617
Process trapping 651–652
Profile Information palette 822–824
Profile Manager 827–828
Profiles 808–813. *See also* Color management (CMS)
Projects and layouts 250–254
Properties dialog box 710, 712
ProScale 183
Punctuation 397–402

Q
Q units 77
Quark License Administrator 45
Quark XTensions. *See* XTensions
Quark.com 843
QuarkCMS. *See* Color management (CMS)
QuarkConverter 460
QuarkXPress
    allocating RAM 46
    early versions 2–5

Environment dialog box 47
folder 45
history of 2–5
installing 44–47
launching 56
learning in 30 minutes 11–42
menu overview 66–67
multi-user packs 45
new in version 5 5–7
new in version 6 7–8
requirements 8–10
QuarkXPress Passport 403
QuicKeys 9, 57, 848
Quotation marks 400–401
QXPort 460

R
Radio buttons 786–787
Raised caps 354, 411
RAM (memory) 9, 46
Range kerning. *See* Tracking
Recycling 678
Redo 80
Reflecting shapes 152–153, 173
Registration
    color 638–639, 685
    marks 401, 683–686
Remove Manual Kerning 328
Rendering styles 812–813
Repeats Every 218
Replace 311. *See also* Find/Change
Repurposing content 741–742
Required Components 45
Resizing and reshaping items 168–171, 182–183, 226–229
Resizing items
    pictures 523–524
    text 315–316
Resolution 505, 507, 548, 698, 704. *See also* Pictures
Restrict To Box 573–574
Reverse Difference 155, 157
Reversed type 321, 610, 659–660
Revert to Saved 79
RGB color 618
Rich black 639, 659
Right Indent 341
Right indent tab 360
Right Point 171
Rivers 362
Robertson, Ray 850
ROBOTS tag 752
Rollovers 767–770
Roman numerals 280
Rosettes 717–718
Rotating 171–172, 524–525
Roth, Steve xi, 505

Rounded corner boxes 123
Rows. *See* Tables
RTF Filter 54, 291–292
Rubber chicken 571
Rule Above/Below 607–612
Rulers 205–206, 343
Rules. *See* Lines. *See* XML: tagging rules
Runaround 33–34, 586–597
    anchored boxes 599
    and vertical justification 340
    both sides of box 596–597
    drop caps 414
    editing 593–596
    inverting 596
    layers 200–201
    Maintain Leading 378
    outset 588
    text paths 594–596
    with no picture 593

S

Safari 761–762
Saturation rendering 813
Save 18, 59–63
    as 5.0 file 61
    as PostScript file 728–729
    books 471
    page as EPS 539–545, 793–795, 829
    page as HTML 789–792
    templates 63–64
    text 452–454
    text as HTML 741–742
    XPress Tags 456
Scaling groups 182–183
ScenicSoft 541, 647
Schulze, Patti xi
Scissors tool 54, 153
Scitex CT 513
Screen redraw 82
Screens. *See* Halftones
Scripting 847–859
    additional software 849
    basics 848–849
    caveats 858–859
    hierarchies 852
    learning 850–851
    object model 851–852
    samples 856–858
    scripts menu 67, 849
Scrolling 83–84, 98
Search/Replace 292–299
Section 278–281, 473–474
Selecting
    anchored items 604
    deselecting 116

    items on layer 197
    Item versus Content tool 115–117
    multiple items 116–117
    points on curve 145–146
    Select All 117
    text 286–288, 332
    through objects 116
    tools 117
Send to Back 180, 197
Separations. *See* Color: separations
Service bureaus 720–731
SGML 865
Shadows
    behind text 418–419
    text style 317–318
Shaffstall, Cyndie xi
Shape menu 160–164
Shape of Things XTension 54
Shape submenu 522
Shape, Edit 145–146
Show All Alerts 97
Single Word Justify 366
Single-sided pages 248
Site Root Directory 748
Skewing 526–527
    objects 173
    text on path 129
Slugs 708
Small caps 319, 381
Smart Quotes 99–100, 400–401, 403
Snap to Guides 209, 248
Son of Bob 843
Sosa, Carlos 552
Source profiles 817
Space Before/After 351–352
Space characters 395–396
Space/Align 185–190
    frames 213
    locked objects 174
Spatulas 841
Special characters 391–408
    accents 403
    ANSI codes 885–890
    carriage return 391
    dashes 397
    dingbats 405–408
    discretionary hyphen 393
    discretionary new line 395
    en space 395
    find/change 293–294
    flex space 396
    formatting 391–397
    indent here 392
    ligatures 398–400, 835
    math 403–405, 836

new column/box 395
new line 30
non-English punctuation 403
nonbreaking hyphen 395
nonbreaking space 395
page numbers 255, 396
punctuation space 396
quote marks 400–401
registration 401
remapping from Mac to PC 834–835
soft return 392
symbols 397–402, 403–405, 885–890
tabs 392
trademark 401
Speed Scroll 98
Spelling checker 299–305
Split Paths 160, 161
Spot colors
basics 616
checkbox in Edit Color 628
converting to process 623, 716–717
DeviceN 697
halftones 628
in EPS files 666
mixing 635–638
Pantone 616, 622–623
swatch books 621
using process in place of 617
versus process 615–617
Spot patterns 582
Spreading frames 213–214
Spreads, multipage 277, 679–681
Spreadsheets 451
Stanley, Shane 850
Stationery Pad 64
Stein, Gertrude 149
Step and Repeat 177, 563
Stimely, Keith xi
Stretch to Corners 219
Strike-thru 319
Stripes 214–222
Style menu 66
Style Sheets 423–448
appending 437–440
applying to text 426–429
based on 440–442, 445–447
benefits of 423–424
character styles 443–448
comparing 440
defining 429–430, 430–434
deleting 440
exporting 453
find/change 445
importing from MS Word 450

in Web layouts 790
libraries of 447
local formatting 424–426, 435
Next Style 442–443
No Style 434–435
Normal 434–435
palette 72–73, 425, 427, 428, 445
redefining 434
tabs 437
XML 861–862
Styles for Print dialog box 713–714
Subscriber options 535
Subtractive colors 618
Suggested Hyphenation 388–389
Suitcase 309
Super Step and Repeat 54, 177
Superscript 319, 379
Suppress Printout 175, 200, 537
SVG format 871
Swann, Greg 459
Swatch books 620–625
Symbols 397–402, 403–405, 885–890
Symmetric bleed 707
Synchronize. *See* Books
Synchronized text 8, 190–193

T

Tab-delimited data 225
Table of contents. *See* Lists
Tables 222–234
adding 227
changing rows and columns 226–229
combining and splitting cells 227–228
combs 231–232
Convert Table to Group 232–233
Convert Table to Text 232–233
Convert Text to Table 224–225
deleting 226
delimiters 223
formatting cells 229–230
gridlines 230–232
in Web layouts 234, 761, 791–792
kerning and tracking 382–387
linking cells 225–226
Maintain Geometry 229
making 223–226
one-celled 231
preferences 233–234
resizing 226
switching rows and columns 233
tab order 225
Tabs 353–360, 392, 437
Tagged text. *See* XPress Tags
Technical documents 463

Templates 63 64
Text
    anchored boxes 598–607
    bullets 290
    convert to table 224
    deleting 288
    drag and drop 288
    exporting 452–454
    Find/Change 292–299
    formatting 22
    greeking 106
    importing 23, 290–292
    linking 24
    paths 127–132, 162–163
    ornamental fonts 213
    outlines 214
    reflow 451
    runaround 586–597
    save as HTML 741–742
    selecting 286–288
    Text to Box 164–166
    typing 22
    word processing 285–305
Text boxes 20
    automatic 248, 259–262
    Bézier curves 138–139
    changing shape 160–164
    changing to picture box 124
    columns 25, 123
    converting to paths 162–163
    default font 261, 435
    in Web layouts 754–757
    insets 123–124
    linking 202–204
    making 119–124
    opaque versus transparent 96, 115
    origin 120, 122
    rulers 343
    synchronized text 190–193
    Text Inset 340
    vertical alignment 335–340
Text fields 780–782
Text Inset 123–124
Text paths 127–132, 162–163
    runaround 594–596
Text to Box 164–166
Text wrap. *See* Runaround
Three-dimensional
    buttons 645–646
    effects 173
    images 527
Thumbnails 90–91, 681–682
TIFF files 509, 513–516, 704, 759
Tiling 687–688
    multiple monitors 64, 94

Tints. *See* Color: tints
Tolbert, Jeff xi, 207
Tool palette 15, 68, 70, 117, 118
    Grabber Hand 84
    preferences 109–111
Tool Tips 101
Tools
    Content tool 21, 114–117
    Item tool 21, 114–117
    Line tools 125
    list of all 118
    Pen tool 136–138
    Scissors tool 153
    selecting 117
Torquemada 459–462
Toyo color 625
Tracking 328–330, 375, 385–387
    text on path 132
Trademark symbol 401
Transparency 552–554, 586, 760
    text boxes when editing 115
Transparent Page 542
Trap Information palette 553, 660–664
Trapping 73, 647–665
    avoiding 656–657
    black 658–659
    color pairs 654–656
    ignore white 653–654
    knockout limit 652–653
    object-level 660–664
    overprint limit 653, 659
    overprinting 647–648, 664, 704
    preferences 111, 649–654
    process color 651–652
    testing 664
    text 657–658
    Trap Information palette 73
TrapWise 541, 647, 650
Trim marks 683–686
Troubleshooting 49, 731–735
TrueType fonts 308–309, 312
TruMatch 615, 621–622
Turning. *See* Rotating
Turpin, Glen xi, 51
Two-position rollovers 770
Type 1 fonts 308–309
Type Tricks 51, 328, 330–331, 390, 409
Typography 307–420
    baseline grid 375–378
    baseline shift 331–332
    changing fonts 72
    character formatting 27
    character-set remapping 834–835
    color and shade 321–322, 617
    fonts 308–313

fractions 408–411
horizontal alignment 333–335
horizontal scaling 322–324, 375
hyphenation and justification (H&Js) 361–372
indents 340–344
initial caps 411–416
Keep Lines Together 373–375
kerning 325–328, 382–385
leading 28–29, 344–351, 377
OpenType 308–309
paragraph formatting 28–29
PostScript fonts 308–309
preferences 379–382
prices 419
reversed type 321, 610, 659–660
Rule Above/Below 607–612
shadows 418–419
size 315–316
space before/after 351–352
special characters 391–408
styles 316–321
tabs 353–360, 392
tracking 328–330, 375, 385–387
TrueType 308–309
typeface 313–314
vertical scaling 322–324
widows and orphans 372–375, 390
wordspacing 330–331

U, V

Umlaut 404
Unanchoring items 605
Underline style 317–318, 610–611
Undo 80–82
Unexpected End of File 58
Ungroup 181
Union 155, 156
Unknown fonts 310
Unlinking text boxes 203–204
Unlocking items 174
Update lists 480
Upgrading 44
URLs. *See* Hyperlinks palette
Usage
    fonts 311–313
    pictures 529–534
    profiles 822–824
Utilities menu 67
Validation code 44
Variable Width Page 746, 754
Version Tracker 844
Vertical justification 335–340
Vertical Measure 205
Vertical rules 605–606
Vertical scaling 322–324

View menu 67, 85
Virgule 409
Visual indicators 195

W

Walrod, Brad 365
Warping text 129
Web documents
    Acrobat PDF files 796–804
    anchors 766–767
    background images 747
    basics of HTML 739–741
    browsers 761–762
    buttons 787–788
    cascading menus 771–774
    checkboxes 786–787
    Convert to Graphic on Export 754–757
    converting print layouts 745
    CSS files 790
    Export File Name 750
    exporting HTML 741–742, 789–792
    File Select tool 779
    folder structure 743–744, 748
    font families 758
    forms 775–788
    full-resolution previews 759
    GIF/JPEG images 755–756, 759
    HTML versus PDF 738–739
    hyperlinks 762–767
    image maps 774–775
    images directory 748–749
    importing HTML 792–793
    lines in 761
    lists 782–786
    menus 771–774, 782–786
    meta tags 750–753
    naming 744
    new 744–753
    Page Properties 749–754
    page sizes 746
    picture boxes in 759–760
    popup menus 782–786
    preferences 748, 761–762
    previewing 761–762
    printing 792
    radio buttons 786–787
    rollovers 767–770
    root directory 748–749
    site management 748–749
    tables in 234, 761, 791–792
    text boxes in 754–757
    text fields 780–782
    title 749–750
Web site, this book's 12, 842, 892
Web-Safe Colors 746–747

Widows and orphans 372–375, 390
Williams, Robin 411
Windows. *See* Documents: window management
Windows Bitmap (.BMP) 512
Windows Metafile 512
Windows XP 7, 9
Word. *See* Microsoft Word
Word processing 285–305, 348, 365, 448–452
Wordspacing 330–331
World Wide Power Company 844
Wrap. *See* Runaround

X, Y, Z

The XChange 844
XCite 844
XML 861–878
    avenue.quark 872–874
    basics 863–864
    DTD file 865–871
    example of 869–870
    exporting XSL 790
    importing 790
    Item Sequence palette 876–878
    placeholders 875–876
    rules 865, 873
    schemas 867
    SVG files 871
    tagging rules 873
    third-party systems 862
    versus HTML 865
    XML Import 875–876
    XSLT 878
    XTensions 862
XPert Tools 190
XPress Preferences 48–51, 387, 834
XPress Tags 454–462, 879–884
    database import 452
    em dashes 398
    Xtags 460–461
XPressobar.com 845
XSLT files 790, 878
XTensions 8, 41, 51–57, 841–845
    AutoPage 843
    BeyondPress 742
    CompassProXT 814, 816
    Cool Blends 642
    disabling 54–55
    DocuSlim 843
    Easypress Atomik 862
    free 843
    FullMeasureXT 843
    ImagePort 844
    import filters 291
    Imposer 680
    InPosition 680

    ItemMarks 686
    MS Word 450
    NAPS NTS 862
    OpenNow XT 843
    PasteboardXT 97
    PrintTools 454
    ProScale 843
    QuarkCMS 816–820
    Redefine Style 434
    RoustaboutXT 862
    ShadowCaster 418
    Sonar Bookends 483
    Type Tricks 328, 330–331, 390, 409, 843
    WebXPress 742
    Xdata 452, 844
    XPert Tools 843
    Xtags 460–461
    XTensions Manager 55–57
    XTensions Manager preferences 102–103
    Xtract 862
Zapf Dingbats 314, 405–408, 885–890
Zero point of ruler 205–206
Zoom tool 86
Zooming. *See* Magnification

Windows Keystrokes
by David Blatner

Fit picture to box	⌃-⇧-F
Fit picture maintaining ratio	⌃-Alt-⇧-F
Move picture one point	Arrow keys
Move picture 1/10 point	Alt-Arrow keys
Negative	⌃-⇧-Hyphen
Halftone Specifications	⌃-⇧-H
Contrast Specifications	⌃-⇧-C

Changing the Picture Box

Resize Picture Box	⌖-handle
Constrain to square or circle	⇧-⌖-handle
Maintain aspect ratio	Alt-⇧-⌖-handle
Scale picture with box	⌃-⌖-handle
Scale picture and constrain box shape	⌃-⇧-⌖-handle
Maintain ratio of box and picture	⌃-⇧-Alt-⌖-handle

Bézier Editing

Edit Shape toggle	F10
Delete Bézier point	Alt-⌖-point or Backspace
Delete active point while drawing	Backspace
Add point	Alt-⌖-segment
Change to corner point	⌃-⇧-⌖-handle or ⌃-F1
Change to smooth point	⌃-⇧-⌖-handle or ⌃-F2
Change smooth to corner while drawing	⌃-⌖-point, then ⌃-F1
Edit while creating item	⌃-⌖
Retract curve handles	⌃-⇧-⌖-point
Expose curve handles	⌃-⇧-⌖-point
Select all points in active box	⌃-⇧-A or ⌖⌖-point
Select all points in active path	⌖⌖-point
Constrain active point/handle to 45° movement	⇧-⌖-point/handle

When Importing Pictures

Get Picture	⌃-E
Import at 36 dpi	⇧-Open
Import color TIFF as grayscale or grayscale TIFF as line art or EPS without adding spot colors	⌃-Open
Force reimport of all pictures	⌃-Open in Open dialog

Lines

Increase width (presets)	⌃-⇧-. (period)
Decrease width (presets)	⌃-⇧-, (comma)
Increase width one point	⌃-Alt-⇧-.
Decrease width one point	⌃-Alt-⇧-,
Other width	⌃-⇧-\ (backslash)
Constrain to 45° or 90°	⇧-⌖
Constrain to existing angle	⇧-Alt-⌖

Function Keys

F1	Help
⌃-F1	Change to corner point
⌃-⇧-F1	Change to straight segment
F2	Usage dialog box
⌃-F2	Change to smooth point
⌃-⇧-F2	Change to curved segment
F3	Maximize or minimize window
⇧-F3	Fit Spread
⌃-F3	Change to symmetrical point
⌃-⇧-F3	Next master page
F4	Show/Hide Document Layout
⇧-F4	Toggle between master pages and document pages
⌃-F4	Close
Alt-F4	Quit
F5	Bring to Front
⇧-F5	Send to Back
⌃-F5	Bring Forward
⌃-⇧-F5	Send Backward
F6	Lock/Unlock
⇧-F6	Thumbnails view
⌃-F6	Previous Document
⌃-⇧-F6	Next Document
F7	Show/Hide Guides
⇧-F7	Snap to Guides
⌃-F7	Show/Hide Baseline Grid
F8	Show/Hide Tools
⇧-F8	Toggle Item/Content tool
⌃-F8	Next Tool
⌃-⇧-F8	Previous Tool
F9	Show/Hide Measurements palette
⇧-F9	Edit font name field
⌃-F9	Next font in list[2]
⌃-⇧-F9	Previous font in list[2]
F10	Edit Shape
⇧-F10	Context (right-button) menu
⌃-F10	Edit Runaround
⌃-⇧-F10	Edit Clipping Path
F11	Show/Hide Style Sheets
⇧-F11	Edit Style Sheets
⌃-F11	Show/Hide Lists
⌃-⇧-F11	Edit H&Js
F12	Show/Hide Colors palette
⇧-F12	Edit Colors
⌃-F12	Show/Hide Trap Information palette
⌃-⇧-F12	Trapping preferences

Peachpit Press
1249 Eighth Street • Berkeley, CA 94710
800/283-9444 • 510/524-2178 • FAX: 510/524-2221
http://www.peachpit.com/blatner/
©2004 David Blatner. All Rights Reserved.

Deleting Text

Previous character	Backspace
Next character	Delete or ⇧-Backspace
Previous word	⌘-Backspace
Next word	⌘-Delete or ⌘-⇧-Backspace

Character Formats

Character format	⌘-⇧-D
Increase point size (presets)	⌘-⇧-. (period)
Decrease point size (presets)	⌘-⇧-, (comma)
Increase point size one point	⌘-Alt-⇧-. (period)
Decrease point size one point	⌘-Alt-⇧-, (comma)
Other Size	⌘-⇧-\ (backslash)
Plain Text	⌘-⇧-P
Bold	⌘-⇧-B
Italic	⌘-⇧-I
Underline	⌘-⇧-U
Word Underline	⌘-⇧-W
Strikethrough	⌘-⇧-/ (slash)
Outline	⌘-⇧-O
Shadow	⌘-⇧-S
All Caps	⌘-⇧-K
Small Caps	⌘-⇧-H
Superscript	⌘-⇧-Zero
Subscript	⌘-⇧-9
Superior	⌘-⇧-V
Increase Scaling five percent›	⌘-]
Decrease Scaling five percent›	⌘-[
Increase Scaling one percent [5]	⌘-Alt-]
Decrease Scaling one percent [5]	⌘-Alt-[
Increase Kern/Track 10 units	⌘-⇧-]
Decrease Kern/Track 10 units	⌘-⇧-[
Increase Kern/Track one unit	⌘-Alt-⇧-]
Decrease Kern/Track one unit	⌘-Alt-⇧-[
Baseline Shift down one point	⌘-Alt-⇧-9
Baseline Shift up one point	⌘-Alt-⇧-Zero

Paragraph Formats

Paragraph Format dialog box	⌘-⇧-F
Left Alignment	⌘-⇧-L
Right Alignment	⌘-⇧-R
Center Alignment	⌘-⇧-C
Justified Alignment	⌘-⇧-J
Forced Justification	⌘-Alt-⇧-J
Leading	⌘-⇧-E
Tabs	⌘-⇧-T
Rules (above and below)	⌘-⇧-N

[5] These keystrokes scale in the direction (horizontal or vertical) which you last selected from the dialog box.

Increase Leading one point	⌘-⇧-"
Decrease Leading one point	⌘ ⇧ ;
Increase Leading 1/10 point	⌘-Alt-⇧-"
Decrease Leading 1/10 point	⌘-Alt-⇧-;
Copy Paragraph Format	Alt-⇧-➤-any paragraph
Apply No Style before applying style sheet	Alt-➤-on style sheet in Style Sheets palette

Special Formatting Characters

One Symbol Character	⌘-Alt-Q
One Zapf Dingbats Character	⌘-Alt-Z
Indent to Here	⌘-Backslash (\)
Soft Return (new line)	⇧-Enter
New Column	Enter on key pad
New Text Box	⇧-Enter on key pad
Discretionary New Line	⌘-Enter
Flush Right Tab	⇧-Tab
Nonbreaking Hyphen	⌘-=
Discretionary Hyphen	⌘-Hyphen
Nonbreaking en dash	⌘-Alt-⇧-Hyphen
Breaking em dash	⌘-⇧-=
Nonbreaking em dash	⌘-Alt-⇧-=
Nonbreaking Space	⌘-5
En Space	⌘-⇧-6
Nonbreaking En Space	⌘-Alt-⇧-6
Flex Space	⌘-⇧-5
Nonbreaking Flex Space	⌘-Alt-⇧-5
Punctuation Space	⇧-Space
Previous text box page number	⌘-2
Current text box page number	⌘-3
Next text box page number	⌘-4

Find/Change Characters

Tab	\t or ⌘-Tab
New paragraph	\p or ⌘-Enter
New line	\n or ⌘-⇧-Enter
New column	\c or ⌘-Keypad Enter
New box	\b or ⌘-⇧-Keypad Enter
Previous text box page number	\2 or ⌘-2
Current page number	\3 or ⌘-3
Next text box page number	\4 or ⌘-4
Wildcard	\? or ⌘-?
Punctuation Space	\. or ⌘-. (period)
Flex Space	\f or ⌘-⇧-F
Backslash	\\ or ⌘-\ (backslash)

Pictures and Lines

Changing the Picture

Increase size by five percent	⌘-Alt-⇧-. (period)
Decrease size by five percent	⌘-Alt-⇧-, (comma)
Center picture in box	⌘-⇧-M

Center picture in box	⌘-⇧-M
Fit picture to box	⌘-⇧-F
Fit picture maintaining ratio	⌘-⌥-⇧-F
Move picture one point	Arrow keys
Move picture ¹⁄₁₀ point	⌥-Arrow keys
Negative	⌘-⇧-Hyphen
Halftone Specifications	⌘-⇧-H
Contrast Specifications	⌘-⇧-C

Changing the Picture Box

Resize Picture Box	Handle
Constrain to square or circle	⇧-
Maintain aspect ratio	⇧-⌥-
Scale picture with box	⌘-
Maintain ratio of box and picture	⌘-⇧-⌥-

Bézier Editing

Edit shape toggle	⇧-F4
Delete Bézier point	⌥-point
Delete active point while drawing	Delete
Add point	⌥-segment
Change to Smooth point	⌃- or ⌥-F2
Change to Corner point	⌃- or ⌃- on handle or ⌥-F1
Change smooth to corner while drawing	⌘-⌃-handle
Edit path while still drawing	⌘-
Retract curve handles	⌃-point
Expose curve handles	⌃-point
Select all points in active box	⌘-⇧-A or ▸-point
Select all points in active path	▸-point
Constrain active point/handle to 45° movement	⇧-point/handle

When Importing Pictures

Get Picture	⌘-E
Low-resolution screen image	⇧-Open
TIFF line art to grayscale	⌥-Open
TIFF grayscale to line art	⌘-Open
TIFF color to grayscale	⌘-Open
Don't import spot colors in EPS	⌘-Open
Force reimport of all pictures	⌘-Open in Open dialog

Lines

Increase width (presets)	⌘-⇧-> (period key)
Decrease width (presets)	⌘-⇧-< (comma key)
Increase width one point	⌘-⌥-⇧->
Decrease width one point	⌘-⌥-⇧-<
Other width	⌘-⇧-Backslash (\)
Constrain resizing at 45°	⇧-
Constrain resizing to angle	⇧-⌥-

[6] *The previous/next font is determined by font name, so you may not get the font you expect.*

Function Keys	
F1	Undo
⌥-F1	Change to corner point
⌥-⇧-F1	Change to straight segment
F2	Cut
⌥-F2	Change to smooth point
⌥-⇧-F2	Change to curved segment
F3	Copy
⌥-F3	Change to symmetrical point
F4	Paste
⇧-F4	Edit Shape
⌥-F4	Edit Runaround shape
⌥-⇧-F4	Edit clipping path shape
F5	Bring to Front
⇧-F5	Send to Back
⌥-F5	Bring Forward
⇧-⌥-F5	Send Backward
F6	Lock/Unlock
⇧-⌥-F6	Thumbnails view
⌘-F6	Font Usage
F7	Show/Hide Guides
⇧-F7	Snap to Guides
⌥-F7	Show/Hide Baseline Grid
F8	Show/Hide Tools
⇧-F8	Toggle Item/Content tool
⌥-F8	Next Tool
⇧-⌥-F8	Previous Tool
F9	Show/Hide Measurements palette
⇧-F9	Edit font name field
⌥-F9	Next font in list[6]
⇧-⌥-F9	Previous font in list[6]
F10	Show/Hide Document Layout palette
⇧-F10	Go between master pages and pages
⌥-F10	Next master page
⇧-⌥-F10	Previous master page
F11	Show/Hide Style Sheets
⇧-F11	Edit Style Sheets
⌥-F11	Show/Hide Lists
⇧-⌥-F11	Edit H&Js
F12	Show/Hide Colors palette
⇧-F12	Edit Colors
⌥-F12	Show/Hide Trap Information palette
⇧-⌥-F12	Trapping Preferences
F13	Font Usage
⌥-F13	Picture Usage

Peachpit Press
1249 Eighth Street • Berkeley, CA 94710
800/283-9444 • 510/524-2178 • FAX: 510/524-2221
http://www.peachpit.com/blatner/

Real World QuarkXPress 6

Deleting Text

Previous character	Delete (Backspace key)
Next character	⌦ or ⇧-Delete
Previous word	⌘-Delete
Next word	⌘-⌦ or ⌘-⇧-Delete
Highlighted characters	Delete

Character Formats

Character format	⌘-⇧-D
Increase point size (presets)	⌘-⇧-> (period key)
Decrease point size (presets)	⌘-⇧-< (comma key)
Increase point size one point	⌘-⇧-⌥->
Decrease point size one point	⌘-⇧-⌥-<
Other Size	⌘-⇧-Backslash (\)
Plain Text	⌘-⇧-P
Bold	⌘-⇧-B
Italic	⌘-⇧-I
Underline	⌘-⇧-U
Word Underline	⌘-⇧-W
Strikethrough	⌘-⇧-Slash (/)
Outline	⌘-⇧-O
Shadow	⌘-⇧-S
All Caps	⌘-⇧-K
Small Caps	⌘-⇧-H
Superscript	⌘-⇧-=
Subscript	⌘-⇧-Hyphen
Superior	⌘-⇧-V
Increase Scaling five percent [5]	⌘-]
Decrease Scaling five percent [5]	⌘-[
Increase Scaling one percent [5]	⌘-⌥-]
Decrease Scaling one percent [5]	⌘-⌥-[
Increase Kern/Track 10 units	⌘-⇧-]
Decrease Kern/Track 10 units	⌘-⇧-[
Increase Kern/Track one unit	⌘-⌥-⇧-]
Decrease Kern/Track one unit	⌘-⌥-⇧-[
Increase "wordspacing" one unit (with Type Tricks XTension)	⌘-⌥-⇧-⌃-]
Decrease "wordspacing" one unit (with Type Tricks XTension)	⌘-⌥-⇧-⌃-[
Baseline Shift down one point	⌘-⌥-⇧-Hyphen
Baseline Shift up one point	⌘-⌥-⇧-=

Paragraph Formats

Paragraph Format	⌘-⇧-F
Left Alignment	⌘-⇧-L
Right Alignment	⌘-⇧-R
Center Alignment	⌘-⇧-C
Justified Alignment	⌘-⇧-J
Forced Justification	⌘-⇧-⌥-J
Leading	⌘-⇧-E
Tabs	⌘-⇧-T

[5] These keystrokes scale in the direction (horizontal or vertical) which you last selected from the dialog box.

Rules (above and below)	⌘-⇧-N
Increase Leading one point	⌘-⇧-"
Decrease Leading one point	⌘-⇧-;
Increase Leading 1/10 point	⌘-⌥-⇧-"
Decrease Leading 1/10 point	⌘-⌥-⇧-;
Copy Paragraph Format	⌥-⇧-➤-any paragraph
Apply No Style before applying style sheet	⌥-➤-on style sheet in Style Sheet palette

Special Formatting Characters

One Symbol Character	⌘-⌥-Q
One Zapf Dingbats Character	⌘-⌥-Z
Soft Return (New Line)	⇧-Return
Discretionary New Line	⌘-Return
Discretionary Hyphen	⌘-Hyphen
Nonbreaking Hyphen	⌘-=
Nonbreaking Space	⌘-Space or ⌃-Space
New Column	Enter
New Box	⇧-Enter
En Space	⌥-Space
Nonbreaking En Space	⌘-⌥-Space or ⌘-⌥-5
Flex Space	⌥-⇧-Space
Nonbreaking Flex Space	⌘-⌥-⇧-Space
Punctuation Space	⇧-Space
Nonbreaking Punctuation Space	⌘-⇧-Space
Breaking em dash	⌥-⇧-hyphen
Nonbreaking em dash	⌘-⌥-=
Current page number	⌘-3
Previous text box page number	⌘-2
Next text box page number	⌘-4
Indent to Here	⌘-Backslash (\)
Flush Right Tab	⌥-Tab

Find/Change Characters

Tab	\t or ⌘-⌃-Tab
New paragraph	\p or ⌘-Return
New line	\n or ⌘-⇧-Return
New column	\c or ⌘-Enter
New box	\b or ⌘-⇧-Enter
Previous text box page number	\2 or ⌘-2
Current page number	\3 or ⌘-3
Next text box page number	\4 or ⌘-4
Wildcard	\? or ⌘-?
Punctuation Space	\. or ⌘-period
Flex Space	\f or ⌘-⇧-F
Backslash	\\ or ⌘-\

Pictures and Lines

Changing the Picture

Increase size by five percent	⌘-⌥-⇧-> (period key)
Decrease size by five percent	⌘-⌥-⇧-< (comma key)